I0063807

Texts and Contexts in Legal History: Essays in Honor of Charles Donahue

Studies in Comparative Legal History

Texts and Contexts in Legal History: Essays in Honor of Charles Donahue

Edited by

John Witte, Jr.

Sara McDougall

Anna di Robilant

The Robbins Collection Berkeley

Printed on acid-free paper.

Robbins Collection Publications
Berkeley Law
University of California at Berkeley
Berkeley, California 94720
(510) 642-5094 fax: (510) 642-8325
www.law.berkeley.edu/robbins

ISBN: 978-1-882239-24-5

Library of Congress Cataloging-in-Publication Data

Names: Witte, John, 1959– editor. | McDougall, Sara, editor. | Di Robilant, Anna, editor. | Donahue, Charles, 1941– honouree.
Title: Texts and contexts in legal history : essays in honor of Charles Donahue / edited by John Witte, Jr., Sara McDougall, Anna di Robilant.
Description: Berkeley : The Robbins Collection, 2016.
Identifiers: LCCN 2016052476 | ISBN 9781882239245 (hardcover)
Subjects: LCSH: Law, Medieval. | Law—Europe—History. | Law—England—History.
Classification: LCC KJ147 .T49 2016 | DDC 340.5/5—dc23
LC record available at https://lccn.loc.gov/2016052476

Contents

Imagining the Past: Foreword in Honor of Charles Donahue

Martha Minow
Morgan and Helen Chu Dean and Professor, Harvard Law School

> *"The past is really almost as much a work of the imagination as the future."*—Jessamyn West[1]

How splendid it is to see these marvelous essays, inspired by the work of Professor Charles Donahue! And how right to see reflected here the qualities and interactions of this superb scholar, devoted teacher and mentor, relentless and effective force in expanding access to original legal materials. I have been honored to be Charlie's colleague for more than three decades and know how lucky Harvard Law School, legal education, and legal history are that his personal history led him to do so much for these worlds.

Superb scholar, influential teacher and indomitable force for archival work and force behind publications of historical materials, Charlie is such a worthy inspiration for the marvelous chapters gathered here. His early teaching on law, history and society influenced his scholarship and then guided generations of scholars to focus on the words, structures, and assumptions embedded in legal texts, and then to ask daring questions about context. For Charlie, context entails the entire situation, and its study compels inquiry into ideas, politics, economics, society, and comparisons across legal systems. To see context requires imagining the people as well as documenting the institutions behind the legal texts. Pursuing context

1. "Jessamyn West Quote." *BrainyQuote*. Xplore, n.d. Web. 15 June 2016.

in Charlie's hands requires examining the parallel and intersecting paths of common law, canon law, and customary continental law. Modest about his own great learning (in a shared study group on the Talmud, Charlie's generously and quietly shared knowledge ranging from the root meanings of Hebrew words to the currency exchanges in 3rd cent. BC–4th cent. AD Palestine), Charlie models what a life of learning and curiosity can be, bringing him into contact with quantitative tools and social science methods, material culture, institutional design, and linguistic study.

Attention to context in Charlie's tradition counsels skepticism about any claims that tempt legal types to make claims about continuities in doctrine or meaning that wipe away context. Similarly, his forays into the digital humanities combine eagerness with cautions about over claiming and about thinking that data determine the questions to ask. Instead, as Hajo Holborn wrote, "[H]istory gives answers only to those who know how to ask questions."[2] Charlie asks great questions—not just how do substance and procedure influence one another, but how did the distinction between substance and procedure emerge?[3] What can be discerned about the institutional context, world view, and assumptions of those who produced a specific document? What are the continuities despite apparent changes, and changes despite apparent continuities?

Always attentive to actual people who produced legal texts, faced the law and administered it, Charlie deploys imagination through both a humanist approach and a lawyerly focus on details and gaps in the evidence.[4] It is Charlie's critical work that has guided the Ames Foundation to expand access to sources through the meticulous preparation of publications and

2. Holborn, Hajo. "History and the Humanities." *Journal of the History of Ideas* 9.1 (1948): 65–69. Web.

3. Kessler, Amalia D. "The Mystery of the "Charitable Arbitrator," or Reflections on a Neglected Old Regime Text and the Intersection Between Status and Practices of Arbitration and Mediation." *Texts and Contexts in Legal History: Essays in Honor of Charles Donahue*. Chapter 24. Print.

4. Donahue served as Assistant General Counsel of the President's Commission on Postal Organization and Attorney-Advisor in the Office of General Counsel in the Office of the Secretary of the Air Force. (Curriculum Vitae. http://hls.harvard.edu/faculty/directory/10220/Donahue)

digitization of manuscripts,[5] and we see Charlie's fine hand in the ongoing work of the American Historical Association, the American Society for Legal History, the Selden Society, and the Harvard Law Library.

Those who love history and those who love law will welcome this volume which wonderfully celebrates and extends the commitments and imagination of Professor Charles Donahue.

5. See, e.g., the *Year Books of Richard II (11th edition)*; an edition of the thirteenth-century treatise *Lex mercatoria*, Joseph Henry Beale's *Bibliography of Early English Law Books*, Robert Bowie Anderson's *Supplement* to Beale, and Bertha Haven Putnam's *Proceedings Before the Justices of the Peace in the Fourteenth and Fifteenth Centuries*; The records of the medieval Ecclesiastic courts, and the Appeals to the Privy Council from the American Colonies.

Foreword

Morris S. Arnold
United States Circuit Judge
United States Court of Appeals for the Eighth Circuit

It is a pleasure for me to reconnect with the Robbins Collection after all these years in this tribute to Charlie Donahue and his many contributions, both substantive and methodological, to the history of law. I spent the better part of a summer more than forty years ago at Boalt Hall attending a seminar on Roman Law taught by the master, David C. Daube, who was at that time the director of the Collection. It was here that I made some tentative and amateurish forays into the works of Bartolus, Baldus, and company.

But apart from these relatively minor brushes with the learned laws, and teaching the occasional readings course on the influence of the civil law on the common law, I am, like Glanvill more than 800 years before me, a thorough-going common lawyer; and so, like him, I have to begin these short observations with a diffident apology for not being better acquainted with much of the subject matter that our distinguished essayists explore here. Luckily, our honorand's historiographical methods and his explanations of them transcend the particular and are sufficiently lucid to allow me to make a few relevant comments that may not be too far off the mark, though I fell from grace some thirty years ago and became a government worker. Charlie's advice about how to write legal history is general enough that even a local antiquary and provincial magistrate can comprehend and profit from seeing how he has worked and how he has influenced the learned company from seven different countries who have produced this impressive volume.

I don't remember exactly when I met Charlie, but it was probably in the late sixties when I showed up at Harvard Law School as a graduate student and he began his teaching career at Michigan. Around that time, there was a rather large meeting of legal historians that I attended at Harvard Law School, which, according to a recent written account, is now supposed to have been some kind of watershed event in the history of our subject (I got a footnote), and perhaps Charlie was there. Or maybe we first encountered each other at a meeting of the American Society for Legal History, of which Charlie later became president. No matter: Whenever we met, it soon became clear that we had a great deal in common, including a training in the languages required for work in the Middle Ages that perhaps counseled pursuing a career in that period rather than a later one.

One of the odd products of the upheavals of the late sixties was a renaissance in the study of legal history, which generated a lot of what I think of as history with a purpose, some of it the product of ransacking the old books and searching the past for friends and enemies. The path that Charlie and I took was decidedly different from that, and perhaps that made our work less relevant in some sense; but as Charlie has argued, and as this book proves, there are very good reasons to study the early period, though some may think those reasons rather subtle and may find the lessons that such study yields are rather hard won.

Charlie thinks his outlook can make our work useful in the real world. Legal phenomena are the product of a particular time and place and so, with Thomas Wolfe, he admonishes his students that you can't go home again. He tells them to be chary of diachronic legal history and legal argument: They are commonly ultra-hazardous enterprises because, despite the occasional legal transplant, legal ideas are not ordinarily prefabricated Lego parts that can be uprooted and transported to some later time and expected to work well. (It would be instructive to hear Charlie expatiate on our Supreme Court's latest efforts to make sense of the Second Amendment to the United States Constitution.) It is nevertheless frequently a lawyer's or judge's job to discern organizing principles in earlier legal events and give those principles present effect. Most of us like to think we live in an ordered world, that what we see behind us is not simply a wilderness of single instances, and one role of the legal system must at least be to give that impression.

Charlie sensibly cautions that historians must usually start with documents, that otherwise their product is, as he puts it, just rubbish, and then they must let the documents speak to them. What are they saying? What are their scriveners or authors trying to tell the reader? Charlie is a highly skillful exegete, but the text is simply the beginning. Context, he allows, is just as important, and by context he means the tenor of the times, the social, political, intellectual, and economic environment that produced the documents. It is by examining these that their true meaning and significance are forced out of the shadows where they can yield their lessons. The result is a look at the law in action, and if that sounds like legal realism that is no accident, for Charlie went to Yale Law School where that outlook was and remains much in vogue.

Charlie's methods also include comparative law, a discipline that to my mind has two main advantages. It allows us to see that a particular moral or legal arrangement is not logically ineluctable, and it allows the features of a particular legal system or event to be more visible because of the way they contrast with features of another one. And Charlie sometime practices comparative law in time, outlining doctrinal shifts and accounting for them as products of broader social changes.

It may be that our field does not lend itself to a great deal of political rumination, but it would not be too hard to imagine, say, critical feminist perspectives on the legal rights of medieval women. For all that I know, there is literature like that out there. But the essays in this book certainly are not likely to raise any ideological hackles. I have noticed only one mention of race and the barest trace of feminist thought in the entire collection; considerations of class, I guess, inevitably intrude when the Statute of Labourers turns up or the Peasants' Revolt becomes relevant. But the iron triangle of race, gender, and class that rules other kinds of historiographical efforts these days is missing here. The essays in this book present an entirely different affect, and many of them bear the imprint of Charlie's sophisticated and engaging methods of describing and evaluating the past. For instance, Elizabeth Kamali's insightful contribution on law and equity in a medieval English manor court is a model of Charlie's insistence that context can make sense of records that at first seem random or discordant. As she puts it, her method is to "combine fine-tuned textual parsing with large-scale contextual pondering."

Toby Milsom taught us, and rightly, that lawyers work with their heads down and he emphasized the role of accident in legal development. But Charlie has (not inconsistently) asked us as historians to lift our heads up and look all around to see what was happening in the external world at the time when particular legal phenomena occurred. He promises that this world-view will be a central feature of his projected history of English law in the fourteenth century, and we all eagerly await its publication.

It is not that more traditional legal history is missing from this volume. John Baker's revealing contribution on Magna Carta in the fourteenth century concerns itself with a traditional theme, but its constitutional and political dimensions guarantee that it is not merely a doctrinal explication. Remarkably, this piece goes some way in rehabilitating that hoariest of Whigs, Sir Edward Coke, and it reminds us that the struggle for individual liberty and against arbitrary government is indeed a central theme in the history of our private and public law.

The last time I spoke with Charlie was in the crypt beneath the Old Hall of Lincoln's Inn following a Selden Society lecture, and he asked me point blank what I was looking for when I began my study of English legal history. I told him I was looking for traces of the importance of liberty to the people of the time and for a clue to what liberties they valued the most. John Baker's article makes me regret, not for the first time, that I abandoned that search. Philip Hamburger's recent book on the legality of American administrative law shows that Magna Carta can still be made to resonate in a context that could hardly be more different from the one that generated it.

Editorial Preface

Leading English legal historian Sir John Baker once wrote that "the guiding logic of the lawyer is different from that of the historian. What the lawyer wants is authority, and the newer the better; what the historian wants is evidence, and the older the better."[1] Professor Charles Donahue has distinguished himself both as a lawyer and as a legal historian of the first rank.

Donahue's record as a lawyer and law professor is impressive enough, particularly his work on property law, which has been a staple of the Harvard Law School curriculum for four decades. He wrote a leading textbook (in three editions) and several long articles on property law, and he offered related courses and seminars on comparative family law, inheritance, family property, and real estate. As anyone who has sat in his classroom knows, here Donahue is very much the lawyer. He presses his students to parse the latest statutes responsibly, to cite or distinguish the latest cases carefully, and to appreciate the policy that is being negotiated and the precedent being set in a given case. "So, what's really going on here," would often be his final "legal realist" question to the class about a case or statute, as he forced us to see the legal text in full context.

While Donahue the lawyer deserves to be celebrated, this volume celebrates his formidable work as a legal historian over the past half century. Here his contributions have been original, weighty, and enduring. Notable are the 100 plus articles, book chapters, and reviews on legal history themes and topics. Included among them are classic articles: "The Policy of Alexander the Third's Consent Theory of Marriage"; "Roman Canon Law in the Medieval English Church: Stubbs v. Maitland Re-Examined"; "Malchus's

1. John Baker, *Collected Papers on English Legal History*, 3 vols. (Cambridge: Cambridge University Press, 2013), 2:761, 763, citing F.W. Maitland, *Why the History of English Law is Not Written* (Cambridge: Cambridge University Press, 1888).

Ear: Reflections on Classical Canon Law as a Religious Legal System"; "*Ius* in the Subjective Sense in Roman Law"; and "Why the History of Canon Law is Not Written." Included as well are searching reviews of new volumes by the leading legal historians of the past two generations – among them, John Baker, Bruce Frier, R.H. Helmholz, and Anne Lefebvre-Teillard who have contributed to this volume.

Even more valuable have been Donahue's volumes on medieval legal records – especially the hard to find and parse case law records of medieval courts. The first major book in this vein was his 1982 Selden Society volume on *Select Cases from the Ecclesiastical Province of Canterbury, c. 1200 – 1301,* a massive work of critical reconstruction of all manner of cases, hitherto available only on frayed rag-paper and almost impossible for anyone but refined specialists to penetrate. Then came the wonderful two-volume guide on *The Records of the Medieval Courts,* anchor texts in the new Dunker & Humblot series that Donahue helped to build on Comparative Studies in Continental and Anglo-American Legal History. Then came critical editions, and sometimes translations, of medieval and early modern texts supported by the Ames Foundation that Donahue directed from 1980 to 2015. Included among these Ames volumes is a very recent title, *Appeals to the Privy Council from the American Colonies,* compiled with another contributor to this volume, Mary Bilder.

Donahue's most important work is his massive 1000 page Cambridge University Press title on *Law, Marriage, and Society in the Later Middle Ages: Arguments About Marriage in Five Courts* (2007). Here, we see him at the height of his powers as a legal historian, showing full command not only of the medieval *ius commune* on marriage and family questions but also of the immense complexities of the English and Continental court systems and their procedures. Using the medieval church court records of York, Ely, Paris, Cambrai, and Brussels as his data set, this book provides a lavish and detailed analysis of all the hard legal questions surrounding marital formation, maintenance, and dissolution that came to these church courts for resolution. General readers come away from this book with a vivid impression of a living family law system in action, every bit as sophisticated as any civil law or common law system of marital family law that came after. Legal historians and family historians must return to this book time and again to check out how their particular topics were worked out by medieval jurists and judges not only in theory but also in action. This book will doubtless be read, mined, and admired for the next century and more.

Donahue the legal historian did not confine himself to his archives and writing desk. He taught wonderful courses and seminars at Michigan, Harvard, as well as several other schools that he visited on Roman law, Continental Legal History, English Legal History, the History of Marriage Law, the History of Canon Law, and the History of the *Ius Commune* in medieval and early modern times. He advised and supervised hundreds of doctoral and professional school students working on legal history themes and has been a generous correspondent with many scholars and a critical reader of many manuscripts for university presses. He involved himself deeply in building and leading the international guild of legal historians, gathered in such societies as the American Society for Legal History, the American Historical Association, the Selden Society, the Medieval Academy of America, the British Legal History Conference, and the Iuris Canonici Medii Aevi Consortio, among others. He has graced distinguished lecterns throughout North America and Europe, and is legendary as a spirited conversationalist and formidable interrogator at professional society roundtables and scholarly panels on legal history.

The theme of "text and context," which typifies Donahue's work as a lawyer, is also on full display in his work as a legal historian – thus inspiring the title to this collection. He writes:

> I try to take a small body of text, drain out of it as much meaning as possible, and then relate it to the context in which it was written and/or in which it was used. Obviously, you can do this with works that are "literary." That's where the method comes from. But it can also be used with the most routine of documents, like court records. Many medievalists are comfortable with this method, but [it] can also help people who are working with other worlds if they want to see comparisons or possible influences. The substantive subjects that I have worked with are principally family law, commercial law, property, and procedure. I try to keep the context as broad as possible: social, economic, political, religious, and strictly legal doctrinal contexts are all fair game.

As his autobiographical chapter herein elaborates, Donahue's legal history writing reveals a deep appreciation for both "nomos and narrative,"[2] both canon and interpretation, both the Ur texts of earlier days and the traditions of interpretation and application they inspired. Whether he is teaching the Twelve Tables or the lex Aquilia, analyzing a decretal of Alexander III or a case from the Yearbooks, rummaging through the matrimonial case laws of medieval York or the marital jurisprudence of an early modern jurist, his method of legal history is constant and consistent. He first has his readers and students go back to the sources. Only after authenticating the original texts and discerning the range of possible original meanings from their original contexts, he insists, can one responsibly assess the layers of interpretation that time and tradition have attached to that text or one's imagination or inspiration might impute to it, especially as a judge or an advocate. In this method, Donahue is very much like the great seventeenth-century English legal historian, John Selden, whom John Baker was describing in his memorable line: "What the lawyer wants is authority, and the newer the better; what the historian wants is evidence, and the older the better." That was Selden in a nutshell, and it's Donahue in a nutshell, too.

As former students of Professor Donahue and happy beneficiaries of his instruction as a lawyer and legal historian, we are delighted to present this Festschrift to him with admiration, appreciation, and affection. We present 26 contributions from leading historians in North America and Europe, and only wish we had space to accommodate contributions from the dozens of other historians who would have liked to contribute. We express our deep appreciation to all the contributors for their splendid chapters and timely delivery.

We express our warm thanks to Dean Martha Minow of Harvard Law School for welcoming and supporting the preparation of this volume, and gracing it with her lovely Foreword alongside the equally lovely Foreword of Judge Morris Arnold. We give special thanks to Max Withers at the Robbins Collection for his masterful work in editing this volume, during an especially difficult year for him, as well as to Laurent Mayali,

2. Robert M. Cover, *Narrative, Violence, and the Law: The Essays of Robert Cover*, ed., Martha Minow et al. (Ann Arbor, MI: University of Michigan Press, 1992), 95–172.

the Director of the Robbins Collection, for publishing this text. And we give special thanks to Amy Wheeler in the Center for the Study of Law and Religion at Emory University for masterminding the administration of this volume from start to finish.

But we owe our greatest thanks to Professor Donahue for his brilliant scholarship, teaching, and mentorship, for his generous humanity, fidelity, and integrity, and for the sterling example he offers to all of us of a gentleman's scholarly life lived well. May it long continue!

John Witte, Jr., Emory University
Sara McDougall, John Jay College
Anna di Robilant, Boston University

Vita of Professor Charles Donahue, Jr.
Harvard University School of Law, Cambridge, MA

Personal

Born October 4, 1941, in New York, New York. American citizen. Married August 1964 with one daughter, born August 1965.

Educational

(1) Portsmouth Priory (Abbey) School, Portsmouth Rhode Island. H.S. diploma, *cum laude*, first in class, 1959.

(2) Harvard College, Cambridge, Massachusetts. A.B. 1962, *magna cum laude*, in Classics and English.

(3) Yale Law School, New Haven, Connecticut. L.B. 1965, Order of the Coif. Articles and Book Review Editor of the *Yale Law Journal*. Special Divisional Program in Legal History directed by W.H. Dunham and Stephan Kuttner.

Honors

Fellow, Royal Historical Society (U.K.), 1986

Docteur h.c., université de Paris II, Panthéon-Assas, 2010

Fellow, Medieval Academy of America, 2011

Honorary Member, Phi Beta Kappa, Chapter Alpha-Iota of Massachusetts, 2012

Fellow, American Society of Legal History, 2014

Fellow, Society of Antiquaries (U.K.), 2015

Employment

(1) Paul, Weiss, Rifkind, Wharton & Garrison, New York, New York, summer 1964.

(2) Attorney-Advisor, Office of the General Counsel, Office of the Secretary of the Air Force, Washington, D.C., 1965–67.

(3) Assistant General Counsel, The President's Commission on Postal Organization, Washington, D.C., 1967–68.

(4) Assistant Professor, University of Michigan School of Law, Ann Arbor, MI, 1968–71.

(5) Associate Professor, with tenure, University of Michigan School of Law, June 1971 to June 1973.

(5a) Academic Visitor, Law Department, London School of Economics and Political Science, September 1972 to June 1973.

(6) Full Professor, University of Michigan School of Law, June 1973 to December 1979.

(6a) Visiting Professor of Law, Vrije Universiteit Brussel, January to June 1975.

(6b) Visiting Professor of Law, Columbia University School of Law, January to June 1976.

(6c) Visiting Professor of Law, University of California School of Law (Boalt Hall), August to December, 1976.

(6d) Visiting Professor of Law, Harvard University School of Law, September 1978 to June 1979.

(7) Full Professor, Harvard University School of Law, since January, 1980. Paul A. Freund Professor of Law, Harvard University School of Law, since June 1995.

(7a) Visiting Professor of Law, Boston College School of Law, January 1987 to June 1987.

(7b) Visiting Professor of Law, Cornell University School of Law, August 1996 to December 1996.

(7c) Visiting Professor of Law, Boston College School of Law, August 2005 to December 2005.

Languages

Classical and Medieval Latin (reading), Classical Greek (some reading), Biblical Hebrew (some reading), French (reading and speaking), German (reading and some speaking), Italian (reading and some speaking), Dutch (smattering), Anglo-Saxon (smattering).

Memberships

New York, Michigan (inactive) and United States Supreme Court bars and the bars of various lower federal courts

American Law Institute

American Society for Legal History (director 1977–79; vice-president 1982–85, president-elect 2004–5, president 2006–7, immediate past president 2008–9, fellow 2014–)

Selden Society (vice-president 1984–87, councilor 1987- , honorary treasurer for the U.S.A. 1987–2014)

American Historical Association

Societé d'histoire du droit

Societé pour l'histoire des droits de l'antiquité

Medieval Academy of America (fellow, 2011-)

Ecclesiastical History Society (Gt. Bt.)

Canterbury and York Society (Gt. Bt.)

Ames Foundation (director 1980– , literary director 1989– , vice-president 1991– , treasurer 2012–14)

Royal Historical Society (Gt. Bt.) (fellow, 1986–)

Iuris Canonici Medii Aevi Consortio (treasurer, 2000–2010)

Courses Taught

Property: Fall 1968, Winter 1969, Fall 1969 & Winter 1970, Fall 1970 & Winter 1971, Fall 1971 & Winter 1972, Fall 1973 & Winter 1974, Summer & Fall 1975, Winter 1976, Fall 1976, Fall 1977 & Winter 1978, Spring 1979, Fall 1979, Spring 1981, Spring 1982, Fall 1985 & Spring 1986, Fall 1987 & Spring 1988, Fall 1992, Fall 1995, Fall 1998, Fall 2000, Fall 2003, Fall 2004, Fall 2006, Fall 2007, Fall 2008, Fall 2009, Spring 2011, Fall 2011, Fall 2012, Fall 2014.

Advanced Property [Family Property Transactions: Wills and Trusts (with some Real Estate)]: Fall 1983, Fall 1984, Fall 1985, Spring 1987, Fall 1988, Fall 1989, Fall 1990, Fall 1991, Fall 1993, Fall 1994.

Wills and Trusts: Fall 1999, Spring 2002.

Regulated Industries: Summer 1968, Summer 1969, Summer 1972.

Federal Anti-trust Laws: Fall 1969, Fall 1970, Fall, 1973, Winter 1975, Fall 1978, Spring 1980, Winter 1981.

Introduction to Roman Law: Winter 1971, Winter 1974, Winter 1976, Winter 1977, Spring 1980, Spring 1981, Spring 1984, Spring 1986,

Spring 1988, Fall 1991, Fall 1994, Fall 1997, Fall 1999, Fall 2002, Fall 2004, Fall 2007.

Reading course in Roman Law: Fall 2010, Fall 2011.

Continental Legal History (survey): Fall 1990, Fall 1993, Spring 1995, Spring 1998, Spring 2000, Spring 2003, Spring 2005, Spring 2008, Spring 2011.

Seminar in Continental Legal History: Fall 1984 & Spring 1985, Fall 1988 & Spring 1989, Spring 1998, Spring 2000, Spring 2003, Spring 2005, Spring 2008, Spring 2011.

Reading course in European Legal History: Fall 2009.

Reading course in the History of Marriage Law: Fall 2014.

Legal Philosophy: Winter 1972.

English Constitutional History to 1485: Fall 1977, Fall 1979, Spring 1991.

English Legal History (survey): Fall 1983, Fall 1984, Winter 1986, Fall 1987, Fall 1988, Fall 1989, Spring 1991, Spring 1992, Spring 1994, Spring 1996, Fall 1996, Spring 1999, Spring 2002, Spring 2004, Spring 2007, Spring 2009, Spring 2012, Spring 2015.

Seminar in English Legal History: Fall 1977, Fall 1979, Spring 1985, Spring 1999, Spring 2002, Spring 2004, Spring 2007, Spring 2009, Spring 2012, Spring 2015.

Reading course in English Legal History: Fall 2008, Fall 2012.

Seminar in Law, History & Society: Winter 1969, Winter 1970, Fall 1971, Fall 1974, Winter 1977, Fall 1978, Fall 1980, Spring 1984, Fall 1990 & Spring 1991, Fall 1991 & Spring 1992, Fall 1994 & Spring 1995.

Seminar in Marital Property: Fall 1975, Winter 1978.

Seminar in Canon Law: Spring 1987.

Seminar in Law, Morals and Theology: Fall, 1996, Fall 1997

Seminar in the History of Marriage Law: Fall, 2005.

Reading course in the History of Marriage Law: Fall 2014.

The course and the seminar in both English Legal History and Continental Legal History are offered in both the Law and the Faculty of Arts and Sciences. In addition, I regularly give reading courses for graduate students in Harvard Faculty of Arts & Sciences and in the Harvard Law School in various aspects of medieval and early modern English and Continental legal and constitutional history. I also serve on doctoral dissertation committees in the same fields in both faculties.

Bibliography

(1) 'An Historical Argument for the Right to Counsel During Police Interrogation', *Yale L.J.* 73 (1964) 1000–1057.

(2) Review, John Honnold, *The Life of the Law*, in *Colum. L. Rev.* 67 (1967) 1353–60.

(3) 'The Alaska Purchase: For a Private Communications System', *Pub. Util. Fortnightly* 82 (Dec. 5, 1968) 40–51.

(4) 'The Supreme Court vs. Section 10(b)(3) of the Selective Service Act: A Study in Ducking Constitutional Issues', *U.C.L.A. L. Rev.* 17 (1970) 908–74.

(5) 'Lawyers, Economics, and the Regulated Industries: Thoughts on Professional Roles Inspired by Some Recent Economic Literature', *Mich. L. Rev.* 70 (1971) 195–220, reprinted in *Corporate Practice Commentator* 14 (1973) App. II, 1–33.

(6) (with J.P. Gordus) 'A Case from Archbishop Stratford's Audience Act Book and Some Comments on the Book and its Value', *Bulletin of Medieval Canon Law* 2 (n.s.) (1972) 45–59.

(7) 'Some Thoughts on Michigan's Copy of the Argentoratene Gratian', *Law Quadrangle Notes* 17 (Fall, 1972) 8–11.

(8) Review, Arthur Schiller, *An American Experience in Roman Law*, in *Mich. L. Rev.* 71 (1973) 1275–85.

(9) Review, John Noonan, *Power to Dissolve*, in *Quis Custodiet?* (Easter, 1973) 59–64.

(10) (with T.E. Kauper and P.W. Martin) *Cases and Materials on Property: An Introduction to the Concept and the Institution* (St. Paul: West Publishing Co., 1974), lxiii, 1501 pp.

(11) 'The Civil Law in England [review article on Brian Levack, *The Civil Lawyers in England*]', in *Yale L.J.* 84 (1974) 167–181.

(12) 'Roman Canon Law in the Medieval English Church: Stubbs v. Maitland Re-Examined after Seventy-Five Years in the Light of Some Records from the Church Courts', *Mich. L. Rev.* 72 (1974) 647–716.

(13) 'Change in the American Law of Landlord and Tenant', *Modern L. Rev.* 37 (1974) 242–63.

(14) (with P. Martin) *A Course in Basic Property* (St. Paul: West Publishing Co., 1975), xv, 392 pp.

(15) 'The Policy of Alexander the Third's Consent Theory of Marriage', in S. Kuttner, ed., *Proceedings of the Fourth International Congress of*

Medieval Canon Law, Monumenta Iuris Canonici, C:5 (Biblioteca Apostolica Vaticana: Città del Vaticano, 1976) 251–81.

(16) Review, Anne Lefebvre-Teillard, *Les officialités à la veille du Concile de Trente*, in *Mich. L. Rev.* 74 (1976) 644–53.

(17) 'Scandal and the Church's New Matrimonial Jurisprudence, *Law and Justice* 52/53 (Hilary/Easter, 1977) 34–51.

(18) 'Comparative Reflections on the "New Matrimonial Jurisprudenceö of the Roman Catholic Church', *Mich. L. Rev.* 75 (1977) 994–1020.

(19) 'The Case of the Man Who Fell Into the Tiber: The Roman Law of Marriage at the Time of the Glossators', *Am. J. of Legal History* 22 (1978) 1–53.

(20) Review, John Barton and T.F.T. Plucknett (eds.), *Doctor and Student*, in *Tijdschrift voor Rechtsgeschiedenis* 47 (1979) 182–86.

(21) 'Comparative Family Law: Law and Social Change? [review article on Mary Ann Glendon, *State, Law and Family*', in *Mich. L. Rev.* 77 (1979) 350–62.

(22) 'What Causes Fundamental Legal Ideas? Marital Property in England and France in the Thirteenth Century', *Mich. L. Rev.* 78 (1979) 59–88.

(23) 'The Interaction of Law and Religion in the Middle Ages', *Mercer L. Rev.* 31 (1980) 466–476.

(24) 'The Future of the Concept of Property Predicted from its Past', in J. Roland Pennock and John W. Chapman (eds.), *Property*, Nomos, 22 (New York: New York University Press, 1980), 28–68.

(25) 'Foreword' to Bruce W. Frier, *Landlords and Tenants in Imperial Rome* (Princeton: Princeton Press, 1980), xi-xv.

(26) 'Proof by Witnesses in the Church Courts of Medieval England: An Imperfect Reception of the Learned Law', in M. Arnold, T. Green, S. Scully, S. White (eds.), *On the Laws and Customs of England: Essays in Honor of Samuel E. Thorne* (Chapel Hill: North Carolina University Press, 1981), 127–58.

(27) (with N. Adams) *Select Cases from the Ecclesiastical Courts of the Province of Canterbury, c. 1200–1301*, Selden Society Publications, 95 (London: Selden Society, 1981), xxx, *119*, 756 pp.

(28) 'Lyndwood's Gloss *propriarum uxorum*: Marital Property and the *ius commune* in Fifteenth Century England', in *Europäisches Rechtsdenken in Geschichte und Gegenwart: Festschrift für Helmut Coing* (C.H. Beck: Muünchen: 1982) 1: 19–37.

(29) Review, Ralph Houlbrooke, *Church Courts and the People during the English Reformation, 1520–1570*, *J. Modern Hist.*, 54 (1982) 550–52.

(30) Review, Alan Watson, *The Making of the Civil Law*, *Mich. L. Rev.* 81 (1983) 972–76.

(31) 'The Canon Law on the Formation of Marriage and Social Practice in the Later Middle Ages', *J. Family Hist.* 8 (1983) 144–58.

(32) (with T. Kauper and P. Martin) *Cases and Materials on Property: An Introduction to the Concept and the Institution*, 2d ed. (St. Paul: West Publishing Co. 1983), lxxviii, 1362 pp.

(33) 'The Dating of Alexander the Third's Marriage Decretals: Dauvillier Revisited after Fifty Years', *Zeitschrift der Savigny-Stiftung für Rechtsgeschichte* 99 (Kanonistische Abteilung 68) (1982) 70–124.

(34) (with T. Kauper and P. Martin) *A Course in Basic Property*, 2d ed. (St. Paul: West Publishing Co., 1983), xii, 317 pp.

(35) 'Prophecy and Politics: Reflections on a Recent Campaign (Mother Elizabeth Seton Lecture, January 17, 1985)', [Portsmouth Abbey School,] *Winter Bulletin, 1985* (Portsmouth [RI]: Portsmouth Abbey School, 1985) 4–10.

(36) 'Church Court Records on the Continent and in England', in H. Coing und K.W. Nörr (eds). *Englische und kontinentale Rechtsgeschichte: ein Forschungsprojekt*, Comparative Studies in Continental and Anglo-American Legal History, 1 (Berlin: Duncker & Humblot, 1985) 63–71.

(37) 'Noodt, Titius, and the Natural Law School: The Occupation of Wild Animals and the Intersection of Property and Tort', in J. Ankum, J. Spruit, et F. Wubbe (eds.), *Satura Roberto Feenstra* (Presses Universitaires de Fribourg: Fribourg [CH], 1985) 609–29.

(38) Review, Antonio García y García, ed., *Constitutiones Concilii Quarti Lateranensis*, *Speculum* 61 (1986) 149–50.

(39) Review, Kenneth Pennington, ed., *Johannis Teutonici Apparatus glossarum in Compilationem tertiam*, *Am. J. Legal Hist.* 30 (1986) 79–85.

(40) '*Animalia Ferae Naturae*: Rome, Bologna, Leyden, Oxford and Queen's County, N.Y.', in R. Bagnall and J. Harris (eds.), *Studies in Roman Law in Memory of A. Arthur Schiller* (Leiden: E.J. Brill, 1986) 39–63.

(41) Review, L. Theo Maes, *Recht heeft vele significatie*, *J. Law & Hist.* 4 (1986) 473–74.

(42) Review, Christopher R. Cheney, *The English Church and its Laws*, *Zeitschrift der Savigny-Stiftung für Rechtsgeschichte*, 103 (Kanonistische Abteilung 72) (1986) 434–35.

(43) *Why the History of Canon Law Is Not Written* (Selden Lecture, July 3, 1984) (London: Selden Society, 1986), 31 pp.

(44) 'Law, Civil--*Corpus Juris*, Revival and Spread', in Joseph R. Strayer, ed., *Dictionary of the Middle Ages* (New York: Charles Scribners Sons, 1987) 7:418–25.

(45) 'On Translating the *Digest* [review essay of Alan Watson, ed., *The Digest of Justinian*]', *Stanford Law Review* 39 (1987) 1057–77.

(46) Review, Brian Tierney, *Religion, Law, and the Growth of Constitutional Thought, 1150–1650*, *J. Legal Educ.* 37 (1987) 444–48.

(47) 'Preface' and 'Introduction' to L.C. Hector and Michael E. Hager (eds.), *Year Books of Richard II: 8–10 Richard II, 1385–1387*, Ames Foundation, Year Books Series, 4 (n.p.: The Ames Foundation, 1987), v-xii.

(48) 'Introduction' to Henry Fielding, *An institute of the pleas of the Crown: an exhibition of the Hyde Collection at the Houghton Library, 1987* (Cambridge, MA: Houghton Library, 1987).

(49) 'Institutional History from Archival History: The Court of Canterbury Rolls', in *The Weightier Matters of the Law: Essays in Law and Religion, A Tribute to Harold J. Berman*, John Witte, Jr., and Frank S. Alexander, eds. (Studies in Religion, 51) (Atlanta, GA: Scholars Press, 1988), pp. 33–55.

(50) (ed) *The Records of the Medieval Ecclesiastical Courts: Reports of the Working Group on Church Courts Records* 1: *The Continent*, Comparative Studies in Continental and Anglo-American Legal History, 6 (Berlin: Duncker & Humblot: 1989), 241 p.

(51) Review, R.H. Helmholz, ed., *Select Cases on Defamation to 1600*, *Speculum: A Journal of Medieval Studies* 65 (1990) 419–23.

(52) 'Property Law', in *Encyclopaedia Britannica: Macropaedia* vol. 26 (1992 ed), pp. 180–205.

(53) 'Comment on R.H. Helmholz, "Conflicts Between Religious Law and Secular Lawö', *Cardozo Law Review* 12 (1991) 729–35.

(54) 'A Legal Historian Looks at the Case Method', *Northern Kentucky Law Journal* 19 (1991) 17–47.

(55) '*Ius commune*, Canon Law, and Common Law in England', *Tulane Law Review* 66 (1992) 1745–80.

(56) 'English and French Marriage Cases: Might the Differences Be Explained by Differences in the Property Systems?', in L. Bonfield, ed., *Marriage, Property and Succession* Comparative Studies in Continental and Anglo-American Legal History, 10 (Berlin: Duncker & Humblot, 1992), pp. 339–66, reprinted in A. García y García and P. Weimar, eds., *Miscellanea Domenico Maffei Dicata: Historia - Ius - Studium* (Goldach: Keip, 1995) 4: 283–310.

(57) '"Clandestine" Marriage in the Later Middle Ages: A Reply', *Law and History Review* 10 (1992) 315–22.

(58) (with T. Kauper and P. Martin) *Cases and Materials on Property: An Introduction to the Concept and the Institution*, 3d ed. (St. Paul: West Publishing Co. 1993), lvii, 1188 pp.

(59) (with T. Kauper and P. Martin) *A Course in Basic Property*, 3d ed. (St. Paul: West Publishing Co., 1993), xiv, 318 pp.

(60) 'Women Plaintiffs in Marriage Cases in the Court of York in the Later Middle Ages: What Can We Learn From the Numbers?', in S.S. Walker (ed), *Wife and Widow in Medieval England* (Ann Arbor: University of Michigan Press, 1993), pp. 183–213.

(61) Review, R.H. Helmholz, *Roman Canon Law in Reformation England*, *Law and History Review* 11 (1993) 442–48.

(62) 'Introduction' to Carol Symes (ed), *History in deed: medieval society & the law in England, 1100–1600: an exhibition of deeds & charters from the Harvard Law School Library, November-December 1993* ([Cambridge]: President and Fellows of Harvard College, c1993).

(63) (ed) *The Records of the Medieval Ecclesiastical Courts: Reports of the Working Group on Church Courts Records 2: England*, Comparative Studies in Continental and Anglo-American Legal History, 7 (Berlin: Duncker & Humblot: 1994), 262 p.

(64) (ed) *Samuel Edmund Thorne: 1907–1994* (Cambridge, MA: Harvard Law School, 1995), 36 pp.

(65) 'Theology, Law & Women's Ordination: *Ordinatio sacerdotalis* One Year Later', *Commonweal*, June 2, 1995, pp. 11–16.

(66) (with T.N. Bisson and Giles Constable), 'Samuel Edmund Thorne', *Speculum* 70 (1995) 732–34.

(67) Review, *Gratian: The Treatise on Laws (Decretum DD. 1–20 with the Ordinary Gloss*, in *Catholic Historical Review* 81 (1995) 427–29.

(68) 'Was there a change in marriage law in the late Middle Ages?', *Rivista internazionale di diritto comune* 6 (1995) 49–80.

(69) (with S.E. Thorne, M.E. Hager and M.M. Thorne), *Year Books of Richard II: 6 Richard II, 1382–1383*, Ames Foundation, Year Books Series, 2 (n.p.: The Ames Foundation, 1996), *213*, 252 (doubled), 253–344.

(70) 'The Monastic Judge: Social Practice, Formal Rule and the Medieval Canon Law of Incest', in *De Iure Canonico Medii Aevi: Festschrift für Rudolf Weigand*, Studia Gratiania 27 (Romae: LAS, 1996), 49–69.

(71) 'Comparative Legal History in North America', *Tijdschrift voor Rechtsgeschiedenis*, 65 (1997) 1–17.

(72) Review, R.B. Outhwaite, *Clandestine Marriage in England, Journal of Modern History*, 70 (1998) 453–55.

(73) (with M.E. Basile, D.R. Coquillette, J.F. Bestor), *Lex Mercatoria and Legal Pluralism: A Late Thirteenth-Century Treatise and its Afterlife* (Cambridge, MA: The Ames Foundation, 1998), *212*, 42 (doubled), 43–118.

(74) 'Biology and the Origins of the English Jury', *Law and History Review*, 17 (1999) 591–96.

(75) 'An Upbeat View of Fourteenth-Century English Justice [review article on Anthony Musson and W.M. Ormrod, *The Evolution of English Justice: Law, Politics and Society in the Fourteenth Century*]', *Michigan Law Review*, 98 (2000) 1725–37.

(76) 'Malchus's Ear: Reflections on Classical Canon Law as a Religious Legal System', in M. Hoeflich, ed., *Lex et Romanitas: Essays for Alan Watson* (Berkeley, CA: The Robbins Collection, 2000), 91–120.

(77) 'Gerard Pucelle as a Canon Lawyer: Life and the Battle Abbey Case', in R. Helmholz, P. Mikat, J. Müller, and M. Stolleis (eds.), *Grundlagen des Rechts: Festschrift für Peter Landau zum 65. Geburtstag* (Paderborn: Schönigh, 2000), 333–48.

(78) '*Ius* in the Subjective Sense in Roman Law: Reflections on Villey and Tierney', in D. Maffei, I. Birocchi, M. Caravale, E. Conte, and U. Petronio (eds.), *A Ennio Cortese* (Rome: Il Cigno Edizioni, 2001), 1: 506–35.

(79) Review, J. H. Baker, *A Catalogue of English Legal Manuscripts in Cambridge University Library, Manuscripta* 43/44 (1999/2000) (published in 2003), 193–94.

(80) 'The Emergence of the Crime-Tort Distinction in England', in *Conflict in Medieval Europe: Changing Perspectives on Society and Culture* (Ashgate: Aldershot, 2003), 219–28.

(81) 'P 265 = JL 16635?: A Mild Heresy Stated and Defended', in M. Ascheri, et. al. (eds.), *"Ins Wasser geworfen und Ozeanae durchquert": Festschrift für Knut Wolfgang Nörr* (Köln: Böhlau, 2003), 165–87.

(82) 'Equity in the Courts of Merchants', *Tijdschrift voor Rechtsgeschiedenis* 72 (2004) 1–35.

(83) 'Medieval and Early Modern *Lex mercatoria*: An Attempt at the *probatio diabolica*', *Chicago Journal of International Law*, 5 (2004) 21–36.

(84) 'Pucelle, Gerard (*d.* 1184)', in *Oxford Dictionary of National Biography* (2004), s.n.

(85) 'Bassianus, That Is to Say, Bazianus?--Bazianus and Johannes Bassianus on Marriage', *Rivista internazionale di diritto commune*, 14 (2003) [published 2005] 41–82.

(86) 'Benvenuto Stracca's *De mercatura*: Was There a *Lex mercatoria* in Sixteenth Century Italy?', in Vito Piergiovanni, ed., *From* lex mercatoria *to Commercial Law*, Comparative Studies in Continental and Anglo-American Legal History, 24 (Berlin: Duncker & Humblot, 2005), 69–120.

(87) 'A Crisis of Law? Reflections on the Church and the Law over the Centuries', *The Jurist* 65 (2005) 1–30.

(88) 'Bassianus, That Is to Say, Bazianus?--Johannes Bassianus on Marriage', in O. Condorelli, ed., *'Panta rei': Studi dedicati a Manlio Bellomo* (Roma: Il Cigno Edizione, 2004) [appeared in 2005], vol. 2, pp. 179–204.

(89) 'Genesis in Western Canon Law', *The Jewish Law Annual*, 16 (2006) 155–84.

(90) 'Johannes Faventinus on Marriage (With an Appendix Revisiting the Question of the Dating of Alexander III's Marriage Decretals)', in Wolfgang P. Müller and Mary E. Sommar, ed., *Medieval Church Law and the Origins of the Western Legal Tradition: A Tribute to Kenneth Pennington* (Washington, DC: Catholic University of America Press, 2006), 179–97

(91) 'Comparative Law Before the *Code Napoléon*', in Mathias Reimann and Reinhard Zimmermann, ed., *The Oxford Handbook of Comparative Law* (Oxford: Oxford University Press, 2006), 3–32.

(92) 'Aggadic Stories About Medieval Western Jurists?', *Diné Israel: Studies in* Halakhah *and Jewish Law*, 24 (2007) 209*–215*.

(93) Review, R. H. Helmholz, The Canon Law and Ecclesiastical Jurisdiction from 597 to the 1640s, Oxford History of the Laws of England, 1, in *Law and History Review*, 25 (2007) 217–19.

(94) Review, Anders Winroth, *The Making of Gratian's Decretum*, in *Law and History Review*, 25 (2007) 401–3.

(95) *Law, Marriage, and Society in the Later Middle Ages: Arguments About Marriage in Five Courts* (Cambridge and New York: Cambridge University Press, 2007). xix, 672 p. (with an additional 304 pp. published 'online' at http://www.cambridge.org/resources/0521877288/5363_9780521877282tc_p673-976.pdf)

(96) 'Private Law Without the State and During its Formation', *American Journal of Comparative Law*, 56 (2008) 541–66, *reprinted in* Nils Jansen and Ralf Michaels, ed., *Beyond the State: Rethinking Private Law* (Tübingen: Mohr Siebeck, 2008), 121–43.

(97) 'Reform, Renewal, Religion and Social Discipline: Reflections of a Medievalist', in Peri Bearman, Wolfhart Heinrichs, and Bernard G. Weiss, ed., *The Law Applied: Contextualizing the Islamic Shari'a: A Volume in Honor of Frank E. Vogel* (London, 2008), 1–21.

(98) 'Reflections on the Editing of Medieval Church Court Records', in Vincenzo Colli and Emanuele Conte, ed., *Iuris Historia: Liber Amicorum Gero Dolazalek* (Berkeley, 2008), 345–53.

(99) 'The Western Canon Law of Marriage: A Doctrinal Introduction', in *The Islamic Marriage Contract: Case Studies in Islamic Family Law*, Asifa Quraishi and Frank E. Vogel ed., Harvard Series in Islamic Law, 6 (Cambridge, MA: Harvard University Press, 2008), 46–56.

(100) 'Whither Legal History', in Daniel W. Hamilton and Alfred L. Brophy, ed., *Transformations in American Legal History: Essays in Honor of Professor Morton J. Horwitz* (Cambridge: Harvard Law School, 2009), 327–43.

(101) 'Papyrology and 3 Caines 175', *Law and History Review*, 27 (2009) 179–84.

(102) '*Ex officio* Cases in the Officiality of Paris, 1384–1387', in Bernard d'Alteroche, et. al., ed., *Mélanges en l'honneur d'Anne Lefebvre-Teillard* (Paris: Éditions Panthéon-Assas, 2009), 393–412.

(103) Review, Jan K. Bulman, *The Court Book of Mende and the Secular Lordship of the Bishop*, in *Catholic Historical Review* 95 (2009), 601–2.

(104) Review, Giuliano Marchetto, *Il divorzio imperfetto: I giuristi medievali e la separazione dei coniugi*, in *American Historical Review*, 115 (2010) 270–71.

(105) Review, Anne Lefebvre-Teillard, *Autour de l'enfant: Du droit canonique et romain médiéval au Code Civil de 1804*, in *Law and History Review*, 28 (2010) 260–62.

(106) 'What Difference Does It Make If Marriage Is a Sacrament? An Historical Approach', in Scott FitzGibbon, Lynne D. Wardle and A. Scott Loveless, ed., *Jurisprudence of Marriage and Other Intimate Relationships* (Buffalo: William S. Hein & Co., Inc., 2010), 15–35.

(107) Review, *The History of Medieval Canon Law in the Classical Period, 1140–1234: From Gratian to the Decretals of Pope Gregory IX*, Wilfried Hartmann and Kenneth Pennington, ed., *Zeitschrift der Savigny-Stiftung für Rechtsgeschichte* 127 (Kanonistische Abteilung 96) (2010).

(108) 'What Happened in the English Legal System in the Fourteenth Century and Why Would Anyone Want to Know?', *Southern Methodist University Law Review*, 63 (2010).

(109) 'Law, Marriage, and Society in the Later Middle Ages: A Look at the English and "Franco-Belgian" Regions', in *Proceedings of the Thirteenth International Congress of Medieval Canon Law (Esztergom-Budapest, August 3–9, 2008)*, ed. Peter Erdö and Sz. Anzelm Szuromi, Monumenta Iuris Canonici C:14 (Città del Vaticano: Biblioteca Apostolica Vaticana, 2010), 17–39.

(110) 'Malchus's Ear Revisited: Reflections on Classical Canon Law as a Religious Legal System', *Law & Justice*, 165 (Trinity/Michaelmas 2010) 144–58.

(111) '*Ius* in Roman law', in John Witte, Jr., and Frank S. Alexander, ed., *Christianity and Human Rights: An Introduction* (New York: Cambridge University Press, 2011), 64–80.

(112) 'The Mysterious Canonist Bazianus on Marriage', in Kenneth Pennington and Melodie Harris Eichbauer (ed.), *Law as Profession and Practice in Medieval Europe: Essays in Honor of James Brundage* (Farnham, Surrey: Ashgate, 2011), 263–92.

(113) 'Comparative Approaches to Marriage in the Later Middle Ages', in Mia Korpiola, ed., *Regional Variations in Matrimonial Law and Custom in Europe, 1150–1600* (Leiden: Brill, 2011), 289–316.

(114) 'Diritto, matrimonio e società nel tardo medioevo: Considerazioni sull'area inglese e area «franco-belga»', *Rivista storica italiana,* 123 (2011) 1129–1179. [Basically a translation of no. 109].

(115) 'The Legal Professions of Fourteenth-Century England', in Susanne Jenks, Jonathan Rose and Christopher Whittick, ed., *Lawyers and Texts: Studies in Medieval Legal History in Honour of Paul Brand,* Medieval Law and Its Practice, 13 (Leiden: Brill, 2012) 227–251.

(116) 'Thoughts on Diocesan Statutes: England and France, 1200–1500', in Uta-Renate Blumenthal, Anders Winroth and Peter Landau, ed., *Canon Law, Religion, and Politics: Liber Amicorum Robert Somerville* (Washington, DC: Catholic University of America Press, 2012), 253–271.

(117) '"The Hypostasis of a Prophecy": Legal Realism and Legal History', in Matthew Dyson and David Ibbetson, ed., *Law and Legal Process: Substantive Law and Procedure in English Law* (Cambridge [UK]: Cambridge University Press, 2013) 1–16.

(118) 'By Way of a Conclusion', in Véronique Beaulande-Barraud and Martine Charageat, ed., *Les officialités dans l'Europe médievale et moderne: Des tribunaux pour une société chrétienne,* Ecclesia Militans, 2 (Turnhout: Brepols, 2014) 325–38.

(119) (with Stuart McManus), 'Philologia ancilla historiae: An Emendation to lex Burgundionum, 42,2', *Zeitschrift der Savigny-Stiftung für Rechtsgeschichte* (*Romanistische Abteilung*) 113 (2014) 414–423.

(120) 'The Role of the Humanists and the Second Scholastic in the Development of European Marriage Law from the Sixteenth to the Nineteenth Centuries', in Jordan Ballor, Wim Decock, Michael Germann, and Laurent Waelkens, ed., *Law and Religion: The Legal Teachings of the Protestant and Catholic Reformations,* Refo500 Academic Series, 20 (Göttingen: Vandenhoeck & Ruprecht, 2014) 45–62.

(121) *Appeals to the Privy Council from the American Colonies: An Annotated Digital Catalogue,* comp. Sharon Hamby O'Connor and Mary Sarah Bilder with Charles Donahue, Jr. (Cambridge, MA: The Ames Foundation, 2014 (online edition), 2014 (paper edition). (Awarded the Joseph L. Andrews Legal Literature Award by the Association of American Law Libraries in 2015.)

(122) 'Ethical Standards for Advocates and Proctors of the Court of Ely (1374–1382) Revisited', in Troy L. Harris, ed., *Studies in Canon Law*

and Common Law in Honor of R. H. Helmholz (Berkeley: The Robbins Collection, 2015) 41–60.

Forthcoming

'Procedure in the Courts of the *Ius commune*', in Kenneth Pennington, ed., *The History of Courts and Procedure in Medieval Canon Law*, History of Medieval Canon Law, forthcoming Catholic University of America Press, 2015.

'The Ecclesiastical Courts: Introduction', in Kenneth Pennington, ed., *The History of Courts and Procedure in Medieval Canon Law*, History of Medieval Canon Law, forthcoming Catholic University of America Press, 2015.

(with Sara McDougall) 'France and Adjoining Areas', in Kenneth Pennington, ed., *The History of Courts and Procedure in Medieval Canon Law*, History of Medieval Canon Law, forthcoming Catholic University of America Press, 2015.

'What Happened to Marriage Law in the Early Modern Period?', forthcoming in a still untitled book on marriage and marriage litigation in the early modern period, edited by Silvana Seidel Menchi.

Unpublished

'Did the Law Achieve Justice in Fourteenth-Century England? There Were Those Who Had Their Doubts', paper given at the New England Medieval Conference, Harvard University, 30 October, 2009, to be incorporated in ongoing work on heading to the volume on the fourteenth-century in the *Oxford History of the Laws of England*.

Marriage, Family and Children: Twenty Years of Research (paper given at the International Congress of Medieval Canon Law, Syracuse, August, 1996).

Was There a Change in Marriage Law in the Late Middle Ages? (paper given at a conference on Family and Society in the Late Middle Ages, Vancouver, BC, November, 1992).

Chaucer's *Raptus* (paper given at the Harvard English Department Medieval Studies Group, March, 1991).

The Code of Canon Law (1983) and the Talmud (paper given at the faculty seminar of the Boston College Law School, May, 1987).

The Case of Two Williams: Alexander III and Social Reality in Thirteenth Century England (paper given at the Roman Law Society, Champaign, IL, May, 1987).

The Use of Computers in Legal Historical Research (paper given at the annual meeting of the American Society for Legal History, Newark, October, 1984).

About the Contributors and Editors

Morris Sheppard Arnold is a judge on the United States Court of Appeals for the Eighth Circuit, retired 2013.

Sir John Baker QC, FBA, is Emeritus Downing Professor of the Laws of England and Honorary Fellow of St. Catharine's College, University of Cambridge.

Robert Berkhofer is Associate Professor of History at Western Michigan University.

Mary Sarah Bilder is Professor of Law and Michael and Helen Lee Distinguished Scholar, Boston College Law School.

Paul Brand is Professor of English Legal History and Emeritus Fellow at All Souls College, Oxford University.

Wim Decock is Research Professor in Legal History at the Law Faculty of the University of Leuven, Belgium, and Associate Researcher at the Max-Planck-Institute for European Legal History in Frankfurt am Main.

Anna di Robilant is Professor of Law at Boston University School of Law.

Charles Donahue is Paul A. Freund Professor of Law at Harvard Law School.

Anne J. Duggan is Emeritus Professor of Medieval History and Fellow at King's College London.

Abigail Firey is a Professor in the Department of History at the University of Kentucky.

Bruce W. Frier is the John and Teresa D'Arms Distinguished University Professor of Classics and Roman Law at the University of Michigan.

Joseph Goering is Professor of History at the University of Toronto.

Thomas A. Green is the John Philip Dawson Collegiate Professor of Law Emeritus and Professor of History Emeritus at the University of Michigan and is an Affiliate Scholar at Oberlin College.

Richard H. Helmholz is the Ruth Wyatt Rosenson Distinguished Service Professor of Law at the University of Chicago Law School.

Paul R. Hyams is Professor Emeritus of Medieval History at Cornell University.

Emily Kadens is Professor of Law at Northwestern University School of Law.

Elizabeth Papp Kamali is Assistant Professor of Law at Harvard Law School.

Amalia D. Kessler is the Lewis Talbot and Nadine Hearn Shelton Professor of International Legal Studies and Professor (by courtesy) of History at Stanford University.

Adam J. Kosto is Professor of History at Columbia University.

Peter Landau is Professor Emeritus at Ludwig-Maximilians-Universität München.

Anne Lefebvre-Teillard is Professor Emerita of Law at University of Paris II.

F. Donald Logan is Professor Emeritus of History, Emmanuel College, Boston.

Sara McDougall is Associate Professor of History at John Jay College and the CUNY Graduate Center.

Shannon McSheffrey is Professor of History at Concordia University, Montreal.

Martha L. Minow is the Morgan and Helen Chu Professor of Law and the Dean of Harvard Law School.

Ken Pennington is Kelly-Quinn Professor of Ecclesiastical and Legal History at The Catholic University of America, School of Canon Law, The Columbus School of Law.

David J. Seipp is Professor of Law and Law Alumni Scholar at Boston University School of Law.

Robert Somerville is Tremaine Professor of Religion, and Professor of History at Columbia University.

Joshua C. Tate is Associate Professor of Law at Southern Methodist University.

Anders Winroth is Forst Family Professor of History, Yale University.

John Witte, Jr. is Robert W. Woodruff Professor of Law, McDonald Distinguished Professor and Director of the Center for the Study of Law and Religion at Emory University.

Methodus ad facilem historiarum cognitionem: Autobiographical and Methodological Reflections

Charles Donahue

I was asked to provide a brief introduction to this volume in which I outlined my "intellectual journey." That sounds just a tad pretentious; perhaps I can rephrase the question: "How did you end up doing what you do?"

Autobiographical

Unlike many of today's students, I was not programmed from the beginning. My parents were both academics, my father a professor of English (with a focus on medieval literature and language, ranging into texts in Germanic and Celtic languages generally) and my mother a high-school English teacher, but neither of them pushed me in the direction of an academic career. Indeed, there were times when my father urged me against it. Dinner-table conversation in the Donahue household, however, frequently focused on literature and language, and my mother was an enthusiastic teacher who talked a lot about what she was doing and why she was doing it. My parents also sat on me to do well in school, an effort that required some sitting. I was not always a diligent student.

My parents were both products of public grammar and high schools, and were great believers in public education. The public schools, however, in the outer suburbs of New York where we lived were not, at that time, particularly good, and my mother ended up as a teacher at the Bedford Rippowam School, a private country-day school near where we lived. The school made up, to some extent, for the modest compensation that it gave its teachers by allowing its teachers' children to attend the school tuition-free; so I went. Rippowam was quite rigorous academically. By the time I graduated from the eighth grade I had excellent preparation in English, good preparation in math, and two years of Latin.

For boys, Rippowam did not go beyond the eighth grade. We were expected to go to boarding school at that point. Our family were practicing Catholics, serious about our religion and committed to the notion that religion could, and should, be approached intellectually. What there was of that at Rippowam—and there was some—was pretty aggressively Protestant. (What Jews there were kept quiet about it.)

Good Catholic schools were quite far from where we lived. Commuting was a possibility but not an attractive one. I ended up going to a boarding school, Portsmouth Priory (now Abbey) School in Rhode Island, at the time a single-sex school. It was located in a monastery of the English Benedictine Congregation, and many, though not all, of the teachers were monks.

Much of what I am today, both personally and intellectually, I owe to Portsmouth. I took four years of both Latin and Greek. I learned some German (not nearly enough). I taught myself French on the side, and was able in my last year to take the third-year French course and audit the fifth. Everyone was required to take four years of what was then called Christian Doctrine, and might be described today, without too much exaggeration, as theology. In the ninth grade, we read most of all four Gospels, and were introduced to what was not called, but what certainly was, the historical-critical method, by a monk who prior to his conversion to Catholicism had taught biblical theology in a Protestant seminary. In the tenth grade we read an elementary seminary textbook in moral theology, and argued with each other and the teacher about the application of rules to particular situations. In the eleventh grade the focus was on Augustine, in the twelfth on Aquinas. It was at Portsmouth that I learned how to listen to and enjoy classical music, how to sing Gregorian chant, and how to practice my religion through participation in the liturgy. All these things have remained with me. Looking back on it, my high-school education was also a bit unbalanced. I got through pre-calculus, but took no more math, and I took no science.

I did well at Portsmouth and was admitted to Harvard College with advanced standing. That meant that I could graduate in three years. Since I was planning to go to graduate school, and money was tight, the opportunity to do so was too good not to take. That also meant that I should concentrate in what I was already well prepared to do, so I concentrated in Classics and English, with a focus in the former on Greek and in the latter on the earlier periods (Chaucer and Shakespeare).

That I was going to go to graduate school seemed foreordained. What I was going to go in was not. I loved Greek literature, but I found the language hard. I was less fond of Latin literature, but the language came easier. Everyone always said that I was whiz at languages, and languages did come easier to me than they do to some people. Looking back on it, however, particularly from the point of view of someone who is noticing some decline in his mental faculties, I think I may not be particularly good at memorizing large numbers of words. Compared to Greek and German, Latin and French have rather limited vocabularies, and I have always been, and remain, better at the latter than the former. That fact, coupled with the fact that jobs in Classics were already difficult to obtain, suggested that I ought to go to graduate school in English, and that was where I was headed until the autumn of my last year in college. I woke up one morning, when interviews for a Wilson fellowship had already been scheduled, and realized that I just did not want to go to graduate school in English.

So what to do? My grandfather had been a lawyer, although he died before I was born. My family knew some lawyers, and I did too. I had some idea of what lawyers did, though not much. I thought of them as wordsmiths, and thought I might be good at it. I had taken a Kuder Preference Test. Professor of English was not one of the categories that it scored, but my score in law was off the charts. So why not?

I applied to both Yale and Harvard and got into both. Yale offered me a scholarship. Harvard's process at the time required that one apply for a scholarship after one had been admitted. I had not been particularly happy as an undergraduate at Harvard. My family had strong Yale connections. So why not?

I knew very little about the difference between the Harvard and Yale law schools, which were, at the time, substantial. I knew that Yale was smaller. I had been to small high school, and had not been particularly good at negotiating gigantine Harvard. Even in high school, I had always wanted to choose my own courses (and did better when I could). Yale had a more flexible curriculum. There was not much more to the choice of Yale than that. I had heard some things about a different approach to law in the two places, but was not in any position to process what I heard, because I had no idea what I was getting into.

It turned out to be a good choice. Yale was good to me and for me. I enjoyed the first year. I thought of it as engineering with words. There were those who had concentrated in the social sciences, and I realized that I was going to have to get more comfortable with that form of reasoning, but language and literature served me well. Despite missing some turns that were pretty obvious to anybody who knew anything about economics or political science (which I did not), and making a glaring error in moral philosophy on one of my first semester exams (which I should not have made), I ended up easily making the law journal at the end of the second semester.

So where is history in all of this? History had come easily to me when I was in grade school. That, of course, is partly the result of the fact that history in grade schools at the time was not particularly demanding. From a very early age I was always uncomfortable with the generalizations that frequently passed for history. Part of this had to do with the fact that I was a Catholic in a school where the dominant culture was Protestant. The Pilgrims had come to America to escape religious oppression, and therefore they espoused religious liberty. That's so far from the truth that we probably ought to say that it's just wrong. But an inquiring little boy, wondering about that, might find on his parents' bookshelves a book that said that the first state to espouse religious toleration was Lord Baltimore's Catholic Maryland. (That's not right either, but it's closer to right.)

I had a quite good American history course in the eighth grade. The history teacher split up the class and got us to debate both sides of the American Revolution. The English teacher picked up on this and got us to produce a school assembly in which we recited quotations from writers on both sides of the issue. Mine was from Edmund Burke; my best friend's was from Samuel Johnson. I did enough work in the standard American history course at Portsmouth that I was able to do well on the American history advanced placement exam. I also took a course in medieval history, where we used Carlton Hayes's college textbook. We did not do much with primary sources in that course, but the teacher was a monk who been an architect before he joined the monastery. He had us go to the library and look at pictures of cathedrals and then describe a couple of them from different periods on the exam. I took three history courses at Harvard. Sterling Dow's Greek History, Carl Friedrich's history of ancient and medieval political thought, and Robert McCloskey's American constitutional history. Dow required papers on puzzles that were presented by primary sources: for example, "Can we rely on Homer's count in the Iliad of the number of ships that went to Troy?" McCloskey had us read the cases. I'm not sure that he even assigned his *American Supreme Court*, though most of us knew about it.

Had I spent four years at Harvard rather than three, I might have moved into history. In that case, I might have gone to graduate school in history, and the whole story would have been different. As it was, I really did not think about a history concentration. Part of it was the desire to get out of Harvard as fast as possible. Part of it was that at that age I did not think that history was challenging enough.

My assignment on the law journal was *Escobedo v. Illinois*, which was pending before the Supreme Court. One could, of course, have analyzed the case from the point of politics, or, perhaps, economics, or just pure legal doctrine. (The latter was not really a possibility at Yale, both because of the nature of the doctrine involved in *Escobedo* and because nobody at Yale at the time, or now, believes that legal doctrine solves problems, or at least not hard ones.) My instinct was to find out as much as I could in the time available about the history of the right to counsel in criminal cases. I began with the *Leges Henrici Primi* (Latin helped; there was no translation at the time). I looked at the debates about counsel in criminal cases in the seventeenth century and at the various forerunners of the Sixth Amendment in the American colonies. I ended up with an argument that counsel had always been provided when the accused was confronted by the state in a situation in which the expertise of the state officers overcame his. (That argument is so far from the truth that we probably should say that it was just wrong.) Now, I argued, that confrontation took place at the time of police interrogation. Police interrogation was unknown at common law. There were no police, just Dogberry and Verges. Hence, the Court today should extend the right to counsel back to police interrogation.

Fortunately, at the time, student pieces in the Yale Law Journal were published anonymously. The historical mistakes that the piece contains would be a considerable embarrassment were it known that I wrote it. The journal also asked W. H. Dunham, the distinguished English constitutional historian in the Yale History Department, to look at the piece. He was, as he should have been, uncomfortable with the diachronic argument that it contained, and urged the editors to leave out the parts about the Middle Ages. He did think that there was something to my use of the seventeenth-century debates about right to counsel, and thought that it might be good to start with those. The editors did not follow his advice. That was bad for the piece as legal history, but great for me. I had caught the bug, and wanted to keep on going with medieval legal history, about which I knew I had a lot to learn.

I had one more year. There was no way in which I could afford to go to graduate school in history. Even if I could have afforded it, I had a military obligation to fulfill. Yale at the time insisted that the students specialize in something in their third year and write a paper about that specialty. I told the dean (and it was the dean himself who made these decisions) that I wanted to specialize in legal history. He said that there were no legal historians on the law faculty (a true statement at the time). I said that the faculty of arts and sciences had two distinguished legal historians (Dunham, and Stephan Kuttner in medieval canon law) and one distinguished legal anthropologist (Leopold Pospíšil). I wanted to work with them. He said "sure," and I spent most of my third year in year-long graduate seminars with the three of them.

It still was not clear that I was going to be an academic. I enjoyed my three years in Washington, two years as an Attorney-Adviser in the Office of the General Counsel of the Air Force and one year as Assistant General Counsel to the President's Commission on Postal Organization—a rather bizarre way to fulfill a military obligation during the Vietnam War. Much as I liked practicing law, however, the legal history bug was still infecting me, and I was not organized enough to do much with it in my off hours. (I published one book review in that period.) So when Mr. Johnson quit and my military obligation was coming to a close, I let it be known that I would be interested in an academic appointment. (That was the way that it was done in those days. One did not apply for teaching jobs, and if one did, one did not get them.) I also interviewed with some law firms and would not have been crushingly disappointed if something did not come through on the academic side.

Something did, however, and I accepted an offer to join the University of Michigan's law faculty in the summer of 1968. Legal history was not on the top of every law school's needs in that period, but Michigan agreed that I could teach one course and write in the area, but, of course, they were also interested in having someone for first-year property (a full-year course at the time). And how about a specialized "real" law course, like Regulated Industries (something that I had done in practice)? Property took some time to learn how to teach. Regulated Industries, and, later, Antitrust, got me into economics, something about which I knew virtually nothing. (One of the great things about a Yale legal education is that the school convinces the students that they can do anything.) I became interested in some pro bono litigation involving the Selective Service system, which led to my arguing a couple of cases in the Sixth Circuit. I was working on a history topic, but I had only three years to get tenure, and I wrote my "tenure piece" on administrative law with particular reference to the Selective Service system.

History was not, however, totally neglected. I began with a seminar that I called "Law, History, and Society." It was modeled, to a great extent, after Dunham's seminar. We dealt with three fairly narrow topics, the deposition of Richard II (a Dunham topic), the formation of marriage in the High Middle Ages (a topic from the Kuttner seminar), and various ways in which medieval and early modern English law had dealt with poverty. The students wrote short papers (no more than five pages) based on primary materials, most of which I translated myself. (Occasionally, it might be a secondary source, but one with a lot of footnotes, so that one could see where the author was getting his or her ideas from.) The students presented the papers in class, and then we went through the documents trying to draw our own conclusions about what they might be saying.

This, of course, was a way for a young teacher who had not taken a graduate degree in history to teach legal history without making a fool out of himself. The method was also well-suited to someone with a background in language and literature. If you want to find out what Shakespeare's sonnets are all about, you read Shakespeare's sonnets. It also focused on the primary sources, without which I was convinced, and remain convinced, that any historical statement is rubbish. It also resonates quite well with what law students learn in the first year of law school, at least if they play the game right. You do not read a treatise, you read the case or the statute, and then you ask what it might mean. I had done well in law school and had never used a commercial outline. The law journal had taught me that what was said in the text was only as good as what the primary sources in the footnotes said, and my job as a law review editor was to make sure that the footnotes supported what was in the text.

Two other things happened in my early years at Michigan that proved quite influential. The dean, Frank Allen, knew that I was interested in legal history, and he asked how he could help. I said that I would like to get to know Willard Hurst. Perhaps Allen could invite Hurst to come to the law school and give a talk. Allen knew Hurst well enough to know that he would not come, but Allen invited him anyway, and said that the purpose of the invitation was, of course, to see if he would come, but also to meet me. Hurst declined the invitation and instead invited me to come to Madison and spend the weekend with him. Hurst was a charming man, and we had a delightful time. At the end of the weekend we sat down and talked about where I might take myself. At that point, there was no particular reason why I should not have pursued American legal history. My history training, such as it was, was almost as good in American as it was in medieval history. (In both areas I had a lot to learn.) Hurst was an American legal historian. He had wondered out loud and in print about why legal historians in America spent so much time on England when there was so much to do on America. I rather thought that he might push me in the American direction. The temper of the times was very much for "relevance" in law schools, and the connections between what happened in the lumber industry in Wisconsin in the nineteenth century and contemporary American problems were a lot more obvious than were those between the rise of novel disseisin and anything that was concerning us today. I was surprised by his answer: "With your languages and your background, you ought to focus on the Middle Ages," he said.

The other influential event that happened in my early years at Michigan began with a phone call that I got from the chairman of the Michigan Classics Department. He had found out that the Law School had appointed an assistant professor who had a degree, at least partially, in Classics. Would I be interested in teaching a course in Roman law? This was a course that the Department had long offered. It was a way to draw in undergraduates who did not immediately think that Classics was something that they wanted to do. The man who had been teaching the course, Frank Copley, was a literary scholar who taught it as a "service course," and he wanted to get out. I had done an independent reading course in Roman law at Yale, so I could not say that I knew nothing about the topic, but I knew that I did not know much. Since the Yale course was an independent reading course, I had no idea how to teach the topic, particularly to undergraduates and graduate students in Classics. I agreed to take a crack at it so long as Copley would teach it with me the first couple of times, and so long as the course would be open not only students in the faculty of arts and sciences but also those in the law school. The course worked sufficiently well that I have tried to open up my courses in any kind of legal history to arts and sciences students ever since. I have also taught Roman law, not every year, but quite regularly, ever since. Teaching Roman law from the beginning of my career gave me the confidence to offer the first paper that I presented to the American Society of Legal History: "The Roman Law of Marriage at the Time of the Glossators."

I got tenure. One of the rewards of a grant of tenure at the Michigan law school at the time was something that was known as "young man's leave." (The gender reference was correct; there were no women faculty in the law school at the time.) With considerable help from colleagues at Michigan who had connections in England, I arranged to spend the year as an "academic visitor" (roughly a visiting scholar) in the Law Department of the London School of Economics and Political Science, one of whose members was S. F. C. Milsom, the most distinguished English legal historian of the period.

In the summer before we went to England, the quadrennial international congress of medieval canon law, a gathering under Kuttner's direction of all the people in world who did Kuttner's kind of work, was held in Toronto. With some trepidation, I proposed to Kuttner that I would give a paper. That paper became "The Policy of Alexander the Third's Consent Theory of Marriage." "Policy," of course, was a Yale word, increasingly used throughout American law schools but not one that was commonly used in the history of medieval canon law. The paper also suggested that one might connect what Alexander did with the roughly contemporary rise of the lyric of "courtly love." That was, of course, pure Harvard English Department, a principal theme in my bachelor's essay on Romeo and Juliet: "Romeo's Sweet New Style." The paper also had some examples, cherry-picked from cases that I had found in the archives at York on a summer trip a year earlier. The paper did not bomb, but there were certainly those who had questions: "Was 'policy' the right way to describe it?" (This from a scholar who had spent his life studying twelfth-century decretal letters written to England.) "Is the connection with 'courtly love' really there (with multiple examples from Chrétien de Troyes that suggested that it was not)?" (This from a scholar who taught broadly in the field of medieval history.) The case examples provoked almost no comment. Historians of medieval canon law in this period did not look at the records of actual cases except when they were embodied in papal decretal letters.

The year in England was roughly the equivalent of the research-in-the-archives year that I would have done had I done graduate work in history. From the time that I had worked with Kuttner, I had become convinced that the contribution, if any, that I could make to the history of medieval canon law was to bring in the dimension of what could be found out about how the law was applied. If Yale had taught me anything, it had taught me that abstract statements of the law can only make sense in the context of actual cases. Many of the papal decretal letters dealt with actual cases, but finding out anything more about the cases was difficult, and in many cases impossible. But records of the ecclesiastical courts did survive, particularly in England. Kuttner had told me that they were particularly rich at York. London and York are not exactly next door, but occasional commuting was possible. I was also aware that there was a somewhat earlier set of records at Canterbury. My short-term goal was to see if I could say anything intelligent about the debate that had flared up in the early twentieth century, and which continued to smolder, about the role in England of the universal western canon law, sometimes called "Roman canon law" or "papal law," if one looked at it from the point of view of what was happening in the ecclesiastical courts. My longer term goal, as yet still imperfectly defined, was to write a monograph on medieval marriage law, once more as viewed from what happened in the church courts.

But I was not a graduate student doing a year of research in the archives, and that had both its advantages and its disadvantages. The advantages were that Sheila and I had more money than most graduate students have; we were able to establish ourselves in London and get some sense of all the things that the city has to offer. I had an office at LSE and was able to get to know my colleagues in the Law Department, particularly Milsom, but also those who had no particular interest in legal history. The major disadvantage was that I could not work full-time in the archives. The first proofs of my property casebook arrived while I was in London, and London is not the best place to check references about what was, and remains, a book about U.S. law. I was expected to give a public lecture at LSE. That turned out to be about the U.S. law of landlord and tenant, a hot topic at the time. Milsom was on leave for one of the three terms. Peter Birks and I taught his seminar in English legal history in that term.

Enough on the marriage paper got done that I was able to fill in some of the major gaps, particularly about the case material, in the paper that had been given in Toronto. It appeared in the proceedings of the Congress. The paper on "Roman Canon Law in the Medieval English Church" began to take shape. It ultimately ended up as a 70-page article that only a law review could, or would, publish. Milsom shared with me Norma Adams' draft of a Selden Society volume on the thirteenth-century Canterbury cases and asked me to help in preparing it for the press. That, too, ultimately got published.

Let me fast forward to my arrival at Harvard in 1980 for what I look back on as, perhaps, the final formative move. Shortly after I arrived, Sam Thorne and Jack Dawson came to me with a request that they did not phrase this way but that boiled down to the proposition that neither of them was getting any younger, and the Ames Foundation needed someone younger to help. The Foundation had not published anything since 1975, but it was sitting on manuscripts of editions of the Year Books of Richard II for the sixth, seventh, eighth and tenth years of his reign (1382–1383, 1383–1383, 1384–1385, 1386–1387). The process of getting those books out ultimately led to my becoming Literary Director of the Foundation (a position from which I have just resigned) and to learning more than I ever expected to want to know about how to code scholarly works in the humanities for both paper and digital publication.

I have focused on the early years and have gone on far too long. Looking back on those early years three things seem particularly striking: First, how serendipitous all of it was. Had it not been for …, and there are a half a dozen or more points where it all could have come out differently. Second, how much I benefited from the generosity of older scholars who helped and encouraged me to do my own thing and then waited for me to do it. The third is more complicated. I had gone to law school, to a certain extent, because I was interested in the practical, in how things worked. I was taught in law school by second-generation legal realists who emphasized, even if they did not always do it themselves, that how things worked was the domain of the social sciences. I worked with a number of economists at Michigan and was attracted to the way in which they explained things. Ultimately, however, I became dissatisfied with exclusively economic explanations of legal phenomena, indeed, more broadly, with exclusively social-science explanations of legal phenomena. This may be because of an influence that I have not yet mentioned: Sheila. She is a thorough-going humanist. A Classics major in college, she keeps up with literature far more than I do. She is broadly interested in, and continues to learn about, the history of art and architecture. We go to concerts together. Over the course of more than fifty years of marriage she has had more influence on the way I think about things than I suspect that she imagines.

Methodus ad facilem historiarum cognitionem

Let me try to summarize what all of this might mean for the legal historian that I have become. I begin with the text (or in a few cases, physical evidence, like a manuscript or even a cathedral). Of course, before I approach the text I have some question in mind, but I try not to prejudge what the answer to that question might be, though, like everyone else, I have inklings as to what it might be. I then try to let the text speak to me. What is it saying? Don't assume that the words mean what you think they mean. Why is the author saying this? What is he (or occasionally she) assuming that I may or may not know? Can I figure out from what the text says what those assumptions might be? Is there other evidence as to what they might be? What is there about the context of the text that might help me to understand the answers to the previous questions? Are there hints in the text about context? As to "context," think broadly. Any element of context—doctrinal, more broadly intellectual, political, economic, social—may help. But judgment is called for; the entire context is, of course, context, but not every element in the context is interesting or explanatory. It is those elements of context that help us to understand what is otherwise puzzling about the text, different from what we expect, that are interesting. And while we are engaged in the process we ought to spell out, at least in our own minds, why we were expecting something that we did not find.

One of the reasons why I enjoy editing unedited texts (of which there are many in my period) is that doing it frequently clears the mind of at least some of the preconceived notions of what one might find. The text exists; it has never been edited. Perhaps some scholars have used it for one or another purpose, but no one really knows in any kind of detail what is in the whole thing. In order to edit the text one has to focus hard on what it says anyway. Thoughts about what it might mean follow naturally.

Getting the text right is the first step. But history does call for generalization, at least if we want to communicate with those who do not spend the time that we do in the weeds. The next step is to ask if there are other texts like this one that may help to answer our question. That, of course, depends on what the question is and on what period we are dealing with. One reason why I have focused on the later Middle Ages is that the documentation is extensive, but it is not overwhelming. For some topics, for example, marriage cases at York, one can spend quite a bit of time on all the cases and still, ultimately, get out a book that deals with them as part of a larger whole.

But any time that one is dealing with a large base of evidence, one has to find ways to summarize it in order to present it. One of the things that I learned something about while it was still possible that I might work in the area of regulated industries was statistics. I know enough to know what I don't know, and to know what simple statistical techniques applied to, let us say, church court records can yield statistically meaningful results.

That gets us some of the way to generalizations that might be interesting to a broader audience, but it does not get us the whole way. There is always going to be a leap between what can be proved by the evidence and what it might mean more broadly. Unlike some historians, I am willing to take that leap, but only if I spell out quite clearly where I am making the leap.

For example, very few defamation cases in the consistory court of Ely in the mid-fourteenth century have a judgment, far fewer than do marriage cases. That *may* mean that the court was encouraging settlement of defamation cases, and there are some features of the procedure in such cases that might lead to that conclusion. If that is right, that may tell us something about the nature of the court and the values that motivated its personnel.

Where does the secondary literature come into this process? Obviously, I will be aware of some of the secondary literature before I start. It may well have shaped the question that I am trying to answer. Unlike some of my history graduate students, however, I do not do a literature search before I start. For me, it's the end of the process, not the beginning. Once I've got something down on paper, I do a literature search to see first, if anyone has said anything about the texts with which I am dealing, and second, if anyone has said anything in the direction of my conclusions. The first process may well lead to modification of what I said, and, of course, citation of the secondary literature either way. The second process is harder, and I'm not sure that I'm particularly good at it. Anyone who ranges as widely as I have runs the risk of reinventing the wheel, or of inventing the wooden wagon wheel when someone else has invented the steel wheel with Michelin tires. I know that the first has happened on occasion. I'm arrogant enough to think that the second has not, but that is for others to decide.

A Bottom Line?

So what does it all add up to in terms of larger themes? Anyone who is as uncomfortable as I am with broad generalizations will find that question a difficult one. One very large theme that I hope gets across, particularly to law students, is the importance of context. In a profession that spends a great deal of its time trying to predict what courts or other legal decision-makers are likely to do, figuring out what elements in the context beyond the rules on the books are likely to affect the decision is crucial. The study of legal history, I hope, makes the law students more sensitive to the elements of context that they should be looking for as lawyers. It also—once more I hope—teaches them that they can't go home. An idea from the past was a product of the context of the past. Contexts change. Be careful of diachronic legal history; be very careful of diachronic legal argument.

To illustrate this, let me close with a few ideas that I try to explore in the last lecture in a course that deals with the development of Continental European law from the fall of Rome to the codifications by examining in some depth the development of three specific bodies of law: that about capture of wild animals, that about formation of marriage, and that about examination of witnesses. Let us raise the broadest question that I dare raise: why did western legal development happen the way it did? If we compare the western legal system to developed legal systems elsewhere (Jewish and Islamic law come immediately to mind), what will strike us is not the difference between the Anglo-American legal system and that of Continental Europe but rather how much the western systems have in common that is not shared by the others.

My answer to the question is eclectic. I am attracted to the notion, which is not original with me, that whenever one is dealing with an activity that is as cut off from the rest of society as much as law has been in the West since the twelfth century, internal explanations of developments should be preferred to external ones whenever they are convincing. Like many historians trained in American law my exploration of internal explanations includes those based on the procedural and institutional, as much as, perhaps even more than, those based on substantive law. There is in my view, however, too much in the comparative history of Western law that cannot be explained internally that we can afford not to look around to what was going on at the time when the developments we are seeking to explain happened. Sometimes these exogenous pieces of context are in the realm of ideas, and perhaps we should always look here first, since we are usually trying to explain a phenomenon that is intellectual, or, at least, the product of conscious choice. Sometimes the exogenous developments are political, and perhaps this is where we ought to look to second, because conscious legal change, at least in the West, has normally been promulgated by political organs. There is enough, however, that lies in the realm of the social and economic that we cannot ignore developments in those areas too. Finally, change is never the product of impersonal forces. Individuals make changes; individuals resist changes. Frequently we cannot find out much about the individuals, but sometimes we can, and sometimes what we learn about them helps to explain what is otherwise quite inexplicable. Let us briefly review the topics that we consider in Continental Legal History in the light of the possible forces that might explain why they were the way they were:

Roman law, and later the *ius commune* generally. There can be no doubt that this was a powerful force in shaping European law, and that much that is different about English law can be explained by the fact that the law taught in universities was less influential in England, particularly in the critical period from 1300–1500, than it was on the Continent. Roman law simply won't go away if that is what every university-trained jurist learns. It affects his habits of thought in ways that he can hardly perceive. The simple divisions of the *Institutes* between public and private law, and within private law among persons, things and actions, and within the law of things among individual things, succession, and obligations have continued to influence everyone who has tried to shape an overall view of law. The Roman law of the occupation of wild animals, to take a particular example, has appeared over and over again, influencing such broad concepts as the relation between ownership and possession, the theory of the origins of property, even the theory of the origins of the state. Two creations of the learned law of the Middle Ages, powerfully influenced by Roman law, Romano-canonic procedure and the consent theory of marriage, have also proven extraordinarily lasting. The former because it provides a means for resolution of any kind of dispute, the latter because it seems so timeless, so reductionist.

Ideas spawned in areas quite outside of what we normally think of as law, however, also impinged on these developments. For example, were it not for the fact that a French theologian named Hugh of St. Victor had espoused a notion of the dual sacramentality of marriage, an idea that was picked up and popularized by Peter Lombard, it is hard to imagine that Pope Alexander III would have come to the conclusions about the formation of marriage that he came to, and even if he had, it is hard to imagine that they would have been accepted. For another example, the humanist movement had been in operation for almost two centuries before it came to affect the lawyers, but when it did so, it did so profoundly. The Roman texts were read more historically, prompting, on the one hand, a search for principle that went beyond the particular but, on the other, study of customary and non-Roman law in their own right. Fascination with the origins of property and the origins of the state in the seventeenth century produced different understandings of the law of wild animals depending on whether one followed Thomas Hobbes, as Pufendorf did, or John Locke, as Barbeyrac did. Only the area of procedure seems relatively immune from such outside intellectual influences, though we certainly may see, as do others, a general concern with individual rights being reflected in procedural ideas about the minimum necessary for a process to conform to natural law.

The rise of the national territorial state. The end result is by no means obvious from the start: by and large we have today a single body of law for each country. The main story from this century that will be told in European legal history in the twenty-second century may be the painful unification of the laws of Europe under the rubric of the European Union. Each of the three topics was affected by the rise of the territorial state in different ways. In the case of wild animals, a Roman-law solution came into conflict with varying local customs about hunting and was finally embodied in the national codes with the important qualification that hunting was subject to national, as opposed to feudal, regulation. In the case of witnesses, national procedural codifications, going back in France to the seventeenth century, were able to impose a uniform practice over a multiplicity of courts with different procedures. The development of marriage law was intimately connected with the church's competing against the monopolization of legal power in secular authorities, a competition that the church ultimately lost. Thus, while in the first two areas the nation-state was able to use pieces of the learned law to unify local custom; in the case of marriage a transnational body of law was dismembered and brought down to the level of the nation-state.

More broadly, the rise of the territorial nation state may be seen in the context of a body of ideas that we call political theory. It is a hard topic to fit into a legal history course because it is rarely the sole preserve of lawyers. John of Salisbury, Thomas Aquinas, William of Ockham, Marsilius of Padua, Jean Gerson, Machiavelli, Jean Bodin, Thomas Hobbes, and John Locke have to be the names we talk about if we want to talk about political theory in the medieval and early modern periods, and only one of these, Bodin, was fully a lawyer. If we do not focus on the individual thinkers, however, but focus instead on schools of thought, lawyers and legal thinking become more significant: supporters of empire vs. supporters of papacy, theorists of papal monarchy, conciliarists, *politiques* and *monarchomachi*, Spanish scholastics, and natural lawyers of the northern school are all, at least in part, participants in legal movements. Whether we focus on the individuals or on the movements, many of the same elements that we saw in dealing with the law in a more narrow sense can be seen to be at play here. Roman law—to which we should add elements of political theory derived from the Christian tradition—play a significant role. But the ancient texts are malleable, particularly when they are applied to political circumstances that the Romans or the fathers of the church could not possibly have imagined. Hence, the gradual emergence of nation states has to be a significant part of any explanation of why the theory came to be the way it was at the end of the seventeenth century. What happened after that is in many ways unpredictable, and the lawyers, by and large, were not a large part of it. Prior to that, however, most of the lawyers seem to be trying to come to grips with a fundamental problem of governance: how to give the power to the governing authority to do what needs to be done in the public interest while at the same time limiting that authority so that it does not become tyrannical. Different ages give different answers to this question, but it is a central problem.

Economic forces. None of the three topics directly deals with much that is of obvious economic concern. Commercial law, about which I have written, is an area where there are some relatively obvious intersections between national and international trade and local and international mercantile custom. I found that most of what is written on the topic is imbued with a kind of mercantile romanticism. It may be good economics; it is rather bad history. There are, moreover, some economic intersection points in the three topics. The relationship between the law of wild animals and the law of poaching is a fairly obvious one. Roman law here provides a poor guide for those who are seeking to restrain poaching in the interests of the lords who claim hunting rights as their economic prerogative. Those who espouse a classical liberal economic view of the origins of property rights would see efficiency as being on the side of the lords, individual ownership of hunting rights encourages conservation, whereas the Roman rule encourages wasteful exploitation. Those who espouse a more Marxian version of economics, on the other hand, also have little doubt as to why it is that the lords' rights gained some recognition, and efficiency is not the reason. The ultimate solution—to recognize the Roman rule but to qualify it with national regulation—is ambiguous in its economic impact. On the one hand, the lords lost big. On the other hand, the effects of national regulation depend on who has the ear of the regulators. Hence, economic interests do get felt in the unlikeliest of areas, but grand economic predictive theories about law tend to fall down in particular examples.

Social forces. Our topics have much more evidence of social forces. The lists of excluded witnesses are a mirror of social attitudes in given periods. The social forces that arranged themselves against Alexander's rules on the formation of marriage tell us much about the formation of what has been called the patriarchal family in the early modern period. The Napoleonic Code reflects a fundamental change in the social structure of France. Perhaps even more pervasive are the ways that social forces work within the interstices of the system. If the rules require that in order for William Smith and Alice Dolling to be married, they must have exchanged words of consent, then the women of Winterbourne Stoke, where William and Alice lived, will testify that they did so, even if we strongly suspect that they did not.

In the case of both the social forces and the economic ones, the phenomena of the law can seem to change in response to them, or the phenomena of the law can seem to remain the same as the forces work their way around them. It is very difficult to predict which reaction will take place. I am more prone than are some to seeing legal change as in some sense caused by such forces. Nonetheless, there are a number of instances in which some piece of Roman learning was picked up wholesale and dumped down in medieval Italy, Renaissance France, or nineteenth-century Germany. Here I must raise a definitional point. The Roman law of the contract of sale, to take a body of doctrine that has remained relatively unchanged across the centuries, was not the same thing in Rome as it was in medieval Italy, Renaissance France, or nineteenth-century Germany. Granted the difference in the economies of the four places, it could not be the same. The same body of rules does not mean the same thing in the context of Roman slave trading wine on behalf of his master with a Greek merchant, as it does in the context of a Florentine merchant trading wool cloth in Bruges using an elaborate system of factors and international credit transactions, as it does with a subsidized and regulated Lyons silk factory making sales across the Alps, or as it does with the sales of an iron foundry in newly-industrialized nineteenth-century Germany. If the rules will not change to accommodate the differences in transactions, the transactions will shape themselves around the sameness of the rules, but the end result in any meaningful social or economic sense will not be the same.

The people. Finally, there are the individuals who have played a role in the story. It is hard to argue that they made a difference. It is altogether too easy to see the law as the product of impersonal intellectual, political, social, and economic forces. Perhaps it is easiest to see the difference that indviduals make in the case of the great political leaders who concerned themselves with law. One can hardly imagine that Western legal history would have been the same if Justinian had not published the *Corpus Iuris Civilis*, if Alexander III had not been so good at deciding cases, if Edward I had not supported a massive effort to reform the common law of England, or if Napoleon had been interested only in war and not also in law. In the case of the intellectuals, the more shadowy figures, the ones about whom legends developed, are the easiest to see as having really made a difference. We know so little about Irnerius and Gratian, in particular, and yet a few years after their deaths everyone perceived their importance. I am not saying that someone would not have gotten on to Roman law if Irnerius, or whoever it was, had not done it, or that someone would not have written a teaching book for canon law to rival the *Corpus Iuris Civilis*, but there is enough about Gratian's book that is idiosyncratic and enough about what we suspect that Irnerius did that is surprising that it may well be that the development would have taken a different course if they had not done what they did.

The practicing lawyers are harder to individualize, harder to show that they made a difference. If, however, one looks at legislative activity, it is remarkable how many legislative products that did make a difference are associated with particular draftsmen. Take away Michel de l'Hôpital, Jean Baptiste Colbert, and Henri-François d'Aguessau, in the sixteenth, seventeenth, and eighteenth centuries respectively, and very few of the *grandes ordonnances* survive. Take away the *grandes ordonnances*, and it is not at all sure that Napoleon's code would have been anything like as impressive as it was. I certainly do not want espouse the "great lawyer" theory of legal history, but I also do not want to end with the notion that the law is as uninfluenced by individuals as is the movements of prices on the Chicago Grain Exchange.

There is a way to get at the people, dangerous for an historian, but irresistible for someone who believes that people matter. We see jurists or lawyers who make unpredictable arguments, judges who have a number of decisions which follow unpredictable patterns, litigants in actual cases who make odd moves. The people behind those arguments, decisions, and moves are not governed by what our abstractions about "forces" predict. Speculations about the personalities and motivations of people about whom we know little or nothing other than what can be a cryptic text may reveal are just that, speculations, but perhaps they are required of those who take a humanistic approach to legal history.

Regulating Incestuous Marriage in the Roman Republic

Bruce W. Frier

Four decades ago Charles Donahue, then my colleague at the University of Michigan, drew my attention to the rich sources on Roman marriage, a subject to which I have often returned. It was the breadth of his approach that I especially admired, his capacity to keep searching for wholly plausible solutions to historical enigmas. The subject of this article is one such enigma, and I very much hope that Charlie will enjoy it, particularly as it aspires to engage with many of the techniques he pioneered in dealing with obviously fragmentary evidence.

In classical Roman law, marriage was permitted between first cousins (or, in Roman terminology, between collateral relatives in the fourth degree: Ulpian, *Tit.* 5.6).[1] However, although details are difficult to come by,

1. *Tituli ex Corpore Ulpiani* 5.6: "Between ascendants and descendants, no matter how distant the degree of kinship, there is no *conubium* (capacity to marry). But between collateral relatives, marriages could once be contracted up to the fourth degree of kinship (i.e., first cousins); now, however, it is also permitted to take a wife of the third degree, although only a brother's daughter...." See also, e.g., Ulpian, D. 23.2.12; Gaius, *Inst.* 1.60–62, to the same effect. (All these sources note the narrow legal exception introduced to accommodate Claudius' marriage to his fraternal niece Agrippina in 50/49 CE.) Degree of kinship, *gradus cognationis*, is determined by counting back by generations from the subject person to the first common ancestor, then forward to the object person. See generally Max Kaser, *Das Römische Privatrecht*, vol. 1 (Munich: Beck Verlag, 1971), 316; Philippe Moreau, *Incestus et Prohibitae Nuptiae: L'Inceste à Rome* (Paris: Belles Lettres, 2002), 187–191; also Percy Ellwood Corbett, *The Roman Law of Marriage* (Oxford: Clarendon, 1930), 47–51; Carla Fayer, *La Familia Romana: Aspetti ed Antiquari: Parte Seconda: Sponsalia, Matrimonio, Dote* (Rome: Bretschneider, 2005), 390–396.

ancient authors appear to have believed that sometime during the Republic the Romans had altered their rules on incestuous marriage, and that the earlier rules had been broader and hence more restrictive. The clearest source for this view is a fawning speech to the Senate in Tacitus' *Annales* (12.6.3). The Senator L. Vitellius (cos. 34 CE) justifies acceding to Claudius' desire to marry his fraternal niece Agrippina the Younger by arguing that times change and we must change with them.

> But, it will be said, marriage with a brother's daughter is with us a novelty. True; but it is common among other peoples, and there is no law to forbid it. Marriages with second cousins (*sobrinae*) were long unknown, but after a time they became frequent. Custom adapts itself to expediency, and this [proposed] novelty will [also] hereafter take its place among recognized usages.[2]

The authenticity of Vitellius' speech cannot be verified, but, as Ronald Syme noticed, several idiosyncrasies suggest that Tacitus may be relying here not on free invention, but on a source such as the *Acta* of the Senate.[3]

The notion that incest rules had formerly been more extensive also emerges in a rather different context: Plutarch's *Roman Questions* 6, discussing the ancient custom whereby Roman matrons were obliged to kiss their close kin on the lips when meeting them. As is his wont, Plutarch supplies several antiquarian explanations (including, what is elsewhere the one most commonly given, that kissing served as a sort of sobriety test);

---

2. Tacitus, *Annales* 12.6.3 (L. Vitellius is speaking to the Senate): "At enim nova nobis in fratrum filias coniugia: sed aliis gentibus sollemnia, neque lege ulla prohibita; et sobrinarum diu ignorata tempore addito percrebuisse. morem accommodari prout conducat, et fore hoc quoque in iis quae mox usurpentur." On the law of incest in the Roman Empire, see Salvatore Puliatti, *Incesti Crimina. Regime Giuridico da Augusto a Giustiniano* (Milan: Giuffrè, 2001); Thomas A. J. McGinn, "Diocletian on Bigamy and Incest," in S. Corrèa Fattori et al., eds., *Estudos em Homenagem a Luiz Fabiano Corrèa* (São Paulo: Max Limonad, 2014), 353–393; Judith Evans Grubbs. "Making the Private Public: Illegitimacy and Incest in Roman Law," in Clifford Ando and Jörg Rüpke, eds. *Public and Private in Ancient Mediterranean Law and Religion*, Religionsgeschichtliche Versuche und Vorarbeiten 65 (Berlin: de Gruyter, 2015), 115–142.

3. Ronald Syme, *Tacitus* (Oxford: Clarendon Press, 1958), 1.330–331, esp. 331 n.2. On the interpretation of this passage, see Karl Ubl, *Inzestverbot und Gesetzgebung: Die Konstruktion eines Verbrechens* (300–1100) (Berlin: de Gruyter, 2008), 179–181.

but his final explanation links the custom with Roman rules on incestuous marriage. As Plutarch states, marriages with close kin had once been unknown. He then narrates a strange, undated tale about a nameless man of admirable character but limited resources, who attempted marriage with his wealthy first cousin (*anepsiá*, = *consobrina*). He was brought to trial over this, but the people refused to hear the case and instead voted a decree (*pséphisma*, = *plebiscitum?*) allowing marriages between first cousins (in Roman legal terminology, relatives in the fourth degree), while banning marriages with closer collateral kin.[4]

Plutarch does not specify the *preceding* degree of prohibited kinship. However, from a snippet of Polybius (6.11a.4), preserved in the early third-century CE author Athenaeus, we know that the custom of kissing extended to sixth-degree collateral relatives of the wife and her husband, therefore up to second cousins.[5] As Riccardo Astolfi notes, close-kinship is identically delimited, outside the context of marital capacity, in a number

4. Plutarch, *Quaestiones Romanae* 6 (*Mor.* B, D–E): "Why do the [Roman] women kiss their kinsmen on the lips? ... Or is it that, since it is not the custom for men to marry blood relations (*sungenidas*), affection proceeded only so far as a kiss, and this alone remained as a token of kinship and a participation therein? For formerly men did not marry women related to them by blood, just as even now they do not marry their aunts or their sisters; but after a long time they made the concession of allowing wedlock with first cousins for the following reason: a man possessed of no property, but otherwise of excellent character and more satisfactory to the people than other public men, has as wife his first cousin, an heiress, and was thought to be growing rich from her estate. He was accused on this ground, but the people (*démos*) would not even try the case and dismissed the charge, enacting a decree that all might marry first cousins or more distant relatives; but marriage with nearer kin was prohibited." On the duty of matrons to kiss their relatives, see also esp. Polybius 6.11a.4 (= Athen. 10.440E), quoted below; Plautus, *Stichus* 89–91; Cato in Pliny, *NH* 14.90; Cicero, *Rep.* 4.6; Propertius 2.6.7–8; Gellius, *NA* 10.23.1; Tertullian, *Apol.* 6.5; Arnobius 2.67.

5. Athenaeus, *Deipnosophistae*, 10.440e: "But among the Romans, as Polybius says in his sixth book, it was forbidden to women to drink wine at all.... And it is impossible for a woman to drink wine without being detected; for, first of all, she has not the key of the cellar; and, in the next place, she is bound to kiss her relations, and those of her husband, down to second cousins, and to do this every day when she first sees them..." See Maurizio Bettini, "Il Divieto Fino al 'Sesto Grado' Incluso nel Matrimonio Romano," *Athenaeum* n.s. 66 (1988), 69–96 at 79–81; republished in translation in *Familie und Verwandtschaft im Antiken Rom* (München: Campus Verlag 1992).

of late Republican and early Imperial statutes, from the *Lex Cincia de donis* of 204 to the *Lex Papia Poppaea* of 9 BCE.[6]

What the accounts in Tacitus and Plutarch have in common is an apparent insistence that the original ban on close-kin marriage was traditional rather than statutory, and that at some point there had taken place a shift away from this tradition, perhaps in the context of legislation limiting incestuous marriage to within the fourth degree of kinship.[7] (Like Vitellius in Tacitus, we know nothing further of this statute, however.) If such a transition occurred, it must have been before the second century BCE, when marriages between first cousins had apparently become, if perhaps never common, still recurrent enough to occasion no particular opprobrium. In the late Republic, close-kin marriages are attested between Scipio Nasica Corculum (cos. 162) and his second cousin Cornelia, and between Scipio Aemilianus (cos. 147) and his first cousin once removed Sempronia, and in the next century the marriages to first cousins of C. Aurius Melinus from the local aristocracy at Larinum, the tyrannicide Marcus Porcius Brutus, the *triumvir* Marcus Antonius, and (probably) M. Aemilius Lepidus son of the *triumvir*.[8] In the Roman Empire, jurists refer to first-cousin marriages quite casually, without perceptible censure.[9]

Perhaps the most compelling source, however, is the proem of a *contio* speech delivered in 171 BCE by the centurion Spurius Ligustinus, in which, while recounting his life, he offhandedly mentions his long-time marriage to his first cousin—although, to be sure, little can be said regarding the

6. Riccardo Astolfi, *Il Matrimonio nel Diritto Romano Preclassico*, 2nd ed. (Padua: CEDAM, 2002), 38–50.

7. It is worth noting that this may not have been the first such transition; literary sources for the regal period and the very early Republic indicate that (perhaps under Etruscan influence) at one time—roughly the seventh to fifth centuries bce—close-kin marriage was permitted. However, the veracity of these sources is suspect: Astolfi, *Matrimonio Preclassico*, 46–47.

8. Alan Watson, *The Law of Persons in the Later Roman Republic* (Oxford: Clarendon, 1967), 38–39; Moreau, *Incestus et Prohibitae Nuptiae: L'Inceste à Rome* (Paris: Belles Lettres, 2002), 190, who at n. 107 (pp. 215–216) adds the inscriptions *CIL* 9.2485–2486 (= *ILS* 915) mentioning the close-kin marriage of the Augustan senator P. Paquius Scaeva from Histonium (Vasto) in Samnium (*PIR*^{2} P 126).

9. Marcellus/Papinian, D. 28.7.23–24.

authenticity of this speech.[10] The well-known article of Saller and Shaw would therefore seem to be wrong were it taken (incorrectly) to imply that close-kin marriages were extremely rare in Roman society.[11]

Most historians have accepted, then, an inward pressure on the accepted boundaries of incestuous marriage, a pressure that manifested itself sometime during, probably, the middle Republic. The sources of this pressure are not easy to identify, but we come a bit further if (alas, a very large if) we accept an odd source commonly called the *Anecdoton Livianum*. Paul Krüger discovered it obscurely lodged in a twelfth-century canon law manuscript, and it was then published in 1870 by Krüger and Theodor Mommsen.[12] The *Anecdoton* purports to be a fragment of the lost twentieth book of the historian Livy, dealing with the interval between the First and Second Punic Wars (240–219 BCE). Here it is, in its entirety:

> *Anecdoton Livianum* (Livy F 12(M), = *Cod. Per. lat.* 3858 C): Livius libro vicesimo: P. Celius patricius primus adversus veterem morem intra septimum cognationis gradum duxit uxorem. ob hoc M. Rutilius plebeius sponsam sibi praeripi novo exemplo nuptiarum dicens sedicionem populi concitavit adeo ut patres territi in Capitolium perfugerent.
>
> Livy, in book 20: P. Celius, a patrician, first violated ancient custom (*veterem morem*) by taking a wife within the seventh degree of kinship. For this, a plebeian named M. Rutilius, claiming that his betrothed had been wrested from him through an unprecedented form

10. Livy, 42.34.3 (speaking of events twenty years before): "cum primum in aetatem ueni, pater mihi uxorem fratris sui filiam dedit" ("As soon as I came of age my father gave me as wife his brother's daughter."). Of the speech, Dominic Rathbone observes, in "Poor Peasants and Silent Sherds," in Luuk de Ligt and Simon Northwood, eds., *People, Land, and Politics: Demographic Developments and the Transformation of Roman Italy, 300 BC–AD 14* (Leiden: Brill, 2008), 305–332 at 308: "spurious undoubtedly, but probably reflecting the reality of the later second century;" this could well be when Roman annalists first composed the speech.

11. Brent D. Shaw and Richard P. Saller, "Close-Kin Marriage in Roman Society," *Man* 19.3 (1984), 432–444, who argue only that: "close-kin marriage does not seem to have been widespread in the Western empire" (p. 436).

12. Theodor Mommsen and Paul Krüger, "Anecdoton Livianum," *Hermes* 4 (1870), 372–376, cited from Mommsen, *Gesammelte Schriften* (Berlin: Weidmann, 1909), 7.163–167.

> of marriage, stirred up such popular resentment that the Fathers (*patres*) fled in terror to the Capitolium.

In this story, the patrician Publius C<a>elius marries a close kinswoman, thereby precipitating a violent public controversy with his wife's jilted fiancé, the plebeian Marcus Rutilius. Most of this sounds exceptionally odd, quite apart from the Caelii not being patrician. (The easiest emendation is *Cloelius*, or possibly *Cornelius*, but the antagonists remain otherwise unidentified.) A patrician/plebeian struggle at this late date may well seem anachronistic; however, other parts of the tale have been modernized to fit subsequent kinship terminology, including the reference to degrees of kinship. Nor is there any easy way to explain how the anecdote could have survived into the High Middle Ages—when, it should be noted, the issue of close-kin marriage was once again being actively debated, a circumstance that certainly might have provided an occasion for either inventing or rediscovering this bizarre story.

So what is to be done with the *Anecdoton*? Most scholars have followed Mommsen's bottom line in finding it extraordinary but still broadly credible.[13] By contrast, a few, like Andreas Schminck and Karl Ubl, have rejected it as a crude medieval forgery.[14] Others, like Philippe Moreau in his recent exhaustive monograph, have thought the story just too compromised to be helpful.[15]

Certainly it would take exceptional courage to stake one's entrance into heaven on the authenticity of the *Anecdoton*. But the story itself may not be entirely beyond redemption. Jürgen von Ungern-Sternberg has vig-

13. Mommsen, *Ges. Schr.* 7.167: *sed ut mirandi causa iusta est, ita nulla est dubitandi.* See the balanced review of the evidence in Gilbert Hanard, "Inceste et Société Romaine Républicaine: Un Essai d'Interpretation Ethnojuridique du Fragment du Libre XX de l'Histoire de Tite-Live," *Revue Belge de Philologie et d'Histoire* 64 (1986), 32–61. It is agreed that the Latin is not a quotation from Livy. For a bibliography, see Gennaro Franciosi, *Clan Gentilizio e Strutture Monogamiche: Contributo alla Storia della Familia Romana*, 6th ed. (Napoli: Jovene, 1999), 86 notes 1–2.

14. Andreas Schminck, "Livius als Kanonist?" *Rechtshistorisches Journal* 1 (1982), 151–164, against whom see Hanard, "Inceste et Société"; Karl Ubl, *Inzestverbot und Gesetzgebung: Die Konstruktion eines Verbrechens (300–1100)* (Berlin & New York: de Gruyter, 2008), 38–39. It counts against this view that the anecdote is not known to have figured in the medieval debate.

15. Moreau, *Incestus* 181–186

orously defended the persistence of patrician/plebeian conflict into the late third century; and, as Ludwig Lange noted in 1879, even the weirdest detail, the retreat of Senators to the fastness of the Capitolium, has an eerie parallel in a passage of Plutarch's *Life of Pompey* (30.4), where Q. Lutatius Catulus, struggling vainly against the *Lex Manilia* in 66 BCE, exhorts the Senate "to seek out a mountain, as their forefathers had done, or a lofty rock, whither they might fly for refuge and preserve their freedom"—obviously, some sort of Senatorial counterpart to plebeian secession.[16]

As Ungern-Sternberg further notes, marriage rules had long been a source of conflict between patricians and plebeians, so that the continued existence of this conflict in the late third century BCE may be less surprising.[17] Indeed, so Bernhard Linke maintains (taking up a line of argument reaching well back into the nineteenth century), the former incest rule might even have been limited to patricians only, a view that is certainly not impossible but that probably presses the *Anecdoton*'s unreliable wording too far.[18]

What strikes me, in any case, as the most arresting aspect of the *Anecdoton* is exactly this part of the story: an *individual's* attempt to depart from traditional marital usage, followed by a *public* uproar over the propriety of this disruption. Here there is, or seems to be, a clear connection to the bizarre story in Plutarch's *Roman Questions*, where the offending party, described as enjoying more popularity with the people than other political leaders, was brought up on charges (presumably for incest) for attempting to marry his wealthy first cousin, but was forcefully acquitted by the *demos*. As Mommsen thought,[19] this popular trial was probably founded not on a statutory norm, but on a supposed violation of the religious duties

16. Jürgen von Ungern-Sternberg, "The End of the Conflict of the Orders," in *Social Struggles in Archaic Rome: New Perspectives on the Conflict of the Orders*, ed. Kurt A Raaflaub, 2nd ed. (Malden, Mass.: Blackwell, 2005), 312–330; German translation: "Das Ende des Ständeskampfes," in Ungern-Sternberg, *Römische Studien: Geschichtsbewusstsein-Zeitalter der Gracchen- Krise der Republik* (Munich: Saur, 2006), 147–169. Ludwig Lange, *Römische Alterthümer* vol. 3 (Berlin: Wiedmann, 1879), 215.

17. Ungern-Sternberg, "The End of the Conflict" 314–315.

18. Bernhard Linke, *Von der Verwandtschaft zum Staat: Die Entstehung Politischer Organisationsformen in der Frührömischen Geschichte* (Stuttgart: Steiner, 1995), 26.

19. Theodor Mommsen, *Römisches Strafrecht* (Leipzig: Binding Verlag, 1899), 683 with notes 1–2.

of citizens; still, the details are fuzzy and impossible to reconstruct. The statute allegedly resulting from this fracas is otherwise unknown, although Moreau credits Plutarch's report.

The other bit of information that the *Anecdoton* may supply is an approximate date for this development: the period between the first two Punic Wars.[20] As we shall see, a date between 241 and 218 is potentially of consequence.

Before I turn to this subject, however, let me briefly discuss the more general handling of incest restrictions in modern scholarship. Although much diversity of opinion persists, there is now considerable agreement on three propositions: first, on the biological level, close-kin reproduction can result in significant genetic damage to offspring, with an incidence and severity that escalate geometrically when kinship is closer than the fourth degree (first cousins);[21] second, not only human children, but higher-order mammals in general, if they grow up together, display fluctuating degrees of natural aversion to subsequent sexual intercourse with one another (the so-called Westermarck effect);[22] and third, all human societies exhibit some form of incest restrictions, which, however, vary widely in their form and scope, with many extending considerably beyond those nuclear family members predictably subject to the Westermarck effect. Although scholars often argue that causal relationships may tie together these three propositions, the exact nature of such causation is murky and still hotly debated; but most scholars assume at least a modicum of underlying natural selection.[23]

20. The date stands so long as we do not follow Robert Develin's attempt to cut the Gordian knot by supposing that Livy was referring, within Book 20, to some much earlier incident. Robert Develin, "Livy F 12(M)," *Latomus* 45 (1986), 115–118.

21. See, e.g., A. H. Bittles, "Consanguinity and Its Relevance to Clinical Genetics," *Clinical Genetics* 60 (2001), 89–98, reviewing the literature. In the ordinary case (supposing no transgenerational inbreeding), first-cousin marriage increases the likelihood of genetic defects from about 2.5% (for exogamous couples) to 5%.

22. Edward Westermarck, *The History of Human Marriage* vol. 2 (1st ed. 1891; 5th ed. New York: Allerton, 1922), 68–91; "Recent Theories of Exogamy," in *Three Essays on Sex and Marriage* (London: MacMillan, 1934), 127–159.

23. See Arthur P. Wolff and William H. Durham, *Inbreeding, Incest, and the Incest Taboo: The State of Knowledge at the Turn of the Century* (Stanford: Stanford University Press, 2005).

Three pertinent points can be made on the basis of this literature. First, if, in fact, the Roman restrictions on incestuous marriage were once fixed at the sixth degree of kinship (second cousins), this would indicate a fairly wide prohibited radius of taboo, although one that is hardly unparalleled; Christian religions, for instance, later experimented with denying marriage between *third* cousins, and curiously extended prohibitions to include, for instance, the relatives of godparents.[24] Second, although in modern law changes in legal regulation of incest and incestuous marriage are largely based on a combination of scientific expertise and public policy (incest within the nuclear family being of special social concern), there has been little convincing discussion of how and why incest regulations changed in pre-modern societies, with the exception of the extraordinary transformations in the Middle Ages.[25]

Third, although structuralist anthropology had often elevated incest restrictions to primacy as an original marker of ordered civilization,[26] most anthropologists today recognize that human societies accord them widely divergent weight, depending on more general patterns of marital strategy normally pursued in these societies. Although endogamy (a preference for marriage *within* predefined social groupings such as families or clans) is obviously consistent with narrowly defined incest borders, the two ideas are not inevitably coupled. Thus, for instance, Americans generally think of marriage as exogamous even though many states permit marriage between first cousins; and first- or second-cousin marriages therefore remain excep-

24. Constance B. Bouchard, "Consanguinity and Noble Marriages in the Tenth and Eleventh Centuries," *Speculum* 56 (1981), 269–270.

25. See, e.g., Elizabeth Archibald, *Incest and the Imagination* (Oxford: Oxford University Press, 2001); Klaus Thraede, "Blutschande (Inzest)," in *Reallexikon für Antike und Christentum*, Suppl. 2 (2002), 38–85; Charles Donahue Jr., "Social Practice, Formal Rule, and the Medieval Canon Law of Incest," in *Law, Marriage, and Society in the Later Middle Ages: Arguments about Marriage in Five Courts* (Cambridge: Cambridge University Press, 2008), 562–597; Ubl, *Inzestverbot* (2008); David D'Avray, "Review Article: Kinship and Religion in the Early Middle Ages," *Early Medieval Europe* 20 (2012), 195–212.

26. See above all Claude Lévi-Strauss, *Les Structures Élémentaires de la Parenté* (Paris: Presses Universitaires de France, 1949), and Meyer Fortes, *Kinship and the Social Order: The Legacy of Lewis Henry Morgan* (Chicago: Aldine Pub. Co., 1969). Subsequent anthropological views are discussed by Maurice Godelier, *Métamorphoses de la Parenté* (Paris: Fayard, 2004), with a review by Jack Goody, "The Labyrinth of Kinship," *New Left Review* 36 (2005), 127–139.

tional, about 0.2% of all marriages.[27] Augustine (*Civ. Dei* 15.16) indicates that something similar had also been true in pagan Rome.[28] (In contemporary Middle Eastern countries, by way of contrast, first-cousin marriages can amount to as much as 25–30% of all marriages.[29])

More generally, it is crucially important to consider the purported rules of incestuous marriage within the broader context of the specific *marital strategies* characterizing historical societies and the social groups within them–Pierre Bourdieu's fundamental insight, which, as Karl Ubl

27. Current law is summarized at https://en.wikipedia.org/wiki/Cousin_marriage_law_in_the_United_States_by_state. Marriage to first cousins is permitted in 19 states and the District of Columbia, prohibited in 25 states, and allowed under some circumstances in 6: http://www.ncsl.org/research/human-services/state-laws-regarding-marriages-between-first-cousi.aspx. Comprehensive world-wide statistics on close-kin marriage are collected by http://www.consang.net/. Data for the United States are sparse but consistent: Newton Freire-Maia, "Inbreeding Levels in American and Canadian Populations: A Comparison with Latin America," *Eugenics Quarterly* 15 (1968), 22-33 (0.2% for Roman Catholics in the USA, 1959–1960); W. J. Dewey, I. Barrai, N.E. Morton , M.P. Mi, "Recessive Genes in Severe Mental Defect," *American Journal of Human Genetics* 17 (1965), 237-256 (0.2% for Wisconsin Roman Catholics, 1941/1955); R. R. Lebel, "Consanguinity Studies in Wisconsin. I. Secular Trends in Consanguineous Marriages, 1843–1981," *American Journal of Medical Genetics* 15 (1983), 543-560 (0.1% for Wisconsin Roman Catholics, 1972/1981, "a clear downward trend since the turn of the century"); D. Sabean, "From Clan to Kindred: Kinship and the Circulation of Property in Premodern and Modern Europe," in S. Müller-Wille H. J. Rheinberger, eds. *Heredity Produced: At the Crossroads of Biology, Politics, and Culture, 1500–1870*. (Cambridge Mass.: MIT Press; 2007), 37–59. But some evidence suggests that rates of close-kin marriage are now rising because of marriage patterns among immigrants to Western nations: Hanan Hamany et al., "Consanguineous Marriages, Pearls and Perils: Geneva International Consanguinity Workshop Report," *Genetics in Medicine* 13 (2011), 841–847.

28. Augustine: "Experti autem sumus in conubiis consobrinarum etiam nostris temporibus propter gradum propinquitatis fraterno gradui proximum quam raro per mores fiebat, quod fieri per leges licebat, quia id nec diuina prohibuit et nondum prohibuerat lex humana." ("And with regard to marriage in the next degree of consanguinity, marriage between first cousins (*consobrini*), we have observed that in our own time the customary morality has prevented this from being frequent, though the law permits it, since divine law did not prohibit it, nor as yet had human law done so.") On this text, see Philippe Moreau, "Plutarque, Augustin, Lévi-Strauss: Prohibition de l'Inceste et Mariage Préferentié dans la Rome Primitive," *Revue Belge de Philologie et d'Histoire* 56 (1978), 41–54.

29. Ghazi O. Tadmouri et al., "Consanguinity and Reproductive Health among Arabs," *Reproductive Health Journal* 6.17 (2009), published online at http://www.reproductive-health-journal.com/content/6/1/17.

observes, ancient historians have not yet fully absorbed.[30] The incest taboo is, in economic terminology, a constraining preference. Most people would never consider breaking the taboo, and not just because of fear of social sanctions, but simply because the taboo is so deeply ingrained within their psyches through the process of socialization. The taboo thus operates simultaneously as an inherent preference against incest and as a social constraint.

All this of course raises the question of what happens when such preferences and social constraints on individual behavior begin to weaken. And it is here that I wish to bring into the discussion the famous divorce of Sp. Carvilius Ruga (cos. 234, 228 BCE). Several ancient accounts of this divorce survive, varying in their details, but the likeliest story is something like the following: In connection (probably) with the Roman census of 230, Ruga divorced his wife because she was physically unable to bear him a child. While claiming to still love her deeply, he asserted that his continued marriage was incompatible with the required censorial oath that his marriage be "for the purpose of bearing children" (*liberorum quaerundorum causa* or the like). This formal explanation was, we are told, accepted as legitimate at the time, but was deeply unpopular because, as Valerius Maximus puts it, even at this early date most Romans "thought that not even desire of children should take precedence over fidelity to a spouse" (*quia ne cupiditatem quidem liberorum coniugali fidei praeponi debuisse arbitrantur*). However, interpretation of the episode was considerably clouded by Carvilius' apparently successful attempt to retain his wife's dowry after the divorce—strongly implying a rapacious motive behind his formal explanation.[31]

30. Pierre Bourdieu, "Les Stratégies Matrimoniales dans le Système de Reproduction," *Annales ESC* 4.5 (1975), 1105–1127 [="Marriage Strategies as Strategies of Social Reproduction," in R. Foster and O. Ranum, eds., *Family and Society: Selections from the Annales* (Baltimore: Johns Hopkins University Press, 1977), 117–144]; *Esquisse d'une Théorie de la Pratique, Précédé de Trois Études d'Ethnologie* Kabyle (Geneva: Droz, 1972), trans. Richard Nice, *Outline of a Theory of Practice* (Cambridge: Cambridge University Press, 1977), 30–71. Ubl, *Inzestverbot* 492.

31. See Valerius Maximus, 2.1.4; Dionysius, *Ant. Rom.* 2.25.7; Aulus Gellius, *NA* 4.3.1–2 and 17.21.44; Plutarch, *Quaest. Rom.* 14, *Theseus-Romulus* 35.3–2, and *Lycurgus-Numa* 25.12–13. In general, see Alan Watson, "The Divorce of Carvilius Ruga," *The Legal History Review* 22 (1965), 38–50, reprinted in *Studies in Roman Private Law* (2003), 23–36. Compare Susan Treggiari, *Roman Marriage: "Iusti Coniuges" from the Time of Cicero to the Time of Ulpian* (Oxford: Clarendon Press, 1991), 442: "Ruga was not the first man to di-

Legal historians generally attach great import to the divorce of Carvilius. As Alan Watson writes,

> It was a big step in the direction of free marriage. Previously, a wife who was divorced for one of certain specified faults lost all of her dowry. Where the wife was divorced and had not committed any of these specified faults—or, it may have been, was merely sent away, divorce of a wife innocent of these misdemeanors being impossible—the husband had to pay her a fixed proportion of his property. The decision in Carvilius' case breached this. In later law, there were no fixed grounds for divorce and the financial penalties for divorce were far less stringent. The exact steps of this development probably cannot be traced, but it recalls the disappearance of the actionability of *sponsalia* [betrothals] during the Republic and the increasing rarity of marriages *cum manu*.

The resemblance between the Carvilius story and the stories of Plutarch and the *Anecdoton* is obvious: an individual transgresses against traditional practices, with considerable public reaction, but in each case the transgressor prevails, with lasting effects for the institution of Roman marriage. To some extent, these stories reinforce each other as part of a single narrative, even if we are ultimately unable to reconstruct that narrative in detail. For instance, the Carvilius story is relatively securely dated, which provides a bit of support to the much maligned *Anecdoton*; for it seems unlikely that a Medieval forger would have accidentally stumbled on this particular dating.

The broader narrative therefore perhaps runs somewhat as follows: Within a generation after the First Punic War, Roman marriage underwent a fairly swift transition toward the more liberal regime associated with classical Roman law—liberal in the sense that it allowed consider-

---

vorce his wife. But his divorce was a landmark. The innovation when he divorced a beloved wife for sterility (because he could not otherwise tell the censors that he was married for the sake of procreating children) was that he suffered no financial penalty. From now on it therefore became necessary to allow the wife action for restoration of dowry." See also Susan E. Looper-Friedman, "The Decline of Manus-Marriage in Rome," *Tijdschrift voor Rechtsgeschiedenis* 44 (1987), 281–296; Annalize Jacobs, "*Carvilius Ruga v. Uxor*: A Famous Roman Divorce," *Fundamina: A Journal of Legal History* 15 (2009), 92–111, at 103–110.

ably greater leeway to personal choice in shaping individual marriages. This transition was not without controversy at the time, and the controversy seems to have had both social and political dimensions; but the controversy was not long-lasting, and in each case it ended with further liberalization. There is no transition from an exogamous to an endogamous marriage regime, and also, probably, there is no major change in pre-existing patterns of exogamous marriage.[32]

If this reconstruction is broadly correct—and our sources, for all their defects, do seem to support it—then the explanation for the transition is fairly readily to hand: it stemmed from, especially, the Roman upper classes having encountered, through the First Punic War and subsequent Roman dealings with the Greek and Hellenistic world, more individualistic aspects of Greek culture; and their subsequent attempt to implement this individualism within the still largely traditional domain of marriage—an attempt with far-reaching consequences for the form and nature of classical Roman marriage law. In this connection, it may be worth noting that it was Carvilius Ruga's freedman who, so it is reported, opened the first Roman elementary school and invented the letter "G."[33]

32. Adolfi, *Matrimonio Preclassico* 38–50 ("Exogamia della famiglia") emphasizes exogamy as an issue in early Rome, but I doubt Romans would have understood the issue this way. Compare Ubl, *Inzestverbot* 496 (of early Medieval marriage): "Die Ehe mit der Cousine, sofern sie außerhalb der hohen Aristokratie praktiziert wurde, war nicht Ausdruck einer tribalen Kultur, sondern eine akzeptierte, aber nicht bevorzugte und deshalp vermutlich auch eher seltene Eheform."

33. Plutarch, *Quaest. Rom.* 54 and 59; Q. Terentius Scaurus, *De Orthographia* 15.15–16.

Property Talk in Old English: Did Anglo-Saxon England Know the Concept of Seisin?

Paul R. Hyams[1]

Two seemingly distinct types of law are known from northern Europe in the early middle ages. The first is Roman law, as it survived the demise of the empire in the West, before fading into a further life as "Vulgar Law."[2] But there is also a second kind of law which may best be called non-Roman, although it was once judged "Germanic," and felt by a wishful leap (not entirely devoid of racism) from the linguistic fact of a family of Germanic languages to spring from a Germanic cultural heritage that reached back into the mists of time. The context was a series of learned debates between Romanists and Germanists that flourished in the nineteenth century and lasted well into the twentieth, energizing on the way a good deal of scholarly research and editorial work on the early middle ages. Many of the issues thus raised are now forgotten, buried beneath our more sophisticated understanding of ethnicity as a social construct. Most participating scholars shared a thorough education in the Roman law on which most Continental

1. I am grateful to the many people who made helpful responses to various preliminary presentations on this subject on both sides of the Atlantic, but especially to Mark Atherton and our honorand. Without them, there would be many more errors.

2. C. Sanchez-Moreno Ellart, "Law, vulgar," in *The Encyclopedia of Ancient History*, ed. R.S. Bagnall et al. (Blackwell: Oxford, 2013), 3975–3978 offers a brief introduction to current opinion. I have myself only the most basic acquaintance with Roman law and have taken my cues from A. Berger, *Encyclopedic Dictionary of Roman Law* (Philadelphia: American Philosophical Society, 1953), B. Nicholas, *An Introduction to Roman Law* (Oxford: Clarendon Press: 1962).

systems are based since the early modern "Reception," and which as a result remained highly relevant to any attempts to study, analyze, modernize, or reform current law. Only England stood apart, confident of its own native tradition that had produced the Anglo-American Common Law.

One central strand of contentious issues concerned notions of property, the ways that people thought, talked, and occasionally wrote about what was "mine" and what "thine." The Germanists had discovered a unitary concept of property known as *Gewere*.[3] Their forefathers had allegedly relied on this instead of the Roman distinction between possession and ownership, which remains to this day central to the common law's understanding of property.[4] Now, all Western legal systems that recognize private property need to allow for two levels of interest in land and other property. A simple view of the Western way to manage this may be illustrated as follows. One may borrow for a time things that you will then possess but not own. The lender surrenders possession while the loan continues, but will continue to own the things. Or take the position of a thief who steals something of yours and has it physically under his control. You would certainly object if he was said to own the object, and would deny that he had even legitimate possession. I use for simplicity's sake examples concerning chattels, things that are usually movable, but the same principles are transferable to immovable land. The concept of *Gewere* (also called "seisin") dealt with the same kind of facts without positing any sharp or clear distinction. It handled all property interests within a single portmanteau notion that carried (as it were) both sides of the possession/ownership distinction whose familiarity in the Western world makes it seem to us like the norm. *Gewere*-seisin enclosed possession, ownership, and perhaps also some kinds of factual control unrecognized by modern law, without the aid of overt lines to separate different kinds of interest. One might say that all degrees of control over property had to be fitted within a single conceptual bag.

3. The French equivalent is *saisine*, and I shall use the English form of this in my text, since seisin is what entered the English legal lexicon.

4. I rely for my understanding of the Germanist argument mostly on the old French scholars cited in notes 5 and 7 below. W. Ogris, "Gewere," in *Handwörterbuch zur Deutschen Rechtsgeschichte* (Berlin: Erich Schmidt Verlag, 2012), 2.2, 347–52 gives a brief statement of the current status quo.

Although Anglo-Saxon England had as good a claim to be considered a Germanic society as any other in northern Europe, nobody in the Germanist heyday or since ever seems to have asked whether it too might have understood and made use of the concept of *Gewere*-seisin, or tried to explain why it did not. There was no Old English noun equivalent of *Gewere* to draw their attention, and the French equivalent, *saisine*, is not found before the Norman Conquest. Scholars perhaps felt that if Anglo-Saxon law were to be considered worthy of standing alongside those of other systems, it too must have used the familiar opposition, so they duly found what they considered Old English equivalents in the lexicon. Though Anglo-Saxon historians, a century ago, knew their German scholarship far better than I do, and some must certainly have pondered my question, I know of no published discussion. There is little enough discussion of seisin *after* 1066, during the "first century of English feudalism," as it used to be known, despite the good reviews received by the 1924 book that explained the concept of seisin and its importance in English legal history.[5]

It is therefore time to ask whether the notion of *Gewere*/seisin (hereafter "seisin") might have been known and used in England before 1066. I shall make the best case I can that it was.[6] I start by asking how a portmanteau concept like seisin *might* have functioned, and use the ancient French literature on the concept to construct the most workable model I can, one that makes most sense of the Continental evidence. I shall then assess this model against what we can know of Anglo-Saxon law, to see if it might have

5. F. Jouon des Longrais, *La conception anglaise de la saisine du xiie au xive siècle* (Paris: Jouve, 1924). The reviews focus almost exclusively on his demonstration that seisin was the term of choice in the eleventh and twelfth centuries. They say little of the rest of the book, which is, indeed, of little value today. Neither the book, nor the later article, id., "La portée des réformes d'Henry II en matière de saisine," *Revue historique de droit français et étranger* 4e s. 15 (1936): 540–71, which defends its argument, are much read today. I have noticed little engagement with its argument, apart from the fine study of S. E. Thorne, "Livery of Seisin," *Law Quarterly Review* 52 (1936), 345–64, before R. C. van Caenegem, *Royal Writs in England from the Conquest to Glanvill*, Selden Society 66 (1959), contested some of Jouon's contentions concerning the importance of seisin's role in the Angevin law reforms of the last third of the twelfth century.

6. Being a specialist neither in Old English nor Roman law, I am incompletely equipped for my self-set task and also, despite editorial kindnesses, constrained in space and time. I therefore rely on J. Hudson, *The Oxford History of the Laws of England*, II (Oxford: Oxford University Press, 2012) in lieu of other secondary literature.

so functioned in England. I shall end with a few remarks about the different kind of law in the period before the legal revolution" of the eleventh and twelfth centuries these seem to indicate. In doing this, I shall try not to beg any questions by using the language of possess/ion and own/ership. This will not be easy. These notions and the distinction between them are as deeply ingrained into our modern English culture as they had been in the Latin language that coined and relied on them. They seem implicit in anything one says on the subject of property.

A Model of Seisin

French authors[7] describe the key to seisin as *jouissance*, enjoyment, a mysterious formulation for many readers. The reference is in fact to the Latin verb *furor* from which we get our word "fruits."[8] One has seisin if one controls the land and exploits it by taking its fruits. This also displays seisin to neighbors and others in ways that they can experience and remember. Visible things represent the best proofs humans can manage in God's lesser, worldly city.[9] Thus seisin uses what can be seen by human eyes as the best indication of the divine verities of right in land and other property; from this humans must establish their rights. The prudent man will take care to ensure that his neighbors do not just see him enjoying his fruits, and will explain in words why he is entitled to do so and on what terms.[10] He will

7. My main source is Ernest Champeaux, *Essai sur la vestitura ou saisine et l'introduction des actions possessoires dans l'ancien droit français* (Paris: Thorin, 1898), but the English literature rests on Jouon, *La conception anglaise de la saisine* (above, n. 5), who studied only the period after 1066, and took much of the theory from his master.

8. This represents Roman law usage. Nicholas, *Introduction to Roman Law*, chap. 3, esp. 107–15, and Berger, *Encyclopedic Dictionary*, 477–8, 755, sketch the law of property. J. C. Tate, "Ownership and Possession in the Early Common Law," *American Journal of Legal History* 48 (2006): 280–95, helpfully assembles the materials available to the twelfth-century schools.

9. See Augustine, *De Civitate Dei*, X. xiv, for the idea that one perceives deep *invisibilia* through the more easily attainable *visibilia*, as noted in the excellent work of Scott Thompson Smith, *Land and Book: Literature and Land Tenure in Anglo-Saxon England* (Toronto: University of Toronto Press, 2012), 27–31, 41–2, 48. Also Ogris, "Gewere," 348, 351.

10. There were as many prudent women in early England as at any other time; I apologize for using male forms.

instruct them what to see and remember, so that future witnesses do not mistake or miss the message. And since seisin is the basis for all claims, anyone who is not known to have been seised by an entitled grantor may have difficulty in persuading any court to grant him title.

Laymen will do their talking in the vernacular, which perhaps encourages them to draw on unlawyerly images and metaphors when they describe their position. So a landholder *sits* on the land.[11] He and his kindred aim to *wear* their land, to be, as it were, *clothed* in it, so that it seems to become part of them or they of it.[12] It is theirs to have and *hold*, to keep in *hand*, under their protection. Notably, much of this imagery makes better sense of movable goods that can be held in the hand than of immovable land, a hint that its distant origin may lie in thought about chattels, perhaps ultimately about theft.[13]

Just as more than one person may possess property, several different people may be seised of it too, as lord, borrower, "owner," possibly even as thief, trespasser, or invader. So people ask how a claimant is seised, what kind of seisin he may have. It can be legitimate, by right, or unjust, perhaps as an invader, or even precarious, as a peasant cultivator holding at his lord's will. Each "enjoys" in his own way.[14] Seisin is thus both crude and simple enough to be handled without too much legal learning, and also flexible enough to treat the variety of situations that arise in property disputes. It covers seamlessly all the conceptual territory modern law treats through the opposition of possession and ownership.

11. The etymology of both Latin *possideo* and "seisin" itself contains this idea.

12. Hence the German term, *Gewere*, for the seisin notion. See further below (at nn. 20–22).

13. The simple distinction between movables and immovables is one that survived the transition between the Roman empire in the West and the successor kingdoms, Nicholas, *Introduction to Roman Law*, 105 ff.; Champeaux, *Essai sur la vestitura ou saisine*, 57–68, 304 ff.

14. The quality of the seisin is then critical. Hence the invention of written, definitive *qualis* clauses from the twelfth century onwards. See, e.g., ibid., 304 ff.; "Summa de Legibus," in *Coutumiers de Normandie*, ed. E.-J, Tardif (Rouen: Impr. de E. Cagniard, 1881–1903), 95. 1. 14.

Human Right is not Absolute

This may help to explain the difficulties historians have experienced in locating full rights of ownership in the early middle ages. Absolute ownership is in fact generally recognized as a chimera, not to be found in any legal system. The divine Maitland was wrong to speak of the "mystery of seisin." The real mystery is right itself, an entity so mysterious that God alone knows for sure what it is and where it lies. Susan Reynolds recently reminded early medieval historians to hedge their bets and talk of something like the fullest right known at the time.[15] I take my cue from the Grand Assize of c. 1179 which added to the standard test of right at the time, judicial battle, a tenant's option of a special high-level jury of knights designed to be as near an exact equivalent as possible. Like battle, this sought God's judgment. Also like it, the question posed was not straight and factual, like "which party has right?" but one that combined factual and normative elements, asking which party had the greater right (*maius ius*).[16] This was a very conservative reform, so formulated as to win over traditionalists. Posing the question in the comparative represents the way those trying to resolve real-life disputes then and in the past had generally understood their task. Certainly, it accords with the ancient and widespread notion that *Gewere* or seisin brought one nearer to proof (*näher zum Beweis*), and posed a question that could be divinely resolved in a single act.[17] Precedents from the learned laws for a comparative formulation[18] show that it was perfectly able to co-exist alongside the distinction between possession and right. But if rivals for property could have greater or lesser right, it might be natural to understand property interest in general as varying as if on a sliding scale through the concept of seisin.

15. S. Reynolds, *Fiefs and Vassals* (Oxford: Oxford University Press, 1994), chap. 3, esp. 53–4, 59–60.

16. *Glanvill*, ed. G. D. G Hall (Oxford: Clarendon Press, 1965, reissued 1993), ii. 14; Hudson, *Laws of England*, 600–03.

17. Ogris, "Gewere," 348; Champeaux, *Essai sur la vestitura ou saisine*, 336–7. *Liber Eliensis*, ed. E. O. Blake (London: Royal Historical Society, 1962), [Hereafter "LE"], ii. 11a (89) speaks of a woman who had "*maius rectum*" in land, apparently through a previous husband.

18. Nicholas, *Introduction to Roman Law*, 155, and cf. the use of *plus iuris* in Digest, 43.17.2 and also in canonical texts.

The Case for Seisin in Anglo-Saxon England

All this is just a model. We must now see if it corresponds to anything that could have existed in early England. But first one more warning. I have talked as if seisin, like possession and ownership, were a definable abstract noun. In fact most of the early medieval texts use verbs not nouns. Seisin should be understood as an action verb, one that expresses an action, that a person (or animal or force of nature) can perform or do. Actors in this model seek to be seised or re-seised; they do not claim seisin. It is not an abstract state of being, still less an institution or definable concept.[19] That came later, if at all. And action verbs favor "Show" as against "Tell"; anything they do or change should in principle be visible.

It is not too surprising then that no Old English noun can be shown to mean seisin, or be etymologically connected with the words *Gewere* or seisin.[20] The Latin *saisire*, used in the generations after the Norman Conquest in an active, transitive sense, is rarely found before 1066.[21] Another verbal absence in Old English is any contrast or opposition between possess and own.[22] There is, indeed, a small group of Old English verbs and some of their cognate nouns which have been thought to fill the gap and signify owning and ownership, *Āgan*, *Agen*, *Agnian*, and the preterite form, *Æhtan*, with nouns such as *Agend*, *Ār(e)* etc. Some of the finest Old English scholars have translated all of these on some occasions as "own," but on others as "possess."[23] Anyone at all schooled in law will find this disturbing.

19. D. Daube, *Roman Law: Linguistic, Social and Philosophical Aspects* (Edinburgh: Edinburgh University Press, 1969), chap. 1, esp. 29 ff., introduced me to the action noun and its verbs. But Jouon, *La conception anglaise de la saisine*, 167–69 dated the arrival of the noun in England to c. 1130, followed by S. F. C. Milsom, *Historical Foundations of the Common Law*, 2d ed. (London: Butterworths, 1981), 120, and nobody has to my knowledge studied the matter in depth since 1924.

20. Ogris, "Gewere," 347 notes the Frankish origins of the seisin word.

21. Jouon, *La conception anglaise de la saisine*, 169 quotes Asser: "quod illi non poterunt *seisinare* vel introducere quemcunque illis placuerit in eorum terras, possessiones et dominio." See also *Leges Henrici Primi*, ed. L. J. Downer (Oxford: Clarendon Press, 1972), 5.26 and notes.

22. On these, Patrick Wormald, "A Handlist of Anglo-Saxon Lawsuits," *Anglo-Saxon England* 17 (1988), 247–281, and idem, *The Making of English Law: King Alfred to the Twelfth Century* (Oxford: Blackwell, 1999), esp. 143–61 remains the authority.

23. Since these all begin with the letter "A", one can study their senses in *The Dictionary of Old English*, ed. A. Cameron, et al. (Toronto: University of Toronto Press,

No good lawyer could easily believe that the same word could denote both sides of so fundamental a legal distinction. It looks as if the Old English language made it close to impossible for its speakers to express the distinction at all, which in its turn makes it hard to see how English men and women could *use* the distinction in their own everyday property dealings.[24] Property, wealth, after all is something which reaches deep down into the life and culture of—at the very least—a nobility greedy for red gold and shining silver, men who did not think twice about listing other human beings among the stock on their estates. This fact alone casts doubt on the received view and justifies this study.

Space does not permit a detailed examination of the lexicography of this word group. It would be beside the point anyway. Though I have scrutinized the dictionary citations from laws and charters in the context of the texts from which they come, these can do no more than establish the possibility of the seisin hypothesis, that it makes as good sense to read the words in the group in its terms as in the more specific received understanding of the possess-and-own distinction. I shall return to this matter, when I discuss what we can know about argument and proof in contested lawsuits. There probably was no ultimate meaning of this ambiguous word group, until God had spoken and His judgment had been received.

There are, however, a few further points that emerge from the words in question which claim attention. One is the fact that *Agend* (another derivative of *agan*), often thought to denote "owner,"[25] is found only in the very earliest laws and in no charter. It is used for the authority that God (and on occasion also the Devil) is said to have over the world and its contents.[26] It

1986–), cited below for letters A–G as DOE from http://doe.utoronto.ca/pages/index.html. Otherwise I have used J. Bosworth and T. N. Toller, *An Anglo-Saxon Dictionary* (Oxford: Clarendon Press, 1921) with supplement, cited from the online version at http://www.bosworthtoller.com/ as BT.

24. Smith, *Land and Book*, 12, n. 34 is the only scholar I have noticed who sees this problem. I am aware that linguistic specialists warn that the different recorded senses of words do not necessarily bleed into each. Indeed the same word (e.g., the verb to cleave) *can* sometime mean both an act or thing and its antonym. The Church's literate elite naturally wrote in Latin much of the time.

25. DOE s.v., and cf. BT, 28, also ibid., 617 for *land-agend(e)*.

26. DOE s.v. *agend* 5. Cf. too DOE s.vv. *āgniend* (Gen. 14:22) and also *æht* 1c, where "the whole world and its contents" are said to be "the property and chattels" of God or the Devil.

is tempting to deduce from this a Christian teaching that God alone could be considered the owner of the earth. To God "the Creator" we should add "God the Owner, Lord of the World," a divine attribute that makes human aspirations to ownership appear positively blasphemous. Here and elsewhere, words that appear to mean "owner" have to be placed not merely in context but within their whole semantic range and judged on patterns of usage. *Agend* fails this test. It is never contrasted to a mere possessor, and it is not used of a human actor in law codes, charters, or narratives, where a lawyer in search of a distinction would demand precision.

None of this need imply that England and its early medieval neighbors were cultures where the private ownership of all kinds of property was not recognized, prized, solemnly transferred in diverse manners, stolen, and fiercely disputed. The sources are full of references to the right to hang thieves or behead them on the spot if caught in the act. Notions of "mine" and "thine" are embedded as deeply in their culture as in our own. Men risked their wealth and sometimes their lives to claim the fullest rights of control they could over land and other property. They engraved on their rings and swords and books that these were Charlie's or Sheila's, and laid anathemas on the villains who stole things or failed to return loans.[27] They handled these issues, apparently, without recourse to that familiar Roman distinction that had passed unchallenged into the legal systems of the modern West. "The past," however, "is a foreign country; they do things differently there." Exactly how differently the English "did" property is too deep a question for the present, but my guess is that all these terms operated within a general sense of the possessive, of the kind that non-lawyers voiced (until very recently at least) by an apostrophe "s."[28]

This would explain why so many of the terms used in both pre-emptive and contested circumstances are far vaguer than modern lawyers would expect. Men have (OE *habban*) their land (OE *land* or *lond*). It belongs to them, and they and their appurtenances belong to it (OE *belimpan*, *gebyrian* etc.). Judging from written texts, they (and their advocates) very often spoke colloquially and tackled matters of property through metaphor and

27. Examples of naming inscriptions in E. Okasha, *Hand-List of Anglo-Saxon Non-Runic Inscriptions* (Cambridge: Cambridge University Press, 1971).

28. See John Hudson, "Milsom's Legal Structure: Interpreting Twelfth-Century Law," *Tijdschrift voor Rechtsgeschiedenis* 47 (1991): 61–2.

visual images. They wear and are clothed in their land, or are clothed in ancestral right to it. This is OE *gewerian* (or sometimes simply *werian*), the verb form behind *Gewere*.[29] Though it may seem as Germanic as could be, the best view now seems to be that it is a vernacularization of Latin *vestire*, from which springs *vestitura* and a slew of English terms prominent in the seisin literature, such as "investiture" and "vested," as in the later emphatic phrase "vested and seised."[30] Yet England is thought to have inherited very little from that Roman law from which Continental notions of "enjoyment" derive.

Gewerian conveys the depth of engagement of a landholder and his (or her) landed property through the relatively superficial attachment of clothes to body. OE *sittan* achieves the same by the even more superficial act of sitting on it.[31] It applies to an occupier who is said to "stay, dwell, sojourn, abide, reside, remain in a place."[32] Or perhaps you grasp it, "hold" it in your hand, as in the phrase to "have and hold."[33] In each case, others

29. For the perfective form, *gewerian*, cf. BT, 466, 677, and Supplement, 449. For simple *werian*, BT, 1169, and for *warian*, note sense 3, citing Beowulf. Many of the 38 matches for *gewer** in the *Dictionary of Old English Web Corpus* online at http://www.doe.utoronto.ca/pages/pub/web-corpus.html, are evidently compatible with the argument in the text.

30. E. Conte, "*Gewere*, vestitura, *spolium*: un' ipotesi di interpretazione," in *Mélanges en l'honneur d'Anne Lefebvre-Teillard*, ed. B. d'Alteroche et al. (Paris: Éditions Panthéon-Assas, 2009), 267–88, argues very cogently that the usage began in papal Latin, during the 7th and 8th centuries and in the context of a drive to restore to bishops and other prelates lost estates of which they and their saints had been despoiled. From these efforts there eventually emerged the influential maxim *nemo placitet dissaisiatus* and the Romano-canonist *actio spolii*. LE ii.18 speaks of land of which the Ely monks were *vestita sive saisita* for many years without challenge. This narrative text, though composed in the twelfth century, reproduces much of a pre-Conquest text, the *Libellus Æthewoldi*.

31. Examples are P. H. Sawyer, *Anglo-Saxon Charters* (London: Royal Historical Society, 1968), nos. 1517, 1539, cited from the updated online version at http://www.esawyer.org.uk/about/index.html [cited hereafter as S followed by charter number].

32. BT, 879, esp. sense 2a. *Gesettan*, the perfective form can also mean much the same, ibid., 440, and supplement, 410. McGovern, "The Meaning of 'Gesetteland' in Anglo-Saxon Land Tenure," *Speculum* 46 (1971), 589–86 takes a different view. And for III Atr 14, cf. below (at n. 57).

33. See, e.g., S 1420; W. H. Stevenson, "An Old English Charter of William the Conqueror in Favour of St. Martin's-Le-Grand, London, A.D. 1068," *English Historical Review* 11 (1896): 741–42 (1068), cited by T.D. Hill, "'To have and hold:' Beowulf Line 658"(unpublished) who brought this and much else to my notice. See now Paul Acker, *Revising*

can see you in occupation and control of land, as a king or bishop sits on his throne visibly radiating legitimacy and authority. Hence too, the use of power words, such as OE *wealden* and *hand*.[34]

But OE *brucan* may be the most significant of the verbs used for occupation. Its prime meaning is to enjoy. But usage includes stocking land and defending it when called upon to contribute to *geld* or *fyrd*, and presumably also if rivals attempt to invade. Its meaning can extend to benefit from, use, and control or exploit land, and can also denote proactive action.[35] It is mostly found in *læns*, leases for one or more lives, which being limited in duration must in principle coexist with another, greater interest to which they ought to revert after the final life. Many of the *læns* written in Old English lay down that the lessee was "to habbane and brucane" the estate, before specifying the lives that defined its term. Many others in Latin use the verb *perfruor*, presumably having the same range of meanings and thrust.[36] The word's use to cover more permanent grants is less easily illustrated but does exist, for example, in the Old English Bede's rendering of *Historia Ecclesiastica*, ii. 3 (142): *territoria ac possessiones in usum eorum … adiecit* as a royal grant him to *brucanne mid heora geferum* and in a number of Latin leases.[37] It is enough to suggest that this "enjoyment" indicated a range of property interests, sometimes still undefined or even allegedly unjust.[38]

This image-laden language seems far from the precision of the terms of art that we find from before 1200 in common law records. Since the texts which preserve them for our examination are, like virtually all written materials from Anglo-Saxon England, the products of a literate elite of churchmen, we must assume that such educated men found the language

Oral Theory: Formulaic Composition in Old English and Old Icelandic Verse (New York: Garland, 1998), 6–14.

34. See, e.g., S 1066, 1116.

35. The evidence is too copious to cite in detail; cf. DOE s.vv. *brucan*, *bryce* 2, *gebrucan*. As for exploitation, one might note the care many leases take to ensure the conservation of the estate's stock in cattle and men, e.g., S 1464 and in DOE *æht* 1b.

36. See, e.g., S 1409, and for *perfruor*, such Worcester leases as S 1321–3.

37. The Bede citation comes from DOE *brucan* 3. 1a. Other apparently permanent grants, some in Old English, others in Latin, direct that the grants be enjoyed, e.g. S 459, 479, 496, 535, 617, 886.

38. S 1195, 1204a, 1508 show that the verb was used of various kinds of occupation, which might even be, as S 1457 indicates, unjust or *on reaflace*.

adequate for the promotion of peace and justice among the English people, including themselves. The literate few and their masters, the power men of the kingdom, apparently found their language, whether vernacular Old English or accompanying Latin, fit for purpose.

PROCEDURE AND PLEADING

We can now see what can be learned of that purpose from records of the way the English argued and resolved their property disputes.[39] The framework around which the dynamic of early medieval trials usually played itself out pivoted around three decisive moments. After someone had been admitted to present his complaint, and this had been discussed, the suitors agreed a preliminary (or "*mesne*") judgment in which the court decided what proof to award and on which party the burden was to lie. This was in many ways the decisive moment of the whole suit. Since proof often, and in land cases almost universally, took the form of an oath, this first judgment set the terms in which it was to be sworn, which party had to swear, and how many oath-helpers were required to support it. This was the human formulation of a question to be put to God, on the community's behalf, as it were. The second decisive moment only followed after a delay for necessary preparations. It consisted of the actual proof, God's judgment. The third such moment is less commented upon in the literature. It consisted of the collective perception of the result, a recognition by those present of what they acknowledged seeing, in order that the presiding officer could pronounce a final judgment as to what they all deemed themselves to know and what was to be done about it.

In the kinds of complex disputes that generated most extant narratives, this must have taken time, weeks rather than days, during which the whole neighborhood rehearsed what they knew of the circumstances, raked up ancient memories and refreshed old prejudices and partialities. Early medieval courts had no rules of admissible evidence or gag laws. Much would seem obscenely foreign to modern lawyers.

39. Hudson, *Laws of England*, chap. 4 is the best survey of procedure. But I also bear in mind a tentative model I first developed for the period before the legal revolution in Paul Hyams, "Henry II and Ganelon," *The Syracuse Scholar* 4 (1983), 23–35.

It is in this context that I would read a famous statement relating to a lawsuit of the 980s naming just three land procedures to which, it says, the English people (*leodscipe*) could commit itself. These are named as *tale ne teames ne ahnunga*.[40] I shall consider each of these in turn, and treat them mainly in the context of secular property interests, even though the statement occurs in an ecclesiastical narrative composed for the Bishop of Rochester.

In the *talu*, a complainant tells his story in his own way. This "statement of claim"[41] is essential to launch the suit in the hope of getting his opponent into court to face the complaint. He may be met by an oral counter-statement (OE *ontalu*) or more probably just a straight denial.[42] Extant narratives often include incomplete hints of what their side said,[43] but say little of counter-arguments. They give few indications of the kind of formality suggested by tracts like *Swerian* and *Becwæđ*.[44] Pleas seem to have differed from twelfth-century practice in three ways. Claimants never assert that they hold "de" or "sub" anyone in the way English *antecessores* are depicted as doing in *Domesday Book*. Though they usually emphasize the rightfulness of their own claim, they seldom trace a hereditary descent of their right in the formalized fashion of actions of right.[45] And they are

40. S 1457 (980/7).

41. Hudson, *Laws of England*, 69–72. The later common law term "count," derived from *conte*, meaning in twelfth-century conversational French much the same as OE *talu*.

42. BT, 742, 971, s.vv. *talu*, *ontalu*; and cf. above [at n. 34].

43. Examples include S 1447 (Archbishop Dunstan emphasizes duty as guardian of child claimant),1456 (reading out the landbooks),

44. F. Liebermann, *Gesetze de Angelsachsen* (Halle: Max Niemeyer, 1903–16), 1.396–8, 400. There is more and stronger evidence for pleading rigor later from treatises like such as *Brevia Placitata*, ed. G. J. Turner and T. F. T. Plucknett, Selden Society 66 (London: 1951), and *Novae Narrationes*, ed. Elsie Shanks and S. F. C. Milsom, Selden Society 80 (London, 1963). Hudson, *Laws of England*, 76 ff. is more inclined than I to believe the OE tracts.

45. S. F. C. Milsom, "Introduction," to Sir Frederick Pollock and F. W. Maitland, *The History of English Law before the time of Edward I*, 2nd ed., repr. ed. (Cambridge: Cambridge University Press, 1968) [hereafter *HEL*], xxxii ff. explained why he understood the twelfth-century norm to be counts founded on hereditary descent, but seems never to have argued his view in detail. See, however, his introduction to *Novae Narrationes*, xxxi ff. and xliv ff. and Milsom, *Historical Foundations of the Common Law*, 119–24. Purchasers, as defined in the next note, were apparently excluded from suing in the right at common law, *Brevia Placitata*, lxxi, ciii, 137–8, 193; W. H. Dunham, ed., *Casus Placitorum and Reports of Cases in the King's Courts, 1272–1278*, Selden Society 69 (London, 1952), 25/55.

comfortable explaining how they acquired the land, whereas later claimants could not usually plead a "purchase," that is a title that did not descend from a father or other close kinsman.[46]

Téam represents the procedure later known as warranty, when someone accused of having stolen property or acquired it illegitimately, summons the person from whom he acquired it to warrant (i.e., confirm and guarantee) his title in court. The burden of defending the case then devolves on this warrantor.[47] If he fails, he must compensate the original defendant by offering an exchange or the value in money. All the extant evidence concerns movables, usually cattle or horses. There is no good evidence for how this procedure, doubtless conceived for use against animal thieves and rustlers, was applied in land cases before 1066.

The third procedure, *ahnung* or *agnung*, is a little more complicated.[48] It is in essence like *talu*, a statement of claim, but addressed more directly to God. The claimant proposes a form of words for an oath to be sworn along with a panel of oath-helpers having personal knowledge of the facts, some chosen by himself, but others nominated by the neighborhood.[49] This is somewhat reminiscent of saga descriptions of negotiations at the Icelandic Thing. The *ahnung* must often have represented a pre-emptive coup to bypass *mesne* judgment and pressure the suitors towards a favorable form of oath, something less bland and peaceful than today's settlement "out of court." As the *witan* suitors are famously and ominously reported to have

46. The term "purchase" here covers non-commercial acquisitions as well as sales made during a litigant's lifetime. OE *sellan* (BT, 861, s.v.) does not discriminate between sales and non-commercial grants of land. OE *bicgan* and *gebicgan* (DOE s.vv.; BT, 98, 137, 377 and supplement, 300) do seem to be restricted to money transactions.

47. Hudson, *Laws of England*, 155–59, sees *team* as similar to but not identical with the later warranty procedure.

48. The word derives from the ambiguous verb *agnian*, discussed above, and has to my knowledge provoked little literature. Hudson, *Laws of England*, 76, glosses it as "ownership."

49. I Ew 1.3; II As 9; II Cn 24–24. (I cite Anglo-Saxon laws by the sigla established in Liebermann, ed., *Gesetze der Angelsachsen*, 1.ix–x. Each of these enactments place the *ahnung* in the context of cattle theft, associating it with the *team* procedure discussed above and the royal requirement that such sales be made before specially appointed witnesses. Quadripartitus translated the words, *ahnung* and *agnian* as *propriare* and *propriatio*, which I understand as declarations that the goods were one's own. That the laws at least sometimes use *gewitnes* to denote personal knowledge as much as formal witness is suggested by the citations in BT, 470 and suppl., 455.

said during one lawsuit around 990, "it would be better for the oath to be set aside now rather than sworn, because thereafter friendship will be at an end."[50] These moments were intrinsically and consciously dramatic. The *ahnung* was a ritual act of power,[51] intended to over-awe the audience and beat down opposition, and one where numbers counted.[52]

There is little evidence in the narratives of fine distinctions or legal tricks and dodges. I see nothing there, which notions of seisin could not handle at least as well as arguments in terms of possession and right. The three procedures just examined were in any event not the only options. The great churches and their dead saints whose concerns dominate our narratives could usually support their claims with a charter, and if necessary create one for the occasion. This conveniently brought its possessor "nearer to the oath."[53] Other things being equal, he could expect to gain a favorable proof. This was not the kind of clear rule which later decided such matters.[54] It could not by itself be conclusive, since it preceded the required proof, and might be countered by the opponent with some counter-plea of the kind that winners' narratives always omit.[55] It must have been more like a legal maxim, an argument to be deployed and rhetorically manipulated toward a favorable judgment,[56] or alongside a demonstration of power. Once the great had agreed what to decide, the rest probably fell into line.

50. S 1454 (990/2). By poetic license I transpose the words into direct speech.

51. Both S 1454 and S 1458 use the verb *gelæden* of the *ahnung* event. Since this usually means to produce, bring forth, the writers were emphasizing the human agency behind the mise-en-scene.

52. In one case, the Abbot of Ely assembled in court all the better sort from six hundreds, and when this failed to convince brought their numbers up to more than a thousand, as *LE*, ii. 25 (99) reports.

53. Cf. *LE*, ii. 25 (99): *quia propior erat ille, ut terram haberet, qui cyrographum habebat qui non habebat*. Cf. Hudson, *Laws of England*, 68, 77–80, and text above, at note 16.

54. Alan Kennedy, "Law and Litigation in the *Libellus Æthelwoldi Episcopi*," *Anglo Saxon England* 24 (1995), 163, 181–82; Ogris, "Gewere," 351 notes that the principle of "*näher zum Beweis*" was current on the Continent.

55. See, e.g., I Ew 1.5, which allows the defense to compel a claimant to choose between *ahnung* and *team*.

56. I discussed in a preliminary fashion of the ways that maxims were used in my "Due Process Versus the Maintenance of Order in European Law: The Contribution of the *Ius Commune*," in Peter Coss, ed., *The Moral World of the Law* (Cambridge: Cambridge University Press, 2000), chap. 5, and especially its appendix. See also S. D. White, "Proposing the Ordeal and Avoiding it: Strategy and Power in Western French Litigation,

Humans had already severely limited God's choices before He gave His judgment as to where justice and right lay.

It not surprising if our narratives always report this divine decision as conclusive, and never make it conditional on any point that could spawn later conflict. Their authors were of course writing for the winners. Losers were often made to renounce all future claims, so that the winners should take the disputed lands *uncwydd 7 uncrafod, unbecweden, unbefliten, unforboden, or unbesacen.*[57] Such declarations of tenure permanently beyond challenge confirm the fullest seisin possible rather than ownership, *ipso nomine.* And the laws only say that claims to land must be put in during a landholder's lifetime and not after his death.[58]

Norman royal writs make an instructive contrast with the Anglo-Saxon materials, for a number end with the injunction that the addressees should act "so that I hear no more about this claim (or dispute) for lack of justice."[59] The obvious intention was that judgment was to be beyond future challenge. In contrast, writs of Henry I and Stephen, still framed in seisin terms, begin to omit this clause to leave open the possibility that a defeated litigant might try again later, suing presumably in what law schools would call "the right." Nothing like this is found before 1066, nor is there any hint that there might be more than a single, unitary level of property interest or any dual process.

1050–1110," in *Cultures of Power,* ed. T. N. Bisson (Philadelphia: University of Pennsylvania Press, 1995), 89–123.

57. III Atr 3 orders that "compromises for love" should be just as binding (*fæst*) as judgments. The range of terms used to express this in charters and narratives suggests a fear that the results might not hold; cf. Hudson, *Laws of England,* 92. For sample illustrations of the words in the text, see S 1460, 1447 and BT s.vv.

58. III Atr 14: "And se the sitte uncwydd 7 uncrafod on his are on life, thæt nan mann on his yrfenuman ne spece æfter his dæge," renewed and extended in V Atr, 32.3, II Cn 72. *LE,* ii. 18, 24 (93–94, 97–98) records a confirmatory case which failed and the claimant fined "because he claimed land, on which he had put in no challenge while Ogga (his kinsman] was alive."

59. *[V]idete ne amplius clamorem audiam....,* first seen in van Caenegem, *Royal Writs,* no. 69 (1087/1100), and later clarified by a reference to *recti penuria.* Ibid., 71/137 (1100/1).

What You See is What You Get

The good lawyer keeps his client out of court by heading off trouble in advance. Landholders are well advised to do the same. We should therefore ask what steps the prudent landholders and their grantors take to ensure that the neighbors[60] understand what they might be needed to remember in time of challenge. They had to arrange the right kinds of visible, memorable events.

The *traditio*, later called "Livery of Seisin," was a ceremonial, public transfer or conveyance that might take place on or near the land itself, at an altar belonging to the recipient church, or at some public assembly or court.[61] We know of no set script and few rules. Explanatory words seem to be optional rather than essential.[62] Though first in importance, this *traditio* was not the first act in the sequence. At least one essential preliminary preceded it, a perambulation to clarify the identity of the property transferred.[63] Once more the accompanying conversations were key. The parties (or their representatives) would surely bring friends and neighbors along as witnesses, and everybody would chat away as they hiked or rode round the estate. In addition to the usual local gossip and farming talk, their conversation might well rehearse the circumstances of the grant and the rules by which such matters had "always" been governed in the area. One such grantor ordered his *geneat*, to ride out with a priest from his adversary's church, and lead him round the bounds of his property while the

60. I use "neighbor" as shorthand for the surrounding community, from which future witnesses and oath-helpers must come. "Friend" might be an alternative term, though OE *neáh-gebúr* does exist, BT, 711.

61. Charters reveal much less of the detail than the occasional narrative source such as *LE*, ii. 11, 19, 25, 31 etc.

62. In *LE*, ii. 18 (94), "Ogga rose up and when he had got silence said: 'I want you know, my very dear friends, that I am giving to St. Etheldreda [i.e. Ely] one hide of land in Cambridge after my days are over.'" But his *traditio* came later. This was the time to enter a challenge to the grantor's right.

63. Champeaux, *Essai sur la vestitura ou saisine*, 66–68, 192–98, 283–84 and Pollock and Maitland, *HEL*, 1.152; Hudson, *Laws of England*, 92, 142–3. Perambulations were just as important after a lawsuit.

priest "read out from the old charters, how they had been determined by the grant of king Æthelbald."[64]

After the grant was completed, the new holder may have put on a third event, later known as an attornment.[65] The idea was to assemble the peasant sub-tenants who were actually to work the land for the new man, as they had for his predecessor, to acknowledge him publicly as their landlord, by an oath of fidelity, or plowing a symbolic furrow, or paying a token penny of rent. Even in the absence of direct evidence this must be a real possibility for the period before 1066.[66]

Individuals might extend at will this short list of events choreographed to demonstrate control over land and men to the world at large, and repeat the acts where and as often as they wished.[67] More everyday sightings confirmed the impression made on locals, for such matters were bound to be part of the dinner conversations in the various halls around, and in casual meetings across fences or on the roads. Many people will have had an opinion long before any dispute came into the open, and sometimes before the principals had even shown their hand.

CONCLUSIONS

Much of the foregoing consists of models. At best they show enough of a congruity with actual evidence to encourage better equipped scholars to pursue the question further. I have come to find the evidence persuasive enough for a prima facie case. I can illustrate why I find the evidence per-

64. S 1441; a comparable occasion is described in S 1449. Cf. also S 1434, S 1460, and R. C. van Caenegem, *English Lawsuits from William I to Richard I*, Selden Society 106 (London, 1990–1991), no. 281 (1133), in which a man proved his land in his lord's court "as his father had better ("*melius*") had it and as the neighbors and those who knew the facts ("*vicini et scientes*") perambulated that land."

65. Pollock and Maitland, *HEL*, 2:97–8; Hudson, *Laws of England*, 365, 659.

66. A writ, S 1242 recalled that King Edgar had "instructed all his thegns who had any land on that estate that they should hold it in conformity with the bishop's wish, or else give it up." Extant estate management documents, few though they are, evidence a managerial mindset that should have seen the point of a public attornment. *LE*, ii. 10 (83) illustrates the kind of trouble it was designed to avoid.

67. Cf. Hudson, *Laws of England*, 141, and for comparison, D. M. Stenton, *English Justice between the Norman Conquest and the Great Charter, 1066–1215* (London: Allen & Unwin, 1965), 24–25, 140–47.

suasive enough from a law of Cnut's that links strong claims to private land to the faithful performance of public obligations due from it. II Cn 79 reads as follows in the original:

> And se đe land gewerod hæbbe on scypfyrde 7 on landfyrde be scire gewitnysse, (7 se nolde ođđe ne mihte, đe hit ær ahte) habbe he unbesaken on dæge 7 æfter dæge to syllanne 7 to gyfane đam đe him leofost sy.[68]

A. J. Robertson, a highly reputed Old English specialist, whose translations of the laws are still much used, renders this as follows:

> And he who, with the cognisance of the shire, has performed the services demanded of a landowner on expeditions either by sea or by land shall hold [his land] unmolested by litigation during his life, and at his death shall have the right of disposing of it or giving it to whomsoever he prefers.[69]

And my own effort:

> And he who has by the witness of the shire been seised of land by [performing the obligations] of ship-fyrd and land-fyrd (which [the previous holder] would not or could not,) is to have it uncontested in his lifetime, and [with power] to alienate and give to whomever he please.

We have been taught to read this in the context of *Domesday* entries a couple of generations later, which suggest that a man who 'defends' his land by paying its share of geld is regarded as "owner."[70] Yet the lawyer historians argue that other evidence for legal ownership remains something like a

68. Liebermann, *Gesetze der Angelsachsen*, 1.366–67, from MS G.

69. A. J. Robertson, *The Laws of the Kings of England from Edmund to Henry I* (Cambridge: Cambridge University Press, 1925) translated from the B text, which omitted the words in brackets, marked by Patrick Wormald, *The Making of English Law*, 350, as a gloss and probably not from Wulfstan.

70. I follow M. K. Lawson, "The Collection of Danegeld and Heregeld in the Reigns of Aethelred II and Cnut," *English Historical Review* 99 (1984), 723–24 on the *Geld* matter,

century away.[71] I would read the judgment of the *Domesday* commissioners as seised with as much right as England knew in the eleventh century.[72] I read the Old English narratives in similar fashion. The winners claimed to dispose of the land as they wished, leave it to their heirs, but without reference to possession or right. It is hard for me to believe that when Wulfstan drafted II Cn 79, using the Old English verb *gewerian*, he was not thinking in very similar terms, and who would know better than the greatest writer of laws in eleventh-century England?

My conclusion, if accepted, ought to provoke some fresh thought on the subject across the Channel too.[73] It would be very odd, indeed, if the area of northern Europe with the lowest documented contact with Roman law in the Early Middle Ages were to prove more deeply influenced by the Vulgar Roman law treatment of property than the rest.

I leave for other occasions the many direct consequences within England, in order to sum up where I now stand. Previous scholarship has, at the lowest, missed a genuine oddity calling for explanation. A key group of Old English words concerning possession and ownership can denote either side of that central distinction. And both the texts that prescribe how property interests were supposed to work and those where winners recorded their litigation and land title against future challenge use this intrinsically ambiguous language. This makes it hard to argue in any specific case for one rather than the other. There is also no indication that any court distinguished between the rights and remedies available on the basis of a distinction it did not know.

None of this should suggest that the Anglo-Saxons were blind to the difference between the claims of, say, a thief in the process of driving off rustled cattle and a proud nobleman surveying his prized ancient

---

but F. W. Maitland, *Domesday Book and Beyond* (Cambridge: Cambridge University Press, 1897; repr. ed. 1907), 55–56 had already shown the way. Neither author mentions seisin.

71. S. E. Thorne, "English Feudalism and Estates in Land," *Cambridge Law Journal* 17 (1959), 193–209; Milsom, *History*, esp. chaps. 2–3 and 171 sq. I recognize that their judgments turn on a definition not universally shared.

72. Cf. above at n. 58 [III Atr 14].

73. Ironically, the characterization of Anglo-Saxon property law argued for here is closer than the received view to current views of Continental property law, based around an understanding of *possessio* in a sense much like that of my seisin model.

patrimony.[74] Nor should we doubt their ability to make much subtler distinctions between competing interests in property. But without the classic distinction, they have to have thought about property and presented their claims in a different style than later law favored. One that relied less on distinctions and definitions and more on qualitative, grey-scale comparisons ranking one claim against another would seem more suitable to the seisin approach suggested here, in which the legitimate interests of different individuals in the same land were distinguished only by their nature and relative strength.

Certainly there existed a small elite of churchmen and a few others, literate enough in Latin to compose and read written charters, whose very language conserved a memory of the Roman law of property. And even in England, some in this elite could have been aware that the Romans had treated these matters in a more rigorous manner.[75] Yet they and their fellows were apparently comfortable enough functioning in a system dominated by the vernacular, which must anyway have served as the prism through which they read and understood their Latin.[76] None of the disputes cited above concerning books suggest that notions of property itself operated any differently on bookright than in other regions of law and culture. Indeed, as we have seen, mere control of relevant landbooks brought litigants nearer to proof, without any sign of a requirement to apply a close reading to the words they contained.

England's reputation as lacking any significant Roman legal legacy goes far to explain why my question has not been asked before. Anglo-Saxon law looks different in character than both our own later Common Law and its distant model of Rome. There is no sign of law schools, little of

74. Tenants could take a much grander view of their tenure than their lords, K. Leyser, *The Gregorian Revolution and Beyond*, ed. T. Reuter (London: Hambledon, 1994), 25.

75. What matters most is how they understood these words. One hint might be the way the plural *possessiones* (with various qualifiers) was sometimes used in charters to denote whole estates, without any obvious opposition to ownership, e.g. S 937, 1065. But the Anglo-Saxons can hardly have discriminated between classical and Vulgar Roman law, and it may well have been the latter which Bede had in mind when making his famous remark about the *exempla Romanorum* behind Æthelbehrt's laws.

76. I suppose that there must be studies of the influence of the vernacular and the oral on the way Anglo-Saxon churchmen read their Latin, but I have noticed none.

full-time lawyers, and I now wonder when or indeed whether a genuine "legal register" entered the Old English language to enable a specifically legal sub-discourse to take place. I very much hope that the specialists will in due course extend my amateur word analysis beyond my restricted text sample and examine the whole Old English corpus to test my suggestions.[77]

One might in fact model Anglo-Saxon law, incompletely but helpfully, from the important aspects of the Roman and Roman-influenced systems which it lacked. In addition to the distinction between possession and ownership or right, I have argued elsewhere that there was in Norman and early Angevin England no clear distinction between crime and tort, no clear differentiation along Roman lines within a more general notion of wrong.[78] I suspect that this argument is similarly applicable to England before 1066.[79] A third distinction, that between real and personal property, seems equally lacking. Not only does much of the material considered above straddle this Roman line, it seems conceivable that many of the ideas were first adopted to deal with chattels, especially livestock, rather than land.[80]

Patrick Wormald showed that one non-Roman distinction *did* affect property thought in Anglo-Saxon England and elsewhere in early medieval Europe. This distinguished inherited land from that acquired within the present generation. It was based on a widely shared sentiment that time

77. Comparisons of Anglo-Saxon England in this respect with the rather fuller legal culture of its Celtic neighbors could also prove helpful.

78. In my *Rancor and Reconciliation in Medieval England* (Ithaca, N.Y.: Cornell University Press, 2003), esp. chaps. 4–5, I call this an "undifferentiated notion of wrong."

79. Thomas Lambert, "Theft, Homicide and Crime in Late Anglo-Saxon England," *Past & Present* 214 (2012), 3–43, has argued persuasively for a very non-Roman organization into the distinctive "conceptual bags" that governed prosecutions of theft and homicide. I am persuaded by his argument. He and other specialists nevertheless continue to believe that the Anglo-Saxons themselves had a notion of "crime" in the period, and that this remains a valid analytical tool to aid our understanding of their practice.

80. Another Roman distinction, between movables and immovables, above, [at n. 12], operated over a similar area. See T. M. Charles-Edwards, "The Distinction between Land and Movable Wealth in Anglo-Saxon England," in *Medieval Settlement*, ed. P. H. Sawyer (London: Edward Arnold, 1976), 180–87. Anglo-Saxon lawmakers and charter draftsmen did take this over. But I cannot see that it made much practical difference.

and the succession of heirs by blood progressively strengthened a family's ties to land and thus the next generation's claims. However, this never hardened into an actionable right or firm rule in Anglo-Saxon times.[81] Thus the exception is more apparent than real.

81. In a lecture, "Bede and the Conversion of England," reprinted with minimal documentation as chap. IV of his *The Times of Bede* (Oxford: Blackwell, 2006), 156. See now Hudson, *Laws of England*, 138–39. Since *Leges Henrici Primi*, 70.21 emphasizes free disposition of acquisitions more strongly than ibid., 48.10; 88.15, it is very possible that pre-Conquest judgments on this capability habitually required *sapientium judicio*. On this, Karl Leyser, "The Crisis of Medieval Germany," in idem, *The Gregorian Revolution and Beyond*, 35–37 offers a suggestive comparison. All bookland started as an acquisition (or "purchase," for which see above text at note 46) and was ipso facto freely alienable. For the distinction after 1066, see J. C. Holt, "Politics and Property in Early Medieval England," in idem, *Colonial England, 1066–1215* (London: Hambledon, 1997), chap. 8, esp. 120–2, and Milsom, *History*, 109, n. 3, 121.

"Death, Where Is Thy Sting?": Locating Capital Punishment in Early Medieval Debates

Abigail Firey

The trouble with homicidal witches, thought the great ninth-century scholar of canon law Hincmar of Rheims, was that they brought into seeming discord the canons of the church. On the one hand, the Council of Elvira clearly and simply prescribed death for them. On the other hand, half a dozen other canons could readily be mustered that clearly affirmed that anyone who repented could not be kept apart from Christian communion.[1] This dilemma encapsulates competing perspectives still evident today in debates over the death penalty: whether there are some crimes so heinous that death seems the obvious response for the protection of society, or whether governments must be bound to respect the preservation of the entire fabric of the living community, even when stained, damaged, and torn. Hincmar was not the only early medieval writer to address the many questions the death penalty raises. As with so much medieval discourse, there are surprising premises (more than one death per person!) and concerns (such as whether torture or death is spiritually more beneficial for the

1. Hincmar of Reims, *De divortio Lotharii regis et Theutbergae reginae*, ed. Letha Böhringer, Monumenta Germaniae Historica. Concilia, tomus 4, supplementum 1; (Hannover: Hahn, 1992), 216–217. The definitive study of Hincmar remains Jean Devisse, *Hincmar, archevêque de Reims, 845–882*, 3 vols. (Geneva: Droz, 1975–1976). See now also the collected studies in *Hincmar of Rheims: Life and Work*, ed. Rachel Stone and Charles West (Manchester: Manchester University Press, 2015).

condemned).[2] Beyond the ethical and spiritual questions, however, early medieval consideration of the death penalty was, as much as anything else, a means of reflecting upon the extent of royal or imperial power. For early medieval writers, the pressing problems arose in the space between increasingly Christian governments that could take blood and an increasingly governmental Church that could not, and their respective prerogatives.

Recent scholarship suggests that early medieval attention to questions about judicial violence tended to coincide with increased royal authority to implement capital punishment. Much of that scholarship has focused on Anglo-Saxon law and related sources, including the archeological evidence of execution cemeteries.[3] Perhaps it is fitting as a tribute to Professor Charles Donahue, therefore, that this essay finds in medieval England—his favored territory—a door through which to pass to wider and deeper antecedents persisting from Roman law, from canon law, and from theology. Charlie has always shown a special willingness to attend to the work of early medievalists, with quizzical patience, as we attempt to elucidate the juridical thought of those he calls "your guys." I hope this exposition elicits that same friendly, raised eyebrow these guys usually prompt.

Anglo-Saxon execution cemeteries have proven useful for understanding early medieval judicial violence for several reasons. They demonstrate the reality of regular, staged executions at particular sites over long periods of time. This shifts our gaze from the putative practices of private vengeance or blood-feud as the fundamental mechanism for addressing capital crimes in the early middle ages, to evidence that public authorities were administering capital punishment in an organized way, from at least

2. On the subject of the multiple deaths that could be experienced by a single person, going beyond the standard duplication of the respective deaths of the body and soul, see Damian Bracken, "Immortality and Capital Punishment: Patristic Concepts in Irish Law," *Peritia* 9 (1995), 167–186; Bracken finds one author who enumerates six possible deaths (182–184), beginning with eternal punishment in hell as a second death.

3. See especially *Capital and Corporal Punishment in Anglo-Saxon England*, ed. Jay Paul Gates and Nicole Marafiote (Woodbridge, Suffolk: Boydell, 2014). For assessment of the correlation of execution cemeteries to state formation that has been proposed by archaeologists, see in that collection Andrew Rabin, "Capital Punishment and the Anglo-Saxon Judicial Apparatus: a Maximum View?," 181–199.

the late seventh century onward.[4] The locations of these cemeteries along boundary lines, away from churches, and separated from other cemeteries, as well as their continued use over several centuries, have led some scholars to conclude both that they were associated with stable administrative or political units, and also were considered unhallowed ground that served to isolate felons from Christian communities, even in death.[5] The execution cemeteries thus indicate that religious ideas about transgression and exclusionary practices, parallel to excommunication or penitential segregation, had permeated the judicial sphere.

The distinction between the sacred and the profane signaled spatially by execution cemeteries has inspired investigations into the relation between Anglo-Saxon secular laws, penitential texts, and insular collections of excerpts of biblical law that refer to judicial violence.[6] These studies reveal an early eleventh-century discourse centered upon the prospects of salvation for those sentenced to die, as well as upon the moral culpability of those sentencing them. When Ælfric, abbot of Eynsham (d. ca. 1010), and Wulfstan, archbishop of York (d. 1023) noted that the prerequisite for absolution from sin was true contrition, they placed responsibility for salvation firmly upon the condemned man, whose remorse could save the life of his soul, even as he forfeited his body to the judge and executioner.[7]

4. For compelling and nuanced arguments about the shift from retributive feud to punishment by public authority, see Daniela Fruscione, "Beginnings and Legitimation of Punishment in Early Anglo-Saxon Legislation from the Seventh to the Ninth Century," in *Capital and Corporal Punishment*, 34–47.

5. J. L. Buckberry and D. M. Hadley, "An Anglo-Saxon Execution Cemetery at Walkington Wold, Yorkshire," *Oxford Journal of Archaeology* 26 (2007), 309–329, at 324–5, with useful references to studies of other Anglo-Saxon execution cemeteries. Note, however, that consecration of holy ground was a mid-tenth century practice, as Marafiote and Gates point out in their introduction to *Capital and Corporal Punishment*, 8, although they concur that the locations of the burials marked the dead as outcasts even prior to formal consecration rites.

6. See Nicole Marafiote, "Punishing Bodies and Saving Souls: Capital and Corporal Punishment in Late Anglo-Saxon England," *The Haskins Society Journal* 20 (2009), 39–57, at 39–40. Hincmar's successor Fulk (882–900) may have transmitted canonistic knowledge to king Alfred (849–899) of England. For review of the arguments that archbishop Fulk of Rheims contributed to the transmission of Frankish penitentials to Alfred's court, see Stefan Jurasinski, "Violence, Penance, and Secular Law in Alfred's Mosaic Prologue," *The Haskins Society Journal* 22 (2012), 25–42, at 40.

7. Marafiote, "Punishing Bodies," 48–50.

This proposition neatly accorded secular authorities the power to administer corporal or capital punishment for actions and spiritual authorities the power to administer penance for intentions, and thus parsed the jurisdictional divisions as relating to body and soul respectively. The division was not a full separation. Wulfstan argued that there was reason to resist destruction of "God's handiwork" (the body). It has also been suggested that the pains of punitive mutilations could have been seen as redemptive, penitential sufferings; although with different logic, Origen had proposed, in neat anticipation of double jeopardy, that execution redeemed the soul, and God would not exact a second punishment.[8]

As a counselor to kings, Wulfstan was close to the realities of royal power and politics, as well as to traditions of both canon and secular law. He was writing his opinions about the death penalty in the context of drafting legislation for kings Æthelred II and Cnut.[9] Ælfric (ca. 955–ca. 1010) was also exposed to canonistic foundations for his views, for his reflections drew upon the work of Abbo of Fleury, a skilled canonist and counsellor to kings, who had written in the 980s at the request of his confrères in England the *Passio Sancti Edmundi*, which Ælfric adapted into Old English.[10] Although Ælfric abbreviated the passage, Abbo had claimed the authority of canon law in his analysis of a case involving a bishop who pronounced a death sentence upon robbers who had tried to steal from the church

8. Nicole Marafiote, "Earthly Justice and Spiritual Consequences: Judging and Punishing in the Old English *Consolation of Philosophy*" in *Capital and Corporal Punishment*, 113–130, at 117–8, 122–5. On Origen's argument, see E. Christian Brugger, *Capital Punishment and Roman Catholic Moral Tradition* (Notre Dame, Indiana: University of Notre Dame Press, 2003), 80. An even more complex logic was proposed by the eighth-century Irish poet Dubthach: the Creator advocates capital punishment because humans must die before their salvation, and human justice should conform to that pattern. Bracken, "Immortality and capital punishment," 179.

9. Marafiote, "Punishing Bodies," 42.

10. Marafiote, "Punishing Bodies," 43–44. For Abbo's biography and analysis of the Passio, see Antonia Gransden, "Abbo of Fleury's 'Passio Sancti Eadmundi,'" *Revue Bénédictine* 105 (1995), 78. It was edited from one manuscript in *Three Lives of English Saints*, ed. Michael Winterbottom (Toronto: Pontifical Institute of Mediaeval Studies, for the Centre for Medieval Studies, University of Toronto, 1972), 65–87. On Abbo's canonistic work, see Franck Roumy, "Remarques sur l'œuvre canonique d'Abbon de Fleury," in *Abbon, un abbé de l'an mil*, ed. Annie Dufour and Gillette Labory (Turnhout: Brepols, 2008), 311–341.

where Edmund's relics lay. Abbo first quoted Proverbs 24:11 ("Deliver them that are led to death: and those that are drawn to death, forbear not to deliver") and 1 Corinthians 6:4 ("If therefore you have judgments of things pertaining to this world, set them to judge, who are the most despised in the church," with the clarifying comment that "those most despised in the church" referred to secular rulers).[11] Abbo then observed, "This is the origin of the canonical precept which forbids a bishop or any one in holy orders to discharge the function of an informer, as it is highly unbecoming that the ministers of the heavenly life should yield assent to the death of any man whatever."[12] Abbo concludes by detailing the bishop's remorse and penance for having ordered the robbers successfully hung.

Abbo's anecdote seems intended to remind readers that although bishops had judicial prerogatives and were accustomed to exercise them, there was a bright line they could not cross. The principle which one scholar has named "the bifurcated teaching" of Roman times, that approved use of the death penalty by non-Christian governmental authorities but, to one degree or another, restricted Christian participation in capital cases, would endure and eventually find expression in the phrase, *ecclesia abhorret sanguinem*.[13] A number of texts from the early middle ages, however, suggest that before that crisp aphorism was to hand, the "bifurcated teaching" gave cause to ponder. Rulers and judges had become Christian, and were wrapped in mantles of Christian ideologies. Further, the western kingdoms and empires of the fifth to eleventh centuries were experiments in government, based on varied understanding of their relation to a Roman past. They lacked stability, their leaders were primarily martial men. Yet there was a broader base of legal materials than had been used in the Roman empire, and the fora for legal action had multiplied. There were thus new ways to think about the death penalty and its place in Christian society.

11. Winterbottom, 84. "'Saecularia negotia si habueritis, contemptibiles qui sunt in aecclesia' (id est, uiros saeculares) 'constituite ad iudicandum.'"

12. Ibid. "Unde canonum auctoritas prohibet ne quis episcopus aut quilibet de clero delatoris fungatur officio, quoniam satis dedecet ministros uitae caelestis assensum prebere in mortem cuiuslibet hominis." See below for the problems in tracing this "canonical precept" to its sources.

13. For the "bifurcated teaching," see Brugger, *Capital Punishment*, 75 f.

The story told by Abbo showed how a bishop might mistakenly think that he did have the ultimate power to deal death in matters under his jurisdiction. Some centuries earlier, Constantine had ruled that secular officials were to enforce ecclesiastical judgments: bishops did not have the power to coerce or punish.[14] Subsequent emperors tried to keep criminal cases, as well as civil ones that might entail corporal punishment, out of ecclesiastical courts. By the sixth century, canon law prohibited corporal punishment by higher clergy of their subordinates or laity. Early medieval councils in the west, however, re-opened the question.[15] Perhaps the intent was to reconcile canon law with provisions for discipline in monastic communities; but both in monastic settings and episcopal judgments, there appears to have been a disjunction between legal norms and practice, with little secular opposition.[16] Two or three ecclesiastical texts refer to stoning offenders, which suggests capital rather than corporal punishment, although other instances seem to represent ecclesiastical punishment as the alternative to the harsher punishments meted by secular courts.[17] The secular elite were, of course, protected from such punishments.[18] Perhaps most telling is a late antique incident in which clerics flogged a man of high social status captured in the act of raping a nun in a church, an event detailed by Augustine in one of his letters. Pope Celestine ordered the clerics prosecuted for *iniuria*; Augustine protested to a friend that there were no secular mechanisms of justice for a crime such as this.[19] In another effort to justify punishment by ecclesiastical authorities, a pseudo-Augustinian text presented the argument that bishops had power as rulers, just as did husbands, fathers, judges, and kings.[20]

By the early middle ages, therefore, a number of issues and traditions were in play, to complicate the questions of who could participate in capital cases, who could be punished, and what textual authorities con-

14. Leslie Dossey, "Judicial Violence and the Ecclesiastical Courts in Late Antique North Africa" in *Law, Society, and Authority in Late Antiquity*, ed. Ralph W. Mathisen (Oxford: Oxford University Press, 2001), 98–114.

15. Ibid., 99–101.

16. Ibid., 102–105, presenting an impressive collection of instances.

17. Ibid., 104, 106 for stoning; as an alternative to harsher punishments, 108.

18. Ibid., 108–110.

19. Ibid., 111.

20. Ibid., 114.

trolled implementation of the death penalty. Abbo's citations of Scripture and "the authority of the canons" reveal the unsettled nature of the situation. The death penalty was among the more problematic topics for writers accustomed to draw upon phrases from Scripture for moral rationales supporting legal precepts. Hebrew Scriptures contain forty prescriptions of the death penalty, and they were not readily discounted as archaic or ritual practices superseded for Christians by the New Covenant.[21] That Abbo chose to cite Proverbs 24:11, 4 Kings 6:18, and 1 Corinthians 6:4 was a conscious and careful act of omission as well as innovative presentation of proof-texts. Earlier compilers and authors had explored the possibilities for deriving legal texts from Hebrew Scriptures for renewed application: the Prologue to king Alfred's Laws of the later ninth century draws upon the *Liber ex lege Moysi*, a set of extracts from Exodus.[22] An eighth-century Irish poem appended to the Irish secular law code the Senchas Már seems to address specifically the problem of reconciling the *lex talionis*, Christian supercession of the Old Law, and a Christian rationale for applying the death penalty.[23]

The canon law offered little clarity. Abbo's seemingly unique citation has been situated by Martin Brett and Antonia Gransden in the context of extensive transmission of canon 31 of the Fourth Council of Toledo (A.D. 633), which limited the capacity of priests to serve as judges if there were the possibility that the sentence would require bloodshed, and its strengthened iteration in canon 6 of the Eleventh Council of Toledo (A.D. 675).[24] Another canon transmitted after the seventh century, attributed to the early fourth century Council of Elvira but believed by many to have been added later to

21. Brugger, *Capital Punishment*, 60.

22. Bryan Carella, "Evidence for Hiberno-Latin Thought in the Prologue to the Laws of Alfred," *Studies in Philology* 108 (2011), 1–26, at 2–3. The Alfredian prologue also drew upon Frankish penitentials, and it has been noted that Alfred's laws showed innovation in their prescriptions for penances rather than traditional punishments; see Jurasinski, "Violence, Penance, and Secular Law," 28, et passim. See also Patrick Wormald, *The Making of English Law: King Alfred to the Twelfth Century, vol. I Legislation and Its Limits* (Oxford: Blackwell, 1999), 416–429.

23. Bracken, "Immortality and Capital Punishment," 168–169, at 180–181.

24. Gransden, 27–28, n. 42. I am grateful to Dr. Simon Corcoran for confirming that Abbo's quotation is not obviously drawn from the Theodosian Code and Novels, nor from the Justinianic Code and Novels.

the original set of decrees, that resonates with Abbo's wording is the canon (c. 73) "Delator si quis extiterit fidelis, et per delationem eius aliquis fuerit praescriptus vel interfectus, placuit eum nec in fine accipere communionem." ["A Christian who denounces someone who is then ostracized or put to death may not receive communion even as death approaches."][25] Both these canons reflect two themes that run through medieval discourse about capital punishment: concern for the spiritual status of those who might be implicated in bringing about someone's death, and concern about the proper administration of sacraments to those whose souls were in jeopardy, whether as a result of their crimes or their participation in a capital case. The condition of victims of crime, their relatives or others bound by ties of affection, loyalty, or need is given no attention; nor is there much interest in the meaning or purpose of the death penalty.

Unlike the seeming meaning of the Anglo-Saxon use of unhallowed ground for burial of those executed, the Carolingian discourse that preceded Abbo's discussion of the problem of the bishop's erroneous execution of the robbers reveals debate over the souls of the convicted that tipped the scales toward reconciliation with the Christian community. The balance of the scales seems to have been precarious, however, even in the writings of Hincmar, with whom this essay began. Hincmar's detailed citation of canon law guaranteeing redemptive penance and communion to anyone who expressed genuine remorse is found in his lengthy analysis of the complicated divorce case of Lothar II and his queen Theutberga.[26] For that explanation, Hincmar seems to have drawn upon the popular canon law collection known today as the *Collectio Dacheriana*.[27] Hincmar cites decretals

25. Again, I thank Dr. Corcoran for pointing out this precedent to me. The English translation is that published by Kenneth Pennington at http://faculty.cua.edu/pennington/Canon%20Law/ElviraCanons.htm

26. See n. 1 supra, for the critical edition.

27. The only printed edition of the *Collectio Dacheriana* remains *Spicilegium sive collectio veterum aliquot scriptorum qui in Galliae Bibliothecis delituerant*, 1, ed. Luc d'Achery and Louis-Francois-Joseph de la Barre, 2nd ed. (Paris, 1723), 509–564. Transcriptions of manuscripts of the *Dacheriana* have been and will be published online in the Carolingian Canon Law project: http://ccl.rch.uky.edu. For a register of manuscripts and bibliography, see Lotte Kéry, *Canonical Collections of the Early Middle Ages (ca. 400–1140: a Bibliographical Guide to the Manuscripts and Literature* (Washington, D.C.: Catholic University of America Press, 1999), 87–92.

from Popes Celestine, Innocent I, and Leo I, and canons from the councils of Nicea and Ancyra. The cited excerpts are among the first canons of Book 1 of the *Collectio Dacheriana*; indeed, the passages from Celestine, Innocent, and Leo begin the collection.[28] Reading the *Collectio Dacheriana* through Hincmar's eyes leads one to wonder whether the compiler of this canon law collection was engaged in debates over punition and penance. The *Praefatio* that often accompanies the *Collectio Dacheriana* has as its usual rubric, *de utilitate paenitentiam agendam*; in it, the author stresses the unconditional mercy given by God to the remorseful confessant, and the need for nothing more than contrition.[29]

In another treatise, however, *De regis persona et regio ministrio*, Hincmar gives only the briefest acknowledgement to protective ministrations to the criminal's soul; he only commented that

> Even for those who must be punished for their crimes, if (in a time of need and urgency of pressing danger, or at their last breath) they seek the protection of repentance and quick reconciliation, penance must not be forbidden, nor reconciliation denied. By evangelical, apostolic,

28. *De divortio*, 216–217. The canons are from the Council of Elvira, can. 6 = *Dacheriana* I.104; Pope Celestine to the bishops of Vienne and Narbonne = *Dacheriana* I.1; Pope Leo 108 to Theodore of Fréjus, = *Dacheriana* I.2 and I.14;. Council of Nicea can. 12 and 13 = *Dacheriana* I.30 and I.18; Council of Ancyra canons 4 and 5 = *Dacheriana* I.28 (can. 5 is not in the printed edition); pope Innocent to Decentius of Gubbio (letter 29) = *Dacheriana* I.21. The library at Rheims during Hincmar's tenure held several copies of the *Collectio Dacheriana*; the shelfmarks of manuscripts with Rheims provenance can be found in Kéry, *Canonical Collections*. On Hincmar's use of the *Collectio Dacheriana* in *De divortio*, see the editor's Introduction, 86–88.

29. In its opening portion, the *Praefatio* proclaims, "...[N]o matter how great our crimes, their forgiveness should never be despaired of in holy Church for those who truly repent, each according to the measure of his sin. And, in the act of repentance, where a crime has been committed of such gravity as also to cut off the sinner from the body of Christ, we should not consider the measure of time as much as the measure of sorrow. For, 'a contrite and humbled heart God will not despise.'" [Sed neque de ipsis criminibus quamlibet magnis in sancta Ecclesia remittendis Dei misericordia desperanda est agentibus poenitentiam secundum modum cuiuscumque peccati. In actione autem poenitentiæ, ubi tale commissum est peccatum ut is qui commisit a Christi etiam corpore separetur, non tam consideranda est mensura temporis quam doloris. Cor enim contritum et humiliatum Deus non spernit. D'Achery, 510] The passage is taken from Augustine's *Enchiridion*, XVII.64: ed. E. Evans (Turnhout: Brepols, 1969), 84.

> and prophetic authority, the sacred canons (and the decrees of the Apostolic See) clearly show that we are able to place no limit on God's mercy nor pronounce any decision on temporal things.[30]

Aside from this statement, *De regis persona* shocked even Hincmar's often sympathetic biographer, Jean Devisse, for its advocacy of punishment over mercy.[31] The chapter on the merits of contrition is one of the shortest in the treatise, and is surrounded by lengthier expositions of the necessity to punish transgressors without wavering.

Two aspects of *De regis persona* require brief comment if we are to understand its place in early medieval discourse regarding capital punishment. First, *De regis persona* is usually classified as a *Fürstenspiegel* ("mirror of princes") text, because of its form as an expression of advice to king Charles the Bald and perhaps because of its frequent citation of Pseudo-Cyprian's quintessential *Fürstenspiegel, De duodecim abusivis saeculi*.[32] There is, however, reason to resist having the genre define the intent. Hincmar's treatise is neither wide-ranging nor general. It is a pointed, argumentative exposition of three topics in a tight sequence: that kings rule by divine disposition; that some wars are just; that rulers should implement capital punishment without fear that they betray Christian injunctions to practice mercy. Hincmar's treatise seems polemical: when he asserts that

30. "Quod etiam his qui pro suis sceleribus puniendi sunt, si in tempore necessitatis, et periculi urgentis instantia, vel in ultimo spiritu, praesidium poenitentiae, et mox reconciliationis petierint, nec satisfactio interdicenda sit, nec reconciliatio deneganda, et sacri canones, et decreta sedis apostolicae, auctoritate sacra, evangelica, et apostolica, et prophetica patenter ostendunt, quia misericordiae Dei nec modum possumus ponere, nec tempora diffinire..." Hincmar, *De regis persona et regio ministro*, cap. 28. *Patrologia Latina* 125, cols. 833–856 (col. 851–852). The translation is that of Priscilla Throop, *Hincmar of Rheims, On Kingship, Divorce, Virtues and Vices* (Charlotte, Vt.: MedievalMS, 2014) 27.

31. Devisse, II.714–721.

32. Hans Hubert Anton, "Pseudo-Cyprian, *De duodecim abusivis saeculi* und sein Einfluß auf den Kontinent, insbesondere auf die karolingischen Fürstenspiegel," in *Die Iren und Europa im früheren Mittelalter*, ed. Heinz Löwe, 2 vols. (Stuttgart: Klett-Cotta, 1982) 2.568–617. For excellent investigation of Carolingian Fürstenspiegels, especially with respect to their advice regarding clemency as among a ruler's virtues, see Andrew J. Romig, "In Praise of the Too-Clement Emperor: the Problem of Forgiveness in the Astronomer's *Vita Hludowici imperatoris*," *Speculum* 89 (2014), 382–409, at 389–394; see also Rachel Stone, *Morality and Masculinity in the Carolingian Empire* (Cambridge: Cambridge University Press, 2012), 27–46.

"the punishment of particular persons who (if acting destructively, are not able to be corrected otherwise) are commanded to be punished with worldly death," he comments that such punishment is "said to be opposed by certain people."[33] That opposition may have been contemporary, or may have been in textual sources of the past. The second characteristic to note about *De regis persona* is that Hincmar assembled most of the text from Patristic sources, excerpting and fitting them together in the typical fashion of Carolingian authors to form a new text.[34] *De regis persona* is even more a compilation of quotations than other Hincmariana, with few *dicta* of Hincmar's own. The intended meaning of the text, and the outline of the argument, lies in the chapter headings, which are presented as propositions. The authorities cited below each chapter heading thus both justify the positions presented and shield the compiler.[35] In light of the sensitive nature of the arguments, whether constructed at Charles' behest or as a result of Hincmar's own cogitation, the decision to use such a highly mediated format is understandable.[36]

Unlike the Anglo-Saxon legislation, in which the death penalty appears to be applied to thieves and robbers, *De regis persona* appears not

33. "Deinde quae debeat esse discretio in misericordia, et de ultione specialium personarum, quae si exitialiter agentes aliter non potuerint corrigi, temporali morte praecipiuntur multari, quod a quibusdam dicitur contradici." PL 125, cols. 833–834.

34. The compositional history of *De regis persona* is complicated by its relation to a collection of excerpts similar to or that of the manuscript Paris, Bibliothèque nationale, lat. 1632, a relation described in the posthumous article by Gerhard Laehr (ed. Carl Erdmann), "Ein karolingischer Konzilsbrief und der Fürstenspiegel Hincmars von Reims," *Neues Archiv der Gesellschaft für ältere deutsche Geschichtskunde* 50 (1935), 106–134. See also the important comments of Devisse, II.710–713. Laehr tentatively proposed that the collection might have been compiled by Jonas of Orléans in the context of a council of 836, and then used by Hincmar. As Laehr himself noted, the correspondence of the excerpts is not direct. The collection may represent a set of citations known and used in episcopal circles for various purposes.

35. In the present analysis, ideas are represented as those of Hincmar, although they are expressed in the words of Augustine, Ambrose, Gregory the Great, and other such sources.

36. The very short preface suggests that Charles requested the work: "Obaudientes praeceptum Domini per prophetam jubentis, 'Interroga sacerdotes legem meam', super quibusdam capitulis me consulere vobis placuit." PL 125, col. 833.

to be treating ordinary, criminal law.[37] It gives particular attention to the problem of punishing family members, and also groups of convicted persons. With regard to sentencing kin to death, Hincmar argues for the importance of impartiality in judgment and also the importance of punishing capital offenses contrary to God, the Church, and the realm.[38] The longest chapter in *De regis persona* has the rubric "When his relatives act perversely, a king ought not to spare them through carnal love."[39] The theme continues into the next chapter, which poses the question, "To what extent a ruler ought to forgive his children, or other close connections, if they sin;" it concludes that "by necessity, the peace of the Church universal and the general welfare ought to take precedence over the love for a beloved person and, even more, over the love for a degenerate child."[40] Adding to the sense that there is a fairly specific set of circumstances that Hincmar had in mind is a chapter dedicated to the problem of a plurality of offenders.

> By chance someone may say that punishment can be competently carried out against one person, but it is seen that, against a great number of sinners (because of the difficulty) punishment must be overlooked or delayed. Saint Innocent in his decretals contradicts this. He says to the Macedonian bishops (letter 22.6) "...But (as often happens when sin is committed by the populace or by a crowd) since it is not possible to punish them all because of their great number, the matter usually passes by unpunished. I therefore say that prior things must

37. Although Marafiote and Gates point to the extensive range of crimes subject to the death penalty (80 of the 97 listed) in Anglo-Saxon England (Introduction, 3), Lisi Oliver, *The Body Legal in Anglo-Saxon Law* (Toronto: University of Toronto Press, 2011), when considering the penalty for theft, focuses on amputation. (pp. 171–174).

38. "Then, on account of the administration of the realm, that the king ought not, with carnal affection, spare those—in any bonds of kinship—who act criminally against God and the holy Church and against the realm," Throop, 2. ["Tum quia rex propter ministerium regium, etiam nec quibuscunque propinquitatis necessitudinibus, contra Deum sanctamque Ecclesiam atque contra rempublicam agentibus criminaliter, affectu carnali parcere debeat." PL 125, col. 834]

39. Chapter 29. Throop, 28–30; PL 125, col. 852–853 ("Quod rex propinquis suis perverse agentibus affectu carnali parcere non debeat.")

40. Throop, 30–31; PL 125, col. 854 ("necessario praeponderare debet pax Ecclesiae universalis, et soliditas generalis, dilectioni etiam dilecti, multo magis autem degeneris filii.")

> be pardoned by God's judgment and care must be taken, with great concern for the rest." And hence likewise, in the decretals of the Apostolic See, it says, "if all priests and the world agree with those who must be condemned, condemnation envelopes those who agree, but consensus does not absolve the transgression. The crime does not diminish, but grows larger when, from some individual act, it becomes general. The God of all indicated this when he destroyed the sinning world by the general flood."[41]

It is almost impossible to read the text without considering the atmosphere at the court of Charles the Bald in the 870s, when *De regis persona* is though to have been composed.[42] Rebellions, often led by his relatives, had been a regular feature of Charles' reign; the brutality with when he suppressed them had at times produced even more disloyalty among his aristocracy and clergy.[43] In 858, Charles had issued a capitulary that declared his assurances that he would not act against individuals, that he would show reasonable mercy to those before him, and that there would be no need to fear his fury, because concerns about his use of royal authority could be discussed with him. The next decade and a half, however, brought further revolts.[44] As a consequence, in 866 Charles had his brother-in-law beheaded; in 873 Charles had his son Carloman condemned and blinded; in the same year, Hincmar's nephew and most bitterly fought opponent, bishop Hincmar of Laon, suspected of conspiracy with Carloman, was also blinded. Charles decreed that counts everywhere in his realm should arrest men and women suspected of witchcraft, and cited the verse from Exodus (22:18) declaring that witches should not live; he also cited the Theodosian

41. Chapter 33. Throop, 33–34. PL 125, col. 856.

42. As is briefly noted by Stone, *Morality*, 72; for more extensive consideration of the possible context and date, Devisse, II.710.

43. Janet Nelson, *Charles the Bald* (London: Longman, 1992), 210–212, 226–229.

44. Nelson, *Charles*, 184: "Charles was a king who inspired fear. So long as wrath was carefully controlled and respected the limits of legitimacy, it was a prime royal asset. It could become a liability if its effects were perceived as arbitrary or unjust." See also her discussion (187) of the famous pact in which Charles promised not to act against individuals, to accord mercy, etc. and the disbelief of nobles, including clergy, who said they could not bear Charles' tyranny.

Code's provisions for condemning to death "those who distort the minds of others."[45]

As was noted earlier, the portion of *De regis persona* preceding the chapters treating the death penalty explains the arguments for a just war. The primary basis for the discussion of the death penalty is that the ruler who orders capital punishment is not violating the Commandment not to kill; the same arguments apply as were set forth for killing in a just war. In Chapter 9, under the rubric,"Those who have waged war under God's authority have not sinned," Hincmar explains, "Thus people who have waged wars by God's authority, or bearing the persona of public authority according to its laws (that is, the rule of very fair reasoning) and those who have punished criminals with death, do not at all trespass against the commandment which says (Ex. 20.13) You will not kill."[46] A similar view is in the next chapter, which also pertains to the just war: "And so, let necessity, rather than your volition, slay the enemy who is fighting against you."[47] The purpose, of course, was the general welfare: "It is necessary for the ruler to compel [the condemned] to undergo the severity of the law, lest he, having refused to take counsel, is able to harm people who wish to live in peace." [48]

The other purpose of the text as a whole was to show how killing, whether in war or as judicial punition, was part of a ruler's responsibility, or at least part of his burden.[49] For this argument, Hincmar drew at length

45. Nelson, *Charles*, 230–231.

46. Throop, 12; PL 125, col. 841 "Sed his exceptis, quos occidi jubet, sive data lege, sive ad personam pro tempore expressa jussione: non autem ipse occidit qui ministerium debet jubenti, sicut adminiculum gladius utenti: et ideo nequaquam contra hoc praeceptum fecerunt, quo dictum est: Non occides, qui Deo auctore bella gesserunt, aut personam gerentes publicae potestatis, secundum ejus leges, hoc est justissimae rationis imperium, sceleratos morte punierunt... His igitur exceptis, quos vel lex justa generaliter, vel ipse fons justitiae Deus specialiter occidi jubet, quisquis hominem, vel seipsum, vel quemlibet occiderit, homicidii crimine tenetur."

47. Throop, p. 13, PL 125, col. 842: "Itaque hostem pugnantem necessitas perimat, non voluntas."

48. Throop, 21; PL 125, col. 847: "...legis severitatem a principe necesse est sustinere cogatur, ne qui sibi consulere noluit, in pace vivere volentibus nocere possit."

49. Chapter 24. Throop, 25: "The idea of killing people lest someone be killed by them, does not please me, unless by chance he is a soldier, or is obliged by public duty...;" PL 125, col. 850: "De occidendis hominibus, ne ab eis quisquam occidatur, non mihi placet consilium, nisi forte sit miles, aut publica functione teneatur, ut non pro se hoc faciat, sed

upon some of Augustine's writings on the value of coerced salvation or compelled virtue.[50] The conclusion was that, "he serves Christ who, with a love of justice, corrects wicked people." Similarly, there are passages stating that kings serve God "by forbidding and punishing with scrupulous severity, things done against the commandments of the Lord" and that "holy men" "in order to inspire fear in those who are living, have rightly punished guilty people with death."[51] In this respect, there is little that moves beyond the Roman position, shared by Christians during imperial times, that secular rulers have the power to punish with death.[52] The innovation, however, is in Hincmar's effort to reconcile that premise with Christian teachings about mercy, and to weave a spiritual dimension into the process of execution, rather than isolating Christians from participation in executions.

For that, Hincmar tried two lines of argument. The first was that execution, or at least punition, would be beneficial for the condemned. Distorting the intent of Paulinus of Nola, who wrote in the Life of Ambrose that, "Confession alone is not sufficient for the one confessing and doing penance, unless correction of the deed follows so that the repentant one does not do things which need repenting," Hincmar seems to say that execution helpfully prevents the penitent from sinning again.[53] In a similar vein, he proposes that for the penitent's sake, one should avoid "useless mercy." That is, using the standard rhetoric of penance as medicine and the confessor as a physician, Hincmar takes the metaphors in new directions and claims that sometimes medicine "covers a wound" that should be open,

---

pro aliis, vel pro civitate, ubi etiam ipse est, accepta legitima potestate, si ejus congruit personae."

50. Chapter 18. PL 125, cols. 845–846.

51. Throop, 17–18, 22–23. PL 125, cols. 845, 848–849 ("Quia enim sancti viri, non solum talium amicitias vitaverunt, sed ad incutiendum viventibus metum, etiam jure reos morte punierunt,")

52. For summaries of references from Roman times in Scriptural and Patristic sources, and their lack of consensus, see Brugger, *Capital Punishment*, 59–95. For Hincmar's demonstration that this was accepted in Christian culture, Chapter 26, quoting pope Innocent's letter to Exsuperius, and ignoring Innocent's lack of enthusiasm form capital punishment.

53. For other traces of arguments for prophylactic use of capital punishment, Brugger, *Capital Punishment*, 90 (Augustine), and Marafiote, "Earthly Justice," 127.

or "opened with a knife".[54] Hincmar also explores the idea that there can be "cruelty in forgiving and mercy in punishing."[55] This brings him the closest he comes to considering those involved in the case besides the judge and the condemned. A lenient judge, says Hincmar, puts the accuser in a dangerous position, because rejecting punishment for the accused "condemns the one trying to prove the case." The second argument was that execution of the condemned would protect society; again one sees an emphasis not on prevention of assaults on potential victims, but on conspiracy: "forgiveness of one unworthy person would cause many to commit a contagious error."[56]

Because Hincmar seems determined to avoid any quotient of retribution in the calculus of execution, and must instead find Christian rationales for an action not readily classified as merciful or forgiving, the plausibility of his case seems strained. Hincmar was aware of the moral imperative for mercy, and includes in his text a passage seemingly describing prisoners of war: "Just as violence is returned to a person who rebels and resists, so mercy is owned to him who is conquered or captured, especially in the case in which disturbance of the peace is not feared."[57] He also acknowledges that "A ruler or judge may lawfully pardon a person," because "under the fair and merciful Judge, who forgives a person who turns back and is pen-

54. Chapter 19; PL 125, col. 846: "Medicus ipse, si serpentis interius inveniat vulneris cicatricem, cum debeat resecare ulceris vitium ne latius serpat, tamen a secandi urendique proposito lacrymis inflexus aegroti, medicamentis tegat quod ferro aperiendum fuit, nonne ista inutilis misericordia est, si propter brevem incisionis vel exustionis dolorem, corpus omne tabescat, vitae usus intereat? Recte igitur et sacerdos vulnus, ne latius serpat, a toto corpore Ecclesiae quasi bonus medicus debet abscidere, et prodere virus criminis quod lateat, non fovere, ne dum unum excludendum non putat, plures dignos faciat quos excludat ab Ecclesia" The popular image of punishment as medicine and the judge as physician whose scalpel prevents spreading infection was developed by Clement of Alexandria; see Brugger, 78–79.

55. Chapter 31; PL 125, col. 855: "Sicuti est enim aliquando misericordia puniens, ita et crudelitas parcens."

56. Throop, 19–20; PL 125, col. 846: "Deinde inter duos, hoc est accusatorem et reum, pari periculo de capite decernentes, alterum si non probasset, alterum si non esset ab accusatore convictus, non id quod justitiae est judex sequatur, sed dum miseretur rei, damnet probantem, aut dum accusatori favet qui probare non possit, addicat innoxium."; "Nonne cum uni indulget indigno, plurimos facit ad prolapsionis contagium provocari?"

57. Throop, 13–14; PL 125, col. 842: "Sicut rebellanti et resistenti violentia redditur, ita victo vel capto misericordia jam debetur, maxime in quo pacis perturbatio non timetur."

itent, it is permissible for a ruler or judge to pardon someone…"[58] Yet even then, Hincmar is reluctant to forego the concept that justice exacts a price: "As Prosper says… "Sins, whether small or great, cannot be unpunished, since they are punished either by the person being penitent, or by the Lord judging."[59]

De regis persona shows how the use of judicial violence as a tool of power was calculated, considered, and yet also apparently questioned in the early middle ages. The calculations and questions, however, seem not to have arisen about routinized corporal and capital punishments for robbery and theft, but about the punishments meted for perceived treachery, rebellion, dissent, resistance. The latter activities would have involved the social and military elite, who were usually immune from such punishments. Hincmar's treatise may have been an attempt to offer approbation or justification of the death penalty in an atmosphere of acute unease about execution and fatal mutilations inflicted upon the elite, and the consequent effects upon the family members of the condemned. Hincmar attempted to supply not only rationales for the death penalty, but also consolation regarding the salvation of the souls of the convicted. Granting religious dignity to the condemned could have political benefits, as well, in potentially helping to repair the relationships between king and surviving kin of the deceased. In an era when monarchs bore more personal responsibility for governing, and there were not the extensive and separate bureaucracies and penal systems for distributing the mechanisms for capital punishment far from royal authority, the monarch's power to pardon was not yet cleanly separated from the power to condemn. In *De regis persona*, the religious condition of both the condemned and the ruler were protected.

While Hincmar's treatise is perhaps the most overt analysis of the death penalty from the early middle ages, other authors and events show precedents for use of the death penalty in times of political instability or danger. Some three and a half centuries earlier, Magnus Felix Ennodius, bishop of Pavia, wrote the *Vita* of his predecessor Epiphanius (bishop of Pavia from 466 to 496), in which he described Epiphanius' embassy to king

58. Throop, 20; PL 125, col. 847: "Cui ergo licite ignoscere liceat principi vel judici, sub justo et misericordi judice, qui convertenti et poenitenti ignoscit…"

59. Throop, 21; PL 125, col. 847: "Peccata, sive parva, sive magna, impunita esse non possunt, quia aut homine poenitente, aut Deo judicante plectuntur."

Theoderic, to plead for civic restoration of the aristocrats who had supported Theoderic's opponent, Odoacer, king of Italy. After explaining that "King Theoderic suddenly decided to grant the right of Roman privileges only to those who had proved their loyalty by joining his party; those whom any necessity had kept from doing so he ordered to be deprived of the right of giving testimony and making free disposition of their property," Ennodius supplies Theoderic with a speech that has striking correspondences to some of Hincmar's perspectives.[60] Although no preceding mention had been made in the text of executions, Theoderic's words clearly refer to them.

The rhetoric credited by Ennodius to Theoderic is thickened with Christian allusions. Theoderic begins by stating that

> The restrictions imposed on one who rules open no access to the mercy which you advocate; and in the midst of the difficulties of a rising power the efficacy of severe measures tends to crush all gentleness and compassion of heart. My assertion is supported by [...] Scripture. We read that a sovereign sinned, who, contrary to the divine prescriptions, saved an enemy from death; his leniency brought upon him that penalty which his severity could have inflicted on another.[61]

Unlike Hincmar, Ennodius does not shy from naming vengeance: Theoderic's speech continues, "He who refuses to take vengeance becomes himself the object of it; he who having his enemy in his power pardons him either makes light of or despises the power of God's commands."[62]

Theoderic's speech parallels Hincmar's arguments about punition and pardon: "[R]ightly should they suffer punishment who have thus failed

60. Facing Latin text and English translation are in Sister Genevieve Marie Cook, *The Life of Saint Epiphanius by Ennodius: a translation with an introduction and commentary* (Washington, D.C.: Catholic University of America Press, 1942), 82–83: "Interea subita animum praestantissimi regis Theoderici deliberatio occupavit, ut illis tantum Romanae libertatis ius tribueret, quos partibus ipsius fides examinata iunxisset…"

61. *Vita Epiphanii*, 84–86: "…regnandi tamen necessitas qua concludimur misericordiae quam suades non ubique pandit accessum, et inter res duras nascentis imperii pietatis dulcedinem censurae pellit utilitas. Exemplorum caelestium testimonio assertio mea nititur. Offendisse legimus principem, qui caelitus destinatum neci inimicum subduxit exitio. Poenam meruit lenitas, quam potuit intulisse districtio."

62. Ibid., 86–87: "Ultionem suscipit qui detractat inferre: vim divini iudicii aut adtenuat aut contemnit qui hosti suo, cum potitur, indulget."

to follow divine favor. He who pardons crimes now committed transmits them to posterity... the milk of kindness is granted to those who are in conformance with the severity of the law."[63] Perhaps most interestingly, Theoderic's speech uses the metaphor of the physician's knife in ways similar to Hincmar's treatise: "For no doctor restores a sick man to perfect health except him who, by cutting away with the knife the putrid members, draws out the filth hidden deep within."[64] Moved, however, by the holiness of Epiphanius, Theoderic declares that "[n]o one shall suffer capital punishment since you can plead so effectively before our God as to cause guilty souls to abandon their wicked ways."[65] Ennodius' text thus lies between patristic segregation of clerical and secular prerogatives and Hincmar's integration of theological and political rationales.

The texts of Hincmar and Ennodius are part of a longer and larger discursive tradition developed in Roman times about clemency and cruelty, leniency and rigor. Severity had long been recognized as a virtue, and the question of how to see clemency as a complementary virtue had taken centuries to resolve. Roman writers had developed an extensive vocabulary and set of rhetorical conventions for discussing the virtues of rulers in this regard, as they examined the question of how to distinguish a tyrant from a good ruler.[66] Andrew Romig has shown how the question was refreshed by the Carolingian writer known as "The Astronomer," who framed his biography of Louis the Pious, the father of Charles the Bald, around the ruler's proclivity to be lenient to those who rebelled against him. Romig has also argued that it was in the 870s that "Charles the Bald's court is precisely where we find the reemergence, in the secular moral philosophical record, of lively debate on the subject of forgiveness," pointing to the *Liber de rectoribus Christianis* and Hincmar's two treatises, *De cauendis vitiis et uirtu-*

63. Ibid. "Iustitia coercendi sunt, quos constat gratiam non secutos. Vitia transmittit ad posteros qui praesentibus culpis ignoscit... illos vere amplecitur lac gratiae, quos austeritas legis informat."

64. Ibid. "Nunquam a medico a plenissimam curationem aeger adductus est, nisi ab illo, qui primum putria ferro membra desecuit et latentem penitus e sinu viscerum produxit inluviem."

65. Ibid. "Nullius caput noxa prosternet, quoniam potestis et apud deum nostrum agere, ut sceleratae mentes a propositi sui perversitate discedant."

66. See the important and detailed study of Melissa Barden Dowling, *Cruelty and Clemency in the Roman World* (Ann Arbor: University of Michigan Press, 2006).

tibus exercendis and the *De regis persona* , as central works in that debate.[67] In this discourse, leniency and severity were subsumed under a guiding principle of equity—*aequitas*—that threads through the corpus of Carolingian meditations upon kingship. Courtney Booker has demonstrated the special interest in defining equity during the reign of Louis the Pious, and sees the fruit of the definitions in the expression *aequitas Petri,* the Petrine power to bind and loose. As pope Leo said in the fifth century, "... neither severity nor leniency is excessive where nothing is bound or loosed unless that which blessed Peter would bind or loose."[68] That passage, Booker observes, was not cited until Hincmar found it. Hincmar quoted it five times—but not in *De regis persona.*[69] It would seem that not even the most agile juridical thinker of the Carolingian era could declare that the death penalty would have been implemented by the saint.

The path toward modern debates over the application to capital punishment of the phrase "cruel and unusual punishment," from the English Bill of Rights of 1689, has been a long and winding one.[70] Early medieval writers were far from casting the argument in such terms: theirs was a cruel world, and there were many unusual turns of fate as kings and kingdoms rose and fell. In a political climate in which enemies were perceived as both beyond and within the borders, borders which were far from stable, and when alliances and loyalties were both valuable and unpredictable, counselors to kings were constrained—whether by fear, tradition, or partiality—to accept harsh measures. In addition, there was a long legacy of both

67. Romig, "In Praise of the Too-Clement Emperor." In the *De regis persona,* Romig sees "an entirely new path," "a distinct challenge to the model of extreme forgiveness" presented by The Astronomer, a shift he suggests may be traced to the trauma of the Battle of Fontenoy. 407–408.

68. Courtney Booker, *Past Convictions: the Penance of Louis the Pious and the Decline of the Carolingians* (Philadelphia: University of Pennsylvania Press, 2009), Chapter 6 (211–246; citation of Leo at 245.)

69. Booker, 382, n. 151 finds Hincmar's citations of the Leonine text in *De presbyteris criminosis, Ep. 26 (ad Adrianum papam), Ep. 32 (ad Ioannem papam), Opusculum LV capitulorum,* and the *Liber expostulationis* (with full references for each).

70. For the realities of Carolingian judicial violence, primarily corporal punishments, their frequency and intent, framed as part of that history, see Patrick Geary, "Judicial Violence and Torture in the Carolingian Empire" in *Law and the Illicit in Medieval Europe,* ed. Ruth Mazo Karras, Joel Kaye, and E. Ann Matter (Philadelphia: University of Pennsylvania Press, 2008), 79–88.

theory and practice since Roman times that punishments were supposed to cause great physical suffering, and that the body was the surface on which punishment was inscribed. Yet the early medieval focus on the inviolability of the soul, the very soul where true guilt inhered, and which could live or die in its own right, complicated the relations of suffering and salvation. Early medieval discourse around the death penalty conserved traditions about the power of the secular sword, but also introduced a new insistence on consideration of the spiritual dangers in capital punishment. That insistence was tied to the canon law, in the passages that stated that no-one on the point of death could be denied the redeeming act of confession. This precept was the foundation for a new teleology of punishment, and an articulation of the relation of body and soul that lay in the interrogation point of the question, "Death, where is thy sting?"

Pope Paschal II's Council of Benevento in 1113

Robert Somerville

The pontificate of Pope Paschal II (September, 1099 - January, 1118), is well known for the complicated events of the years 1111-1112S involving the Emperor Henry V and the pope. The events have been described and their significance debated from the early twelfth century to the present, and the issues are generally beyond the scope of this presentation. The conciliar decisions of the first dozen years of this pontificate have been edited and analyzed by Uta-Renate Blumenthal, but no comprehensive treatment exists of Paschal's acta for the period after the Lenten Synod of 1112 to the pope's death.[1] Professor Blumenthal once was asked if she planned to prepare a second volume of her work on Paschal's councils, and she replied that as far as she could see the sources were so scattered and episodic that such a work would be virtually impossible. One of those scattered, post-1112 sources for the reign of Paschal is the text which is the focus of the present work, and it is a pleasure to dedicate it to a colleague whom the author first met many years ago at Yale when CD was an advanced Law School student of seemingly encyclopedic knowledge and RS was a green, first-year doctoral candidate in Religious Studies.

1. The following works can provide basic orientation especially for Paschal's councils: Uta-Renate Blumenthal, *The Early Councils of Pope Paschal II, 1100-1110* (Toronto: Pontifical Institute of Mediaeval Studies, Studies and Texts 43, 1978); I.S. Robinson, *The Papacy, 1073-1198* (Cambridge: Cambridge University Press, 1990); Georg Gresser, *Die Synoden und Konzilien in der Zeit des Reformpapsttums in Deutschland und Italien von Leo IX. bis Calixt II., 1049-1123* (Paderborn: Fredinand Schöningh, 2006), especially 333-431.

Paschal II presided over a Church council at Benevento in the first part of February, 1113, although the precise date is unknown. This assembly is very poorly documented, but the importance of the city of Benevento, given its location in the Papal States, for the eleventh-/twelfth-century Reform Papacy is well known. Popes Victor III and Urban II held councils there, and Paschal himself convoked synods in this city in 1108, 1113, and in 1117.[2] The pontiff thus was in and out of Benevento at several points, and came to the city once more on December 2, 1112.[3] Seemingly he remained there until Spring, 1113, and in early February presided over the first papal council assembled outside of Rome since his own gathering at Benevento in 1108. This synod was in session in the second week of February, 1113.[4]

The Beneventan council is hardly prominent in the secondary literature, and biographies of Paschal by Servatius and Cantarella have little to say about it.[5] The reason why is not hard to see, given the paucity of primary source material at hand. Georg Gresser's summary, along with the entries in Jaffé's *Regesta pontificum*, summarize the little that is known. As Gresser notes, the gathering was concerned with southern Italian questions and problems related to the Holy Land.[6] Perhaps involvement with those matters afforded Paschal welcome relief from replaying the complicated events that had troubled him a year earlier. In the early decades of the twelfth century, of course, issues about the Latin presence in the East readily might arise in papal synods, and evidence for one remarkable episode of this sort survives for Benevento.

The item in question is a fragmentary text that is not unknown. It seemingly was edited for the first time in 1781 by P.A. Paoli in a work on the Hospitalers. Paoli's text was reprinted in London in 1852; Pflugh-Hartung

2. And maybe also in 1102, as Carlo Servatius thinks (*Paschalis II.* [Stuttgart: Anton Hiersemann, Päpste und Papsttum 14, 1979]99, although Blumenthal, *Councils*, 130-31, and Gresser, *Synoden*, 343-44, are dubious.

3. *Italia pontificia*, ed. Walther Holtzmann (Berlin: Weidmann, 1962) 9.206, no.*14.

4. Ibid., ed. Paul Fridolin Kehr (1935) 8.28, no.*97.

5. See n.2 above for Servatius; cf. Glauco Maria Cantarella, *La costruzione della verità. Pasquale II, un papa alle strette* (Rome: Istituto Storico Italiano per il Medio Evo, Studi Storici 178-79, 1987).

6. Gresser, *Synoden*, 406ff. See also Phillipp Jaffé, *Regesta pontificum Romanorum*, 2nd ed., vol. 1 (Leipzig: Viet & Co., 1885) 749.

re-edited it in his *Acta pontificum Romanorum inedita* in 1884; and thirty years ago Rudolf Hiestand again re-edited the account.[7] The text recounts the appearance at the Council of Benevento of two emissaries from Antioch who presented a complaint before the pope on behalf of the Latin Patriarch Bernard and Prince Roger of Antioch. At issues was jurisdiction over churches claimed by Sboth Antioch and Jerusalem. Pope Paschal dismissed the Antiochene petition quickly. In doing so he reached back to the year 1095, to Pope Urban II, and referred to a ruling which he said was known to have been decreed at the Council of Clermont when the First Crusade was proclaimed. Urban is thus reported to stipulate that after non-Christian practices were suppressed, restored churches should belong to the principalities of the princes who conquered "the provinces and cities from the heathen" (*prouincias uel ciuitates supra gentiles*). Paschal declared that he was not about to countermand such a weighty decree, and the Antiochene legates, being reduced to silence, prepared to go home.

As noted, this text has been available for more than 200 years. It was analyzed fifty years ago by J.G. Rowe, then by Alfons Becker, twice by Robert Somerville, in an interpretive article by Hiestand, and more recently by Gresser, and this may be an incomplete list because Crusade historiography is a growth industry. It is, however, against Hiestand's study that all other discussions must be set. After considering whether or not the text was a forgery and deciding that it is not, he offered a new interpretation. Hiestand proposed that Pope Paschal, in his response to the Antiochene legates, applied to the Holy Land a statement from the Council of Clermont that Urban II formulated for the Christian re-conquests in Spain.[8]

This analysis is ingeniously elegant, and Hiestand solves problems that have perplexed investigators for years. For example, could Urban at Clermont have envisioned political entities in conquered Eastern lands?

7. *Papsturkunden für Kirchen im Heiligen Lande* (Vorarbeiten zum Oriens pontificius III) (Göttingen: Göttingen Abhandlungen, Dritte Folge 136, 1985) 119-21, no.15, where earlier editions and printings are listed. A portion of this account is also found in a cartulary of the Church of the Holy Sepulcher in Jerusalem: see n.6 in the article by Hiestand cited in the following note..

8. Rudolf Hiestand, "Les canons de Clermont et d'Antioche sur l'organisation ecclésiastique des Etats croisés. Authentique ou faux?", *Autour de la première croisade*, ed. Michel Ballard (Paris: Society for the Study of the Crusades and the Latin East, Byzantina Sorbonensia 14, 1996) 29-37.

Furthermore, Paschal has Urban refer to both "principalities" (*principatus*), and "princes" (*principes*), yet in November, 1095, no prince was as yet lined up for the Crusade other than Raymond of St.-Giles. Hiestand's suggestion is the most recent in a series of works considering the Beneventan text through the lens of the Crusade and the Antioch-Jerusalem territorial quarrels in the first decades of the twelfth century. But what else might be gleaned from this fascinating vignette? Other perspectives also are possible, and three can be offered here.

I) In the first place, what can be said about manuscript where the Benevento account survives?

II) Secondly, the text can be analyzed from both a Crusading *and also* from a conciliar angle, and the discussion to follow will not touch on the portion that delineates the specifics of Antioch's jurisdictional claim.

III) Thirdly, looking backward from 1113 to 1095 and the Council of Clermont, what could the Benevento text reveal about Clermont, and about Urban II and the launching of the First Crusade?

Consider, therefore, the manuscript where the Beneventan fragment is preserved. Biblioteca apostolic Vaticana, MS Vat. lat. 1345, is a mid-twelfth-century composite manuscript, written by five similar hands, and described by Stephan Kuttner and Reinhard Elze.[9]

Fols. 1r-3r: Canons of the Council of Nablus, 1120, cf. new ed. by

Benjamin Z. Kedar, "On the Origins of the Earliest Laws of Frankish Jerusalem: The Canons of the Council of Nablus, 1120", *Speculum* 74 (1999): 330-35.

Fols. 3r-v: Pope Paschal II: JL 6456, JL 6467[10]

Fol. 3v: *Definitiones verbi "territorium"* (unedited; see Kuttner-Elze)

Fols. 4r-211v: *Sententiae Sidonenses (Sentences of Sidon)*

Fols. 212r-13v: Canons of Innocent II's Lateran Council, 1139

9. *A Catalogue of Canon and Roman Law Manuscripts in the Vatican Library* I (Città del Vaticano: Biblioteca Apostolica Vaticana, Studi e testi 322, 1986)98-100.

10. See Jaffé, *Regesta* (as in n.6), with entries calendared by Samuel Loewenfeld (=JL), and see n.13 below.

Fol. 214v: Excerpt from the Council of Ephesus, 431
: Excerpt from the Council of Benevento, 1113
Ex concilio pie memorie pape Paschalis apud,
Beneventum habito.

After this summary of the MS 1345's contents the Beneventan text will be presented, both in Hiestand's edition (see above n.7), and in an English translation by RS.

Council of Benevento, February, 1113 -- account of appearance of Antiochene emissaries

Ex concilio pie memorie pape Paschalis apud Beneuentum habito.

Finito sermone post inclinationem tanto primati debitam conscensis gradibus ad eius pedes me reddidi. Surrexerant, antequam sedissem, uiri duo crinibus et barbis concreti, calamistrati non ex industria, sed ut apparebat, ex incuria, etate comparabiles, habitudine uenerabiles et pronati coram domno papa post salutacionem se legatos esse dixerunt Anthiocheni principis Rogerii Bernardique ciuitatis eiusdem patriarche, qui domno pape sicut patri supplicabant petentes, ut ecclesie suum ius [Antioch]ene restitui iuberet.

... [Details of Antioch's boundary dispute are omitted.]

Ad hoc papa: Non soleo de tractatibus ecclesiarum cito respondere sed petitioni uestre, quia de longe uenistis et longa uos uia redituros expectat, non est differendum, quod habemus uobis respondere paratum. Sancte memorie uenerailis Urbanus papa, quando concilium populosissime congregationis in Monte Claro celebrauit uiamque Ierosolimitanam suscitauit, decreuisse memoratur et scitur, quod quicumque principes prouincias uel ciuitates supra gentiles conquirerent, eorum principatibus eliminatis gentium ritibus ecclesie restitute pertinerent. Quod discretissimi patris decretum rescindere non audemus, Accepto legati responso tacuerunt et repatriandi prouidentie uacauerunt.

From the council held at Benevento by Pope Paschal of pious memory.

When the sermon was over, after making the bow that was owed to such a primate, upon climbing the stairs I returned to my place at his feet. Before I could sit down two men arose, plastered down with hair and beards, curly-headed not due to styling but, as it appeared,

> from neglect. Comparable in age, venerable in bearing, and bowing before the lord pope, after a greeting they said that they were legates of Prince Roger of Antioch and Patriarch Bernard of the same city who were petitioning the lord pope, seeking that he order that to the Antiochene church its own rights be restored.
>
> ...
>
> To this the pope replied: "I am not accustomed to respond quickly about the management of churches, but what we have prepared to respond to your petition should not be deferred because you came a long way and a long road awaits you as you are about to set off to return. When at Clermont he celebrated a council, a very well attended assembly, and opened the road to Jerusalem, venerable Pope Urban of holy memory is remembered and known to have decreed that after the practices of the heathen have been suppressed, restored churches would pertain to the principalities of whichever princes conquer [the] provinces and cities from the heathen. We dare not to rescind that decree of a most illustrious father." Having received the response, the legates were silent and busied themselves with making preparations for returning home.

The text describing Antioch's petition at the Council of Benevento is an excerpt of something longer, now lost. Vat. lat. 1345 contains the only known copy of the *Sententiae Sidonense*, and although they are unedited they have been studied. The most recent investigator dates them after the year 1138, obviously with an eye on the canons of Pope Innocent II's Lateran Council of 1139 (see fols. 212-13). Although MS 1345 derives, in all probability, from the church of Sidon in the Latin Kingdom of Jerusalem, by the fourteenth century it formed part of the papal library in Avignon, whence it came into the Vatican Library.[11] Kuttner and Elze note that the *Sententiae* conclude with a colophon that may read *Bernardus scripsit.* – i.e., "Bernard

11. The author is grateful to Dr. John Wei for generously sharing the results of his doctoral dissertation on Gratian's *De penitentia*, a work written under the auspices of History Dept. at Yale University. For MS 1345's origin in the church of Sidon see Kuttner-Elza, whose description is based on the work of Annaliese Maier, "Die Handschriften der 'Ecclesia Sidonensis'", *Manuscripta* 11 (1967): 39-45 (repr. in *Ausgehendes Mittelalter* III, ed. Agostino Paravicini Bagliani [Rome: Storia e letteratura 138, 1977]). Maier emphasized that her conclusions are "likely", but required further investigation, but to the best of this author's knowledge the matter has not been investigated more recently.

wrote it" - although the scribe's name is unclear. Be he *Bernardus* or someone else, the scribe's identity is unknown, nor is it clear whether he was the actual copyist or whether the colophon was simply imported into MS 1345 from its model.[12] Notwithstanding their lengtht, however, the *Sententiae* are only one among a series of interesting elements contained in MS 1345. As the tabulation provided above indicates, flanking the *Sententiae* at both the beginning and the end are other items copied soon after the main text by various mid-twelfth-century hands.

Pondering why this particular set of supplements was added to MS 1345 does not yield obvious answers. It is hard to discern clear patterns either in the attributions or in the content, other than the fact that five of six are conciliar and/or papal texts, and that all exhibit general concern with issues of Church jurisdiction. The letters of Paschal II, for example, on fol.3, also survive elsewhere, and although dealing with issues of ecclesiastical rights, they do not speak about the Holy Land.[13] The canons of the Second Lateran Council of 1139, on fols.212-13, cover a multiple of issues but contain nothing specific about the Crusader States, although the Latin patriarch of Antioch attended this synod, and thus someone in his delegation could have been responsible for bringing these decrees to the East.[14] In short, while the array of texts surrounding the fragment from Benevento could possibly suggest a context for its presence in Vat. lat. 1345, such a connection certainly cannot be proven or even presumed.

Yet, identifying the church of Sidon as the probable home for the manuscript implies that the Beneventan excerpt survived in a mid-twelfth-century codex written in the Latin East, even if its author, copyist, and its rationale for composition are unknown and may never be known. The description of the book in Kuttner-Elze is very useful, but does not provide a full codicological or paleographical analysis. Five different hands account for the main text of the *Sententiae* and the supplements, but other hands

12. The colophon seems not to be listed in *Colophons de manuscrits occidentaux des origines au XVIe siècle* (Fribourg: Editions Universitaires Fribourg Suisse, Spicilegii Friburgensis subsidia 2, Fribourg 1965).

13. JL 6456 and JL 6467: (=*Gallia pontificia*, eds. Bernard Vregille, René Locatelli, et Gérard Moyse [Göttingen: Vandenhoeck und Ruprecht, 1998])1.1.53-54, no.53, and 1.1.55-56, no.55), but with no mention of MS 1345.

14. Georgine Tangl, *Die Teilnehmer an den allgemeinen Konzilien des Mittelalters* (Weimar: Hermann Böhlaus, 1922) 207

are discernible too in the marginal glosses of the *Sententiae*.[15] An interesting but difficult question thus suggests itself. Can any of those glossing hands be matched with the hand of the fragment from Benevento, and if so, is there a pattern to be seen in the subjects covered in the glosses written by that hand? Furthermore, Kuttner-Elze indicate that at the very end of the manuscript, following the Beneventan text, on 214v, two additional rubrics were begun but never completed. They are, *Ex con'* - that is "From the council" - and *Ex concilio pie memorie pape I.* - that is, "From the council of Pope I. of pious memory". *Pie memorie pape I.* - note the similarity to the Beneventan rubric - may refer to Pope Innocent II, who died in September of 1143. These fragmentary rubrics are curious and prompt the question of whether they were written by the same hand as the Benevento text. The question may not have a clear answer, but until MS 1345 is examination further the matter is left open.

With this series of comments about MS 1345 as background, consider the Beneventan fragment as a sources for conciliar history. The text's inscription as translated reads, "From the council held at Benevento by Pope Paschal of pious memory". Paschal II died in January, 1118, so this text is no early than that date. Its author is unknown, although he seems to have been a high ranking member of Paschal's entourage who delivered a sermon in the council. The procedures that governed papal councils during the early twelfth century are not clear. Various textual snapshots can be found which offer pieces of information about activities therein, but it is impossible to gain anything like a full picture of what happened. The liturgical *Ordines de celebrando concilio* provide information about how the ceremonial aspects of synods were conducted; but getting descriptive information about the workings of these gatherings is a haphazard process. For example, despite later chroniclers' recreations of what he said, there is no accurate information that describes Pope Urban II's famous Crusading sermon at Clermont in 1095. Where in town it was delivered, who was on hand to hear it, what rituals if any accompanied the speech are all unknown.

Among the fullest accounts of what transpired in papal synods of this time are two descriptions of Pope Calixtus II's Council of Reims in

15. See Kuttner-Elze, *Catalogue*, 100.

1119. These accounts were written by a man designated as Hesso "Scholasticus" (that is, "Hesso, a man of the schools"), and by the Norman monastic chronicler Ordericus Vitalis. Hesso says he was at Reims and Ordericus may have been too, but even if not he had excellent information about the assembly.[16] These writers are not stingy with details, for example, a description of pope and curia seated on a raised platform at the front of the gathering; renditions of sermons delivered during the conciliar sessions; accounts of visitors who came forward to plead cases before the pope; and several interventions and judgments rendered from the pontifical throne. Similar nuggets exist for other papal synods of the time, but the narratives by Hesso and Ordericus for Reims, 1119, are especially rich in detail.

Looking at the fragment from Benevento in terms of conciliar activity reveals parallels to the reports from Reims six years later. In the first place, as is true for the texts of Hesso and Ordericus the anonymous Beneventan description is a private account, not a product of the papal chancery. The author, as did Hesso, describes himself as an eyewitness, and he was important enough to have a seat on the papal platform that was erected for the synod. In the center of that dais would have been the elevated papal throne, and note the Beneventan narrator's remark that he was seated at the pope's feet. At Reims, Ordericus described Pope Calixtus II and five members of the curia with their assistants seated on the platform. No enumeration is given for Benevento, but the cleric responsible for preserving this text, whoever he was, was a prominent churchman in Paschal II's entourage.

The sermon that this prelate delivered at Benevento does not survive, at least not in MS 1345. Sermons were usual features of Church councils,

16. *Hessonis scholastici relatio de concilio Remensi*, ed. Wilhelm Wattenbach, Monumenta Germaniae Historica, Libelli de lite III (Hannover: Hahnsche Buchlandlung, 1897) 21-28; *The Ecclesiastical History of Orderic Vitalis*, XII.21, ed. and transl. Marjorie Chibnall (Oxford: At the Clarendon Press, 1978) 253-77. For Hesso and Odericus see also Robert Somerville, "The Councils of Pope Calixtus II: Reims 1119", *Proceedings of the Fifth International Congress of Medieval Canon Law* (Salamanca, 1976) (Città del Vaticano: Biblioteca Apostolica Vaticana, Monumenta iuris canonici, Subsidia 6, 1980) 35-50 (repr. in Robert Somerville, *Papacy, Councils and Canon Law in the 11th-12th Centuries* [London: Ashgate, Variorum Reprints CS 312, 1990; 2nd ed. 1993]). See also idem, *The Councils of Urban II, Vol. 1: Decreta Claromontensia* (Amsterdam: Hakkert, Annuarium historiae conciliorum, Supplementum 1, 1972), chapt.ii, and idem, "Pope Calixtus II and Canon Law", *"Panta rei": Studi dedicati a Manlio Bellomo*, ed. Orazio Condorelli (Rome: Il Cigno Edizioni, 2004) 5.235-43 (at 236).

as Hesso and Ordericus confirm, although the themes developed in the Beneventan homily are unknown. The address was delivered at the front of the assembly, but not from the papal platform because the preacher recounted ascending stairs up to that platform after he finished speaking. Parallels for the ceremonial bowing to the pope after the sermon and also when the Antiochene ambassadors turned up seem to be obvious markers of respect for the Roman pontiff, and other instances of the same or similar gestures probably can be discovered in narrative sources of the time.

With an eye on Pope Paschal's negative decision at the end of the account regarding the plea from Antioch, it can be noted that papal statements couched in the first person singular are not unusual in conciliar sources of the eleventh and twelfth centuries. Calixtus II, for example, speaks thus at Reims, although it is unclear to what extent, at Reims or at Benevento, the words put into the pope's mouth represent authentic papal statements rather than narrative inventions. Most likely they were a combination. Finally, it is worth noting that the uncertainty about Paschal II's orthodoxy that arose as a result of the events of the years 1111-1112 at Rome is completely absent at Benevento. Paschal's authority seems not to be diminished in this synod which was convened less than a year after the Lateran Council of March, 1112, where the pope was compelled formally to affirm that he was not a heretic who permitted lay investiture.[17] Paschal at Benevento is *tantus primas* - "such a great primate". He is a figure of great authority capable of rendering judgments about churches as far away as Antioch. Even Pope Paschal's invocation of a president from Pope Urban II could be an effort to place himself in the tradition of a venerable, "most illustrious", predecessor.

The appearance of the Antiochene legates also was the occasion for a bit of theater. The description of these bearded sojourners with their disheveled hair has, perhaps, a whiff of disapproval about it. Those travel-worn ambassadors are not named, but in a papal privilege issued at Benevento on February 13, 1113, among the subscribers are *Rollandus An-*

17. Uta-Renate Blumenthal, "Opposition to Pope Paschal II: Some Comments on the Lateran Council of 1112", *Annuarium Historiae Conciliorum* 10 (1978): 95-96 (repr. In Uta-Renate Blumenthal, *Papal Reform and Canon Law in the 11th and 12th Centuries* [Aldershot: Ashgate, Variorum Collected Studies CS618, 1998]).

tiochenae Ecclesiae legatus, and *Pontius*, designated in the same manner.[18] This document probably was issued after the conclusion of the synod, and if Rollandus and Pontius were the Eastern emissaries who appeared in the synod, which seems likely – how many pairs of *legati* from Antioch were on hand in February, 1113 at Benevento? – they did not head home as soon as Paschal dismissed them in the synod but remained at the papal curia while "making preparations for returning home", as the Beneventan fragment concluded. Did they hang around hoping for another hearing? There is evidence of that, but the Antioch-Jerusalem disputes continued for years, and it is not impossible that these two men reappear somewhere in that history.

The climax of the episode which is recounted at the end of MS 1345 was a synodal judgment rendered by Paschal II. The pontiff reached back to 1095 and cited what Pope Urban II at the Council of Clermont "is remembered and known to have decreed" about the disposition of churches in the Crusaders' lands. Whatever Paschal might have remembered, no such ruling from Clermont is known, but the survival of the acts of Clermont is chaotic, hence absence of such a provision does not mean that it never existed. Furthermore, Paschal at Benevento was ready, uncharacteristically, as he himself noted, to deliver his ruling at once: "I am not accustomed to respond quickly about the management of churches, but what we have prepared to respond to your petition should not be deferred". But did the situation at Benevento in fact play out in this impromptu manner? It is impossible to say, and little is known of how papal sentences were rendered *in concilio* in Paschal's day. It also is impossible to know what the pontiff meant in being "prepared" to answer. This implies he knew what was coming and was ready. But in the first decades of the twelfth century the papacy certainly was being requested to deal with questions of jurisdiction in the Latin East, and from that perspective the scenario depicted at Benevento seems not impossible, even if the details of the process are murky.

If Paschal at the assembly cited what Urban at Clermont is remembered and known to have decreed, would he have been referring to a written text or would he and his advisers be relying on memory? Uta Blumenthal has shown that Paschal's chancery used canonical collections,

18. JL 6340 (=*Italia pontificia*, ed. Kehr [1935] 8.161-62, no.174).

including the compilation of Cardinal Deusdedit, in formulating synodal acts.[19] Decrees from Clermont are not part of Deusdedit's compilation, at least in the form in which it has been edited.[20] But other than a canon law book, what type of authoritative reference, written or unwritten, might have undergirded the Benevento statement? Paschal, as Cardinal Rainerius of St. Clemente, may have been at the Council of Clermont in 1095. The evidence for his presence there is unclear, but as Urban II's chancellor John of Gaëta certainly was at Clermont. John served as chancellor for much of Urban's pontificate and throughout the pontificate of Pope Paschal, until his own elevation to the papacy as Gelasius II after Paschal's death. John must have had a good idea of what was known and remembered about Clermont. Unfortunately, nowhere did he reveal it, nor did he list the documents and books which he carried along to Benevento from Rome in the autumn of 1112 when the papal chancery moved south.[21]

In conclusion, a final speculation can be permitted regarding another possible source at Benevento about memories of Clermont. Several French clerics were on hand at Paschal's synod in February, 1113, among them Bishop Aimeric of Clermont. Aimeric, formerly abbot of La Chaise-Dieu not far from Clermont, became bishop in 1111 and had a long episcopate, dying in 1150 (or 1151).[22] No information is at hand about his activities early in his episcopacy, nor is his reason for being in southern Italy in 1113 known. Was Aimeric carrying archives from his church with him during his southern Italian trip? Would he have been considered an authority on the history of his see, that is, an authority on the church at Clermont and perhaps also of the 1095 council in that city? Would Bishop Aimeric have been in a position to help Paschal II and his advisers remember what Pope Urban II is known to have decreed at Clermont in November, 1095?

19. Blumenthal, *Early Councils*, passim (see 165).

20. *Die Kanonessamlungen des Kardinals Deusdedit*, ed. Victor Wolf von Glanvell (Paderborn: Ferdinand Schöningh, 1905).

21. For Rainerius and John see Robert Somerville, "Council of Clermont and Latin Christian Society", *Archivum historiae pontificiae* 12 (1974): 80-1 (repr. in RS, *Papacy, Councils and Canon Law, as in n.16 above*).

22. See *Dictionnaire d'histoire et de géographie ecclésiastiques* 12 (1953) 1457, and Abel Poitrineau, *Le diocèse de Clermont* (Paris: Letouzey et Amé, Histoire des diocèses de France 9, 1979) 52ff.

Forgery and Pope Alexander III's Decretal on *Scripta authentica*

Robert F. Berkhofer III

In his scholarship and teaching, Professor Charles Donahue often stressed a comparative approach to legal history.[1] In particular, he taught that medieval laws often studied as separate traditions—canon law, Roman law, English common law, and customary continental laws—were connected in their development. This article emerges out of a desire to affirm the enduring value of this approach. Some influences across legal traditions were direct borrowings and so can be traced through traditional textual analysis, but others emerged out of responses to common legal problems. Of course, social, political, and cultural factors were also important in shaping medieval legal practice and ideas. In particular, during the twelfth century, increasing literacy and use of documents in all forms of administration challenged older legal practices, which had stressed the spoken word, witness testimony, and memory rather than written record.[2] This story has long been known, but this article seeks to address a particular issue raised by the increased use of documents in medieval courts: the problem of forgery. To this end, it will focus on forgery and Pope Alexander III's

1. Notably in relation to marriage, Charles A. Donahue, Jr., "Conclusion: Comparative Approaches to Marriage in the Later Middle Ages," in *Regional Variations in Matrimonial Law and Custom in Europe, 1150–1600*, ed. Mia Korpiola (Leiden: Brill, 2011), 289–316.

2. Michael T. Clanchy, *From Memory to Written Record: England, 1066–1307*, 3rd ed. (Oxford: Wiley-Blackwell, 2012).

(1159–81) decretal *Scripta authentica* (1167–9), concerning the authenticity and admissibility of written documents. While a traditional legal history approach might (rightly) study this decretal in relation to rules of evidence, a comparative perspective reveals the potentially larger significance of what otherwise might be regarded as an obscure ruling.

The Challenge of Forgery

As monasteries dominated the teaching of reading and writing in the early Middle Ages, it is unsurprising that monks were the leaders in using both writing and forgery in their appeals to legal authorities. By the mid-twelfth century, forgery of monastic privileges had been practiced for so long that it was almost an established tradition. Papal reform in the mid-eleventh century had encouraged monks (and others) to look to the Bishop of Rome as a final arbiter in disputes and so provided an incentive for monastic houses to ask that older privileges—either authentic or fabricated—receive papal confirmation.[3] When such petitioning grew more common in the early twelfth century, the papal chancery began to be inundated with copies of supposedly ancient monastic privileges. Whether such privileges were confirmed (and, if forged, thereby effectively granted for the first time) depended on many factors, including notions of monastic "reform," the influence of a house, preexisting arrangements with secular lords, and the discretion of the papacy, to name only a few. But it also depended on if such privileges were believed to be genuine.

Authenticity had become an increasing concern, especially with rising numbers of petitions arriving at the papal chancery by the early twelfth century. For English papal acts, Holtzmann's *Papsturkunden in England*, which effectively covered the mid-eleventh century to 1200, indicated that less than 1% of acts were forged.[4] But more recent work by Harald Zimmermann, who edited papal acts throughout all of Europe from 896 to 1046, indicated that, out of 566 documents, 168 look suspicious and 68 were forged,

3. Monastic forgeries are the focus of the author's forthcoming book, *Rewriting the Past*.

4. Walther Holtzmann, ed., *Papsturkunden in England*, 3 vols. (*Abhandlungen der Akademie der Wissenschaften in Göttingen. Philologisch-Historische Klasse*, 3 Folge, nos. 13–14, 43) (Göttingen: Vandenhoeck and Ruprecht, 1931–1952).

together 41.7% of the total. Notably, out of the authentic papal acts less than 6% [5.47], survive as original charters.[5] While such counts have manifest flaws, the results suggest that forgery of papal acts may have already been a serious concern before the twelfth century. Furthermore, the issue of determining which documents were acceptable had been raised by some relatively "high profile" cases involving forgery. One of these was the death bed confession of Guerno the forger, revealed before Pope Innocent II at a very large council in northern France in October, 1131. This confession, which I have analyzed elsewhere, revealed that at least three (and perhaps more) monastic houses in France, Normandy, and England had employed Guerno's services to forge charters, in order to have supposedly ancient "liberties" confirmed in new papal bulls.[6] Such incidents raised at least one obvious problem: how to tell if older documents were authentic before confirming them.

A technology of validation, which came into broad use in northern Europe in the eleventh and twelfth centuries, was the sealed charter. Wax seals (or metallic bulls) provided physical signs of validation and, thus, provided one means of detecting or preventing forgery. During the 1120s, the papal chancery began to employ new forms of validation, including scripts and formulae, as well as lead bulls, when issuing papal letters. During Innocent II's tumultuous pontificate (1130–1143), the papal curia adopted even more rigorous procedures for issuing privileges, which were aimed in part at reducing forgery.[7] The curia was adapting to the press of business, including frequent petitions from England for reconfirmation of ancient (and dubious) privileges.[8] By 1148 cardinal-legates had begun to refuse older pa-

5. Harald Zimmermann, *Papsturkunden 896–1046* (Vienna: Österreichische Akademie der Wissenschaften, 1988–1989), x found that of 566 papal documents, 168 "als Fälschungen verdächtigt sind" and another 66 "verfälscht wurden." Of the remaining 332 charters, only 31 are originals.

6. Robert F. Berkhofer III, "Guerno the Forger and His Confession," *Anglo-Norman Studies* 36 (2013), 53–68.

7. For the evolution of the "simple privilege" under Innocent II and forgery, see Reginald Lane Poole, *Lectures on the History of the Papal Chancery* (Cambridge: Cambridge University Press, 1915), 112–22.

8. Charles Duggan, "'*Improba pestis falsitatis*': Forgeries and the Problem of Forgery in Twelfth-Century Decretal Collections (with Special Reference to English Cases)," in *Fälschungen im Mittelalter*, ed. Horst Fuhrmann, MGH Schriften, 33, 6 vols. (Hanover: Hahnsche Buchhandlung, 1988–90) 2.319–61.

pal privileges which did not have bulls. These were administrative, practical measures taken in response to (ever increasing) daily business as well as the potentially disruptive problem of forgery. But a statement of the reasons or ideas behind such practices had yet to be explicitly expressed as rules or laws. Since a massive transformation in the study, teaching, and practice of canon law, alongside other legal traditions, was occurring in twelfth century, perhaps it is not surprising to find that such a statement emerged within a few decades.

POPE ALEXANDER'S DECRETAL *SCRIPTA AUTHENTICA*: WORDS AND MEANING

In early September, in the years 1167, 1168, or 1169, Pope Alexander III sent a long letter, or probably two letters, containing responses to queries about law and procedure made by Bishop Roger of Worcester, a papal judge delegate (1163–1179).[9] In those years, as part of the fallout from the disputes between Henry II and Thomas Becket, Roger was in self-imposed exile from England and was residing at Tours, where he may have been improving his knowledge of law.[10] Pope Alexander's responses dealt with various subjects of which the final three concerned the validity of written grants. The final response addressed the issue of what documents would be acceptable as evidence in church courts. Although the text of the letter is transmitted in various versions in canonical collections, Alexander's response is worth scrutinizing because key features of its wording remain consistent:

> It does not seem to us that original (or authentic) writings (*scripta autentica*) have any force if witnesses to their writing are deceased,

9. *Meminimus nos ex* and *Super eo quod*, edited together in Philip Jaffé and Samuel Loewenfeld, et al., eds., *Regesta pontificum Romanorum*, 2nd ed., 2 vols. (Leipzig, 1885–8; repr. Graz, 1956), 2:328–9, no. 13162 (hereafter: JL). See Mary G. Cheney, *Roger, Bishop of Worcester, 1164–1179* (Oxford: Clarendon, 1980), 172–80 for analysis and ibid., 364, no. 91 and 349–50, no. 63 for lists of clauses. See also Mary Cheney, "JL 13162 'Meminimus nos ex': One Letter or Two?" *Bulletin of Medieval Canon Law* 63 (1974): 66–70.

10. Cheney, *Roger of Worcester*, 40.

> unless by chance they were made by a public hand (*manum publicum*) or have an original (or authentic) seal (*sigillum autenticum*).[11]

The complex textual tradition and the peculiar wording of this passage, which make it difficult to translate into English, should not conceal its potentially revolutionary character.

First of all, one must consider the meaning of the words themselves at the time. Alexander's ruling meant that, if there were no living witnesses to an "original document" (*scriptum autenticum*), it could only have legal force if it met two conditions:[12] If it had been written by a public hand (*manum publicum*), that is by a notary, or if it possessed an original (or authentic) seal (*sigillum autenticum*).[13] This response neatly reflected the two main types of written records in use in medieval western Europe: notarial records, which predominated around the Mediterranean, and sealed charters, more usual in north-western Europe.[14] Notarial records were established as legitimate evidence following Roman law traditions. They became widely used in pleas and debates by increasingly professionalized advocates and judges from the 1140s and 1150s in both urban senatorial and papal courts in Rome.[15] The significant departure in the pope's response (and the

11. JL 13162: *Scripta autentica, si testes inscripti decesserint, nisi forte per manum publicam fuerint facta, aut sigillum autenticum habuerint, non videri sibi alicuius firmitatis robur habere.*

12. For "*aut(h)enticum*" as meaning "original," see Oliver Guyotjeannin, "Le vocabulaire de la diplomatique," *Vocabulaire du livre et de l'écriture au Moyen Âge*, ed. Olga Weijers (Turnhout: Brepols, 1989), 128 and Bernard Guenée, "'Authentique et approuvé. Recherches sur les principes de la critique historique au Moyen Âge," *La lexicographie du latin médiéval et ses rapports avec les recherches actuelles sur la civilisation du Moyen Âge* (Paris: CNRS, 1981), 215–29.

13. *Manum publicum* was the standard phrase for a notarial act. Cheney, *Roger of Worcester*, 179 observed: "It would be interesting to know whether the pope or the bishop imported into the discussion the reference to the deed drawn up *per manum publicum*."

14. Luc Chassel, "L'usage du sceau au XIIe siècle," in *Le XIIe siècle: Mutations et renouveau en France dans la première moitié de XIIe siècle*, ed. Françoise Gasparri (Paris: Le Léopard d'Or, 1994), 73–8. Compare Cheney, *Roger of Worcester*, 179: "The bishop had put his finger on a problem common throughout Europe, in this period of transition from Germanic to Roman, or romanized law."

15. Chris Wickham, "Getting Justice in Twelfth-Century Rome," *Zwischen Pragmatik und Performanz: Dimensionen Mittelalterliche Schriftkultur*, ed. Christoph Dartmann, et. al (Turnhout: Brepols, 2011), 103–131 at 113–14 and 116–18, treated Rome's early use of Justinianic law and notaries.

one most relevant for Bishop Roger in England) was requiring non-notarial documents to have an original seal (*sigillum autenticum*). Thus, Pope Alexander raised the evidentiary bar for those presenting written documents as proof: the possession of original sealed charters was henceforth required.

One should appreciate how innovative the response and its wording were. Alexander, almost certainly in consultation with his learned legal advisors, chose his words carefully.[16] They were not just using prior decretals or recycling the learned law of either Gratian's *Decretum* or the Roman law texts, though these sources had been increasingly consulted by the curia from the 1150s onward.[17] As Brigitte Bedos-Rezak has argued, Alexander's letter to Bishop Roger contains the first use of the phrase *sigullum autenticum*, which seems to have been invented for this response.[18] In a detailed study, she reviewed all early canon law references to seals and authenticity of documents, building on the extensive work on seals in canon law by Mariano Welber.[19] While Gratian and earlier legal treatises often considered written evidence and its credibility, they did not mention seals in this context.[20] So, while the papal chancery had been concerned with authenticating papal acts for more than a generation, "It was Pope Alexander III (1159–1181) who, apparently for the first time in canon law, considered physical criteria for a investigation of spurious seals and documents."[21]

16. Cheney, *Roger of Worcester*, 179: "The final section rules, in more cautious terms than usual, upon the evidential value of charter (*scripta autentica*) of which the witnesses are dead."

17. For use of the *Decretum* by the Roman curia from the 1150s, see Peter Landau, "Gratian and the *Decretum Gratiani*," in *The History of Medieval Canon Law in the Classical Period, 1140–1234*, ed. Wilfried Hartmann and Kenneth Pennington (Washington, D.C.: Catholic University of America Press, 2008), 22–54 at 48–49. For Roman law in the 1150s, see Wickham, "Getting Justice," 37, esp. n. 27 for bibliography.

18. Brigitte Bedos-Rezak, "The Efficacy of Signs and the Matter of Authenticity in Canon Law 800–1250," in *Zwischen Pragmatik und Performanz*, 199–236 at 217: "Alexander III, however, was the first to coin the expression *sigillum authenticum* in a letter addressed (ca. 1167–1169) to Bishop Roger of Worcester."

19. Mariano Welber, *I sigilli nella storia del diritto medieval italiano*, vol. 3: *Sigillografia: Sigillo nella diplomatica, nel diritto, nella storia, nell'arte* (Milan: Guiffré, 1984), esp. 91–229, ch. 23 "Il sigillo nel diritto canonico."

20. Bedos-Rezak, "Efficacy of Signs," 207 n. 23 provided references to Gratian on documentary credibility; see also Welber, *I sigilli*, 97–107, 165–7. Note: Seals were mentioned in contexts other than authenticity of documents.

21. Bedos-Rezak, "Efficacy of Signs," 216 esp. n. 40–1 where instances were listed.

One can see that the wording of Alexander's response had at least two important features. First, although previous concerns of the curia about forgery had focused on beneficiaries—that is on petitioners submitting forged documents and making untruthful requests—the new response focused on the physical aspects of the document (and its author) as guarantors of authenticity.[22] Secondly, the wording itself was oddly repetitive, using *authenticus* twice, as if trying to insist upon it. As Bedos-Rezak explained, the meaning of the word may not have been the same in each instance:

> One is surprised by the awkward formulation of the decretal, in which the same adjective, *authenticus*, is used to describe both the documents and their seals. When applied to the *scripta, authentica* alludes primarily to the fact that they are original documents. When applied to the seal, the meaning of *authenticum* becomes less clear.[23]

Further, she argued: "the problem with this formulation is that it seeks to establish the seal as self-referential sign, as a sign that can signify absolutely, without reference to contextual parameters." But this was a reductive and potentially troubling view of seals, which had rich and heavily contextual meanings in this period. Unsurprisingly, this phrase was heavily glossed by later canonists, seeking to establish a clearer meaning.

Scripta authentica in Canon Law

One must consider the contexts in which Alexander's response on *Scripta autentica* was composed. An important context was that of preventing or detecting forgeries. Of course, the response does not mention monastic forgery, but it would certainly have an effect on its practice: monastic forgers seeking to confirm ancient privileges would now need to produce a document with an *autenticum sigillum*, either an original seal (which could be recycled by attaching it to a forged charter) or a forged seal designed to look genuine. Moreover, there is some indication that this response about *scripta autentica* was written with monastic activities in mind, as the two

22. Ibid., 217: "In this construction, authenticity, just as authority, was distanced from the beneficiaries and situated in the hands of the author of the document."

23. Ibid., 222.

prior responses about written grants dealt, respectively, with the issue of a convent protesting a grant made by an abbot alone and the issue of donor trying to revoke a conditional gift to a church.[24]

I say "some indication" because the manuscript context of Alexander's response, like so many of his decretals, is fraught with complexity and some uncertainty. In this case, the actual letter or letters sent by Alexander do not survive, though their contents were often copied. The origins and dating of Alexander's decretals has never been easy to determine because of his massive legal activity.[25] In addition to influential conciliar decrees at Tours (1163) and the Third Lateran Council (1179), Pope Alexander issued at least 700 legal letters (decretals) in his reign (approximately 68 per cent of the total recorded output of the twelfth century), more than 400 of which found their way into the official promulgation of church law by Gregory IX in 1234, the *Liber Extra*.[26] The response on *Scripta autentica* was one of those.

Likewise, understanding the early development of canon law matters greatly. The emergence of learned law was greatly stimulated by the compilation of the *Concordia discordantium canonum* ("The harmony of discordant canons"), commonly called the *Decreta* or *Decretum Gratiani* (c. 1125–41x48), and the recovery of Justinian's *Corpus Iuris Civilis* (Corpus of [Roman] Law) in the early twelfth century. By the late 1150s, the *Decretum* had become the main (though not the only) source of canonical texts used in litigation and judgments.[27] However, the *Decretum* had no official standing as law. What was important was its method: the new dialectical technique used to harmonize different canons (hence its title). Meanwhile, learned arguments were increasingly brought to the popes in cases, with the result that mid-twelfth-century popes appointed more and more cardinals who

24. *Meminimus nos ex § Super eo quod*, JL 13162.

25. See Charles Donahue, Jr., "The Dating of Alexander the Third's Marriage Decretals: Dauvillier Revisited after Fifty Years," *Zeitschrift der Savigny-Stiftung für Rechtsgeschichte, kanonistische Abteilung*. 99/68 (1982): 70–124.

26. Anne J. Duggan, "Master of the Decretals: A Reassessment of Alexander III's Contribution to Canon Law," *Pope Alexander III (1159–1182): The Art of Survival*, Peter D. Clarke and Anne J. Duggan, ed. (Farnham: Ashgate, 2012), 365–417 at 365.

27. Duggan, "Master of the Decretals," 366–68.

had legal training.[28] During Alexander III's pontificate, a standard legal shorthand for the core arguments of cases was developing and bishops (and especially judge delegates) began to seek papal advice about legal issues, necessitating definitions and clarifications. As a result, teachers, lawyers, or judges started to collect such papal rulings for future use in similar cases. This process is particularly well known for England in the 1160s and 1170s because certain English prelates, who were often papal judge delegates, requested clarifications from Alexander III and placed his responses in their collections.[29]

In many ways, *Scripta autentica* was a precociously early and exceptional decretal. It was one of the first so-called "multiple subject" decretals, which dealt with otherwise unconnected legal or procedural problems raised by judge delegates. It was an early example of what would become an increasingly common type of decretal after the 1170s, as popes and their judges delegate dealt with burgeoning mass of cases.[30] Moreover, very soon after the two letters were sent to Roger of Worcester in 1167–1169, they were copied in the earliest canonical collections in England. *Scripta autentica* itself appeared in both the *Wigorniensis altera* (probably compiled by 1173–4) and the *Belverensis* (probably compiled before 1175).[31] Consequently, *Scripta autentica* had a remarkably successful afterlife, being picked up in at least twelve canonical collections of the later twelfth and early thirteenth centuries.[32] Given the challenge of forgery and the innovative character of *Scripta autentica*, it makes sense that later canonists (notably Huguccio)

28. James A. Brundage, *The Medieval Origins of the Legal Profession* (Chicago: University of Chicago Press, 2010), 131–32.

29. Charles Duggan, *Twelfth-Century Decretal Collections and their Importance in English History* (London: Athlone, 1963), 111–12 mentioned Bartholemew of Exeter, Roger of Worcester, Baldwin of Forde/Worcester/Canterbury, and Richard of Canterbury. See also Cheney, *Roger of Worcester*. One should add Gilbert Foliot, see Adrian Morey and C. N. L. Brooke, *Gilbert Foliot and His Letters* (Cambridge: Cambridge University Press, 1965), 230–44.

30. Cheney, *Roger of Worcester*, 179–80.

31. Wig. alt. 5§e (British Library MS Royal 11 B 2, f. 98v); Belv. I.10§o (Bodleian MS e Musaeo 249, f. 123r). See Duggan, *Twelfth-Century Decretal Collections*, 69–73 and 152–9 for contents.

32. See Walther Holtzmann's card file, no. 649, under letter l, available digitally at the Stephan Kuttner Institute of Medieval Canon law, http://www.kuttner-institute.jura.uni-muenchen.de/holtzmann_formular_english.htm.

glossed Alexander's response in an attempt to arrive at criteria for detecting forgeries and that later popes (especially Innocent III) devoted substantial attention to the matter.[33] Eventually, through classifying and harmonizing, a modified version found its way into a section of the *Liber Extra* entitled *de fide instrumentorum*: "on the faithfulness of written instruments," which dealt with the validity and admissibility of various forms of written evidence.[34] Thus, what had begun as a response to a legal query in the later 1160s was refined and reified as law and legal principle by over sixty years of legal commentary.[35] But sixty years is a long time, especially during a time of rapid shifts in literacy and law.

Was Forgery of Charters a Crime?

To understand the wider significance of Alexander III's decretal on *Scripta autentica* beyond canon law, one must return again to forgery. In particular, one must consider medieval notions of forgery as a crime. The study of seals has traditionally been subsumed by modern scholars under the "auxiliary science" of diplomatic, the analysis of charters, since they were understood as mere signs of authentication of documents. Less commonly, seals have been treated as a distinct area of study, sigillography. But the manner in which seals provided authentication was part of, not distinct from, the documents which bore them. A sealed charter created meaning as an integrated or unified set of signs, which should not be disaggregated.[36] In addition, sealed charters drew on the earlier medieval tradition of exchanging symbolic objects (e.g., knives, rods, or rings) to effect agreements or property transfers. Thus, seals physically and symbolically joined oral and ritual practices with literate ones. As Bedos-Rezak observed:

33. Duggan, *Twelfth-Century Decretal Collections*, 41–2; Clanchy, *From Memory to Written Record*, 325–6; Bedos-Rezak, "Efficacy of Signs," 217.

34. *Decretales Gregory IX (Liber Extra)*, ed. Emil Friedberg, *Corpus juris canonici*, 2 vols. (Leipzig: Tauchnitz, 1879, repr. ed., Graz, 1959), 2.22.2 (hereafter: X): "Scripta vero authentica, se testes inscripti decesserint, nisi forte per manum publicam facta fuerint, ita, quod appareant publica, aut authenticum sigillum habuerint, per quod possint probari, non videntur nobis alicuius firmitatis robur habere."

35. Compare Duggan, "Master of the Decretals," 383.

36. Brigitte Bedos-Rezak, *When Ego Was Imago: Signs of Identity in the Middle Ages* (Leiden: Brill, 2011), esp. 26–31.

> The medieval seal, thus standing at the junction of literate and oral tradition, encouraged trust in the written word by incorporating participatory, tactile, and iconic practices associated with an orality that remained throughout the Middle Ages the framework in which literacy and documentation functioned.[37]

Thus, the sealed charter was important in assuring trust in writing.

Even so, forging seals seems not quite the same as forging text of charters, since—as authenticating signs—seals had a different (though related) function and meaning than mere text alone. They were "visible and tangible objects symbolizing the wishes of the donor," as Michael Clanchy argued, and so "the seal could be significant even without the document."[38] They were powerful symbols of the identity/personality of the owner. In the medieval west, especially from late Carolingian times onwards, seals bore images of their owners: kings, emperors, and popes. The images and written legends on seal impressions thus conveyed the owners' authority to documents to which they were affixed.[39] Furthermore, the process of making seals also opened up possibilities for forgers. Because the seal was a technology of replication, the very ability to make standard impressions repeatedly was—in itself—potentially disruptive to the authenticity seals purportedly assured.[40] Impressions in various colors of wax (and for bulls in metal) were made using a matrix, usually itself made of metal, which bore the negative (or intaglio) of the image to be produced in the wax or lead. The seal matrix was designed, therefore, to be able to make a similar (or the same) impression multiple times. It was a means of replication and so was open to forgers' abuse—like any copying technology. So, through-

37. Brigitte Bedos-Rezak, "Seals and Sigillography," in *Medieval France: An Encyclopedia*, ed. William W. Kibler, et al. (New York: Garland, 1995), 865–68 at 868.

38. Clanchy, *From Memory to Written Record*, 261.

39. Bedos-Rezak, *When Ego Was Imago*, 31; "Seals, in embodying the characters of their owners, their fame, their authority, their authenticity (all three qualities are interchangeable in the period under consideration), impressed the charter with their strength." For personality and identity, see ibid., ch. 6 and 7.

40. Bedos-Rezak, "Efficacy of Signs," 217, n. 43: "The standardized features of genuine seals, which rested upon replication, blurred the distinction between truthful and false reproduction."

out the Middle Ages seal matrices were closely guarded and often ceremonially destroyed when their owner died.[41]

Although modern diplomatists have treated seals as part of charters, medieval people often regarded seals as similar to coins, because of their physical production and especially their way of representing rulers. Indeed, the process of making coins was similar: coins were impressions in metal made using dies, which were the equivalent to seal matrices. Both were inscribed surfaces, combining legends with images. This mental association of seals with coins was important, because faking coins was counterfeiting—a crime recognized throughout the Middle Ages in a way that forgery of texts was not. Medieval laws against counterfeiting had been adapted from an imperfect understanding of the Roman law of counterfeiting, transmitted at first through the Theodosian Code in the early Middle Ages and later known from Justinian's Digest. The Roman law of counterfeiting had its origins in the late Republic in the *Lex Cornelia de falsis* of Sulla (81 BCE), now lost.[42] During the late Republic and early Empire, counterfeiting was punished as a criminal fraud (with banishment for free men and death for slaves), but later imperial refinements distinguished different types of counterfeiting based on whether the coins were gold or silver (and issued in the emperor's name with his image) or other metals, such as bronze (initially issued under the authority of the Senate).

In the later years of the principate, penalties against counterfeiting gold coins with the imperial image and superscription seem to have become more severe: free men were condemned to the beasts in the amphitheater and slaves to crucifixion.[43] This change slowly began a process whereby counterfeiting (at least of imperial money) came to be regarded not merely as criminal, but an offense against the ruler's person and, ultimately, a form of sacrilege. The *Theodosian Code* incorporated many changes along these lines that occurred in the fourth century, when the penalty for coun-

41. Michael Pastoreau, *Les Sceaux (Typologie des sources du Moyen Âge occidental, 36)* (Turnhout: Brepols, 1981), 40.

42. See summary of Ulpian in the Digest 48.10.9. See also reference to *Lex Cornelia de falsis* in the *Institutes* 4.18.7, in which the falsification of documents and seals was discussed. See Philip Grierson, "The Roman Law of Counterfeiting," *Essays in Roman Coinage Presented to Harold Mattingly*, ed. R. A. G. Carson and C. H. V. Sutherland (Oxford: Oxford University Press, 1956), 240–61 at 242–43, on which this paragraph is based.

43. As prescribed by Ulpian, Digest 48.10.9.

terfeiting gold coins was raised to being burned alive, although the *Lex Cornelia de falsis* still seems to have applied to silver and bronze coin counterfeiters.[44] Theodosius himself issued a constitution in 389, in which the crime of *falsa moneta* was deemed equivalent to treason.[45] Though the full rigor of capital punishment seems not to have been applied even by Theodosius himself, it was this more "political" view of counterfeiting—that it was treason against the ruler—which survived into the laws of the early medieval west, stripped of any nuances.[46]

Thus, the association of counterfeiting with treason (and its severe penalties) became common throughout medieval Europe. This view was at first transmitted by the various law codes of the early medieval kingdoms, and later persisted despite the recovery of Roman law during the twelfth century. Because seals also bore the ruler's image and were inscribed like coins, the forging of seals (at least royal seals) may have been more harshly regarded than the forging of documents, which seem to have been regarded differently. Even in the later twelfth century, after the rediscovery of Justinian's Digest, vestiges of the older interpretation of the Roman law of counterfeiting as treason remained. So, for example, the common law treatise known as *Glanvill* (ca. late 1180s) in its initial description of criminal pleas in Book I, listed the *crimen falsi* as one of the crimes that constituted *lèse-majesté*, or treason, for which the penalty was death or loss of limbs, which in effect preserved the stern view of the early middle ages.[47] Although earlier English law codes (Canute, Henry I) had only condemned counterfeiting, *Glanvill* (under the influence of the learned law) defined pleas involving the *crimen falsi* more broadly than counterfeiting:

44. Theodosian Code, Book 9, Title 21 *De falsa moneta* dealt with various aspects of counterfeiting, including 9.21.5, a constitution of Constantius II of 343 which referred to the penalty of burning. See Grierson, "The Roman Law of Counterfeiting," 249.

45. Theodosian Code 9.21.9: "Falsae monetae qui, quos vulgo paracharactas vocant, maiestatis crimine tenentur obnoxii."

46. Grierson, "The Roman Law of Counterfeiting," 240–41 and 255–56 argued the Romans were previously inclined to view counterfeiting as an ordinary crime.

47. *The Treatise on The Laws and Customs of Realm Commonly Called Glanvill*, ed. and trans. G. D. G. Hall, 2nd ed. (Oxford: Clarendon, 1993), 3, I.2 (hereafter: *Glanvill*): "Crimen quod in legibus dicitur crimen lese maiestatis.... crimen falsi et si qua sunt similia."

The general crime of falsifying (*crimen falsi*) includes several specific crimes such as the making of false charters (*falsa carta*), false measures or false money (*falsa moneta*), and other similar offences of which one element is falsifying for which a person ought to be accused and, when convicted, condemned.[48]

Yet *Glanvill* observed distinctions in regard to false charters, noting that:

> If anyone is convicted of making a false charter, it is necessary to distinguish whether it is a royal or a private charter. If it is a royal charter, the convicted person shall be condemned as for the crime of *lése-majesté*. But if it is a private charter, then the convicted is to be more leniently dealt with as in other minor crimes of falsifying, where punishment of the guilty involves only loss of limbs to an extent dependent on royal will and clemency.[49]

Forging royal charters was doubtless seen as more serious because they bore the king's seal and so, like coins, the king's image. Such forging was, therefore, condemned as *lèse-majesté*. Although one should not regard *Glanvill*'s categorization of crimes as systematic, these passages indicate that the challenge of forgery led to refinements of legal ideas in England within a generation of Alexander's decretal on *Scripta autentica*.[50] Nevertheless, counterfeiters of coins and forgers of royal seals in later medie-

48. Ibid., 176, XIV.7: "Generale crimen falsi plura sub se continet crimina specialia, quemadmodem de falsis cartis, de falsis mensuris, de falsa moneta, et alia similia que talem falsitatem continent super quam aliquis accusari debet et convictus condempnari." The Assize of Northampton, cl. 1, added forgery (*falsoneria*) to the offenses presented in 1176.

49. Ibid., 177, XIV.7: "Si quis convictus fuerit de falsa carta, distinguendum est utrum fuerit carta regia an privata. Quia si fuerit carta regia, tunc is qui super hoc convincitur condempnandus est tanquam de crimine maiestatis. Si vero fuerit carta privata, tunc cum convicto micius agendum sicut in ceteris minoribus criminibus falsi, in quorum iudiciis consisit reorum condempnatio in membrorum solummodo amissione, pro regia tamen voluntate et principalis dispensationibus beneficio."

50. John Hudson, *The Oxford History of the Laws of England: Volume 2, 871–1216* (Oxford: Oxford University Press, 2012), 712: "Overall, the picture is of a lack of universally applied, strictly defined categories."

val England continued to receive very harsh sentences, though these were sometimes commuted to the king's profit.[51]

Overall, it seems that counterfeiting coins and forging royal seals carried considerably greater risk for those intent on fraud, because their functional importance as graphic symbols of authority was regarded more highly than the texts of documents. Furthermore, it was recognized that the technology of reproduction itself (the seal matrix, the coin dies) could be used to spawn many fraudulent copies, and accordingly those who dared to exploit them were always severely punished when detected. Interestingly, forging of ordinary charters (without seals) remained distinct. The same distinction one finds in *Glanvill* seems to have persisted in canon law also. So, while Alexander's response about *Scripta autentica* was rephrased and placed in section two of the Decretals of Gregory IX (on *iudicium*, relating to issues of procedure and judgment), forgery was still treated as a crime, and thus placed under section five (on *crimen*).[52]

Towards a Comparative Approach to *Scripta authentica*

So how are we to understand Pope Alexander III's decretal on *Scripta autentica* in comparative context? One important factor was the documentary revolution, which was transforming many aspects of rule, administration, and law in the twelfth century. In particular, concerns about forgery help explain the reasoning behind Alexander's response to Roger of Worcester. Alexander's response attempted to deal with both the burgeoning documentation and the problem of forged charters by limiting the use of documents as evidence or proof. In the first place, he preferred witness testimony, which restricted document use overall. This move both preserved

51. G. E. Woodbine and S. E. Thorne, eds., *Bracton de legibus et consuetudinibus Angliae*, 4 vols. (Cambridge, Mass.: Harvard University Press, 1968–77) 2.337 (*crimen falsi*, mentioning both coins and seals, as *lèse-majesté*); 3.307 (case of forfeiture of property for forging king's seal). See Henry Summerson, "Counterfeiters, Forgers and Felons in English Courts, 1200–1400," *Expectations of the Law in the Middle Ages*, ed. Anthony Musson (Rochester: Boydell, 2001), 105–116.

52. Raymond de Peñafort arranged the *Liber Extra* in five books: *iudex, iudicium, clerus, sponsalia*, and *crimen*. Forgery was covered under the title *De Crimine Falsi*, esp. X 5.20.4 and 5.

earlier medieval stress on orality while remaining consistent with learned law, especially Roman law, about witnesses. But if the witnesses were dead, then Alexander indicated that original documents (*scripta autentica*) did not have legal force unless they were drawn up by notaries or bore original seals (*sigillum autenticum*). This distinction acknowledged the different documentary cultures of northern and southern Europe, but proved difficult in both theory and application. Tying the validity of written evidence to sealed charters was a self-referential move which was inherently unstable, because seals were a technology of replication and, hence, facilitated forgery even as they allowed for its detection and prevention. Indeed, later canonists attempting to gloss Alexander and systematize the decretal corpus remained troubled by his ruling for this very reason.[53] In addition, one must consider the circumstances in which the original response arose. It was no accident that Alexander was asked about the validity of documents by Bishop Roger, an English judge delegate. It has long been known that the rapidly growing royal law under King Henry II (1154–1189) (the rise of what would become the English common law) and the emergent canon law influenced each other's development. Friction between two overlapping jurisdictions generated both contestation (of which the Becket controversy was the most obvious) and creativity. Consequently, the early and large output of decretal collections in England, and the judges delegate who inspired their compilation, had a disproportionate role in shaping the development of church law.[54] *Scripta autentica* was just one instance of this ongoing reciprocal process.

Overall, scholars working on medieval legal history in the 1160s and 1170s must take into account that it was a time of massive and continuous change. Separating analysis by legal tradition—be it canon law, English common law, Roman law, or continental law—may obscure the causes of those changes as much as it reveals them. Another way of thinking about this same point is to understand that law and culture before 1200 should

53. Bedos-Rezak, "Efficacy of Signs," 222–36 traced later decretalist and papal use of *Scripta autentica*.

54. Charles Duggan, "Twelfth-Century Decretal Collections," 21–22 and idem, "Papal Judges Delegate and the Making of the 'New Law' in the Twelfth Century," in *Cultures of Power: Lordship, Status, and Process in Twelfth-Century Europe*, ed. Thomas N. Bisson (Philadelphia: University of Pennsylvania Press, 1995), 172–99.

not be studied as separate things.[55] These legal traditions were mutually influential partially because a separate legal profession and specialized legal education were only nascent before 1200.[56] As legal professionals and legal education emerged out of the (predominantly clerical) literate elites in medieval Western Europe, they shared some of the concerns of those elites. One shared issue was how to respond to the increased use of writing—especially the use of documents in courts as proof or evidence. The problem of forgery was multi-faceted, since forgery both relied on and simultaneously undermined the authority of writing generally. Moreover, it was especially troubling for nascent legal professionals seeking to adapt to the rapid and disruptive effects of the twelfth-century documentary revolution.

Such observations underscore the central importance of the "Donahue approach": analyzing the development of legal ideas and practices comparatively, across legal traditions, and within the larger social, political, and cultural context of their development. Of course, using such an approach is difficult because it requires very broad reading in many languages. However, this comparative approach is ultimately rewarding because it allows scholars to understand more fully how—and more importantly why—rulings like Pope Alexander III's *Scripta autentica* were made.

55. This idea inspired by a series of panels organized by Paul Hyams on "Law and Culture in the Middle Ages," aptly held at the International Medieval Congress in Kalamazoo.

56. Brundage, *The Medieval Origins*, esp. chaps. 4 and 5, on the rise of professional lawyers and judges in the late twelfth and early thirteenth centuries.

Written Agreements and Civil Wars: The Catalan and Anglo-Norman Examples

Adam J. Kosto

One the many things I learned sitting at Charlie Donahue's feet—or at least at the feet of the ominously precarious towers of books in his Langdell office—was the virtues of historical comparison. The History Department bureaucrats didn't quite know what to make of an orals field in Late Medieval *and* Early Modern England *and* France. They could have warned future editors about a tome on marriage practices in York *and* Ely *and* Paris *and* Brussels *and* Cambrai. But students surely appreciated the way he structured Continental Legal History clearly by leading a merry chase after wild animals (and witnesses and weddings) through lawbooks and court cases from diverse times and places. There is a method here. In seeking to "impose patterns on the variety"[1] the historian can generate the significant commonality *and* the telling difference—happily lumping and splitting at the same time and, ideally, finding an intellectually productive mean. History is rarely simple, but "it's complicated" is never good enough.

As an exercise in Donahue-inspired historical comparison, this essay examines the relationship between conflict and documents in eleventh-century Catalonia and twelfth-century England. These were each periods

1. Charles Donahue, Jr., *Law, Marriage, and Society in the Later Middle Ages: Arguments about Marriage in Five Courts* (Cambridge: Cambridge University Press, 2007), 6. An earlier version of this study was presented at a colloquium at the University of Bergen; I thank the participants, especially Bjorn Weiler, for helpful feedback, and Thomas Roche for sharing his work in advance of publication.

of profound political disorder. In England, the succession crisis following the death of Henry I in 1135 led to the "anarchy" of the reign of Stephen. By 1138, a unified opposition coalesced behind the empress Matilda and Robert of Gloucester. The next fifteen years are a catalog of strategic, tactical, and diplomatic blunders on both sides, neither of which was strong enough to turn temporary advantage into clear victory. The civil war did not come to a close until Stephen named Matilda's son, the future Henry II, as his heir as part of the Treaty of Winchester of 1153 and then, to everyone's great relief, died in 1154.[2]

Catalonia's crisis of a century earlier is clearest in the county of Barcelona. After the death of Borrell Ramon I in 1017, the dowager countess, Ermessenda, was unable to consolidate control, and the period saw a marked decline in public order to the benefit of viscomital lineages, powerful castellans, and even local strongmen. The death of her son Berenguer Ramon I in 1035 opened the door to the revolt of Mir Geribert against the new count, Ramon Berenguer I, who fought both the rebel and his grandmother until the resolution of the conflict in 1058–59. From then on, the count worked effectively to reestablish and even to extend comital control over the region, laying the foundations for Barcelona's dominance of the Iberian northeast.[3]

The differences between the English and Catalonian situations are substantial. Most notably, the struggle in the Catalan counties was not over control of a single powerful position, but rather over the organization of political power itself. And while the key circumstance determining the course of the English conflict was the afterlife of the Norman Conquest, which featured families with property interests on both sides of the channel, in the Catalan counties, the geography of power was more clear cut. Still there are very striking parallels, including the one which will be analyzed in what follows: the spread in both periods of conflict of written agreements. The agreements in question appear under a variety of names throughout medieval Europe—*conventio, concordia, conventum, convenien-*

2. David Crouch, *The Reign of King Stephen, 1135–1154* (Harlow: Longman, 2000); Edmund King, *King Stephen* (New Haven: Yale University Press, 2010).

3. Pierre Bonnassie, *La Catalogne du milieu du Xe à la fin du XIe siècle: Croissance et mutations d'une société*, 2 vols. (Toulouse: Publications de l'Université de Toulouse–Le Mirail, 1975–76); Santiago Sobrequés, *Els grans comtes de Barcelona*, 4th ed. (Barcelona: Editorial Vicens-Vives, 1985).

tia—but from a diplomatic standpoint they do stand out as a distinct class of document. Their roots go back into the Early Middle Ages, but their numbers unquestionably increase in the eleventh and twelfth centuries, and it is the coincidence of that increase with periods and places of disorder that demands closer attention.[4]

Documents in the form "Hec est conventio" appear in England from the 1080s, likely drawing on models from across the Channel, although parallel language does appear in Anglo-Saxon diplomatic.[5] In whatever form, they become common only from the 1120s. Edmund King has argued that the roots of the *conventiones* of Stephen's reign lie in the land dispute settlement practices of local communities in Anglo-Norman England. Henry II's rejection, as reflected in Glanvill, of *privatae conventiones* may have led to the loss of many earlier written agreements. But that does not explain the fact that "Stephen's reign is jam full of *convenciones*"; there is something more going on here than vagaries of archival survival.[6] David Crouch, in

4. Adam J. Kosto, "The *convenientia* in the Early Middle Ages," *Mediaeval Studies* 60 (1998), 1–54.

5. Julia Barrow, "What Happened to Ecclesiastical Charters in England 1066–c. 1100?," in *Myth, Rulership, Church and Charters: Essays in Honour of Nicholas Brooks*, ed. Julia Barrow and Andrew Wareham (Aldershot: Ashgate, 2008), 229–48, at 238; Thomas Roche, "'Des conventions infiniment variées': Normes et coutumes dans les concordes des moines de Saint-Wandrille (XIe–XIIe siècles)," in *Coutumes, doctrine et droit savant*, ed. Jean-Marie Augustin and Véronique Gazeau ([Paris]: LGDJ, 2007), 13–42; Emily Zack Tabuteau, *Transfers of Property in Eleventh-Century Norman Law* (Chapel Hill: The University of North Carolina Press, 1988), 31–33. Documents that might date to the late 1070s include: *English Episcopal Acta*, vol. 33, *Worcester 1062–1185*, ed. Mary Cheney et al. (Oxford: Oxford Univeristy Press, 2007), nos. 5 (a. 1072x95), 6 (a. 1077x81 or a. 1091x95). In the text of the agreement between Bishop Gundulf of Rochester and Eadmer *anhænde* (a. 1077x87) preserved in the *Textus Roffensis*, fol. 210v (online at http://enriqueta.man.ac.uk/luna/servlet/s/08hh75), "Hęc est conventio..." is part of the rubric, not necessarily the original document. *English Lawsuits from William I to Richard I*, ed. R. C. Van Caenegem, 2 vols., Selden Society 106–7 (London, 1990–91) [=*English Lawsuits*, cited by document number] 136 (=*Textus Roffensis*, fol. 175) is dated 1085x88 (*English Episcopal Acta*, vol. 28, *Canterbury 1070–1136*, ed. Martin Brett and Joseph A. Gribbin [Oxford: Oxford University Press, 2004], no. 9). On *conventiones* in Domesday, see below, n. 47.

6. Edmund King, "Dispute Settlement in Anglo-Norman England," *Anglo-Norman Studies* 14 (1991), 115–30, quotation at 119; *Tractatus de legibus et consuetudinibus regni Anglie qui Glanvilla vocatur* 10.8, 18 (ed. G. D. G. Hall, Oxford Medieval Texts [1993], 124, 132).

contrast, sees these early *conventiones* as essentially political documents. He identifies a tradition of such agreements in Wales and along its frontier, and analyzes a Norman *conventio* drawn up in the context of the crisis in England, but he also accepts the significance of the flourishing of English *conventiones* during Stephen's reign.[7] Crouch is correct that the political context of *conventiones* outweighs in importance their formal roots in practices of dispute settlement and conveyances. It seems impossible, however, when dealing with written agreements concerning lands and rights, to separate those with a "political" intent from those without one. Furthermore, the high-profile written *conventiones* from this era do draw, at least in part, on the traditions of dispute settlement and conditional grants of land that King identifies.

Conventiones from the reign of Stephen appear in three overlapping types.[8] The first are those generated by disputes, whether judicial or extrajudicial. Despite a series of earlier *conventiones* explicitly growing out of formal lawsuits,[9] only two survive from Stephen's reign: one concerning the priory of Southwick heard in the court of the lord of Portchester ("hec conventio... facta fuit"), the other a settlement between Roger de Mowbray and the abbey of St. Mary of York, heard in the former's court ("Hanc conventionem et pactionem," in the *subscriptio*).[10] Other settlements that employ the language of *conventio* were extrajudicial: Duke Henry's confirmations of compensation made by the earl of Chester to Lincoln Cathedral in 1153, for example, or agreements between Chester and Robert Marmion

7. David Crouch, "A Norman 'conventio' and the Bonds of Lordship in the Middle Ages," in *Law and Government in Medieval England and Normandy: Essays in Honour of Sir James Holt*, ed. George Garnett and John Hudson (Cambridge: Cambridge University Press, 1994), 299–324. Most of the references to English material in what follows are drawn from the rich notes of King, "Dispute Settlement," and Crouch, "A Norman 'conventio.'"

8. Cf. the functional typology in King, "Dispute Settlement," 121–23. The agreements discussed here do not necessarily adhere to the "Hec est conventio..." form.

9. *English Lawsuits* 15E (a. 1086, "Hec est confirmatio conventionis...Hujus conventionis testes"), 136 (a. 1085x89, "Haec est conventio"), 252 (c. 1121x27, "Hec est convencio... fecit concordiam"), 272B (a. 1127, "hec conventio... prescriptas conventiones").

10. *English Lawsuits* 343 (a. 1151x54), 345 (1142–c. 1154).

in 1145x46.[11] Many more *conventiones* concerning grants of land may conceal broader disputes behind the language of agreement.[12]

The second category of *conventiones* comprises those agreements by which leaders attempted to build up power by entering into relationships with magnates. Few such texts survive, but they are thought to be representative. In a pair of documents from shortly after his accession, Stephen confirmed to Miles, sheriff of Gloucester, the whole *honor* that he held in Gloucester and Brecon, as well as those rights held by his father, notably custody of the castle of Gloucester, to be held directly from the king. Unusual use of the term *conventio* signals the novelty of the documents. In one, the king states that he has entered into an agreement—*convencionavi*—with Miles that he will not bring suit against him concerning his rights. In the other, he notes that he is "in agreement with him" ("ego ei in conventionem habeo").[13] The documents were far from effective, as Miles switched to the empress's allegiance just three years later. But they were something

11. *Regesta regum Anglo-Normannorum 1066–1154*, vol. 3, *Regesta regis Stephani ac Mathildis imperatricis ac Gaufridi et Henrici ducum Normannorum 1135–1154*, ed. H. A. Cronne, R. H. C. Davis, and H. W. C. Davis (Oxford: Clarendon Press, 1968) [*RRAN*, cited by document number] 491–92 (a. 1153, "hujus conventionis / Conventionavit... hanc conventionem... facta fuit hec conventio"); R. H. C. Davis and Robert Bearman, "An Unknown Coventry Charter," *English Historical Review* 86 (1971), 533–47, at 534 (a. 1145x46, "eisdem conventionibus que prescripte sunt... hac conventione"). Cf. *RRAN* 58 [=*Earldom of Gloucester Charters: The Charters and Scribes of the Earls and Countesses of Gloucester, to A.D. 1217*, ed. Robert B. Patterson (Oxford: Clarendon Press, 1973), no. 6] (a. 1146, "ista compositio et concordia"), a settlement between Robert of Gloucester and the bishop of Bayeux before the empress. The "Westminster charter" (*RRAN* 272, a. 1153), which promulgated the terms agreed at Winchester, refers to the latter as "conventiones inter nos prolocutas, que in hac carta continentur"; see J. C. Holt, "1153: The Treaty of Winchester," in *The Anarchy of King Stephen's Reign*, ed. Edmund King (Oxford: Clarendon Press, 1994), 291–316, at 293–96. The language used to describe such treaties in the narrative sources is worth study. See, e.g., William of Malmesbury, *Historia novella* 3.56 (ed. Edmund King, Oxford Medieval Texts [1998], 106): "aequis conditionibus et rex et ipse absoluerentur, nullo pacto alio interueniente." Cf. agreements with the king of Scotland, e.g.: John of Hexham, *Symeonis Historia regum continuata*, s.a. 1139 (ed. Thomas Arnold, Rolls Series 75.2 [1885], 300); Richard of Hexham, *De gestis regis Stephani*, s.aa. 1136, 1139 (ed. Richard Howlett, Rolls Series 82.3 [1886], 146, 177). See also below, n. 17.

12. Similarly, Crouch, "A Norman 'conventio,'" 308.

13. *RRAN* 386–87 (c. 1136). A more likely punctuation for *RRAN* 387 is: "sicut patrimonium suum; et totum honorem suum.... fuit vivus et mortuus. Et ego ei in conventionem habeo sicut rex...."

significant and different. The empress entered parallel agreements by which she lured Geoffrey de Mandeville to her side, probably in 1141. The second of these refers to itself as a *conventio*—"Hanc autem conventionem et donationem... istam supradictam conventionem"—and again uses the verb *conventionare*. These agreements were even less effective than the one between Stephen and Miles of Gloucester; within the year, Geoffrey had switched his allegiance back to the king.[14] The empress tried the same approach with Aubrey de Vere, granting him an earldom with a document that uses identical language: "Hanc autem conventionem et donationem"; "supradictam conventionem;" and in promising to assemble weighty sureties, "conventionavi."[15] De Vere switched to Stephen's allegiance by 1145. In the run-up to the final settlement, in April 1153, Duke Henry reached an agreement—"Hec est conventio... Hanc supradictam conventionem et pacem"—with the bishop of Salisbury over control of the castle of Devizes.[16] Thus each of the three major leaders of the war made deals for support and put them in writing; not every document used the language of *conventio*, but many did.[17]

The third type of agreement brought together not a leader and a magnate whose allegiance was being sought, but instead two magnates looking out for their own interests. A few of these come from the early years of the war: the Meulan-Neubourg agreement of 1141x42 ("hanc conuentionem");[18] and the treaty between Earls Robert of Gloucester and Miles of Hereford

14. *RRAN* 274–75 (a. 1141). For the date, see Crouch, *The Reign of King Stephen*, 182n36. *Conventionare* seems to appear first precisely in this time and place. The earliest citation in *Dictionary of Medieval Latin from British Sources*, 17 vols. (London: Oxford University Press, 1975–2013), s.v. is to 1130, from the Pipe Roll of 31 Henry I (ed. Judith Green, Pipe Roll Society 95, ns 57 [2012], 114), in reference to a debt contracted in Normandy; the form *conventionati* is cited from William Thorne, *Chronica*, s.a. 1144 (ed. Roger Twysden [London, 1652], col. 1805), although the date of composition of the passage in question is not at all clear.

15. *RRAN* 634 (c. 1141); cf. 635 (a. 1141).

16. *RRAN* 796 (a. 1153); cf. 795 (a. 1149), which is not referred to as a *conventio*.

17. See also *RRAN* 68 (a. 1141), 178 (a. 1146), 267 (a. 1144x45, "concordiam"), 276 (a. 1141). Cf. Robert of Torigny, *Chronica*, s.a. 1141 (ed. Richard Howlett, Rolls Series 82.4 [1889], 142, "concordiam fecit"); John of Hexham, *Symeonis Historia regum continuata*, s.a. 1150 (ed. Arnold, 323, "in unam sententiam convenerunt").

18. Crouch, "A Norman 'conventio,'" 321–23. Cf. the Warwick-Clinton agreement of 1137x38 (323–24), which does not similarly refer to itself as a *conventio*. Crouch also refers (309) to Marshal-Salisbury and Northampton-Maudit alliances secured by marriages.

from 1142, a *confederacio amoris* and *convencio* in which Robert undertook not to make alliances with anyone who injured Miles, "especially in that war that is now taking place between the empress and King Stephen." Notably, while the two earls promised to remain on the same side in the conflict, their agreement did not rule out switching sides together. The agreement was about them, not about their lords.[19]

The so-called "magnates' peace" of the late 1140s and early 1150s—when instead of bringing the civil war to a head, the great men of the realm seemed to wait for the clock to run out on Stephen's reign—best illustrates the operation of this third category of *conventiones*. A flurry of agreements survive from the years 1148 and 1149. Some are between magnates nominally on the same side of the conflict, such as the renewal of the Gloucester-Hereford agreement (*confederacio amoris*),[20] and others between putative enemies, such as the agreement between the earls of Chester and Leicester ("Hec est conventio... et finalis pax et concordia").[21] Good evidence suggests that there were also a Leicester-Gloucester agreement and a Hereford-Leicester agreement, although no texts have survived.[22] And we have texts from these years of at least two others that extend outside this tight circle: a Gloucester-Salisbury agreement ("firmam pacem") and one between Roger of Hereford and William de Braose ("Convencionem...

19. R. H. C. Davis, "Treaty between William Earl of Gloucester and Roger Earl of Hereford," in *A Medieval Miscellany for Doris Mary Stenton*, ed. Patricia M. Barnes and C. F. Slade, Pipe Roll Society [74], ns 36 (London, 1962), 139–46, at 145–46 ("Et nominatim de hac guerra que modo est inter imperatricem et regem Stephanum se cum comite Hereford' ad unum opus erit"). See also the Chester-Marmion agreement of 1145x46 (above n. 11), which might also be considered in this context, and Paul Dalton, "*In neutro latere*: The Armed Neutrality of Ranulf II Earl of Chester in Stephen's Reign," *Anglo-Norman Studies* 14 (1991), 39–59.

20. Davis, "Treaty," 144–45 (a. 1147x49).

21. *The Charters of the Anglo-Norman Earls of Chester, c. 1071–1237*, ed. Geoffrey Barraclough, Record Society of Lancashire and Cheshire 126 (Gloucester, 1988), no. 110 (a. 1149x53); cf. no. 82 [=Davis and Bearman, "An Unknown Coventry Charter," 537] (a. 1145x47).

22. Davis, "Treaty," 144 ("Salvo hostagio in quo Rogerus comes Herefordie posuit Willelmum comitem Gloec' erga Robertum comitem Legrecestrie"); David Crouch, *The Beaumont Twins: The Roots and Branches of Power in the Twelfth Century* (Cambridge: Cambridge University Press, 1986), 85.

istam").[23] These agreements mapped out futures concerning military aid against enemies, control of castles, and proper responses to possible actions by third parties. They added up to a structure, represented graphically by R. H. C. Davis in his discussion of these years.[24]

Cutting deals during a civil war is hardly surprising. Writing them down may be. Even in the realm of international diplomacy, written treaties are rare before the twelfth century; for England, only two—the Anglo-Flemish agreements of 1101 and 1110—survive before the reign of Henry II. Notably, these are themselves both *conventiones* ("Conventio inter…"), and they share the chirographic form and mirror the content of several of the *conventiones* discussed above, thus forming part of the background for the flourishing of those documents in King Stephen's reign.[25] But in the domestic as in the international context, putting pen to parchment certainly did nothing to guarantee adherence to the terms recorded, as all the switching of sides shows. Everyone involved was surely aware of the likelihood of betrayal and could hardly expect such documents to "hold up in court." But they wrote them down nonetheless and took pains to signal their novelty.

Despite the different circumstances and the absence of a royal center, Catalonia offers the same three overlapping types of written agreements: dispute settlements, conventions that leaders used to ally themselves with more-or-less subordinate supporters, and treaty-like conventions among equals.[26] In the context of the long-running political conflict in the region in the eleventh-century, the latter two in particular served to articulate order.

23. *Earldom of Gloucester Charters*, no. 171 (c. 1147–48); Z. N. Brooke and C. N. L. Brooke, "Hereford Cathedral Dignitaries in the Twelfth Century—Supplement," *Cambridge Historical Journal* 8 (1946), 179–85, at 185 (a. 1148x54).

24. R. H. C. Davis, *King Stephen, 1135–1154*, 3rd ed. (London: Longman, 1990), 110. For an important revision, see Dalton, "*In neutro latere*," and Paul Dalton, "Allegiance and Intelligence in King Stephen's Reign," in *King Stephen's Reign (1135–1154)*, ed. Paul Dalton and Graeme J. White (Woodbridge: Boydell, 2008), 80–97.

25. Pierre Chaplais, *English Diplomatic Practice in the Middle Ages* (London: Hambledon and London, 2003), 1–74, esp. 41–45, 50–56; *Diplomatic Documents Preserved in the Public Record Office*, vol. 1 (only), *1101–1272*, ed. Pierre Chaplais (London: HMSO, 1964), nos. 1–2.

26. Cf. the typology in Pierre Bonnassie, "Les conventions féodales dans la Catalogne du XIe siècle," *Annales du Midi* 80 (1968), 529–61 (trans. Jean Birrell, "Feudal Conventions in Eleventh-Century Catalonia," in Pierre Bonnassie, *From Slavery to Feudalism in Southwestern Europe* [Cambridge: Cambridge University Press, 1991], 170–94).

Although the rise of the *convenientia* and the decline of adjudicated settlement before the comital tribunal coincided chronologically, the former were not a substitute for the latter.[27] Indeed, very few of the *convenientiae* involving Ramon Berenguer I can be tied explicitly to traditional processes of dispute settlement. The closest is a *convenientia* of 1058x71 in which Guillem Bernat de Queralt promised Ramon Berenguer and his wife to return by a certain date charters concerning castles under dispute or guarantee by oath and ordeal that he did not have them destroyed.[28] Outside the immediate orbit of the count, the written *convenientia* found a more regular place in disputing procedures, in conflicts about, for example, the alienation of cathedral property, an adulterine castle, or possession of a church.[29] But these dispute-settlement *convenientiae* are in the minority in the eleventh century.

The *convenientia* recording a wartime alliance between de facto equals was instead the first to emerge. The earliest to survive is so complex that it can hardly be the first one, but it must be among the first. Its political context is very clearly the outbreak of Catalonia's eleventh-century political crisis. It is an agreement—"Haec est convenientia"—between Berenguer Ramon I and his cousin Ermengol II of Urgell, dating from around 1021. Ermengol became the commended man of Berenguer Ramon and swore fidelity and aid to him, gaining in return extensive grants in fief in the terri-

27. Adam J. Kosto, *Making Agreements in Medieval Catalonia: Power, Order, and the Written Word, 1000–1200* (Cambridge: Cambridge University Press, 2001), 75–76; cf. Bonnassie, *La Catalogne*, 2.560–74.

28. *Els pergamins de l'arxiu comtal de Barcelona de Ramon Borrell a Ramon Berenguer I*, ed. Gaspar Feliu et al., 3 vols. (Barcelona: Fundació Noguera, 1999) [=*Els pergamins* I, cited by document no., with abbreviated archival reference] 824 (RBI sd 6). For dispute settlement *convenientiae* generally, see A. J. Kosto, *Making Agreements*, 101–7; for the *convenientiae* of Ramon Berenguer I in particular, see Kosto, "The 'convenientiae' of the Catalan Counts in the Eleventh Century: A Diplomatic and Historical Analysis," *Acta historica et archæologica mediævalia* 19 (1998), 191–228, at 212.

29. *Diplomatari de l'Arxiu Capitular de la Catedral de Barcelona: Segle XI*, ed. Josep Baucells i Reig et al., 5 vols. (Barcelona: Fundació Noguera, 2006), no. 1357 (LA 1.393, a. 1079); *Els pergamins de l'arxiu comtal de Barcelona, de Ramon Berenguer II a Ramon Berenguer IV*, ed. Igansi J. Baiges et al., 4 vols. (Barcelona: Fundació Noguera, 2010) [=*Els pergamins* II, cited by document no., with abbreviated archival reference] 77 (RBII 21, a. 1077); Cebrià Baraut, ed., "Els documents, dels anys 1076–1092, de l'Arxiu Capitular de La Seu d'Urgell," *Urgellia* 7 (1984–85), 7–218, no. 1043 (a. 1088).

tory of Barcelona and a payment in gold. The agreement is best read as the young count making an alliance in an attempt to get out from under the control of his mother, Ermessenda.[30] Another of the earliest agreements concerns the same Ermengol and the bishop of Urgell, again about military aid. From the early 1040s—that is, the height of the crisis—comes a *convenientia* in which the count of Berga and his brother promise to fight with the bishop of Urgell against the count of Cerdanya; the bishop made the same promise to them.[31] The new count of Barcelona, Ramon Berenguer I, also made an alliance with the count of Urgell against the same count of Cerdanya.[32] As Pierre Bonnassie wrote, "... war led to *convenientiae*... through the coalitions it produced. A close analysis of the clauses of these treaties would amount to a political history of eleventh-century Catalonia."[33] The same, of course, could be said of Stephen's England, where it is often the case that *conventiones* provide the only way to start to make sense of the political history.

Convenientiae recording magnate treaties, are, however, far outnumbered by the third and most characteristic of the Catalonian agreements: those used by magnates to establish relationships with subordinates, particularly those detailing terms for the custody of castles. These articulate clearly what seems to be the much-maligned standard model of feudalism: grants of land in return for military service, coupled with oaths of fidelity and acts of homage, with all of the key vocabulary (*hominaticum, fevum, fidelis*...).[34] For present purposes, what is interesting is how these agreements begin to be written down in a particular form in a particular political context.

From the date of the first *convenientia*, around 1021, to 1050, there survive about fifty *convenientiae* of all types. Of those, twenty-eight concern castles in some way.[35] One of these, from 1041, involves the rebel Mir Geribert. He and his wife received the castle of Ribes from the hand of the bishop, his cousin. In return, they promised to remain in homage and to swear

30. *Els pergamins* I 177 (RBI extra. 2001, a. 1018x26).
31. *Els pergamins* II 25 (Extra. 3151, c. 1050).
32. *Els pergamins* I 334 (RBI sd 1, c. 1046); cf. 391 (RBI sd 2, c. 1050).
33. Bonnassie, "Les conventions féodales," 538 (trans. Birrell, 180).
34. Kosto, *Making Agreements*, 85.
35. Kosto, *Making Agreements*, 68–69, 71–73; cf. 81–97.

fidelity; not to replace the castellans without the bishop's permission; not to let the castellans hand over the castle to Mir's heirs until they, too, had done homage and sworn fidelity to the bishop; and that the castle would revert to the bishop after that next generation. Ribes was a frontier castle, and this agreement was part of Mir's systematic development of control over military strongholds in that region.[36]

This particular example is relevant here because of its connection to a known rebel, but it is in fact out of the ordinary for a castle-holding agreement in that the power disparity between the parties was minimal. Yes, Mir was doing homage to his cousin the bishop, but what did that mean when Mir was arguably the most powerful man in the region? Much more common were *convenientiae* that show the commendation of a castle to a true political inferior. In the same way that networks of "horizontal" agreements articulated structures of order beneath disorder in England, networks of these "vertical" agreements articulated structures of order beneath disorder in Catalonia.

The most detailed example of this phenomenon concerns the castle of Talarn in the county of Pallars, for which a group of five *convenientiae* detail what can only be called a "chain of command," with each layer in the hierarchy related to the one directly above it through commendation and homage and to the top (the count) through *solidantia*, the regional version of "liege homage."[37] Many other *convenientiae* suggest the existence of networks of power that are similarly dense, if less completely attested in the surviving documentation. This is how power was organized in the midst of a conflict, and it was done on parchment.

One other set of these castle-holding agreements deserves mention because of its close parallels to the English situation: the *convenientiae* by which Ramon Berenguer I reestablished his power after quashing Mir Geribert's revolt. Like the principals in England, Ramon Berenguer built up a network of support through individual agreements. Unlike the English principals, he did it at the end of the war rather than in the midst

36. *Diplomatari... Barcelona*, no. 606 (ACB 4-70-413, LA 4.371–72, a. 1041); cf. nos. 607 (ACB 4-70-411, LA 4.377, donation, a. 1041), 608 (LA 4.373, oath, a. 1041). See Kosto, *Making Agreements*, 191–93; Bonnassie, *La Catalogne*, 2.627–28.

37. *Els pergamins* II 103–4, 109–10, 123 (RBII 42.1–4, 55, a. 1079x81); Kosto, *Making Agreements*, 86–89.

of the conflict, and from a position of strength. Seventy-one *convenientiae* involving Ramon Berenguer I survive from the forty-one years of his reign. In the year 1058, coincident with the death of his grandmother and with the negotiations for the capitulation of Mir Geribert, two things change with respect to these agreements: a sharp increase in number, and a change in formula that suggests a change in substance. Earlier agreements began "Hec est convenientia que facta est inter N. et N." The new style read "Hec est convenientia que facit N. ad comitem." There was a shift, in other words, from agreements presented as between equals to agreements presented as between a superior and a subordinate. The bulk of these new-style agreements concerned castles. Ramon Berenguer began to purchase castles from their castellans and to bind them to him by means of written oaths and *convenientiae*—at least eighteen castles within ten years. In short, he saw in the written agreement for control of a castle a perfect way to consolidate his power.[38]

Both mid-twelfth-century England and mid-eleventh-century Catalonia experienced civil wars, and, in both places, there appear at just that point written agreements with novel diplomatic form, *conventiones* and *convenientiae*. In both places these agreements served a variety of functions that make sense during conflict: settlement of disputes, but more significantly the formation of offensive and defensive alliances among magnates, and construction of networks of subordinate supporters. There are other parallels, too: the use of extraordinary guarantees, such as hostages, appears in agreements from both regions, as do feudo-vassalic elements.[39] Both places manifest the interesting phenomenon of multiple documents being drawn up for what seems to be a single transaction.[40] Differences there are, as well. Ramon Berenguer I used *convenientiae* to build up his power after the

38. Kosto, *Making Agreements*, 161–63; Kosto, "The 'convenientiae' of the Catalan Counts," 192–214.

39. Kosto, *Making Agreements*, 81–97, 124–33; King, "Dispute Settlement," 122–23, 129; Crouch, "A Norman 'conventio,'" 315, 320; Marjorie Chibnall, "Anglo-French Relations in the Work of Orderic Vitalis," in *Documenting the Past: Essays in Medieval History Presented to George Peddy Cuttino*, ed. J. S. Hamilton and Patricia J. Bradley (Woodbridge: Boydell, 1989), 5–19, at 17.

40. E.g.: *RRAN* 386–87; King, "Dispute Settlement," 120 and n. 28; Kosto, *Making Agreements*, 191–93.

cessation of hostilities, while Henry II did not, at least in domestic affairs.[41] Similarly, *conventiones* involving King Stephen are rare, while comital *convenientiae* are by far the most numerous in Catalonia. Many more agreements survive from Catalonia than survive from England. A consistent diplomatic form for such documents developed very quickly in Catalonia, but not in England. And on the interpretive rather than the descriptive level, Bonnassie sees in these documents the beginning of feudalism in Catalonia, but Stenton sees in them "The End of Norman Feudalism."[42] That is a puzzle that badly needs sorting out. But these differences do not distract from the striking parallels. What to make of them?

Surely not all civil wars in the Central Middle Ages witnessed this phenomenon. Bonnassie, analyzing the Catalonian case, pointed to other mid-eleventh-century examples of aristocratic assaults on older power structures: in Lombardy, the Ile-de-France, and notably the Normandy of Duke William before the Conquest.[43] In none of those regions do written agreements of the type being examined here flourish. Why, then, in these places, at these times? In asking this question of the evidence from Catalonia generally, rather than with reference to the period of crisis, I have argued that it had to do with the fact that these written agreements were not so much records of past acts as visions of how the future should look—that administrative writing was not simply a replacement for memory, as argued by Clanchy, but something that made possible the imagining and shaping of a complex future as never before.[44] This obviously applies to the period of crisis specifically: in a period of great disorder, imagining order makes perfect sense. The same argument applies, mutatis mutandis, to the English material. Furthermore, in making the argument about the material from Catalonia, I have stressed that a realist approach is not necessary: it did not really matter whether or not the agreements were kept, or whether the structures of order that they articulated worked as planned.[45] The English

41. W. L. Warren, *Henry II* (Berkeley: University of California Press, 1973), 54–81.

42. Frank Stenton, *The First Century of English Feudalism, 1066–1166*, 2nd ed. (Oxford: Clarendon Press, 1961), 218–57; Bonnassie, *La Catalogne*, 2.566–73.

43. Bonnassie, *La Catalogne*, 2.611–12.

44. Kosto, *Making Agreements*, 289–94; cf. M. T. Clanchy, *From Memory to Written Record: England, 1066–1307*, 3rd ed. (Chichester: Wiley-Blackwell, 2013).

45. Kosto, *Making Agreements*, 271.

case reinforces this point: most of the agreements that survive were quickly violated, but parties nonetheless continued to write them down.

Yet if arguing that *convenientiae* and *conventiones* were as much as anything written visions of future order suggests why a civil war would bring forth written agreements, it does not explain why disorders in Italy, or Normandy, or the Ile-de-France, or anywhere else in an increasingly politically volatile medieval Europe do not witness the same phenomenon. Here again, what I have argued in analyzing the evidence from Catalonia seems reinforced by the English material: that these agreements are connected to the spread of written administrative practices generally. Catalonia and England were sites of precocious administrative development, meaning that the eleventh and twelfth centuries were not too soon for war to have administrative consequences.[46] But the comparison between England and Catalonia also highlights the fact that their respective civil wars took place during an *early growth phase* of administrative development, when notarial competencies and imagination were certainly present, but not yet fossilized. In fact, the development of the diplomatic forms of the *conventio* and the *convenientia* follow similar trajectories. The language of *conventio/convenientia* appears first in documents from both regions in *narrationes* and conditional clauses; it then begins to be applied to the document as a whole, usually in the eschatocol; and it ends up in the characteristic opening of the form, "Hec est conventio/convenientia."[47] *Convenientiae* and *conventiones* flourish in both England (from about the 1120s) and Catalonia

46. Kosto, *Making Agreements*, 272–85; Clanchy, *From Memory to Written Record*; W. L. Warren, *The Governance of Norman and Angevin England, 1086–1272* (Stanford: Stanford Univeristy Press, 1987).

47. Kosto, *Making Agreements*, 35–43. For England, the earlier stages of this transition can be seen in the (mostly Norman) *acta* of William I (*Regesta regum Anglo-Normannorum: The Acta of William I [1066–1087]*, ed. David Bates [Oxford: Clarendon Press, 1998]), where *conventio* appears in conditional clauses (nos. 173, 179, 236, 246, 290, 324), in narrative passages (nos. 212, 217, 290, 317, 324), and in the *eschatocol* or closing passages (nos. 9, 143, 234, 245, 341, 349). The sole appearance of the phrase "Hec est conventio" is likely a later rubrication (no. 257), although *conventio* does appear in a narrative phrase in the protocol of a confirmation (no. 142). Cf. Robin Fleming, *Domesday Book and the Law: Society and Legal Custom in Early Medieval England* (Cambridge: Cambridge University Press, 1998), nos. 632, 834, 1172, 1609, 1666, 2767, 2944, 3201 (narrative passages); nos. 478–79, 625, 630, 2767, 2937, 2946, 3049, 3127, 3182 (conditional clauses). See King, "Dispute Settlement," 116–17; Roche, "Des conventions," 21.

(from a century earlier) for a wide variety of conditional transactions that have nothing to do with high politics.[48] In both regions, however, the form becomes a major instrument in those politics.

Finally, the comparison between the crises in England and Catalonia shows that in these two regions at these particular stages in their administrative development, writing as an instrument of power was by no means limited to the royal or comital chancery. When the earls of Leicester and Chester wrote a *conventio*, or Mir Geribert and his episcopal cousin drew up a *convenientia*, they were exercising the same species of power as the king, or the count. They were able to do so because the written agreement as an instrument, and as an expression, of power was available to them. Henry II's lawyers made *privatae conventiones* irrelevant. Ramon Berenguer I from 1058, and his successors after him—who renewed these *convenientiae* into the late twelfth century—made sure that they remained in control. But during the crises in England and Catalonia, the written agreement was available to all. That thought may suggest a revision of our understanding of political culture in the Central Middle Ages: law, administration, and the written word were certainly boons to central—usually royal—governance, but it is worth stressing that those sitting atop political hierarchies did not have a monopoly on them. In periods of civil war, writing a *convenientia* or a *conventio* was a prerogative, perhaps even a marker, of membership in the political class.

48. Kosto, *Making Agreements*, e.g. 107–19. By the early twelfth century, the scribes of Burton and Ramsey Abbeys and Bath Cathedral, for example, had adopted the "hec est conventio" form for conditional grants: G. Wrottesley, ed., "The Burton Chartulary," *Collections for a History of Staffordshire* 5.1 (1884), 1–101, at 31–36, etc.; *Cartularium monasterii de Rameseia*, ed. William Henry Hart and Ponsonby A. Lyons, 3 vols., Rolls Series 79 (1884–93), nos. 36, 40, 72, 78–79, etc., cf. nos. 35, 55, 71, etc. (no. 51 is an extrajudicial dispute settlement); *Two Chartularies of the Priory of St. Peter at Bath*, ed. William Hunt, Somerset Record Society [7] (London, 1893), CCCC MS, nos. 51–52, 54, 70, 76; cf. no. 1.

Glanvill and the Development of the English Advowson Writs

Joshua C. Tate[1]

I am most grateful to the editors of this volume for the opportunity to honor Professor Charles Donahue, known affectionately to his many students, colleagues, mentees, and friends simply as "Charlie," who has served as a mentor for me throughout my academic career. In keeping with the theme of this volume and with Charlie's general analytical approach, this article will focus on a single text—the twelfth-century English legal treatise commonly called *Glanvill*—and explain how a particular technical discussion therein acquires new significance when carefully examined and situated in the broader contemporary social and legal context.

The text traditionally known as *Glanvill* was completed between 29 November 1187 and the death of Henry II on 6 July 1189.[2] Although various distinguished authors have been proposed for the treatise (including the royal justiciar Rannulf Glanvill, the traditional choice), it is more likely to have been written by a young man who had a strong understanding of the procedures employed in the royal courts, but who had not yet reached

1. I am grateful to Paul Brand as well as Professor Donahue for their input on the problems discussed in this article.

2. The treatise makes clear (both in the Prologue and in the substance of the discussion) that it was written during the reign of Henry II, and it includes two final concords dating from 1187, the later of which dates to 29 November. See G. D. G. Hall, ed. and trans., Introduction to *The Treatise on the Laws and Customs of the Realm of England Commonly Called Glanvill* (London: Nelson, 1965) [hereinafter "*Glanvilll*"], xxxi.

the pinnacle of his career.[3] It is evident that the author had some understanding of Romano-canonical learning, and especially of Justinian's Institutes.[4] The prologue reads like an apology for the disorganized and unwritten nature of English law, as though it were addressed to an audience who considered systematization and writing to be essential components of an advanced legal system.[5] An audience of men with a Romano-canonical background, whose previous practical experience lay in the ecclesiastical courts, would fit this description. For this reason, Paul Brand has suggested that the treatise was meant to be "a kind of 'conversion kit'" for men with some Romano-canonical training "that would allow them to operate in the rather different world of the royal courts in addition to (or perhaps even in place of) the ecclesiastical courts."[6]

In describing the law of the royal courts, *Glanvill* follows a method that F. W. Maitland characterized as "dilemmatic."[7] When beginning a new topic, *Glanvill* offers two or more possibilities of what might occur: e.g., either the defendant appears in response to a summons, or he does not appear. The author first describes what happens if the former occurs, and then moves on to the second possibility. The first bifurcation of this kind occurs in Book I, where *Glanvill* divides all pleas into the categories of "criminal" and "civil."[8] After delineating the criminal pleas, *Glanvill* further divides civil pleas into those that "are to be pleaded and determined only in the court of the lord king," and those that "belong to the sheriffs of counties."[9] Finally, with regard to the pleas that belong in the king's court, *Glanvill* makes a distinction between pleas that "concern solely claims to the property in the disputed subject matter (*placita solummodo super pro-*

3. Ibid.; Sarah Tullis, "*Glanvill Continued*: a reassessment," in Andrew Lewis et al. eds., *Law in the City: Proceedings of the Seventeenth British Legal History Conference, London, 2005* (Bodmin, Cornwall: MPG Books, 2007), 15 n. 2.

4. Hall, Introduction to *Glanvill*, xxxvi–xl.

5. *Glanvill*, Prologue, 2–3.

6. Paul Brand, "Legal Education in England before the Inns of Court," in Jonathan A. Bush and Alain Wijffels, eds., *Learning the Law: Teaching and the Transmission of Law in England 1150–1900* (London: Hambledon Press, 1999), 53–55.

7. F. Pollock and F. W. Maitland, *The History of English Law before the Time of Edward I* (Cambridge: Cambridge University Press, 2nd ed. 1898, repr. 1968, 2 vols.), 1.166.

8. *Glanvill*, I, 1, p.3.

9. Ibid. I, 3, p. 4 (trans. Hall).

prietate rei prodita)" and those "in which the claim is based on possession, and which are determined by recognitions (*illis autem que super possessione loquuntur et per recognitiones terminantur*)." The former pleas are discussed first, while treatment of the latter is postponed until later in the treatise.[10]

Following his classification of pleas, *Glanvill* begins a discussion under the heading "the writ for making the first summons," in which he discusses the *precipe* writ of right for land.[11] This writ, which would later be invalidated by clause 34 of Magna Carta,[12] ordered the defendant to render a certain tract of land to the plaintiff; if the defendant failed to do so, he was to be summoned by good summoners to appear before either the king or his justices at a specific place and on a specific day, at which point he could explain why he had failed to follow the command in the first clause of the writ.[13]

After concluding his discussion of the *precipe* writ of right for land, *Glanvill* moves on to pleas concerning advowsons. *Glanvill* begins this discussion by stating that an advowson plea "is begun sometimes when the churches are vacant, sometimes when they are not vacant (*moueri solet tum ecclesiis ipsis uacantibus tum ecclesiis non uacantibus*)."[14] For this reason, *Glanvill* explains, "I distinguish between a dispute about the advowson itself—that is, the right to present a parson—and a dispute about the last presentation, that is, seisin of the right to present a parson (*distinguo utrum fiat contencio super aduocatione ipsa, id est super iure ipso presentandi personam, uel super ultima presentatione, id est super saisina iuris presentandi personam*)."[15]

If the plaintiff claimed the last presentation to a vacant church, or asserted that some third party last presented to a vacant church, and the defendant claimed the last presentation for himself, the issue would be decided by an assize (recognition) concerning the last presentation, not by

10. Ibid. (trans. Hall).

11. Ibid. I, 6, p. 5.

12. M. T. Clanchy, "Magna Carta, Clause Thirty-Four," *English Historical Review* 79 (1964), 543.

13. *Glanvill*, I, 6, p. 5.

14. Ibid. IV, 1, p. 43 (trans. Hall).

15. Ibid. (trans. Hall).

the writ of right.[16] The party who prevailed at that assize "thereby recovers seisin of the presentation of the vacant church in dispute, and so he may lawfully present a parson to that church, saving the right and claim of the other party as to the right of advowson (*eo ipso saisinam presentationis ecclesie uacantis super qua contentio est dirationabit, ita quod personam ad eandem ecclesiam presentabit, saluo iure et clamio alterius super iure aduocationis*)." On the other hand, if the plaintiff claimed "only the right of advowson (*ius aduocationis tantum*)," then he would "add to his claim (*adiciet*)" either that he or one of his ancestors presented the last parson, that the defendant or one of his ancestors did, that a third party did, or that he does not know who did. If the plaintiff conceded that the defendant or his ancestors made the last presentation, "then, without any recognition, the [defendant] shall present one parson at least (*sine recognitione unam personam presentabit ad minus*)."[17] In all other cases, the dispute would be resolved by the recognition.[18] In other words, according to *Glanvill*, if the church is vacant, there are only two possible outcomes: either the dispute will be resolved by the recognition, or the defendant will be allowed to present the next parson without any recognition.

Glanvill's introduction to the law of advowsons seems to raise more questions than it answers, at least for a modern reader. Given that, when the church is vacant, it will inevitably be the party successfully claiming the last presentation who presents the next parson, why does *Glanvill* not simply state that the appropriate way to resolve a dispute over a vacant church is by recognition? Moreover, what sort of procedure is envisioned in this discussion? Before these questions can be answered—if indeed they can be answered—it is necessary to continue with *Glanvill*'s account of advowson writ procedure.

Once the issue of the last presentation was decided, either by recognition or otherwise, and the church was no longer vacant, *Glanvill* tells us that the party claiming the right of advowson would have "the writ for making a summons concerning advowsons of churches":

16. Ibid. IV, 1, pp. 43–44. The assize in question is the assize of darrein presentment, discussed *infra*.

17. Ibid. IV, 1, p. 44 (trans. Hall).

18. Ibid.

> The king to the sheriff, greeting. Command N. justly and without delay to release the advowson of the church in such-and-such a vill to R., who claims that it belongs to him and complains that N. unjustly withholds it from him. If he does not do this, summon him by good summoners to be at such-and-such a place on a certain day before me or my justices, to show why he has not done it. And have there the summoners and this writ. Witness, etc.[19]

The wording of this writ is very close to the *precipe* writ for land, replacing the words regarding land with references to the advowson. *Glanvill* explains that the procedure associated with the advowson writ is identical with that concerning its counterpart for land, except that a unique procedure is required to take the right of presentation into the king's hand in the event that the summoned party fails to appear when required.[20] In order to accomplish this, the sheriff would go to the church in the presence of trustworthy men (*coram probis hominibus*) and announce that he was seizing (*se saisiasse*) the presentation of the church into the king's hand, which gave seisin (*saisina*) to the king.[21] Through this fiction, the common law overcame the problem that the advowson, as an intangible, could not be physically controlled. When the defendant had exhausted his essoins (if applicable) and both parties were present in court, the plaintiff would appear and state his claim, which would be followed either by battle or by the grand assize, at the election of the defendant.[22]

Three points can be made at this stage about the *precipe* writ of right of advowson as described in *Glanvill*. First, the writ itself, like the *precipe* writ for land, does not use the word *ius*, and the only indication that the writ concerns right rather than seisin is in *Glanvill*'s discussion. Second, the count made by the plaintiff uses both terms, referring to the advowson

19. "Breue de summonitione facienda de aduocationibus ecclesiarum. Rex uicecomiti salutem. Precipe N. quod iuste et sine dilatione dimittat R. aduocationem ecclesie in illa uilla quam clamat ad se pertinere, et unde queritur quod ipse ei iniuste difforciat. Et nisi fecerit, summone eum per bonos summonitores quod sit ibi eo die coram me uel iusticiis meis ostensurus quare non fecerit. Et habeas ibi summonitores et hoc breue. Teste etc." Ibid. IV, 2, p. 45 (trans. Hall).

20. Ibid. I, 7, pp. 5–6; IV, 3–6, pp. 45–46.

21. Ibid. IV, 5, p. 46.

22. Ibid. IV, 6, p. 47.

as *ius meum* but also stating that the plaintiff or his ancestor was seised (*saisatus*) of the advowson in the reign of the specified king, and that this seisin was on account of having presented a parson. It is quite possible that the language of the writ and of the count were quite older than the treatise itself. Thus, while the distinction between *ius* and *saisina* with regard to advowsons may have been better understood by *Glanvill*'s day, the concept of seisin of an advowson was already established by the time the treatise was written. This is also shown by the statement of the sheriff, in taking the advowson into the king's hand, that he is "seizing" (*se saisiasse*) the presentation of the church, a relatively advanced concept when applied to an intangible.

Finally, there is nothing in either the writ or the count to indicate that the plaintiff claims (or does not claim) the last presentation. This suggests that the procedure *Glanvill* describes as taking place before the issuance of the *precipe* writ, in which the plaintiff makes his claim concerning the last presentation, is not part of the actual pleading under the writ. Rather, it appears to be a kind of preliminary hearing to determine whether the writ will be issued in the first place. The earliest plea rolls, however, give no indication that such preliminary hearings took place, although it is possible that preliminary hearings may lurk behind some entries that appear to record assizes of darrein presentment. *Glanvill* may have described this imagined hearing merely in an effort to help the reader understand the difference between disputes over right and disputes over seisin. The actual procedure may rarely have been used in *Glanvill*'s day, if indeed it was ever used.

The remainder of Book IV of *Glanvill* is devoted to three other advowson writs: the writ of *quo advocato*, by which a clerk is summoned to explain by which of two patrons he claims to hold the church; and two writs of prohibition to prevent advowson disputes from being held in the ecclesiastical courts.[23] *Glanvill* describes the writ of *quo advocato*, as a way of initiating an advowson dispute when the church is not vacant.[24] Through this writ, the king summons the clerk holding the benefice to explain by

23. Ibid. IV, 8–14, pp. 47–53.
24. Ibid., IV, 7, p. 47.

what patron (*quo advocato*) he claims to be parson.[25] If the clerk names the plaintiff as his patron, or if the defendant claims no right in the advowson, then the lawsuit in the king's court terminates, and the plaintiff may institute a proceeding in the ecclesiastical court against the clerk if he so chooses.[26] On the other hand, *Glanvill* explains, if the clerk names the defendant as his patron, and the defendant contests the plaintiff's claim, the case will proceed as under the *precipe* writ of right.[27]

Glanvill next addresses the question of what to do with the current occupant of the benefice if he claims to have been presented by the defendant but the plaintiff prevails in the royal action. *Glanvill* answers it by explaining that "nothing more will be done in the lord king's court beyond what is decided between the patrons as to the advowson; but the patron who has just proved his right of advowson shall proceed against the clerk in an ecclesiastical court... and if it appears that at the time of presentation he who presented was believed to be patron, then the clerk will keep the church for the rest of his life."[28] Moreover, *Glanvill* explains, "it has been ordained in the realm of the lord king that clerks presented to churches by patrons who have usurped the advowsons of those churches in time of war shall not lose those churches as long as they live."[29] The treatise author then mulls over the possibility that a decision on the right might be followed by an action concerning the last presentation, ultimately proposing that the

25. Ibid. IV, 8, pp. 47–48. The writ given in *Glanvill* actually summons both the clerk and the rival patron, but Hall suggests that this form of writ might have been used following an earlier writ directed specifically against the clerk. Ibid. at p. 47, n. 3.

26. Ibid. IV, 9, pp. 48–49.

27. Ibid. IV, 9, p. 49.

28. "Et quidem in curia domini regis nihil amplius inde agetur, nisi quod de aduocatione ipsa inter aduocatos iudicabitur; sed in curia christianitatis aduocatus qui de nouo ius aduocationis euicit uersus clericum ipsum coram episcopo suo uel eius officiali placitabit, ita quod si tempore presentationis credebatur patronus is per quem fuit presentatus, tunc remanebit ei ecclesia illa omnibus diebus uite sue." Ibid. IV, 10, p. 50 (trans. Hall).

29. "Statutum est eciam super hoc in regno domini regis de clericis illis qui ecclesias obtinent per tales aduocatos qui se in aduocationes ecclesiarum tempore werre uiolenter intruserunt, ne ecclesias ipsas quamdiu uixerint amittant." Ibid. IV, 10, p. 50 (trans. Hall). This may be a reference to the settlement reached at the beginning of Henry II's reign, or to a more recent settlement following the rebellion of the young king.

judgment in the action of right, to the extent it can be proved, will constitute a defense to any subsequent assize.[30]

Much later, in Book XIII, the treatise writer discusses the several "recognitions" devised during the reign of Henry II, all of which summoned a jury-like body called an "assize" composed of freemen from a particular area to resolve a question or questions specified in the writ.[31] In the recognition pertaining to advowsons, the question put to the assize jurors was "which patron [in time of peace] presented the last parson who is now dead to the church in that vill, which is alleged to be vacant and of which N. claims the advowson (*quis advocatus presentavit ultimam personam que obiit ad ecclesiam de illa villa, que vacans est ut dicitur et unde N. clamat advocationem*)."[32] Thus the assize concerned the last presentation, i.e. the *ultima presentatio*, or, in contemporary French, the "darrein presentment."

Like the assize of mort d'ancestor and the assize of novel disseisin, the assize of darrein presentment summoned an assize of twelve.[33] The defendant was allowed two essoins, but on the third day the assize would be taken whether the defendant appeared or not.[34] Once he appeared, the defendant might offer an exception to the assize, such as that the plaintiff's ancestor gave him the fee to which the advowson is appurtenant by some good title, or that the plaintiff or his ancestor made the last presentation as of wardship and not of fee.[35] If the defendant offered an exception on the

30. Ibid. IV, 11, pp. 50–51.

31. Ibid. XIII, pp. 148–70.

32. Ibid. XIII, 19, p. 161 (trans. Hall). The Latin word *villa* in this writ (which Hall renders into English as "vill") is difficult to translate, but here it seems to mean "village," although, in an earlier part of the writ, the king summons men *de visneto de illa villa*, "from the neighborhood of that village." Interestingly, book XIII of *Glanvill* does not mention the requirement found in later versions of the writ that the presentation have been in time of peace (*tempore pacis*), although a reference is made to the requirement in *Glanvill*, IV, 1, p. 44. For early examples of the writ with the *tempore pacis* requirement, see 1 PKJ nos. 3497, p. 373 (1199), 3533, p. 402 (1199), 3534, p. 403 (1199); see also Elsa de Haas and G. D. G. Hall, eds., *Early Registers of Writs*, Selden Society 87 (London, 1970), 4 (Hib. no. 9), 28 (CA no. 40). It is not clear why the requirement was omitted from the discussion in *Glanvill*.

33. *Glanvill*, XIII, 3, p. 150; 19, p. 161; 33, p. 167. Not all recognitions involved a jury of twelve; the recognition to determine whether a particular man was underage summoned a jury of eight. Ibid. XIII, 16, p. 159.

34. Ibid. XIII, 7, p. 152; XIII, 20, p. 161.

35. Ibid. XIII, 20, p. 162.

basis of the alleged gift, the parties would join issue on the exception; or, if the defendant claimed that the last presentation was by reason of wardship, a separate recognition on that point would be summoned by writ.[36] Otherwise, the assize would proceed, and the person or persons found to have presented the last parson (or whose ancestor or predecessor was found to have presented the last parson) recovered seisin of the advowson and were entitled to present the next parson.[37]

Glanvill's account of the procedure that is followed in a dispute over the right of presentation to a vacant church may not have reflected any actual practice at the time he wrote the treatise. It is possible, in fact, that *Glanvill* may have been summarizing what happened before the assize of darrein presentment was created in 1180, making necessary (if clumsy) amendments to address the assize and leaving out key details. Before the creation of the assize, it might have been useful for the court to hold a kind of preliminary hearing to address the issue of the last presentation whenever process was initiated by the *precipe* writ set out in *Glanvill* IV, 2. Although the assize had not yet been invented, the king's court might have had the authority to deal on an *ad hoc* basis with the issue of the last presentation before proceeding under the *precipe* writ, if it deemed the vacancy sufficiently important (and the matter sufficiently urgent) to warrant such special treatment. A preliminary hearing of the sort alluded to in *Glanvill* would force the plaintiff to specify his claim with regard to the last presentation at the outset, giving the royal justices the chance to decide whether some extraordinary intervention was necessary in order to fill the vacancy pending the dispute. The details of this older procedure, however, might have been forgotten or misremembered by the time *Glanvill* wrote his treatise.

Although no direct evidence survives that the royal courts intervened on an ad hoc basis to determine possession in advowson disputes prior to 1180, two early records concerning the churches of Shinfield and Swallowfield (Berks) quoted in the cartulary of Carisbrooke are worthy of consideration. In the first, a royal writ that Raoul Van Caenegem dates to be-

36. Ibid. XIII, 20–21, p. 162.
37. Ibid. XIII, 20, pp. 161–62.

tween March 1164 and 15 March 1166,[38] King Henry orders Osbert of Bray to "seise without delay the monks of Lire of the church of Swallowfield and its appurtenances, as was recognized at Wallingford by the oath of jurors before my justice and adjudicated to them (*Precipio tibi quod sine dilatione saisas monachos de Lira de ecclesia de Swalewefeld et de pertenentiis suis sicut recognitum fuit apud Walengeford sacramento juratorum coram justicia mea et adjudicatum eis.*)." If Osbert will not do it, the king decrees, the sheriff of Berkshire is to do it (*Et nisi feceris, vic(ecomes) de Berchesira faciat*).[39] The writ does not state that the dispute involved an advowson, but a royal notification issued about a decade later referring to the same church does use that word. This notification, dating to either 1173 or 1177,[40] is directed by the king "to his archbishops, bishops, earls, barons, and justices, and ministers of England." In it, Henry II proclaims that "it was recognized and deraigned in my court before my barons that the churches of Shinfield and Swallowfield belong to the advowson and donation of the abbot and monks of Lire (*in curia mea coram baronibus meis recognitum et dirationatum fuit quod ecclesie de Sinigefeld et Swalewefeld sunt de advocatione et donatione abbatis et monachorum de Lira*)."[41]

The wording of both the writ and the notification calls to mind later writs used to enforce an assize judgment. The first of these is *Glanvill*'s writ for restoring seisin to a plaintiff who prevails following the grand assize:

> The king to the sheriff, greeting. I command you to put M. without delay in seisin (*Precipio tibi quod sine dilatione saisas M.*) of one hide

38. Van Caenegem's date is based on the fact that the writ was witnessed by Simon fitz Peter (who appears in records from 1158–66) at the castle of Porchester, where Henry II was in 1164 and 1166. R. C. van Caenegem, ed., *English Lawsuits from William I to Richard I*, Selden Society 107 (London, 1991), 286–87; Robert William Eyton, *Court, Household, and Itinerary of King Henry II* (London: Taylor and Co., 1878), 70, 91–92, 340. S. F. Hockey, the editor of the Carisbrooke cartulary, proposes an earlier date of 1155–58, but this seems unlikely. S. F. Hockey, *The Cartulary of Carisbrooke Priory* (Southampton: Camelot Press, 1981), 14.

39. Van Caenegem, *Royal Writs in England from the Conquest to Glanvill*, Selden Society 77 (London, 1959), 462, no. 97; Van Caenegem, *English Lawsuits*, 466, no. 433 (trans. Van Caenegem).

40. The writ was issued at Verneuil, which means a date of 9 Aug. 1173 or 1 Oct. 1177. See Eyton, *Court, Household, and Itinerary*, 176, 220.

41. Van Caenegem, *English Lawsuits*, 555, no. 500 (trans. Van Caenegem).

> of land in such-and-such a vill which he claimed against N., and in respect of which the said N. has put himself upon my assize (*posuit se in assisam meam*), because the said M. has recovered that land in my court as the result of the recognition (*dirationauit terram illam in curia mea per recognitionem*). Witness Rannulf, etc.[42]

Second, although *Glanvill* does not reproduce the writ of *quod admittas*, by which the bishop is directed to institute a parson following an assize of darrein presentment, the early thirteenth-century register "Hib" gives it as follows:

> The king to such-and-such a bishop, greeting. Know that A has deraigned in our court, by a recognition of last presentation (*disracionauit in curia nostra per recognicionem ultime presentacionis*), his seisin (*seisinam*) of the presentation to the church of N. And therefore we command you that on his presentation you admit a fit parson to that church. Witness etc.[43]

The similarities in language between these writs and the royal writ and notification in the Carisbrooke cartulary are apparent. The notification uses the phrase "*in curia mea... dirationatum*" to indicate a final judgment in the king's court, while *Glanvill*'s writ says that M. "*dirationauit terram illam in curia mea*," and "Hib" says that "A *disracionauit (seisinam) in curia nostra.*" Moreover, both of the Carisbrooke records use the word *recognitum* in connection with the earlier royal proceedings, while the writs in *Glanvill* and "Hib" refer to a *recognitionem*. It is clear from both Carisbrooke records that

42. "Rex uicecomiti salutem. Precipio tibi quod sine dilatione saisas M. de una hida terre in illa uilla quam petiit uersus N. et unde idem N. posuit se in assisam mean, quia idem M. dirationauit terram illam in curia mea per recognitionem. Teste Rannulfo etc." *Glanvill*, II, 20, p. 36 (trans. Hall).

43. "Rex episcopo tali salutem. Sciatis quod N. disracionauit in curia nostra per recognicionem ultime presentacionis seisinam presentacionis sue ad ecclesiam de N. Et ideo uobis mandamus quod [ad] presentacionem ipsius ad ecclesiam illam idoneam personam admittatis. Teste etc." Haas and Hall, *Early Registers of Writs*, 5 ("Hib" no. 12) (trans. Haas and Hall).

they refer to prior proceedings in the royal courts, proceedings that did not involve trial by battle.[44]

Notably, neither of the Carisbrooke records specifically refers to *ius* or suggests that the royal proceedings concerned the abbey's right, even though the 1164–66 writ has a *nisi feceris* clause where such a reference could have been inserted. Instead, the 1164–66 writ orders the addressee to seise (*saisas*) the monks, although the object of the *saisas* command is the church (*de ecclesia de Swalewefeld*) rather than the advowson. By contrast, an earlier 1155–58 writ concerning the abbey of St. Benet's Holme refers to the *ius* of the abbot in the *nisi feceris* clause but makes no reference to seisin.[45] One may doubt whether the 1155–58 writ used the term *ius* in any technical sense, but its omission from the Carisbrooke records should be noted.

There are also important differences between the Carisbrooke records and the later writs in *Glanvill* and "Hib." To state that a decision *recognitum fuit* in the royal court, as Henry II did in the Carisbrooke records, is not quite the same as to refer to a *recognitionem*. The Carisbrooke writ is not specifically addressed to the bishop of the diocese, the most likely addressee of a writ following an assize of darrein presentment, as shown in "Hib." Finally, neither of the Carisbrooke records refers to "my assize (*assisam meam*)," as does the writ in *Glanvill*, or to a "recognition of last presentation (*recognicionem ultime presentacionis*)," as does the *quod admittas* writ in "Hib." Thus, the proceedings with regard to Shinfield and Swallowfield could have been *ad hoc* in nature and not associated with a formal assize of darrein presentment. One would, of course, expect as much if the assize of darrein presentment was invented in 1180.

This is not the only possible explanation for the Carisbrooke evidence. R. C. Van Caenegem, in his discussion of the 1164–66 writ, suggests that it was issued in connection with the campaign that followed the king's famous royal assize (ordinance) on disseisin, from which others have traced the later writ of novel disseisin.[46] Van Caenegem's evidence is a pipe roll

44. Compare *Glanvill*'s writ for delivering seisin after a battle, which specifically notes that a battle has taken place. *Glanvill*, II, 4, p. 26.

45. *Et nisi feceris, archiepiscopus Cantauriensis faciat fieri ne pro penuria recti vel plene justicie ius suum amittat.* Van Caenegem, *Royal Writs*, 514–15 no. 196.

46. Ibid. at 283–87.

entry recording a 40 s. fine assessed on Osbert of Bray in connection with a plea in Berkshire.[47] Van Caenegem explains that, although the entry does not mention that the fine was for a disseisin, the amount of the fine "was very common for disseisins and the eyre was concerned with disseisins."[48] One might add that the fact that the 1164–66 Swallowfield writ refers not only to the church, but also to its *pertinentiis,* implies that the plea was not simply about an advowson, but also involved some land. It is clear from the subsequent notification, however, that there was later some dispute over the advowson to the church, whether or not it involved Osbert of Bray. Moreover, if the dispute over Swallowfield involved the king's assize on disseisin, one would expect to see some reference to the assize in the writ itself.

Whatever may be the context for the Carisbrooke writ, the later notification clearly concerns an advowson, and the fact that the king addressed it "to his archbishops, bishops, earls, barons, and justices, and ministers of England" might suggest that the judicial proceeding in question was extraordinary in nature, although one should not read too much into such formulaic language. At the least, the notification is consistent with the theory that *ad hoc* proceedings were used to resolve advowson disputes before 1180. The preliminary hearing suggested in *Glanvill* might have served to identify those disputes that were sufficiently important to be decided through such *ad hoc* proceedings rather than by the regular action of right. Some of those *ad hoc* proceedings could have focused on the last presentation, although neither Carisbrooke record indicates as much. Once the assize became available, on the other hand, a preliminary hearing would have been unnecessary, as a plaintiff who claimed the last presentation to a vacant church would simply begin with the assize.

After 1180, *Glanvill's* procedure would have been useful only when a plaintiff claimed the advowson of a vacant church but was willing to concede that the defendant made the last presentation. In such a case, however, the plaintiff could allow the defendant to present the next parson, but subsequently challenge the defendant's right by bringing a writ of *quo advocato* during the plenarty of the church. Most plaintiffs, in any event, would not have conceded the last presentation if they had any chance of recovering by

47. *Pipe Roll 13 Henry the Second,* 10; Van Caenegem, *Royal Writs,* 287.
48. Van Caenegem, *Royal Writs,* 287.

the assize, because canon law protected the clerk whose patron made the last presentation.[49] A plaintiff who conceded the last presentation might not have another chance to present for a generation. In short, the preliminary procedure described by *Glanvill* may already have been obsolete by *Glanvill*'s day, which would account for the absence of references to that procedure in the early plea rolls. Nevertheless, *Glanvill* still recalled the outlines of the earlier procedure (or had talked to someone with such a recollection) and used it to introduce the concepts of right and seisin as applied to advowsons.

Whatever its origins may be, the assize of darrein presentment offered plaintiffs in advowson cases the possibility of a swifter judgment in comparison with the writ of right. It also provided a fixed mode of dispute resolution in the form of a jury drawn from the locality, which undoubtedly attracted plaintiffs who did not wish to face the possibility of a battle and who thought that representatives drawn from the community would decide in their favor. In light of these advantages, it is perhaps unsurprising that the assize of darrein presentment is the most common type of advowson action in the early plea rolls. The assize, however, did not provide a final answer as to who had the superior right to the advowson; only the writ of right could offer the successful plaintiff some assurance that the matter would not be taken up again in the king's court.

If judgment was given against the defendant in the assize, the defendant could subsequently bring a writ of right.[50] Whether a party who lost by writ of right could subsequently bring the assize was a closer question, or at least the author of *Glanvill* pretended it was for the sake of argument. As mentioned above, *Glanvill* ends his discussion of the writ of *quo advocato* by addressing the question of whether a judgment in an action of right precludes any later assize of darrein presentment. The treatise writer suggests that, in principle, a plaintiff should be able to bring the assize on the basis of his ancestor's seisin "notwithstanding anything that may have been decided about the right to present (*non obstante aliquo quod factum*

49. See Joshua C. Tate, "The Third Lateran Council and the *Ius Patronatus* in England," in Peter Erdö and Sz. Anzelm Szuromi eds., *Proceedings of the Thirteenth International Congress of Medieval Canon Law: Esztergom, 3–8 August 2008* (Vatican City: Biblioteca Apostolica Vaticana, 2010), 589, 595.

50. *Glanvill*, XIII, 20, p. 161.

sit super iure ipso presentandi)."[51] At the same time, however, allowing the assize to be brought by the party who lost the advowson by writ of right would mean that "it does not seem that disputes which have once been ended by judgment in the court of the lord king are firmly settled forever (*non uidetur quod perpetuo firma sint ea que in curia domini Regis per iudicium semel sunt terminate negocia*)," and judgment in the action on the right ought to conclude the matter.[52]

Resolving this apparent conundrum, *Glanvill* concludes that a plaintiff who lost an action of right could subsequently prevail by the assize only if the defendant failed to plead and prove the earlier judgment. If the defendant was able to demonstrate by a record in the king's court that the plaintiff lost by royal judgment whatever right he or his ancestors may have had, the plaintiff would lose his case and would be liable for amercement.[53] In other words, a party who lost by the assize could subsequently bring a writ of right, but not vice versa, so long as the party who prevailed in the action of right was able to prove the earlier judgment. Such a result, at least in the absence of new facts, is unsurprising, and the surviving plea rolls do not suggest that the problem arose with any frequency in the royal courts. *Glanvill*'s discussion of the point has a slightly academic tone that suggests his interest may have been scholarly rather than practical, or that the passage was written for teaching purposes.[54] This would be consistent with Paul Brand's theory that the treatise was written as a "conversion kit" for men trained in the schools of Roman and canon law who wished to begin a career in the royal courts.[55] In any event, *Glanvill*'s discussion of the English advowson writs illustrates how a technical analysis of legal procedure can take on a different meaning when viewed in its broader context.

51. Ibid. IV, 11, p. 51 (trans. Hall).

52. Ibid. (trans. Hall).

53. Ibid.

54. The discussion begins with a hypothetical question (*numquid igitur eo ipso remanere assisa?*) followed by an analysis of the arguments pro and con, and then a resolution (*Respondetur ad hoc . . .*). Ibid.

55. Brand, "Legal Education in England," at 53–55.

"Tempering the Wind": Moderation and Discretion in Late Twelfth-Century Papal Decretals[1]

Anne J. Duggan

It is a special pleasure and honor to be able to record my immense regard for the scholarship of Charlie Donahue, whom I first heard at the Fourth International Congress of Medieval Canon Law in Toronto in 1972, where he discussed "The Policy of Alexander the Third's Consent Theory of Marriage." It was a *tour de force*. Since then, of course, he has made the study of medieval marriage law very much his own. He brings to it an incisive legal intelligence and special subtlety in commentary and interpretation, whether in presenting (with Norma Adams), *Select Cases From the Ecclesiastical Courts of the Province of Canterbury, c. 1200–1301* (1981) or surveying *Law, Marriage, and Society in the Late Middle Ages* on the basis of cases from five jurisdictions, York, Ely, Paris, Cambrai, and Brussels (2007), a monumental study by any standards. Among his many articles, my particular favorites are: "The Case of the Man Who Fell into the Tiber: The Roman Law of Marriage at the Time of the Glossators" (1978) and "Johannes Faventinus on Marriage (With an Appendix Revisiting the Question of the Dating of Alexander III's Marriage Decretals)" (2006), the latter with a fine translation of a passage from Rufinus's *Summa* on Gratian's *Decretum*, where his earlier classical education has served him well.

1. First published in *Discipline and Diversity*, ed. K. Cooper and J. Gregory, (Woodbridge: Boydell and Brewer, 2007), 180–90; reprinted here with minor corrections.

Medieval canon law has generally had a bad press. Its professionalization in the period c. 1140 to 1234 can easily be caricatured as the emergence of a rigid, centralized, and authoritarian system which paid small heed to the needs of the people it was supposed to serve. This conclusion is readily sustained by perusal of the *Liber Extra*, the Gregorian *Decretales* of 1234, which enshrined the legal developments of the period, from about 1140, which followed the establishment of Gratian's *Decretum* as the principal authority for the teaching and practice of canon law. The genesis of the *Liber Extra* is well known. Pope Gregory IX commissioned Raymond of Peñafort to compile an authoritative collection of papal decretals and conciliar legislation to supplement to Gratian's *Decretum*, and it drew, principally but not exclusively, on the so-called *Quinque compilationes antique* which had been compiled for teaching purposes in Bologna between *c*. 1189–91 and 1226.[2] And when the work was completed, it was authorized by the bull *Rex pacificus*, which ordered that "everyone should use *only* this compilation in judgments and in the schools" (*ut hac* tantum *compilatione universi utantur in iudiciis et in scholis*);[3] and a copy was duly dispatched to the canon law school in Bologna. The image of centralized, authoritarian lawmaking could not be clearer; and that perception is reinforced by an examination of its structure, where the individual extracts are organized systematically under Titles, which define the subject matter.[4] Such a compilation, like the *Quinque compilationes* themselves, was the result of an analytical method, which totally obscured the processes of consultation which had preceded many of the decisions, as well as depriving them, in many cases, of their historical context in terms of the identity of the pope, the recipient, the litigants, and the local circumstances.[5] What emerged was a disembodied

2. *Quinque compilationes antiquae necnon collectio canonum Lipsiensis*, ed. E. Friedberg (Leipzig, 1882; repr. Graz, 1956), for *Compilatio prima* and *Compilatio secunda*: cited below as *1 Comp.* and *2 Comp.*

3. *Decretales Gregorii IX* (= X), *Corpus iuris canonici* (= CIC), ed. E. Friedberg, 2 vols. (Leipzig: ex officina Bernhardi Tauchnitz, 1879–81), 2.3.

4. E.g., *De officio et potestate iudicis delegati* (X 1.29); *De appellationibus, recusationibus, et relationibus* (X 2.28); *De matrimonio contracto contra interdictum ecclesiae* (X 4.16); *Qui filii sint legitimi* (X 4.17), etc.

5. Note that Raymond's compilation contained only the excerpts printed in Roman font in Friedberg's edition; it was the latter who inserted, in italics, the often extensive passages which Raymond had omitted: X, xlv, "Ut vero quae inserui a Gregoriano textu discerni possent, illa italicis quos vocant typis exprimenda curavi."

code, shorn of the nuances and hesitations which had characterized the decisions which it enshrined.

But a very different picture emerges when one examines the original letters from which the *canones* were extracted or constructed. In the overwhelming majority of cases, the decisions or directives had emerged either from specific litigation or from episcopal requests (consultations) for advice or judgment on matters which had arisen in their dioceses. If it had not been for the willingness of numerous bishops, lesser ecclesiastics, and lay people to seek clarification or judgment from the papal curia, the creation of this decretal law could not have taken place; and the problems arose both from the more searching analysis to which Gratian's compilation was subjected in the schools and from the ambiguities revealed in application. The Curia thus found itself inundated with appeals and queries which demanded clarifications of and often adjustments to the written law.

An early example of this process was Adrian IV's highly important declaration on the right of serfs to marry without their master's consent. The decretal, *Dignum est*, which responded to a lost letter from Archbishop Eberhard of Salzburg, silently corrected Gratian's C.29, q.2, c.8. This had declared that "the marriages of serfs may not be dissolved, even if they have different lords...." But the rider, "This is to be observed in those instances where there was a lawful marriage, and with the lords' approval,"[6] added a significant limitation, which implied that the absence of prior consent on the part of the lord of the estate constituted an impediment to the lawful matrimony of the unfree. Without reference to the *Decretum*, Adrian directed that:

> [M]arriages between serfs (*inter seruos... matrimonia*) should not be forbidden on any account, and if they are contracted against the prohibition and against the wishes of lords they should not for this reason be dissolved by ecclesiastical law, although the service due to their lords should not be reduced on this account.[7]

6. *Decretum Gratiani, CIC*, 2: C.29 q.2 c.8, "Coniugia servorum non dirimantur, etiam si diversos dominos habeant [...] Et hoc in illis observandum est, ubi legalis coniunctio fuit, et per voluntatem dominorum."

7. *Regesta pontificum romanorum: ab condita ecclesia ad annum post Christum natum MCXCVII*, ed. P. Jaffé, 2d ed. (Leipzig: Veit et comp., 1885–88) [hereafter cited as JL], 10445; X 4.9.1. A. J. Duggan, "*Servus servorum Dei*," in *Adrian IV. The English Pope (1154–*

Here was an example of the pope taking the opportunity of a specific question from a German archbishop to define a universal right to Christian marriage, and the two key sentences which expressed the principle found their way into Gregory's *Decretales* (*Liber Extra*), and thus into the very fabric of the marriage law of the West.[8]

Numerous similar instances could be drawn from the "avalanche of decretal legislation" of Adrian's successor, Alexander III (1159–1181),[9] but two particularly striking examples may be cited from answers to questions raised by Bishop Bartholomew of Exeter. In the first, *Sicut dignum est* (1172), the pope made important modifications to Canon 15 (*Si quis suadente*) of the Second Lateran Council (1139). This had decreed that anyone who laid violent hands on a cleric or religious should be automatically excommunicated and compelled to seek absolution in person from the Holy See.[10] The canon was so widely drawn, however, that it embraced everything from minor scuffles to serious assault, and Alexander allowed a series of exceptions: for students; for monks and canons regular who strike one another within the cloister; for secular doorkeepers and other laymen who strike clerks found in questionable circumstances with a wife or close female relative or in self defense. In all these instances, suitable penance could be imposed by the relevant ecclesiastical authority, without recourse to the

1159). *Studies and Texts*, ed. B. Bolton and A. J. Duggan (Aldershot, Hampshire: Ashgate, 2003), 181–210, at 189–90, 204 no. 2.

8. C. N. L. Brooke, *The Medieval Idea of Marriage* (Oxford: Oxford University Press, 1989), 51–52, 264–65; Peter Landau, "Hadrians IV. Dekretale 'Dignum est' (X 4.9.1) und die Eheschliessung Unfreier in der Diskussion von Kanonisten und Theologen des 12. und 13. Jahrhunderts," *Studia Gratiana* 12 (1967) = *Collectanea S. Kuttner*, 2.511–53; idem, "Frei und Unfrei in der Kanonistik des 12. und 13. Jahrhunderts am Beispiel der Ordination der Unfreien," in *Die abendländische Freiheit vom 10. zum 14. Jahrhundert*, ed. J. Fried (Sigmaringen: Thorbeke, 1991), 177–96, at 178; A. Sahaydachny Bocarius, "The Marriage of Unfree Persons: Twelfth-Century Decretals and Letters," in *Studia Gratiana*, 27: *De iure canonico medii aevi: Festschrift für Rudolf Weigand* (Rome: LAS, 1996), 481–506, at 485, 489–95.

9. A. J. Duggan, "Making the Old Law 'New', II. Canon Law in New Environments: Norway and the Latin Kingdom of Jerusalem," *Medieval Canon Law Collections and European Ius commune (Középkori kánonjogi gyűjtemények és az európai ius commune)*, ed. S. A. Szuromi (Budapest: Szent István Társulat, 2006), 236–62, at 243.

10. For the implications of excommunication *latae sententiae* in this context, see E. Vodola, *Excommunication in the Middle Ages* (Berkeley: University of California Press, 1986), 28–31.

Apostolic See.[11] Even more important was the declaration, in *Meminimus nos* (1162–1181), of what became known as the principle of *legitimatio per subsequens matrimonium*. "So great is the power of matrimony (*tanta est vis matrimonii*)," Alexander wrote, that children born before marriage are legitimized by their parents' subsequent matrimony.[12]

In these cases Adrian and Alexander modified the application of the canonical norms for marriage and violence against clerks and religious, not in the manner of ecclesiastical autocrats but in response to queries presented to them by local bishops who had experienced the problems of the written law first hand.

Not all issues were as easy of solution as these; not all environments were as relatively settled as the Austria of Eberhard of Salzburg or the England of Bartholomew of Exeter. In more remote regions like Norway and the disintegrating Latin Kingdom of Jerusalem, for example, the Church and its leaders often found themselves confronted by complex and difficult situations which defied the easy application of the *ius commune*. For conscientious churchmen, the tension between the law of the canons and the social, political, or personal predicaments of the time raised questions of conscience as much as law; and in its responses the popes again and again held back from imposing global solutions.

The twelve decretals which Alexander III addressed to Archbishop Øystein of Trondheim between 1163 and 1173,[13] for example, reveal a pope

11. JL 12180; X 5.12.6(a), 5.39.1(b)–2(c)–3(d); cf. C. Duggan, "St Thomas of Canterbury and Aspects of the Becket Dispute in the Decretal Collections," *Mediaevalia Christiana XIe–XIIIe siècles. Hommage à Raymonde Foreville*, ed. C. E. Viola (Paris: Editions universitaires, 1989), 87–135, at 110–11 no. 23; repr. with the same pagination in C. Duggan, *Decretals and the Creation of 'New Law in the Twelfth Century: Judges, Judgements, Equity and Law* (Aldershot, Hampshire: Ashgate, 1998), no. II.

12. JL 13917; X 4.17.6: *Tanta est vis matrimonii, ut qui antea sunt geniti post contractum matrimonium legitimi habeantur.* Cf. C. Duggan, "Equity and Compassion in Papal Marriage Decretals to England," in *Love and Marriage in the Twelfth Century*, ed. W. Van Hoecke and A. Welkenhuysen (Leuven: Leuven University Press, 1981), 59–87, at 77; repr. with the same pagination in idem, *Decretals and the Creation of 'New Law'*, no. IX.

13. For this revised dating, see A. J. Duggan, "The English Exile of Archbishop Øystein of Nidaros (1180–83)," in *Exile in the Middle Ages: Selected Proceedings from the International Medieval Congress, University of Leeds 8–11 July 2002*, ed. L. Napran and E. van Houts (Brussels: Turnhout, 2004), 109–30, Appendix. These important texts are treated more fully in A. J. Duggan, "The Decretals of Archbishop Øystein of

who was particularly sensitive to the predicament of Christian communities on the periphery of the Latin world. On the problem of the inhabitants of an island more than twelve days' sailing from the mainland,[14] who found it difficult to observe the canonical rule which forbade marriage up to the seventh degree of consanguinity, Alexander declined to lay down a general principle "because our letters have not usually made law on such matters" (*quoniam scripta nostra super talibus legem facere non consueuerunt*); but he allowed Øystein and his suffragans to permit marriages within the fifth, sixth, and seventh degrees, "until such time as the Almighty removes the pressing need" (*donec omnipotens dominus tantam ab eis aufert necessitatem*).[15] In the same way, when Øystein asked him to determine the penance for homicide, he reiterated the general rule of seven years' penance, but declared that "he could not give a definitive ruling" (*nullam tibi certitudinem possumus respondere*), since individual circumstances are "matters of judgment" (*quoniam arbitraria sunt*). The archbishop was told that he could increase or decrease the penance, according to the facts of the case

Trondheim (Nidaros)," in *Proceedings of the Twelfth International Congress of Medieval Canon Law, Washington, D.C., 1–7 August 2004*, ed. U.-R. Blumenthal, K. Pennington and A. A. Larson, Monumenta Iuris Canonici, Series C, Subsidia, 13 (Città del Vaticano: Biblioteca Apostolica Vaticana, 2008), 491–529; cf. W. Holtzmann, "Krone und Kirche in Norwegen im 12. Jahrhundert," *Deutsches Archiv* 2 (1938), 341–400, at 383–95 nos. 1–11.

14. This estimate of distance strongly suggests Greenland: see A. Forte, R. Oram, and F. Pedersen, *Viking Empires* (Cambridge: Cambridge University Press, 2005), 330, quoting the *Landnámabók*: "Learned men state that from Stad [north of Bergen] in Norway it is seven days' sail west to Horn in the east of Iceland; and from Snæfellsnes, where the distance is shortest, it is four days' sea west to Greenland."

15. *Ex diligenti: Decretales Ineditae Saeculi XII*, ed. S. Chodorow and C. Duggan, Monumenta Iuris Canonici, Series B: Corpus Collectionum, 4 (Città del Vaticano: Biblioteca apostolica vaticana, 1982), 149–51 no. 86, at 149; cf. Holtzmann, 'Krone und Kirche', 383–4 no. 1. A similar dispensation was made on the grounds of the *duritiam populi* to Archbishop Gerard of Split/Spalato (Dalmatia, then in Hungary) in 1168–70: C. Duggan, "Decretal Letters to Hungary," *Folia Theologica* (Budapest) 3 (1992), 5–31, at 23–4 no. 10; repr. with the same pagination in idem, *Decretals and the Creation of New*, no. V: "Verum super eo quod quarto vel quinto gradu consanguinitatis in provincia tua dicuntur esse coniuncti, propter duritiam populi talia matrimonia, licet sint contra sacrorum canonum institutionem contracta, sub silentio et dissimulatione poteris preterire (But on the point that people in your province are said to be married within the fourth or fifth degree of consanguinity, because of the obduracy of the people, you may pass over such marriages in silent dissimulation, even though they are contracted contrary to the institution of the sacred canons)."

and the "quality" of the person.[16] Similarly, on the appropriate penance for the death of young children under the age of seven, killed in fire or water, Alexander held back from giving specific instructions, because individual cases must be judged according to circumstances (*secundum qualitas casuum et personarum*).[17]

Local conditions also had a bearing on general ecclesiastical discipline. Where the absence of bread made fasting on bread and water almost impossible (Norway had to import much of its corn from England), penitents might eat fish or other alternatives, so long as they "avoided rich fare and consumed only what was necessary to sustain life" (*non ad delicias, sed ad necessariam solummodo sustentationem*).[18] Similarly, strict observance of the prohibition of "servile work" on Sundays and feast days caused hardship where living conditions were severe, and where people lived from the fruit of the sea: so, "except for the major festivals of the year, at times of need your parishioners may catch fish (? Herring) if they turn towards the land on Sundays and other feast days."[19] Equally, the timing of festivals, which should run "from evening to evening" (*de uespera ad uesperam*), caused problems of interpretation in the land of the midnight sun: so Øystein was instructed to consider the custom of the region and the length of the days.[20] Even on matters relating to liturgical celebration, Alexander held back from "making law." He refused to issue instructions for the observance of the feast of the Holy Trinity, for example, since it was celebrated at "different times in different places" (*secundum diuersarum consuetudinem regionum*), and the Roman Church itself did not have such a feast: so, "he could not give a definitive answer" (*certum nequaquam potuimus dare responsum*.[21] Nor could he speak authoritatively on the lections on the *Inventio S.*

---

16. Holtzmann, "Krone und Kirche," 388–90 no. 6 (*Quoniam in parte*, now dated 1163–73), at 389, § 2.

17. Ibid., 391–92 no. 8 (*Audiuimus quod*, 10 Dec. 1169), at 392, § 2.

18. X 2.9.3 (*CIC*, 2.271–2), here wrongly addressed "Triburiensi Archiepiscopo"; cf. Holtzmann, "Krone und Kirche," 388 no. 5, without text (*Licet tam ueteris*, 1164–81).

19. X 2.9.3 (*CIC*, 2.271–2): "liceat parochianis vestris diebus dominicis et aliis festis, praeterquam in maioribus anni solennitatibus, si alecia terrae se inclinaverint, eorum captioni ingruente necessitate intendere."

20. Ibid., 388–90 no. 6, at 388–9, § 1.

21. Ibid., 389, § 4.

Stephani martyris[22] used in Norway, since he had not seen them, but he confirmed that those on Lucian of Antioch were read in the Roman Church.[23] This pope was certainly not afraid to make changes in the law—as we have seen in the case of the punishment of violence against clerks—but while he responded with sympathy to difficult situations, he was anxious to ensure that temporary concessions relating to unusual circumstances should not be used to change the general law. His declaration that his letters "have not usually made law on such matters" implied a recognition that they could.[24]

A similar discretion characterized the decretals of Pope Celestine III (1191–98), the former Cardinal Hyacinth who was elected pope at the age of eighty-five. In his case, one example addressed to the Holy Land must suffice. In *Laudabilem pontificalis officii*, Celestine responded in 1192–1193 to a series of questions posed by Bishop Theobald of Acre on various legal matters, including the validity of marriages contracted in bizarre circumstances between Christians and converted Saracens.[25] Bishop Theobald had asked what should be done about Saracen captives who killed their captors, with the connivance of their captors' wives, and then, having been converted to Christianity by the same women, wished to or had married them. Relying on Gratian's *Decretum*, Celestine's answer cited the "Council

22. *Bibliotheca hagiographica latina antiquae et media aetatis*, ed. Société des Bollandistes (Brussels: Société des Bollandistes, 1898–1902; repr. in 2 vols 1949), nos. 7850–56.

23. Holtzmann, "Krone und Kirche," 384–86 no. 2 (*Uestre discretionis*, now dated 1163–73), at 386, § 6. But Alexander pointed out (ibid., § 5) that it was [Pope] Sylvester, not Eusebius, who had baptized the emperor Constantine!

24. Decisions addressed to one recipient in one context could enter the tradition of written law and be circulated as authoritative definitions through the schools and courts of Europe. For the rapid transmission of some of Adrian IV's decretals, see A. J. Duggan, "*Servus servorum Dei*," 185–90, 202–07, esp. nos. 1, 2, 6, 7, 8, and 9.

25. Fulcher of Chartres, *Historia Hierosolymitana (1095–1127)*, ed. H. Hagenmeyer (Heidelberg: Carl Winters Universitätsbuchhandlung, 1913), iii, 37, cc. 3–4 (pp. 748–9) recorded that Latin men married converted Syrian, Armenian, and Saracen women after the First Crusade. For conditions in Acre following the Christian defeat at Hattin (1187) and the loss of the greater part of the Latin kingdom to Saladin, see B. Hamilton, *The Latin Church in the Crusader States. The Secular Church* (London: Variorum Publications, 1980), 243–44, 301. Theobald, the recipient of this letter, former Prior of the cathedral of Nazareth and a canon in Nazareth from 1174, was elected Bishop of Acre on 17 Aug. 1191; he died *c.* 1200.

of Tribur" (a mistake for Meaux, 845),[26] to the effect that women who compassed their husbands' deaths could not marry the agents. To the question of what should happen where Saracens or Christians married the wives of those whom they had killed in battle and where the wives, subsequently learning of the manner of their husbands' deaths, sought to have the marriage dissolved, Celestine replied that since there had been no conspiracy to kill the husbands, the marriage contracts were lawful.

In another very difficult case, Bishop Theobald sought advice in the same letter on the appropriate action where a Christian husband had abandoned his wife and married a pagan, and the abandoned wife, with the approval of her archdeacon, had married another husband. What was to be done if the first husband returned to Catholic unity, with his now converted wife and children? This was not a theoretical case presented in a law school but an extraordinary human predicament which involved two families. Celestine was being asked to make a judgment of Solomon: not, indeed, to decide which mother should have the baby they both claimed, but which man should be declared the lawful husband of the Christian woman. Celestine's reply was that the Christian woman's second marriage was lawful, because she had been abandoned in contempt of Christ and had remarried with ecclesiastical permission; that the returned husband could, if he wished, enter a monastery; or he could, when his first wife died, lawfully marry the second: in both cases, *tanta est uis matrimonii*[27]—here citing the words of *bone memorie Alexandri* (Alexander III)—the children were legitimate.[28]

Underlying this complicated decision was the commitment to defend the bond of Christian marriage while permitting a humane solution to an intractable problem. The last thing Celestine wanted, was to create a precedent which enabled disgruntled Christian husbands (or wives) to use the device of temporary abandonment of Christianity to marry a non-Chris-

26. Gratian, C.31 q.1 c.4 (*CIC*, 1.1109). "Tribur" was a mistake. The council was held at Meaux in 845 (*Sacrorum conciliorum nova et amplissima collectio*, ed. J. D. Mansi, cont. I. B. Martin, L. Petit, 53 vols. [Florence/Venice, 1759–98; Paris, 1901–27; repr. Graz, 1960–61], 14.835, c. 69).

27. JL 13904; *I Comp.* 4.18.6, X 4.17.6 (*CIC*, 2.712).

28. X 3.33.1, *ad fin.* (*CIC*, 2.588), supplied by Friedberg from earlier collections, including 2 *Comp.* 3.20.2.

tian and, after returning to the faith, enter into lawful Christian marriage while the first spouse still lived. It is highly significant, nevertheless, that this judgment was not included in the *Liber Extra*. Although Raymond of Peñafort put most of the decretal, which he received from *Compilatio secunda*, into the *Decretales*, he excluded the two segments relating to this unusual case.[29] The reason for its omission is not far to seek. The circumstances were too unusual and, despite Celestine's careful language, the legal experts who shaped the law at Bologna considered that the risk of providing an opportunity for collusive action to circumvent the marriage law was too great. Indeed, Bishop Hugh of Ferrara, better known as the great canonist Huguccio of Pisa, raised this very question with his former pupil Innocent III[30] in 1199, and the new pope took the opportunity to rescind the decision of *quidam predecessor noster*, and declared that a lawful Christian marriage could not be dissolved when one spouse "lapsed into heresy or the error of paganism" (*vel labatur in heresim, uel transeat ad gentilitatis errorem*), partly on the ground of the binding character of the Christian sacrament, and partly to avoid the trickery of those who might feign heresy in order to escape from their marriage commitments.[31]

Another issue treated in Celestine's advice to the bishop of Acre related to a marriage whose validity was challenged by the couple themselves after twenty years of matrimony, on the ground of spiritual relationship, in that the father of the wife was the god-father of the husband. They claimed that their consciences had troubled them for five years before the matter

29. 2 *Comp*. 2.9.2 = X 2.16.2 (Clem. III); 2 *Comp*. 4.12.3 = X 4.18.4; 2 *Comp*. 4.4.2 = X 4.6.6 (Celest. III); 2 *Comp*. 3.20.2 = X 3.33.1 (omitting the passages cited here, which were supplied by Friedberg); 2 *Comp*. 2.12.4 = X 2.20.27; 2 *Comp*. 4.9.3 = X 4.15.5; 2 *Comp*. 2.11.un = X 2.25.1.

30. The assumption that Innocent had been a pupil of Huguccio was challenged by K. Pennington, "The Legal Education of Pope Innocent III," *Bulletin of Medieval Canon Law* 4 (1974): 70–77; but compare J. C. Moore, "Lotario dei Conti di Segni (Pope Innocent III) in the 1180s," *Archivum Historiae Pontificiae* 29 (1991): 255–58.

31. *Die Register Innocenz' III., 2. Pontifikatsjahr, 1199/1200. Texte*, ed. O. Hageneder, W. Maleczek, A. A. Strnad (Rome/Vienna: Verl. des österreichischen Akademie der Wissenschaften, 1979), 2.88–9 no. 48 (50), *Quoniam te novimus*, to Hugh, bishop of Ferrara, "Per hanc autem responsionem quorundam malitie obviatur, qui in odium coniugum, vel quando sibi invicem displicerent, si eas possent in tali casu dimittere, simularent heresim, ut ab ipsa nubentibus coniugibus resilirent." It was this correction which entered the legal tradition as X 4.19.7 (*CIC*, 2.722–23 at 723).

was brought before an ecclesiastical court, which duly annulled the marriage. In this case, Celestine declared that since there was no ambiguity about the spiritual relationship, the couple must separate, but he added humane conditions. Not only were they to be mutually responsible for one another's welfare thereafter, but he "judged" that the children should be regarded as legitimate, "if nothing stands in the way." This highly significant rider acknowledged that practical obstacles might impede his compassionate judgment. The verb *censemus* expressed a pastoral opinion rather than a directive; and his *si aliud non obsistit* allowed the demands of compassion to be weighed against familial circumstances.

Running through these letters is a profound sense of the pastoral responsibility of bishops and of the pope as chief bishop. Where one might have expected an automatic application of the general law (*ius commune*), irrespective of circumstance, one finds popes struggling to find workable solutions to sometimes intractable problems. Unusual and difficult circumstances required delicate handling; at the same time, Alexander and Celestine were reluctant to allow changes to ecclesiastical law and practice on the basis of "hard" or unusual cases; but ameliorations and dispensations could be allowed, *moderata discretione*, in the light of necessity (*necessitas*). These were not new ideas. They grew from the philosophy of pastoral care which had been circulated through the writings of canonist-bishops from Burchard of Worms (1000–1025) onwards,[32] and was summed up in the Prologue with which Bishop Ivo of Chartres (d. 1116) had prefaced his *Decretum* and *Panormia*.[33] One passage in particular, a quotation from a

32. His great work was the *Decretum* (1008–1012; 1023): PL 140, 537–1065 (from Jean Foucher's 1549 edition); cf. E. van Balberghe, "Les éditions du Décret de Burchard de Worms," *Recherches de Théologie ancienne et médiévale* 37 (1970), 5–22; G. Fransen, "Le Décret de Burchard de Worms: Valeur du texte de l'édition. Essai de classement des manuscrits," *Zeitschrift der Savigny-Stiftung für Rechtsgeschichte, Kanonistishe Abteilung* 63 (1977), 1–19, at 3; H. Fuhrmann, *Einfluss und Verbreitung der Pseudoisidorischen Fälschungen*, 3 vols., Schriften der Monumenta Germaniae Historica 24 (Stuttgart: Hiersemann, 1972–74), 2.442–85, 576–82.

33. See now Bruce Brasington's edition and commentary, *Ways of Mercy. The Prologue of Ivo of Chartres*, ed. B. C. Brasington, Vita Regularis. Ordnungen und Deutungen religiosen Lebens im Mittelalter, Editionen, 2 (Münster: LIT, 2004).

letter of Pope Leo I (440–61) to Rusticus of Narbonne (427/430–61), contains the essence of his concept of dispensation:[34]

> Just as there are certain things which cannot be overturned for any reason, there are many things which may be tempered either because of the necessity of the moment (*pro necessitate temporum*) or in consideration of the times (*pro consideratione etatum*), always bearing in mind that we should recognize that in those things which may be doubtful or obscure we must follow what is not contrary to the Gospel precepts or found to be against the decrees of the Holy Fathers. But such dispensation should be limited to the circumstances which gave rise to it, and "should cease when the necessity ceases (*cessante necessitate*)," nor should something be considered as law which either utility has urged or necessity imposed.[35]

These principles were widely disseminated, not only in Ivo's works, which continued to be copied and read throughout the twelfth century, but through their absorption into Gratian's *Decretum*, which transmitted a summary of the limit of dispensation[36] as well as the Leo letter,[37] and thus exercised a profound influence on the evolving canonical jurisprudence. From this perspective, canon law could be seen as an instrument of discipline tempered with mercy. The law was not abandoned when particular historical circumstances made it difficult or impossible to apply, but it could be temporarily disre-

34. Ibid., 58–59, 126: Sicut quedam sunt que aut pro necessitate temporum aut pro consideracione etatum oportet temperari illa semper consideracione seruata ut in his que dubia fuerint aut obscura id nouerimus sequendum quod nec preceptis euangelicis contrarium nec decretis sanctorum patrum inueniatur aduersum;" cf. PL 54, 1197–1209, no. 167, at 1202. There is an unresolved debate about whether Ivo composed the *Prologus* for the *Panormia* or for the *Decretum*: see the summary in *Ways of Mercy*, 9–10.

35. Ibid., 90, 140: "cessante necessitate, debent et ipse cessare, nec est pro lege habendum quod aut utilitas suasit aut necessitas imperauit." On this principle, see H. Krause, "Cessante causa cessat lex," *Zeitschrift der Savigny-Stiftung für Rechtsgeschichte, Kanonistishe Abteilung* 49 (1960), 81–111.

36. Cf. Gratian, C.1 q.1 c.41: "Quod pro necessitate temporis statutum est, cessante necessitate debet utique cessare quod urgebat: quia alia est ordo legitimus, alia usurpatio, quam ad presens fieri tempus impellit."

37. Gratian, D.14 c.2.

garded. As Alexander III had written to Thomas Becket in August 1165, "Because the days are evil, and many things should be tolerated because of the temper of the times" (*Quoniam dies mali sunt, et multa sunt pro qualitate temporis toleranda*).[38] At the same time, with charitable understanding of the weakness of the human condition—*considerata fragilitate uasis*,[39] room could be found for adjustment to new and difficult circumstances, subject, of course, to the fundamental principle that "nothing was done contrary to the Gospel or to the teaching of the Apostles"—*nichil contra euangelium nichil contra apostolos usurpauerit.*[40]

38. *The Correspondence of Thomas Becket, Archbishop of Canterbury 1162–1170*, ed. and trans. A. J. Duggan, 2 vols. (Oxford: Clarendon Press, 2000), 1.224–25, no. 54 (Melgueil, *c.* 22 August 1165).

39. *Ways of Mercy*, ed. Brasington, 117, 116.

40. Ibid., 141–42. Cf. J. Van Engen, "From Practical Theology to Divine Law," in *Proceedings of the Ninth International Congress of Medieval Canon Law: Munich, 13–18 July 1992*, ed. P. Landau and J. Müller, Monumenta Iuris Canonici, Series C: Subsidia, 10 (Città del Vaticano: Biblioteca Apostolica Vaticana, 1997), 873–96.

Texts and Parisian Context of the *Licentia Docendi* at the Beginning of the Thirteenth Century

Anne Lefebvre-Teillard

The *licentia docendi* has long received the attention of historians either as part of a scholarship on medieval universities, particularly the university of Paris,[1] or more specifically on the subject of the *licentia docendi* itself. Who does not know the study Gaines Post devoted to it in 1929?[2] Since that time studies on the medieval universities have built upon Post's analysis on this point. In this study, Gaines Post, whose work relies particularly on the

1. Many thanks to Sara McDougall for her help with this English translation. The solid foundations of a critical historiography of the birth of universities and their development appears from the late nineteenth century onwards especially with Heinrich Denifle's work: *Die Entstehung der Universitäten des Mittelalters bis 1400* (Berlin, 1885; repr. Graz, 1956) and Hastings Rashdall's *The Universities of Europe in the Middle Ages*, 3 v. (Oxford, 1895; new ed. by F. M. Powicke and A. B. Emden, Oxford, 1936). Since then, the history of medieval universities has continued to flourish. For the beginnings of university teaching in Paris to which our study will refer, Jacques Verger has taken stock of the existing scholarship in his article: "Que sait-on des institutions universitaires parisiennes avant 1245?," *Les Débuts de l'enseignement universitaire à Paris (1200–1245)*, J. Verger and O.Weijers ed. (Turnhout: Brepols, 2013), 27–47.

2. G. Post, "Alexander III, the *licentia docendi* and the Rise of the Universities," in *Anniversary Essays in Mediaeval History by Students of Charles H. Haskins* (Boston: Mifflin, 1929), 255–277. The author quotes Rashdall several times but seems to ignore, like the latter, Georges Bourdon's study: "La licence d'enseigner et le rôle de l'écolâtre au Moyen Age," *Revue des questions historiques* v. 19 (1876), 515–553, which cites the London council of 1138 and contains on p. 527 ff. some interesting details about *scolastici*.

Chartularium Universitatis Parisiensis of Denifle and Chatelain,[3] emphasizes the importance of papal legislation in the history of *licentia docendi*. The action of Alexander III rightly appears to him to have been decisive in the matter.[4] He especially stresses the decretal *Quanto* addressed "to the French bishops," which he published in the text *in extenso* in a transcription from the *Chartularium Universitatis Parisiensis*.[5]

This decretal is indeed one of the three fundamental texts referring to the *licentia docendi* collected in the first compilations of decretals.[6] In the *Compilatio prima* of Bernard of Pavia, a text of recognized importance for the development of a new teaching based on the *ius novum*, it appears as chapter 3 of Book V, title IV. This title also includes two other texts: the decretal *Prohibeas* (c.2) addressed by Alexander III to the bishop of Winchester and canon 18 of the Third Lateran Council (1179) placed first (c.1: *Quoniam*).

As we know, Bernard of Pavia devoted his Book V to criminal law; it is thus through this lens that the question of *licentia docendi* was considered. This situating of our topic will remain in the subsequent collections up to and including the Decretals of Gregory IX.[7] Narrow apprehension for a purpose, one clearly expressed by the rubric of Title IV: *De magistris et ne aliquid exigatur pro licentia docendi*. This restricted meaning can also

3. *Chartularium Universitatis Parisiensis*, ed. H. Denifle and E. Chatelain, v. I (Paris, 1889) and v. II (Paris, 1891).

4. Alexander III's legislation, writes Post (264), "was the real beginning of active control of the teaching organization by the papacy, if only as a precedent." On its increase in the thirteenth century, see A. E. Bernstein, "Magisterium and License: Corporate Autonomy against Papal Authority," *Viator* 9 (1978), 291–307.

5. Post, 261. The author was still quite unfamiliar with canonical sources.

6. The three fundamental texts that would appear in Bernard of Pavia's *Compilatio prima* existed already in 1183 in the French collection: *Francofurtana*, cf. P. Landau, G. Drossbach, *Die Collectio Francofurtana: eine französische Decretalensammlung*, M.I.C. series B, v. 9 (Città del Vaticano, 2007), respectively 22,14 for *Prohibeas*, 22,16 for *Quanto* and 22,19 for *Quoniam* (= canon 18 of the Third Lateran Council). *Prohibeas* and *Quanto* also appeared in the English collection *Appendix Concilii Lateranensis* of 1180 (2,17 et 2,18).

7. L.V, t. V: *De magistris et ne aliquid exigatur pro licentia docendi* where we find our three texts: *Quoniam* (c.1), *Prohibeas* (c.2) and *Quanto* (c.3). The area of concern will expand with canon *Quia Nonnullis* (c.4= c.11 of the Fourth Lateran Council, 1215) and especially with Honorius III's famous decretal *Super Specula* (1219 = c.5).

be connected to the one effected by the Title II: *De simonia et ne aliquid pro spiritualibus exigatur vel promittatur,* of which it is a particular case.

This narrow understanding of one aspect of simony nonetheless had great importance: the churches' progress (*ecclesiasticum profectum*) itself linked to the souls' progress (*animarum profectum*) that the Church "*sicut pia mater*" must ensure through teaching. This progress was prevented by those who greedily sold *licentia docendi.* This is expressed *in fine* in the canon *Quoniam,*[8] which does not limit itself to the sanctioning of such a practice but tries also to provide greater access to knowledge. For this purpose it prescribes in effect that in each cathedral church a sufficient benefice must be attributed to a master who will teach *gratis* the clerics of that church and the poor schoolchildren,[9] "so that the opportunity to study and progress is not denied to the poor who can not be helped by their parents' resources."[10] The desire to avoid any obstacle to the granting of the *licentia docendi* goes along with this capital provision. Not only would no money be required from the person requesting the licence nor, on behalf of any custom, from those who teach, but also, "*petita licentia,*" one would not prohibit from teaching anyone who is capable of instruction.[11] This canon *Quoniam,* adopted in the reforming Third Lateran Council, is undoubtedly the most important of our three texts.

A few years earlier, Alexander III in the decretal *Quanto* (c.3), addressed to the archbishops and bishops *per Galliam,*[12] had denounced with

8. The text even says that by such sales the offender strives to prevent this progress: "...qui cupiditate animi, vendit docendi licentiam, ecclesiasticum profectum nititur impedire."

9. "Per unamquamque cathedralem ecclesiam magistro qui clericos eiusdem ecclesiae et scholares pauperes gratis doceat, competens aliquod beneficium tribuatur quo docentis necessitas sublevetur."

10. "...ne pauperibus qui parentum opibus iuvari non possunt legendi et proficiendi opportunitas subtrahatur."

11. "Pro licentia vero docendi nullus omnino pretium exigat vel sub obtentu alicuis consuetudinis ad eis qui docent, aliquid quaerat nec docere quemquam qui sit idoneus, petita licentia, interdicat."

12. The address only appears in some manuscripts, cf. *Corpus iuris canonici,* ed. E. Friedberg, 2 vols. (Leipzig: ex officina Bernhardi Tauchnitz, 1879–81), note under X 5.5.3. It is absent in the manuscripts used by Parisian canonists and would be added by its annotator in the *Francofurtana.* The probable date of this decretal (JL 11925) is October 1170 or 1171.

particular vigor the greed at the root of this "*prava et enormis consuetudo*" of the *magistri scolarum* who only deliver the *licentia docendi* in exchange for money.[13] Maintaining the same tone, Alexander III had ordered the bishops to act vigorously to eradicate this custom from their churches. They must prevent those who exercise this dignity [to deliver the *licentia*], if dignity there is, he says, to dare require any money *sub anathematis interminatione*.[14] They must rigorously enjoin them to accept that those who, *idonei et literati*, want to govern *studia litterarum*, do so *sine molestia et exactione qualibet*.[15] Violators will be deprived of their offices and dignities. The decretal finally ends with a warning against bishops who would prove negligent in fulfilling the task that the pope entrusted to them.[16]

In a much more moderate tone, the same injunction would be made in 1177 by Alexander III to the bishop of Winchester in the decretal *Prohibeas* (c.2).[17] If the candidate has paid or merely promised to pay, he will be capable in the first case of recovering his money and in the second of being relaxed from his promise.[18] The second part of the decretal states that if, because of this prohibition, "somebody"[19] delays introducing masters *in locis congruis*, it will be permitted to the bishop, *de concessione nostra*, to

13. "...tanto vehementiori dignos eos esse animadverstione censemus qui nomem magistri scolarum et dignitatem assumunt in ecclesiis vestris et sine certo pretio eclesiasticis viris docendi alios licentiam non impendunt."

14. "Mandamus quatinus consuetudine ipsa de vestris ecclesiis extrirpata sub anathematis interminatione hoc inhibere curetis ne qui dignitate illa, si dignitas dici potest, fungentes pro prestanda licentia docendi alios ab aliquo quidquam amodo exigere audeant vel extorquere."

15. "...sed eis districte precipiatis ut quicunque viri idonei et litterati voluerint regere studia litterarum, sine molestia et exactione qualibet scolas regere patiantur."

16. "...negligentiam vestram gravem habebimus et ad ea corrigenda manum extendere compellemur."

17. "Prohibeas attentius de cetero ne in parochia tua pro licentia docendi ab aliquo exigatur aliquid aut etiam promittatur." *Prohibemus* often appears as this decretal's incipit in the manuscripts owned by the Parisian canonists. I thank my colleague Anne Duggan for the help she has given me in the dating of this decretal which forms the § b of the decretal *Nuntios* addressed to Richard bishop of Winchester (JL 14157).

18. "... remittti promissum facias et restitui appellatione cessante solutum, sciens quod scriptum est: gratis accepisti, gratis date." [=Matthew 10,8].

19. Alexander III cautiously uses the vague term *si quis*: "Sane si quis occasione huius prohibitionis distulerit magistros in locis congruis instituere, tibi liceat... ibi aliorum instructioni praeficere viros providos, honestos et discretos."

establish there prudent, honorable and discerning men, *omni contradictione et appellatione postposita.*

Texts and context

The texts above suggest that Paris is the privileged target of the battle led by Alexander III against this particular species of simony, especially because of the significant development of theological studies in that city.[20] We know how quickly that the decretal *Quanto,* although addressed in general to archbishops and bishops *per Galliam,* had been solicited *contra cancellarium parisiensem.* Does not Huguccio already allude to it in his *Summa* on the *Decretum?*[21]

It is therefore particularly interesting, it seems to me, to learn how these texts were received by the Parisian canonists, what their glosses can teach us regarding the context in which one enters the *licentia docendi.* We are lucky in fact to have several manuscripts recording their teaching during the first decade of the thirteenth century, on both the *Decretum* and the *Compilatio prima.*[22]

20. Gilbert Dahan's introductory study on "L'enseignement de la théologie," in Verger and Weijers, *Les débuts de l'enseignement universitaire à Paris,* 249–253; Ricardo Saccenti, "Questions et Sentences: l'enseignement entre la fin du XIIe et le début du XIIIe siècle," ibid., 278 ff., gives a clear statement of the various controversies agitating Paris, which are an important source of concern for Alexander III, who reiterates in 1177 in his decretal *Cum christus* (Ia 5.6.5 = X 5.7.7) the condemnation of Peter Lombard's ambiguous Christological doctrine. *Adde* S. C. Ferruolo, *The Origins of the University, The Schools of Paris and their Critics* (Stanford: Stanford University Press, 1985), 289.

21. Huguccio on di. 37 c.12 , v. *quia in hiis*: "...Similiter turpe lucrum est et peccatum mortale si quis accipit pecuniam ut det alicui licenciam docendi quod parisius olim fiebat, non enim cancellarius permictebat ibi aliquid regere scolas nisi dato precio quod vicium Alexander graviter reprehendit et sub pena anathematis prohibuit ne deinceps fieret, ut in extra Quanto gallicana [Ia 5.4.3 = X 5.5.3] et in concilio romano Quoniam ecclesia dei [Lateran III c.18, Ia 5.4.1 = X 5.5.1]" (MS Paris B.N. latin 3892, fol. 46va).

22. On these diverse manuscripts, cf. A. Lefebvre-Teillard, "La lecture de la *Compilatio prima* par les maîtres parisiens du début du XIIIe siècle," *Proceedings of the Twelfth International Congress of Medieval Canon Law* Washington, D.C. 1–7 August 2004 (Vatican City, 2008), 223–250. *Adde* "Petrus Brito, auteur de l'apparat *Ecce vicit leo?*" *Proceedings of the Thirteenth International Congress of Medieval Canon Law* Estergom, 3–8 August 2008, (Vatican City, 2010), 117–135. On the *Apparatus* on the Decretum *Animal est substantia,* slightly later than the previous, I can only refer to Chris Coppens's efforts over

The first thing reflected in our manuscripts, not surprisingly, is the very real existence, at least at the time of Alexander III, of the custom to only deliver *licentia docendi* in return for the payment of a sum of money. The Lilienfeld manuscript that most faithfully reports the teaching of Petrus Brito, the magister who then dominated the Parisian school of Law,[23] contains a gloss on *Quanto* that not only confirms that this decretal had been solicited against the chancellor of Paris but also gives us the name of the person who has obtained it, Jean du Petit Pont:[24] *Magister Iohannes de parvo ponte hanc decretalem contra cancellarium parisiensem obtinuit qui nullum parisius legere permissit nisi duas marcas daret et hoc longa consuetudine fuit obtentum* (ms. Lilienfeld, Stiftsbibl. 220 fol. 59 vb, v. *Quanto*).[25]

Practice is the result of a *longa consuetudo* that was not easy to remove in a social context dominated by custom. Shortly after the decretal *Quanto*, was not Alexander III forced to grant a derogation to the Parisian chancel-

---

many years to provide a transcription on the website: www.medcanonlaw.com. See most recently his contribution in *Les débuts de l'enseignement universitaire à Paris*, op. cit supra n. 1, 329–343, esp. 334–336.

23. Cf. A. Lefebvre-Teillard, "La voix de son maître. Etude sur le manuscrit Lilienfeld Stiftsbibliothek 220," *Revue historique de droit français et étranger* 86 (2008), 305–330.

24. The name of Jean du Petit Pont is also remembered in the gloss of the Brussels manuscript 1407–09 in this same decretal: "Et est decretalis magistri Iohanni de parvo ponte contra cancellarium parisiensem impetrata" (fol. 76 vb). Jean du Petit Pont was a Master of Arts of whom I have found mention in the *Karolinus* of Gilles de Paris, famous poem finished on September 3, 1200 and published by M. L. Colker in *Traditio* 29 (1973), 199–325. In a *captatio* located at the end of the poem, Gilles lists the names of some famous Parisian masters and adds: "Nec memoro cunctos. aliquos quoque transeo sicut/ Sepe retemptatis auctorum excursibus illum / Vasis inexhausti parvo de ponte Iohannem / Iam tot propositis magnatibus unde resisti " (cf. 321, l. 73–76). Bulaeus (Du Boulay) in his *Historia Universitatis Parisiensis* (Paris, 1665–1673), II.526–27, had already published verses 8–75 of the *captatio*. On Gilles himself cf. Colker, 200–202.

25. This gloss is probably the source for the gloss of Vincentius Hispanus cited in a note by Denifle and Chatelain, *Chartularium*, under number 4 (= text of the decretal *Quanto*) of the *pars introductoria*, according to manuscript Vat. lat. 1377 (citation taken again by Post, "Alexander III," 260, n. 23). This manuscript does not contain Vincentius' *apparatus* on the *Compilatio prima* but instead Tancred's, who took from Vincent this gloss: "Hoc capitulum fuit impetratum contra cancellarium Parisiensem qui a quolibet docente marcam unam exigebat." It ends with the initial of the latter as we have verified in MS Paris B.N. Latin 3931 A, fol. 65 rb. We will notice here that our Parisian glossator's *duas marcas* have halved!

lor who was none other than the important theologian Petrus Comestor?[26] He does it though not without reluctance[27] and under certain conditions.[28] It is understandable that he wished to renew the ban at the Third Lateran Council.

Through the gloss developed around 1205–06 on the word *consuetudinis* of the canon *Quoniam* in the Saint Omer manuscript, we perceive the resistance that might have occurred in the name of this *antiqua consuetudo*, even if its author speaks in the past tense:

> Consueverint enim magistri scolarum scilicet cancellarium pro licencia docendi pecuniam querere et est argumentum contra pravam

26. The text reproduced by Post, "Alexander III," 273, appears in Denifle and Chatelain, *Chartularium*, pars intr. n° 8, who date it to October 29, 1174. The theologian Petrus Comestor, pupil and successor of Peter Lombard, was chancellor of the bishop of Paris from 1168 to 1178. After giving up his office and retiring to the Abbey of Saint Victor, he died on October 22, 1178. On the importance of this personage in the schools of Paris, cf. G. Dahan, *Pierre de Troyes dit Pierre le mangeur, maître du XIIe siècle* (Troyes, 2011). It is likely that Alexander III, then very concerned about Peter Lombard's Christological doctrine (cf. supra n.20), was forced to grant the derogation, probably requested by Petrus Comestor himself, and perhaps with the support of the archbishop of Sens, Guillaume aux Blanches Mains, "William White Hands" (see infra n.28). On the links between Petrus Comestor and William to whom he had dedicated his *Historia scholastica*, cf. Dahan, 19. On William of the White Hands, uncle of the future king Philip Augustus, cf. P. Desportes, "Guillaume de Champagne" *Fasti ecclesie Gallicanae* (Turnhout, 1998), 3.151; *adde* J. R. Williams, "William of the White Hands and Men of Letters," *Anniversary Essays in Mediaeval History by Students of Charles H. Haskins* (Boston, 1929), 365–387.

27. The letter addressed to cardinal-priest *Sancti Chrysogoni*, legate in France since 1174, begins with a rehearsal of the rule and speaks of special prerogative: "Licet mandaverimus ut hi qui volunt docere nihil pro scolis regendis ab aliquo exigant, iuxta illud: veni et audi, volentes tamen honestati et litterature magistri Petri, cancellarii Parisiensis, quantum salva honestate possumus, prompta benignitate deferre, quem speciali prerogativa diligimus et volumus honorare...."

28. The legate to whom he entrusts the task of controlling the amount of the sum to be collected, must do it "habito concilio cum venerabilibus nostris Wilhelmo Senonensi archiepiscopo, apostolice sedis legato et H[enrico] Remensi archiepiscopo et aliis et honestis personis super regimine scolarum Parisiensum quod tibi visum fuerit;" and this in a way "quod personam dicti Petri non excedat quod exinde feceris...quod non videaris modum excedere et illi qui scolas rexerint non debeant immoderate gravari." Archbishop Henry of Reims, younger brother of King Louis VII, was close to Alexander III, cf. P. Demouy, "Henri de France," *Dictionnaire d'histoire et de géographie ecclésiastiques*, v. XXIII (1990), col. 1129–1130.

> consuetudinem quamvis antiquam supra *De consuetudine* c.1 [1.3.1 = X 1.4.1] et *De symonia, Non satis* [5.2.7 = X 5.3.8]. Sed queritur cum liceat magistris artium vendere laborem docendi, quare non liceat eis emere a cancellario? Dicimus quod aliud est officium docendi, aliud labor docendi quia labor temporale quid est et vendi potest; officium autem docendi spirituale est et ita symonia constituetur si vendam; vel officium illud temporale est, non spirituale, nec potest vendi cum sit prohibitum propter honestatem et magistrorum vitandam multitudinem et secundum hoc si officium illud vendatur non est symoniam sed tamen est peccatum mortale (MS B.M. St Omer 107, fol. 95 vb).

In his *apparatus* to the *Decretum* on the canon *De quibusdam* [D.37 c.12] to which glosses over the *Compilatio prima* commonly refer,[29] Petrus Brito, after recalling the rule, asks a question that hints that the practice *de facto* had perhaps not completely disappeared:

> ...Item nec magistri cancellarii scolarum possunt ab huiusmodi magistris aliquid petere ut extra *De magistris, Prohibemus* (= *Prohibeas*). Sed quid si de facto vendant licentiam docendi sacras litteras ut theologiam et decreta? Symonia est et tenentur restituere et est crimen concussionis; si alias litteras non est [symonia] sed tamen crimen concussionis.
>
> Quid si episcopus vendet clerico licentiam eundi ad scolas? Solutio: non est symonia. Sed [quid] si episcopus accipiat pecunias ut ca-

29. Here is the text, particularly conducive to the development of glosses on our subject: "De quibusdam locis ad nos refertur, neque magistros neque curam inveniri pro studio litterarum. Idcirco ab universis episcopis subiectis plebibus et aliis locis in quibus necessitas occurrerit, omnino cura et diligentia habeatur ut magistri et doctores constituantur qui studia litterarum liberaliumque artium dogmata assidue doceant quia in his maxime divina manifestantur atque declarantur mandata" (Ex sinodo Eugenii II Papae, ab anno 826). On this text's transmission in earlier canonical collections cf. the recent study by Thierry Kouamé, "La réception de la législation scolaire carolingienne dans les collections canoniques jusqu'au Décret de Gratien (IXe–XIIe siècle)," *Universitas scolarium, Mélanges offerts à Jacques Verger*, ed. C. Giraud and M. Morard (Geneva: Droz, 2011), 27–29 and 37.

nonicus in scolis prebendam suam habeat? Solutio: non est symonia (Sankt Florian Stiftbibl. XI 605, fol. 16vb).[30]

There is in this text a distinction also found in the gloss above on the canon *Quoniam*. It slightly reduces the pontifical legislation's scope: selling the *licentia* to those who want to teach the "sacred letters or *decreta*" is simony: *symonia est*, but selling it to those who want to teach the other letters: *non est symonia sed tamen crimen concussionis*, [31] and in any event a mortal sin as emphasized by the gloss on *Quoniam*.

The second part of this gloss on the *Decretum* refuses to condemn as simoniacal two likely commonplace practices that illuminate the context of the sale of *licentia docendi*. They raise two issues that greatly preoccupied our canonists. The first is that of *licentia eundi ad scolas*. Is it essential for the cleric who wishes to pursue his studies? Some have tried to interpret a passage of the decretal *Relatum* under the title *De clericis non residentibus in ecclesia prebendata* (Ia 3.4.4 = X 3.4.4) as authorizing, in this case, the clerk to do so without a license from his bishop, which Petrus Brito clearly rejects:

> ...[D]icunt quidam quod ex iusta causa abesse potest sine consensu sui prelati et presertim causa studii cum sciencia sit res inestimabilis et iustissima sit absencia studii ut ff Quibus ex causis maiores integrum restituuntur, l. Necne § I [= Necnon, D. 4.6.28 §1] et infra extra *Alex. Fraternitatis* [= *Fraternitati*, Gilb. 3.2.1 = X 3.4.5] argumentum: ubi peregre, idem dicitur quod hic; non credo quod clericus peregre proficisci non potest sine licentia sui episcopi ut de consecratione di. V, *Non oportet* [c.37] et quantum favoris habet scientia et peregrinatio tamen hoc non potest, ergo nec illud (Lilienfeld, Stiftsbibl. 220, fol. 26 vb, v. *studio*).[32]

30. On *De quibusdam* di 37, c.12, v. *assidue doceant*.

31. Huguccio in his gloss on this same canon followed the passage cited supra note 21 with a sentence limiting simony to the case of a sale in order to teach theology: "*forte in tali casu symonia commictebatur si magister debebat docere theologiam*." Nothing was said about the *decreta*.

32. The attribution to Petrus Brito is especially made by his pupil, author of the gloss on the text contained in Lambeth Palace MS 105, fol. 171 ra, v. *sine consensu*. Here is the passage that led to this questionable reading: "nisi forte de licentia suorum prelatorum

The interpretation was indeed questionable but it would be used, with lots of nuance, a few years later by the author of the *apparatus* on the *Decretum*, *Animal est substantia*, in favor of the cathedral churches' clerics, if the bishop had not introduced a *doctor* to instruct the clerics:

> [E]rgo tenentur episcopi instituere doctores in ecclesiis cathedralibus qui clericos instruant, ex quo videtur quod si episcopus neminem providerit eis doctorem quod ipsi possunt recedere ab ecclesia causa studii, petita tamen licentia ab episcopo etsi non impetrata, extra De clericis non residentibus, Relatum.[33]

It is clear that the *licentia eundi ad scolas* and the "simoniacal" practices that might possibly accompany it, preoccupied our canonists just as much as those concerning the *licentia docendi*.

Hence this double question: *Quid si episcopus vendet clerico licentiam eundi ad scolas? [Quid] si episcopus accipiat pecunias ut canonicus in scolis prebendam suam habeat?*

To understand the relative leniency of the answer: *non est symonia*, one has to think that the absence could last several years and that many cathedrals did not have the resources to meet the needs of both those present as well those absent. Our canonists plead for those who are absent *causa studii* to keep their prebends *si habundantes sint ecclesie*, when these "absents" do not possess sufficient inheritance;[34] but the bishop may also

vel studio literarum vel pro aliis honestis causis contingerit eos abesse." This interpretation was made *disiunctive* as noted by the author of the gloss on the v. *studio* in the manuscript Paris BN lat. 15398: "Quidam hic adheret litere et intelligit lectionem disiunctive ita scilicet quod causa studii facienda, abesse possit sine prelati litera. Sed videtur quod numquid abesse nisi de litera prelati..." (fol. 238 vb).

33. On *De quibusdam* [d.37, c.12] v. *ab universis* (Chris Coppens's transcription available online).

34. Petrus Brito on *De quibusdam* [d. 37 c.12], *v. instituantur* : "Si ergo in magistris debet clericis providere episcopus, ergo multo magis scolaribus canonicis prebendas suas debent dare unde ar. quod clerici in scolis debent habere prebendas suas ar. XXXII d. *Si quis vero* [c.3] ar. extra *De magistris* c.I [Ia 5.4.1 = X 5.5.1], et hoc tantum in favorem litterarum dei, extra *De clericis non residentibus*, c.ult. [Ia 3.4.4 = X 3 4 4] ...si ita sit decimis ecclesia quod reditus non sufficiant et servientibus et absentibus tunc locus habent contra; sed si habundantes sint ecclesie tunc qui in scolis sunt, plenos debent habere reditus et hoc intellige nisi forte absentes sufficiens habeant patrimonium ar. extra *De prebendis*,

be tempted to seek some kind of compensation in return. From the years 1181–86, a *summa* on the *Decretum* begun in England and finished in Paris, the *Summa omnis qui iuste iudicat,* had asked the same question:

> Item essetne simonia, si quis daret episcopo aliquid ut permitteret eum licite prebendam habere et fructus moram faciens in scolis? Et videtur quod non quia nichil det episcopo ob prebendam vel usum prebende set ideo ut habere permittatur, episcopus tamen turpiter accipit set ille turpiter non dat.[35]

It is no simony for the bishop, but it still turpitude, a turpitude from which the author, Rodoicus Modicipassus, exempts the one who gave the money.[36] That is pretty much what Huguccio will say in his turn.[37] The author of the *apparatus Animal est substantia,* very well disposed, as we have seen, to the encouragement of studies, seems to show even more indulgence with regard to this practice.[38]

Episcopis" [Ia 3.5.4 = X 3.7.4], c.XII q.III *Si sacerdos* [= *Sacerdotes* XII q.IV c.1] (Sankt Florian Stiftbibl. XI 605, fol. 16 vb).

35. *Summa omnis qui iuste iudicat sive lipsiensis*, ed. R. Weigand, P. Landau, W. Kozur, Monumenta Iuris Canonici, series A, Corpus glossatorum 7, (Vatican City 2007) 154 on *De quibusdam* (di.37 c.12). Concerning the author of this *summa*, cf. P. Landau, "Rodoicus Modicipassus—Verfasser der *Summa lipsiensis*?," in *Zeitschrift der Savigny Stiftung für Rechtsgeschichte, Kanonistische Abteilung* 92 (2006), 340–354.

36. Honorius of Kent who taught in Paris and wrote his *Summa de iure canonico* between 1185 and 1191, contented himself with writing on this same canon *De quibusdam*: "Hinc argumentum scolari habenti stipendia permitti debere... Nec erit simoniacus si quid dederit pro licentia habenda," *Summa omnis*, ed. R. Weigand et al., 126.

37. In a passage preceding the one cited supra note 21: "Sed ecce: episcopus non vult dare licentiam clerico eundi ad scolas nisi data peccunia, datur ei peccunia est ne simonia? Non credo, est tamen turpe lucrum et mortaliter peccat episcopus cum precio dat quod gratis dare debuit eis ar. I q.III vendentes [c.10] et XI q.III qui recte [c.66]." "Turpe lucrum" for the bishop but what about the cleric? Huguccio says nothing.

38. On *De quibusdam, v. episcopis*: "Argumentum ad illam questionem utrum si clerico volenti ire ad scolas licentia denegetur utrum possit episcopo pecuniam offere ut licentiam obtineat? Et dicimus quod sic, quia episcopus tenetur ad hoc, quia cum dat quod debet non facit ei beneficium. Si autem deneget facit ei iniuriam, ff De aqua cottidiana adestiva (sic = et estiva), l.1 § penult. [D. 43.20.1.45]. Ergo potest iste redimere vexationem suam I q.III Quesitum [c.4]." (transcription by Chris Coppens).

Parisian canonists therefore reserve the qualification of the act of simony only to the sale of *licencia docendi de theologia vel canonibus*. But in the other cases, if there is no simony there is nevertheless a turpitude that they call, using the Roman law, *crimen concussionis*:

> Si dederit pro licencia legendi de artibus, non est simonia sed est crimen concussionis et ideo repeti potest ar.I q.I l. Iubemus [c.126= C. 9.27.4] ; si vero dederit pro licencia legendi de theologia vel canonibus, simonia est, tamen potest repetere ar. I q.III Quesitum [c.4].[39]

The restitution of the amount foreseen by the decretal *Prohibeas* is for these *legum et canonum magistri parisienses*[40] the opportunity to present their knowledge of Roman law. This is especially the case for the author of the gloss contained in the Saint Omer manuscript:

> Sed fiet ne restitutio magistri qui dedit? Videtur quod non quia turpitudo versatur ex utraque parte et quotiens turpitudo versatur ex utraque parte cessat repetitio, ff De condictionibus ob turpem causam, l. Ubi autem [D. 12.5.3] et dantis et accipientis turpitudo versatur non posse repeti dicimus, veluti si pecunia detur ut male iudicetur ut l. Si ob turpem causam [D. 12.5.8]: Si promiseris titio quamvis, si petit, exceptione doli mali vel in factum submovere, eum possis tamen, si solveris, non posse [te] repetere quoniam sublata proxima causa stipulationis que propter exceptionem inanis esset, si (sic) pristina causa, id est turpitudo, superesset: porro autem si et dantis et accipientis turpis causa sit, possessorem potiorem esse et ideo repetitionem cessare videtur et si ex stipulatione solutum est. Verba legis. Aut si promisserit ex exceptione doli mali, retinere possit cum exigatur ff. De conditionibus ob turpem causam l.IIII [D. 12.5.4]: si ob stuprum datum sit vel si aliquis in adulterio deprehensus se redemerit, cessat repetitio. Item si dederit fur, ne proderetur, quoniam utriusque turpitudo versatur, cessat repetitio quotiens autem solius accipientis turpitudo versatur, Celsus ait repeti posse, veluti, si tibi dedero ne ini-

39. Paris BN lat. 15398, fol. 269 va, on *Prohibeas v. restitui*.

40. This is how they describes themselves in a consultation held at the Abbey of St Bertin between 1205 and 1211, cf. our study: "La lecture ," op. cit. supra n. 22, 244.

uriam mihi facias. Verba legis. Sed videtur quod illi ecclesie in cuius iniuriam collatam est, illa pecunia sit restituenda, supra *De symonia, De hoc autem* (Ia 5.2.10 = X 5.3.11)? R/ casus illud spiritualis est et restituenda magistro pecunia quod dedit et ita subvenitur ei non in favorem sui sed in odium alterius ut supra dictum est De eo qui duxit in matrimonio c.i [Ia 4.7.1 = X 4.7.1] unde bene dicitur restitui quod ipse de iure suo repetere non potest quia in paria causa turpitudinis melior est condictio possidentis et notendum quod auctoritate huius decretalis non tantum potest ipse [habere] exceptionem qui promisit sed liberationis condictionem sicut ff Quod metus causa, l. Metum [D. 4.2.9]. Sed est ne idem de quolibet magistro? Videtur quod non Co. Libro X De confessis (sic=de professoribus) et medicis, l. Poete [C. 10.52.3]: nulla immunitatis prerogativa iuvantur. Item Augustinus in libro De civitate dei ait Platonem precepisse ut de civitate quam ordinaverat poete quasi inimici eiicerentur pro arbitrio enim suo intervenitur et hominibus miseris docere facta mutanda proposuit R/ quo ad hoc et pro licencia docendi nichil dare debent et si dederint et repetere possint; eodem privilegio gaudent quo et alii sed quo ad multa alia non (MS 107, fol. 95 vb v. *restitui*).

The original gloss attributable to Petrus Brito was more sober but did contain, in addition to the solution, the references to the *Poete* law and to Saint Augustine's *De civitate Dei,*[41] but did not take up however the latest of our Parisian *apparati* on the *Compilatio prima,* by the author of the *apparatus Militant siquidem patroni.*[42]

41. The original gloss we cannot reproduce here for lack of space, it is found in the manuscript of Lilienfield Stiftsbibl. 220 fol. 59 vb. The gloss of Lambeth Palace manuscript 105 on the same word (fol. 201 va) expressely attributes to Petrus Brito the solution of giving back the outlay to the master. The passage of *De civitate Dei* that has been the basis for our glossators is in book II, ch. XIV (in Bibliothèque Augustinienne (Paris, 1959), 33.344).

42. It is subsequent to 1207 and prior to the *Compilatio tertia.* Here is the gloss on v. *facias restitui*: "Ergo iste habet actionem ad repetendum quod dedit; sed obicitur hoc dare fuit symonia vel non? Hoc fuit symonia, ergo uterque est in crimine turpitudinis ergo meliorem condictionem possidentis ut ff De conditione ob turpem causam, l. VI [sic= Ubi D. 12.5.3] et XIII q.V Non sane [c.15]. Si non fuit symonia tamen iste sciens solvit indebitum ergo similiter non potest repetere ut c. De condictione indebiti, l. Indebitum [C. 4.5.9]; scienter solvit repeti non potest. Solutio: si dedit pro licentia docendi artes

It is difficult to know if this "privilege" was of any efficacy in removing what remained of the practices examined above and of which Innocent III would affirm, regarding at least the sale of *licentia docendi*, that it was no longer occurring at the time he was studying in Paris.[43] It would not stop, it seems, John of Candelles who in 1210 would succeed as chancellor to Prevotin of Cremona.[44]

Our canonists in any case sought to carefully distinguish between the sale of the *officium docendi* from the *labor docendi*.[45] Restitution can only take place in the first case. The *labor docendi* that is theirs deserves to be remunerated *quia nemo cogatur suis expensis militare*. They show indeed some concerns about the provisions contained in the canon *Quoniam*. They wish to specify that the gratuity applies only if the prebend given to the teacher is sufficient. Otherwise, they consider it normal to receive remuneration from the "foreign" or "wealthy" clerics:

---

vel auctores non est symonia sed crimen concussionis et ita potest repetere, ut I q.I lex Iubemus [c. 126 = C. 9.27.4]. Si pro licentia docendi decreta vel theologia symonia est et tunc etiam potest repetere quia non est in turpitudinem, ex parte enim accipientis tantum est symonia, non ex parte dantis, iste enim quasi ius suum reddiunt unde non pecant ar. I q.III Quesitum [c.4]; ita est quod nichil potest exigere a discipulis pro eis docendis; ad hoc dicimus quod si habeat beneficium super hoc assignatum ut supra eodem c.1, nichil potest exigere ar. supra eodem c.1; si non, potest exigi moderate tamen habito respectu ad qualitatem discipulorum quia nemo propriis stipendiis etc ut XII q.II Caritatem [c.45] et supra *De censibus*, *Cum apostolus* [Ia 3.34.6 = X 3.39.6]."

43. "Cum igitur tempore quo vacavimus Parisius studio litterarum, numquam scolares viderimus sic tractari," he writes in his decretal *Miramur* of January 20, 1212 the text of which is reproduced in Denifle and Chatelain, op. cit. supra n. 3, pars I n° 14. It is not possible to give the exact dates of Lotario dei Conti di Segni's years of study in Paris. The major part of it might have been during the 1180s; it seems indeed that he left France around 1186–1187 at the latest, cf. J. C. Moore, "Lotario dei Conti di Segni (pope Innocent III) in the 1180s," *Archivum historiae pontificiae* 29 (1991), 255–258.

44. Cf. infra note 48. John of Candelles (Iohannes Candelis) probably succeeded in the end of 1209– early 1210 to Prevotin, who is though to have died on February 25, 1210, cf. G. Lacombe, "La vie et les œuvres de Prévostin," in *Prepositini, cancellarii Parisiensis (1206–1210)*, Bibliothèque Thomiste XI, (Paris, 1927), 46. He does so in a context marked by the condemnation, as heretical, of the supporters of Amaury de Bène, Master of Arts, which would be pronounced by the council of Paris in 1210. On this context, cf. N. Gorochov, *Naissance de l'Université. Les écoles de Paris d'Innocent III à Thomas d'Aquin (v.1200–v.1245)* (Paris, 2012), 257 et s.

45. Cf. the gloss of the manuscript of St Omer 107 on *Quoniam* v. *consuetudinis* cited above in the text.

> Per argumentum a contrario sensu videtur quod a clericis advenientibus et extraneis aliquid possit et hoc verum est si non habeat ad hoc stipendia assignata... quia nemo cogatur suis expensis militare, supra *De simonia, Cum sit* [5.2.9 = X 5.2.10] et XXVII q. I Iam nunc [c.8]. Si vero haberet stipendia et exigeret, ecclesie concussor [est] et mortaliter peccaret, XXIII q.I Militare [c.5]. Idem est de magistris liberalium artium, theologi vero vel decretiste, omnes nichil possunt petere ; si tamen indigeant possunt recipere XVIII d. De eulogiis [c.8] immo clerici tenentur eos sustentare, unde apostolus: si nobis spiritualia seminamus magna est si a nobis metamus carnalia ut XIII q.I [Iam nunc=c.8].[46] (MS Bruxelles 1407–09, fol. 76 va v. *eiusdem ecclesie*).[47]

Is the master who has received a prebend to teach *gratis* bound to accept everyone who comes to him? Here is what the gloss on *Quoniam* contained in the Lilienfeld manuscript says:

> Sed tenetur ne docere omnes qui veniunt? Non nisi quos sunt eadem ecclesie clericos commode poterit et sine magno detrimento sui corporis. Ita tenendum est de magistris laborantibus, sed scolastici cancellarii qui aliis proponuntur a illo sive docante sive discante aliquid accipere [non] debent hoc pretextu et si fecerint mortaliter peccant et potest ab eis repeti tanquam indebitum ut infra eodem capitulo proximo". (MS Lilienfeld, Stiftsbibl. 220, fol. 59 vb, v. *Quoniam*).

46. The text in c. *Iam nunc* referenced successively to several passages of Paul's first letter to the Corinthians, but not directly to v.11 ch.9 which is referenced here. There is nothing on the issue that concerns us in Petrus Brito's gloss on this canon *Iam nunc* (MS Sankt Florian Stifbibl. fol. 102 va).

47. Before the student's text, the argument was developed by Petrus Brito whose gloss is reported by his student in the Lilienfeld manuscript: "...Sed potest ne advenientibus aliorum pecuniam exigere si stipendium ad hoc deputat sibi non sufficiat? Bene potest accipere et ab habundantibus quia si eis seminat spiritualia, non est inhibitum si metat carnalia ut XIII q.I [Iam nunc=c.8] Et si sufficiens stipendium ad hoc deputat, sic gratis docebit." (ms Lilienfeld, Stiftsbibl. 220, fol. 59 vb v. *Quoniam*).

Gratuity is limited to clerics *eadem ecclesie* and the master must be able to teach *commode* and without any detriment to his health *sine magno detrimento sui corporis*.

A final important question is pointed out by our canonists, still regarding the canon *Quoniam*: the conferral of the *licentia docendi*. No one disputes that it belongs to the bishop's chancellor. But this canon *Quoniam* already set a limit to the chancellor's power. He could not prevent the candidate *idoneus, licentia petita* from beginning to read before the license was even granted to him. This canon is exploited by our canonists to assert that whoever wishes to read in Paris could, *licentia petita*, do it:

> Si dignus est legere, potuit incipere cancellario invito, licentia petita ar XIX q.II, Due [c.2 in fine]; debet enim prius petere licentiam, supra *De iure patronatus, Nullus* [3.33.21 = X 3.38.17] ar., et XIX q.I c.I. (MS Paris. BN latin 15398, fol. 269 va, v. *interdicatur sic = interdicat*).

> Patet quod cancellarius parisiensis non potest prohibere legere volentibus parisius dum modo ydonei sint infra eodem c. ult. [c.3] (MS Lilienfeld 220, fol. 59 vb v. *interdicat*).

"Si dignus est legere," "dum modo ydonei sint": Our canonists, as with Alexander III in the decretal *Quanto*, are silent as to the subject of who ought to judge this ability even though they admit that *licentia petita* it is possible to start reading. None of them seized on the words *qui sit idoneus* of the canon *Quoniam* or *viri idonei et literati* of the decretal *Quanto* to make a clarification on this subject. Yet, if we judge by the contents of Innocent III's decretal *Miramur* which is slightly subsequent to their teaching, the masters already possessed the assertion of this ability: "Miramur… quod, sicut ex dilectorum filiorum scolarium Parisiensium querela didicimus, a volentibus scolas regere quos etiam magistrorum assertio idoneos asserit ad regendum… ".[48]

48. Cf. Denifle and Chatelain, op. cit. supra n. 3, pars I n° 14. The conflict might have begun no later than in 1211 since the decretal answers the complaint of 20 January 1212 of Parisian *scolares* against the chancellor Jean de Candelles who "a volentibus scolas regere… iuramentum fidelitatis vel obedientie ac interdum pecunie precium… nititur extorquere." The pope ordered Hervé Bishop of Troyes, the dean and the archdeacon of

The compromise that would put an end to this conflict triggered by the Parisian *scolares* against the chancellor John of Candelles (1210–1215) would confirm the masters' role in this matter.[49] In addition it went further and would also provide an answer to another essential question: What if the chancellor refuses the *licentia?*

This is indeed a question that torments our canonists. The gloss of the Lilienfeld manuscript referred to above seems to say that formally he could still read, but today it was no longer possible *propter magistrorum multitudinem:* "Sed esto de facto quod neget licentiam, puto quod expetita licentia etsi non prestita, legere possit? Hoc tamen hodie non fit propter magistrorum multitudinem."[50]

In reality one can not overrule the chancellor's refusal, even once he had started reading. This will increase the tension between the chancellor and the masters who use the decretal *Quanto* to affirm that the chancellor cannot forbid to read those who are *ydonei:*

> [A]r. quod cancellarius parisiensis non potest inhibere volentes legere parisius ne legant dummodo sint ydonei, infra eodem c. ult. [c.3] ff De aqua [et aque] pluvie arcende, l. In summa [D. 39.3.2] Si petam a te quod tibi non nocet et mihi prodest equitas est illud tribui." (BM St Omer 107, fol. 95 vb on *Quoniam* v. *interdicat*).

---

this same church to compel by ecclesiastical censures the chancellor to correct himself if he does not do so.

49. Cf. Denifle and Chatelain, op. cit. supra n. 3, pars I n° 16. These letters emanating from Peter [de Nemours] Bishop of Paris, dating back to August 1213, publicize the content of the compromise reached between the masters and students on the one hand and John of Candelles on the other hand. It results of the arbitration made by six arbiters at the instigation of Peter, as John of Candelles will recognize it himself in the text by which he promises to respect "compositionem illam quam venerabilis pater P. Parisiensis episcopus... procuravit." (cf. ibid., n°17, text also dated August 1213).

50. I am not sure that Petrus Brito's opinion has been properly reported by his student; the gloss is unclear. However the author of the *apparatus Militant siquidem patroni* attributes to Petrus Brito the view that previously the *"ydoneus"* cleric could still read: "Sed quid si magister scolarum nolit ei dare licentiam potestne ipse sibi assumere? Videtur quod non... tamen p.b' dicit quod si ydoneus est legere potest magistro scolarum invito, sicut et presbiter ruralis potest transire ad religionem prelato suo invito, si nolit dare ei licentiam ut XIX q.II Due [c.2 in fine]" (MS BM Troyes 385, fol. 82 vb).

Yet at the same time they recognize that, if the chancellor refuses *licentia,* the only recourse possible for the moment is to address themselves to the chancellor's superior, *id est* to the bishop, and read with his consent:

> Sed esto de facto quod contradicat: ne legat, legeret ne auctoritate sua? Videtur quod non, nisi maioris et superioris consensu IX q. III Cum simus [c.3]. Dicit p.b' quod expetita licentia de iure incipere potest non licenciatus ab eo.[51]

The author of the *apparatus Militant siquidem patroni* will insist in turn on this as the only possibility, on behalf of the *bonum obedientie:*

> Ergo non est interdicenda licentia docendi ydoneo. Sed quid si magister scolarum nolit ei dare licentiam potestne ipse sibi assumere? Videtur quod non propter bonum obediencie propter quod etiam bonum aliquando omittur ut XI q.III Quid ergo [c.99]... vel dicatur quod non debet legere, sed debet conqueri superiori sicut et monachi si episcopi nolint eis dare licentiam accipiendi decimas a laicis ut supra *De iure patronatus, Nullus* [3.33.21 = X 3.38.17]. (MS BM Troyes 385, fol. 82 vb, v. *interdicat*).

The compromise of 1213 will not only provide an answer to the *scolares'* complaint, asserting that the chancellor will not be able to demand anything "ab aliquo lecturo Parisius," "pro licentia danda," but it will go further, affirming that the chancellor will no longer be able to refuse the *licentia* to the one of which the masters have assured *quod idoneus sit,* according to terms specified for each discipline.[52] This last measure having

51. Continuation and end of the gloss of the manuscript BM St Omer 107, fol. 95 vb, v. *interdicat.* This opportunity for the bishop to grant *licentia docendi* that would have refused the chancellor will be recalled in the compromise of 1213: "/-/ quod si forte denegaverit ex tunc quandocumque voluerit auctoritate nostra habeat legendi licentiam ," cf Denifle and Chatelain, op. cit. n. 3, pars I n°16.

52. Denifle and Chatelain, op. cit. n. 3, pars I n°16: "Porro petenti licentiam de theologia non poterit cancellarius denegare licentiam si maior pars theologorum legentium perhibuerit ei testimonium et asseruerit pro vero quod idoneus sit ad hoc, salvo hoc ipsi cancellario quod ipse possit dare licentiam cui viderit esse dandam etiam non habito testimonio aliquorum magistrorum vel alicuius magistri... Petenti quidem licentiam legendi de decretis vel legibus non possit cancellarius denegare si maior pars legentium

been taken *ad tempus... quamdiu videlicet predictus cancellarius cancellariam tenebit,* will be confirmed by Cardinal Robert de Courçon, papal legate, in the "Statutes" of 1215 which on this point will refer expressly to the compromise.[53]

Our canonists, if they were still alive, must have rejoiced.

de decretis vel legibus dicant in verbo veritatis quod idoneus sit ad hoc... ." On modalities regarding the other disciplines, cf. ibid. The compromise will officially be promulgated by Bishop Hervé of Troyes and the dean of the chapter of Troyes, cf. ibid., pars I n°18.

53. Robert acts "cum domini pape speciale mandatum ut statui Parisiensium scolarium in melius reformando" (cf. Denifle and Chatelain, op. cit. n.3, pars I n° 20 [August 1215]) and uses some precedent regulations as S. Ferruolo remarks in his study "The Paris Statutes of 1215 reconsidered," *History of Universities* 5 (1985), 1–14. Robert specifies the examination's modalities by referring to the compromise for those who want *legere de artibus,* but no doubt he implies the compromise also for the others: "examinetur quilibet secundum formam que continetur in scripto domini P. Parisiensis episcopi ubi continetur pax confirmata inter cancellarium et scolares a iudicibus delegatis a domino papa, scilicet ab episcopo et decano Trecentibus et a P. episcopo et J. cancellario Parisiensis approbata et confirmata." On the statutes of 1215 which were the subject of an abundant scholarship, cf. most recently N. Gorochov, op. cit. supra n. 44, 299–316.

The Fourth Lateran Council, Its Legislation, and the Development of Legal Procedure

Ken Pennington

Pope Innocent III sent his letter *Vineam domini Sabaoth* to every prelate in Christendom on April 19, 1213 in which he summoned them to attend a "general" council in Rome during November of 2015.[1] He admonished them to appear at the council without pomp and circumstance in accordance with the rules governing episcopal visitations established by canon four of the Third Lateran Council, which mandated that a bishop's retinue should not contain more than thirty horses nor should it have hunting dogs and birds.[2] Charles Donahue made two important points about the legislation of the Fourth Lateran Council when he reviewed García y García's edition of the canons and the commentaries on them:[3]

1. The Latin text is printed and translated in *Selected Letters of Pope Innocent III concerning England (1198–1216)* (London: Thomas Nelson and Sons, 1953), 144–147. See also Paul B. Pixton, *The German Episcopacy and the Implementation of the Decrees of the Fourth Lateran Council, 1216–1245: Watchmen on the Tower* (Leiden: Brill, 1995) 1–3. A "generale concilium" meant a papal council, see Atria A. Larson, "Early Stages of Gratian's *Decretum* and the Second Lateran Council: A Reconsideration," *Bulletin of Medieval Canon Law* 27 (2007), 21–56, at 28–36.

2. Canon 4, *Cum apostolus*, 1 Comp. 3.34.6 (X 3.39.6), Atria A. Larson and K. Pennington, "Concilium lateranense III 1179," *Conciliorum oecumenicorum generaliumque decreta*, 2.1: *The General Councils of Latin Christendom: From Constantinople IV to Pavia-Siena (869–1424)*, ed. Alberto Melloni et al. (Turnhout: Brepols, 2013), 115–147, at 130.

3. Charles Donahue, Jr. Review of Antonio García y García, *Constitutiones Concilii quarti Lateranensis una cum Commentariis glossatorum* in *Speculum* 61 (1986), 149–150, at 150.

> By the quantity of commentary, the canon on inquisitorial procedure (c.8) and that on pluralism (c.29) were recognized as important... The canon on ordeals (c.18), on the other hand, received relatively little commentary and nothing of any note on what is to us its key provision.... It... was, at least for the canonists, the death knell of a moribund institution.

Donahue was right on each point. The canonists were particularly interested in the rules and norms governing inquisitorial procedure, which at this time had nothing to do with heresy, and they welcomed the prohibition that clerics could not hold multiple ecclesiastical benefices.[4] He correctly noted that the ordeal was dead in church courts. He was also right that the law professors who wrote commentaries on the canons, Vincentius Hispanus, Damasus Hungarus, and Johannes Teutonicus, differed from the pope's agenda that Innocent had itemized in *Vineam domini Sabaoth*. In his letter the pope had emphasized that reforms must be made in the Church and that a new crusade to the Holy Land must be launched. The crusade was the centerpiece of his letter. As Innocent proclaimed in another letter written about the same time, "a greater necessity exists now than ever that the Holy Land be succored."[5] The canonists, however, did not find the Fourth Lateran canon, *Ad liberandam terram sanctam* that called for a new crusade, particularly important for canon law. While Johannes immediately incorporated all the other Fourth Lateran canons into his decretal collection, *Compilatio quarta*, that was taught in the schools until it was replaced by Pope Gregory IX's *Decretales* in 1234, he omitted the long, complex crusade canon. When Damasus glossed *Ad liberandam*, he did not think the canon merited any discussion. "This constitution is temporary, and I do not care to gloss it," he wrote. Johannes Teutonicus had glossed it sparsely; Vincentius Hispanus was the only canonist to give the canon a detailed examination.[6] Although *Ad liberandam* was excluded from the *libri*

4. Pennington, "Pluralism and the Canonists in the Thirteenth Century," *Speculum* 51 (1976), 35–48

5. PL 216.819: "Quia major nunc instat necessitas quam unquam existerit ut terrae sanctae necessitatibus succurratur..." Potthast 4725, April 1213. García, *Constitutiones* has noted that sections of this letter were incorporated into *Ad liberandam*, pp. 314–316.

6. García, *Constitutiones* 380–384.

legales before 1234, Raymond de Peñafort reached back to the original text and selected a small section in which Innocent had threatened excommunication to those who supplied ships, arms, and other war materials to the Saracens for his edition of the *Decretales* of Gregory IX.[7] By the middle of the thirteenth century, Hostiensis rehabilitated the canon and argued for its continuing relevance to the crusading movement.[8] He placed the entire text and an extensive commentary on it into his massive commentary on the *Decretals* of Gregory IX.

Many historians, including myself, have misled students in our lectures about the main themes of the Council. When presenting the conciliar canons to them in our lectures and in our textbooks we have focused on the calling of a new crusade, the abolishing of the ordeal, the changes in the rules governing consanguinity, and the mandate to take communion and confess sins to a priest once a year. If we take the program in *Vineam domini Sabaoth* as a guide to Innocent's agenda, what he wanted in 1213 was reform of the Church, the stamping out of heresy, establishing peace and liberty (*libertas ecclesiae?*), and calling for a new crusade. The Council's seventy-one canons touched on those issues and many more.

The story, however, is even more complex. If we take into account the report of eyewitnesses, the appointment of a patriarch to the See in Constantinople, Toledo's claims of primacy, the prosecution of Count Raymond IV of Toulouse, Otto IV's request for absolution from his sentence of excommunication, proclamation of the two dogmatic constitutions that dealt with the heretical teachings of Joachim of Fiore and Amaury de Bène,[9] the excommunication of the English barons and annulment of *Mag-*

7. X 5.6.17; on the *libri legales*, see Michael H. Hoeflich and Jasonne M. Grabher, "The Establishment of Normative Legal Texts: The Beginning of the *Ius commune*," *The History of Canon Law in the Classical Period, 1140–1234: From Gratian to the Decretals of Pope Gregory IX* (Washington, D.C.: The Catholic University of America Press, 2008), 1–21.

8. See Uta-Renate Blumenthal, "A Gloss of Hostiensis to X 5.6.17 (*Ad liberandam*)," *Bulletin of Medieval Canon Law* 30 (2013), 89–122, at 101: "Ut ergo quod textus omisit glossa suppleat, quia et multi quotidie ipsam querunt nec inveniunt eadem, quantenus tangit hunc articulum duximus his apponendam."

9. The two dogmatic canons were *Firmiter credimus* c.1, and *Dampnamus* c.2, and entered canon law in 4 Comp. 1.1.1 and 1.1.2 and later in Gregory IX's *Decretales*, X 1.1.1 and 1.1.2, under the title *De fide catholica et summa trinitate*.

na carta, the confirmation of Frederick II as German emperor, and finally, the crusade were most important.[10]

The conciliar canons were promulgated during the last session of the council. An eyewitness reported their promulgation with a cryptic and short sentence: "Finally the constitutions of the Lord Pope were read."[11] Other reports leave no doubt that most of the constitutions were not drafted in the sessions of the council. *Ad liberandam* and the two dogmatic canons were probably shaped to some extent by the discussions of the participants. The remaining sixty-eight were not. Two important questions arise from these facts: how were the canons distributed to the participants and what was Innocent III's role in drafting them? If we compare the promulgation of the Fourth Lateran's canons to how the canons of the Third Lateran Council (1179) circulated, we see a sea change in how conciliar constitutions entered canon law. We can undoubtedly attribute this change to Innocent's rigorous reorganization of the papal curia. There had been no official collection of the Lateran III canons; they circulated in manuscripts that had no order and even omitted some of the canons. Eventually, the canonists haphazardly placed them in various canonical collection.[12] Twenty years after the council, Bernardus Papiensis incorporated all of them into his *Compilatio prima.* His collection was adopted by the canonists, was taught in the schools, and took its place alongside the other *libri legales.* Without papal encouragement or approval, the Lateran III canons became a part of canon law.

In contrast Innocent III ordered the Lateran IV canons to be placed in the papal registers. At almost certainly his mandate, the canons immediately circulated as a collection and were glossed by three jurists who were teaching in Bologna.[13] Within no more than a year, Johannes Teutonicus

10. Stephan G. Kuttner and Antonio García y García, "A New Eyewitness Account of the Fourth Lateran Council," *Traditio* 20 (1964), 115–178 have analyzed the sources that reported the activities of the sessions of the council.

11. Ibid. 128: "Deinde leguntur constitutions domini pape."

12. See Anne Duggan, "Conciliar Law 1123–1215: The Legislation of the Four Lateran Councils," *The History of Canon Law in the Classical Period, 1140–1234: From Gratian to the Decretals of Pope Gregory IX* (Washington, D.C.: The Catholic University of America Press, 2008) 338–339.

13. There is no direct evidence that Innocent sent the canons to the law schools, but the fact that the canonists immediately glossed them as a separate collection is good indirect proof.

incorporated them into his *Compilatio quarta.*[14] Did Innocent's vision of papal power include a grand conception of the pope's conciliar legislative authority as well as a plan to bring his legislation into the schools and the courts?

The evidence is perplexing and contradictory. Johannes Teutonicus' efforts to include the Lateran IV canons in his new collection of Innocent's decretals provoked gossip at the papal curia and in legal circles. A short history of canonical collections in Vatican and Breslau manuscripts contains the following information:[15]

> After the *Compilatio tertia* Master Johannes Teutonicus received the constitutions of Innocent [III] and certain decretals which Pope Innocent issued in six years of his pontificate up to the council. He compiled and glossed them. However, because the Lord Pope did not want to approve (authenticate) the compilation, Johannes left the curia in anger.

Some evidence of Johannes Teutonicus' anger exists in his opening gloss in his commentary on *Compilatio tertia* that was written shortly after these events:[16]

14. Pennington, "Decretal Collections 1190–1234," *The History of Canon Law in the Classical Period, 1140–1234: From Gratian to the Decretals of Pope Gregory IX* (Washington, D.C.: The Catholic University of America Press, 2008) 314–315.

15. Vatican, Borghese lat. 45, fol. 23r–23v (V) and Breslau, Universitätsbibliothek I.Q.102, fol. 201v–202r (B): "Processu temporis magister Johannes (Joan. V) Theutunicus (Theothonicus V) accepit constitutiones concilii Innocentii et quasdam decretales quas (idem *add.* V) Innocentius sexto anno sui regiminis usque ad concilium fecit (fecerat V) in sex annis sui regiminis usque ad concilium et V), compillavit (eas *add.* V) et glosavit, et vocatur (vocatus fuit V) quartus liber decretalium. Set quia dominus Innocentius noluit (illam compilationem *add.* V) actenticare (approbare V), ira succensus recessit de curia." See the augmented essay of Stephan Kuttner, "Johannes Teutonicus, das vierte Laterankonzil und die Compilatio tertia," *Medieval Councils, Decretals, and Collections of Canon Law* (London: Variorum Reprints, 1980), no. X, 625–626; Pennington, "The Making of a Decretal Collection: The Genesis of Compilatio tertia," *Proceedings of the Fifth International Congress of Medieval Canon Law, Salamanca 1976*, Monumenta iuris canonici, Series C 6 (Città del Vaticano: Biblioteca Apostolica Vaticana, 1980), 67–92, at 76, n.23

16. Johannes Teutonicus to *Devotioni vestrae*, Innocent's letter introducing *Compilatio tertia*, ed. Pennington, *Johannis Teutonici Apparatus in Compilationem tertiam*, Monumenta iuris canonici 3.1 (Città del Vaticano: Biblioteca Apostolica Vaticana, 1981, 1: "Licet

> Although here you call yourself the servant of the servants of God, in another decretal you sound like a god when you scorn to be called the vicar of Peter... Jerome called you the successor of the fisherman.

Those who read Johannes' gloss understood his pointed comment exactly. It was deleted from later manuscripts. Innocent had his defenders.

What does this evidence tell us about Innocent's relationship with Johannes, about his plans for his legislation, and his vision of papal legislative authority? The first point would be that Johannes had connections with the papal curia. He knew the pope. Is the very short history of *Compilatio quarta* correct? Did the pope deliver the Lateran constitutions and other decretals to Johannes that he placed in *Compilatio quarta*? In spite of the evidence from the two histories, the manuscript evidence would indicate no. Innocent had other ideas.

Innocent distributed his constitutions but not solely or exclusively to Johannes. The evidence is that Innocent wanted his conciliar canons to circulate as a collection. The canonists understood his intention. Three of them wrote commentaries on them immediately. Johannes finished his commentary on them very quickly as did Vincentius Hispanus. Vincentius eventually wrote two recensions of his commentary. Damasus Hungarus also wrote a commentary. The most likely explanation of this evidence is that Innocent sent his constitutions to Bologna, and the canonists lectured on them and provided the texts with glosses. If we are to believe any of the facts in the Borghese and Breslau histories, we could conclude that Johannes finished his commentary before Innocent died in July of 1216. That means he completed a quite extensive commentary within six months; most likely even sooner. Did Innocent send Johannes other decretals that he issued after ca. 1210? That seems unlikely. As Stephan Kuttner has shown, the decretals that Johannes placed in *Compilatio quarta* had already been singled out as important legal texts in other small collections. Johannes simply included what others had already chosen as well as some of his own choices.

---

hic te appelles serum seruorum dei, altius tamen intonas, cum dedignaris dici uicarius Petri, ut infra de translat. episc. Quanto (3 Comp. 1.5.3 [X 1.7.3]), et a Ieromino appellaris successor piscatoris, xxiii. q.i. Quoniam uetus (C.24 q.1 c.25]). jo."

Two manuscripts provide crucial evidence for Innocent's legislative intentions in the month before he died. Florentine and Graz manuscripts both contain the text of the Fourth Lateran constitutions and decretals that Johannes collected for inclusion into *Compilatio quarta*. I will call this text the *Proto-Quarta*.[17] In Graz the constitutions precede and in Florence they follow *Proto-Quarta*. Both manuscripts are Italian and date to the early thirteenth century. The manuscripts are identical in their method of indicating where the Lateran canons should be placed among the decretals of *Proto-Quarta*. The numbers of the constitutions is given in Roman numerals and their incipits.[18]

Florence, Biblioteca Laurenziana Santa Croce IV sin. 2 omits 18 decretals that Johannes later added to *Compilatio quarta*.[19] The other *Proto-Quarta* manuscript, Graz, Universitätsbibliothek 138 omits none of the decretals from the final version of *Compilatio quarta* but adds the full text of Lat. IV c.70 = 4 Comp. 5.4.2, instead of just the incipit. Florence gives only the incipits of all the Lateran constitutiones.[20] This evidence would indicate that the Florence manuscript was an early draft of *Compilatio quarta* and that the Graz manuscript is a later, pre-*Compilatio quarta*, augmented text. The Florence manuscript contains a marginal gloss to Innocent's decretals that appears to be contemporary with the main text. There is no evidence that the gloss was excerpted from Johannes's Ordinary Gloss on

17. Firenze, Biblioteca Mediceo-Laurenziana, Santa Croce IV sin. 2 (F), fol. 239r–253v (*Proto-Quarta*) and fol. 255r–265v (IV Lateran constitutions); Graz, Universitätsbibliothek 138 (G), fol. 233r–246v (IV Lateran constitutions) and fol. 246v–268r (*Proto-Quarta*). Another explanation for these two manuscripts could be that the *scriptoria* extracted the *Proto-Quarta* decretals from a complete *Compilatio quarta*. I think that explanation is improbable and violates Ockham's *Lex parsimoniae*. One has to make far more complicated assumptions about how the *Proto-Quarta* would have been created in two different manuscripts in two different Italian *scriptoria* for an unknown purpose than the simple assumption that it was Johannes' original work that he presented to Innocent III. For a discussion of the sources of the decretals Johannes placed in *Compilatio quarta*, see Kuttner, "Johannes Teutonicus" 617–622.

18. E.g. F, fol. 241r, G, fol. 249r: "Constitutio xxiii. Ne profectu, Const.' xxiiii. Quia propter diuersas, Const.' xxv. Quiquis election, Const.' xxvi. Nichil est quod ecclesie', placed after 4 Comp. 1.3.7 (X —).

19. 4 Comp. 1.14.2, 2.3.2, 2.4.1, 2.6.1, 2.7.5, 2.9.2, 2.10.1, 2.11.3, 3.2.1, 3.3.3, 3.9.4, 3.12.1, 3.13.2, 4.1.2, 5.6.1, 5.6.4, 5.12.2, 5.15.4.

20. G, fol. 264r.

Compilatio quarta. A later rubricator noted that there were two decretals missing in the Florence manuscript.[21] His notations indicate that he knew the *Proto-Quarta* of the Graz manuscript or a completed *Compilatio quarta*.

Consequently, the evidence would suggest that the Florence manuscript very likely reflects the text that Johannes asked Innocent to authenticate.[22] In other words Johannes did not present the pope with *Compilatio quarta* when he asked for authentication but a possible draft. There are good reasons for this scenario. Johannes and the other canonists would have begun glossing and teaching the IV Lateran canons in the Spring of 1216. The Graz manuscript has Johannes' commentary on the constitutions but not on the *Proto-Quarta*; the Florentine manuscript has glosses on the *Proto-Quarta* and the constitutions. The glosses on the *Proto-Quarta* are slightly different from his Ordinary Gloss to *Compilatio quarta*, possibly indicating that these glosses in Florence also pre-date his apparatus to *Compilatio quarta*.[23]

There can be no doubt that Johannes wanted Innocent's approval (authentication) for a decretal collection that included the IV Lateran constitutions in one form or another. In this context Stephan Kuttner's seventy-year-old speculation that Innocent denied Johannes' petition because he wished that his constitutions circulated separately looks completely plausible.[24] Kuttner's theory was supported by the fact that three canonists immediately glossed them. His observation is further buttressed by the rubric of a Florentine manuscript of the constitutions with the gloss of Damasus Hungarus. At the beginning of the text of the constitutions, the rubricator called the constitutions "novellae," imitating the name that was given to Justinian's legislation after his codification.[25] That title had never been given to papal legislation. We may not know what Innocent thought,

21. F, fol. 242v and 244r. The rubricator is not a trained hand and is a later and cruder than the text of F.

22. F and G have differences in rubrication and, most importantly, in the order of the texts.

23. This observation is based on a limited comparison of the apparatus in F with Johannes' Ordinary Gloss; a collation of F would be necessary to substantiate my tentative conclusion.

24. Kuttner, "Johannes Teutonicus" 628.

25. Florence, Biblioteca Laurenziana, Santa Croce III sin. 6, fol. 97r: "Prima pars (MS: pas with a line through the descender of the p) nouellarum de fide catholica et sum-

but we can have a good idea how the jurists interpreted his intentions. Innocent, they thought, conceived of his constitutions as legislation that supplemented the collections of canon law in the schools and courts; possibly they thought of him as a new Justinian. Imitating the great emperor would certainly have fit well with Innocent's vision of the papal office.

Over fifty years ago Christopher Cheney called attention to three pre-*Compilatio quarta* collections of Innocent III's decretals. Cheney conjectured that they were supplements to Petrus Benevantanus' *Compilatio tertia*. In any case they are examples of collections that were similar to those from which Johannes gathered his texts for his new collection.[26] In fact, five of the eighteen decretals that Johannes did not include in the *Proto-Quarta* and later added to *Compilatio quarta* can be found in Cheney's three collections.[27]

After returning from Rome and after Innocent's death, Johannes Teutonicus did not abandon his collection but did what canonists had been doing for centuries: he put together a private collection that began to circulate throughout Europe. He drew the decretals he included in the *Proto-Quarta* of Florence, Biblioteca Laurenziana Santa Croce IV sin. 2 from other small collections similar to those examined by Cheney. Most importantly, Johannes worked on *Compilatio quarta* in stages. First, he attempted to honor Innocent's mandate that the constitutions be preserved as an independent collection. His solution was to preserve the Lateran constitutions as a separate collection and append other Innocentian decretals that had not been included in *Compilatio tertia* to the constitutions. For reasons we cannot know with certainty, Innocent objected to this new collection. After Innocent's death and without an imperious pope peering over this shoulder, Johannes expanded his collection to create what came to be known as *Compilatio quarta*.

ma trinitate. Innocentius tertius." Noted by Kuttner, "Johannes Teutonicus, das vierte Laterankonzil," 618, but without commenting on the small problem of "pars."

26. A comparison of the inscriptions in F and G show that Johannes did not take decretals from the papal registers.

27. Christopher R. Cheney, "Three Decretal Collections before Compilatio IV: Pragensis, Palatina I, and Abrincensis II," *Traditio* 15 (1959), 464–483. The evidence of the inscriptions preclude these collections from being Johannes' sources.

The collection was a success. Contrary to the opinions of some scholars, *Compilatio quarta* was accepted by the canonists and the schools. Although *quarta* circulated ca. 6 fewer years than *tertia* and was considerably smaller, there are a surprisingly large number of extant manuscripts. A comparison of the number of manuscripts of Petrus Beneventanus' "authenticated collection," *Compilatio tertia* ca. 1210, to *Compilatio quarta* is revealing: ca. 90 of the *tertia* to 60 of the *quarta*. Like the *tertia*, the canonists taught and glossed the *quarta*. We have signed glosses of Phillipus of Aquileia, Jacobus, another Johannes, and Marcoardus, as well as Johannes' commentary that became the Ordinary Gloss.[28] Further, only 20 years later, Raymond de Peñafort included most of the decretals that Johannes selected into the *Decretals of Gregory IX*. A comparison to Tancred's *Compilatio quinta* compiled at the command of Pope Honorius III in 1227 is instructive. Raymond omitted 91 decretals from Honorius III's official collection but only 15 from Johannes'. Those numbers hardly support the contention that there was "great resistance in the schools" to *Compilatio quarta*.[29]

The second part of the question about Innocent's vision and role in shaping and promulgating the IV Lateran canons is whether Innocent had a hand in drafting the constitutions. In the most recent edition of the IV Lateran canons, Alberto Melloni states unequivocally that the canons "were written before that assembly, by the canonist and theologian Pope Innocent III." He writes that proof of Innocent's authorship is the fact that the collections of canon law gave all the canons an inscription "Innocentius iii. in concilio generali."[30] Melloni's conviction raises two interrelated prob-

28. Winfried Stelzer, "Österreichische Kanonisten des 13. Jahrhunderts," *Österreichisches Archiv für Kirchenrecht* 30 (1979), 57–81, at 78–80.

29. Quotation from Giulio Silano, "Of Sleep and Sleeplessness: The Papacy and Law, 1150–1300," *The Religious Roles of the Papacy: Ideals and Realities, 1150–1300*, ed. Christopher Ryan (Toronto: Pontifical Institute of Mediaeval Studies, 1989), 343–361, at 359. I do not find Silano's other arguments about *Compilatio tertia* and *quarta* convincing, particularly his assertion that *Compilatio tertia* was "official" rather than as I have argued "authenticated."

30. Alberto Melloni, "Concilium lateranense IV 1215," *Conciliorum oecumenicorum generaliumque decreta, 2.1: The General Councils of Latin Christendom: From Constantinople IV to Pavia-Siena (869–1424)*, ed. Giuseppe Alberigo and Alberto Melloni (Turnhout: Brepols, 2013), 154–155.

lems: how much did Innocent participate in the judicial activities of the Roman curia and whether he drafted judicial decisions or conciliar canons.

The question whether the inscriptions of the canons in canonical collections can be used to determine authorship can be easily resolved. They cannot. When the constitutions circulated as a collection, they had no inscriptions, just an indication at the beginning of the entire text of the constitutions that Innocent was the pope. In *Compilatio quarta,* the inscriptions do not mention Innocent. They are labeled with their number, e.g. "Constitutio xxii." as an inscription.[31] Raymond de Peñafort gave all the canons the inscription "Innocentius in concilio generali," but Raymond cannot have meant to convey to his readers that Innocent drafted all of them.

The question of which of his decretals Innocent himself drafted is much more difficult. I raised doubts about the common assumption among scholars that Innocent drafted all his decretals forty years ago. My doubts were met with skepticism. Stephan Kuttner and Christopher Cheney, two people who knew Innocent's letters much better than I at that time, were convinced I was wrong. Since then I think scholarly opinion has changed.[32] Most scholars would concede that Innocent could not have written all the legal decisions produced by his curia and would no longer consider Innocent the first great lawyer pope. We do know he sat in judgment over important cases and wrote significant decretals. It is not always easy to

31. E.g. Admont, Stiftsbibliothek 22, Cordoba, Bibl. del Cabildo 10, Munich, Bayerische Staatsbibl. 3879 are very good manuscripts and have the same style of inscriptions to the Lateran constitutions. Munich occasionally has "Idem (i.e. Innocentius) Const. xxii." as do other manuscripts.

32. See my "The Legal Education of Pope Innocent III," *Bulletin of Medieval Canon Law* 4 (1974) 70–77 with "Further Thoughts on Pope Innocent III's Knowledge of Law," *Popes, Canonists, and Texts 1150–1550* (Aldershot: Variorum, 1993) II, 1–14; "Pope Innocent III's Views on Church and State: A Gloss to *Per venerabilem*," *Law, Church and Society* (Philadelphia: University of Pennsylvania Press, 1977), 49–67; Innocent III and the Ius commune, *Grundlagen des Rechts: Festschrift für Peter Landau zum 65. Geburtstag*, herausgegeben von Richard Helmholz, Paul Mikat, Jörg Müller, Michael Stolleis (Paderborn: Verlag Ferdinand Schöningh, 2000), 349–366. The most important piece of evidence for Innocent's legal skills as judge in the papal court, if not for his legal training, is chapters 41–45 of the *Gesta Innocentii*; see James M. Powell, *The Deeds of Pope Innocent III by an Anonymous Author* (Washington, D.C.: Catholic University of America Press, 2004), 55–61.

decide which ones. For me a clue to his authorship is the presence of biblical citations, particularly if the citations are used to make clever and unusual points. Quite obviously that subjective judgment is not a certain and sure standard. The same problem confronts the authorship of the Fourth Lateran constitutions. There are very few passages in which one might detect the mind of an author with Innocent's theological background in the procedural canons. A quest for Innocent's mind in the procedural canons is further complicated by the fact that many of them have their origins in earlier decretals.

The procedural canon that has attracted the most attention from modern scholars is canon 18, *Sententiam sanguinis*, in which clerical participation in the ordeal was prohibited. Yet, for all the scholarly attention this constitution has received, the short sentence on the ordeal, inserted at the end of the canon, seems like an afterthought. It probably was. The canon began by prohibiting clerics to render sentences that shed blood, moved on to those people who injured churches or clerics, and instructed clerics that they could not draft documents ordering the shedding of blood. In secular courts laymen should perform that task. Clerics should also not be in command of soldiers nor should they perform surgery. Finally, almost as an addendum, clerics were forbidden to administer the rites for the ordeal of cold or hot water and the glowing hot iron.[33]

A significant number of scholars have not, however, seen Innocent III's rejection of the ordeal as an afterthought. They see it as either a revolution or a sudden halt to accepted court practices or both.[34]

33. García, *Constitutiones* 66.

34. Robert Bartlett, *Trial by Fire and Water: The Medieval Judicial Ordeal* (Oxford: Oxford University Press, 1986) and most recently following Bartlett, Scott L. Taylor, "Survival of Customary Justice," *Crime and Punishment in the Middle Ages and the Early Modern Age*, ed. Albrecht Classen and Connie Scarborough (Berlin: De Gruyter, 2012), 109–130, at 114–115. There are other variants on this theme in the literature; see e.g. Richard M. Fraher, "IV Lateran Revolution in Criminal Procedure: The Birth of Inquisitio, the End of Ordeals, and Innocent III's Vision of Ecclesiastical Politics," *Studia in honorem Eminentissimi Cardinalis Alfonsi M. Stickler*, ed. Rosalio Iosepho Card. Castillo Lara (Rome: Libreria Ateneo Salesiano, 1992), 97–111; Winfried Trusen, "Das Verbot der Gottesurteile und der Inquisitionsprozeß: Zum Wandel des Strafverfahrens unter dem Einfluß des gelehrten Rechts im Spätmittelalter," *Sozialer Wandel im Mittelalter: Wahrnehmungsformen, Erklärungsmuster, Regelungsmechanismen*, ed. Jürgen Miethke und Klaus Schreiner (Sig-

If one explores Innocent's registers a very different picture emerges. In the Summer of 1199 the Archbishop Johannes of Antivari and Dioklea (Bar, Montenegro) sent a set of canons from the Synod of Antivari to Innocent for his approval. They were endorsed by Johannes the papal legate and seven of Archbishop Johannes' suffragan bishops. Canon five stated:[35]

> Similarly we prohibit under ban of excommunication that any layman presume to bring a cleric to a judgment of the country, such as the hot iron or water or any other judgment of this sort.

This text confirmed what had already become standard practice in the church: the ordeal should not be imposed upon clerics and clerics should not participate in ordeals. I have argued that church courts abandoned the ordeal during the twelfth century.[36] Gratian included canons that had forbade the procedure.[37] No twelfth-century jurist argued that the ordeal was a legitimate procedure in ecclesiastical courts, although some conceded that it could be used to judge the unfree. At the end of the twelfth century, the greatest canonist of the age, Huguccio, condemned the ordeal categorically.[38] Although the twelfth-century jurists were more or less united in their objections to the ordeal on legal and theological grounds, historians, encouraged by the paucity of good evidence, have created a ca-

maringen: Jan Thorbecke Verlag, 1994), 235–247; Finbarr McAuley, "Canon Law and the End of the Ordeal," *Oxford Journal of Legal Studies* 26 (2006), 473–513.

35. *Die Register Innocenz' III. 2: 2. Pontifikatsjahr*, ed. Othmar Hageneder, Werner Maleczek, and Alfred A. Strnad (Wien: Verlag der Österreichischen Akademie der Wissenschaften, 1979), no. 169, 326–330 at 329: "Similiter sub excommunicatione prohibemus ne aliquis laicus clericum ad peregrina iudicia trahere praesumat, veluti candentis ferri vel acque vel cuiuslibet alterius judicii. Non enim pertinet ad laicum clericum iudicare."

36. Kenneth Pennington, *The Prince and the Law: Sovereignty and Rights in the Western Legal Tradition* (Berkeley: University of California Press, 1993) 132–136, where I also discuss the literature on the ordeal to ca. 1990.

37. Gratian, *Decretum* C.2 q.5 c.7 and c.20, in which the ordeal of the hot iron and water is mentioned and rejected. Compurgation continued to be accepted.

38. As John W. Baldwin, "The Intellectual Preparation for the Canon of 1215 against the Ordeals," *Speculum* 36 (1961), 613–636, at 618–626, illustrated more than sixty years ago that the canonists were unanimous that the ordeal could not be used in ecclesiastical courts and were unsure only whether the ordeal could be used in secular courts. However, by ca. 1190 Huguccio was adamant that ordeals were not legitimate or valid modes of proof.

cophony of opinions about the ordeal. I still think an essay by Paul Hyams is the most balanced analysis of the place of the ordeal in pre-Lateran IV medieval society.[39]

The first decretal in Innocent's registers in which the papal curia heard a case in which the ordeal was an issue took place in the Fall of 1202. In its decision the court ordered the Archbishop of Besançon not to drag Cistercian monks into secular courts where they would be forced to undergo ordeals of the hot iron and water. Judicial combat was also forbidden. These practices were superstitious.[40] In July of 1204 in a decretal sent to Comita, a judge in Torres, Sardinia,[41] the papal curia made crystal clear the norm in canon law that would be repeated in canon 18 of the IV Lateran. The situation in Sardinia was intolerable:[42]

> Where poor priests are compelled to bless and be present in judgments of the hot iron, cold water and similar modes of proof that canon law does not permit, and if those priests who have been compelled do not want to obey, the magistrates who have jurisdiction over them smite them with monetary punishments.

39. "Trial by Ordeal: The Key to Proof in the Early Common Law," *On the Laws and Customs of England: Essays in Honor of Samuel E. Thorne*, ed. Arnold S. Morris, Thomas A. Green et al. (Chapel Hill: University of North Carolina Press, 1981), 90–126.

40. *Die Register Innocenz' III. 5: 5. Pontifikatsjahr, 1202/1203*, ed. Andrea Sommerlechner with Christoph Egger and Herwig Weigl (Wien: Verlag der Österreichischen Akademie der Wissenschaften, 1994), no. 106 (107), 214–215, at 214: "qui ad ea que Dei sunt, respectum debitum non habentes, eos ad secularia pertrahere iudicia non formidant et examen aque frigide, ignisque candentis vetitumque duellum subire compellunt, nullatenus attendentes sacros canones non censere confessionem a quolibet per huiusmodi extorquendam, et quod sanctorum Patrum non est documento sancitum, non esse superstitiosis adinventionibus praesumendum."

41. Evandro Putzulu, "Comita," *Dizionario biografico degli italiani* 27 (1982), 600–602.

42. *Die Register Innocenz' III. 7: 7. Pontifikatsjahr, 1204/1205*, ed. Othmar Hageneder and Andrea Sommerlechner, with the collaboration of Christoph Egger and Rainer Murauer (Wien: Verlag der Österreichischen Akademie der Wissenschaften, 1997), no. 113, 176–178, at 177: "Cumque candentis ferri et aque frigide ac similia iudicia lex canonica non admittat, benedicere ac interesse talibus compelluntur miseri sacerdotes, et si compellentibus parere noluerint, a curatoribus, in quorum habitant jurisdictione, poena pecuniaria percelluntur."

The decision left judge Comita no wiggle room:[43]

> Therefore you must strive to abolish the evil of this practice and abuse from your land and preserve the liberty of clerics and churches. You must leave ecclesiastical judgments to them.

These decretals are proof that it was settled canon law that clerics could not be judged by the ordeal, and they could not participate in them or even be present when they were carried out. Is there further proof that the ordeal was settled law by the beginning of Innocent's pontificate? The proof is an argument from silence but convincing. The canonists inside and outside the papal curia combed Innocent's registers for letters that made important points of law. The significant appellate decisions of Innocent's curia circulated individually and in small collections. Rainer of Pomposa was the first canonist to compile a collection of Innocent's decretals ca. 1202. Between 1202 and 1210 Albertus, Gilbertus, Alanus, and Bernardus Compostellanus followed suit. None of them bothered with the decretals in which ordeals were discussed.[44] The reason they did not collect these decretals is simple. The ordeal and clerical participation in the liturgy of the ordeal no longer attracted their attention. It was not important. When the ordeal was included at the end of canon 18, it was an afterthought not a revolution. It was, as Donahue observed, a "moribund institution" and a legal procedure that had long ago fallen into desuetude. A further proof of that conclusion, albeit again from silence, is that Johannes, Vincentius, and Damasus did not discuss the ordeal when they glossed the canon. It is impossible to imagine their silence if they thought a revolution was about to occur in the ecclesiastical courts of Christendom.

IV Lateran's most important procedural canons were those that established the rules for inquisitorial procedure and for the courts' obligation to create and preserve written records of its proceedings.[45] Canon 8,

43. Ibid. 178: "Sic igitur praesumptionis et abusionis huiusmodi vitium de terra tua studeas extirpare, sicque viros ecclesiasticos et ecclesias in sua libertate conserves, ecclesiastico iudicio relinquens eosdem."

44. Pennington, "Decretal Collections" 303–310.

45. c.8 *Qualiter et quando* rules for conducting an "inquisition" = 4 Comp. 5.1.4; c.35: *Ut debitus*, rules for appeals = 4 Comp. 2.12.3; c.36: *Cum cessante causa*, no appeals from interlocutory decisions = 4 Comp. 2.12.4; c.37: *Nonnulli gratia*, defendants should not

Qualiter et quando, which laid down the rules for prelates to conduct an investigation into clerical behavior has generated a debate similar to the controversy surrounding the ordeal. Winfried Trusen and Richard M. Fraher have maintained that Pope Innocent III established inquisitorial procedure in ecclesiastical courts. This new procedure offered an alternative to accusatorial procedure, which required that an accuser was essential to a criminal trial. Inquisitorial procedure granted a judge the authority to investigate wrongdoing and summon defendants to his court.[46] There is no question that the introduction of inquisitorial procedure marked a sea change in court procedure that has lasted until the present day.

Did Pope Innocent and his jurists impose this new mode of proof on ecclesiastical courts? Until recently that was the received opinion. However, the recent research of Lotte Kéry has shown that *inquisitiones veritatum* begin to be used in episcopal courts in the second half of the twelfth century.[47] These *inquisitiones* formed the foundation for the development of inquisitorial procedure. Her conclusions are supported by the silence of the canonists when they commented on the primary source of the IV Lateran's *Qualiter et quando* in *Compilatio tertia*, a decretal that was also had

---

be burdened by excessive summons of witnesses more than two days distant without the agreement of both parties = 4 Comp. 1.2.5; c.38: *Quoniam contra falsam*, all the proceedings of a trial must be recorded in writing = 4 Comp. 2.6.2, 2.12.5, and 3.2.4; c.48: *Cum speciali sit*, Recusing a judge = 4 Comp. 2.12.5. Although some scholars have assumed otherwise, *Qualiter et quando*'s rules had nothing to do with the inquisitions into the crime of heresy.

46. Winfried Trusen, "Der Inquisitionsprozeß: Seine historischen Grundlagen und frühen Formen," *Zeitschrift der Savigny-Stiftung für Rechtsgeschichte*, Kanonistische Abteilung 74 (1988), 168–230; Trusen, "Das Verbot der Gottesurteile und der Inquisitionsprozeß: Zum Wandel des Strafverfahrens unter dem Einfluß des gelehrten Rechts im Spätmittelalter," *Sozialer Wandel im Mittelalter: Wahrnehmungsformen, Erklärungsmuster, Regelungsmechanismen*, ed. Jürgen Miethke and Klaus Schreiner (Sigmaringen: Jan Thorbecke Verlag, 1994), 235–247. Richard M. Fraher, "IV Lateran Revolution in Criminal Procedure: The Birth of Inquisitio, the End of Ordeals, and Innocent III's Vision of Ecclesiastical Politics," *Studia in honorem Eminentissimi Cardinalis Alfonsi M. Stickler*, ed. Card. Castillo Lara, 97–111, was his last word on the subject; he cited his earlier essays in his notes.

47. Lotte Kéry, "Inquisitio—denunciatio—exceptio: Möglichkeiten der Verfahrenseinleitung im Dekretalenrecht," *Zeitschrift der Savigny-Stiftung für Rechtsgeschichte: Kanonistische Abteilung* 87 (2001) 226–268; idem, *Gottesfurcht und irdische Strafe: Der Beitrag des mittelalterlichen Kirchenrechts zur Entstehung des öffentlichen Strafrechts: Konflikt, Verbrechen und Sanktion in der Gesellschaft Alteuropas* (Köln: Böhlau Verlag, 2006).

the incipit *Qualiter et quando*.[48] None of them noted or complained that the decretal was establishing a new and unknown procedure. Inquisitorial procedure should rather be understood as having organically emerged from practice rather than as a mode of proof having been imposed on ecclesiastical courts by Rome. Johannes Teutonicus, however, did note one innovation in the conciliar canon. At the beginning of the part of the conciliar canon that was not copied from the decretal in *Compilatio tertia*, the canon mandated that "the defendant must be present during the inquisition." To which Johannes noted: "Only this <point> is new and cannot be expressly found in any other place."[49] Vincentius agreed and said he had always thought the defendant should be present but observed that other jurists felt that the defendant could be absent."[50] These glosses do not prove that the inquisition pre-dated Innocent's pontificate but do indicate the procedure had been around for some time.

The other significant procedural canon that the IV Lateran Council promulgated was canon 38, *Quoniam contra falsam*, which established that all the proceedings of a trial must be recorded in writing.[51] The drafters of the canon also borrowed from the language of an earlier letter dated January, 1211 that Johannes Teutonicus included in *Compilatio quarta*.[52] Since it repeated the points made in canon 38, Raymond de Peñafort placed an extremely truncated text in the *Decretals of Gregory IX*.[53] If the Florence manuscript of what I have earlier dubbed Johannes' *Proto-Quarta* can be relied on, Johannes did not include the earlier decretal in his first draft of *Compilatio quarta*, but he added it after Johannes' unsuccessful trip to the

48. 3 Comp. 5.1.4 (X 2.1.17 and 5.1.17). Two-thirds of the decretal in *Compilatio tertia* was placed into the conciliar canon word for word.

49. Johannes Teutonicus, *Commentary* to IV Lateran c.8, ed. García, 201: "*sub verbo: Debet igitur esse praesens is, contra quem facienda sit inquisitio*: Hoc solum novum est nec alibi hoc ita expresse inveniebatur. jo."

50. Vincentius Hispanus, *Commentary* to IV Lateran c.8, ed. García p. 299, sub verbo: *Qualiter et quando*: "Item quod presens debeat esse ille contra quem fit inquisitio, hodie expressum est in hoc capitulo... et semper idem sensi, licet alii sentirent contra."

51. Ed. García, 80–81.

52. 4 Comp. 2.6.1 (X 5.37.11), *Dilectus filius Jacob*, dated January 1211. The sections "contra falsam assertionem—prevaleat equitati" and "quantenus hoc adhibitio—iustitia non ledatur" were quoted word for word in *Quoniam contra falsam*.

53. X 5.37.11.

papal curia.[54] We do know from papal letters of the twelfth century that the testimony of witnesses, summons, and other documents were often mentioned in court cases.[55] They were required for any appeal to Rome. Nonetheless, *Quoniam contra falsam* was an important step in protecting the rights of litigants from arbitrary or criminal judges.[56]

Finally, one last example of how the drafters of the IV Lateran canons borrowed from earlier papal decretals. The relationship of ecclesiastical and secular courts and their jurisdiction had been an issue and would remain an issue for church and state relations long after IV Lateran. Innocent may have sent a letter to Bishop Peter des Roches, an ardent supporter of John and royal government. That Peter was the recipient is probable but not certain. The letter forms an appendix to Thomas de Capua's collection of model letters in a Parisian manuscript.[57] With appropriate doubts, Hampe conjectured that it was sent to Peter in Winchester; Cheney and Semple accepted his reasons. Hampe's arguments were good if not conclusive. Bishop Peter had an usually interesting career. He rose from being the archdeacon in the diocese of Poitiers to become Lord Chamberlain under Richard the Lionheart, then elected to the see of Winchester in 1205, and John chose him to be chief justice of the realm in 1213.[58] In the Spring or Summer of 1215 Innocent sent a letter to Bishop Peter in which the pope told the bishop that he should prevent his court from hearing suits' belong-

54. Florence, Biblioteca Laurenziana Santa Croce IV sin. 2, fol. 244r does not contain the decretal. The Graz manuscript contains it.

55. Christopher R. Cheney and Mary Cheney, "A Draft Decretal of Pope Innocent III on a Case of Identity," *Quellen und Forschungen aus italienischen Archiven und Bibliotheken* 41 (1961), 29–47, discovered a document that was based on the written testimony of witnesses. A document of this type is rare before the thirteenth century.

56. The theory of Finbarr McAuley, "Canon Law and the End of the Ordeal," 501: "*Quoniam contra falsam* (IV Lat. c. 38) appears to have been passed to deal with the problem of corrupt judges... a judge who opted to remit a case *ad judicium Dei* would have complied with the statute [*Quoniam contra falsam*]," is partially right about corrupt judges—but the major thrust of the canon is to protect litigants when they wished to appeal their case. His second idea is completely implausible. No ecclesiastical judge after the IV Lateran Council would dare to consider remitting a case to a trial by ordeal. As I have argued earlier, they would not have done so before IV Lateran as well.

57. Paris, Bibliothèque Nationale de France, lat. 11867, fol. 30r–45v, at 37vb–38ra.

58. Nicholas Vincent, *Peter des Roches: An Alien in English Politics, 1205–1238* (Cambridge: Cambridge University Press, 1996).

ing in secular courts. He also informed him that he will promulgate rules at the upcoming council about the issue.[59] Innocent also mentioned that he asked John to send proctors to the council to defend his rights.

Most importantly for our purposes is the wording of the letter. It begins:

> Sicut volumus et ut iura clericorum laici non usurpent ita velle debemus ne clerici iura sibi vendicent laicorum... ut que sunt cesaris cesari et que sunt dei deo recta distributione reddantur... quod hactenus obtentum.
>
> We wish that laymen should not usurp the rights of the clergy, so we ought to wish that clerics do not take rights away from laymen in court... follow those things that have previously been observed and render those things which are Caesar's to Caesar and those that are God's to God in their proper and correct division.

Canon forty-two of the council adopted the wording of Innocent's letter with only a slight shifting of the clauses.

> Sicut volumus ut iura clericorum laici non usurpent, ita velle debemus ne clerici iura sibi vendicent laicorum... contentus existat constitutionibus scriptis et consuetudinibus que hactenus sunt optente, ut que sunt Cesaris Cesari, et que sunt Dei Deo recta distributione reddantur.
>
> We wish that laymen should not usurp the rights of the clergy, so we ought to wish that clerics do not take rights away from laymen in court... be content with written constitutions and customs that have previously been observed that those things which are Cesar's to Caesar and those that are God's to God should be rendered in their proper and correct division.

59. The Latin text is printed and translated in *Selected Letters of Pope Innocent III* 205–206. Karl Hampe, "Aus verlorenen Registerbänden der Päpste Innocenz III. und Innocenz IV." *Mitteilungen des Instituts für österreichische Geschichtsforschung* 23 (1902), 545–67, at 556–557.

Bishop Peter was a staunch defender of King John and of royal jurisdictional rights.[60] It may be the canonists knew the back story of the canon and realized that its purpose was too narrow and that its main principle had long been established as a general maxim of canon law. Although the canonists did not see fit to include canon forty-two into any of their collections, its admonitions lived on. It was quoted in full well into the early modern period.[61]

I would conclude by making three points. The first is that the two most significant procedural canons of the Fourth Lateran Council had histories and were not bursts of creative energy during Pope Innocent III's pontificate or just before the council and imposed by the papacy on lower ecclesiastical courts. Innocent's jurists codified what had been established court procedure. It is, rather, another example of legislation following practice. Second, and perhaps most important, the procedural norms established by the canons of IV Lateran were adopted by the secular courts of continental Europe during the thirteenth century. By the year 1300, IV Lateran rules of procedure were European rules of procedure. Third, Innocent III probably did not draft the Lateran constitutions. As I have shown, *Sententiam sanguinis*, *Qualiter et quando* and *Quoniam contra falsam*, and *Sicut volumus* borrowed exact language and norms from earlier decretals. This is good evidence that the jurists in Innocent's curia were the authors of the constitutions, not Innocent. More searching in Innocent's registers for language and norms found in other Lateran IV canons will, I am sure, reveal even more.

60. Vincent, *Peter des Roches*, 95–100.

61. E.g. Diego Lainez, *Disputationes tridentinae*, ed. Hartmannus Grisar (Innsbruck: Felicianus Rauch, 1886) 67; William Cobbett, *Political Register*, 5 (London: 1804), 739; Petrus de Marca, *Dissertationum de Concordia sacerdotii et imperii seu de libertatibus ecclesiae gallicanae* (Bamberg: Vincentius Dederich, 1788), Book 4, chapter 21, vol. 2, p. 326.

Law and Empowerment at the Fourth Lateran Council

Joseph Goering

In June of 2015 I was invited, along with Charlie Donahue and others, to take part in a learned symposium at St. Louis University celebrating the 800th anniversary of Magna Carta and of the Fourth Lateran Council. In thinking about my remarks I quickly found myself stymied: What could I bring to this discussion? I had no new manuscript discoveries to pull out of a hat; nor did I have new texts to illuminate the mysteries of Charter or Council; I didn't even have Powerpoint slides to delight and instruct. What could I do? In the midst of this "dark wood," I found myself, unaccountably, thinking about Power. This is not a topic that has held much fascination for me; in fact, I have spent a good deal of time encouraging students to be wary of power and its pursuit as an explanatory tool in the practice of medieval history. Nevertheless, in reading over the canons of the Fourth Lateran Council once again I was struck, for better or worse, with thoughts of power, and it is a record of those thoughts that I would like to dedicate here to Professor Donahue.

It is something of a commonplace for us to say, with Lord Acton, that "Power Corrupts," and we are quick to add the corollary: "Absolute Power Corrupts Absolutely." As obvious as these sentiments may seem to us today, they are not ones that were obvious to our medieval forebears. With a moment's reflection we will recall that "absolute power" in the Middle Ages was not a bad thing, nor was it thought to be a source of corruption. Rather, absolute power (*omni-potentia*) was one of the primary attributes of God. *Firmiter credimus*, "We firmly believe," begins the famous creed of the Fourth Lateran Council, "and simply confess... one true God, eternal, immeasurable [and] all powerful—*omnipotens*."[1] Power and might (*potestas*) are praised everywhere in the scriptures and in the liturgy. It is just as difficult to find a negative use of the term "power" in medieval writings as it is to find a positive use in our contemporary discourse.

A recent issue of *The New Yorker* magazine carried letters to the Editor under the headline: "Reading Magna Carta."[2] One of the letters captures well our popular conception of medieval power. "Magna Carta... attested to King John's reconciliation with the Church in Rome. It reflected an ambitious Church bent on expanding its hegemony by means of an astute political strategy." Such a concatenation of law, politics and hegemonic power, is, of course, the everyday stuff of our popular discourse.

But it is not only in the popular press that such suspicious views of Law and Power are to be found. Without wishing to give undue credit to a single author, it would be hard to overstate the influence of R. I. Moore's 1987 monograph, *The Formation of a Persecuting Society: Power and Deviance in Western Europe: 950–1250*, on scholarly opinion about medieval ecclesiastical power and its hegemonic nature.[3] A careful and circumstantial restatement of Moore's views as applying precisely to the decrees of the Fourth Lateran Council is Richard Fraher's fine article entitled "IV Lateran's Revolution in Criminal Procedure: The Birth of *Inquisitio*, the End of Ordeals, and Innocent III's vision of Ecclesiastical Politics."[4] Fraher begins his study with the salutary suggestion that R.I. Moore's book might better have been titled: "The Formation of a Prosecuting Society," thus acknowledging the importance of law and legal procedure in this "revolution." But Fraher ends his study with a conclusion quite in keeping with R.I. Moore and the New Yorker. He writes:

1. *Decrees of the Ecumenical Councils*, ed. Norman P. Tanner, Giuseppe Alberigo, et al., 2 vols. (London: Sheed and Ward, 1990) 1.230 (c. 1).

2. "The Mail," *The New Yorker*, 1 June 2015.

3. R. I. Moore, *The Formation of a Persecuting Society: Power and Deviance in Western Europe: 950–1250* (Oxford: Blackwell, 1987).

4. Richard Fraher, "IV Lateran's Revolution in Criminal Procedure: The Birth of *Inquisitio*, the End of Ordeals, and Innocent III's Vision of Ecclesiastical Politics," in *Studia in Honorem Eminentissimi Cardinalis Alphonsi M. Stickler* (Rome: LAS, 1992), 97–111.

> Finally, and all pervasively, the decrees [of the Council] marked a programmatic assertion of the hierarchy's authority over the Church, at the expense of the laity and of local clerical autonomy.[5]

Some twenty-five years before the publication of Moore's "persecuting" (or "prosecuting") thesis, in 1961, the great Italian ecclesiastical historian Michele Maccarrone published an article in the Italian journal, *Divinitas*, entitled simply "Il IV Concilio Lateranense."[6] This little article of some thirty pages quickly was recognized as one of the best and, paradoxically, given its brevity, the most comprehensive studies of the Fourth Lateran Council published at that time. It is still today, page for page, one of the best introductions to the Council. Among Monsignor Maccarrone's many astute observations, perhaps the one that is most surprising is his insistence that the great work of Innocent III in the Council was that of using the law not as a tool of hegemonic and centralizing rule, but rather as a means of decentralization! Maccarone presents this paradox as follows:

> Canon law is extended by the Council to all fields of Church life; sectors and aspects of ecclesiastical structures which until then had been independent or isolated are now regulated and disciplined. Furthermore, this does not bring about an increase in centralization of the Roman Curia; this is a very important result of the Fourth Lateran Council which has not been sufficiently stressed, and merit for it is to be attributed to Innocent III. Indeed, although the cases of interventions and controls on the part of the Papacy and its organs multiply, the conciliar canons clearly manifest a tendency to limit those cases and to avoid abuses.... Without doubt, Innocent III in this manner.... followed a program of his own, which he had been following from the very beginning of his pontificate; its intent was to lighten the heavy and ever-growing weight of the Curia, seeking to develop instead some forms of decentralization of papal authority.[7]

5. Ibid., 111.
6. Michele Maccarrone, "Il IV Concilio Lateranense," *Divinitas* 5 (1961), 270–298.
7. Ibid., 293.

It is this paradox that I wish to explore in this paper. According to Maccarrone, the spread of papal law initiated at the Council resulted not in a loss of power on the peripheries, but rather in an empowerment of local clergy and laity alike. It is as if the cliché about "power corrupting" had been turned on its head. One can almost imagine Innocent III as the witty inventor of the counter proposal (often attributed to the old and wily Italian Christian Democrat, Giulio Andreotti, now deceased) that "Power corrupts... those who don't have it." As if aware of this proposition, Innocent and his Council went about the task of reform by empowering those who were without power and who therefore might be especially prone to various forms of corruption.

Pope Innocent announced the calling of a new general council in a series of letters that went out from the papal curia in April of 1213. The council was called for November of 1215, thus giving notice of more than two year's time for participants to prepare. The first set of letters went out to all archbishops and bishops, both East and West, requiring their attendance, and asking for suggestions, *propositi*, to be considered in anticipation of the Council. In an important innovation, Innocent also sent letters inviting representatives of the cathedral chapters and other collegiate churches to attend. A second set of letters went out at the same time to abbots and priors of the Cistercian and Premonstratension Orders (perhaps, in Innocent's view, the only true religious "orders" in the modern sense), as well as to the Crusading Orders of the Hospital of Jerusalem and of the Temple. Another series of letters went out to all the sovereigns of Europe, inviting them to send ambassadors, not to take part in the deliberations of the Council, but to be present and to be able to make their needs known to the pope, "for their own honor and advantage."[8] Finally, other secular powers, in particular the Italian cities, were invited to send representatives to the Council. The breadth of the invitation was unprecedented in conciliar (or any other) history.[9]

8. Ibid., 278

9. For a calendar of these letters, see Augustus Potthast, ed. *Regesta Pontificium Romanorum inde ab a. post Christum natum MCXCVIII ad a. MCCCIV* (Berlin: Rudolph de Decker, 1874), 1.407–412, nos. 4706–4727. For the Latin texts of the letters, see PL 216.817–832.

According to Maccarrone, Innocent imagined the Council as "a convocation of the Estates General of the Church." This is true, he insists, "not because Innocent conceived the Church as a religio-politico organism, like the so-called *Christianitas* (or *Christendom*) of which one speaks nowadays, but precisely because he considered the Council as the appropriate locus for restoring the Church in its function as an organized religious society (*società religiosa organizzata*)."[10] This vision of the Council as a solemn assembly of all of the "Estates" of the Church, both ecclesiastical and lay, convoked and orchestrated by the pope, was a fruitful one, rich in innovation, with something for everyone.

As vicar of Christ and acting head of the Church, Innocent III could think of himself as a law-giver on the model of a Roman Emperor, a new Justinian, and the decrees of the Council as "constitutions." Already in 1198 Innocent had used the word *constitutio* to designate a particular law that had universal validity.[11] Now at the Council he could exercise the power of an emperor in making new laws to meet new situations. The wording of many of the canons makes clear that Innocent was their author, in the sense that he, like Justinian, is the promulgating authority behind the canons. Throughout he uses the first-person plural to designate his own role: *credimus et confitemur, prohibemus, statuimus, sanccimus, diffinimus, confirmamus,* etc. In doing so, he was fulfilling, consciously or not, one of the rubrics of the so-called "Dictates of the Pope" from the registers of Gregory VII. The seventh Dictum proposes: "That the pope alone is able to make new laws according to the needs of the Church" (*Quod illi soli licet pro temporis necessitate novas leges condere*).[12] Maccarrone suggests that this claim should be read alongside the assertion in a Dictum of Gratian [denying that councils of bishops have the power to make laws (*non habent vim constituendi—sunt invalida ad constituendum*).[13] Taken together, we can see the emergence of something that can be called "new law" (the *ius novum*), in the modern sense promulgated by the pope as vicar of Christ, who had a kind of absolute power to make laws as necessary for the good of the Church.

10. Maccarrone, "Il IV Concilio Lateranense," 275–76.
11. Ibid., 283, n. 16 bis.
12. Ibid.
13. Ibid., citing *Decretum,* C.16 q.1 d.a.c.19.

The old law (*ius vetus*), by contrast, was not *ad hoc* and not promulgated by a ruling authority. Rather it was discovered in the spirit-led decisions of the authentic synods and in the writings of the Holy Fathers of old. If new situations arose, the old and good laws would be searched, creatively and professionally, to find apt or adaptable answers to the new questions.

The old law was characterized especially by its gravity (*gravitas*). The new law, at least the constitutions of Innocent III in the General Council, strike me rather with their playfulness. It is difficult, for example, to read the "scientific" justification for reducing to four the prohibited degrees in marriage (c. 50) without imagining Innocent with his tongue firmly in cheek: "The number four," he writes, "agrees well with the prohibition concerning bodily union... because there are four humors in the body, which is composed of the four elements."[14] Or what should be made of Innocent's "theological" justification of the new criminal procedure of inquisition by appealing to authorities in the Old and New Testaments. In Genesis God, in the guise of an inquisitor, says of Adam and Eve, "I will go down and see whether they have done as the outcry which has come to me suggests." And from the Gospels Innocent invokes the parable of the bad steward to whom the Lord, like the judge in an inquisition, says "What is this I hear about you?"[15] Then there is canon 41, in which Innocent seems to justify the novel requirement of good faith possession in claims of prescription by quoting the Apostle Paul, "Whatever does not proceed from faith is sin."[16]

Even more than their playfulness, I am struck by what I would call the "experimental" nature of many of the conciliar canons. A good deal of experimentation is permitted because, unlike the old law, these new laws are not written in stone, but rather are open to development and refinement both by the legislator himself and by the jurists whose task it is to formulate, interpret and apply them. Thus, as we shall see, canon 8, "On Inquisitions," did not begin at all as a canon aimed at ferreting out heretics, but rather as an experimental attempt to find a way for subjects safely to

14. *Decrees of the Ecumenical Councils*, 1.257 (c.50, On the Restriction of Prohibitions to Marriage).

15. Ibid., 1.237–38 (c.8). Fraher seems to overreach when he says, dismissively, that "Innocent claimed that the *inquisitio* was based on the parable of the unjust steward." Fraher, "IV Lateran's Revolution," 108.

16. *Decrees of the Ecumenical Councils*, 1.253 (c.41, On Good Faith in Prescription).

bring their offending superiors to account. So, too, canon 10, "On Appointing Preachers" in the dioceses to help bishops in this relatively new pastoral task, must have been an improbable suggestion at the time. Who could have predicted that the Dominican friars would emerge almost immediately as an Order of Preachers eager to fulfill the spirit (and the letter) of the Canon? The same can be said about many other canons. Who would have predicted that these pie-in-the-sky constitutions could realistically be instituted? Examples might include: the forbidding of new religious orders (canon 13), the expectation that physicians would call in a priest before treating a sick patient (canon 22), the mandating of annual provincial synods (canon 6), and of provincial chapters of monks to be held every three years (canon 12). Perhaps the most "experimental" of all the canons and the one seemingly least likely to succeed, was canon 21, "*Omnis utriusque sexus,*" on annual confessions to one's proper priest. The canon provided that everyone—women as well as men, teenage boys and girls and, peasants and servants of both sexes, as well as nobles, both clerical and lay—should be given the opportunity to appear before their parish priest once a year, and should be asked to search their consciences (after learning, of course, that they had consciences to search) and confess their sins of thought, word and deed to the priest. Such an innovation must have seemed almost unimaginable at the time. Equally unimaginable must have been the idea that simple parish priests might develop the skill, the resourcefulness, and the prudence (or jurisprudence) to hear such confessions and to assign an appropriate penance to each person in his parish. It is hard to know how long it took for this audacious experiment to bear fruit, but we know that, by the end of the Middle Ages it had done so. In the sixteenth century the Council of Trent could proclaim that "almost all Christians are convinced that everything holy and pious conserved in the Church at this time is to be attributed, in large part, to confession."[17]

So playfulness and experimentation mark the canons of the Lateran Council. I would add a third hallmark, namely a certain generosity of spirit, especially when it comes to distributing power among the various estates of the Church. This is not a self-abnegating generosity. There is no sense

17. See Joseph Goering, "The Internal Forum and the Literature of Penance and Confession," in *The History of Medieval Canon Law in the Classical Period, 1140–1234* (Washington DC: Catholic University of America Press, 2008), 379–428, at 427.

that the pope's power must decrease in order for others to increase. Rather one sees in the canons Pope Innocent using the fullness of his power in order to legislate on behalf of those who are lacking in power. Medieval power politics, it seems, is not a zero-sum game.

And this brings us back to our central theme, law and empowerment in the canons of the Council. Let me begin with canon 8, "On Inquisitions."[18] This canon is one of the most famous (or infamous) of the council's provisions. The new form of criminal procedure outlined in this canon would come to be universally associated with one particular type of inquisition, namely the "Inquisition concerning heretical depravity." As such it is seen as a black spot in the history of the medieval church, and as one of the things (along with crusades) that even popes have recently felt it necessary to apologize for. But it was not always so. Although the new inquisitorial procedures, invented and developed by Innocent III from the first years of his pontificate and promulgated at the Council, would come to be used in criminal investigations of heresy, the place of *inquisitio* in the conciliar canons themselves was primarily as a means of empowering subjects to be able to hold prelates and higher clergy accountable for their misdeeds. A reading of canon 8 leaves no doubt as to this primary intention.

The Canon begins with a long verbatim quotation from a letter of Innocent written in 1206,[19] which says, in part:

> From these authorities [of the Old and New Testament] it is clearly shown that not only when a subject has committed some excess but also when a prelate has done so, and the matter reaches the ears of the superior through an outcry or rumor which has come not from the malevolent and slanderous but from prudent and honest persons, and has come not only once but frequently... the superior ought diligently to seek out the truth... [and] the offender should be subjected to canonical punishment.

And a little further on:

18. *Decrees of the Ecumenical Councils*, 1.237–39.

19. Incorporated into the *Corpus Iuris Canonici* in book five of the *Liber Extra* of Gregory IX (1234) at X 5.1.17. See Emil Friedberg, ed., *Corpus iuris canonici*, (1879; repr. ed., Graz: 1955), 2.738–39.

> The holy fathers... wished to ensure that prelates are not accused unjustly, and yet that at the same time they take care not to sin in an arrogant manner.... Degradation [of a prelate] shall in no wise be allowed unless it is preceded by a charge in lawful form. But when someone is so notorious for his offences that an outcry goes up which can no longer be ignored without scandal or tolerated without danger, then without the slightest hesitation let action be taken to inquire into and punish his offences, not out of hate but rather out of charity.

This rehearsal of Innocent's letter is followed in the conciliar constitution by a series of safeguards protecting the rights of defendants, for example, that the defendant must be present in person; he must be informed of the charges against him; the names of the witnesses and their testimony must be made known to him, etc.[20] It was especially by ignoring such safeguards that the inquisitorial procedure became infamous later in the century in its use in the *inquisitio de haeretica pravitate*. In a manner familiar to us today in legislation like the so-called "Patriot Act" and in the Guantanamo incarcerations, fear of terrorism, as of heresy, is seen easily to lead to abuses of procedure and curtailment of legal protections.

Nevertheless, on its face, canon 8 of the Lateran Council is intended to facilitate the prosecution of powerful churchmen. As such, it serves to empower both laity and lower clergy who are under authority and are unable to call that authority to account for criminal behavior. It is famously difficult, and intentionally so in canon law, to bring charges against an ecclesiastical superior. Neither the accusatory procedure of Roman Law nor the denunciatory procedure of the canons provides much protection for the one accusing or denouncing a superior. But by introducing the notions of public infamy (*fama*) and of outcry (*clamor*) coming to the ear of the judge and taking the place of personal accusation and denunciation, it becomes possible to call to account even the most powerful and vindictive of local superiors. We may be skeptical about how effective this new tool was in actually calling superiors to account, but it would be a mistake to ignore the obvious thrust of the canon and the judicial empowerment of subordinates that it entails.

20. *Decrees of the Ecumenical Councils*, 1.238–39.

Other groups can also be identified who were newly empowered by the introduction of the procedure of *inquisitio*. Most obvious were judges, who now had the responsibility of evaluating the quantity and quality of *fama* and of *clamor* to determine whether there was just cause to carry out a judicial inquiry. Judges were increasingly supported in their work by a learned cadre of jurists, who had studied Roman law and Canon law in the schools. These *jurisperiti*, standing at arms length both from the legislator (the pope), on the one hand, and from the local powers, on the other, were newly empowered to interpret the law in the schools and to apply it in judging cases.

Another canon that deserves mention in this light is canon 38, "On Preserving Judicial Acts in Writing" (*De scribendis actis ut probari possint*).[21] At the same time as the canon on inquisitorial procedure increases the power and the autonomy of the judge, so the Council makes provision for protecting and empowering litigants against the abusive exercise of a judge's power. It does this in c. 38, not by restricting the judge's power, but rather by increasing the power of litigants and their ability to appeal improper judgments. The canon provides that a written record must be kept of all judicial proceedings. Copies are to be given to all parties in the case and the originals kept by the notary or scribe responsible for the written record. If a dispute should arise about the way in which the judge conducted the case, the truth can be established from the original documents. In this way, the canon affirms, "*aequitas* can triumph over *iniquitas*, and the innocent can be saved from harm done by imprudent or wicked judges."

Examples of such extension of power in the canons of the Council can easily be multiplied. Canons 47 and 48, for example, concern appeals of unjust excommunications and challenges of suspect judges. They carry forward the empowerment of litigants and defendants with respect to abusive judgments that we saw in canon 38, while at the same time protecting judges from frivolous or malicious appeals.

This extension of power from the center to the peripheries can be found at all levels of the ecclesiastical hierarchy. At the top, according to canon 5 ("On the Dignity of Patriarchs"), is the Roman Church, the *mater et magistra* of all Christ's faithful, which has a "primacy of ordinary

21. Ibid., 1.252 (c.38).

power" (*ordinarie potestatis principatum*) over all other Churches.[22] Having set forth his own authority in the hierarchy, Innocent then is able to take the unusual step of recognizing and renewing the privileges of the other ancient Patriarchal Sees. First after the Roman Church is the Church of Constantinople, followed by the Churches of Alexandria, Antioch, and Jerusalem. The heads of these churches, once they have received the pallium from the Roman pontiff and promised fidelity and obedience to him, enjoy "the fullness of the pontifical office" (*plenititudo officii pontificalis*) in their respective domains. This explicit recognition of the privileges of the Eastern patriarchs may seem to us a gratuitous and empty gesture, but it is paradigmatic of Innocent's hopeful approach to even the most intractable problems. Innocent is here offering his support, his *subsidium*, to the Eastern patriarchs in the best way he is able. By linking this canon with canon 4, On the abuses of the Greeks against the Latins, and with canon 9, On diverse rites within the same faith, it is easy to see how Innocent might welcome renewed and empowered patriarchs in the East who would make it their business to address locally these pressing issues.

At the other extreme of the ecclesiastical hierarchy, monks and nuns, for example, receive special attention from the Council. One of the most ambitious and innovative provisions was canon 12, "On General Chapters of Monks."[23] Innocent himself stressed the experimental nature of this canon, referring to it repeatedly as a "novelty" (*novitas*). Although it would take more than a century before any of its provisions would be widely enacted, the canon is a rich evocation of the many ways that power could be fostered and distributed. It begins with a call for a general chapter of the abbots and priors of every kingdom or province to be held every three years, on the model of the Cistercian Order. At the chapter, inquisitors (*visitors*) should be appointed who, in the name of the pope(!) (*vice nostra*) are to visit every abbey of monks and of nuns in the kingdom or province, correcting abuses there. Diocesan bishops, too, have a role to play. They are given the clear authority to reform the monasteries under their diocesan jurisdiction, but taking care not to "weigh down the monasteries with any unjust burdens."

22. Ibid., 1.236 (c.5, On the Dignity of Patriarchs).
23. Ibid., 1.240–41 (c.12, On General Chapters of Monks).

Of all the beneficiaries of power distributed by the Fourth Lateran Council, perhaps the parish priest should head the list. A good example is Canon 66, on the avarice of clerics, which is a model of canonical reasoning.[24] The Holy see has learned from frequent reports that some clerics demand payments for celebrating funeral rites, for blessing marriages, and the like, and if they don't receive such payments, they refuse the sacraments on fictitious grounds. Such "wicked exactions," Innocent declares, are strictly forbidden by the Council. On the other hand, he notes that some lay people, stirred up by heretical depravity, have attempted to infringe on a praiseworthy custom introduced by the pious devotion of the faithful. This praiseworthy custom is not further specified in the canon, but it is surely the custom of making a free offering to the priest for providing marital and burial services. The canon wisely provides that the church's sacraments are to be given freely, but also that the bishop of the place should restrain anyone who maliciously seeks to deny the priest the fruits of a praiseworthy custom.

More straightforward empowerment of the parish priest can be found, for example, in canon 51, prohibiting clandestine marriages.[25] This canon makes clear that the parish priest is to be the primary administrator of marriage discipline in the local community. He is to announce publicly the marriage banns in the parish, and to investigate whether there are any legal impediments. The specialized canonical knowledge required of the priest and the authority granted to him to enforce the new marital discipline goes a long way toward establishing the parish priest as a powerful presence in the local community.

Even more transformative in this regard, was canon 21, *Omnis utriusque sexus*. It placed the primary responsibility for the Church's new penitential discipline squarely in the hands of the local priest. By insisting on annual confession to one's "proper" priest, and annual communion in his church, the Council enhanced the power and the stability of the parish community, and the authority of its pastor.

This same canon 21 was also transformative for the power of the laity. The requirement that everyone confess to his or her proper priest at least

24. Ibid., 1.265 (c.66, On Simony with Regard to the Avarice of Clerics).

25. Ibid., 1.258 (c.51, On the Punishment of Those Who Contract Clandestine Marriages).

once a year meant that many people (including women, children, peasants and other *miserabiles personae*) now had the right to have confession and communion made available to them individually, and thus to take an active part in the religious life of the community. This empowerment of the laity in the so-called "court of penance" or of "conscience" (*forum penitentiae* or *conscientiae*) had another consequence deserving of note. By confessing their sins in this judicial forum, lay people, even those who had never been to school, were able to gain a sometimes-sophisticated knowledge of the law and of canonical jurisprudence as it related to practical cases of conscience, especially their own.[26]

Examples of the empowerment of laity, and of the other estates of the church as well, could easily be multiplied. But I will end here with what may be the most unusual and least expected canon of the Council, canon 42, "On the Rights of the Laity." In this canon Innocent defends the rights of the laity against encroachments by the clergy. Innocent may be the first (and the last) pope to issue such a decree. The canon reads in full:

> Just as we desire lay people not to usurp the rights of clerics, so we ought to wish clerics not to lay claim to the rights of the laity. We therefore forbid every cleric henceforth to extend his jurisdiction, under pretext of ecclesiastical freedom, to the prejudice of secular justice. Rather let him be satisfied with the written constitutions and customs hitherto approved, so that the things of Caesar may be rendered unto Caesar, and the things of God may be rendered unto God by a right distribution.

Not surprisingly, perhaps, this is the only canon of the Council not included by Johannes Teutonicus in his *Compilatio quarta*, and one of only two canons not included by Raymond of Peñafort in Gregory IX's authoritative collection of the laws of the Church, the *Liber Extra* of 1234.[27]

What are we to make of this canon? If it is a canon of the Council but excluded from the *Liber Extra* is it still the law of the Church? Is it playful?

26. See Goering, "The Internal Forum."

27. The other canon of the Fourth Lateran Council omitted from the *Liber Extra* is c.49, *Sub interminatione*, on the punishment for excommunicating someone unjustly and then expecting a money payment for absolving the excommunicate.

Or is it *ad experimentum*? Is it an empowerment of the laity? Or of the clergy? Or both? Or is it perhaps a sign of Innocent's own particular generosity of spirit? It could, of course, be all of these things. But, in this anniversary year of two great legal documents, it is worth considering whether canon 42 of the Fourth Lateran Council might have something to do with Magna Carta, the "Great Charter" of England. We know that already in July of 1215, just a month after its signing, Pope Innocent III had condemned the charter as a diminution of the rights and powers of the English King. Innocent described the Charter as being: "not only vile and unseemly, but also illicit and iniquitous, a great diminishment and derogation of the king's rights, and of his honor, extorted from him by force and fear such as would move even a most constant man."[28]

Is this perhaps a context in which canon 42 of the Lateran Council, held later in the same year, might make sense? Might Pope Innocent here be protecting the rights of the secular power (the king), against encroachments of the English Church, as well as of the barons? This is not the time or place to try to answer these questions. But I trust that this is enough at least to suggest that a more generous view of power, and of law as its distributive mechanism, is called for if we are fully to appreciate the spirit and the letter of the Fourth Lateran Council.

28. *[N]on solum vilem et turpem, verum etiam illicitam et iniquam, in nimiam diminutionem et derogationem sui iuris pariter et honoris,"* and extorted from the king *"per vim et metum qui cadere poterat in virum etiam constantissimum." Selected Letters of Pope Innocent III Concerning England (1198–1216)*, ed. C. R. Cheney and W. H. Semple (London: Thomas Nelson and Sons, 1953), 212; cf. ibid., 15 n. 4; and *Councils & Synods, with Other Documents Relating to the English Church,* AD *1205–1313*, ed. F. M. Powicke and C. R. Cheney, 2 vols. (Oxford: Clarendon Press, 1964), 1.43.

Bertrandus and Guido de Baysio: Commenting on the *Decretum Gratiani* between 1234 and 1300

Peter Landau

Among the many studies Charles Donahue wrote in the field of medieval canon law, we find two essays dealing with canonists who wrote during the second half of the twelfth century. The first is concerned with Gerard Pucelle, the canon lawyer who taught for some time in Cologne. The other contribution is devoted to the Bolognese canonist Bazianus, identified by Annalisa Belloni with the civilian Johannes Bassianus; here Donahue is comparing the doctrines of both jurists in marriage law with the result that it is unlikely, though not impossible, that Bassianus would be the same person as the canonist Bazianus.[1] For Donahue, Bassianus "had a sharp legal mind," whereas Bazianus was only "second rate by comparison." My own contribution to Charles's *Festschrift* will compare two canonists of the thirteenth century: Betrandus during the pontificate of Gregory IX, and Guido de Baysio in the time of Boniface VIII.

The latest comprehensive commentary on the text of the *Decretum Gratiani* is certainly the "Rosarium" written by the Bolognese canonist Guido de Baysio during the final years of the thirteenth century and

1. Charles Donahue, "Gerard Pucelle as a Canon Lawyer: Life and the Battle Abbey Case," in *Grundlagen des Rechts. Festschrift für Peter Landau zum 65. Geburtstag* ed. Richard H. Helmholz et al. (Paderborn: Ferdinand Schöningh, 2000), 333–348; idem, "Bassianus, that is to say Bazianus? Johannes Bassianus on Marriage," in *Panta rei. Studi dedicati a Manlio Bellomo II*, ed. Orazio Condorelli (Rome: Il Cigno Edizioni, 2004), 179–203.

completed in 1300.[2] Guido became Archdeacon of Bologna in 1296 and then left the city in 1305 for Avignon, having been appointed Auditor of the Audientia litterarum contradictarum in 1304, where he died nine years later, in 1313.[3] The main work of this famous canonist was his "Rosarium" intended as a supplement to the *Glossa ordinaria* and collecting many texts from earlier canonists not taken into consideration by the ordinary gloss.[4] Among the authors quoted by Guido we find the names Huguccio,[5] Laurentius Hispanus,[6] and Vincentius Hispanus.[7] But we also have texts in the "Rosarium" that refer to glosses by a canonist called Bertrandus, who must have taught in Bologna shortly after 1234.[8] Bertrandus is mentioned by Johannes Andreae around 1348 in his *Additiones* to the *Speculum* of Duranti among the important canonists.[9] Kuttner discovered those glosses in a Berlin manuscript, where they are usually quoted with the logogram "Bert" or "Bt."[10] In the last few years I transcribed these glosses in Berlin with financial support from the Bavarian Academy of Sciences. I published a first report on these glosses in the *Liber Amicorum* for E. C. Coppens in 2012.[11] I offer here a survey of the influence of Bertrandus on Guido de Baysio.

2. For the Rosarium cf. Johann Friedrich v. Schulte, *Die Geschichte der Quellen und Literatur des canonischen Rechts II* (Stuttgart, 1877; repr. Graz: Ak. Druck- und Verlagsanstalt, 1956) 187.

3. For the biography of Guido de Baysio see Filippo Liotta, "Appunti per una biographia del canonista Guido da Baysio, archidiacono di Bologna," *Studi Senesi* 76 (1964) 7–52.

4. For the quotations of Huguccio by Guido cf. Schulte (n.2) 188.

5. P. Antonio García García, OFM, *Laurentius Hispanus*, Cuadernos del Instituto Juridico Espanol 6 (Roma-Madrid, 1956), 47, n. 121.

6. Javier Ochoa Sanz, CMF, *Vincentius Hispanus*, Cuadernos del Instituto Juridico Espanol 13 (Roma-Madrid, 1960), 118, n. 21.

7. For Betrandus and his glosses cf. Peter Landau, "Bertrandus, ein vergessener Kanonist des 13. Jahrhunderts," in *Recto Ordine procedit Magister. Liber amicorum E. C. Coppens* ed. Louis Berkvens et al. (Brussels, 2012), 175–179.

8. Cf. Johannes Andreae, "Additio ad Speculum Guil. Durantis," in Schulte, *Geschichte I*, n. 3 (Stuttgart, 1875; repr. Graz, 1956), 241 and 242 between Rodoycus and Guilelmus Naso.

9. For the glosses by Bertrandus in MS Berlin Staatsbibl. lat. fol. 2 cf. Stephan Kuttner, *Repertorium der Kanonistik* (1140–1234) *Studi e Testi* 31 (Citta del Vaticano: Biblioteca Apostolica Vaticana, 1937), 100 s.

10. See n. 10.

11. See n. 8.

While studying the Berlin manuscript I found nearly 300 glosses by Bertrandus. A remarkable number among them were included in Guido's "Rosarium."

I offer here a few examples:

1. MS Berlin ad D.28, c.11 v. "castitate" (fol. 30ra): "B id est propter castitatem servandam, sc. ut caste vivat. Ei intellige que in ordinationem viri vovet expresse vel tacet, in orientali est statutum, propter reverentiam ordinum, unde presumitur."

Guido ad D.28, c.11 v. "castitate" (fol. 37vb): "id est propter castitatem servandam, sc. ut caste vivant. Et intelligitur secundum hoc de illa, que in ordinatione viri vovet vel tacet, unde presumitur vovere."

An explicit or silent vow of chastity is taken by a man's wife at the time of his ordination.

2. MS Berlin ad D.37 Dict. p.c. 7 § 2, v. "sive aurum" (fol. 36va): "Bertr. Nam per aurum sapientia, per argentum eloquentia intelligitur, ut hic habes. Unde quidam peritus vir elegit eloquentiam, ut ff. l. II, § Furt. Alias aurum designat caritatem ut De pe. D. II Principium (D.2 c.45 de pen.). Alias viros caritate et virtutibus parat, De pe. Di. I, § Non aliter."

Guido ad D.37 d.p.c. 7 (fol. 48ra): "Aurum sapientie. Sic etiam sumitur aurum pro sapientia, De pe. Di. II, Principium. Verum aurum ibi etiam sumitur pro charitate. Alibi viros claritate fulgentes..."

Gold means wisdom or charity.

3. Ad D.45 c.4 v. "Licet plerumque" (fol. 40va): "Bertr. iudicasset. Id est condempnasset. Et est ar. quod non semper est statim fulminandum in aliquo, ar. D.L XXXII, c. ult."

Guido ad D.45 c.4, v. "iudicasset" (fol. 56ra): "id est condemnasset. Et est ar. quod non statim est fulminandum in aliquem, ar. XCIII Di. c. ul. (D.94, c.3?)."

Judging someone means condemning them. It should not be like lightning.

4. Ad D.46 c.6 v. Clericum scurrilem (fol. 42rb): "Bt. Clericum scurrilem. Scurrilia verba assidue proferentem."

Guido ad D.46 c.6 (fol. 58va): "Clericum scurrilem, id est scurrilia verba proferentem assidue."

A scurrilous cleric is always making ludicrous statements.

5. Ad D.50 c.5 (fol. 44vb): "Bert. Occiderit. Subaudi in bello et sponte. Preter necessitatem. Si enim aliquem interficeret, non promoveretur ad maius, ut infra De hiis clericis (D.50 c.6), ubi plene distinguitur de homicidio."

Guido ad D.50, c.5 (fol. 62rb): "Clericum occiderit. Sponte Ber."

Homicide means spontaneous killing.

6. Ad D.50 c.37 (fol. 47va): "Bertr. Clerico. Iste clericus dedit operam rei licite etiam expellendo porcos de agro suo, tunc intellige quod initiis diligenter hec fecerit, ar. in nullo puniretur, ut supra XI Di. c. De hiis (D.50 c.34) et Extra de homicidio, Johannes quidam (X 5.12.23)."

Guido ad D.50, c.37 v. "Clerico" (fol. 67ra): "In I. gl. ibi, licite adde sub quod non faciebat secundum Ber. Ut no. extra de homicidio."

Expelling pigs from your field is allowed and should not be punished.

7. Ad D.61 c.15 (fol. 54rb): "Bt. Providere. Supple non per electionem, sed per deliberationem, quia prima non cassata non debet fieri electio secunda, ut Extra de electione, Consideravimus (X 1.6.10)."

Guido ad D.61 c.15 (fol. 79ra): "Studii providere. Sub. Non per electionem, sed per deliberationem, quia prima electione non cassata, non debet secunda electio celebrari, extra de electione. Consideravimus. Ber. hodie dicit."

If a first election is not invalidated, a second election should not take place, but rather a close examination.

8. Ad D. 62 c.1 (fol. 54vb): "Bt. Habeantur. Id est remaneant quantum ad dignitatem vel executionem, sed ordinem episcopalem amittere non possunt, ut I, q.I, Quod quidam (C.1, q.1, c.97)."

Guido ad D.62 c.1 (fol. 79va): "Habeantur. Id est remaneant quantum ad dignitatem et officii executionem, sed ordinem episcopalem amittere non possunt, I, q. I, Quod quidam. B."

Bishops can lose their dignity and executive power, but not their episcopal *ordo*.

9. Ad D.63 c.3 (fol. 55ra): "Bt. Ad hesperias. Id est pralitas. Hesperia dicta est pralia ab Hesperio rege, qui ibi regnavit."

Guido ad D.63 c.3 (fol. 80rb): Hesperias id est Italicas. Hesperia dicta est ab Hespero rege, qui ibi regnavit. B."

Here Bertrandus explains that the word Hesperia refers to King Hesperus.

10. Ad. D.63 c.9 (fol. 55va): "Bt. Voluntate. Quia patronus erat illius ecclesie, et propter hoc allegatur c. et ideo interesse debet electioni."

Guido ad D.63 c.9 (fol. 80vb): "Voluntate. Quia patronus erat illius ecclesie, et ideo debebit interesse electioni, aut absens consentire, et propter hoc allegatur c."

The patron of a church should participate in church elections.

11. Ad C.11 q.1 c.15 (fol. 129va): "Bt. Experientie, Istud capitulum loquitur de causis civilibus, nam coram seculari clericus non potest agere

> criminaliter contra laicum. Sed civiliter potest sive de crimine siue de alia re."
>
> Guido ad C.11 q.1 c.15, v. Experientie (fol. 203va): "Nam hoc c. loquitur de civilibus causis. Nam coram seculari iudice clericus non potest agere criminaliter contra laicum, sed civiliter potest siue de crimine siue de alia re."

A cleric can bring an action in civil cases before a secular judge, but not in a criminal case.

> 12. Ad C.11 q.1 c.39 (fol. 331ra): "Bt. Facias. Exactionem vocat. Rome enim est generale forum, et ex eo ad legatum eius sicut ad papam omnes clerici possunt deferre causas, tam per querimoniam quam per appellationem."
>
> Guido ad C.11 q.1 c.39 (fol. 206ra): "Facias. Coactionem notat. Romana ecclesia est generale et commune forum omnium. Et ideo ad legatum eius sicut ad papam omnes clerici possunt suas causas deferre tam per querimoniam quam per appellationem omisso quolibet medio iudice."

The Roman church is the general court for everyone. This means that each cleric can bring his legal affairs by complaint or by appeal to the pope or his legate without having to first consult any intermediate judge.

These twelve examples may be sufficient to prove that Guido de Baysio knew and used the glosses of Bertrandus for his "Rosarium." Bertrandus and his work must therefore have been well known in Bologna around 1300. An edition of the glosses in the Berlin manuscript would certainly increase our knowledge about the development of canon law between 1234 and 1300. The history of canon law between Gregory IX and Boniface VIII should take into account the accomplishments of rather unknown contemporary canonists as well as the achievements of papal legislation.

The article deals with a canonist in Bologna during the thirteenth century, who wrote numerous glosses to the *Decretum Gratiani* after 1234. Some of them were taken over by Guido de Baysio in his "Rosarium" around 1300. The author of the glosses had the name Bertrandus and was almost forgotten in modern scholarship on the history of canon law, until he was rediscovered by Stephan Kuttner. Research on canon law after 1234 has recently concentrated on the practice of the courts and brought many results, especially by Charles Donahue. But we need also to know much more about the development of literature in canon law during that period, a neglected field of research until now.

The Secular Consequences of Annulment of Marriage for Precontract in England c. 1300

Paul Brand

Much of Charlie Donahue's work has been concerned with the medieval canon law and its courts and in particular with the exercise of the jurisdiction of those courts over matrimonial causes. He has also had a long-standing interest in the growth and development of the English common law in the middle ages and in the early history of law reporting. The following paper explores a particular area where canon law and common law courts and jurisdiction overlapped in England in the years around 1300: a small group of common law cases for which we have enrolled records and some law reports that deal with the secular consequences of annulments for precontract which had been made in the canon law courts.

In the first of these cases, the story begins in 1286 when Alan Waldeshef married Avelina atte Cruche.[1] Avelina was the daughter and the eventual heiress of Geoffrey *de Cruce* or de la Croyz, lord of a manor in Walton on Thames in Surrey and of lands in Oxfordshire and Herefordshire, and she had probably been born in the early or mid-1240s.[2] Avelina

1. The judgment annulling the marriage (below, n. 14) makes it clear that this was a "clandestine" marriage, without any prior calling of the banns and probably without any marriage at the church door.

2. *The 1235 Surrey Eyre*, vol. I, ed. C. A. F. Meekings and David Crook, Surrey Record Society 31 (Guildford, 1979), 177–8. A local jury in Essex in 1278 found that she was aged 40 or more, but a different jury in Oxfordshire at around the same time found that she was aged 30 or more: *Cal. Inq. Post Mortem*, ii, no. 248 (and C 133/18, no. 11). Atte Cruche is an English version of *de Cruce*.

had previously been married to Roger *de la Legh* and had a son named John by him.[3] Roger had died some time after June 1281.[4] We know nothing of Roger's own land holdings or of the land Avelina will have held as dower after his death. We do know that her father Geoffrey had died in 1260; that his son and heir Nicholas was dead by 1269; that within ten years Geoffrey's grandson Nicholas was also dead; and that by 1279 Avelina had then succeeded to her father Geoffrey's inheritance.[5] We also know that two further manors were inherited by Avelina shortly before her first husband's death, the Essex manor of Shelley by Ongar and the Oxfordshire manor of Lashbrook, in Shiplake. Avelina inherited these manors from a more distant female relative, Joan de Saunford, the widow of Waleran de Mounceaus, who had died without issue shortly before the end of March 1278. Joan and Avelina shared a great-grandfather, Oger fitzOger.[6] These manors had been Oger fizOger's wife Amy's share of the inheritance of her father, Michael of Shelley. The other coheiress was her younger sister Sara, who had been married to Oger's brother, Michael fitzOger, and who obtained other lands belonging to her father's inheritance as her share.[7] Lashbrook was valued at £10 a year in 1278 and was held of Robert de Vere, earl of Oxford, for one knight's fee; Shelley was valued at £15 a year and was held of the earl of Hereford for one knight's fee. The Oxfordshire inquisition *post mortem* on the death of Joan made Avelina Joan's sole heiress for Lashbrook, but the

3. See the jury verdict in KB 27/173, m. 6d. The son is the John son of Roger de la Leye who is mentioned as the first of those who accompanied Avelina in entering the manor of Shelley in the 1303 assize and who was described as her son and heir in the inquisition post mortem after her death (below, n. 26).

4. When Avelina had been referred to as his wife: *Cal. Fine Rolls, 1272–1307,* 149.

5. *The 1235 Surrey Eyre*, I.188.

6. *Cal. Inq. Post Mortem,* ii, no. 248 (and TNA: PRO, C 133/18, no. 11). Oger fitzOger was one of the royal justices of the reign of Richard I. Joan was Oger's great granddaughter and heir through his son Peter and Peter's daughter and Joan's mother, Amy. Avelina was Oger's great grand daughter through his daughter Mirabel and her son Geoffrey.

7. An initial final concord made in 1182 between the brothers and their wives for the division of the inheritance shows how heavily indebted the inheritance had been: *Feet of Fines, Essex,* vol I, 1. This was revised in a second final concord made in 1198 after Oger's death: ibid., 18.

Essex inquisition mentioned a coheir for Shelley.[8] That coheir seems soon to have dropped out of the picture.[9] Less is known about Alan Waldeshef. Alan had become a knight by May 1281 when he is so named as a witness to a charter of the king's brother, Edmund of Lancaster. This charter suggests that he may already by then have entered Edmund's service.[10] An existing connection with Edmund would also help to explain why, shortly in advance of the marriage, Avelina granted the manors of Shelley and Lashbrook by charter to Edmund and handed over physical possession of the manors to Edmund's agents. They retained possession of the manors for forty days before Edmund resettled them (probably again by charter) on Alan and Avelina and the heirs of their bodies with a remainder over to her

8. The 1278 inquisition (above, n. 6) calls him sir William de Clovile knight, but the 1281 mandate to hand over the lands to the coheirs once they have performed fealty calls him William de Knoville: *Cal. Fine Rolls, 1272–1307*, 149. The inquisition suggests he is the descendant of a sister of Mirabel, the daughter of Oger fitzOger. The 1281 mandate mentions land in Cornwall belonging to the same inheritance. An inquisition held in 1279 found that Joan a year before her death had enfeoffed Robert de St Melano of the manor of Trenant in Cornwall: *Cal. Inq. Post Mortem*, ii, no. 327. This manor is also mentioned in an agreement made between William de Clovill and queen Eleanor of May 1280 in which he promised that, if he established his entitlement to a share in Joan's lands at Trenant, Lashbrook and Shelley, he would transfer it to the queen in return for a payment of up to 250 marks, reserving to himself Joan's lands in Suffolk: *Cal. Close Rolls, 1279–88*, 53. This agreement seems not to have been effective.

9. In 1288, soon after Avelina and Alan were married, they made a final concord with John of Bakewell and his wife Cecily on the manor of Shelley under which John and Cecily quitclaimed all right to this manor for a nominal consideration: *Essex Feet of Fines*, ii.63. There seems to be no obvious connexion, however, between Cecily and the William de Clovile/Clovill/Knoville mentioned in the 1278 inquisition, 1280 agreement and 1281 mandate (above, n. 8) and no trace of Queen Eleanor transferring her claims (above, n. 8) to her.

10. *Cal. Pat. Rolls, 1272–81*, p. 436 (as "Alan de Waldesepf knight"). Alan was later given a one year protection when going overseas with Edmund of Lancaster on the king's service in April 1292 (*Cal. Pat. Rolls, 1281–92*, 486) and appointed an attorney for a year when going abroad with Edmund in May 1293 (*Cal. Pat. Rolls, 1292–1301*, 9). Edmund's son Thomas granted Alan lands at Donington and Goulsby in Lincolnshire not long before September 1300: *Cal. Close Rolls, 1296–1302*, 365. Alan may also be the Alan de Waldechef, then married to a coheiress named Lucy, who is named as a vouchee to warranty for land at Alsop in the 1281 Derbyshire eyre: *The Rolls of the 1281 Derbyshire Eyre*, ed. Aileen M. Hopkinson, Derbyshire Record Society 27 (Chesterfield, 2000), nos. 169, 366.

right heirs.[11] Perhaps a little after this, in Trinity term 1286, a final concord was made in the Common Bench at Westminster between Alan and his wife Avelina and Edmund on the two manors, recording the resettlement in the same terms.[12] The net effect of the resettlement was to ensure that Alan would retain a life interest in the manors if he survived Avelina, even if they did not have any children (if the manors had not been resettled, Alan would only have had a life interest as a tenant in curtesy if a live child had been born to the marriage) and that any children Alan and Avelina might have would succeed to the manors after the death of their parents rather than Avelina's son John by her first marriage, who would take only if there were no children or those children died without issue.

Alan and Avelina remained in joint possession of these two manors as a married couple (which probably means that Alan was in effective control of them) for a little over ten years. There were evidently no children of the marriage,[13] perhaps because even at the time of their marriage Avelina was close to being beyond the age for childbearing. After ten years of marriage, Avelina sued for an annulment of her marriage to Alan before Robert of Winchelsea, archbishop of Canterbury, apparently in his court of audience, on the grounds that she had previously made a binding contract of marriage by words of mutual consent followed by intercourse (*carnali copula subsecuta*) with John *de Pouns* and that her marriage to Alan had only been a "clandestine" one, without any banns being called. She succeeded in obtaining an annulment (*divorcium*). The sentence also included an order for the restitution of all her "movable and immovable goods" (*bona mobilia et immobilia*). Winchelsea's register contains a copy of the judgment annulling the marriage pronounced by master Hugh of Mowsley in the church of Chartham three miles outside Canterbury on 2 May 1297.[14] John *de Pouns*

11. There is a detailed account of the process of granting Shelley to Edmund and his agent taking and retaining possession and then resettling the manor in the two assizes of novel disseisin discussed below. There is no similar account relating to Lashbrook but the sequel suggests a similar sequence of events took place there as well.

12. *Essex Feet of Fines*, ii.57.

13. This is specifically stated by the assize jury in answer to a question put to it by the assize justices in the first assize of novel disseisin of 1297 (see below).

14. *Registrum Roberti Winchelsey*, vol. I, ed. Rose Graham, Canterbury and York Society 51 (Oxford, 1952), 163–5. Avelina's suit was brought under the name of her first husband as "Avelina de la Legh". A related mandate for publication went to the archdea-

is called John *de Ponte* by an assize jury in 1303. If that is his name then it seems possible that he is to be identified with the John *de Ponte* who was a canon of the prebend of Wellington in Hereford cathedral from 1294 or earlier until his death in 1303.[15] It seems rather more likely, however, that he is the John of Bridgwater (alias *de Ponte*) who had been in the service of the future Edward I before he became king, who then served queen Eleanor as her bailiff in Somerset, as her constable of Leeds castle in Kent and became her under-steward just before her death, before moving to Ireland to take up a legal career as king's serjeant there (from 1292 to 1300) and as a justice in eyre and of the Dublin Bench between 1301 and 1306, though none of the references to this man specifically identify him as a clerk.[16] There are also a small number of references in the 1280s to a John *de Ponte*, king's clerk, as being given custody of the "manor" of Leominster, a cell of Reading abbey, for four years (in 1285);[17] being appointed to the custody of the lands which Maud widow of Robert Walerand had held in dower and as joint feoffee (in 1288);[18] and being given a safe conduct in taking cloth and other necessities to Gascony for the use of the chancellor, Robert Burnel (also in 1288).[19] This might be either of the previous two men or a third man of the same name. The fact that the annulment, despite its assertion that John was at the time it was given still living, does not seem to have led to a (third) marriage with him may point to the "Irish" John as the most likely candidate since, if he was in Ireland, he was effectively out of reach of the English ecclesiastical courts.

---

cons of London (and rural dean of Ongar) and Oxford (and rural dean of Henley) whose jurisdiction covered the manors of Shelley and Lashbrook. Publication was also ordered by the rural dean of Guildford (in Winchester) evidently because of Avelina's tenure of the manor in Walton on Thames within that deanery, and that of Elham (in Canterbury) for reasons that are not clear.

15. *Cal. Pat. Rolls, 1292–1301*, 91; *Reg. Ricardi de Swinfield*, ed. W. W. Capes, Canterbury and York Soc. 6 (Hereford, 1909), 337–8, 534; TNA: PRO, CP 40/130, m. 222d, /133, m. 43.

16. Paul Brand, *The Making of the Common Law* (London: Hambledon Press,1992), 34–5, 41, 47–8.

17. *Cal. Pat. Rolls, 1281–92*, p. 197. A "John de Ponte" (not identified as "clerk") had been given the custody of the English lands of the abbey of Fecamp during a vacancy in 1284–5 (*Cal. Pat. Rolls, 1281–92*, 135, 149).

18. *Cal. Pat. Rolls, 1281–92*, 301.

19. *Cal. Pat. Rolls, 1281–92*, 302.

Once the annulment was finalized Avelina took control of the manor of Shelley.[20] She retained control for three months,[21] and then granted Shelley to master James de Mohun to hold for his lifetime.[22] Not long afterwards Alan Waldeshef brought his first assize of novel disseisin for the manor against his former wife Avelina, her grantee master James, and twenty three other defendants before the regular Essex assize justices, Robert of Retford and Henry Spigurnel, at their session at Stratford at the end of June 1297. Master James vouched her to warranty and she warranted. Avelina claimed to be in by succession from Joan de Saunford, not disseisin. The assize verdict recounted the facts of the resettlement and the eventual annulment of the marriage and Avelina's seizure of control of the manor. The justices asked a number of supplementary questions (including one on the reason for the annulment), but the assize justices, perhaps sensing this was a difficult case, adjourned the case to the Common Bench at Westminster for the octaves of Michaelmas. In Hilary term 1298 only Alan and master James appeared in court. James objected that Alan was under major excommunication and so was not entitled to be answered. Alan's attorney said that Alan belonged to the king's household and the king was privileged in respect of the members of his household, but his excommunication meant that the case was effectively suspended until Hilary term 1302. We are not told why he had been excommunicated. It may conceivably

20. The first assize of 1297 speaks of Avelina sending men to the manor; the second of 1303 of her entering the manor with a group of named men including John son of Roger de Leye, her son by her first husband. They removed the existing reeve and bailiff and appointed replacements. She does not seem to have taken control of Lashbrook at the same time. In Michaelmas term 1297 the serjeant and future royal justice William Inge was suing Alan Waldeshef in an action of covenant relating to the manor of Lashbrook, commonly a preliminary to the levying of a final concord (TNA: PRO, CP 40/121, m. 260). If Inge was already in possession of Lashbrook that would explain why Avelina was bringing suit against him as well as her ex-husband and the named rector of Shelley before archbishop Winchelsea's commissioners in May 1298 (*Register... Winchelsey*, I.256) and why in Easter term 1299 Inge was suing an action of prohibition against master Robert de Ros (the archbishop's chancellor) and against Avelina for holding and suing pleas in court christian on his lay chattels: TNA: PRO CP 40/127, m. 143.

21. This is the period of time indicated only by the second assize of 1303.

22. Master James was the rector of the church of Shepperton in Middlesex at this time, just across the river from Avelina's manor in Walton on Thames: A.B. Emden: *A Biographical Register of the University of Oxford to A.D. 1500* (Oxford, 1958), vol. II, p. 000.

have been because he was impeding the restitution of Avelina's property as required under the original sentence. Alan was then able to show he had been absolved from the excommunication by John, bishop of Winchester, acting as a papal judge delegate. Writs were issued for the appearance of the defendants in the following Easter term.[23] Alan was then non-suited for reasons that are not clear but perhaps because his ex-wife had died.[24] Certainly when he renewed his suit through a second assize of novel disseisin for the same dispossession of the manor of Shelley at a hearing before the same two Essex assize justices at Chelmsford in mid-January 1303, she was no longer on the list of defendants, but her son John son of Roger de Leye had taken her place at the head of a shorter list. Both pleading and assize verdict were similar, but not identical, to those in 1297. This time judgment on the assize was adjourned to subsequent sessions of the assize justices and the assize then removed not into the Common Bench but into the court of King's Bench, for Trinity term 1303.[25] The justices of King's Bench seem to have been quick in making up their minds.[26] They showed no doubt that the 1286 resettlement had been valid.[27] They deduced that the resettlement had entitled Alan to at least half of the manor after the annulment and that Avelina and John by taking sole control of the whole of the manor had disseised Alan unjustly of "his" half and they awarded him possession of that half plus damages back to the time of the disseisin. That was not all. The court pronounced that "according to the custom of the realm" (*juxta consuetudinem regni*) in certain cases of annulment judgments ought to follow the cause (*in quibusdam casibus divorcii judicia causam sequi debent*) and so judgment was to be respited on the other half of the

23. TNA: PRO, CP 40/121, m. 92.

24. She had apparently died before 17 June 1299 when orders were given for the seizure of the lands of Avelina de la Leghe, tenant in chief: *Cal. Fine Rolls, 1272–1307*, 415. The inquisition post mortem mentions only the manor in Walton on Thames and land in West Molesey held by her son John, aged 30 and more: *Cal. Inq. Post Mortem*, ii, no. 515. Her lands were released to him by a writ of late August 1299: *Cal. Fine Rolls, 1272–1307*, 417.

25. TNA: PRO, JUST 1/1323, m. 54d. It is also copied in full onto the King's Bench roll (see note 21).

26. TNA: PRO, KB 27/173, m. 6d. One report of the same case (in BL MS. Stowe 386, fol. 173r) specifically ascribes the judgment to the court's chief justice, Roger Brabazon.

27. Despite the fact that the questioning of the justices of the second group of assize jurors had provided rather more evidence for doubts on this score.

manor (and related damages) until the jurors had provided further information about the "cause, manner and form" (*causa, modo et forma*) of the annulment. The jurors appeared in late August before Gilbert of Rothbury, the junior justice of King's Bench, at Shapens [in Great Chishall] in Essex. They said that the reason for the annulment (*causa divorcii*) was the precontract Avelina "said she had made" (*dicebat se fecisse*) with John *de Ponte* and that the case had been "initiated, propounded and prosecuted" by her (*per ipsam Avelinam mota fuit, proposita et prosecuta...*) at the cost and expense of Avelina and her "friends" (probably her kin) (*ad custus et misas ejusdem Aveline et amicorum suorum*) by her procurement. Alan on the other hand had been unaware of the precontract and had "defended" the case to the best of his ability (*pro viribus suis*). On the basis of this information the court held that because Avelina ought not to have benefited from her own malice or wrongdoing (*nec... de malicia sua aut pro delicto suo commodum consequi de jure debeat*) and because after her death Alan was entitled to the whole of the manor under the settlement, he should now recover the other half of the manor for his lifetime and the associated damages.

It is tempting to see in this a hasty, and perhaps even a biased, judgment. Neither the plea roll enrolment nor the two surviving law reports of this case[28] cite any previous judgments, merely a generic "custom of the realm," to support the general proposition that after an annulment the decision as to the division of property given to, or settled on, a married couple should, or might, depend on the reason for the annulment and who had prosecuted that annulment. Moreover, Roger Brabazon, the chief justice of King's Bench, had been a leading legal adviser of Edmund of Lancaster before he became a justice and later the chief justice of King's Bench, this at the time when Alan Waldeshef was in Edmund's service and Edmund had assisted the resettlement of the manor, and had perhaps a further reason for favoring Alan, now that he had become a member of the king's household.

28. The reports are in short sections of reports for this term in BL MSS. Stowe 386, fol. 173r and CUL MS. Ee.6.18, fol. 84r. Neither gives any of the argument of counsel that probably preceded the judgment and both seem to record the chief justice's summary of the case plus his judgment. There is also a note on the general principle involved with a reference to the names of the parties in BL MS. Harley 25, fol. 60v.

There is, however, at least one earlier case in which the decision looks to be markedly similar to that in Alan's case. This is another assize of novel disseisin brought by Lucy the wife of John Lumbard (and her husband) against Lucy's former husband, John of Ruxley, heard before William of Saham and his fellow Surrey assize justices at Lambeth in July 1287.[29] Lucy's claim was to a messuage, thirty acres of arable, ten acres of meadow and one water-mill at Shawford in Ewell and Long Ditton. John denied having disseised her. He said his title to the lands came from a grant made by Henry Picot of Chessington (who, it later appears, was Lucy's father) whose charter he produced in court. This showed that the grant had been made to John and Lucy and her lawful issue, with a life remainder to John if they had no issue but he survived her, with reversion to Henry (and his heirs). Lucy admitted that the tenements had been so given but said that after the annulment she had tried to take possession of the tenements and John had prevented her from doing so and thereby disseised her. She subsequently spelled out the underlying basis of her claim: she was the daughter of the grantor and had been the reason for the gift (*et fuit causa donacionis predicte*) and had both free tenement (a life interest) and fee tail (since the land had been granted to her and her issue) and had been prevented by John from taking possession. John's answer focused partly on the life interest he had been given under the grant and partly on the fact that she had only been given an interest in the land as his wife (with the implication, perhaps, that once she had ceased to be his wife, she ceased to be entitled). More radically (and more relevantly in our context), he pointed out that the annulment had been made on Lucy's initiative and by reason of a precontract between her and her current husband (*ad suggestionem ipsius Lucie racione precontractus inter ipsam et predictum Johannem Lumbard*) and thus it was her wrongdoing (or her "sin") that was the reason for the divorce (*et sic peccatum ipsius Lucie fuit causa divorcii*). The implication seems to be that John ought not to be prejudiced by his ex-wife's wrongdoing, when he himself had done nothing wrong. The assize justices evidently felt the need to take additional advice. Judgment was not given until January 1288 and Thomas Weyland, the chief justice of the Common Bench, was present to give the assize justices his assistance in the making of their judgment.

29. TNA: PRO, JUST 1/880, m. 5d (and there is also a copy in C 260/186, no. 61).

The justices noted that the charter had provided that John should hold for the remainder of his life if he survived Lucy, even if there was no issue, and seem to have considered that an annulment was in effect analogous to death. They also noted that she was the reason (*occasio*) for the annulment. They therefore adjudged that the assize should not proceed during his lifetime and amerced John and Lucy for a false claim.

This decision seems to be a departure from earlier practice. In a case heard in the 1249 Wiltshire eyre, Parnel, the daughter of Roger *de Molendinis*, claimed a small holding of land at Corsley in the county against Richard Cruc as that which her mother Christine *de Molendinis* had given to Richard in marriage with Parnel and which ought now to revert to Parnel because her marriage to Richard had been annulled. The assumption seems to be that under these circumstances the ex-wife would be entitled to all of the land thus given. Richard kept the land, however, because he was able to show to the satisfaction of a jury that he had acquired the land after their marriage from a third party, not in the way Parnel had suggested.[30] In a second case, an assize of novel disseisin brought by Alice the daughter of Walter of Kenningford against John Abel and Thomas of Castle Holgate in the 1272 Shropshire eyre seeking to recover three messuages and one and a half virgates of land in Nether Stanway, John admitted that the land had once belonged to Alice's mother Margery but claimed he had received it and taken possession partly by the grant of Margery, partly by the grant of a third party to whom Margery had granted it.[31] The assize jury found that the land had all been given by Margery to John in frankmarriage with her daughter. The court adjudged that because the land was Alice's frankmarriage and there had been an annulment all the land now belonged to Alice and that John had disseised her and she should recover the land and the damages. Nothing was recorded of the reason for the annulment and no enquiry apparently made as to who obtained it and which of the parties bore any culpability for it. The land was the former wife's marriage portion and on the annulment of her marriage the land was assumed to belong rightfully to her. In a third case, again an assize of novel disseisin, brought in the 1281 Devon eyre, Joan *de Houlesham* alleged that William de

30. *Civil Pleas of the Wiltshire Eyre, 1249*, ed. M. T. Clanchy, Wiltshire Record Society 26 (Devizes, 1971), no. 53.

31. TNA: PRO, JUST 1/736, m. 8.

Benlegh', Alexander of Blakewell and Richard Futerel had disseised her of a messuage, a ferling and eight acres in *Benlegh*" and Blakewell.[32] The assize verdict found that the land had been acquired by Wymund of *Benetknolle* chaplain, who had then given them to William in frankmarriage with his daughter Joan. When the marriage was annulled William had ejected her and retained the land. The court held that since William had no interest in the tenement except because of the said Joan (*racione predicte Johanne*), whose marriage portion it was, and since he was now a total stranger to her by reason of the annulment, she was to recover it all plus damages. Again nothing is said of the reason for the annulment and nothing said about who sued it and who, if any one was culpable. The judgment was on similar grounds to that in the 1272 Shropshire eyre.

There is only a single case in the king's courts known to me from the later thirteenth or early fourteenth century which deals with the consequences of annulment for precontract on a grant of movables (chattels) made by the father of the wife to the future husband. This detinue of chattels case was brought by Agnes, daughter of Richard de Brok, in the Common Bench in 1290 against her ex-husband Edmund of Navestock to claim movables to the value of £66 given by her father as a marriage portion, and there are two independent, unofficial law reports of the case as well as the official enrolment.[33] The basis of the claim was that, immediately after marriage, Edmund began suing for a dissolution of the marriage on the grounds of a precontract with another named woman and had obtained a dissolution of the marriage to Agnes on those grounds in the Court of Arches in London,[34] but had then refused to return the chattels her father had given. Edmund's counsel tried a variety of arguments in his defense. They included one suggesting that, at best, Agnes could claim only half of what had been given since the chattels had been given to them both. Her counsel argued that she was entitled to all of them both because she had

32. TNA: PRO, JUST 1/185, m. 24d.

33. I have previously discussed this case at greater length in "The Equity of the Common Law Courts" in *Law and Equity: Approaches in Roman Law and Common Law*, ed. E. Koops and W.J. Zwalve (Leiden: Martinus Nijhoff, 2014), 43–53 at 39–41.

34. The eventual jury verdict in the case found that it was the other woman who had brought the suit for the annulment but also found that it was at Edmund's instigation. This came to much the same thing.

been the reason for the gift (and the chattels had come from her father) and because the annulment had been procured by Edmund. Edmund was eventually driven to what was probably always going to be an unsuccessful denial of having received any of the chattels, whose truth was then tested by a jury, not (as Edmund had wished) by compurgation. One of the two reports tells us that the court drove him to accept jury trial out of favor for a woman who had been "deceived and lost her virginity." The outcome, then, in this case was in part determined by a similar bias to those found in Alan Waldeshef's case for the "innocent" party, who had been deceived by the partner who had made a precontract and then procured an annulment on its basis, but also partly on the basis of the initial reason for the grant of the chattels, which aligns this case more with the earlier decisions that returned marriage portions in land to the partner with whom they were given.

The annulment of marriages in later medieval England was a matter for the ecclesiastical courts alone. But the secular courts might deal with the aftermath of annulments in sorting out property transactions which had been made in connection with the marriage but with no prior provisions for what should happen in the case of annulment. The case on which this paper has mainly concentrated shows the king's court taking an almost equitable approach to this problem. The court of King's Bench did not in 1303 simply undo the sequence of transactions which had settled the manor of Shelley on Alan Waldeshef and his wife Avelina atte Cruche, one possible option which would have ensured that Avelina or her heir got her manor back. Nor did it simply split the manor between the two of them (or between Alan and Avelina's heir), a second possible option, and one that the court seems to have considered as the baseline for the minimum to which Alan was to be entitled before it considered the question of responsibility for the annulment. It chose instead to proceed on the basis of the prior conduct of the two parties: the fact that Avelina had entered into the marriage knowing she was precontracted to John *de Ponte* or had persuaded the ecclesiastical court that this was the case in order to have her marriage annulled and had then herself initiated the proceedings and prosecuted the suit for the annulment of the marriage, while Alan had known nothing of the precontract and had defended the validity of his marriage to Avelina for as long as he could. It was not, of course, that Alan was going to keep any of the property for longer than his own life. It was all going to pass on his death to John, Avelina's son by her first husband. But Alan's freedom from any responsibility for the annulment and the fact that Avelina was by now dead persuaded the court that he should be entitled to both halves, as he would have been had the marriage not been annulled. The court did not take any account in its judgment of the fact that the manor had originally been Avelina's own property, not that of Alan. The decision is similar to that in the 1287 Surrey assize where again the king's court decided that the guiltless ex-husband was entitled after an annulment for precontract prosecuted by his ex-wife to retain the whole, and not just half, of the land which had been settled on him and his ex-wife and her issue by her father for the remainder of his lifetime. These are two decisions which happen to favor the ex-husband in a relationship dissolved by an annulment. In the 1290 Common Bench detinue of chattels case it was the ex-wife who benefited from a generically similar approach to the question of what should happen to movables settled on a couple just in advance of a marriage that was dissolved not long afterwards on the initiative of the husband in ensuring that a second woman successfully claimed him as her rightful husband by virtue of a precontract. In this case the ex-wife recovered all the movables given to the couple once she had got a jury to find that the movables really had been given as she had claimed. It may have helped her, however, that the chattels had been given to the couple by her father. All three of these cases were recorded on the plea rolls of the king's courts and the first and the third were also reported in the unofficial law reports which had begun to circulate among members of the English legal profession. We cannot be certain how clearly or how accurately they were remembered or whether they affected future decisions on similar matters or the advice lawyers may have given their clients when such situations occurred in future, but it seems more than likely that they did. The English Common Law courts did not challenge the right of ecclesiastical courts to annul marriages but they certainly did on occasions assert their right to determine what should happen to the couple's property and developed and applied their own rules in doing so.

Chapter 29 of Magna Carta in the Fourteenth Century

Sir John Baker

Historians are much beholden to Professor Donahue, both for his own scholarship and for his generous encouragement of the scholarship of others. Equally renowned in France, in England his work on the ecclesiastical courts and their records has earned the gratitude of English legal historians as well as historians of Church and society. Especial credit is due to him for starting to open up the fourteenth century, a period much neglected in English legal history despite the wealth of surviving sources. His seventy-fifth year happened to be a year much celebrated throughout the world as the eight-hundredth anniversary of Magna Carta, a subject which has certainly not been neglected by historians. The celebrations may have obscured the fact—for most people, that is, other than historians—that the charter of John had a very brief official life. The only legal judgment passed upon it was that of Pope Innocent III, who on 24 August 1215 threatened King John with eternal anathema should be presume to honor the promises extorted from him only seventy days earlier.[1] John was only too pleased to repudiate what he had been coerced by force of arms into approving. And that was the end of the charter of 1215, which was not called Magna Carta and never took legal effect. Most of its content, however, was incorporated in the Great Charter issued by the young King Henry III in 1225, and

1. The original bull is in the British Library [BL], Cotton MS Cleopatra E. I, fol. 155. There are also two copies of the 1215 charter of John in the Cottonian collection, one of which was damaged in a fire in 1731 and is almost illegible.

that was the version which, if not itself an act of Parliament, was enacted into statute at Marlborough in 1267 and confirmed by successive kings in Parliament. One of the most important provisions, still notionally law in England, was that known in the statutory numbering as chapter 29:[2]

> No free man shall be taken or imprisoned, or disseised of any freehold or of his liberties or free customs, or outlawed, or exiled, or in any way destroyed, nor shall we go upon him or put upon him, except by the lawful judgment of his peers or by the law of the land; to no one shall we sell, to no one deny or delay, right or justice.

By the early seventeenth century this noble provision was on everyone's lips, and it has been hailed ever since as a clear declaration of the core principles of constitutional government and the Rule of Law. But it is far from clear that it had as much clout in the medieval period. There are remarkably few references to chapter 29 in the medieval law reports. In one of the earliest of them, in 1311, objection was taken to a generally worded writ of protection on the grounds that the king had promised not to deny or delay right or justice. Chief Justice Bereford responded that "The king, in whose place we are, has commanded us that the defendant should be quit of all pleas... how, then, can we hold pleas against his command?"[3] And so the great Bereford, with impeccable logic, laid the *nulli deferemus* provision

2. Translated. The original charters were not written with distinct paragraphs, let alone divided into numbered chapters. In medieval references the numbering varies, but it became fixed in the printed editions. The clauses of the 1215 charter corresponding to chapter 29 of the statute were those now numbered 39 and 40. Some historians still refer to clauses 39 and 40 as if they had a life beyond the summer of 1215; the text is the same, but the usage is legally misleading.

3. *Abbot of Croyland's Case* (1311) Year Book [YB] Mich. 5 Edw. II, Selden Society 63 (London, 1944), 6, pl. 4 (translation slightly paraphrased). A regular writ of protection placed a defendant temporarily beyond the reach of legal process while he was engaged, or about to be engaged, in the king's service outside the realm. The protection in question did not disclose the cause. The scope of ordinary writs of protection was repeatedly circumscribed by judicial decisions, beginning in the fourteenth century; there are 116 entries in Sir Anthony Fitzherbert's *Graunde Abridgement* (London: 1514–16) under the title "Protection."

to rest for nearly two hundred years.[4] As to *nulli vendemus*, selling justice most obviously meant making people pay for access to royal justice. In 1351 the Commons complained that writs which gave such access were "the first part of [the king's] law, which law is the supreme right of his realm and his Crown (*quele leie est soverein droit de son roialme et de sa corone*)," and that to charge fees for them was against chapter 29; but the king's response was that he was entitled to charge for writs of grace, albeit the chancellor could show grace in ease of the people.[5] A similar complaint was given even shorter shrift when it was raised in Parliament in 1381. King Richard II responded that he was not willing to abandon a source of revenue which had been enjoyed by all his forebears, both before and after the charter.[6] Lecturers in the late-medieval inns of court, attempting to reconcile the reality with the wording of chapter 29, concluded that "right" only meant writs of right, and that "justice" only meant writs of *justicies*, a perverse interpretation which led to the miserable consequence that this noble guarantee of justice applied only to certain proceedings in inferior courts.[7]

Magna Carta was not, of course, a written constitution. It did not address limits on legislative power, because it did not contemplate future legislative change. Its purpose was more immediate, to restore and preserve the ancient common law, and many of its provisions took immediate effect through the king's compliance. It did not specify in general terms what the king's government could or could not do in the future, nor could it provide any remedies by way of an action at law against the Crown if the government acted despotically.[8] Some of the wording was unclear, and in the fourteenth century open reference was made in high places to its

4. Except as against lesser authorities: see *R. v. Gisors* (1321) in the *Eyre of London 1321*, ed. H. M. Cam, Selden Society 85 (London, 1968), 67, where an alleged custom to bail prisoners for felony until the next eyre was held bad because, eyres having become rare, it would delay justice; it was just as well, since there never was another eyre of London.

5. *Rotuli Parliamentorum, ut et Petitiones et Placita in Parliamento* (London, 1767–77) [Rot. Parl.] 2.241, no. 30. Cf. a similar petition and response in 1377: ibid., 370, no. 51.

6. Rot. Parl. 3: 116, no. 88. See further F. Thompson, *Magna Carta: Its Role in the Making of the English Constitution* (Minneapolis: University of Minnesota Press, 1948), 98–9.

7. See J. Baker, introduction to *Selected Readings and Commentaries on Magna Carta 1400–1604*, Selden Society 132 (London, 2015), lxxxi.

8. No action at law could be brought against the Crown until 1947.

doubts and obscurities.[9] Although *Bracton* had proclaimed that the king was under the law, because it was the law which made him king,[10] the inns of court seem not to have been aware of this doctrine. Shocking as it is to relate, the *glossa ordinaria*—which probably brought together the common learning of the fourteenth century—actually declared that the king was beyond the law. *Rex est supra legem.*[11] Whether this negative approach to chapter 29 reflected the virtual absence of reported case-law on the matter, or vice versa, can only be a matter for conjecture. What is clear is that Magna Carta was still being treated as an ordinary statutory text, to be read and analyzed according to its wording. It had not yet acquired its magical symbolic power, which has depended on not reading the words too closely, and therefore it is hardly surprising that chapter 29 was not yet considered to contain forensically useful law. Its underlying objects would be attained in other ways, and then retrospectively attributed to Magna Carta. That story lay largely in later centuries.[12] Nevertheless, chapter 29 was far from dormant in the fourteenth century, and there are a few strands in its story which deserve attention.

9. E.g. the Ordinances of 1311, Rot. Parl. 1: 281 (doubtful points to be clarified by the lords ordainers), 286 (doubtful points to be clarified in the next Parliament by the baronage, justices, *et autres sages gentz de la lei*); *Statutes of the Realm* (London: Record Commission, 1810–28) 1.158, no. 6; 167, no. 38. In 1327 the Commons petitioned that the points of *la chartre du franchises* which were in need of clarification (*que unt mestier destre esclarsys*) should be clarified in Parliament: Rot. Parl. 2: 7, no. 3. This probably referred to the earl of Lancaster's case, discussed below.

10. *Bracton on the Laws and Customs of England*, ed. G. E. Woodbine and S. E. Thorne (Cambridge, Mass.: Harvard University Press, 1968–77), 2.33 (*rex non debet esse sub homine sed sub deo et sub lege, quia lex facit regem*). Amongst Professor Donahue's many achievements was making this text accessible online, via the website of Harvard Law School Library.

11. *Selected Readings and Commentaries on Magna Carta*, 92. For the date of this text see the introduction, in ibid., xli–xlii. Cf. YB Mich. 8 Hen. IV, fol. 9, pl. 12, *per* Stourton (*potestas principis non est inclusa sub legibus*).

12. See J. Baker, "The Legal Force and Effect of Magna Carta," in *Magna Carta: Muse & Mentor*, ed. R. J. Holland (Washington, D.C.: Library of Congress, 2014), 65–84, at 80–3.

Chapter 29 in Parliament and Council

The king could not be sued in his own courts, not so much because he was king as because no one had a peer in his own land.[13] It was a privilege shared with every inferior lord. In the case of the king, however, there was no superior court in which he could be sued. One of the earliest ways in which a remedy could be achieved against the Crown, without suing the king, was to sue *to* the king. The formal way of doing this was the petition of right, which was used where a subject's property came into the hands of the Crown. It was a well established procedure in the fourteenth century. Such petitions were dealt with in the Chancery, but could be sent to the King's Bench for trial of facts.[14] The issue in a petition of right was usually one of title rather than due process, and it was the usual principle that the king's title could only be established by matter of record.

Besides the formal procedure for recovering property, it was possible to seek administrative justice in Council or legislative justice in Parliament by invoking chapter 29. Magna Carta was often mentioned in petitions to Parliament and the Council in the first half of the fourteenth century,[15] usually meaning chapter 29, and broad claims were sometimes made as to its scope. Perhaps the broadest was made in 1319. An attorney of the Sheriffs' Court in the city of London complained that one of the sheriffs' clerks had refused to allow him to act as an attorney, against the law of the land (*vileynment, a tort e encountere ley de terre*), and had thereby taken away his living, in breach of the king's great charter of the liberties of the land (*en blemisement de la graunt chartre nostre seygnur le roy de fraunchises de la terre*). He claimed damages of £100.[16] The complaint was addressed to the king and his *enquerours*, but no outcome is recorded. It is an interesting document for four reasons. First, because the plaintiff relied on the Mag-

13. *Hadelow's Case* (1348) YB Hil. 22 Edw. III, fol. 3, pl. 25, *per* Thorp C.J. (in Parliament).

14. E.g. *Gervaise Clifton's Case* (1348) YB Pas. 22 Edw. III, fol. 5, pl. 12.

15. See also A. Musson, "Magna Carta in the Later Middle Ages," in *Magna Carta: the Foundation of Freedom*, ed. N. Vincent (London: Third Millennium Publishing Ltd, 2015), 92–3.

16. *Moumby v. Hardyngham* (1319) Public Record Office, London [PRO], SC 8/320/E455. Attorneys were lesser practitioners attached to the court and regulated by the court. The attorneys of the city courts were doubtless, as in slightly later times, professionally separate from those of the royal courts, who in turn were inferior to learned counsel.

na Carta of the current king, Edward II, rather than that of 1225, thereby showing that the king was thought to be especially bound by his own confirmation. Second, chapter 29 was treated as applying not only to the king and feudal lords, but also to minor civic officials such as a sheriff's clerk. Third, the provision was treated as applying not only to freehold land and franchises but also to a professional person's means of earning a living. Finally, the plaintiff assumed that a remedy could be given in damages. In all these respects the humble London attorney had seen far into the future; but his ideas were not yet to be, either in his own century or the next. Although seemingly sanctioned by chapter 5 of the Statute of Marlborough 1267, actions for damages founded on chapter 29 are not found until 1501 and never became numerous.[17]

Chapter 29 was not usually mentioned in Chancery petitions, but there was an instance in 1397. The defendants were alleged to have arrested several chaplains while they were robed and attending divine service, showing contempt of a Chancery subpoena by casting it down, and violently disturbing a consistory court when it subsequently investigated the arrests.[18] The background is unclear, but the case was probably rooted in local politics or even in popular religion. The plaintiff was a Chancery clerk suing on the king's behalf, and this seems to be a downward use of Magna Carta by the king against his subjects, in dealing with troublesome townsmen, rather than an upwards complaint about governmental power. The rarity of appeals to chapter 29 might have a number of explanations. It was only a confirmation of the common law, and once the legal system was more settled there was less point in referring to it. Another may have been the teaching of the inns of court, mentioned above, which found it upon analysis to have little or no specific meaning. In any case, for the Chancery or Council to award damages would itself have been contrary to due process.

17. Baker, "The Legal Force and Effect of Magna Carta," 82–3.

18. *Pokelyngton v. Exebrigge and others* (1397) PRO, C 1/68/7. This was drawn to our attention by N. Le Poidevin Q.C. The proceedings in the consistory are mentioned in F. C. Hingeston-Randolph, *Register of Edmund Stafford* (A.D. *1395–1419*)*: An Index and Full Abstract of its Contents* (Exeter: William Pollard & Co., 1889?), 134. The matter is further complicated by the fact that Bishop Stafford was also lord chancellor.

The jurisdiction of the Council was restricted in the fourteenth century precisely because it was against Magna Carta.[19]

The story is different in the world of Parliament, at any rate in the fourteenth century. Here the king could be personally challenged to honor his obligations as a constitutional monarch. Magna Carta was confirmed many times by the king in Parliament. Edward III confirmed it no less than fifteen times, and in 1331 chapter 29 was paraphrased or explained in the following words: "no man from henceforth shall be attached by any accusation, or forejudged of life or limb, nor his lands, tenements, goods or chattels seised into the king's hands, against the form of the great charter and the law of the land."[20] The word "accusation" here probably referred to proceedings before the king's Council, as was made more explicit later in the reign. The measure was further expounded in 1354: "no man, of whatever estate or condition he be, shall be put out from land or tenement or arrested, imprisoned or disinherited or put to death without being brought to answer by due process of law."[21] The words "no man" (or person) brought villeins more clearly within its compass, and this was reinforced by "whatever estate or condition." Villeins could hardly be excluded from the Great Charter, especially after the social upheaval of the Black Death,[22] though they could still be imprisoned by their own lords, since that was the law of the land. The right to be heard, and "due process of law," were easier to understand than the obscure language of 1215 and 1225, though they only codified the previous understanding. Also helpful was the transition from

19. 25 Edw. III, stat. 5, c. 4 (no one to be arrested upon a petition or suggestion to the king or Council except by indictment or presentment, or by process made by writ original at the common law). Cf. also 37 Edw. III, c. 18 (concerning false suggestions to the king, contrary to c. 29); 42 Edw. III, c. 3 (to eschew the mischiefs arising from false accusations before the king's Council, and otherwise, no one to be put to answer without presentment, or matter of record, or due process and writ original according to the old law of the land). Some ingenuity would later be required to square the coercive powers of the Chancery and Star Chamber with these statutes.

20. 5 Edw. III, c. 9. This did not replace c. 29, which remained in force as part of the 1225 charter.

21. 28 Edw. III, c. 3.

22. In *Russell v. Hirde* (1388) a bondman of the king complained in Chancery that he had been put out of his unfree tenement in Tintagel by bailiffs, acting without due process of law, and the matter was referred to the sheriff and escheator of Cornwall to investigate: *Calendar of Patent Rolls [CPR] 1385–9* (London: HM Stationery Office, 1900), 474.

the royal first person. By using passive language, Parliament clarified the general application of the legislation. These statutes were to prove very important in the seventeenth century. Remarkably, however, they were not made the subject of any known lectures in the inns of court, where the curriculum seemed—until the Tudor period—immovably rooted in the *statuta antiqua,* the legislation prior to Edward III, the old testament of English law. There are therefore no learned commentaries on "due process," though it is apparent from conciliar petitions that it was merely an encapsulation of the received sense of chapter 29 as protecting what is now known as the Rule of Law. For example, in 1328 the countess of Pembroke petitioned the king in Council that no writ should issue to oust her from a castle without her being summoned by due process according to the law of the realm.[23] This was presumably an allusion to Magna Carta, which in the same year was reinforced by the parliamentary enactment that the judges should not desist from doing justice by reason of any command under the great or petty seal.[24] And in about 1330 the archbishop of York complained to the king in Council that the king's bailiff had seized the franchises of the port of Hull without judgment or due process, contrary to Magna Carta, again presumably referring to chapter 29.[25] Due process was not an arcane constitutional mystery, but the ordinary procedure of the common law as opposed to the arbitrary whim of those in power. It was well understood that people should not be dispossessed of their property without regular legal proceedings to establish the true title, and should not be condemned to death or prison without an opportunity to be heard before a court of law following the procedure of the common law.

Repeated confirmation might be seen as a sign of the precarious impermanence of Magna Carta in the fourteenth century rather than of its firm entrenchment. In the records of Parliament, however, may be found a number of successful invocations of chapter 29 in real cases. In 1322 the

23. *Countess of Pembroke v. Robert de Holand* (1328) PRO, SC 8/11/510.

24. 2 Edw. III, c. 8. This was repeated in 14 Edw. III, stat. 1, c. 14, and inserted in the judges' oath in 1344 (18 Edw. III, stat. 4; recited in 20 Edw. III, c. 1; confirmed by 8 Ric. II, c. 3). The precise bearing of this prohibition requires further investigation. It looks like an attempted check on the nascent equitable jurisdictions of the Council and Chancery.

25. PRO, SC 8/11/515. The allusion to c. 29 rather than c. 9, which guaranteed the liberties of towns and ports, is shown by the reference to judgment and due process.

exile and disinheritance of Hugh le Despenser, the elder, was reversed in Parliament, on a writ of error, upon complaint (*inter alia*) that it was against the provision in Magna Carta that no man should be exiled[26] or ruined in any way destroyed except by judgment of his peers or by the law of the land; the former decision had been made without summoning[27] Hugh to any court to answer, and in the absence of the bishops, who were peers of the realm, and no record was made of the prosecution.[28] The reversal was promptly annulled after Edward III's accession in 1326, but confirmed in 1397. The legal interest, however, lies more in the wording of the parliamentary record than its effect. It demonstrates again that, well before the statute of 1354, chapter 29 was understood to guarantee a right to be heard and to due process of law. It was also understood to guarantee that peers of the realm should be tried by their peers.

Similar use was made of chapter 29 in 1327, by the opposite political faction, in order to reverse the attainders for treason of Thomas, earl of Lancaster, Bartholomew, Lord Badlesmere, and Roger Mortimer, earl of March, in 1322.[29] Lord Badlesmere had been sentenced to death on 14 April before Lord Cobham, Edmund de Passeley (king's serjeant at law) and other justices at Canterbury on the basis of common knowledge and "the king's record." The king's record was a privy seal instrument, in French, setting

26. The text says "forjugge," which the editors of the new edition of *The Parliament Rolls of Medieval England 1275–1504* (Leicester: Scholarly Digital Editions and the National Archives, 2005) have rendered as "judged," but in view of the prefix *for-* (from the Latin *foris*) it more naturally means exiled or outlawed, following the wording of chapter 29. The judgment in the same record actually uses the word "exile" in paraphrasing chapter 29, and unlawful exile was part of the complaint. (References to Rot. Parl. here are to the more usable eighteenth-century edition.)

27. The text says *appeletz en court*, which the editors of the new edition have rendered in one place as "appealed in court" and in another as "summoned to court." The latter interpretation seems preferable, especially since the judgment uses the phrase *sauntz appeler... en respouns*."

28. *Hugh Le Despenser's Case* (1322), record in French recited in the 1397 proceedings in Rot. Parl. 3.361–7; *Calendar of Close Rolls [CCR] 1318–23* (London: HM Stationery Office, 1898), 542–6; L. W. Vernon Harcourt, *His Grace the Steward and Trial of Peers* (London: Longmans, 1907), 324–6 (French text from the close roll). The Despensers had been granted a safe-conduct on 8 Dec. 1321 to pursue their petition: CPR 1321–24: 45.

29. The records of all three cases are printed, in their original languages, in Harcourt, *Trial of Peers*, 327–34.

out Badlesmere's offences and directing the judges to pronounce judgment. There was no trial. In the first term of Edward III's reign the judgment was reversed in Parliament on three grounds.[30] The first was that judgment had been pronounced without the accused being arraigned for any felony, or given an opportunity to be heard, contrary to the law and custom of the realm. The second was that the king could not make a record of such crimes except in respect of his enemies in time of war, when the king rode out with banners displayed, and not in time of peace, whereas at the time of the judgment the chancellor and the justices of both benches were sitting to administer justice.[31] And the third was that Badlesmere was not tried by his peers as required by Magna Carta. It will be noted that chapter 29 was cited only in respect of trial by peers. The right to be heard, before judgment of death could be pronounced, was on this occasion treated as common law.[32]

In the same term Parliament heard the case of Thomas, late earl of Lancaster. On 22 March 1322 the earl had been charged with treason and murder before the king, seven earls, and others of the Council, at Pontefract, and because the treason and murder were notorious (*manifesta, notoria et nota*) to the earls, barons, magnates and people of the realm, and were recorded by the king, judgment of death was given. The earl's son, Henry of Lancaster, now in 1327 presented a petition in French, seeking the removal of the record into Parliament because his father had been adjudged to death unrighteously (*nounresonablement*). When it was removed he assigned two specific errors: (1) whereas every subject arrested for treason, homicide, robbery, arson and other felonies in time of peace should be arraigned for such offences by the law and custom of the realm, put to answer, and convicted according to law, before he can be adjudged to death; and although Thomas was a subject of the king's father and arrested in time of peace, and brought before the king himself, the king recorded that he was guilty of treasons and felonies without his being arraigned or put to answer as is customary according to the law and custom of the realm, and so the judgment of death was erroneous, especially since the Chancery and other

30. Harcourt, *Trial of Peers*, 332–4; *CPR 1338–40*: 208–10 (record exemplified in 1339).

31. For this understanding of peace-time see also *Countess of Kent v. Abbot of Ramsey* (1340) YB Pas. 14 Edw. III (Rolls Series), 127, pl. 54.

32. In the statute of 1354, mentioned above, it was also treated as implicit in chapter 29.

courts were open all the time and doing justice, and the king was not riding with banners displayed; (2) whereas Thomas was one of the peers and great men of the realm, and it is provided in the *Magna Carta de Libertatibus Angliae* that no free man should be destroyed except by lawful judgment of his peers or by the law of the land, Thomas was erroneously adjudged to death as aforesaid without arraignment, or answer, or lawful judgment of his peers, against the tenor of Magna Carta. Judgment was given in Parliament by the king, peers, magnates, and the whole community of the realm, that the judgment should be reversed as erroneous.[33] The reasons were the same as in Badlesmere's case, though reduced to two in such a way that the right to be properly charged and heard was now attributed to chapter 29 as well as the common law.

The third case heard by Parliament in Hilary term 1327 was that of Roger Mortimer.[34] He had been sentenced to death without trial at Westminster on 3 August 1322, by a commission including two justices of the Common Bench (William de Herle and John de Stonore), following a similar direction from the king, though he had escaped to France. The judgment was reversed on the same grounds. A Latin document in very similar words, conjecturally assigned to 1327,[35] concerned Lancaster's associate John, Lord Mowbray, who had likewise been executed in 1322 following the battle of Boroughbridge. The Mowbray heirs were told to sue for their inheritance by due process, as was customary (*processu debito inde faciendo prout moris est*). However colored they may have been by the politics of the moment, these were decisions of the first importance. Trial by common notoriety was no longer thought consistent with the Rule of Law.[36] A person

33. Harcourt, *Trial of Peers*, 327–9 (printed in Latin from the exemplification on the patent and close rolls); Rot. Parl. 2.55–6, no. 13; *CCR 1327–30*, 105–6; PRO, KB 27/418, m. 49.

34. *CPR 1327–30*, 141–3; Latin text in Harcourt, *Trial of Peers*, 329–32. He had been convicted by the peers on the ground that his offenses were notorious: Rot. Parl. 2.52, no. 1.

35. PEO, SC 8/196/9788.

36. Plucknett considered that it had previously been common, and that it might have been the origin of impeachment, though Thompson questioned this: T. F. T. Plucknett, "The Origin of Impeachment," *Transactions of the Royal Historical Society* (4th series) 24 (1942), 47–71; Plucknett, "The Impeachments of 1376," *Transactions of the Royal Historical Society* (5th series) 1 (1951), 153–64; reprinted in Plucknett, *Studies in English Legal History* (London: Hambledon Press, 1983), ch. 8; Thompson, *Magna Carta*, 75–6.

accused of a capital offence was entitled to a summons and an opportunity to be heard before judgment was given. Moreover, the king could not record a person's guilt without trial, except by martial law on the field of battle, and it was unlawful for his judges to obey his command to give judgment upon such a record.[37]

These important decisions were temporarily forgotten or laid aside in 1330 when Roger Mortimer, earl of March, was again condemned to death on account of the notoriety of his guilt, *sanz nul accusement et sanz estre mesne en juggement ou en respons*, and this time he was executed. But justice of a sort prevailed in 1354, when the judgment of 1330 was reversed for that reason.[38] In 1330 also John Mautravers (or Maltravers), first Baron Maltravers (d. 1364), was condemned to death by Parliament for complicity in the death of the earl of Kent, and fled abroad. His exile is briefly alluded to in the year books.[39] His disgrace was of a modified nature, since he acted on behalf of Edward III while in exile in Flanders, and in 1339 and 1345 he petitioned to be allowed to return. The reason given in the first petition was that by the law and custom of the realm, and the ordinance lately made therein in Parliament, no one ought to be condemned unheard, that he had been condemned without any appeal or indictment, and that he was willing to come back and be tried by his peers.[40] The petition was not immediately successful, and Maltravers tried again in 1348, alleging that he had been sentenced to death in his absence, *nient endite, nient atteintz ne apele a re-*

37. Conviction by the king's record alone was used after the battle of Blackheath in 1497 and was considered to be good law by Edward Hales in 1512: reading in the Inner Temple on Magna Carta, c. 11, printed in *Selected Readings and Commentaries on Magna Carta*, at 148.

38. Rot. Parl. 2.255–6, no. 8–12.

39. Rot. Parl. 2.53, no. 3 (record of the judgment only, omitting to mention any process against him); YB Mich. 10 Edw. III, fol. 53, pl. 37 (referring to her husband's exile "for a certain cause"). See also *Oxford Dictionary of National Biography [ODNB]*, ed. H. C. G. Matthew and B. Harrison (Oxford: Oxford University Press, 2004), *sub nom.* Maltravers, John.

40. *Rotuli Parliamentorum hactenus Inediti*, ed. H. G. Richardson and G. O. Sayles (London: Royal Historical Society, 1935), 285–6 (1339 petition); *CPR 1343–5*, 535 (and see 541). As the 1339 petition made clear, the ordinance referred to was the clarification of Magna Carta in 1327 in the context of the earl of Lancaster's case: *Rotuli Parliamentorum hactenus Inediti*, 117 (*qe desormais soit nul mys a la mort par record le roy saunz responz iugez*).

sponse, contre les leis de roialme et les usages aprovez.[41] There is no recorded response to this petition either, but he was finally pardoned in 1352 and returned to England.[42] What is particularly notable about the case is that the claim was made, and seemingly accepted, that even Parliament could not override the requirement of natural justice. The same conclusion was reached in the earl of Arundel's case in 1330, when a judgment confirmed by Parliament in 1327 was held to be erroneous and void in that it had been given without due process of law.[43] For jurisdictional reasons, however, it was for Parliament alone to set aside its own erroneous judgments. Since there was no higher court, only the king in Parliament could redress an error or injustice committed by an earlier Parliament.

In 1340 Chief Justice Willoughby was arraigned before commissioners for misconduct in office. He was said to have perverted and sold the laws as if they were cattle, though the precise background to his prosecution remains unclear. He challenged the proceedings because the king had not been informed of the accusation by indictment or by suit of a party with pledges, but Chief Justice Parving responded that the king had been informed by the clamor of the people, as if that were sufficient.[44] Willoughby was clearly appealing to the requirement of due process, though it is not obvious that it was denied in a substantive sense. The accusations were indeed made without pledges or good suit, and therefore fell short of an action of trespass. Clamor of the people, however, was effectively equivalent to an indictment by grand jury, especially since the accusations had been put into written bills. The defendant was given an opportunity to be heard, and was even allowed counsel, since no felony was alleged. How he would be tried did not become a question, because in the end he said he would not plead with the king and threw himself upon the king's mercy. After a heavy fine, Willoughby was pardoned,

41. Rot. Parl. 2.173, no. 65. The word *atteintz* seems to be an error for *arreine*.

42. Rot. Parl. 2.243, nos. 54–6.

43. Rot. Parl. 2.55–6, no. 13; ibid. 256–7, nos. 13–15; *CCR 1330–3*, 291–3. Cf. the case of John Mountagu, earl of Salisbury, who was murdered by a mob in 1400 and attainted. His son's petition of 1409 to reverse the attainder, relying on chapter 29, was adjourned: Rot. Parl. 4: 18, no. 12. The son was nevertheless summoned to Parliament as earl of Salisbury in 1409.

44. *R. v. Willoughby* (1340) YB Mich. 14 Edw. III (Rolls Series), 258–63, pl. 109; G. O. Sayles, introduction to *Select Cases in the Court of King's Bench under Edward III*, vol. 6 Selden Society 82 (London, 1965), at xvii.

and the king reappointed him to the bench in 1343. The case was therefore not such an aberration as might at first sight appear.

CHAPTER 29 IN THE YEAR BOOKS OF 1368–9

Later in the reign of Edward III two notable cases were reported in the year books, and they appear to be the only reported cases before Tudor times in which chapter 29 was given effect, albeit not in ordinary legal proceedings.[45] The first is known only from the *Liber Assisarum*, an atypical year book which reported cases occurring before royal justices away from Westminster.[46] A commission of oyer and terminer was opened in June 1368 at Chelmsford in Essex before the two chief justices, John Knyvet and Robert Thorp,[47] and Chief Baron Ludlow, and it was presented before them that one John Clerk of Ewell together with Sir John atte Lee[48] had arrested Thomas "Scuryngge" of "Toll,"[49] with certain goods and chattels,

45. Cf. an obscure case of 24 Edw. III (1350), abridged in Brooke Abr., *Commissions*, pl. 3: "Nota que commissions al certain persons de prendre tous que sont notoriousment sclaunders pur felonie et trespas, coment que ils ne fueront endites, hoc est contra legem: et concordat anno 42 Ass. 5 et 12" (punctuation added). This is the case cited by Fleetwood in his discourse on the Bridewell commission: *The Oxford Francis Bacon*, I: *Early Writings 1584–96*, ed. A. Stewart (Oxford: Oxford University Press, 2012), 60 (untraced by the editor).

46. *Sir John atte Lee's Case* (1368) 42 Edw. III, Lib. Ass. 5; corrected from Cambridge University Library MS Mm.2.16, fol. 96 (which supplies the missing names) and BL MS Harley 6691, fol. 66. The report is missing from most other manuscript texts of the *Liber Assisarum*, which contain only an abridged version of the year 42 Edw. III. The record of the commissioners' session in Hertfordshire, which included other proceedings against Lee, are preserved in PRO, JUST 1/339; the Essex rolls seem not to have survived.

47. Knyvet was chief justice of the King's Bench, and Thorp chief justice of the Common Bench. They were acting under a special commission of oyer and terminer issued on 3 June, which extended to five counties (Norfolk, Suffolk, Cambridgeshire, Essex and Hertfordshire): *CPR 1367–70*, 189–90. Only the previous year Lee himself had served on a similar commission with the same judges: *CPR 1364–67*, 438.

48. This name might be modernized as Attlee, but that form, though made famous by a prime minister, was an uncommon survival. Just as atte Style became Style, so atte Lee usually became Lee.

49. These names are only in the Cambridge manuscript. The Harleian manuscript says "S. de T.," while the vulgate has "T. S. de S." "Toll" might be Tolleshunt, Essex, or perhaps Colchester.

taken him to Colchester castle,[50] and imprisoned him there for four weeks until he had made fine to them in £40, half of which was paid for his deliverance. Lee produced in court a commission from the Chancery, issued to him and others, to arrest Thomas and his goods and chattels and take him to Colchester castle, which is what he did, and said that he handed Thomas over to John Oliver, the sheriff,[51] by indenture, "without this that he took any fine." Thereupon the justices, evidently with a note of outrage, exclaimed that "this commission was against the law, to take a man and his goods without indictment or suit of a party, or other due process," and said they would take the commission away with them and show it to the king's Council. Magna Carta was not expressly mentioned, but the principle relied on was evidently that enshrined in chapter 29 and the statute of 1368. As reported in the *Liber Assisarum*, this was a notable precedent, the importance of which would not be lost on Sir Edward Coke.[52] But it was no ordinary case. Sir John atte Lee (d. 1370) was steward the household and had been imprisoned in the Tower of London a month earlier after various complaints, presented to the king by Chief Justice Thorp, of his high-handedness and extortion.[53] A little earlier in the same Parliament a petition had been presented "that no man shall be put to answer without presentment before justices, or matter of record, or by due process and original writ according to the ancient law of the land, and if anything henceforth shall be done to the contrary it shall be void in law and treated as being in error." The king assented to this on the grounds that it was one of the articles of

50. The printed *Liber Assisarum* says Gloucester, but this is obviously a mistake for "Colcestre" (as it is spelt in the manuscripts). Colchester is in Essex.

51. John Oliver was sheriff of Essex 1366–8, and according to the *Liber Assisarum* was himself indicted for extortion.

52. It was cited in his memorandum on c. 29 (1604): *Selected Readings and Commentaries on Magna Carta*, 395 (where Coke corrected the name of the castle to Colchester); and in E. Coke, *Second Part of the Institutes of the Lawes of England* (London: M. Flesher and R. Young, 1642), 46.

53. Rot. Parl. 2, 297–8, nos. 20–28; *ODNB, sub nom.* Lee, Sir John (d. 1370); and see now W. M. Ormrod, "Parliamentary Scrutiny of Royal Ministers and Courtiers in Fourteenth-Century England: the Disgrace of Sir John Atte Lee (1368)," in *Law, Governance and Justice: New Views on Medieval Constitutionalism*, ed. R. W. Kaeuper (Leiden: Brill, 2013), 161–88, and the sources cited there (without reference to the proceedings at Chelmsford).

Magna Carta.[54] It seems, therefore, that the justices of oyer and terminer at Chelmsford were not challenging the king's government but were simply implementing the recent confirmation of Magna Carta in the context of investigations prompted by Parliament itself. Yet the case had a greater significance. It was not so much that it uncovered another instance of Lee's manifold offenses against the Rule of Law, which was merely a historical event, but rather that the judges could overturn a commission issued by the Chancery. The mere fact that someone acted under the authority of the great seal of England, and therefore at least notionally with the authority of the king's chancellor (in this case William of Wykeham), did not prove that they had followed due process.

Commissions which bypassed due process nevertheless remained a grievance. In 1378 the Commons complained that the commissions authorized by a statute passed in the last Parliament, which empowered the commissioners to arrest troublemakers without indictment or other process of law, were *tres-horrible et perillouse*, and threatened every free man with slavery (*servage*), contrary to Magna Carta and the statutes of due process. The statute was thereupon repealed.[55] A less successful petition was presented in 1415 by the men of Sandwich, who complained of a commission to charge them with a supposed debt to a Flemish widow, without giving them an opportunity to answer, contrary to chapter 29. The response this time was that the lord chancellor should proceed in accordance with the terms of the treaty with Flanders.[56]

The second case in the *Liber Assisarum* occurred the year after Lee's case, but in an entirely different context.[57] Mary de Valence (née de St. Pol),

54. Rot. Parl. 2.295, no. 12. This followed a petition to confirm Magna Carta generally. The resulting statute was 42 Edw. III, c. 3. The Commons had complained in 1341 and 1369 that people were often imprisoned without due process, contrary to Magna Carta: Rot. Parl. 2.129, no. 21; 130, no. 28; 15 Edw. III, stat. 2, c. 3; Rot. Parl. 2.270, no. 12; cf. 37 Edw. III, c. 18. It was again a grievance in the 1390s and 1400s: Rot. Parl. 3.319, no. 37; 4.470, no. 60.

55. 2 Ric. II, stat. 1, c. 6; Rot. Parl. 3.65, no. 46; 2 Ric. II, stat. 2, c. 2.

56. *Kalewartes v. Town of Sandwich* (1415) Rot. Parl. 4.67; PRO, SC 8/303/15127 (petition); SC 8/23/1145 (answer); CPR 1413–16: 110 (commission).

57. *Valence Mary Hall, Cambridge v. Regem* (1369) PRO, CP 40/440, m. 590 (petition of right, in French, and its outcome, pleaded in the replication in a *quare impedit* against Bardolf and the presentee, Humberston); 43 Edw. III, Lib. Ass. 21 (the petition of right in the Chancery); YB Mich. 44 Edw. III, ff. 35–6, pl. 24; PRO, C 44/5/20 (petition of

countess of Pembroke, was in 1345 granted the advowson of Tilney, Norfolk, with an acre of land, by John Bardolf (d. 1363), the third baron, and the grant was confirmed by a final concord levied in Hilary term 1346. In 1347 the countess founded Valence Mary Hall in Cambridge, now Pembroke College,[58] and amongst many other endowments gave them the advowson, with a mortmain license, in 1358. After Lord Bardolf's death in 1363 the king seized his heir as a ward and later (on 14 October 1369) presented to the benefice, which had fallen vacant during the wardship, on the footing that the advowson had descended to the heir;[59] the king's clerk, William Humberston, was then admitted by the archbishop of Canterbury *sede vacante*. The College immediately presented a petition of right. According to the report in the *Liber Assisarum*, the College's complaint was that they had been ousted of their presentment without an opportunity to object ("sans responder"), which was absolutely contrary to the Great Charter and other statutes to the same effect (*purement contre la grande chartre et auters divers statutes de ceo faits*). The Crown argued that the parol should demur[60] until the boy came of age, but it was decided that, since the petition was in the nature of a *quare impedit*, the form of action for recovering an advowson against a disturber, the case should proceed. It was then suggested that John Bardolf had been a tenant in tail, and therefore had no power to bar his issue by final concord. A hearing was held in Chancery on 19 November 1369, in the presence of Chief Justices Knyvet and Thorp, and other judges. The king's serjeants on this occasion declined to aver that John was a tenant in tail, presumably because they could not prove it, and judgment was therefore given against the king. The king thereupon revoked the presentation, and the College was able to recover the advowson by an ordinary writ of *quare impedit*. The College records show that a writ was sent to the

right); Cambridge, Pembroke College Archives, B.1–20 (located with the help of Dr. Jayne Ringrose, the College archivist).

58. In the *quare impedit*, Serjeant Kirton pleaded misnomer in that the plaintiffs' true name was Pembroke Hall. This was disputed, and the point seems to have been abandoned.

59. The presentation was enrolled in Chancery: *CPR 1367–70*, 310.

60. I.e. that the proceedings should stand over during the minority, which was the usual course in real actions brought against infants.

bishop to give effect to the judgment;[61] the king regranted the advowson to the College, and Humberston was granted a pension and a room in college in return for his loss. The reference in the petition to Magna Carta must have been to the disseisin clause of chapter 29, and the "sans responder" looks very like the principle of natural justice encountered in the cases of the 1320s. Coke so cited it, adding: "*nota bene*, the usurpation to an advowson is within this Act."[62] Thus, although no action could be brought against the Crown, and no execution of judgment could be awarded against the Crown, a remedy was obtained by due process against the usurper on the principle that the king could do no wrong.[63] It was by no means a unique or even a new case,[64] but its inclusion in the year books gave it greater prominence than any other of its kind.

THE DEPOSITION OF KING RICHARD II

In 1399 the great charter played its part in the greatest case of all, the deposition, or forced abdication, of a king.[65] It was not such a prominent part as might be expected, since the case against Richard II was framed chiefly in

61. Pembroke College Archives, B.16–17. The presentation by the king was revoked by patent on 8 December: *CPR 1367–70*, 332. Whether this patent was effective was one of the matters discussed in the Common Bench: YB Mich. 44 Edw. III, fol. 36, pl. 24.

62. Coke, *Second Part of the Institutes*, 46, margin.

63. For the importance of this principle see Baker, "The Legal Force and Effect of Magna Carta," at 80–2.

64. See, e.g., *The Earl of Surrey's Case* (1346), in which John de Warenne complained that the escheator of Norfolk had seized his manor of Thetford without warning or calling him first, contrary to Magna Carta: CCR 1346–9: 29; PRO, C 54/179, m. 7 (quoted in Thompson, *Magna Carta*, 77 n. 29). Two other Chancery cases mention due process, evidently alluding to Magna Carta. In *Robert de Barton's Case* (1348) a collation to a prebend in York cathedral, made by the king *sede vacante*, was revoked when the chancellor decided that the king's right could not be proved, and Barton was told to pursue his right by due process of law: *CPR 1348–50*, 102–3. And in *John de Lile's Case* (1355) a grant of the custody of a priory was revoked upon the prior's complaint that, since he had been inducted into the freehold, he could not be deprived without being brought to answer by due process of law: *CPR 1354–8*, 266.

65. Edward II's deposition in 1327 was less formal and did not use judicial forms: *Taswell-Langmead's English Constitutional History*, ed. T. F. T. Plucknett (London: Sweet & Maxwell, 1960), 487–9. The "six articles" against him, drawn up by Robert Stratford, bishop of Winchester, did not mention Magna Carta.

terms of the king's obligation, arising from his coronation oath, to uphold the laws of the realm in general. The case was set out in a series of charges (*Objectus contra regem*) which formed part of the formal record of the deposition.[66] The king, it was alleged, had been unwilling to preserve and protect the just laws and customs of the realm, in accordance with his oath, but had claimed that the laws lay in his mouth, or in his breast, and that he alone could change and make laws.[67] He had said that the life, lands, and goods of his subjects were subject to his will (*ad voluntatem suam*), contrary to the laws always used in former times with respect to *liberi homines*.[68] He had forced the judges to give an opinion as to the law of treason against their better judgment,[69] and by color of that had proceeded to the destruction of the duke of Gloucester, the earls of Arundel and Warwick, and Lord Cobham, without due process, "contrary to justice and the laws of his realm, and his oath."[70] Furthermore, Archbishop Arundel had been sentenced to exile, in his absence, without any process of law.[71] How far these allegations were meritorious it is difficult to say. There is no evidence that the judges had approved of conviction without trial. According to the record, the earl of Warwick had pleaded guilty, while the earl of Arundel and Lord Cobham had been arraigned in Parliament and asked what they had to say.[72] But the opportunity to speak seems in their case to have been in the manner of an *allocutus*, that is, the calling upon a convict after verdict to say why judgment should not be given according to law; this would explain why Arundel relied on nothing other than a pardon, which the king rejected as void for misrepresentation. The real gravamen must have been that they were not tried by their peers, upon a specified charge and with ev-

66. Rot. Parl. 3.418–21.

67. Ibid., 419, no. 33.

68. Ibid., 420, no. 43.

69. As to this see S. B. Chrimes, "Richard II's Questions to the Judges," *Law Quarterly Review* 72 (1956): 365–90; N. Saul, *Richard II* (New Haven: Yale University Press, [1997]), 173–5.

70. Rot. Parl. 3.418, nos. 19, 21. Cobham's sentence was commuted to exile, since what he had done had been with the king's express authority.

71. Rot. Parl. 3.421, nos. 47, 50. Tresilian C.J. had also been sentenced *in absentia*: ibid. 238.

72. *Complete Collection of State Trials*, vol. I, ed. T. B. Howell (London: R. Bagshaw, 1809), at 129, 174. The duke of Gloucester, having already been murdered, was attainted posthumously.

idence given openly. Impeachment had been veering in the wrong direction, under royal pressure.[73]

All these accusations against the king contain echoes of chapter 29, but the statute was not expressly cited until the forty-fourth charge, which was that men had been accused before the earl marshal's court (*in curia militari*), and only allowed to defend themselves by battle, even when they were old and their accusers young and fit, contrary to chapter 29 (which was recited in full) and to the king's oath.[74] One other explicit breach of the statute, in this case the first chapter, was that the king had sent prohibitions to church courts under his signet seal, contrary to the ecclesiastical liberties approved in the great charter.[75] This complaint was not about prohibitions in general, but about prerogative writs of prohibition without involving any court; indeed, the charge was that the king had sent them after the chancellor had refused to grant a regular prohibition. Some of these grievances undoubtedly had substance, while others may have been exaggerated or distorted. That is not the point. The great point of principle was that the Rule of Law, which had found expression in the broadest provisions of the great charter, did not spare kings. It was not Magna Carta itself which justified deposal, since the 1225 version provided no such remedy. The true justification had to be that kings took a solemn oath, before they were crowned, to uphold the laws, and it followed that arbitrary government outside the law amounted both to perjury and to a breach of the conditions on which they were crowned. Nevertheless, the constitutional principle that kings were under the law, a law which protected life, liberty and property, had also come to be associated indelibly with Magna Carta. It would in future be taken for granted, without the need for repeated confirmation.

73. For the development of more regular procedure earlier in the reign see Plucknett, "The Impeachments of 1376" (above, n. 36). For the later proceedings see *Studies in English Legal History*, ch. 9–10.

74. Rot. Parl. 3.420, no. 44. See A. Tuck, *Richard II and the English Nobility* (London: Edward Arnold, 1973), 197–8.

75. Rot. Parl. 3.421, no. 46.

Conclusion

How far Magna Carta entered the popular consciousness in the fourteenth century is difficult to gauge. The peasants who revolted in 1381 were not Magna Chartists.[76] But the charter certainly had a potentially subversive quality. John Wycliff regarded the liberties of the *ecclesia anglicana* guaranteed by chapter 1 as including a measure of freedom from interference by the Roman Curia,[77] a notion perhaps reflected in the twenty-seventh charge against Richard II,[78] but hardly the orthodoxy of the day. He wrote scathingly in the 1370s that

> much treasure, and much time of many hundred clerks in universities, is foul wasted about books of the emperor's law and study about them.... It seemeth the curates should rather learn and teach the king's statutes, and namely the Great Charter, than the emperor's law or much part of the pope's; for men in our realm are bound to obey the king and his rightful laws and not so the emperor's, and they might wondrous well be saved though many laws of the pope had never been spoken....[79]

It is doubtful whether the university doctors would have been more successful in their exegesis of Magna Carta than the laymen in the inns of court, or what parts of it might have helped the cause of religious freedom. It helped the Lollards no more than it did the aggrieved peasants. For most purposes, Magna Carta was still the property of the upper levels of soci-

76. As to whether they had any legal ideals or were essentially anarchic see A. Musson, *Medieval Law in Context: The Growth of Legal Consciousness from Magna Carta to the Peasants' Revolt* (Manchester: Manchester University Press, 2001), 241–55. Wat Tyler had demanded, rather puzzlingly, that there should be no law other than "the law of Winchester."

77. See E. Tatnall, "John Wyclif and *Ecclesia Anglicana*," *Journal of Ecclesiastical History* 20 (1969), 19–43.

78. Rot. Parl. 3.419, no. 27. The grievance was stated to be that, whereas the realm had always been so free that neither the pope nor anyone else outside the realm could meddle with it (*se intromittere debeat*), Richard had petitioned the pope to confirm certain acts of Parliament, contrary to his royal crown and dignity and against the statutes and liberties of the realm. The *regnum*, of course, did not necessarily comprehend the *ecclesia*.

79. Quoted in F. W. Maitland, *English Law and the Renaissance* (Cambridge: Cambridge University Press, 1901), 53 (here modernized).

ety and their lawyers. In the fifteenth century, chapter 29 would disappear almost completely from the law reports, except in relation to the trial of peers of the realm. And it disappeared from petitions. The bill jurisdiction of the Star Chamber and Chancery was in its infancy, though over the next century it would grow until it seemed to challenge the common law itself. The procedure by subpoena, English bill and depositions was not the due process contemplated in Edward III's reign, but it would be accommodated as part of the law of the land.

As for the inns of court, their teaching in the fifteenth century would minimize the practical effectiveness of chapter 29. Yet it is evident from the cases discussed above that the underlying notions of due process and the rule of law had been kept alive in appropriate cases during the fourteenth century. The inns of court were a professional law school, and their mode of teaching—borrowed from the universities—was to gloss texts, word by word, as a way of inculcating a critical approach to written law and its interpretation. They did not provide lectures on constitutional law or human rights, or try to read into statutes what was obviously not there. Participants in their exercises of learning were introduced to the problems and opportunities raised by looseness of language, and it was left to the real world to circumvent the problems or seize the opportunities. A glimpse of that real world is provided by the parliamentary and conciliar records, and the exceptional *Liber Assisarum* for 1368. They do not yet show judges, independently of Parliament, daring to challenge the ministers of a ruling government, as Sir Edward Coke was to do in the time of James I. Indeed, in the cases of 1322, 1327 and 1336 it was the king himself who took advantage of chapter 29 to benefit political favorites. They nevertheless show that, by the middle of the century, the judges seem to have been confident enough in suitable cases to invoke the principle of due process against royal officials on behalf of private subjects and institutions. Coke has often been criticized for his bold misuse of history. But his court might not have succeeded in establishing judicial review of prerogative or administrative action without reliance on Magna Carta, and so the words had to be imperceptibly reinterpreted. In achieving an appearance of continuity, old precedents were vital. And that is where Coke would be very grateful for the steps that had been taken in the reign of Edward III.

Law and Equity in a Medieval English Manor Court[1]

Elizabeth Papp Kamali

The ambitious title given this brief contribution belies the nature of the exercise, which is a close textual reading and contextual analysis of a short series of early fourteenth-century manorial court roll entries regarding a messuage (dwelling house) and half yardland in the Buckinghamshire manor of Great Horwood. Perhaps it is unreasonable to think that one might derive conclusions about law and equity in a manor court from a tiny sampling of texts.[2] Yet it is in the nature of the methodology imparted by Charlie Donahue to his many students that one might place a seemingly minute detail from a court roll under the legal historian's microscope, trace the threads that come into view, and ultimately draw macro-level conclusions, sometimes tentative and occasionally provocative, about the nature of law and society in medieval England. It is a methodology I first encountered as a freshman preparing weekly response papers in Charlie's course on the "Legal and Constitutional History of Medieval England," a class that inspired my subsequent career choices. But for now let us return to that messuage and half yardland.

In late October 1317, during harvest time, an inquest at Great Horwood—likely a jury of twelve tenants—declared that Robert de Salden, a

1. My thanks to Charles Donahue for a first introduction to the fascinating world of manorial court records, and also to John Goldberg, Tom Green, Tom Johnson, Eric Nemarich, and John Witte for reading earlier drafts.

2. On the allure of the "interesting case," see Charles Donahue, "Female Plaintiffs in Marriage Cases," in *Wife and Widow in Medieval England*, ed. Sue Sheridan Walker (Ann Arbor: University of Michigan Press, 1993), 184–85.

villein, was "a fugitive and of ill repute" (*fugitivus et male fame*).[3] Due to his fugitive status, Robert "entirely forfeited" (*omnino… forisfecit*) his land, an ostensibly permanent forfeiture that allowed the lord to transfer the tenements to a person of his choosing, to hold without any danger of a future claim by Robert or his issue.[4] The record was unequivocal: the forfeiture was to be permanent. Yet Robert's interest in the land did not vanish with this proclamation by the manor court. Instead, the ensuing fourteen years witnessed a series of claims by interested parties, including Robert's widow and son, ending ultimately in recovery by the fugitive's heir. What explains this reversal of the court's 1317 judgment, which supposedly precluded all claims *in perpetuum*? A close reading of the roll, combined with consideration of the broader historical context, reveals: (1) competing interests among various members of the Great Horwood community; (2) the selective marshaling of written evidence, manorial custom, and common law rules; and (3) the exercise of equitable discretion in selecting the "rightful" tenant, possibly guided by extra-legal factors, such as the exigencies of famine. Each of these themes will be treated in succession in Parts III–V following a brief timeline of possession in Part I and a description of the tenements in Part II. In addition to making a claim about the inherent flexibility of custom and the various tactics employed in this particular manor court to resolve a complex dispute, I hope to advance a methodological claim regarding the importance of the deep, textual and contextual history familiar to Charlie's students.

The Successive Holders of Robert de Salden's Lands, 1317–1331

According to Maitland's pithy definition, a manor was "an estate which could be and was administered as a single economic and agrarian whole."[5]

3. L.R. Poos and Lloyd Bonfield, eds., *Select Cases in Manorial Courts* (London: Selden Society, 1998), 3. I rely gratefully on these excerpts from rolls housed at New College, Oxford. For analysis of the core dispute, see ibid., xcvii–xcix.

4. Ibid., 3 ("…dominus tenementum illud tradere potest cuicumque voluerit tenendum absque reclamatione predicti Roberti vel alicujus alterius de exitu illius in perpetuum.")

5. Frederic Maitland, *Select Pleas in Manorial and Other Seignorial Courts*, Selden Society 2 (London: B. Quaritch, 1888), xl.

Manorial tenants plowed and reaped in common to supply their needs and those of the lord.[6] A manor court was a periodic gathering of tenants and manorial officers to register land transfers, respond to violations of manorial custom, and adjudicate disputes among tenants. Decisions were often made by all those gathered at court, i.e., the body of suitors or "the homage," although over time it became more common for this power to be delegated to smaller juries.[7] Rolls often refer to "the lord" (*dominus*) making specific grants and receiving tenements into his hands; however, he might be represented in court by his steward, an administrative officer who, as part of the lord's council (*consilio domini*), likely held great sway in adjudication. Manorial rolls are the parchment records of the manor court, written in the same secretarial hand as the plea rolls of the central royal courts, with fines typically enumerated in the left margin.

To return to the specific dispute here, upon Robert's condemnation as a fugitive in 1317, the lord transferred his tenements to Walter Hogges, who died within a year of taking possession.[8] In 1318, the lord assigned the land to Stephen le Carter, who appears to have held it peacefully for the next decade. Then, in 1329, Robert de Salden's widow, Isabel, appeared in the manor court; she successfully claimed her dower in the messuage and half yardland.[9] It is unclear when Robert died, and whether Isabel remained in Great Horwood following her husband's initial forfeiture, but Isabel brought her dower claim against Stephen with the contention that her late husband never actually forfeited the said tenements (*ea tenementa numquam forisfecit*).[10]

Just months later, Stephen le Carter's son-in-law, John le Carpenter, perhaps alarmed by the court's resolution of Isabel's dower claim, approached the manor court for confirmation of his right to succeed to the tenements. The lord granted to John that the land currently held by Stephen le Carter and Isabel de Salden (i.e., her dower portion) should descend

6. Ibid.

7. See Poos and Bonfield, *Select Cases*, xxiii.

8. Ibid., 3–4.

9. Ibid., 4–5. Dower is a widow's life estate in a portion, typically one-third, of the land held by her husband at the time their marriage was contracted. See Theodore Plucknett, *Concise History of the Common Law*, 5th ed. (Boston: Little Brown, 1956), 566.

10. Poos and Bonfield, *Select Cases*, 4–5.

Timeline of Events	
October 1317	Robert de Salden declared a fugitive; forfeits land. Walter Hogges takes possession, pays 100s., and does fealty.
June 1318	Walter Hogges reported dead.
June 1318	Stephen le Carter pays 100s. entry fine and takes possession.
June 1329	Isabel, widow of Robert de Salden, claims her dower successfully.
October 1329	John le Carpenter, Stephen's son-in-law, secures assurance that he and his wife, Joan, will succeed to the tenements following Stephen's death; pays 6s. 8d.
August 1330	Thomas, son of Robert de Salden, makes his first claim and loses.
January 1331	Thomas again makes a claim and succeeds, paying a 66s. 8d. entry fine. Henry Bicon pays a 15s. entry fine for a leasehold of 6.5 acres.

to John and his wife Joan and their heirs, "to hold in villeinage (*in villenagio*) according to the custom of the manor" following the deaths of Stephen and Isabel.[11] This result contravened the wishes of Stephen himself, who preferred the land to devolve upon his younger daughter instead of Joan, who had married John against her father's wishes.[12] According to the rolls, passing the tenement to a younger daughter would be "completely against manorial custom" (*contra consuetudinem maneri* [sic] *omnino*). The court roll does not identify Stephen's younger daughter by name, but other entries indicate that Stephen may have been in financial straits within years of acceding to Robert de Salden's forfeited tenements, and that he owed debts in conjunction with a daughter named Agnes; in fact, Stephen appears to have had at least three daughters and no sons, a circumstance that may have

11. Ibid., 16.
12. Ibid., 16–17.

further strained his finances as the daughters reached marriageable age.[13] Following Stephen's death in 1329/30, John successfully took possession of the land, performing fealty for the two-thirds not subject to Isabel's dower. Yet John and Joan's success was short-lived. In 1330, Thomas de Salden, the son of Isabel and the late fugitive Robert, appeared in the manor court to claim the tenements as his father's heir.[14] This initial attempt proved unsuccessful. A few months later, however, Thomas reasserted his claim and succeeded in recovering the land allegedly forfeited by his father over a decade earlier. In less than a decade and a half, Robert de Salden's lands had passed through a variety of hands, ultimately coming full circle to rest with Robert's first-born son, Thomas. What might explain this series of events?

Background Information on the Nature and Value of the Tenements

Robert de Salden's land consisted of a customary (as opposed to freehold) messuage and half yardland (*mesuagium et dimidiam virgatam terre*), the former likely referring to a dwelling-house, subsidiary structures, and perhaps a garden, and the latter to a plot of land that may have been roughly thirty acres in extent.[15] We know from the rolls that

13. In May 1320, Stephen was fined 6d. for violating the assize of ale and, along with his daughter Agnes, was the target of a debt plea brought by a Little Horwood resident. W. O. Ault, *Open-Field Farming in Medieval England* (London: Allen and Unwin, 1972), 162–63. Stephen had at least one more daughter, Johanna, for whom he paid the lord one-quarter of oats for permission to marry her to John of Westbury, also in 1320. Ibid., 163. A few years later, in 1323, Stephen le Carter paid a small 2d. fine for default.

14. Poos and Bonfield, *Select Cases*, 5–6.

15. In 1320, Great Horwood had eight freehold and forty-two customary messuages, and eleven cottages without attached farmland; it had fifty-eight tenants, likely heads of household with multiple dependents. See Matthew Tompkins, *Peasant Society in a Midlands Manor* (Ph.D. Diss. University of Leicester, 2006), 179. A virgate (from Latin *virga*, rod), or yardland (Old English *gięrd-land*), varied in measurement. See *OED*, s.v. virgate; A. W. Barsby and Clare Barsby, *Manorial Law* (Epsom: Barsby Legal Research and Publ., 1996), 18. On the word "acre" in medieval records, see P. D. A. Harvey, "Manorial Records," in *Medieval Manorial Records*, ed. Margaret L. Faull (Leeds: Medieval Section of the Yorkshire Archaeological Society, 1983), 6–8. On villein lands, see Frederick Pollock and Frederic W. Maitland, *History of English Law*, 2nd ed. (Cambridge: Cambridge University Press, 1898), 1.364–65.

the tenements contained not just a single dwelling house, but multiple buildings.[16]

The tenements were valued, for entry fine purposes (an entry fine being a sum paid by a new tenant upon assuming possession), at a surprisingly high 100 shillings, or £5; this was the amount paid by Walter Hogges and Stephen le Carter in 1317 and 1318, respectively, suggesting that these men were relatively well off.[17] The entry fine of 6s. 8d. prepaid by John and Joan le Carpenter in 1329 represented a substantial discount, likely due to the fact that the couple could not occupy the entire property until Joan's father and the widow Isabel had both died.[18] The discount may also reflect the court's awareness of the implications of Isabel's successful dower claim a few months earlier; there may even have been foreknowledge of Thomas de Salden's imminent suit. The entry fine paid in 1331 by Thomas de Salden—66s. 8d. (i.e., five marks), or two-thirds of 100s.—suggests that he may have only gained immediate entry to two-thirds of the full property at the time, perhaps due to his mother's continued dower stake in the remaining one-third.[19]

Competing Interests in Robert de Salden's Messuage and Half Yardland

Creditors and other tenants, possibly overlapping categories, likely shared an interest in Robert de Salden's tenements. Thanks to the work of Chris Briggs, we know that Robert was saddled with debts in the decade preced-

16. See Poos and Bonfield, *Select Cases*, 4 ("domos et edificia"). "Messuage" might be translated as "farmstead." See Tompkins, Peasant Society, 60.

17. Poos and Bonfield, Select Cases, 3–4. Tom Johnson (private correspondence) speculates that Great Horwood's tenants may have included relatively well-off yeomen in light of these sizable £5 entry fines, which may also reflect the inflationary impact of the famine years. On the use of local courts by wealthier peasants at Great Horwood and elsewhere, see generally, Chris Briggs, "Seignorial Control of Villagers' Litigation," *Historical Research* 81 (2008), 399–422. Briggs specifically describes Robert de Salden as a significant landholder in light of his possession of a half virgate. See Chris Briggs, *Credit and Village Society in Fourteenth-Century England* (Oxford: Oxford University Press, 2009), 173–74.

18. Poos and Bonfield, *Select Cases*, 16.

19. Ibid., 7.

ing his forfeiture.[20] When he forfeited his tenements in 1317, other Great Horwood tenants may have clamored for an opportunity to benefit from the newly available lands. Assigning a new tenant swiftly was also in the lord's interest: he would receive customs and services (*consuetudines et servicia*) with little interruption, ensure the maintenance of any buildings, and receive a 100-shilling fine from the new tenant.[21] During a time of crop failure, a circumstance to be discussed below, the lord and his tenants alike may have been particularly interested in a speedy conveyance.

A whole series of tenants—from Walter Hogges, to Stephen le Carter, to John and Joan le Carpenter, to Thomas de Salden—gained access to the tenements between 1317 and 1331. Another subset of individuals leased an arable 6.5-acre portion of the tenements, thereby providing a source of ready income to the lessor. Emma Isoude held the 6.5 acres for a term of years as of 1329, although her tie to the land may have been established prior to that date. For instance, the rolls reveal that Emma's husband, John, served as a pledge for Stephen le Carter in 1318 when the lord first granted Stephen the tenements.[22] Perhaps Emma and John's interest predated Stephen's accession to tenure: they may have been farming the plot during the tenure of Walter Hogges, or perhaps even before Robert de Salden's forfeiture. This same 6.5-acre portion would be leased again in 1331, when Thomas de Salden, upon regaining his father's lands, immediately demised the arable piece to one of his pledges, Henry Bicon, for a fourteen-year term.[23]

Beyond these tenants and lessees, another group of manor court participants may have had some interest in the outcome of these successive moments of litigation. Ralph, son of Richard the Reeve, for example, served

20. See Briggs, *Credit and Village Society*, 153 (describing Robert's declining fortune in the 1310s, when he appears in the rolls as a lessor and, on six occasions, as a debtor).

21. Poos and Bonfield, *Select Cases*, 4. The new tenant, Walter Hogges, promised to perform the customs and services and to maintain the buildings in the same or better condition than before, as was typical in such land transfers. Tompkins observes that vacancies were relatively rare at Great Horwood due to the manor's favorable landholding conditions, including low rents. Tompkins, *Peasant Society*, 56.

22. Poos and Bonfield, *Select Cases*, 4. In 1331, John Isoude was described as the former holder of the 6.5-acre arable plot, ibid., 7. It was not uncommon for an individual to serve as pledge before leasing a portion of a newly acquired tenement, as will be seen below with Thomas de Salden and Henry Bicon.

23. Ibid., 7. Henry paid an entry fine of 15s.

as a pledge for both Walter Hogges in 1317 and Stephen le Carter in 1318,[24] supporting both men in their commitment to maintaining the property and performing the customary services once owed by Robert de Salden. Of greater interest is Robert Saunders, who appeared as a pledge for Walter, Stephen, and John le Carpenter in 1317, 1318, and 1329, respectively.[25] Perhaps Robert was simply a man of local good repute and significant enough means to serve as pledge for his neighbors. Yet his involvement may not have been entirely impartial. In fact, Robert was "challenged by the parties" when the court summoned the whole homage, presumably all the tenants attending the court,[26] to determine the outcome of Thomas de Salden's claim.[27] Logic tells us that Thomas likely challenged Robert, although matters are complicated by the fact that Robert then proceeded to serve as a pledge for Thomas when the court decided in the latter's favor.[28] Nevertheless, his exclusion from the homage suggests that his impartiality had somehow been tainted by his prior participation in the lord's grants.

Supporting this conclusion is the fact that Walter Stevenes, who served as pledge for Stephen le Carter in 1318 and John le Carpenter in 1329, was likewise excluded from the homage's deliberations in 1331.[29] Walter apparently had an even greater financial tie with Stephen: the 1318 roll reveals that Walter owed Stephen a sizable 60s. debt, which was immediately applied to cover more than half of Stephen's entry fine.[30] Perhaps there was some greater *quid pro quo* involved in Walter's willingness to serve as pledge; this, in turn, could have inspired Thomas de Salden to challenge his participation in the homage in 1331.[31]

24. Ibid., 3–4.

25. Ibid., 3–4, 17. This assumes that the same Robert Saunders was involved in all three instances, and not, for example, his son.

26. See *OED*, s.v. homage ("the body of tenants attending a manorial court, or the jury of such a court."); John Beckerman, "Procedural Innovation and Institutional Change in Medieval English Manorial Courts," *Law and History Review* 10 (1992), 242–3.

27. Poos and Bonfield, *Select Cases*, 6.

28. Ibid., 7.

29. Ibid., 4, 6, 17.

30. Ibid., 4.

31. For the idea that pledging frequently involved payment, see Martin Pimsler, "Solidarity in the Medieval Village?" *Journal of British Studies* 17 (1977), 5, 11. At Great Horwood, we may be dealing less with monetary payments and more with promises regarding interests in the land at issue.

While the evidence is inconclusive, the rolls hint that pledges might have directly influenced the outcome of a dispute by serving on an inquest jury or through participation in the homage. For example, William Baynard served as pledge for Walter Hogges in 1317 when Robert de Salden was first condemned as a fugitive, and then participated thirteen years later in an inquest assigned to determine whether Robert had indeed been a fugitive; the inquest answered in the affirmative.[32] William may have been selected for the inquest due to his direct knowledge of the 1317 events. He may also have been a regular actor, along with his kinsmen, in the Great Horwood court.[33] Finally, we have evidence that John le Carpenter may have shored up his case through recourse to a third party, Ralph Burdet (identified in the roll as *dompno* and therefore possibly the prior of Newton Longville Priory, a Cluniac house that had held the manor since the twelfth century), to whom he paid 12d.[34] Burdet, whose identity is unclear but who may have been the lord of the manor, registered a small monetary gain when John succeeded in acquiring a right to his father-in-law's tenements.

32. Poos and Bonfield, *Select Cases*, 5–6. William may have been related to Sabina Baynard, to whom Robert de Salden acknowledged a 19s. debt in 1312. See Briggs, *Credit and Village Society*, 153.

33. See, e.g., William's participation on other occasions, as well as that of Richard Baynard and Richard Baynard "the younger" in the 1330 inquest. Poos and Bonfield, *Select Cases*, 5, 18, 51–52.

34. Ibid., 17 and n. 1. "Dompno" is an honorific frequently attached to abbots and priors. On the early history of Great Horwood, located less than three miles from the Bletchley Park of World War II fame, see H. E. Salter, *Newington Longeville Charters* (Oxford: The Society, 1921), xii; William Illingworth, ed., *Placita de Quo Warranto* (London: G. Eyre and A. Strahan, 1818), 96; "Parishes: Newton Longville," in *A History of the County of Buckingham*, ed. William Page (London: St. Catherine Press, 1927), 4.425–29. The prior was lord of the manor as of 1316, the year before Robert de Salden's forfeiture. See "Parishes: Horwood," in *A History of the County of Buckingham*, 3.372–76; *Inquisitions and Assessments Relating to Feudal Aids, 1284–1431* (London: Her Majesty's Stationery Office, 1899), 1.112. See also "Alien Houses: Cluniac Priory of Newton Longville," in *A History of the County of Buckingham*, 1.395–96; David Knowles and R. Neville Hadcock, *Medieval Religious Houses: England and Wales* (London: Longmans, Green, 1971), 101; David Smith and Vera London, eds., *Heads of Religious Houses, England and Wales, 1216–1377* (Cambridge: Cambridge University Press, 2001), 242–3. Newton Longville did not have a monastic house; rather, Longueville in Normandy may have routinely sent a monk or two to manage the Buckinghamshire properties. Salter, *Newington Longeville Charters*, xvi.

From tenants to lessees, and pledges to inquest jurors, several Great Horwood residents had a stake in the outcome of the dispute over Robert de Salden's messuage and half yardland.

SELECTIVE USE OF MANOR ROLLS AND CUSTOM

Despite the involvement of third parties, we cannot attribute the outcome of the successive claims solely to self-interested human intervention, or "jiggery-pokery," to borrow a phrase from Charlie's teaching lexicon.[35] Rather, the manor rolls themselves, as a source of written precedent, and manorial custom, as a source of oral precedent derived from collective memory, may have helped determine the outcome of the litigation.[36] Manor court participants made selective use of both these devices. And written records alone were not necessarily dispositive. For example, when Robert de Salden's widow, Isabel, staked her dower claim to a third of Stephen le Carter's tenements, the roll states that Stephen was unable to assert that Robert had clearly forfeited the tenements.[37] Yet the 1317 roll, had it been consulted, would have informed the court that Robert had indeed "entirely forfeited that land."[38] Did Stephen fail to anticipate the value that a search of the rolls might hold for his claim? Might a roll search have proven too costly or cumbersome? Did Stephen perhaps anticipate that the equities weighed too heavily in favor of Robert's widow to make a forceful challenge to her claim unseemly or unlikely to succeed?[39] Did illness or dementia weaken

35. A phrase, incidentally, which has since crept into Supreme Court jurisprudence. See Justice Scalia's dissent in *King v. Burwell*, 135 S.Ct. 2480, 2500 (2015) (describing the Court's "interpretive jiggery-pokery" in parsing the Affordable Care Act).

36. Beckerman observes that it became common to vouch the rolls as proof during the second half of the thirteenth century. Beckerman, "Procedural Innovation," 224. On the benefits thereby accruing to villeins, see R. M. Smith, "Some Thoughts on 'Hereditary' and 'Proprietary' Rights in Land under Customary Law," *Law and History Review* 1 (1983): 110.

37. Poos and Bonfield, *Select Cases*, 5.

38. Ibid., 3.

39. On the role of equity, see Lloyd Bonfield, "The Nature of Customary Law in the Manor Courts of Medieval England," *Comparative Studies in Society and History* 31 (1989), 521, 531. See also J. A. Raftis, *Tenure and Mobility: Studies in the Social History of the Medieval English Village* (Toronto: Pontifical Institute of Mediaeval Studies, 1964), 207, n. 3. My thanks to Tom Johnson for the latter reference.

his effectiveness in responding to Isabel's dower claim, given the fact that Stephen died shortly after? Perhaps everyone knew that the earlier judgment against Robert de Salden and his issue had been wrongly decided, assuming we can speak of "right" and "wrong" with regard to custom,[40] in which case a search of the rolls might have only complicated matters.

In contrast, the rolls were searched less than a year later when Robert de Salden's son, Thomas, first brought a claim. According to the 1330 roll, "it was found by the rolls of the court" from 1317 that Robert was indeed a fugitive who "entirely forfeited" the land;[41] the use of direct quotations from the 1317 roll confirms that an actual search transpired, as opposed to relying on the memory of individuals present at the earlier court session. In fact, the roll search must have been thorough, as the court proceeded to describe the devolution of tenure from Robert to Walter Hogges, Stephen le Carter, and ultimately John and Joan le Carpenter, "as nearer of the blood of the same Stephen."[42] In light of the outcome, one suspects that John and Joan may have petitioned for an examination of the rolls. Yet after all the trouble of a thorough search of the rolls, the written record was not held as unimpeachable evidence of the failure of Thomas' claim. Rather, the court then held an inquest of twelve men, who concluded that Robert had been a fugitive and had forfeited his tenements, and that neither Robert, were he alive, nor any of his issue could hold the tenements "according to custom" (*secundum consuetudinem*).[43] A jury, representing local knowledge and testifying under oath, supplemented the evidence of the rolls with statements of fact related to Robert's status and inheritance custom, and the matter appeared to have been settled conclusively.

Yet what explains the turn of events a few months later when the court awarded possession of the tenements to Thomas de Salden? Neither the court's declaration in 1317 that Robert de Salden had permanently forfeited his tenements, nor its assertion in 1330 that Robert's son, Thomas,

40. On the nature of custom, see Beckerman, "Procedural Innovation," 216; Bonfield, "Nature of Customary Law," 519, 522, 526–7; Smith, "Some Thoughts on 'Hereditary' and 'Proprietary' Rights," 98, 102.

41. Poos and Bonfield, *Select Cases*, 5.

42. Ibid.

43. Ibid., 5–6. Had memory perhaps triumphed over the written record? See, generally, Michael Clanchy, *From Memory to Written Record* (Oxford: Blackwell, 1993).

could not legitimately claim the tenements, precluded revisitation of the issue when Thomas decided to try his luck again. What appears, from our perspective, to have been *res judicata,* was in actuality still open for reconsideration, suggesting that if Thomas did indeed have a right to his father's tenements, then that right could not be eliminated by a prior court decision. Finality does not appear to have been of overriding concern in Great Horwood's court.[44] Inspired by Charlie's example, we might imagine some legal realist motivations for the court's reconsideration of Thomas' plea. For instance, perhaps a claim brought during the harvest season, in August 1330, was viewed less favorably than a claim brought in midwinter, in January 1331, when fields were lying fallow, thereby simplifying a transition in tenancy. Thomas may also have brought more persuasive arguments and evidence to bear in his second appearance. For example, Thomas argued that the court had previously endowed his mother, Isabel, in the same tenements, and a search of the rolls confirmed this point.[45] Thomas apparently felt the court was bound by its earlier decision to admit Isabel to her dower, as this amounted to a concession that Robert de Salden's right in the land had not evaporated in 1317. Had Robert truly forfeited his land permanently, then his widow might have had no viable claim to dower in the tenements.[46]

Once again, the roll evidence could not stand alone. Instead, the whole homage was sworn to testify. The homage confirmed that Robert had indeed been a fugitive, both "of ill fame and behavior" (*male fame et conversationis*).[47] Rather than stating that Robert had entirely forfeited (*omnino forisfecit*) his holdings, as the 1317 roll indicated, the 1331 roll entry indicated more ambiguously that he "relinquished" (*reliquidit*) the tenements, and

44. A further study might explore the role of finality in manorial court decisions. Was Thomas' relitigation of this issue a rare exception to a normal rule of preclusion, or was this instead a fairly common practice in Great Horwood and elsewhere?

45. Poos and Bonfield, *Select Cases,* 6.

46. This appears to have been the case at common law. Henry de Bracton, *On the Laws and Customs of England,* trans. and ed. Samuel E. Thorne (Cambridge, Mass.: Belknap Press, 1977), 3.360–61.

47. The word "conversatio" might denote the nature of the people with whom Robert associated or, alternatively, his general manner of life. See Latham, ed., *Dictionary of Medieval Latin from British Sources* (London: Oxford University Press, 1975–2013), Fasc. II, s.v. *conversatio.*

that the lord transferred them to Walter Hogges "for lack of tenants."[48] This left open the possibility that Robert's kin may have had standing to assert a claim to the land at the time of the fugitive's alleged forfeiture; most likely Thomas was still a minor in 1317, and perhaps the family departed abruptly due to Robert's local infamy. The homage was then asked (it is unclear by whom) whether Robert had been indicted or convicted, answering in the negative and expressing confusion over whether fugitive status alone, without a conviction, would be grounds for forfeiture. This may have been the first time the issue had arisen in recent memory in Great Horwood's court, in which case the relevant custom, assuming there was any, may not have been readily known. The question was submitted by the homage "to the discretion of the lord's council" (*super discretionem consilii domini*).[49] Three weeks later, Thomas de Salden and John and Joan le Carpenter returned to the court to hear the decision. The council declared that Robert de Salden's withdrawal from the manor and his fugitive status were not reason for forfeiture, thereby contradicting the court's earlier written decision.[50] John was to recover expenses incurred in maintaining the tenements, valued at 7s., while Thomas would now be liable for all future fines, maintenance of the premises, and services.

Equitable Considerations

Did Thomas succeed based on a reinterpretation or reinvention of manorial custom, a determination that the 1317 forfeiture had been in error, or the court's perception of the equities of the case? Charlie might encourage us to ask what else was going on in England in 1317. The fourteenth century, as Charlie reminds us,[51] was punctuated by cataclysm, most notably the

48. Poos and Bonfield, *Select Cases*, 6.

49. On this procedural move, see Beckerman, "Procedural Innovation," 218.

50. For the idea that the written record gave greater fixity to custom, see John Beckerman, "Toward a Theory of Medieval Manorial Adjudication," *Law and History Review* 13 (1995), 12. Perhaps this was less true for more obscure custom, such as how to deal with forfeiture by fugitives; it is also possible Great Horwood did not have established custom on this issue.

51. See, e.g., Charles Donahue, "What Happened in the English Legal Justice System in the Fourteenth Century and Why Would Anyone Want to Know?" *Southern Methodist University Law Review* 63 (2010), 949–52.

Black Death in mid-century, but also an earlier stretch of famine. Considering the timing of Robert's forfeiture, it takes little imagination to paint a Jean Valjean-like image of a desperate father's efforts to provide for his family after a third consecutive year of miserable harvests.[52] "I heard men in that place make much moan," reads a contemporary poem, "How they are miserable in their tilling; good years and grain are both gone, and they keep not here any saying nor sing any song."[53] These were not easy years for England's farming communities. An early fourteenth-century poem described the plight of the fugitive outlaw as especially dire, as he dared not approach his own hearth: "I may not return to the peace among my kindred," bemoaned the literary outlaw, who observed that "the rich are ransomed, while the poor are emasculated."[54]

Admittedly, the 1317 harvest marked an improvement over the previous two years, although England would not experience its first post-famine bountiful harvest until 1318.[55] Nevertheless, desperation may have inspired Robert's alleged wrongdoing, even if a somewhat improved harvest may have constrained the inquest's tolerance of unlawful behavior. In fact, there is some evidence that the Great Horwood community historically took a fairly unforgiving stance toward those who failed to earn their keep.[56] Of course, this is all speculation. Another possibility is that Robert simply

52. See, generally, Ian Kershaw, "The Great Famine and Agrarian Crisis in England, 1315–1322," *Past & Present* 59 (1973), 3–50. Kershaw observes that robberies, particularly of foodstuffs, dominated criminal prosecutions in Kent in 1316–1317: ibid., 12. See also Barbara Hanawalt, "Economic Influences on the Pattern of Crime in England, 1300–1348," *American Journal of Legal History* 18 (1974), 281–97.

53. Thomas Wright, ed., *Political Songs of England From the Reign of John to that of Edward II* (London: J. B. Nichols and Son, 1839), 149 ("Ich herde men up mold make muche mon, / Hou he beth i-tened of here tilyynge, / God yeres and corn bothe beth a-gon, / Ne kepeth here no sawe ne no song syng.")

54. Ibid., 231–236 ("...n'os à la pes venyr entre mon lignage; / Les riches sunt à raunsoun, povres à escolage.")

55. Kershaw, "Great Famine," 13.

56. See, e.g., the decision in late July 1305, followed by similar rulings a year later, by Great Horwood's free and villein tenants that "no one shall go about gathering grain who can earn half a penny a day and his food," and that no one should "harbour such as carry away grain unlawfully." Ault, *Open-Field Farming*, 86. These concerns continued in the immediate post-famine years and beyond: ibid., 88–90. See also W. O. Ault, "The Vill in Medieval England," *Proceedings of the American Philosophical Society* 126 (1982), 196; Ault, *Open-Field Farming*, 103.

abandoned his tenements, and perhaps his family, in Great Horwood to seek greener pastures elsewhere and avoid paying his debts; he was named as a debtor in an action as late as December 1318, more than a year after his forfeiture.[57] The rolls hint at this possibility, referring to Robert's "withdrawal" (*subtractio*) from the tenements and ultimately concluding that this did *not* work a forfeiture.[58]

Robert's condemnation as a fugitive in 1317, although recorded in stark terms in the manor roll, remains laden with ambiguity. The roll fails to record what, if any, offense he allegedly committed, and whether any action had been taken within or beyond the manorial court in response.[59] This was not likely a deliberate omission, but rather reflects the terse style of clerical prose employed in manorial records; the reason for Robert's fugitive status may not have appeared to be relevant when the 1317 roll was prepared, as no one in the court may have anticipated a later challenge to the court's decision to declare Robert's tenements permanently forfeit. Yet the reason for his fugitive status may have actually mattered. At common law, mere flight after an alleged felony did not result in immediate forfeiture of one's lands.[60] Typically land did not escheat to one's lord unless one were convicted of a felony, although if contumacy ripened into outlawry,

57. On Robert's debts, see Briggs, *Credit and Village Society*, 153, n. 12. Robert may have married into the Great Horwood community; his surname likely derives from the hamlet of Salden, roughly five miles away in the parish of Mursley. See "Parishes: Mursley," in *History of the County of Buckingham*, 3.401–6. Pushing against this is the appearance of a "Thomas de Salden" in the 1279–1290 hundred rolls for Great Horwood, possibly an ancestor of Robert. See *Rotuli hundredorum temp. Hen. III & Edw. I* (London: G. Eyre and A. Strahan, 1818), 2.336. Surname evidence is, admittedly, quite unreliable. Most intriguingly, Robert de Salden was cited by the Great Horwood court in 1311 for having drawn a customary tenant from the manor into an "alien court" a few miles away at Winslow, suggesting that Robert engaged in business outside Great Horwood and perhaps despaired of securing justice in his local manor court. See Briggs, "Seignorial Control," 415, n. 47. For this citation and hypothesis, I am grateful to Tom Johnson.

58. Poos and Bonfield, *Select Cases*, 6. Note that "fugitivus" did not necessarily refer to a fugitive from justice, but could also signify a runaway villein who abandoned a tenement. See Howlett, ed., *Dictionary of Medieval Latin from British Sources*, Fasc. IV, s.v. *fugitivus*.

59. I have been unable to find any record of Robert de Salden in the surviving Buckinghamshire gaol delivery records.

60. It could result in forfeiture of chattels, however. See Bracton, *Laws and Customs*, 2.362.

then escheat of lands and forfeiture of chattels might follow.[61] As *Bracton* described it, an outlaw "forfeits everything pertaining to right and possession," both inheritance rights and tenements, while also dissolving any bonds of homage or fealty.[62] According to *Britton*, a late thirteenth-century treatise, a felon's heirs were to be entirely disinherited (*desheritez de chescun heritage*), and a felon's wife would also not be able to hold any land in dower. Evidence from the plea rolls suggests that these rules were taken seriously.[63] Of course, Robert was a villein holding customary lands, so it is unclear that common law rules would have governed or whether, in the alternative, his lord could have taken his lands under conditions that would not have merited escheat at common law.[64]

If the court did take cognizance of mitigating circumstances surrounding Robert's alleged misdoing, this might explain its willingness to turn a blind eye to the 1317 "forfeiture"—perhaps no longer considered a forfeiture upon reexamination by the manor court—when Robert's widow, Isabel, staked her dower claim in 1329. It may further explain the rapid turn of events in 1331, when the court made an about-face in upholding Thomas's claim after he pointed out the court's earlier willingness to grant his mother her dower in the tenements. Of course, the court may also have had limited patience for the calculated maneuvers of John le Carpenter, whose efforts to secure the tenements were undertaken in defiance of the wishes of his dying father-in-law and may have been motivated by financial

61. See ibid., 366–67. See also G. D. G. Hall, ed., *The Treatise on the Laws and Customs of England, Commonly Called Glanvill* (Oxford: Clarendon Press, 1993), 90. On outlawry's effects, see Pollock and Maitland, *History of English Law*, 2.581.

62. Bracton, *Laws and Customs*, 2.363.

63. Francis Morgan Nichols, ed., *Britton: The French Text Carefully Revised with an English Translation* (Oxford: Clarendon Press, 1865), 1.37; Susan Stewart, "Outlawry as an Instrument of Justice," in *Outlaws in Medieval and Early Modern England: Crime, Government, and Society, c. 1066– c. 1600*, ed. John Appleby and Paul Dalton (Farnham: Ashgate, 2009), 48–49.

64. See, e.g., Ault, "Community of the Vill," 194–95 (describing how a miller was banned from a vill and had his lands confiscated after a jury found that he was "a very rebellious neighbor and a common malefactor unworthy of living in the vill"). See also Smith, "Some Thoughts on 'Hereditary' and 'Proprietary' Rights," 107, 114. See also Poos and Bonfield, *Select Cases*, xcv, for examples of manor courts alternatively willing and unwilling to regrant land to heirs after forfeiture for felony.

troubles of his own.[65] In addition, the 1317 forfeiture had been declared by an inquest, most likely twelve men, and an inquest was again employed in 1330 when Thomas initially tried to claim his father's tenements; in 1331, on the other hand, the whole homage was consulted, and in turn consulted the lord's council for guidance. It is possible that the extra procedural steps taken in the latter instance helped facilitate an optimal conclusion, all things considered.[66] Recourse to the homage, and its deference, in turn, to the lord's council, likely reflected continuing uncertainty about the justice of the matter and a desire to reach an acceptable consensus.[67] Finally, the court may have been unwilling to hold a law-abiding widow and her son accountable for Robert's misdeeds over a decade earlier. The same compassion that drove common law juries to undervalue felons' chattels so as not to subject their families to excessive forfeiture may in this instance have pushed in favor of allowing Robert de Salden's tenements to revert to his family's possession.

Conclusion

Manorial rolls continue to hold great promise for illuminating how medieval English farming tenants understood the law, asserted legal rights, and accessed remedies for wrongs.[68] Many breakthroughs in legal-historical understanding will result from wide-reaching data collection and analysis as historians mine court rolls for empirical evidence of manorial life and custom. The methodological approach I have taken here, combining fine-tuned textual parsing with large-scale contextual pondering—considering

65. See Ault, *Open-Field Farming*, 172 (John fined 12d. for default).

66. Beckerman has highlighted the first quarter of the fourteenth century, as "the heyday of jury trial in English manor courts," arguing that juries were seen to be ideal at bringing closure to disputes because they were well situated for "laying bare the truth of a matter and reaching a reasonable conclusion." See "Procedural Innovation," 212–14. Here, an inquest's testimony may have paled in authority compared with the deliberation of the whole homage.

67. On the production of custom from the consensus of the homage, see Beckerman, "Toward a Theory of Medieval Manorial Adjudication," 20.

68. For some hypotheses, see Paul Hyams, "What did Edwardian Villagers Understand by 'Law'?" in *Medieval Society and the Manor Court*, 92–9.

issues of scribal phrasing alongside the exigencies of famine—prompts insights that might not be unearthed by quantitative analysis. By tracing a single narrative thread through the rolls and supplementing this analysis with recourse to other sources, one gains a sense of the deeply contextualized nature of local dispute resolution and the competing strategies used by litigants and adjudicators in the manorial court setting. In the case of this modest messuage and half yardland, we find the employment of a variety of fact-finders and adjudicators, whether inquests, the whole homage, or the lord's council, at various stages of a dispute. An inquest might be well suited to finding particular facts and resolving specific narrow issues, such as whether Robert de Salden had been designated a fugitive and consequently forfeited his tenements at a previous session of the manor court. However, the whole homage might be the preferred adjudicator when a dispute raised issues that were more complex and involved issues of fundamental justice, issues that might therefore prove disruptive to the communal life of the manor, such as whether Robert's son and wife should have any claim upon tenements allegedly forfeited years earlier. Where custom proved to be uncertain or had to be reconciled with the common law—as with regard to the question of whether fugitive status alone, without a felony conviction, might work a forfeiture—the homage might seek expert guidance from the lord's council; this may also have taken pressure off the homage should a final verdict prove controversial. As one might expect in an early fourteenth-century setting, oral statements of custom were reinforced with recourse to the written record of past court proceedings. However, tenants did not always vouch the rolls and, even when they did, the rolls did not necessarily serve as the final word on a dispute. Rather, if the equities pushed in an alternative direction—in this instance, in favor of Robert's widow and son—the rolls might offer simply one of many avenues toward resolution of a dispute.

This case study of a single thread of evidence from Great Horwood reveals a manor court that, by design, allowed for tremendous flexibility and discretion in handling disputes, involved a wide cross section of local society in resolution of a contentious claim, and combined respect for the rule of customary law with a commitment to promoting equitable outcomes, even at the expense of reversing a purportedly final prior decision. We might indeed conclude that Great Horwood customary law incorporated within itself a notion of justice and equity, such that an outcome backed by oral custom and the written record might be rejected in favor of an alternative path that promoted fundamental fairness.

Custom and Law in the Medieval Court Records of the Province of Canterbury

R. H. Helmholz

Historians invited to contribute to this volume were asked to pick a topic that coincided with Professor Donahue's interests. They had a lot to choose from. I was one of them, and I knew how widely his scholarship had ranged. That made the invitation an easy one to accept. It presented little difficulty in choosing a topic. My choice was the place of custom as it is found in the records of the English ecclesiastical courts of the southern province of Canterbury during the later Middle Ages.[1] That it fit the invita-

1. The names of the dioceses or archdeaconries from which records have been used are found today in the repositories named below. The cases were collected by the author over a number of years, and in some cases their classifications have now been changed slightly. However, they should remain identifiable under the older forms in the archives given below:

Bath and Wells	Somerset Record Office, Taunton
Buckingham	Buckinghamshire Record Office, Aylesbury
Canterbury	Canterbury Cathedral Archives and Library
Carlisle	Cumbia Record Office, Carlisle
Chester	Cheshire Record Office, Chester
Chichester	West Sussex Record Office, Chichester
Ely	Cambridge University Library, Cambridge
Hereford	Herefordshire Record Office, Hereford
Lincoln	Lincolnshire Archives Office, Lincoln
London	London Metropolitan Archives, London
Norwich	Norwich and Norfolk Record Office, Norwich
Salisbury	Wiltshire Record Office, Trowbridge
Winchester	Hampshire Record Office, Winchester

tion's requirements is not open to doubt. Professor Donahue's two volume guide to these records, a praiseworthy effort that extended to archives from across the English Channel, is the fundamental introduction to its subject,[2] and his own interest in custom's place in Western law is manifest in his scholarship.[3]

The topic is also a significant one for historians of the law of the medieval church.[4] Although the *Liber Extra* contained a title devoted to custom as a source of law (X 1.4.1–11), and although modern scholarship has demonstrated that a legitimate place for custom was preserved within the medieval canon law,[5] the common view among historians has been that canon lawyers regarded laws based purely upon custom with suspicion. Not without reason. The place custom had long occupied in the church's governance presented problems for the Gregorian reformers. Many customary practices stood as an obstacle to be overcome.[6] The motivation for their suspicion was that during the period of Gregorian reform, powers long exercised by lay rulers over ecclesiastical institutions stood in the way

2. Charles Donahue, ed., *The Records of the Medieval Ecclesiastical Courts, Part I: The Continent*, Charles Donahue, Jr., ed. (Berlin: Duncker and Humblot, 1989); idem, *Part II: England* (Berlin: Duncker and Humblot, 1994). See also his "Reflections on the Editing of Medieval Church Court Records," in *Iuris Historia: Liber Amicorum Gero Dolezalek*, Vincenzo Colli and Emanuele Conte eds. (Berkeley: The Robbins Collection, 2008), 345–53.

3. E.g., Charles Donahue? "Introduction," *Lex Mercatoria and Legal Pluralism: A Late Thirteenth-Century Treatise and its Afterlife*, ed. Mary Basile et al. (Cambridge, Mass.: Ames Foundation, 1998), 154–56.

4. See, e.g., Jean Porter, "Custom, Ordinance and Natural Right in Gratian's Decretum," in *The Nature of Customary Law*, ed. Amanda Perreau-Saussine and James Murphy (Cambridge: Cambridge University Press, 2007), 79–100.

5. E.g., René Wehrlé, *De la coutume dans le droit canonique* (Paris: Recueil Sirey, 1928); John Gilissen, *La coutume* (Turnhout: Brepols, 1982), esp. 24–33; Udo Wolter, "Die consuetudo im kanonischen Recht bis zum Ende des 13. Jahrhunderts," in *Gewohnheitsrecht und Rechtsgewohnheiten im Mittelalter*, ed. Gerhard Dilcher (Berlin: Duncker and Humblot, 1992), 87–116.

6. See Harold Berman, *Law and Revolution: The Formation of the Western Legal Tradition* (Cambridge, Mass.: Harvard University Press, 1983), 112–13. See also Gerd Tellenbach, *The Church in Western Europe from the Tenth to the Early Twelfth Century*, trans. Timothy Reuter (Cambridge: Cambridge University Press, 1993), 234, 239, 316; K. J. Leyser, "The Polemics of the Papal Revolution," in *Trends in Medieval Political Thought*, ed. Beryl Smalley (Oxford: Oxford University Press, 1965), 42–64, at 58–59.

of securing the liberty of the church. They permitted long-standing practices by which laymen exerted what seemed to be undue influence in clerical affairs, and they no longer seemed tolerable to the clergy. So Pope Gregory VII is said to have reminded the Emperor Henry IV that Christ had said, "I am the truth," not "I am the custom." That dramatic statement found a place in the canon law texts.[7] It also had real consequences, not least in a later decretal of Pope Gregory IX capable of drastically restricting custom's place in the church's law.[8]

The struggle against customs regarded as unlawful had been raised in England in a dramatic way during the struggle between King Henry II and Archbishop Thomas Becket over the trial of clerks accused of crimes. Henry invoked what he described as the customs of the realm to claim temporal jurisdiction over them. Becket countered with the law of the church.[9] When it came to a conflict between the church's law as found in the *Corpus Iuris Canonici* and local custom, even long established custom, in the eyes of the archbishop the latter necessarily took the back seat.[10] The custom was invalid. That conclusion is confirmed by a recent compilation listing those customs that were treated as invalid perversions of a system of justice under the medieval canon law. That list is significantly longer than the corresponding record which lists those that were sustained.[11] The operative test was always whether a local custom was contrary to the canons and to

7. Dist. 8 c. 5. See, e.g., Colin Morris, *The Papal Monarchy: The Western Church from 1050 to 1250* (Oxford: Oxford Universtity Press, 1989), 110–11.

8. X 1.4.11. See also the entry on the subject, "Coutume" by A. Van Hove, in *Dictionnaire de droit canonique*, ed. R. Naz (Paris: Letouzey et Ané, 1935–65), Vol. 4, cols. 731–56.

9. John Hudson, *Oxford History of the Laws of England, Volume II, 871–1216* (Oxford: Oxford University Press, 2012), 768–75.

10. E.g., X 1.4.11; *gl. ord.* ad X 3.24.3, v. *consuetudo* (authorizing some use of local custom only if not contrary to the canons); See also Antonio Padoa Schioppa, *Storia del diritto in Europa: Dal medioevo all'età contemporanea* (Bologna: Il Mulino, 2007), 192–97; F. W. Maitland, *Roman Canon Law in the Church of England* (London: Methuen, 1898), 10, 41; Walter Ullmann, "A Decision of the Rota Romana on the Benefit of Clergy in England," *Studia Gratiana* 13 (1967): 457–89, esp. 471–78.

11. See Francis Germovnik, *Indices ad Corpus iuris canonici* (Ottawa: Facultas iuris canonici, Universitas Sancti Pauli, 2000), 200–203.

principles of justice established by the church's law. If not, they were to be set aside, minimized, and wherever possible abolished.[12]

This negative treatment of custom found in the texts of the medieval canon law suggests two things we should expect from the act books and other records of the ecclesiastical courts in medieval England. First, local customs overall would have played a much smaller role in practice within the courts than would the law of church found in the *Corpus Iuris Canonici*. Then, as now, litigants had to align their claims with the law in force, and it makes sense to suppose they would have hesitated to rest their claims upon purely customary practices. Particularly would this have been so for customs open to challenge as illegitimate, unreasonable, or contrary to religious principles. Second, when customary rights were introduced into litigation, as they were bound to be from time to time, disputes over their legality under the canon law would have ensued. They would have been challenged as contrary to sound principles of religion and justice. Disputes over the validity of local customs were what lay behind many of the cases found in the Gregorian Decretals, and it is logical to assume that this same characteristic would have been echoed in practice. Determining the legitimacy of particular customs would not always have been an easy task, but the canon law texts invited and even required it. Cases raising the question of custom's reach and validity is what historians should expect to find within the court records.

However logical, that is not what one does find, at least within the medieval courts of the southern English province. What one actually reader finds is the reverse: a regular citation of customs as legal authority and an absence of challenges to them based on their illegitimacy under the canon law. Such challenges did occur, but to all appearances they occurred very rarely. Instead, lawyers repeatedly acted on the assumption that custom was a legitimate source of law, one not open to challenge. In these cases, the formal law was not wholly irrelevant. It controlled many aspects of the procedure used in the courts, but its actual effect on the substance of customary law was small. It determined how customs were to be proved, but

12. See David Ibbetson, "Custom in Medieval Law," in *The Nature of Customary Law*, 151–75.

it did not undermine their legal legitimacy. Custom retained a hold on the law of the church as it was put into practice.[13]

Evidence from the Court Records

Before looking at specific examples drawn from the act books, one should first call to mind that a consequential share of the overall jurisdiction of the English ecclesiastical courts depended upon custom, rather than upon texts found within the *Corpus Iuris Canonici*. Unlike the law of marriage,[14] in which the English courts followed the formal canon law with minor deviations, the laws of defamation and testamentary succession—both mainstays of ecclesiastical jurisdiction—depended upon local custom.[15] So in a sense did the implementation of canonical rules concerning "breach of faith" that brought so many disputes about ordinary contracts before the spiritual courts during the late Middle Ages.[16] Representing a large share of the litigation that came before the consistory courts, the existence of areas where custom's force was recognized may have opened the door a little wider to the admission of local custom in other areas of practice. But it was the canon law itself that opened the door in the first place, and practice shows that the opening was not small.

Of course, it is important to note that none of these areas of ecclesiastical jurisdiction proves by its existence that the English church had the right or the desire to separate itself from the rest of western Christendom.[17]

13. See Eric W. Kemp, *Introduction to Canon Law in the Church of England* (London: Hodder and Stoughton, 1957), 25–29; R. N. Swanson, *Church and Society in Late Medieval England* (Oxford: Basil Blackwell, 1989), 160.

14. For a broader European perspective, however, see the essays, and in particular the conclusion by Charles Donahue, "Comparative Approaches to Marriage in the later Middle Ages," in *Regional Variations in Matrimonial Law and Custom in Europe, 1150–1600*, Mia Korpiola ed. (Leiden: Brill, 2011), 289–316.

15. For jurisdiction over defamation, see R. H. Helmholz, *Select Cases on Defamation to 1600*, Selden Society 101 (London, 1985), xiv–xx. For testamentary jurisdiction, see Michael Sheehan, *The Will in Medieval England* (Toronto: Pontifical Institute of Mediaeval Studies, 1963), 163–76.

16. Brian Woodcock, *Medieval Ecclesiastical Courts in the Diocese of Canterbury* (London/ Oxford: Oxford University Press, 1952), 89–92.

17. It was not unique; see Paul Ourliac, "La juridiction ecclésiastique au Moyen-Age," in *Mémoires pour l'histoire du droit et des institutions des anciens pays bourguignons,*

Nor were they products of a desire to "oust" the canon law from its rightful place in practice. Few English jurisdictional practices contradicted express canonical norms. Nor were they regarded as attacks on the formal law. However, a great deal of what actually happened in the courts did stand outside that law. Neither the law of testaments nor that of defamation was claimed as a *causa spiritualis* by the canonists. Neither was based upon texts found in the Gregorian Decretals or in the *Liber Sextus*. Both were governed by provincial constitutions which put English customary practice into written form. It was therefore natural that the English law sometimes deviated from practice on the Continent. If anything, the English church's basic jurisdictional boundaries prepare us for the strong hold of local custom on several other areas which were in fact part of the formal canon law.

Tithes and other Monetary Offerings.

One of these was the church's law of tithes. It was stated in texts collected in the *Liber Extra*, the *Liber Sextus*, the *Clementines*, and the *Extravagantes*.[18] Not the simplest of laws as it was worked out, in theory it stated a relatively simple duty owed by all persons to church and clergy. The tithe consisted of the payment of one tenth of the fruits of the earth (the predial tithe) and also one tenth of the income of every man's labor (the personal tithe). This obligation was regarded as the product of God's command to his people (Deut. 12:6). It was not the product of benevolence. Like modern taxes, payment of the tithe was a duty, one stated in the formal law and worked out in detail by generations of canonists.

Although this was true of the canonical tithe, it was a duty shaped by custom. In practice, libels brought to collect arrears of tithes commonly alleged a defendant's failure to pay "according to the manner and custom of the country."[19] Where defendants in tithe cases refused to pay some part of the tithes allegedly owed to a clerical claimant, a common reason offered

---

comtois et romands 34 (1977): 13–20, at 17.

18. X 3.30.1–35; VI 3.13.1–2; *Clem.* 3.8.1–2; *Extrav. Comm.* 3.7.1.

19. E.g., *Harmer c. Walter & Downe* (Salisbury 1555), Act book 1, fol. 20a: "recusaverunt solvere decimas vitulorum et agnorum secundum modum et consuetudinem patrie." See also *Ex officio c. Swayne* (London 1512), Act book MS. 9064/11, fol. 72v: the allegation was of a failure to pay "iuxta ratam et consuetudinem."

was that "the custom was to the contrary."[20] Witnesses in disputed cases were also commonly required to testify "in order to prove the custom and manner of paying tithes within the parish."[21] Resistance in principle to payment of tithes among the laity is not a visible theme often found within the early records, but insistence on the validity of customary rights in meeting the obligation is.[22]

The predominance of custom in some measure grew out of the character of what was owed in tithe. Many of the disputed cases arose out of agreements about the form of payment between clergy and people. It would have been quite inconvenient if all tithes had in fact been paid in kind, and once an agreement about a substituted form of tithing had been reached, that agreement was likely to last. Called a *modus decimandi*, the agreement easily became an established custom. Hostiensis confirmed their importance in practice, noting that while the tithe itself was owed *iure divino*, it was nonetheless paid "according to the approved custom of the place."[23]

There were limits, of course. An agreement or custom of paying no tithes at all was regarded as unlawful under the canon law, even where it had sometimes happened over the course of many years. In fact, the only case so far discovered in the records in which a customary freedom from making any payment was pleaded ended with a judicial declaration that this particular tithing custom was "illegitimate, wholly null and irrational."[24] It was a singular case, however, a reminder that custom's hold on

20. E.g., *Vicar of Shalfleet c. Barnard* (Winchester 1529), Act book 5, fol. 142: "non tenetur solvere ex eo quod consuetudo est contraria." See also *Ex officio c. Whichcote* (Lincoln 1517), in *Episcopal Court Book for the Diocese of Lincoln 1514–1520*, ed. Margaret Bowker, Lincoln Record Society 61 (Lincoln:, 1967), 36.

21. E.g., *Vicar of Wickham c. Hostler* (Ely 1542), Act book D/2/3, fol. 40: "ad probandum consuetudinem ac modum solvendi decimas vitulorum infra dictam parochiam." See also *Vicar of Stoke c. Bute* (Rochester 1438), Act book DRb Pa 1, fol. 42v: assignment "ad proponendum materiam consuetudinariam."

22. See also the evidence found in Giles Constable, "Resistance to Tithe in the Middle Ages," *Journal of Ecclesiastical History* 13 (1962), 172–85, at 179, and Norma Adams, "The Judicial Conflict over Tithes," *English Historical Review* 52 (1937), 1–22.

23. Henricus de Segusio, *Summa aurea* (Venice, 1574), Lib. III, tit. *De decimis*, no. 15.

24. *Vicar of Carisbrooke c. Fleitt et al.* (Winchester 1517), Act book 1, fol. 114v: "pronunciavit dictam consuetudinem fore illegitimam et omnino nullam ac irrationabilem." One other possible example is found in *Ex officio c. Vicar of Westley Waterless* (Ely 1376),

tithe law, though strong, was never complete.[25] Most tithing customs found in the records were not tested and found wanting in medieval practice. Tithe payers depended on their validity.

Once one has moved beyond tithes, however, the place of custom in justifying obligatory payments made to the clergy within the province of Canterbury seems to have been dominant. The mortuary provides a prominent example.[26] In rural areas typically the best (or second best) beast owned by the decedent, or in cities a similar item of clothing, a mortuary was due from the estate of every parishioner, payable at death to the parochial incumbent. Principled objections could be raised against it under the canon law. However in practice its legality was repeatedly justified as a long-standing and pious custom. Local custom determined what was owed as the mortuary.[27]

The obligation did remain controversial. In response, the church's lawyers hit upon justifications to distinguish the mortuary from simoniacal payments for religious services. It was suggested, for instance, that the obligation might take the place of tithes that had been forgotten and unpaid during the dead person's lifetime. However, no proof that the deceased person had forgotten to pay tithes was required (or even admitted) in suits brought to collect mortuaries, and no evidence of faithful payment was admitted to excuse the requirement that the mortuary be paid at death. The most direct and honest justification offered was a simple one: that payment of the mortuary was a "pious and laudable custom." It was so described in the act books,[28] and as such it could be distinguished from simony with the support of texts from the law of the medieval church.[29]

Act book D/2/1, fol. 39v, where a rural dean was forbidden to allege a new custom because it would have been "in magnam depressionem et preiudicium cleri et populi."

25. This is confirmed in William Lyndwood, *Provinciale (seu Constitutiones Angliae)* (Oxford: n.p.,1679), 199, v. *consuetudini locorum*. "in magnam depressionem et preiudicium cleri et populi."

26. This subject is treated at length in R. H. Helmholz *The ius commune in England: Four Studies* (New York/Oxford: Oxford University Press, 2001), 135–86; see also R. N. Swanson, *Church and Society in Late Medieval England* (Oxford: Blackwell, 1989), 215–17.

27. E.g., *Wyot c. Andrewes* (Norwich 1510), Act book 1, s.d. 17 July, alleging a failure to pay the mortuary "iuxta consuetudinem ibidem."

28. E.g., *Malt c. Felding* (Ely 1380), Act book EDR D/2/1, fol. 142, dealing with question of whether the mortuary was owed where a child had died.

29. See X 5.3.42 and DD ad id.

The history of this controversial mulct does not exhaust the subject of custom's hold on monetary obligations. Parish rates, which were normally obligatory payments to sustain the church fabric, were paid according to a combination of agreement and custom supposedly settled from time immemorial.[30] When a dispute arose about them, as it did in a typical instance at Canterbury in 1421, the churchwardens offered proof of the obligation's legitimacy and its extent by producing "a roll of ancient assessments."[31] In an earlier dispute over a payment allegedly due to the hospital at Hythe, proof was sought "by faithful men and the country according to what had long been in use."[32] It was the custom that counted in these cases, not the formal law drawn from the Decretals.

Particular customary oblations also existed in many individual parishes—for example a requirement that owners of particular lands maintain the churchyard,[33] and (perhaps more frequently) small money payments with names like "Christesdole" or "garthpenny" or "maynpott."[34] True, most of these monetary obligations could be amended or forgiven. They were subject to variation by agreement of the parties, and this sometimes happened.[35] However, long established customs were the starting points for argument in the disputes over allegedly unpaid tithes and the other

30. *Redhill c. Pole et al.* (Lichfield 1464), Act book B/C/1/1, fol. 1v: "a tempore immemorata." See also John Ayliffe, *Parergon juris canonici Anglicani* (London: D. Leach, 1726), 406–07.

31. *Churchwardens of Challock c. Simon Amys* (Canterbury 1421), Act book Y.1.3, fol. 173v: "pars decorum yconomorum exhibuit unum rotulum antique assedationis."

32. Petition (Canterbury ca. 1290), Sede Vacante Scrapbook III, no. 182: "per viros fidedignos et patriam et secundum quod diu usitatum fuit tempore multorum archiepiscoporum."

33. *Ex officio c. Fygone and Spede* (Winchester 1524), Act book 2, fol. 26: the obligation said to be "secundum consuetudinem antiquam."

34. These are mentioned (in order) in: *Ex officio c. Richard de Grangia* (Norwich 1305), in Lambeth Palace Library, London, Act book MS. 244, fol. 59; *Rector of Stapleton c. Harlie* (Carlisle 1629), Act book DRC 3/62, s.d. 30 January; *Ex officio c. Croft* (Lincoln 1346), in *Lower Ecclesiastical Jurisdiction in Late-Medieval England*, L. R. Poos, ed. (Oxford: Oxford University Press, 2001), 202.

35. E.g., *Ex officio c. Chever* (London 1486), Act book MS. 9064/2, fol. 134v, a suit brought because the defendant "recusat solvere iuxta taxacionem factam per parochianos electos ad necessaria ecclesie per parochianos supportanda."

oblations that came before the courts throughout the medieval period. In them, custom was the principal source of legal obligation.

Testamentary Practice

The English church's jurisdiction over testamentary succession to personal property, itself founded upon custom, also admitted local customs that deviated from the prevailing norms.[36] Subject to the requirements of the law of proof, these exceptions were pleaded and accepted in the spiritual courts. For example, the custom of a particular location might itself justify an exception from ecclesiastical jurisdiction – usually in favor of the court of a local lord, a town, or other secular authority. In 1470, for example, the widow of John Tyly of Leadbury alleged in the consistory court of Hereford that "she was not bound to prove the testament by virtue of the custom of the country."[37] The judge then awarded her a court day to prove the existence of that exception. A similar plea was entered at Winchester a few years later in favor of the testamentary jurisdiction said to be held by/over? the countess of Salisbury. Her right to jurisdiction was said to be justified by a custom established "from time immemorial."[38] These pleas were not always successful of course. Alleging a custom was not the same thing as proving it. In a case early in the sixteenth century a defendant, brought before the Hereford court for a refusal to appear to prove a testament, advanced his claim to exemption based upon a customary right. However, he later admitted that he had alleged the custom only in order to avoid the probate fees paid in the ecclesiastical forum. He submitted to the court and introduced the document. Happily for him, the judge then dismissed him

36. This was not peculiar to England, of course. See Philippe Godding, "Dans quelle mesure pouvait-on disposer de ses biens par testament dans les anciens Pays-Bas méridionaux?" *Tijdschrift voor Rechtsgeschiedenis* 50 (1982), 279–86.

37. *In re testament of Tyly* (Hereford 1470), Act book O/9, p. 55: "[C]omparet et allegat se non teneri ad probacionem testamentorum ex consuetudine patrie et habet terminum ad probandum." Similar is *Ex officio c. Pembur* (Hereford 1447), Act book O/4, p. 12, where the servile status of the deceased was proffered as the justification for refusal of ecclesiastical probate.

38. *Ex office c. Eristhe* (Winchester 1524), Act book 2, fol. 27: "consuetudo ibidem fuit et est a tempore immemorato." Similar is *Ex officio c. Newman* (Winchester 1528), Act book 4, fol. 91v: "ex antiqua consuetudine usi fuerunt per tempus immemoratum."

without imposing a fine or penance "because he was a pauper."[39] But, as in other cases, it was his failure to prove a custom's existence that defeated his claim, not its irrationality or its lack of congruence with the written law.

The act books show that the details of what might be called "the probate process" were themselves subject to regulation by custom. Provincial constitutions attempted to control abuses—fraudulent transfers before death for example[40]—but a great deal was left to agreement or local custom. William Lyndwood, England's greatest medieval canonist, himself endorsed custom's importance in probate practice.[41] There could be, he noted, a special customary way of compiling and filing the inventory of the estate of a testator.[42] It was also possible to file a claim against an urban estate based upon "the custom of the city of London."[43] Most famously, of course, the right of children to take a share of the estate of their fathers—the so called *legitim*—was almost always based upon the custom of specific places.[44] For a time it prevailed in most areas of England, but by the fifteenth century it had been abandoned (except for pockets of resistance) within the province of Canterbury. It lasted longer in the northern province of York. Its history serves as an indication of both the force and the flexibility that accompanied admission of local custom as a legitimate source of law. This particular custom seems to have succumbed only to a growing sentiment in favor of freedom of testation.

39. *Ex officio c. Dowle* (Hereford 1474), Act book O/12, p. 2: "Thomas asseruit se allegasse huiusmodi consuetudinem propter paupertatem qua laborabat ad evitandum solucionem consuetam."

40. See Archbishop's Stratford's constitution, *Cordis dolore*, attempting to prevent inter vivos gifts made to deprive family members, the church, and creditors of their just claims. It is printed with Lyndwood's gloss in *Provinciale*, 161–65.

41. *Provinciale*, 172, v. *mobilibus*: "potius in his standum est regni legibus et consuetudinibus." See also his comments at 174, v. *probatis*. Valuable on this subject is Brian Ferme, *Canon Law in late Medieval England* (Rome: LAS, 1996), esp. 141–44.

42. E.g., *In re testament of Pake* (Canterbury 1519), Act book Y.2.10, fol. 62: "inventarium secundum consuetudinem ville Dovor'." Acceptance of this result is confirmed by Lyndwood, *Provinciale*, 176, v. *inventarium*.

43. *In re estate of Sutton* (London 1486), Act book MS. 9064/2, fol. 147v: "iuxta consuetudinem civitatis London."

44. For more information see Sheehan, *The Will*, above note 15, at 293–95; R. Helmholz, "Legitim in English Legal History," *University of Illinois Law Review* (1984): 659–74.

Ecclesiastical Sanctions.

It is sometimes said that the only sanction available to the English ecclesiastical courts was excommunication.[45] That is true in a sense. The judges could not directly apply afflictive sanctions to even the most obdurate of defendants, and judicial power even to impose monetary fines was quite limited in England. However, the statement is incomplete in failing to recognize the variety of intermediate sanctions employed in practice by the judges. They appear frequently in the act books. Behind all of them of course lay the threat of excommunication, a threat backed up in England by regular intervention by "the secular arm" (the royal Chancery and the sheriff). The church's invocation of secular aid led to imprisonment until the person excommunicated had secured absolution by the church.[46] In theory, however, its penalties were not imposed by the judges of the spiritual courts, but by the royal officials.

Once one looks at the records, however, the generalization that excommunication was the church's sole effective sanction all but melts away. The measures meted out to offenders against the ecclesiastical law included a considerable range of sanctions designed to fit specific offenses.[47] They were justified by both reason and local custom. One such technique was to submit disputes to negotiation before a selected group of men from the parish to which the parties adhered. Arbitration, formal or informal, was a normal expedient.[48] It was most frequently employed in settling disputes about parochial and patronage rights,[49] but Frederik Pedersen has also

45. E.g., Christopher Hill, *Economic Problems of the Church* (Oxford 1956), 86–87.

46. The standard work is F. D. Logan, *Excommunication and the Secular Arm in Medieval England* (Toronto: Pontifical Institute of Mediaeval Studies, 1968). See also William Holdsworth, *History of English Law*, 7th ed. (London: Sweet & Maxwell, 1966), 1.630–32.

47. For discipline of the clergy themselves, see Michael Burger, *Bishops, Clerks, and Diocesan Governance in Thirteenth-Century England* (Cambridge, 2012), 136–66.

48. E.g., *Rector of Wexham c. Corbette* (Archdeaconry of Buckingham 1488), in *The Courts of the Archdeaconry of Buckingham 1483–1523*, ed. E. M. Elvey, Buckinghamshire Record Society 19 (1975), no. 82.

49. E g., *Ex officio c. Villeins of Halton* (Chester 1525), Act book EDC 1/3, fol. 28: "Et iudex decrevit xii viros iurandos ad inquirendum de consuetudine." Many examples are found in my "Canonical 'juries' in Medieval England," in *"Ins Wasser geworfen und Ozeane durchquert": Festschrift für Knut Wolfgang Nörr*, ed. Mario Ascheri et al. (Cologne: Böhlau, 2003), 403–18.

uncovered evidence of its use even in settling matrimonial litigation.[50] Although mostly after 1550, custom was also employed as a legitimate source of right in dealing with problems arising out of the individual erection of pews in parish churches.

The remedies used in deciding defamation cases also varied from the remedy of excommunication authorized by the provincial constitution on the subject. More often than not, the goal of the judges was to restore harmony between neighbors. This aim called for a variety of sanctions: sometimes a simple order that a defamer keep silence in the future;[51] sometimes a requirement of public penance and apology in the parish church; sometimes a private apology and reconciliation before a group of parishioners; and on one occasion even a "sentence" requiring the parties to drink a cup of beer together.[52] In dealing with repeated sexual offenses, the courts also adopted what seems to have been something like a "sliding scale" of penalties—from a sentence requiring offenders to perform public penance, to an injunction that they avoid each other's company in all private places, and even in extreme cases to an order of banishment from the parish or diocese against one of the offenders.[53] All of these were matters of custom and choice.

Of course, the *stylus curiae* was a legitimate authority in the *ius commune*. It permitted some deviation from the texts, supplying perceived defects in their contents. Its existence importance was not regarded as threatening to the formal canon law, at least if it rested upon just, lengthy, and widely recognized observance. What the English consistory courts did in administering the penal law also fit the oft-stated principle that "the best

50. Frederik Pedersen, *Marriage Disputes in Medieval England* (London: Hambledon, 2000).

51. E.g., *Ex officio c. Lewys* (Hereford 1493), Act book I/1, p. 78: "...unde iudex imposuit eidem silencium."

52. See *Select Cases on Defamation*, above note 15, at xxxviii–xli. The "sentence" involving beer is *Olyver c. Carr* (York 1523), Act book D/C.AB 2, fol. 307: "et cum dicta uxore simul bibat denariatum cervisie."

53. E.g., *Ex officio c. Fullbyke* (Chichester 1507), Act book Ep I/10/1, fol. 70v: "Ideo iudex iniunxit sibi quod decetero non frequentetur consorcium dicte Alicie sub pena iuris." Anon. (Hereford 1454), Act book O/5, p. 62: "[M]ulier iuravit se dictam parochiam in perpetuum relinquere et nunquam redire ad eandem." *Ex officio c. Dawes* (Rochester 1514), Act book DRb Pa 6, fol. 50: "Dominus iniunxit eidem quod recedat a diocesi Roffen."

interpreter of a law" is the custom of the place where it was applied.[54] The practices just described did not, therefore, necessarily conflict with the spirit of the canon law. They may even have fulfilled its larger purpose. However, most of them were not found in the *Corpus Iuris Canonici*. Not everything could, or should, have been. They rested on custom. The medieval canonists recognized this, and so should we.

Parochial Law

Much of the administration within English parish churches was also determined by customary rules. The obligation of English parishioners to keep the nave of their church in repair, for example, was based upon custom. Under the general law of the church, the duty fell upon the rector, but English practice diverged from the canons on this point.[55] Maitland himself took notice of the divergence, though he saw no constitutional principle at work within it.[56] In minimizing its significance, he was certainly right, but he ought to have acknowledged the force of local custom as something recognized and allowed under the canon law. The medieval act books certainly did. When the question arose in practice, their wording tracked the common form for recognizing the force of a custom, not recognizing any special need to justify its legitimacy.[57] This was no attempt "to set up a schismatical law" on their part.[58] It was simply an example of the force that local custom long held in English practice. Maitland's account of the matter, written before he (or almost anyone else) had examined the records of the ecclesiastical tribunals unfortunately overlooked that point.

It is also a point for which evidence is found in many such cases that were brought before the courts. At Lincoln, the duty to provide a chaplain to officiate in a chapel in Stragglethorpe was alleged to belong to the rector of Beckingham "both by an agreement and according to a laudable custom

54. "Optima legume interpres [est] consuetudo."

55. Lyndwood, *Provinciale*, 53, v. *reparatione*.

56. Maitland, *Roman Canon Law*, 42.

57. E.g., *Provost of Backford c. Inhabitants of Wallington* (Chester 1503), Act book EDC 1/1, fol. 18: alleging that "parochiani ecclesie parochialis de Bakford reparaverunt ab antiquo et iam reparunt ipsam ecclesiam." The suit was described as a "causa recusationis onerum parochialium."

58. Maitland, *Roman Canon Law*, 43.

established by lawful prescription."[59] In London, payment of the stipend of the sidesmen was fixed by habitual practice.[60] The division of revenues between clerics derived from the payment of tithes was determined "by prescription time out of mind" in a case originating in Gloucester. The custom alleged was itself proved by written instruments in a 1306 cause heard in the archbishop's court, but it was a custom all the same.[61] Indeed the English custom by which the parishioners were responsible for repair of a parish church's nave was itself subject to variation where a contrary custom had been established "by long usage."[62] The influential position of churchwardens in the administration of parochial life in English churches itself seems also to have been based on convenience and prescription.[63]

Conclusion

Act books were records of the cases brought before the consistory courts. They were not intended to state the law, and the cases cited in the body of this contribution are limited in what they can tell the legal historian. Nevertheless, on this special subject—the place of custom in the medieval ecclesiastical courts—they are articulate enough to establish two things. First, custom served as a source of obligations in a surprisingly large number of the cases that came before the courts in the province of Canterbury during the later Middle Ages. As a source of law, custom mattered more than is usually allowed in most general histories of the medieval church. Second, in practice custom was rarely challenged as contrary to the formal canon law. Whether because most of the customs alleged were on matters of indifference to the clergy or actually stood in favor of the church's in-

59. *Inhabitants of Stragglethorp c. Simon Yates* (Lincoln 1517), Act book Cj/2, fols. 39v–41: "tam ex compositione quam ex consuetudine laudabili legitimeque prescripta." See also *Vicar of S. v. Parishioners of S.* (Lincoln 1518), Act book Cj/2, fol. 67: "in dicta parochia est consuetudo quod vicarius exhibebit ididem sibi ministrare."

60. *Ex officio c. Agerlay* (London 1510), in *Series of Precedents and Proceedings in Criminal Causes 1475–1640*, ed. W. H. Hale (Edinburgh: Bratton Pub., 1973), no. 293.

61. Anon. (Gloucester 1306), Lambeth Palace Library, London, Act book, MS. 244, fol. 78v: "per instrumenta que exhibent et per prescriptionem temporis longissimi."

62. *Provost of Backford c. Inhabitants of Mollington* (Chester 1503), Act book EDC 1/1, fols. 18–19: "ab antiquo... et semper fuit divisa."

63. Thomas Deutscher, *Punishment and Penance: Two Phases in the History of the Bishop's Tribunal of Novara* (Toronto: University of Toronto Press, 2013), 86.

terests, few were challenged as inconsistent with canonical principles or texts in the formal law. The many cases where the legitimacy of a custom was challenged as wicked or unreasonable in the *Corpus Iuris Canonici* give a quite misleading impression of the significant place custom occupied in court practice.

It is tempting, therefore, to trumpet this finding as a discovery. It is tempting, but it would be quite unwarranted. Why? It would be inappropriate because this survey has reached virtually the identical conclusion to that which Professor Donahue himself reached in an article that appeared in the *Michigan Law Review* more than forty years ago.[64] The principal difference is that his article was devoted to the court records of the province of York. This essay had been based on those of the province of Canterbury. To have uncovered a similarity between the two is not a discovery worth trumpeting.

64. "Roman Canon Law in the Medieval English Church: Stubbs vs. Maitland Re-examined after 75 Years in the Light of Some Records from the Church Courts," *University of Michigan Law Review* 72 (1974), 647–716.

Interdict at Lynn, Norfolk: Canon Law Anomalies

F. Donald Logan[1]

"We have recently heard of a dreadful crime, a wicked and detestable event in the diocese of Norwich." This was Simon Sudbury, Archbishop of Canterbury, writing on 18 June 1377. He said that the crime touched his heart deeply with a sorrow beyond measure. It was a crime unheard of in his time in the Province of Canterbury.[2]

Archbishop Sudbury was writing about the physical assault on his suffragan, Henry Despenser, Bishop of Norwich. In Sudbury's telling, Bishop Despenser, the spiritual and temporal lord of Lynn (hence Bishop's Lynn and now King's Lynn), was beset by townspeople, their names unknown (to Sudbury). They closed the gates of the town, not permitting Despenser and his companions to proceed to his manor at Gaywood. These satellites of Satan attacked, struck, and even fired arrows, wounding the bishop and some of his clergy and servants. These armed men forced Despenser and his companions to return through the center of town to the Benedictine Priory of Lynn. Thus spoke Simon Sudbury.

1. The author would like to record his appreciation for assistance with this paper from Peter D. Clarke, Karen Corsano, Christopher Harper-Bill, David M. Smith, and Daniel Williman.

2. "[H]orrendus et detestabilis sceleris flagicium... super quo turbamur non immerito per intima cordis nostri.... In ea latus nostre Cantuariensis ecclesie sensimus grauiter uulneratum," London, Lambeth Palace Library, Register of Simon Sudbury, fol. 38 (hereafter Reg. Sudbury). The text with some minor variations appears in David Wilkins, *Concilia Magnae Britanniae et Hiberniae*, 4 vols. (London: Sumptibus R. Gosling, 1737), 3.118–19.

Archbishop Sudbury's account should not be allowed to stand alone. From other contemporary accounts a fuller story emerges. Friction had for some time existed between the Bishop of Norwich and the town of Lynn, and it was to continue into the fifteenth century.[3] On this occasion, Bishop Despenser, described by the chronicler Thomas Walsingham as "youthful and impetuous" (*juvenis et effrenus*) insisted on having the mace carried before him in Lynn, a custom reserved for the mayor, and a custom strongly held by the townsfolk.[4] Walsingham related how the elders of the town tried to dissuade the bishop from usurping this honor which belonged solely to their mayor. Despenser was warned that there could be hostile reaction by townsmen who understood this to be an attack on their liberties. The warnings were to no avail: Despenser proceeded with the mace carried before him by one of his party. The attack on the bishop and his party followed with the bishop himself being struck and his horse killed. On 16 June 1377, a commission of oyer and terminer was issued at the petition of Despenser, who named 23 men and others unknown for assaulting him at Lynn and following him to Lynn Priory, where they threatened to kill him. He also said that he had lost twenty horses and that his company had also been assaulted.[5] In another action, the royal council on 12 July 1377, just four days before the coronation of the boy king Richard II, while admitting that there was blame on both sides, wrote to the sheriffs of Norfolk and Cambridge and the mayor and bailiffs of Lynn that they should proclaim a fine of £2,000 for anyone harming the bishop of Norwich; the council

3. Kate Parker, "A Little Social Difficulty: Lynn and the Lancastrian Usurpation," in *Medieval East Anglia*, ed. C. Harper-Bill (Woodbridge, Suffolk: Boydell Press, 2005), 115–29, and her unpublished Ph.D. Diss. "Lordship, Liberty and the Pursuit of Politics in Lynn, 1370–1420" (University of East Anglia, 2004).

4. Thomas Walsingham in his *Chronicon Angliae ab anno domini 1328 ad annum 1388*, ed. E. M. Thompson (London: Longman and Co., 1874), 139–40, where he related this incident. At the time of his appointment as bishop in 1370, Henry Despenser, being perhaps 27 years old, was in need of a papal dispensation. He had studied law at Oxford. See A. B. Emden, *A Biographical Register of the University of Oxford to A.D. 1500*, 3 vols. (Oxford: Oxford University Press, 1957–1959) 3.2169–70, (hereafter *BRUO*) and the article by R. G. Davies in *Oxford Dictionary of National Biography*, ed. H. C. G. Matthew and Brian Harrison (Oxford: Oxford University Press, 2004), 15.910–13 (hereafter *ODNB*).

5. *Calendar of the Patent Rolls, 1327–77* (London: H.M.S.O., 1891), 16.502.

added that it would look into the matter. There the matter seems to have rested, as no further action was taken by the council.[6]

In the meantime, the disciplinary arm of the church had inflicted the extreme penalty of interdict on the town of Lynn, in effect, closing churches to the faithful and severely limiting access to the sacraments.[7] There automatically came into force the penalty of Pope Clement V's constitution *Si quis suadente diabolo*, which made excommunication and interdict automatic (*a iure* or *late sententie*) penalties for assaulting a bishop.[8] Archbishop Sudbury stepped in on 18 June and wrote the letter quoted above.[9] He ordered the archdeacon of Norwich and the official of Lynn to publish the excommunications and to enforce the observance of the interdict.[10] This paper concerns the latter.

Sudbury acknowledged that a severe application of interdict could be harmful to souls. He was echoing the words of Pope Boniface VIII, whose crucial constitution *Alma mater* (1298) he cited and quoted in part. The archbishop insisted that the interdict be observed without fraud or deception but with the moderation introduced by Boniface's decretal. Al-

6. *Calendar of the Close Rolls, 1377–81* (London: H.M.S.O., 1914), 85.

7. The classic work on interdict is Peter D. Clarke, *The Interdict in the Thirteenth Century: A Question of Collective Guilt* (Oxford: Oxford University Press, 2007) (hereafter, Clarke, *Interdict*). See also idem, "Two Constitutions of Boniface VIII: An Insight into the Sources of the Liber Sextus," *Bulletin of the John Rylands Library* 83.3 (2001), 115–28; and idem, "Reflections on *The Interdict in the Thirteenth Century*," in *Droit et exclusion religieuse dans les socités chrétiennes (XIe–XVIe siècle): Les mechanismes de jurisdicisation de l'excommunication*, ed. E. Rosenblieh (Besançon: Presses universitaires de Franche-Comté, forthcoming). See also Richard C. Trexler, *The Spiritual Power: Repulican Florence under Interdict* (Leiden, 1974), and Martin Kaufhold, *Gladius spiritualis: das päpstliche interdict über Deutschland in dre Regierungszeit Ludwigs des Bayern (1324–1347)* (Heidelberg: Universitätsverlag C. Winter, 1994).

8. *Clementis Papae V Constitutiones* 5.8.1, in *Corpus Iuris Canonici*, ed. E. Friedberg, 2 vols. (Leipzig: ex officina Bernhardi Tauchnitz, 1879–81) 2.1187–88: "quemvis pontificem iniuriose vel temere percusserit, aut ceperit seu banniverit vel haec mandaverit fieri aut facta ab aliis rata habuerit... terra quoque ipsius... necnon locus aut loca in quibus episcopus detinebitur... ecclesiasico subiacerunt interdicto." For interdicts *a iure* and the Clementine constitution, see Clarke, *Interdict*, 126–28.

9. See supra n. 2.

10. The Archdeacon of Norwich was William Swynflet. See John LeNeve and Thomas Duffus-Hardy, *Fasti ecclesiae anglicanae, 1300–1541*, vol. 4: *Monastic Cathedrals, Southern Province*, ed. B. Jones (London: Athlone Press, 1963), 27.

though not specified in this letter, the modifications of Boniface VIII allowed masses and other divine offices to be celebrated by clergy in churches but with voices muted, doors shut, and bells silent. It also distinguished between the culpable and the non-culpable. On four feast days a year (Christmas, Easter, Pentecost and the Assumption of the Virgin) all could attend with voices raised, doors open and bells ringing, but only the non-culpable could receive communion.[11] There the matter stood on 18 June 1377.

Two days later Archbishop Sudbury, a trained and experienced canonist well conversant with the canon law on interdict, went a step further than Boniface's constitution.[12] Whereas Boniface allowed the innocent to attend mass and receive communion on four feasts, Sudbury now extended the mitigation to allow the attendance of the innocent on every day and permitted them to receive other sacraments. He wrote two letters to this effect, one, on 20 June 1377, to the Prior of Lynn Priory and another, on 26 June, to the same prior and to Ivo, Rector of Babingley, and a certain John Peie, Chaplain of Norwich diocese.[13] They carried the same message: a further mitigation beyond that of Boniface VIII, and all the more remarkable in that he mitigated a sentence of interdict imposed not on his own judicial authority but *a iure*, thus, in effect, on papal authority. In view of later developments it may be useful to quote his exact words:

> We wish, however, that as for those inhabitants of the said village who were and are in no way culpable for the aforesaid excesses, and who did not offer them counsel, aid, or favor, the said interdict notwithstanding, you should graciously admit them to the divine services in your church and the other churches of the said village, with the doors closed and all interdicted and excommunicated persons entirely excluded, according to the tenor of the aforesaid Decretal

11. *Liber sextus decretalium dommini Bonifacii Papae VIII* 5.11.24, in *Corpus Iuris Canonici*, 2.1106–07.

12. For Sudbury's training and experience as a canonist see *BRUO* 3:218 and particularly Simon Walker's article in *ODNB*.

13. The Prior of Lynn was Ralph of Martham. See David M. Smith and Vera M. London, eds., *Heads of Religious Houses: England and Wales*, vol. 2 (Cambridge: Cambridge University Press, 2001), 116. Peie is also called John Peye. See Dorothy Owen, *The Making of King's Lynn: A Documentary Survey* (London: Oxford University Press, 1984), 135, n. 126, and 137–38, n. 127.

(*Alma mater*), and to the other ecclesiastical sacraments allowed by the aforesaid Decretal.[14]

Almost precisely the same words were used in the second letter of mitigation.[15] In justification Sudbury repeated the sentiment of Boniface that the severity of preceding statutes could result in diminished devotion, harm to souls and innocent churches being deprived of divine services. Yet the matter did not end there.

Several weeks later, on 12 July 1377, Archbishop Sudbury wrote a strong—one is tempted to say angry—letter to all the clergy of the diocese of Norwich, but especially to those in Norwich and Lynn.[16] Some of the clergy, he wrote, had allowed "indiscriminate admission" (*indies indifferenter*) to all who came, not distinguishing the innocent from the guilty. As a consequence, after consulting suffragans, he revoked the mitigations which he had added and ordered that the interdict be inviolably observed. This left in place the penalties of *Alma mater* with its more moderate mitigations. Could the words quoted above from Sudbury's letter be construed in a way that allowed wholesale, undifferentiated admission to sacred services? Sudbury accused some of the clergy of "a cunning interpretation of his letters."[17] Do words like "in no way culpable" (*nullatenus culpabiles*) admit of a broad interpretation, one that blurs the usual meaning? And Sudbury carefully insisted that "in no way culpable" includes past and present guilt, thus excluding any participants in the attack who were now penitent. That said, difficult practical problems must have presented themselves to parish priests in trying to distinguish the guilty from the innocent and to admit only the latter.[18] With this revocation Archbishop Sudbury's at-

14. Reg. Sudbury, fol. 38v: "Volumus tamen quod dicte uille inhabitatores qui in premissis excessibus nullatenus cuplabiles extiterint aut existent nec eis prebuerunt consilium, auxilium uel fauorem, dicto interdicto non obstante, ad diuina officia in uestra ecclesia et aliis dicte uille ecclesiis audienda, ianuis clausis ac interdictis et excommunicatis penitus exclusis iuxta tenorem decretalis predicte [*Alma mater*], et ad alia sacramenta ecclesiastica per prefatam decretalem concessa graciose admittatis."

15. Ibid.

16. Ibid.

17. "[P]er hastutam ipsarum interpretacionem literarum."

18. For the failure of parish clergy to enforce interdict see Clarke, *Interdict*, 86ff.

tempt to allow broader modification had failed. And with that revocation the interdict at Lynn disappears from his register, but questions remain.[19]

By what authority did Sudbury intervene in a suffragan's diocese in the matter of an interdict which had been imposed *a iure*? Nowhere did he justify his intervention, but twice he said that he had conferred with suffragan bishops. As metropolitan of the province of Canterbury, did he have the power to mitigate the severity of such an interdict? Dr. Churchill refers to Sudbury's first letter as not an unusual "commission" to publicize the automatic excommunications, which, however, does not explain his subsequent mitigations.[20] Yet he made no claim to be acting by his authority as metropolitan in acting beyond the provisions of *Alma mater*. While it is true that a metropolitan could intervene if a suffragan appealed to him, there is no mention of such an appeal in Sudbury's letters.[21] A clue might be found in this initial letter, where he said he had heard of the recent events at Lynn from trustworthy persons.[22] Could Bishop Despenser, the victim of the assault, have been one of his informants, perhaps even the major informant? As has been seen, on 16 June 1377 a commission of oyer and terminer was granted at Despnenser's request. Two days later Sudbury issued his first letter. It would seem quite likely that Despenser sought Sudbury's assistance at this time and stimulated his intervention with the letter that gave an account of the assault, which was clearly favorable to Despenser. That narrative would explain the archbishop's involvement but does not explain his authority for granting mitigations beyond those granted by Boniface VIII..

The Franciscan chronicler of Lynn was a contemporary and no doubt witness to much of what happened in Lynn at this time. He wrote

> That same year [1377] the interdict was imposed upon the town of Lynn from the fifth ides of June [9 June] until the vigil of St. Law-

19. Curiously, Despenser's episcopal register is entirely silent about both the attack and the interdict. See Norwich, Norfolk Record Office, DN/REG 3 book 6.

20. Irene J. Churchill, *Canterbury Administration: The Administrative Machinery of the Archbishopric of Canterbury Illustrated from Original Sources*, 2 vols. (London: S.P.C.K., 1933), 353, n. 1.

21. For the reasons for the intervention of a metropolitan see Clarke, *Interdict*, 91–2.

22. "[E]x quorundam fidedignorum insinuacione clamosa nostris insonuit auribus" (Reg. Sudbury, fol. 38r).

> rence [9 August] of that same year, on account of the violence done by some fools of that town upon the person of Lord Henry Despenser Bishop of Norwich.[23]

The interdict, thus, was imposed (*supposita*) on 9 June 1377 for two months, ending on 9 August. There can be little doubt that it was Bishop Despenser, acting by ordinary authority, who imposed the interdict just days before he petitioned oyer and terminer and probably wrote to the archbishop. One may ask why Despenser imposed an interdict when an interdict was already in place *a iure*. Unlike Sudbury, was he unfamiliar with *Si quis suadente diabolo* of Clement V? No further reference has come to light concerning the lifting of the interdict at Lynn, and we should perhaps conclude that it ended on 9 August, relaxed by the authority of the ordinary.

What we seem to have here at Lynn are two puzzling canonical anomalies. The first is the archbishop of Canterbury apparently acting beyond his authority in extending the terms of a papal constitution by further mitigating the penalties for an interdict, and the other is the imposition of two simultaneous interdicts on the same place, one *a iure* (by Clement's constitution) and one *ab homine* (by Despenser's action).

As Professor Donahue said in another context, canon law is complicated.[24]

23. Antonia Gransden, "A Fourteenth-Century Chronicle from the Grey Friars at Lynn," *English Historical Review* 72 (1957), 278: Item eodem anno [1377] fuit villa Lenn' supposita interdicto a quinto idibus Iunii usque ad vigiliam sancti Laurencii eiusdem anni, propter violenciam factam per quosdam fatuos eiusdem ville in personam domini Henrici Dispensariis episcopi Norwyc.

24. *Law and Society in the Later Middle Ages* (Cambridge, 2007), 1, 14.

Canon Law in the Arctic: A Marriage Case in the Register of Bishop Jon of Hólar

Anders Winroth

Charles Donahue has done more than anyone to throw light on how canon law was understood and applied in local courts.[1] His great work on marriage cases focuses on five local courts in England, France, and the Low Countries, where unusually rich documentation survives. His results are particularly valuable since they provide a context through which to understand other surviving but less detailed sources about marriage litigation. This article will focus on such a source preserved from the northernmost cathedral in the medieval world.

The Arctic Circle touches the furthest outposts of the diocese of Hólar in northern Iceland, but it was still a viable bishopric, thanks to the rich stocks of fish available in the waters surrounding the island. The fifteenth century is known as "the English age" in Iceland, since this was a period when Iceland enjoyed close commercial and cultural contacts with England.[2] During the fifteenth century, many of the bishops at Iceland's two bishoprics were Englishmen. In 1426, Pope Martin V appointed the English friar John Craxton bishop of Hólar. He arrived in Iceland in 1427

1. Charles Donahue, Jr., *Law, Marriage, and Society in the Later Middle Ages: Arguments about Marriage in Five Courts* (Cambridge, 2007). I wish to thank Jóhanna Friðriksdóttir and Elizabeth Walgenbach for their help.

2. Björn Þorsteinsson, *Enska öldin i sögu íslendinga* (Reykjavik, 1970); Björn Þorsteinsson, Guðrún Ása Grímsdóttir, and with contributions by Sigurður Líndal, "Enska öldin," in *Saga Íslands*, ed. Sigurður Líndal (1990), 3–216.

and instead of riding to his cathedral in the north, he went to the national assembly known as the Althing to show his papal appointment letters. Icelanders prefer patronymics, so they knew him as Jón Vilhjálmsson; I suppose his father would have been called William at home in England. When Jón arrived in Iceland in 1427, his diocesans did not like him, so he sailed back home to safety in England the same summer, but only after ordaining four priests and some deacons.[3] Episcopal acts were much needed since no bishop had visited Iceland for several years. Jón came back in 1429 and was finally able to sing his first mass in the cathedral of Hólar on Assumption Day, 15 August. He would stay in Hólar for six years until Pope Eugen IV in 1435 promoted him to Iceland's senior and larger bishopric at Skálholt in the south. That see had become vacant after some inhabitants in the diocese drowned the incumbent, suggesting that bishop Jón might have been wise not to try to get to his cathedral as long as his diocesans disliked him. Jón eventually retired from this bishopric and moved back to England, where he appears to have invested in trade on Iceland (the identification is somewhat uncertain).[4]

Soon after arriving in Hólar, Jón began a register, known as the *Bréfabók Jóns biskups Vilhjálmsonar,* in which he had copied letters and judgments issued by him.[5] The book remained in Hólar after his promotion to Skálholt and was used by several subsequent bishops. It contains many traces of the bishop's judicial activities, and much of this in marriage cases.

3. Gustav Storm, *Islandske annaler indtil 1578* (Christiania, 1888), 294.

4. The basic facts of Jón's biography are found in Oluf Kolsrud, *Tillægg till Syttende samling,* Diplomatarium Norvegicum, vol. 17 B (Christiania, 1913), 267 and 278. The only evidence for his possible post-episcopal career is a memoranda roll from the English chancery, edited in *Diplomatarium Islandicum: Íslenzkt fornbréfasafn,* (Copenhagen and Reykjavik, 1857–1972), 16.357–362.

5. Reykjavik, Þjóðskjalasafn Íslands, Bps B. II 3. The individual items in the volume are printed under their respective dates in *Diplomatarium Islandicum,* vols. 4–5. See also 4.363–371 and Kristian Kålund, *Katalog over de oldnorsk-islandske håndskrifter i Det store kongelige bibliotek og i Universitetsbiblioteket (udenfor den Arnamagnæanske samling) samt den Arnamagnæanske samlings tilvækst 1894–99)* (Copenhagen, 1900), 504–505. The manuscript collector Árni Magnússon borrowed this manuscript from the bishop of Hólar in 1727 and it was stored in his library under the shelfmark AM 235 4:0, until the University of Copenhagen returned the book to Iceland in 1918. To my knowledge, no overdue fees were ever calculated. I wish to thank the staff of the Icelandic national archives for making the volume accessible to me.

Most of the texts are in Icelandic, although there is an occasional text in Latin. Usually, the curious scholar is frustrated by the brevity of the notices, which simply hint at interesting stories, as for example this case that is only mentioned in a brief marginal note:

> Et super hoc publicus adulter est deuictus quod incestum perpetrauit priuignam suam stuprando violan<do> et defl<orendo?>//[6]

In one of the most fully described cases in the register, in 1429, Bishop Jón annulled the marriage between Þorleifr Þórðarson and Þorgerðr Böðvarsdóttir. The register contains an account of some of the testimony in the case. The final verdict is reproduced both in Latin and in the vernacular, while the rest of the documentation is given only in Icelandic.

Þorgerðr first testified that she never had wanted to marry Þorleifr; she only wished to stay without a husband for all her life. She had uttered "that little yes-word" (*þat litla jayrdæ*) only because others had persuaded and threatened her, and because she was afraid of her father.

Next, the bishop interrogated the groom, who swore on the Bible to tell the truth. The text reproduces questions and answers, and may be quoted in full:

> My lord the bishop first asked him whether he first spoke with her father or with her herself. And Þorleifr responded that he first had spoken about it with her father and later with her. And when he spoke with her, then she neither said no nor yes. And thereafter when he spoke with her later, during the wedding, then she said yes, that her father should decide. Then the lord bishop asked him whether he had (*hafdæ*) her or not. And Þorleifr answered that he had not betrothed/wed (*hafua fæst*) her.[7]

6. Bps B. II 3, fol. 8v (the space is in the manuscript), above a probably unrelated text dated to 11 January 1434. *Diplomatarium Islandicum*, 4.535, n. 533 prints this notice with several incorrect readings, including *peregrinam* ("pilgrim") for *privignam* ("step-daughter").

7. Bps B. II 3, fol. 13r, ed. *Diplomatarium Islandicum*, 4.394: "fyrst spurdæ herra biscupæn han huortt han taladæ fyrr med faudr hennar ædr hana sealfa. En þorlæifr sagdizst fyrr hafua taladh med faudr hennar þar vm en sidar med hana. Ok þa han taladi med hana þa sagdæ hon huorcki næi næ ia. Ok þar æfter er han taladæ sidar med hana þa kaupit

It is striking how the actions, as reported in Bishop Jón's register, follow the standard pattern that Charles Donahue has excavated from a 1387 Paris marriage case. The groom and the bride's father first agreed to the marriage, and the bride then agreed to do the will of her father. Afterwards, in court, the bride claimed that she does not want to marry the groom, nor anyone else. It is as if Þorgerðr Böðvarsdóttir in northern Iceland was following the same script as Jacquelotte fille de Michel Tybert in Paris.[8]

The last sentence in the account of Þorleifr's testimony is prima facie puzzling; how can he say that he had not betrothed or wed Þorgerðr, when the entire case is about whether or not their marriage was valid? The previous sentence confuses further: what is the bishop asking? The editor of the text took *hafdæ* (had) to be an auxiliary verb; he supplied the missing main verb from the next sentence and read *hafdæ (fæst)* ("had betrothed/wed"), which does not help our understanding. Seen from the perspective of the legal issue at stake, it would seem clear that the one question the bishop needed clarified at this point was whether the marriage had been consummated or not. Whether it could be declared void depended entirely on the answer; Charles Donahue has shown that courts were usually unwilling to dissolve consummated marriages,[9] so the question of whether Þorgerðr and Þorleifr had had sex should have been essential for the outcome of the case. Is it possible to read the last two sentences in this light? Could *hafdæ* have the same sense that the verb "have" may carry in modern English? Did the bishop ask Þorleifr whether he "had" Þorgerðr? No such sense of the verb *hafa* seems to be known to the standard dictionaries of Old Norse, most of which, however, were compiled during the Victorian period. For what it is worth, the English word "to have" could certainly mean "to have sexual intercourse with" in both Old and Middle English.[10]

If my suggestion about the meaning of *hafdæ* carries conviction, we still have to explain what Þorleifr meant when he responded that he had not *fæst* her. If we understand the word in one of its usual meanings, "to wed,"

for fram þa sagdi hon jaa ath fader hennar skuldæ rada. æi sidr spurdi herra biscuppenn hann huortt han hafdæ hana ædr æi, en þorlæifr sagdizst ecki hafua fæst hana."

8. Donahue, *Law, Marriage, and Society*, 339–342.

9. Donahue, *Law, Marriage, and Society*, 43.

10. *Oxford English Dictionary*, s.v. "have," vb, II 13 a, at oed.com.

the writer would in a sense have included in Þorleifr's response the legal meaning of the sexual act: it was only through that act that an undissolvable marriage would have been created. We could also take *fæst* (infinitive *at festa*) in its basic meaning, "to fasten": Þorleifr had not bound Þorgerðr in wedlock. Whichever interpretation we chose, the response establishes that the two had not engaged in sexual intercourse.

The register includes testimony from two witnesses, Sölvi Arngrímsson and Sigurðr Þórðarson, who testified that they had heard Þorgerðr say "yes" and that they saw that she was willing to wed him.[11] Before the ceremony, her father Böðvar spoke to Þorgerðr, telling her not to go through with the wedding unless she was willing, and that she then said that she was happily willing to have Þorleifr.

The bishop must not have given much weight to the testimony of these two men, for on 1 November 1429, he issued a letter of separation.[12] He found that Þorgerðr and Þorleifr had not been lawfully joined together with both consenting, since Þorgerðr had never consented and continued to withhold her consent. In canon law, sexual intercourse counted *de jure* as a presumption of consent,[13] which must mean that Bishop Jón had ascertained that Þorgerðr and Þorleifr had not consummated their union. The bishop then declares them free to marry elsewhere, as long as God's law permits. He threatens anyone who tries to prevent his judgment from gaining force with excommunication.

The letter follows some of the usual forms, except that it is in Icelandic. The Latin version, in contrast, is problematic, starting with how difficult it is simply to read it in the manuscript. One gets the impression of a scribe who is confident in copying Icelandic but much more uncertain

11. The edition misrepresents the order in which the texts appear in the register, fol. 13r–v. The testimony of Þorgerðr and Þorleifr (no. 433 in the edition) is there followed by the Latin version of the bishop's decision (no. 435 A). Then comes the testimony of Sölvi and Sigurðr (no. 434), and finally the decision in Icelandic (no. 435 B). The heading "skilnadarbref þorlæifs þordarsonar oc þorgerdar boduarsdottur," which the edition prints before no. 435 B is in fact the page heading of fol. 13v.

12. Agnes Arnórsdóttir, *Property and Virginity: The Christianization of Marriage in Medieval Iceland 1200–1600* (Aarhus, 2010), 167–168, interprets the case differently, as being entirely about consent. She states that, since two witnesses testified that Þorgerðr had consented, "the marriage was not declared illegal." I find her conclusion puzzling.

13. Donahue, *Law, Marriage, and Society*, 43.

in Latin, especially with the system of abbreviations. The Latin is poorly formulated (unless we are to blame all infelicities on the scribe), and the text does not employ the most common formularies.[14] The bishop wants to say that both Þorgerðr and Þorleifr are free to marry other people, which in Latin becomes *a hincinde,* when the adverb (uncommon but not extremely rare; it means "on both sides") does not require a preposition. Similarly, when he says that they may marry at any place that to them seems suitable, the Latin ties itself into knots attempting to use the verb *video* (corresponding to Icelandic *synizt*), but is not very successful: *vbicumque locorum viderent vel viderint contrahendi.* The sense is obviously that Þorgerðr and Þorleifr may marry anywhere they see fit (as in the Icelandic), but it is difficult to construe thus the actual words.

Even if the Latin of the letter of separation leaves something to be desired, the decision seems in line with European practice. Even if the verdict is brief, it touches the essential points: the marriage is declared void, because there was no freely given consent; the parties are free to get married elsewhere; and the bishop threatens sanctions against anyone who counteracts his decision.

It is in fact not surprising that the bishop of Hólar knew the law, for his library was far from devoid of canonical literature. An inventory of the property of the cathedral in Hólar from 1396 shows that the church owned two copies of Gratian's *Decretum,* two copies of the *Liber Extra,* as well as single copies of the *Liber Sextus* and the *Clementines.* There is also a small selection of commentaries: two copies of Goffredus (one in two volumes), the *Casus Bernardi,* and two books by Raymond of Peñafort (one of them explicitly identified as a *Summa*).[15] None of these books survives today.

What is striking about this case is that it suggests that the canon law of marriage, including the rules of consent, were taking root (or: had taken root) in Iceland. We can, of course, not know whether Bishop Jón's verdict was respected. One may read his strong words about excommuni-

14. Charlie Donahue generously makes available on the internet great comparative material in the form of a searchable file with source quotations and comments supplementing his great marriage book: http://www.cambridge.org/download_file/202931.

15. *Diplomatarium Islandicum,* 3.612–613; Sigurður Líndal, "Um þekkingu Íslendinga á rómverskum og kanóniskum rétti frá 12. öld til miðrar 16. aldar," *Úlfljótur* 50 (1997), 241–273.

cating anyone disobedient as acknowledging that it might not, except that such formulations are common in medieval letters. That the bride should give her unforced consent when married had in fact been the law of the land ever since the Althing in 1275 accepted a lawbook for church matters (*Kristinréttr*) that had been composed by Bishop Árni of Skálholt. Árni is quite specific, one might even say pedagogical: "Good men should hear the yes-word of the maiden or the woman who is being married. And that condition is fixed, because God's help prohibits that any man marry a maiden or a woman who has been forced."[16]

Despite Árni's clear words, maidens and women continued to be forced into marriages, in Iceland as well as on the European continent. Strategic marriages served to preserve the patrimony of landed families, and also to create and maintain political alliances.[17] The Icelandic secular lawbook *Jónsbók*, which became valid in 1280, states that a father has the right to disinherit a daughter who gets married without his agreement. The saga literature shows that in many of the stories that Icelanders told each other during the later Middle Ages, the will of the bride mattered little; in fact, late medieval sagas are often ruthlessly and violently misogynistic.[18] If we take stories as symptomatic of society—at best a problematic proposition—it was a brave woman who stood up for her rights, as Þorgerðr did in 1429.

Appendix: Bishop Jón's verdict

Bishop Jón's letter declaring the marriage between Þorleifr Þórðarson and Þorgerðr Böðvarsdottir void, edited after *Brefabók Jóns Vilhjalmsónar*, Þjóðskjalasafn Íslands, Reykjavík, Bbs II:3 (AM 4:o 235), fo. 13r–v (= B). Previously edited in *Diplomatarium Islandicum: Islenzkt fornbréfasafn*, 4 (Copenhagen, 1897), 395–396, no. 435 (= D).

16. "[H]eyra scolu oc goðir menn iayrði meyiar þeirrar eþa kono sem fest verðr. oc scilorð þess er festir. fyrir þvi at þat forboðat af guðs halfu at noccor maðr festi mey eða cono nauðga." Rudolph Keyser et al., *Norges gamle love indtil 1387* (Christiania, 1846), 5.37.

17. Jenny Jochens, "Consent in Marriage: Old Norse Law, Life, and Literature," *Scandinavian Studies* 58 (1986), 142–176.

18. Jóhanna Katrín Friðriksdóttir, *Women in Old Norse Literature: Bodies, Words, and Power* (New York, 2013), esp. ch. 5.

Latin version

Nos Johannes Dei et apostolice sedis gracia episcopus Holensis exhaminimus perite(?)[19] diligenter tam in publico quam secreto et non invenientes matrimonium contractum nec inter(?)[20] nec etiam in personis vt oportet uoluntatem contrahendi inter thorlafum thorderi et thorgerde boduari; item vna pars thorgerda non consentire, nec wlt adhuc consentire / ipsas disiungimus et discopulamus ac disiunctas et dijscopulatos denunciamus per presentes. / Et liberos facimus contrahere alibi, vbicumque lex divina permiserit a hinc<i>nde[21] // Per presentes insuper omnibus nostris subditis in virtute sa<c>re[22] obediencie iniungimus // et sub pena excommunicationis precipimus vt nullus jmpediat seu impedire faciat istas predictas partes seu alterum ipsarum qui[23] nubere uel matrimonium contrahere poterit vbicumque locorum viderent vel viderint contrahendi Coram hijs facta est hec separacio videlicet abbate asberno de thingeyr domino sigwardo domino hermanno preposito in hunavatzthingh johanni egilli publico notario johanni johannis[24] johanni thorgrimsson ~~mattheo~~ halloni thorgrimi[25] et beroni Amundi et alijs pluribus notabilibus personis presentibus

Icelandic version

Wær jon med gudz nadh biscup a holum skodadom græinoliga opinberliga oc leyinliga hionaband þorlæifs þordarsonar oc thorgerdar boduarsdottur ecki logliga saman bundit vera þeirra j millom suo sæm ber med bæggia þeirra vilia af þui ath sogdh thorgerdr af sinnæ halfuo hefuer æigi med sinom fullom vilia oc ecki en vil samþyckia // Þui sundr skilium wer oc sundr slitom oc sundr sægium þeirra hiona bandh med[26] ollo laust gerom þeim mæga giptazst j huern stadh annan er gudz logh þeim lofuar // huar

19. *p̲tt'* D.

20. *n^c^itit* D.

21. *aliunde* D, who reads C as saying *atjende*.

22. *sare* B, but with a superfluous minim.

23. A line above this word makes it look not unlike an abbreviated *quoniam*.

24. This man is not mentioned in the Icelandic version.

25. A minim is missing. Hallr Þorgrimsson is one of the witnesses mentioned in the Icelandic version.

26. D supplies (*oc*) before *med*.

firir wer biodum ollum worum vnder monnum vnder heilaga hlydnæ oc skyldu vnder bans pino ath þær hindræt ædr talme þessa fyrsagda lutæ ath þau mæga giptazst oc hiona bandh binda huar þau uilia oc j huern stadh er þeim synizst. Nerverandom þesse worre giordh oc hion skilnadæ asbirnnæ abota a þingeyrom sira siugurdæ jonssyni sira hermannæ jonssyni profasti i hunavatzþingi[27] jonæ egilssyni publico[28] notario jonæ þorgrimssyni. hallæ þorgrimssyni oc biorne amundasyni oc flæirom uæl kændom monnum datum a þingeyrom allra heilagra messo aftan anno domini m°cd°xx°nono

27. *i hunavatzþingi* added above the line B.
28. The scribe of B has first written *buplico,* then crossed it out.

When Lawyers Lie:
Forging an English Constitution in 1399

David J. Seipp[1]

Charlie Donahue was my teacher in the Fall of 1980, my friend thereafter, and my literary director as I undertook, beginning in 1999, a project for the Ames Foundation to compile a database of printed Year Book reports. Year Books are the case reports of England's courts of common law from 1268 to 1535. I started my database project beginning with the first reign for which there were no modern scholarly editions, the reign of Henry IV. A total of 22,316 case reports are now translated from the Law French and indexed forty different ways.

This is the story of the very first case I compiled for the database. The case involves politics roiling around Henry IV's usurpation of the crown. The case was sparked by the earliest rebellion against his rule, while his predecessor Richard II was still his prisoner. Coincidentally, Henry IV's deposition of Richard II was the first topic in the seminar in which I was Charlie's student in 1980. The case is a longstanding puzzle of English legal history, a whodunit about the lawyers' Year Book report of a case that didn't happen.

The first Year Book report of the first year of Henry IV, 1399.001 in my database,[2] as first printed in 1553 is reproduced on the following page. I will translate it and intersperse some commentary on the report:

1. I delivered a longer version of this to the Oxford Law Faculty as the Youard Lecture in Legal History for 2015.

2. Mich. 1 Hen. 4, pl. 1, fol. 1 = 1399.001 in www.bu.edu/law/seipp, first printed by Richard Tottell in 1553 (Lincoln's Inn copy), last printed in Vulgate edition of 1679.

E Countey de. H. fuit endicte dell hault Treason en Londres per un commission deuaunt le Mayre et Justices, de ceo que il oue auters parsons accord de fayre un Mummyng en la nuycte del Epiphanie, en quel ils entendant de tuer le Roy donques estant all Wyndesore. Et puis le Roy fesoit commission a le Countie de. D. recitant que lou. G. le Coūte de. H. fuit endicte del hault Treason par luy fait concernant sa parson, et que il vouloit ceo que droit est, et pur ceo que loffice dell Scenescall del Angleter est ore voyde il graunta cest office a le dit counte de. D. pur fair droyt all dit Counte de. H. commaundant par mesme le commission toutes Seigniours de estre attendant sur luy. Et cōmādāt auxi par mesme le commission le Constable dell Toure pur estre attendant sur luy, et pur conueyer le prysoner .s. le dit Counte de. H. deuant le dit Countie de. D. a quell iour ill serra a ceo assigne. Et sur ceo a certayne iour le dit Counte de. D. sept en le sale de Westminster south un cloth de estate a par luy. Et le counte de Westmerlād et toutes auters countees et seigniours la sederūt par un graund space de luy, mes nemy sur mesme le banke, mes sur auters formes downeward en la dit sale. Et tous les Justices et barons del Excheker sederunt en le mulnes circa un Table par enter les dictes seigniours. Et puis trois *Oyes* fuerunt solempnemēt faits per le Crier, et le dit cōmission fuit lie. Et puis les Justices deliueront lenditement a le dit Scenescal, le quell ceo deliuer all Clerke del Corone, le quell ceo lia a le dit Counte de. H. le quel il confes, pur que Thil un des seriants le Roy pria que le dit Seigniour Senescall voil doner iudgement, sur quel il rehersa le dit matter, et puis done iudgement que il alera a le Toure de Londres, et de ceo que il serra trahe a les furkes et la pend, et let down arere uncore viuant, et que donques il serra decolle et quartere. *Et sic Deus propicietur animæ suæ.* Et touts les Justices dions que si le dit Counte voil auer denie le Treason, donques le Scenescall demaundera de chescun Seigniour a par luy apartement quel il esteme en sa conscience, et il commencera enprimes oue le puisne Seigniour. Et si le pluis nombre dira culpable, donques le iudgement serra done *ut supra*. Et nul Seigniour serra iure sur ceo, &c.

Corone. Treason

Coment un seigniour serra trie per ses pares.

A.ii. Nostre

> The earl of H. was indicted for High Treason in London, by virtue of a commission, before the Mayor and Justices, for this, that he with other persons agreed to perform a "Mumming" on the night of Epiphany, in which they intended to slay the king, the king then being at Windsor.

Mumming is an old word for acting out a mime show or a play, or in this case for staging a tournament.

The report goes on to say that the king sent a commission setting up a special court. This commission document recited that "G., earl of H." was indicted for high treason, and it ordered four things. First, the king appointed "the earl of D." to the office of Steward of England, because the office was then vacant.[3] Next the king ordered the earl of D. to "do right" to the accused traitor, the earl of H.[4] Third, the king commanded all lords to appear before the Steward, the earl of D., at the trial of the earl of H. (This tells us that Parliament was not in session. The same dukes, earls, barons, and lords who made up the House of Lords in Parliament, and maybe also the bishops and abbots, were specially summoned for this special trial.) Finally, the king commanded the Constable of the Tower of London (Thomas Rempston, one of Henry IV's closest supporters) to convey the prisoner, the earl of H., to appear before the Steward, the earl of D., when he assigned a day for the trial.

The Steward convened his proceeding in the obvious place, Westminster Hall.[5] Next the report states that the earl of D., presiding as Steward of England, sat in Westminster Hall under a cloth of state, a canopy and backdrop with the royal coat of arms. He sat by himself, because this was his court. The report then says that the Earl of Westmorland (Ralph de Nevill, Lord Marshal of England) and all the other earls and lords sat at a distance from the Steward, not on the same bench but on other wooden forms set up down the length of the hall, probably on

3. This was a high office of state, usually held by a member of the nobility, with duties to perform at coronations.

4. This was the usual sort of language for setting up a court of law.

5. This was where the king's courts of Common Pleas and King's Bench were both set up at opposite ends of the room four times a year for three-week sittings. And it was where coronation banquets, state trials, and state funerals were held.

two sides facing each other. (Forty-eight temporal lords had been summoned for Henry's first parliament just two months before, and about forty of them attended. The report does not say whether spiritual lords—archbishops, bishops and abbots—were summoned, but that would have been another forty-some.)

Next the report says that the justices of Common Pleas and the justices of King's Bench and the barons of the Exchequer—all thirteen of the king's justices of common law—were also there. The justices sat around a table in the middle between the two rows of earls and lords. Seating arrangements are not usually mentioned in the Year Books, but this was not an ordinary legal proceeding. Lawyers wanted to remember who was there and what places and roles they took.

Now with the Steward presiding and the lords and the justices all seated, the report supplies the script, the props, and the stage directions: "And then three cries of "Oyez" were solemnly made by the Crier, and the commission was read," as described earlier. The report goes on to say: "And then the Justices delivered the indictment to the Steward, who delivered this to the Clerk of the Crown."

Now the report finally starts to get interesting from a legal point of view: "The Clerk of the Crown read the indictment" to the accused traitor, the defendant earl of H., "which he confessed." He pleaded guilty. This was not going to be one of those dramatic state trials where we get to hear juicy evidence and the verdict was in doubt until the last minute.

The report next says, "Thereupon Hil, one of the King's Serjeants..." There was a Robert Hill, one of seven Serjeants at Law practicing in the Court of Common Pleas in 1399. But Hill was never a king's serjeant, specially called to plead on the king's behalf, nor was he the king's attorney or attorney general. So perhaps these others were absent and Serjeant Hill volunteered or was specially appointed to speak on behalf of the king in this case. Anyway, the report says that a lawyer, speaking on behalf of the king, "prayed that the Lord Steward would give judgment."

"The Steward rehearsed the matter and then gave judgment that the confessed traitor, the earl of H., would go to the Tower of London and from there that he would be drawn to the gallows and there hanged, and let down again yet living." In 1605 and thereafter we find added words: "that then his entrails would be drawn out of his body and burned, "and that he would be beheaded and quartered."[6] The report then departs from law French with the following in Latin: "And so may God be gracious to his soul."

Now the report, back in law French, adds a note, which may have been from that day or some time afterwards: "And all the Justices said that if the said earl [the accused traitor] were to have denied the treason, then the Steward would have asked each lord separately, one by one which [verdict] he deemed[7] in his conscience, and he [the Steward] would begin with the junior lord. And if the greater number would say guilty, then the judgment would be given as above, (then) and no lord would be sworn on this, etc."[8]

Finally we hear from the king's justices of common law, all of whom have been in the hall watching and listening. Previously they had delivered the indictment to the Steward, who presided over the court. But otherwise they had taken no part. Now the justices said what would have been the order of proceeding if the earl of H. had pleaded not guilty. All the other earls and lords of England would have acted as something almost like a jury. The justices said nothing about the presentation of evidence against the earl of H., or in his favor. There had long been an assumption in the common law that the jury would come to court already informed, already knowing the answer to the question they would be asked.[9] These lords were certainly expected to have their opinions already formed about the guilt or innocence of the earl of H. The Steward would ask them each of them separately "on their conscience" what verdict they would give, but unlike a jury, the lords would not be sworn. And unlike a jury, they did not have to be unanimous in their verdict. So a majority of lords could convict an indicted traitor, if he too was a lord. And not being sworn, they would not need to risk their immortal souls if they voted the way the king wanted them to (or the opposite way). The Steward would start with the "junior lord," who I assume was the lord of the lowest degree whose title was the most recent.

6. To be hanged, drawn, and quartered was a particularly disgraceful and symbolic death sentence used in treason cases at least since William Wallace in 1305.

7. The French is "esteemed."

8. This last phrase is added as an afterthought.

9. On persistence of the self-informing jury, see Seipp, "Jurors, Evidences, and the Tempest of 1499," in *"The Dearest Birthright of the People in England": The Jury in the History of the Common Law*, ed. John Cairns and Grant McLeod (Oxford: Hart, 2002), 82–85.

I suppose this was so that the senior peers with the oldest titles would not influence the junior lords.

Trial of the peers of England by their peers, their fellow members of the House of Lords, was a cherished privilege in the Middle Ages. A bishop complained in 1329 that he ought to be judged by his fellow peers in Parliament, and not arraigned in the ordinary Court of King's Bench.[10] A statute in 1341 confirmed that no peer of the land could be put to answer nor be judged, except by award of his peers in the Parliament.[11] Magna Carta's most famous clause 39, numbered 29 in the 1225 version found in statute books, provided that "No free man shall be taken or imprisoned or disseised or exiled or in any way destroyed, nor will we (the king) go upon him nor send upon him, except by the lawful judgment of his peers or by the law of the land." This clause of Magna Carta was quoted in fifteenth century Year Books, but only to make the point that an indictment of an earl or baron could only be tried in Parliament by his fellow lords. Arguments were made on this point in a 1442 trial, an appeal of robbery against a baron. They were noted by Statham's Abridgement in an entry dated 1456 and by Justice Littleton in a Year Book case in 1470.

But this privilege, trial by peers, was also a disability. The earl of H. was tried by the list of lords who were summoned by the king and who showed up for the trial. The earl of H. did not have the power that every ordinary criminal defendant had to challenge prospective jurors for cause and to challenge up to 35 prospective jurors "peremptorily," without having to explain any cause. Clause 39 of Magna Carta said famously and oddly that trial at the king's suit could only be either "by judgment of peers or by the law of the land." It has always been easier to think that "or" (in Latin *vel*) meant "and," as in "by judgment of peers and by the law of the land." Much ink has been spilled about whether "or" meant "or" in this most famous clause of Magna Carta. In the fifteenth century, England's noblemen understood the tradeoff between judgment of their peers, whom they did not have the power to choose, and "the law of their land," which gave them a jury of mere commoners whom they could challenge for good cause or for no cause.

10. Pasch. 3 Edw. 3, pl. 32, fol. 18b–19a (King's Bench 1329) = 1329.071.
11. 5 Edw. 3, stat. 1, ch. 2 (1341).

Now, why do I claim that this report was a lie? The Year Book does not say who this "G., earl of H." was. It was common in Year Books to identify a party with only a letter or a first name, and not always the right name. Lawyers didn't care about such details. But the treason committed by this defendant earl and his confederates was to perform a "mumming" on the night of the Epiphany at Windsor, and in the course of that to try to kill the new king Henry IV. This treason can be identified with certainty.

The "Epiphany Rising" was a conspiracy in the first months of Henry IV's reign, while his predecessor Richard II was still alive and Henry's prisoner. Loyal supporters of Richard II wanted to kill the usurper and restore the deposed former king. Richard's supporters included Thomas Holland, Earl of Kent; John Montagu, Earl of Salisbury; Thomas le Despenser, formerly Earl of Gloucester; Edward of York, Earl of Rutland (son of the Duke of York); and John Holland, Earl of Huntingdon. John Holland, who was an "Earl of H.," was Richard II's older half-brother on his mother's side. John Holland's wife was one of Henry IV's sisters, which didn't stop him from plotting to kill his brother-in-law. We can understand his loyalty to Richard, who had showered John, his half-brother, with honors and riches, had made him Lord Chamberlain of England for life, Admiral of the Fleet in the Western Seas, and Duke of Exeter. After seizing the throne Henry IV stripped John Holland of his dukedom, but this still left him Earl of Huntingdon.

Holland and the other conspirators plotted to stage a tournament when the new king was at Windsor for the feast of Epiphany, "Twelfth Night"—the evening before Tuesday January 6th—and to kill Henry during the tournament. The timing was freighted with meaning. Richard II had been born on Epiphany, and this one was his thirty-third birthday. Shakespeare portrayed the dramatic discovery of this same conspiracy in his play *Richard II*, Act 5. Edward of York, Earl of Rutland, first cousin to Richard II and to Henry IV, revealed the conspiracy to his father Edmund, the uncle of both kings. Henry was forewarned. He did not go to Windsor. He and his men chased down the rest of the conspirators. The earls of Salisbury and Kent fled west to try to join Richard's queen and to start a rebellion. They were chased to Cirencester, where the townsmen dragged them from the abbey and beheaded them on January 8th. The Earl of Huntingdon, John Holland, was in London, waiting to seize control of the city once news of Henry's death came from Windsor. When the attempt to kill Henry failed, the Earl of Huntingdon tried to escape to France. But the wind was blowing the wrong way and his ship was driven ashore in Essex. He was arrested at Prittiwell and imprisoned by the king's mother-in-law, the Countess of Hereford, in Pleshey castle. The Earl of Huntingdon, if that's our earl of H., was beheaded by an angry mob of commoners in the courtyard of Pleshey castle probably on January 9th or 10th. No hanging, no drawing, no quartering, no trial, no judgment. Despenser, a former earl, got as far west as Bristol, where he was seized and summarily executed on January 13th. All the earls who rose against Henry on Epiphany in the first year of his reign were killed without benefit of judicial proceedings. By mid-February, Richard II himself was dead.[12]

A multitude of historical sources—chronicles, letters, and official documents—trace this story now well accepted by historians of the period. No historical trace has been found—other than this Year Book report—that any of the conspirator earls received any form of trial, in Westminster Hall or anywhere else, before they were killed. The office of Lord Steward of England was not vacant, at least it hadn't been three months earlier at Henry IV's coronation. Henry's second son, twelve-year-old Thomas, was Lord Steward on that occasion, and again afterward. But Henry probably would not have wanted his twelve-year-old son to preside over the trial of an earl who had plotted to kill him. Edward de Courtenay was Earl of Devon, and probably the Earl of D. who, according to the report was appointed Lord Steward for this purpose, though there is no record evidence of this grant of the office. Courtenay was a loyal supporter of Henry IV. So too was the Earl of Westmorland, Ralph Neville, who had been instrumental in bringing Henry IV to the throne, and was mentioned by name in the report.

The report of this trial that never happened was first printed in 1553 by Richard Tottel. It was printed again in 1563, 1576, 1605, and 1679. It was

12. I have kept describing this as a report of 1399, though the events were all in January and February following December 1399. For the participants at the time, it was still 1399. New Year's Day was March 25th, not January 1st. And the report itself is found in print in front of the reports for September and October, Michaelmas Term of 1399, perhaps given pride of place as the most notable legal proceeding before the next term of court began.

cited in William Staunford's *Plees del Coron* in 1557 and Sir Edward Coke's *Institutes*, probably written by 1628. David Jenkins excerpted it in his *Eight Centuries of Reports* in 1661. It was presented with a good translation by Bertrand Clover in the *Columbia Jurist* in New York City in 1886,[13] and was paraphrased by Luke Owen Pike in his *Constitutional History of the House of Lords* in 1894.[14]

Then in March 1907, a book was published in London that denounced this report as "an absolute forgery" (p. 416) a "most iniquitous... forged report" (p. 434) "a gross fraud" (p. vii), and "quite the most interesting fraud in the whole legal history of England" (p. 399).[15] The book was entitled *His Grace the Steward and Trial of Peers*. The title page went on to say that it was "A Novel Inquiry into a Special Branch of Constitutional Government, Founded Entirely upon Original Sources of Information, and Extensively upon Hitherto Unprinted Materials."

The author of this exposé was L. W. Vernon Harcourt. Leveson William Vernon Harcourt was a 35-year-old barrister of Gray's Inn, an Oxford man, son of a Professor of Civil Engineering at University College London, grandson of an admiral, and great-grandson of an archbishop of York. He was one of those scholarly barristers in the circle of Frederic William Maitland. The great Maitland had just died, only three months before Vernon Harcourt finished his book. Vernon Harcourt had rounded up fifteen hitherto unknown Year Book manuscripts of the 1313 Eyre of Kent in the time of Edward II, most of them better manuscripts than the one that Maitland had been using.[16] Then two years after he published *His Grace the Steward*, Vernon Harcourt died suddenly, age 37, just four days before the birth of his only son. That 1907 book *His Grace the Steward and Trial of Peers* became the only thing for which we remember L. W. Vernon Harcourt.

As a prosecuting barrister, Vernon Harcourt built the case against his prime suspect, Henry VII, the first Tudor king, or the lawyers working

13. "From the Year Books of the Reign of Henry IV," *Columbia Jurist* 3 (Dec. 11, 1886), 139–140.

14. Luke Owen Pike, *Constitutional History of the House of Lords* (London, 1894), 209–211.

15. L. W. Vernon Harcourt, *His Grace the Steward and Trial of Peers* (London, 1907).

16. He was collating these manuscripts for the Selden Society.

for him. He said that they must have forged this Year Book report and inserted it among those of a century earlier. The forgery, he said, must have happened, in or shortly before 1499, a full century later. It was forged, he said, in order to provide a precedent for the 1499 trial of the 24-year-old Edward Plantagenet, Earl of Warwick. Young Warwick's crime was that he was perhaps the last legitimate descendant of King Edward III through a male line of descent, and thus a potential claimant to the throne of Henry VII. And so he was executed, after a proceeding that tracked the procedure described in our Year Book report of 1399.

Vernon Harcourt argued that the lawyers of 1399 and thereafter could not have accepted this spurious report into their manuscript collections of Year Book cases, because they would have known that there was no meeting of the Steward, the lords, and the justices that year in Westminster Hall for the treason trial of any earl. They would have known that all the Epiphany conspirators were killed within a week and without benefit of legal proceedings.

Vernon Harcourt pointed out that there was no surviving early manuscript of this report. And none has been found since. But we also don't have a manuscript for the other ten cases in that first year of Henry IV, although they do appear in printed Year Books. Manuscripts of years immediately following do exist, but frequently ascribe cases to different terms and different years than does the printed report. Vernon Harcourt also said that our suspect case was not included in Anthony Fitzherbert's Grand Abridgement of cases in 1514 to 1516, or any other early printed abridgement. But the same could be said of eight other cases out of ten in the first year of Henry IV. Our case also does not appear in the seventeenth-century index to the printed collection of the Year Books of Henry IV, which appears to have been compiled from abridgement entries.

Vernon Harcourt did not make it easy for himself. He blasted eminent, established scholars with whom he disagreed, such as those who concluded that "or" meant "and" in that famous clause of Magna Carta. He called Luke Owen Pike, who in 1907 was the pre-eminent living editor of Year Book material, "a blind leader of the blind" (p. 343). The *Law Quarterly Review* then asked Pike to review the book, and not surprisingly,

Pike rejected Vernon Harcourt's conclusion.[17] Pike said that the Earl of Huntingdon could have been sentenced in Westminster Hall as the Year Book said, then escaped from the Tower, then gotten caught again and murdered by commoners at Pleshey. Barnaby Keeney, who wrote a little book in 1952 on *Judgment by Peers,* agreed with Pike that the Earl could have been tried as the Year Book stated and, even so, killed at Pleshey as the chroniclers all agreed.[18]

T. F. T. Plucknett in 1932 was more willing to credit Vernon Harcourt's accusation of a later forgery.[19] Plucknett surmised that fifteenth-century Year Books must have circulated quite narrowly, just among the half-dozen serjeants at law active at any one time, so few that they could have kept the secret of a new report introduced into their manuscripts. Brian Simpson in 1957 also accepted that our 1399 case was "very probably," "fairly certainly" a forgery (p. 56).[20] But Simpson drew the opposite conclusion from Plucknett's. Simpson wrote that manuscript Year Books must have circulated very widely in the legal profession in the fifteenth century, so widely that no one lawyer's manuscript looked exactly like any other lawyer's manuscript. Cases that had never been seen before were turning up all the time, Simpson thought, so the forgery could be slipped in once enough time had passed so that no one was likely to remember that no such trial had happened.

I suggest that the Year Book report about the Earl of H.'s trial was certainly forged, but it was forged in 1399 or very soon thereafter. It was forged by lawyers and for lawyers who were very well aware that it never happened, but who wanted it to have happened, and wanted future lawyers always to remember that it had or should have happened that way.

At my request, Benjamin Niehaus, a Ph.D. candidate in French Literature with a subspecialty in medieval French linguistics, has studied this suspicious Year Book report, along with the next half dozen cases that

17. L. Owen Pike, "The Trial of Peers," *Law Quarterly Review* 23 (1907), 442–447.

18. Barnaby C. Keeney, *Judgment by Peers* (Cambridge, Mass., 1952), 104–106, 180–181.

19. T. F. T. Plucknett, "The Place of the Legal Profession in the History of English Law," *Law Quarterly Review* 48 (1932), 328, 337–338.

20. A. W. B. Simpson, "The Circulation of Yearbooks in the Fifteenth Century," *Law Quarterly Review* 73 (1957), 492, 495.

follow it from the year 1399, and has compared them to the first half-dozen cases of the year 1499, the year in which Vernon Harcourt thought our case was forged. Niehaus found that our suspect report was linguistically similar to other 1399 Year Book reports in ways that differed from the 1499 reports. His conclusion is based on such matters as the presence of the letter "u" before nasal consonants when followed by dental plosives, and the use of epinthetic "e's" at the beginning of words that start with "s," among other spelling peculiarities. When 1499 cases tend to spell "in" with an "i," our suspect case spells "en" with an "e," as did other cases a century earlier. Niehaus and I both note that there are more English words in our suspect case—"mumming," "cloth," "downward," and "let down"—than we would expect. But four Year Book reports in the next decade similarly introduce English words amidst the French, and more do so in succeeding decades. If Henry VII's lawyers forged this a century after it was supposed to be written, they did a surprisingly good job.

I don't have a manuscript confirming or refuting Vernon Harcourt's accusation of Tudor forgery. The supposed "commission" has not turned up, nor has the "indictment." We do see, in the Parliament Rolls, more than a year after the attempted rebellion, that "all the lords temporal present in parliament"—25 named lords—"by the assent of the king," confirmed the forfeiture of the lands of the Earl of Huntingdon and the other conspirators, who had been, the Roll says, "seized and beheaded in their armed uprising by the loyal lieges" of the king (not by judgment of their peers before the Steward).[21] The king and lords in Parliament in March 1401 also "declared and adjudged" the Earl and the other conspirators to be traitors, presumably for the first time, well after their deaths. Our 1399 Year Book report is surely a detailed account of a trial that didn't happen.

The report itself has not been tracked any earlier than that first 1553 printing, but there is a widely known and well circulated Year Book report of 1470, also found in three manuscripts and excerpted in Fitzherbert's and Brooke's Abridgements, that suggests that the 1399 report was known in 1470 and perhaps earlier.[22] In this report, Thomas Littleton, a Justice of

21. *The Parliament Rolls of Medieval England, 1275–1504*, ed. Chris Given-Wilson) (London, 2005), 8.109–110 (3 Rot. Parl. 442a–442b).

22. 1470.035ss = Pasch. 10 Edw. 4, pl. 17 fol. 6b–7a (C.P.) and 47 SS 63 (pl. 16), excerpted in Fitzherbert, Corone 34; Brooke, Corone 152; briefly excerpted in Statham

Common Pleas, told about a private accusation of robbery against a baron in 1442, and how it was tried before Chief Justice Fortescue. According to Littleton—and perhaps also from Fortescue almost thirty years earlier—if a lord, a peer of the realm, had been indicted for felony or treason, this would be sent into Parliament and the Steward would require the defendant lord to answer. If the defendant lord pleaded not guilty, he would be tried by his peers. The spiritual lords (the bishops and abbots in the House of Lords), who could not consent to the death of a man, would appoint a proctor in Parliament to represent them. Then, Littleton said, the Steward ought to examine first the most junior lord present as to whether the defendant lord be guilty, and then ask in turn each other lord present. What Justice Littleton described was a proceeding in Parliament, whereas this 1399 report was of a trial when Parliament was not in session. But what Littleton said about the order of taking separate verdicts from individual lords, starting with the junior lord, should sound familiar now. This was different from how common law juries conferred together and spoke through a foreman. This 1470 case suggests strongly that Littleton knew about the 1399 report and based his remarks on it. It has that fingerprint—separate verdicts, junior lord first—though there is no mention of needing only a majority vote to condemn. Vernon Harcourt would argue, of course, that his Tudor forgers in 1499 knew of Littleton's 1470 dictum, and incorporated some of its details into their later backdated forgery of the 1399 case.

Justice Littleton's note in 1470 may have been prompted by events of that year. In the middle of 1470, lawyers were writing at the tops of the pages of their Year Books and other records that it was Easter and then Trinity Term of the 10th year of the reign of Edward IV. Then in October the Earl of Warwick freed the previous king, Henry VI, from captivity in the Tower and put him on the throne. Lawyers shrugged, turned over the leaf of parchment, and wrote at the top of the new page that it was now Michaelmas of the 49th year of Henry VI, as if Edward IV had never been king. Hilary term followed, still dated 49 Henry VI, but by the next spring, Warwick and Henry VI had both been killed, Edward IV was back on the throne, and lawyers shrugged once again, turned over the leaf of parchment, and wrote at the top of the page that it was Easter Term of

---

Triall 45, fol. 178r, dated Pasch. 34 Hen. 6 = 1456.106abr.

the 11th year of Edward IV. By 1470, the comings and goings of kings of the rival dynasties meant little more than the headings on the pages of the lawyers' manuscripts. The king's court was the court of whoever happened to be king at the moment.

There is also a hint that a longer variant manuscript of the 1399 report once existed. Sir Edward Coke, in the Third Part of his *Institutes*, probably completed around 1628, added many more details about the procedure before the Steward in a treason trial of a peer, but Coke cited only the 1399 case.[23] In the Fourth Part of his *Institutes* Coke identified our Earl of H. from the 1399 report as John Holland, Earl of Huntingdon, and our Earl of D. as Edward, Earl of Devon. This suggests that Coke may have had a manuscript, now lost, that gave more details and more identifications than the version we now have, first printed by Richard Tottel in 1553. Or maybe Coke was just interpolating procedures followed in 1499, in 1521, and afterwards. And then, like a good historian, Coke filled out the initials with the obvious historical characters from two centuries earlier. In a sidenote in the Fourth *Institutes*, Coke said that he believed the Year Book account to be true and rejected what Thomas Walsingham and the other chroniclers had written about Huntingdon's murder at Pleshey.

As others have noted, Vernon Harcourt's case is at its weakest when he insisted that in 1499 Henry VII needed a venerable precedent for the trial of the Earl of Warwick. Vernon Harcourt admitted that in August 1415 Henry V had ordered his brother Thomas, Duke of Clarence, Steward of England, to convene a court, consisting of eighteen to twenty peers, at Southampton to try Henry Scrope, Baron Scrope of Masham, and Richard of Conisbourgh, Earl of Cambridge, for the Southampton Plot to put Edmund Mortimer on the throne in place of the Lancasters. This 1415 trial should have been precedent enough for what Henry VII proposed to do to the Earl of Warwick in 1499. And since when did a Tudor king care about precedent?

When you think about it, a Year Book report was an odd thing for a king and his henchmen to have forged. If there were skeptics or critics of the way Henry VII was proceeding against the Earl of Warwick in 1499, the

23. Edward Coke, *The Third Part of the Institutes of the Laws of England* (1644), 28–29; *The Fourth Part of the Institutes of the Laws of England* (1644), 59.

kind of precedents that they would have expected were official documents, maybe entries in the rolls of Parliament, not in the manuscript collections of individual lawyers. Kings and their henchmen would be more likely to forge official documents, over which the king had pretty good control, not the private, completely unofficial manuscripts that were traded around by lawyers. Putting such a report in a manuscript perhaps at one of the Inns of Court did not guarantee that it would get copied into other collections and eventually printed. And if Henry VII or his lawyers were introducing a never-before-seen report about a high matter of state and treason, wouldn't they more likely have slipped it into the middle or the end of the series of reports of humdrum 1399 cases? Wouldn't they have written it on the blank back page of an older manuscript, rather than giving it pride of place as the first case of the whole reign, out of chronological order with reports of matters from previous months, as if it were a sign of things to come in the new reign just starting?

Also, there were many uprisings against Henry IV in the first six years of his reign, several of them led by earls or other lords. It seems unnecessary for forgers a hundred years later to have specified the Epiphany Uprising in their fake Year Book report, in such unnecessary detail, when any trial of any earl while Parliament was not in session would suffice.

So I am saying yes, the 1399 case was a lie. But no, it was not forged a century later, or so I believe. It was forged at the same time it didn't happen, because that was when lawyers needed it to have happened. It was forged to solve a problem for the legal profession and for English law and governance.

The problem was this: An unsuccessful challenger to the reigning king was a traitor, but a successful challenger to a king became the next reigning king. Henry IV had proved that a king, Richard II, could be deposed and replaced by a challenger, Henry IV, who was not the deposed king's nearest heir. The throne of England was up for grabs. Winners would leave it to their lawyers to come up with claims to legitimate authority—often tendentious and unconvincing claims—pretending hereditary right, parliamentary ratification, popular acclaim, holy consecration, or a combination of any or all of these. But this shaky claim to royal authority meant that Henry IV had to fight off many challenges to his position, as did his son. His grandson lost his crown to a challenger, Edward IV, who took it because he could. Judges and lawyers did not want to be in, or anywhere near, a decision-making position about which of the great and powerful men of England were or were not traitors. Judges who gave judgment that a challenger's uprising was an act of treason could themselves be executed for treason if the challenger succeeded, or if the challenger's son or brother succeeded in the next uprising.

This lesson had been brought forcefully to lawyers' attention in England in the dozen years before Henry IV's successful coup d'etat of 1399. Opponents of Richard II, including his cousin the future Henry IV, when they had the upper hand in Parliament, first used impeachment to attack King Richard's favorites and supporters. Then in 1387 Richard II turned the tables. His Chief Justice, Robert Tresilian, propounded a series of ten questions to the other justices,[24] asking whether opponents of the king could employ impeachment in Parliament without the king's consent? No, they could not. Tresilian asked his fellow justices whether the opponents' actions in the previous Parliament amounted to treason? Yes, they did. And whether the opponents' actions should be punished by death? Yes, they should. But Richard didn't manage to kill all of his opponents. Just a year later, Richard's opponents got the upper hand again, they tried a new tactic devised by lawyers, private accusations called "appeals of treason," brought now for the first time in 1388 directly in Parliament as a court of law.[25]

The six judges who had, in the previous year, answered Tresilian's question as Richard II had wanted them answered were now all removed from office. The lawyer who had drafted and written out the questions for Tresilian, a man named John Blake, was appealed of treason and hanged. Tresilian himself, the Chief Justice of England, was appealed of treason for obtaining from his fellow justices a false opinion calling the king's opponents traitors. Tresilian was arrested, brought into Parliament, tried, and sentenced. Parliament didn't listen to any of his learned legal arguments. He was hanged, and four others of Richard's chief supporters were also executed. The other judges, whose only offence was that they answered the questions propounded by the Chief Justice a year before, were impeached,

24. See S. B. Chrimes, "Richard II's Questions to the Judges, 1387," *Law Quarterly Review* 72 (1956), 365–390.

25. See Alan Rogers, "Parliamentary Appeals of Treason in the Reign of Richard the Second," *American Journal of Legal History* 8 (1964), 95–124.

they were removed from office, they were charged with treason, they were put on trial for their lives. They ultimately were not put to death, but were banished for life to Ireland. The judges said in their defense that they were forced to answer the questions as the king commanded. But this did not help them. The events of 1387 and 1388 taught that judges and lawyers risked their own lives when they took sides in the new games of power in England. This was true even if they played relatively minor roles. Remember lawyer John Blake, who was hanged simply for drafting the questions that Chief Justice Tresilian wanted to ask the other justices.

Appeals of treason in Parliament continued after 1388. Shakespeare's play *Richard II* opens with cross-appeals between two of the king's opponents, the future Henry IV and Thomas Mowbray, Earl of Nottingham, each accusing the other of treason. Richard II stopped the fight and took the occasion to banish both of them. This began the string of grievances for which Henry returned from banishment, deposed his cousin Richard, and took the crown for himself. Parliamentary appeals of treason were then abolished by Henry IV's first Parliament in 1399. That left indictments of treason, one of which we have seen in our 1399 case.

Judges and lawyers needed to prescribe a procedure that would provide an orderly way to decide accusations of treason against powerful noblemen. But judges and lawyers desperately wanted to get out of the way and leave these difficult, dangerous decisions to others. The obvious and ideal choice was to leave such momentous decisions to the collective body of lords. Henry IV soon found that, in practical terms, holding onto the throne in England depended on keeping the greater number of peers of the realm on his side. Who better to decide, then, which power grabs were treason and which were politics than the same powerful magnates whose support made it possible for the king to keep his shaky hold on power? Unlike ordinary jurors, peers didn't even need to swear an oath to give their true verdict. Peers could switch loyalty as necessary in future roundabouts of the Wars of the Roses.

Were the lawyers who fabricated this Year Book report trying to fool anyone? This is a difficult question. The Year Books are filled with hypothetical arguments, and some entire reports are phrased in hypothetical terms. No other report, setting out so many specific details as if they had actually happened, has been found to lack any historical basis. But this report could have been meant as a kind of legal fiction. Legal fictions were a convenience to the legal system. They did not deceive the court, nor opposing counsel. They usually introduced innovations while making the paperwork appear as if nothing had changed. This legal fiction of 1399 allowed the courts and lawyers to pretend that a procedure had been settled for the trial of peers of the realm, whether or not Parliament was in session. An indicted lord would be tried by majority vote of temporal lords, with lawyers and judges playing only the most minor of roles. And if it appeared to nonlawyers that the sort of proceeding the lawyers were recommending had already happened, this was not the lawyers' fault. Their Year Books were not meant to be read by those outside the profession.

Vernon Harcourt found it impossible, offensive, and outrageous that lawyers might include in their reports the account of a trial that didn't happen. But lawyers wrote down these words—the Year Books—for their own professional reasons. Year Books were not written for us. They were not written to be historically accurate. They were written to be useful. Sometimes this probably meant improving on what a particular lawyer really did argue in court in order to let it be remembered what the lawyer should have said, or wished he had said.

When lawyers lie, they do so to solve a problem. The Epiphany Uprising of four earls in the first months of Henry IV's reign and the swift extra-legal beheading of all the main conspirators provided an ideal opportunity. The earls were all dead. This was the right moment to say and remember how one of those dead earls should have been tried—by majority vote of his fellow lords before the Steward of England. The lawyers who forged this Year Book report—and I nominate for the leader of the group that lawyer Robert Hill named in the Year Book—could not be accused of taking sides in a pending case. The lawyers wrote that the accused earl had pleaded guilty. I can think of no obvious legal or practical advantage for the earl to have done so. On the other hand, the advantage for the lawyers to say that the earl pleaded guilty was obvious. By having the accused earl conveniently confess his guilt, the lawyers avoided the awkward need to list which earls voted guilty and which voted innocent in their report of the trial that didn't happen.

So lawyers lied. They reported that a trial had occurred (though it hadn't), and they reported how it had occurred in a way that made it appropriate for the justices to say what procedure would have been followed had the accused earl made a different choice, to plead not guilty. This was their best way to influence what procedure would be followed when the next accused traitor pleaded not guilty and forced a verdict of his peers. Lawyers forged a report of the trial that could and should have happened in order to recommend prospectively a procedure that should be followed when the need next arose. And it arose again in 1415, in 1499, in 1521 (when the Year Book once more gave a very full account of the proceedings, matching our case precisely), and several more times in the sixteenth century, even more often when we include trials before the Steward when Parliament was in session. Lawyers and judges in 1399 saw and helped articulate, in this lie, how governmental power in England was constituted. A majority of the dukes, earls, and great lords of England could and would decide who next challenged the king and failed, and who next challenged the king and replaced him. This was, for better or worse, part of England's constitution in 1399 and through the lawless fifteenth century that followed.

Lawyers lied, but in a good cause. They lied to save their own necks, but did so heroically, trying to steer forces much larger than themselves to a mutually acceptable end. To quote the Year Book: "and so may God be gracious to their souls." I wish every case in the database that I compiled with Charlie Donahue's generous support and advice had such an interesting puzzle behind it. What puzzles remain have become easier for all scholars to reveal thanks to his wise direction of the Ames Foundation.

The Murder of Mistress Lacey's Maid: Ad Hockery and the Law in England circa 1530

Shannon McSheffrey

On 20 June 1530, John Laurence, former servant to a London widow named Lucy Lacey, and Robert Turner, a Lancashire man, made a confession regarding their parts in a heinous crime committed about two months before. In late April of the same year, the two men and two other confederates had conspired to rob Mistress Lacey's house and had callously killed her maidservant in the process. The two men admitted their roles in the felony under examination at Cardinal Wolsey's residence at the manor of Southwell, Nottinghamshire. As those who examined Laurence and Turner no doubt knew, Mistress Lacey was a widow of advanced years—perhaps as old as eighty—and the attack upon her, not to mention the cruel slaying of her maidservant, was an especially heinous crime.

Laurence and Turner were likely in custody awaiting trial when they were examined at Southwell, but this was not an official questioning; it was instead an ad hoc interrogation, undertaken at the residence of a man no longer in the king's service, by examiners who had no official standing in the case. We know, of course, that alongside the formal legal processes of late medieval and Tudor England a range of informal and under-the-table negotiations and maneuvers took place, but by their nature such practices were usually undocumented. Sometimes, however, they were documented and sometimes, usually by accident, those written records survive, as is the case for Laurence's and Turner's examination, the record of which made its way into the State Papers series at the National Archives when it was seized in a later unrelated treason attainder.[1] Taking apart this curious record and putting it into its context—considering how the men came to be at Southwell and what the purpose of the interrogation was—allows this usually shadowy behind-the-scenes world to come partially into the light. Unsurprisingly, backchannel strategies in Tudor England depended heavily on networks of power and influence. Though a woman of humble birth, the elderly Mistress Lacey had through her long life built up impressive connections that she could call upon in this moment of crisis. Those connections helped her with both formal legal processes and the informal and even illegal tactics upon which the success of those formal legal processes depended.

The document written at Southwell consists of records of John Laurence's and Robert Turner's interrogations and an inventory of the stolen goods. Three men were named as examiners: one, Sir John Dunham, was a local gentleman; and the other two, William Disney and Hugh Fuller, were administrators in the cardinal's household. As Mistress Lacey's servant, Laurence, was clearly a lynchpin in the conspiracy, the record of his questioning is the longer and more detailed of the two. He told his examiners a version of events in which he distanced himself from the most terrible part of the crime—he insisted that he had had no role in the murder of the maidservant—while admitting his part in the planning and execution of the robbery, itself a capital offence. Laurence gave the examiners a narrative of events: he had been in Mistress Lacey's service in the parish of St. Antholin in London for about nine months when he became acquainted with a certain rather shady priest named Sir Richard (surname unknown). Sir Richard, Laurence hastened to clarify, was by no means respectable and perhaps not really in holy orders: he was a sanctuary man of St. Martin le Grand, and he lived there with a woman named Charity, meaning that she was "either a concubine orellis [he] falsely profess[ed] the order of priesthod." Sir Richard put Laurence in touch with a certain "unknowen person" who was an accomplished thief. Although both Laurence and Turner claimed that they never learned the second man's name, they described him in some detail for the examiners so that they could hunt him down:

1. Kew, The National Archives [TNA], SP 1/57, fols. 179r–181v. The details of the examination below come from this document. They were part of Cromwell's papers seized in 1540 on his attainder.

> A yong man about xxxii yeres of aege, meane of stature, whitely visaged, with sharpe nose, light abren heare, a litle berde nere of the same colour, comunely accustomed to were a Spanysshe Cape and sumtyme a cote of Orange Tawny and white hosen / most parte haunting to Saynt Martyns Saynctuary.

The man brought with him to his meeting with Laurence certain irons "mete to pike locks," hidden underneath his "Spanissh cloke."[2]

Although Laurence did not immediately enter into a coven with the white-visaged man, soon thereafter his mistress's high-handed ways caused him to consider his new acquaintance's criminal expertise. Lucy Lacey was a formidable woman who was not inclined to take nonsense from her servants, and whose servants sometimes resented it.[3] Laurence outlined to his examiners at Southwell why he felt ill-treated: he had ridden out to Kent to Mistress Lacey's daughter, Mistress Knyvett, who usually lived with her mother in London but had gone to her own property in Kent for a week. On his return to London Mistress Knyvett sent back with Laurence a small gift for her mother, a "bowed noble," a bent coin that served as a good luck charm or a token of faithfulness, but which nonetheless still carried the value of a noble coin, 7s 6d. Laurence duly brought it to Mistress Lacey, but she refused to acknowledge that she had received it, and he began to worry that she would report him for theft. Because of this, he said, he conceived "inwarde grefe ayenst his Mistress."[4] In that resentful state, he set out to St. Martin's to find the mysterious man in the Spanish cloak. On the morning of 25 April 1530 the two men, together with Robert Turner, Laurence's co-examinee, met in the Leopard's Head tavern, and the three of them agreed that they would rob Mistress Lacey's house.

Laurence and Turner explained to the examiners that the robbery, which a later record dates to 28 April (a Thursday), was accomplished in this fashion: first, at about ten o'clock in the morning John Laurence se-

2. TNA, SP 1/57, fols. 179r, 181r.

3. In an undated case in the court of Requests, a priest who had been in her employ complained in a petition of the "Ryall power" (regal pretensions?) she exhibited in withholding of his wages, a gown, and his "letters of his orders" when he wanted to leave her employ. TNA, REQ 2/6/101.

4. TNA, SP 1/57, fol. 179v.

cretly brought Robert Turner and the unknown man into the house, and hid them in a cellar until such time as Mistress Lacey left the house to hear mass, as she did daily. While she was at church, they took her maid and bound her hands and feet and gagged her with a cloth so that "she should not crye or make any noyse." They then took her up to a chamber and cast two featherbeds on top of her to muffle her cries. Once downstairs again, however, they could still hear her and feared others would, too. The unknown man returned to the chamber where they had left her, and "what so ever he dyd unto her these deponents can not say, but crye they herde her no more."[5]

When the time came for Laurence to go to the church to escort Mistress Lacey home again after mass, he left the unknown man and Turner, warning them not to hurt the maid. When he brought Mistress Lacey into the house, they tied her up, too, binding her hands and feet and putting a blindfold over her eyes. They used her keys to enter into her chamber where she kept her valuables, using sheets to wrap up her plate, money, jewellery, and other goods. Laurence and Turner, both probably originally Lancashire men,[6] then apparently fled to the north with their share. At Ripon in Yorkshire and in Lancashire and Westmorland, they fenced the stolen goods with a number of men named on the inventory—an esquire, a barber, a "Master Cettle" of the collegiate church of Ripon. Where the man in the Spanish cloak went, Laurence and Turner did not know, and they had, or so they claimed, only partial knowledge of the goods that he had taken. Their interrogation ended with the examiners asking Laurence and Turner if they had ever before been accessory to any murder or felony other than what they had just confessed, to which the two men fervently swore that indeed they had not.

This examination was recorded neatly in a secretary hand, with a heading detailing the names of the men examined, the names of the examiners and their positions, the place, and the date, in the "xxii^{ti} yere of the reigne of our Sovereigne lorde King Henry the viiith." The confessions and inventories take up three sheets of paper, which survive today as part

5. TNA, SP 1/57, fols. 179v–180r.

6. Turner is identified in his examination as of Warton, Lancashire, and John Laurence, too, seems to have originally hailed from the same area, as some of the goods were delivered to a Lancelot Laurence of Yealand, Lancashire, near Warton.

of the State Papers series at the National Archives. These papers are not, however, state papers in the sense that they represent some kind of formal, governmental legal process; they are instead the record of an unofficial examination undertaken in the residence of Cardinal Wolsey, by a local gentleman and two of the cardinal's servants. Although Wolsey had held very high administrative and judicial offices in the king's service from the early 1510s until November 1529, in June 1530 he was simply the cardinal archbishop of York, without secular office of any kind, living theoretically in retirement at his manor at Southwell.[7] How, then, came John Laurence and Robert Turner to undergo this examination in the cardinal's household regarding their part in a London crime, outside both Wolsey's authority as a bishop and his ecclesiastical province of York? Why would this crime, heinous as it was, pique the concern of the cardinal? What was this extra-judicial examination meant to accomplish? How did the records find their way into the State Papers?

Some of these questions are answered relatively easily. The records came into the Crown's possession when Thomas Cromwell's papers were seized in 1540 on his attainder for treason. They had come into his possession because he was acting as the widows' main legal counsellor in the case; he kept the records probably because he kept everything, for which historians of Henry's reign should be truly thankful. Wolsey's involvement is also fairly easy to explain; although he was in disgrace, and with hindsight we know he would never recover his former position, he still had hope in the summer of 1530 while he was resident at Southwell that he could salvage his career as royal servant. He was certainly busy around this time attempting to build good will: his biographer George Cavendish reported that in June and July he "made many agrementes and concordes" amongst disputing parties who came to him at Southwell.[8] This intervention in Mistress Lacey's case was similar in some ways to the arbitration and mediation that was commonplace in legal disputes over land or other kinds of litigation.[9]

7. On Wolsey's last year, see Peter Gwyn, *The King's Cardinal: The Rise and Fall of Thomas Wolsey* (London: Pimlico, 1992), 599–639.

8. George Cavendish, *The Life and Death of Cardinal Wolsey*, ed. Richard S. Sylvester, Early English Text Society 243 (London: Oxford University Press, 1959), 138.

9. J. H. Baker, *The Oxford History of the Laws of England*, Volume VI, 1485–1558 (Oxford: Oxford University Press, 2003), 333–34.

Unlike those other kinds of unofficial facilitations of concord, however, this dispute would not have been brought to Wolsey by the two parties. Laurence and Turner were felons, not litigants, and they were presumably brought there in some kind of custody. The case had to have been brought to Wolsey's attention through strings the victims, Mistress Lacey and her daughter Anne Knyvett, were able to pull. Thus the identities and connections of the two widows are crucial to understanding how this examination came about. Over her long lifetime Lucy left traces in different kinds of records and, as it turns out, her life journey is an interesting story in itself.

The Networks of Mistresses Lacey and Knyvett

Mistress Lucy Lacey was likely born about 1450 or a few years after, and she died in 1541, at the age of about ninety.[10] She was not born into the kind of family that presaged the high connections she was able to call upon at the end of her life. Her father, Lewis Brampston, was a provincial brewer of modest means, married to a woman named Katherine, and they had at least three children, a son Lewis and two daughters, Mary and Lucy. Brampston was, however, a brewer in a university town, Cambridge, and after his death in the late 1460s, his widow Katherine's remarriage about 1470 to a university-trained physician, Walter Lemster, seems to have provided access to a quite different world, both for the widow and for her daughter Lucy.[11] (Lewis's and Katherine's other two children make only brief appearances in the records, in small bequests in later decades from Walter and Katherine, suggesting that they played a much less central part

10. Her date of birth is inferred from her having entered into a betrothal c. 1469 (see TNA, C 1/61/584, discussed below), when she would have been no younger than her later teens according to contemporary marriage patterns for non-elite women (as she was then). Her will (TNA, PROB 11/28/631) was probated in 1541.

11. Corpus Christi College Cambridge Archives (through online calendars at http://janus.lib.cam.ac.uk), CCCC 09/06/1A–1C; CCCC 09/07/46; CCCC 09/07/104; CCCC 09/09/32; TNA, PROB 11/8/40, Will of Walter Lemster, 1487; A. B. Emden, *A Biographical Register of the University of Cambridge to 1500* (Cambridge: Cambridge University Press, 1963), 362–63. C. H. Talbot and E. A. Hammond, *The Medical Practitioners in Medieval England: A Biographical Register* (London: Wellcome Historical Medical Library, 1965), 369–70, mistakenly considers Lemster's "daughter-in-law" (in our terms, stepdaughter) to be distinct from his "daughter," Lucy.

in the Lemsters' lives.)[12] Walter Lemster would have been amongst the earliest academically-trained physicians in England to marry, part of a shift of university-trained medical men away from their clerical roots towards a lay identity.[13] Walter, Katherine, and Lucy settled in St. Antholin's parish in London while Walter, or all of them, maintained connections with Cambridge.

In the years that followed, Walter's medical career advanced. Probably through Cambridge connections he became physician to the bishop of Ely and to Elizabeth Mowbray, dowager duchess of Norfolk, whom he named in his will as "his singular lady and renowned princess [*meam singularem dominam et inclitam principissam*]."[14] As an academic who may well have started his career assuming he would never marry but then acquired a wife and daughter, Lemster straddled the lay and clerical worlds. His will shows that he had a "chamber" at the Carthusian house at Sheen, and that he had ties to the lay literary circle in London that formed around William Caxton in the 1480s. Amongst his most precious bequests were his books, most of which were given to King's College, Cambridge, while several others were bequeathed to individuals, including a copy of the fourteenth-century Latin horticultural text *Ruralia commoda* by Petrus de Crescenciis, which he intriguingly left to the wife of William Pratt, mercer, a close friend of Caxton, "as her own book [*ut suum librum proprium*]."[15] By the mid-1480s, Lemster's ties to episcopal, noble, and London civic circles were crowned by an appointment as royal physician, first to Richard III in 1484 and then

12. TNA, PROB 11/8/40, Will of Walter Lemster, 1487; and TNA, PROB 11/11/211, Will of Katherine Bentley alias Lemster, 1497.

13. On English physicians and marriage, see Carole Rawcliffe, *Medicine and Society in Later Medieval England* (Stroud, Gloucestershire: Sutton, 1997), 110–12.

14. TNA, PROB 11/8/40; see also C 1/147/56, on a ring the duchess had given to Lemster, which he devised back to her in his will but which Lucy had lent to another man who refused to return it.

15. Ibid. William Pratt and his wife Alice, who was likely a silkwoman in her own right, were close friends with William Caxton. See Anne F. Sutton, "Caxton Was a Mercer: His Social Milieu and Friends," in *England in the Fifteenth Century: Proceedings of the 1992 Harlaxton Symposium*, ed. Nicholas Rogers (Stamford: Paul Watkins, 1994), 118–48; Anne F. Sutton, "Alice Claver, Silkwoman (d. 1489)," in *Medieval London Widows, 1300–1500*, ed. Caroline M. Barron and Anne F. Sutton (London: Hambledon Press, 1994), 133–42. A fifteenth-century English manuscript copy of Petrus de Crescentiis is Harley MS 3662 (which is available online at www.bl.uk); it was also printed in Augsburg in 1471.

to Henry VII in 1486.[16] He was not able to enjoy his new position for long, however, as he died in March 1487. His epitaph in St. Antholin's church highlighted his final career triumph: "Under this black marble stone lieth the body of Master Walter Lemster, doctor of physic, and also physician to the high and might prince Henry VII."[17]

Of Katherine's children with Lewis Brampston, Lucy clearly had a special place, both with Walter and with her mother, probably owing to her continuing to live with them through much of her young adulthood. This circumstance arose because of an ambiguous marital situation in which she found herself in the decade following her mother's marriage to Walter Lemster. Lucy made her first appearance in surviving records in a Chancery bill dating from 1481, in a suit by Walter Lemster against Richard Narborough. As the bill states, in 1469 Lucy entered into a future contract of marriage with Narborough, then a young Cambridge scholar, before he left for what was supposed to be a two-year stint in Padua to study civil law.[18] He did not return, however, for ten years, and when he did return, as a newly minted Doctor of Civil Law, he refused to go through with the marriage. Given the binding nature of such promises of marriage, Lucy had been left through the 1470s with little choice but to wait for his return, probably through the entirety of her twenties, her most marriageable decade. Narborough's repudiation of the contract was a caddish act. One might imagine that Lucy (with the help of Walter and her mother) sued Narborough in the ecclesiastical court to enforce the contract, but if so, it was not successful. We do know that Walter Lemster successfully sued Narborough in Chancery for Lucy's room and board and the costs of a maidservant over ten years, and that he was awarded the sum of 300 marks. This was a mitigated victory for Lemster and Lucy Brampston, however: Narborough could not pay and was thus incarcerated in Ludgate, the London debtors' prison, from which he was subsequently able to escape. At the time of his death, Lemster had a

16. *Calendar of the Patent Rolls Preserved in the Public Record Office, 1476–85 (Edward IV, Edward V, and Richard III)* (London: HMSO, 1901), 482; *Calendar of the Patent Rolls Preserved in the Public Record Office, 1485–94 (Henry VII, Vol. 1)* (London: HMSO, 1914), 482.

17. John Weever, *Antient Funeral Monuments, of Great-Britain, Ireland, and the Islands* (London: William Tooke, 1767), 190.

18. On Narborough, see Emden, *BRUC to 1500*, 419.

suit pending against the sheriffs of London, whose negligence had allowed the escape, to recompense him for the full sum. (The outcome of the suit is unknown.)[19] In any case, however, Narborough's career was apparently ruined, as he disappears from the records, and no doubt Lucy and her parents took some comfort in that.

When Lucy's stepfather Walter Lemster died in 1487, he left substantial bequests in his will to his still-unmarried stepdaughter.[20] Some time soon after that, Lucy finally did marry, taking as her husband another Cambridge-educated physician, Walter Lacey, who presumably knew Lucy through Walter Lemster. Given the dates of his university career, Walter Lacey was likely born about 1450,[21] and thus both he and Lucy embarked on this marriage when they were in their mid- to late-thirties; for her it was certainly her first marriage (not counting the abortive relationship with Narborough), and likely also for him. Walter and Lucy Lacey settled in St. Antholin's parish, where Katherine and Walter Lemster had lived. Katherine herself remarried after Walter Lemster's death to a John Bentley, but that marriage was either very short in duration or highly unsatisfactory according to Katherine's 1497 will (which pointedly names Lewis and Walter as "beloved" husbands, but not John).[22]

Although relatively little is known of Walter and Lucy Lacey's early married life, various records give us some hints. Like Walter Lemster, Walter Lacey was tied to the book-centred elite lay circles in London; he was associated with the family of the mayor Sir Thomas Hill and with the lawyer and future King's Bench justice John More.[23] He also had a particular interest in Syon Abbey, then an important locus for a style of literate lay piety. The extent to which the wives of the two Walters—Katherine and her daughter Lucy—shared their husbands' interest in the current styles of literate devotional piety is unknown; both Walters bequeathed their whole libraries to others on their deaths, and neither Katherine nor Lucy

19. TNA, C 1/61/584; PROB 11/8/40.

20. TNA, PROB 11/8/40.

21. Emden, *BRUC to 1500*, 346; Talbot and Hammond, *Medical Practitioners*, 369.

22. TNA, PROB 11/11/211. It is possible that John Bentley was still alive when Katherine made her will; she did not call herself widow, and she bequeathed only her paraphernalia. Lucy was named executrix.

23. R. A. Latham, ed., *Calendar of Close Rolls, Henry VII, Vol. 2, 1500–1509* (London: HMSO, 1963), 25, 45.

left books in their wills.[24] Lacey, like Lemster, maintained his academic links: he was a man of considerable learning and proud of his connections to Cambridge, especially desiring in his will that he be remembered as a fellow of Peterhouse and "that I may be putt in their boke the better to be hadde in memorie ons a yere what tyme they doo their obsequies."[25] Walter Lacey's occupation as physician allowed him an entrée into court circles, too. Walter was listed among those who walked in Henry VII's funeral procession in May 1509, and then was among the "Squires of the Body" in the coronation procession for Henry VIII and Katherine of Aragon the following month.[26]

As Walter wrote his will in 1509 but did not die until 1513, it is possible that he fell ill in the first year of Henry VIII's reign, when he was about sixty. Walter's and Lucy's marriage was apparently very affectionate, at least on his part, for he emphasized in his will the "verey love" that he found in her and urged the overseers who were to help her in the execution of the will to see that "noon wrong her in her right."[27] Lucy did not subsequently remarry and was thus a widow of considerable means for about the last three decades of her life. At Walter's death, he and Lucy had only one surviving child, Anne, although both Walter and Lucy asked for masses to be said for other children, indicating there were others who had died as infants or young children. Walter left Anne a significant sum, 300 marks, to be used to buy property for her marriage.[28] The high status that Walter and Lucy Lacey had established for themselves by the time of his death is perhaps best illustrated by Anne's marriage, which occurred some time subsequent to the writing of Walter's will: Anne married the Norfolk gentleman Charles Knyvett, who as grandson of the first duke of Buckingham was quite a match for the granddaughter of a provincial brewer. Knyvett served in the household of Edward Stafford, the third duke of Buckingham, in the 1510s and played a crucial role in the latter's fall, testifying against him

24. TNA, PROB 11/11/211; PROB 11/28/631, Will of Lucy Lacey, 1541.

25. TNA, PROB 11/18/1, Will of Walter Lacey.

26. J. S. Brewer, James Gairdner, and R. H. Brodie, eds., *Letters and Papers, Foreign and Domestic, of the Reign of Henry VIII* (London: Longman, Green, Longman & Roberts, 1862), 1/1.13, 1/1.42.

27. Ibid.

28. TNA, PROB 11/18/1; PROB 11/28/631.

in his trial for treason in 1521.[29] Knyvett subsequently entered into the service of Lord Berners, but was dead by about 1526.[30] Anne and Charles had at least six children together, three sons, Richard, Anthony, and William; and three daughters, Lucy, Anne, and Alice.[31] Anne Knyvett later married the gentleman John Sebyll or Sybley, probably fairly soon after the 1530 robbery and murder.[32]

In 1530, then, Mistress Lucy Lacey was at least in her seventies, and perhaps eighty, and her daughter, Mistress Anne Knyvett, was a widow aged forty or so with six children. In the aftermath of the traumatic robbery and murder, Lucy and her daughter, who lived with her mother at least some of the time, were able to call upon the networks of influence that they had collectively inherited from their husbands and perhaps themselves had nourished. The point of contact between the two widows and Cardinal Wolsey seems to have been Wolsey's former servant Thomas Cromwell, still faithful to his master through the summer of 1530 and in close touch with him. Cromwell had reason to be loyal to Mistress Knyvett in particular; it had been her husband Charles Knyvett's engagement of his services in the early 1520s, in the aftermath of Buckingham's fall, that brought Cromwell to the attention of Cardinal Wolsey and in effect launched his career in government.[33] Cromwell may have been personally present at the interrogation of Laurence and Turner, as documents place him with the cardinal at Southwell on or about the day in question.[34] And Cromwell was not the only man with high connections the two widows knew; records of Lucy's activities in the courts in 1520 and 1529 relating to a manor she

29. Roger Virgoe, "The Earlier Knyvetts: The Rise of a Norfolk Gentry Family, Part II," *Norfolk Archaeology* 42 (1990), 251–52, 262–63; Barbara Harris, *Edward Stafford, Third Duke of Buckingham, 1478–1521* (Stanford: Stanford University Press, 1986), 180–89; *Letters and Papers*, 3/1.49.

30. *Letters and Papers*, 3/1.513. The will of his brother, Edward Knyvett [Knevet], dated 1528, shows him as already deceased: Sir Nicholas Harris Nicolas, ed., *Testamenta vetusta* (London: Nichols and Son, 1826), 2.635–40.

31. These are all named in Lucy Lacey's will, dated 1534, proved 1541. TNA, PROB 11/28/631.

32. See the Chancery bill, between 1529 and 1532, which dates from after the marriage: TNA, C 1/677/29.

33. Howard Leithead, "Cromwell, Thomas, Earl of Essex," *ODNB*, 2004.

34. He wrote with his own hand a draft of a letter from Wolsey responding to a letter from the king dated 21 June. TNA, SP 1/57, fol. 168; *Letters and Papers*, 4.2906.

held in Sussex indicate that Sir Thomas More—named as chancellor only months before the attack on Mistress Lacey's maid and house—served as a feoffee for the property.[35] The tie between Mistress Lacey and Sir Thomas may well have dated back to More's father John's relationship with Lucy's late husband Walter during the reign of Henry VII. Even though More was presumably busy with his new post, he nonetheless had his hand in this situation; Cromwell mentioned in a letter to Wolsey that More had discussed the case with him, apparently representing Mistress Lacey's interests.[36]

None of this tells us explicitly how John Laurence and Robert Turner came to be examined at Cardinal Wolsey's residence on 22 June 1530, so we must make some inferences. Following the robbery, Mistresses Lacey and Knyvett must have called upon the men of influence they knew—Cromwell, More, possibly others. Having escaped to the north with their ill-gotten goods and fenced them to various men in Yorkshire, Lancashire, and Westmorland, John Laurence and Robert Turner must have been arrested for the felony. That arrest must then have been brought to the attention of the widows' counsellors. Laurence and Turner were—somehow—brought from wherever they were being held to the cardinal's manor to be questioned. The interrogation was not part of the normal criminal process, but it was undertaken with the knowledge and even the authority of the current chancellor More and his predecessor Wolsey. Laurence and Turner were presumably induced to tell their story by threats or promises, or a combination of the two. They could easily have believed, even if no one promised them directly, that their cooperation would entail an escape from the noose—a pardon from the king, perhaps.

If the two men hoped to avoid execution, however, that hope was vain, as likely both were hanged. Unfortunately I have not been able to locate any records of the formal prosecution of the felony; most ordinary records of processes against felons do not survive for this period.[37] There is, howev-

35. This dated from at least 1520 to 1529: TNA, CP 40/1060, mm. 568d, 632; Edwin Hadlow Wise Dunkin, ed., *Sussex Manors, Advowsons, Recorded in the Feet of Fines, Henry VIII*, Sussex Record Society 19 (London: Sussex Record Society, 1914), 87–88.

36. *Letters and Papers*, 4.2913–14.

37. I searched through the KB 27 and KB 29 records for two years following the date of the robbery, and found nothing.

er, evidence, if somewhat unspecific, that they were prosecuted in London, convicted, and hanged. An anonymous London chronicle contains three entries related to executions for this felony. In the first, the chronicler states that on 5 July 1530 "was one hangyd in chayns in Fynsbery fyld for kyllynge mastres knevytt's mayd in sente Auntolyns paryshe." The second, dated 14 July 1531, reads: "maystre Lacis servant was hangyd in Fynsbery fylde for ye morderynge of a mayde, & for ye robynge of this sayd mistar Lacie." The third, dated 28 June 1532, indicates that "The xxviij day of June was one othar man hangyd in chaynes in Fynsbery fylde for ye kylynge of mystris Lacis mayd."[38] This indicates that three men were executed for the crime, although some of the information the chronicler had was somewhat imprecise. The second, named as servant of "Master" Lacey, must have been John Laurence, while the first and third were presumably Robert Turner and the man with the Spanish cloak. (Sir Richard would have been able to claim benefit of clergy.) The first was executed about two weeks after the interrogations at Southwell, while there were apparently delays before Laurence was executed a year later and the third man two years later. The chronicler indicates not only that the men were executed, but that at least two of them were "hangyd in chayns." This was a type of execution reserved for particularly notorious crimes, by which the body would not be taken down from the gibbet after the hanging but would instead be left there, suspended by chains, to decompose, as an example to others. John Bellamy notes that normally the order for such an execution was made by the king or his council, as it was in effect an extra-judicial punishment.[39]

Although the confession Laurence and Turner made before the examiners at Southwell on 22 June 1530 was presumably not used in the felony process, the information the two gave about the man in the Spanish cloak could well have allowed those counselling Mistress Lacey and her daughter to identify him. That they did in fact learn the names of the third conspirator, along with that of the priest Laurence and Turner knew only as Sir Richard, is shown by a Star Chamber suit, likely launched by the

38. Charles Lethbridge Kingsford, ed., *Two London Chronicles from the Collections of John Stow*, Camden Third Series 18 (London: Camden Society, 1910), 4–6.

39. John G. Bellamy, *The Criminal Trial in Later Medieval England: Felony Before the Courts from Edward I to the Sixteenth Century* (Toronto: University of Toronto Press, 1998), 154.

two widows soon after the examination at Southwell manor. One of the purposes of the Southwell interrogation seems to have been to gather information for that suit, the goal of which was recovery of the stolen goods. In the only surviving record from the suit, Lucy Lacey and Ann Knyvett outlined in a bill the terrible robbery and murder, which they said was committed by Laurence, Turner, and two other men: Richard Hudson, clerk—presumably the priest Sir Richard—and Thomas Brode, who must be the hitherto-unnamed man in the Spanish cloak. (The bill also gives a name to the slain maidservant: Joan Cake.) Those men took away money, plate, apparel, and jewels worth 500 marks, the widows said, and afterwards they fled, and some of them were still at large (presumably meaning at least Brode and perhaps also Hudson). The account of the crime was a prologue, however, to the object of the suit: that the chancellor should issue a subpoena to seven men of Yorkshire, Westmorland, and Lancashire, who had come into possession of the goods Laurence and the other felons had stolen. The widows, the bill indicated, knew not how, nor by what means, the said goods had come into the possession of the seven defendants; they therefore prayed that the men be summoned to appear in the Star Chamber to explain themselves.[40]

As alleged receivers of stolen goods, these men could have been indicted as accessories to the robbery and murder. It is thus interesting that the widows (presumably through the advice of the men counselling them) instead take a much softer approach, requesting that the men be summoned to the Star Chamber to explain how the goods came into their hands. Although retribution was evidently the goal regarding Laurence, Turner, and Brode, regarding the receivers the strategy instead seems to have been to ask, firmly, for the return of the (presumably fenced) goods. Felony charges against the receivers would in fact have been counter-productive if the goal was return of the goods; once convicted of a felony, all the felon's moveable property, including any stolen goods in his or her possession, became property of the Crown.[41] A victim might petition the Crown for the goods' restitution, but that might take some time and the request might not be grant-

40. TNA, STAC 2/25/65.

41. K. J. Kesselring, "Felony Forfeiture and the Profits of Crime in Early Modern England," *The Historical Journal* 53/2 (2010): esp. 273–77; K. J. Kesselring, "Felony Forfeiture in England, c. 1170–1870," *The Journal of Legal History* 30/3 (2009), 201–26.

ed; if the widows were willing to forego punishment of these men, then this more oblique method of the Star Chamber suit was the best tactic to pursue. The objective, presumably, was for the men to appear in Star Chamber, profess ignorance as to the goods' provenance (they fell off a wagon), and agree to return them to the widows. This may have been what happened: some of the jewellery and plate Lucy Lacey bequeathed to her relatives in her will, written in 1534, seems to correspond to the similar items listed by Laurence and Turner in their interrogation, although the descriptions on both lists are too generic to be certain.[42] There is every reason to think, however, that it would have been a successful strategy.

Ad Hockery and the Law in Henry VIII's England

What does all this tell us about the operation of law in Henrician England? One of the great gifts that Cromwell left behind for future historians in his papers is the lifting of a veil on what had hitherto either gone altogether unrecorded or for which documents usually do not survive. Backroom negotiations and end-runs around the courts and the letter of the law were nothing new in Henry VIII's reign, but because of Cromwell's obsessive paper-keeping we are able to take apart a number of interesting instances of it, for he had his fingers in many cases before and during his period of power. In Mistress Lacey's case, we see men of great influence, including the Lord Chancellor Thomas More himself, using back-door processes. How we might characterize the questioning of Laurence and Turner by Cardinal Wolsey's men is not quite clear to me: quasi-legal? Illegal? Was it secretive or a perfectly legitimate activity? Was its departure from the normal process of felony prosecution problematic, or did the chancellor's involvement (and even perhaps his mandate) *make* it legitimate? The utility of the interrogation is clear: it was meant to elicit from the suspects information that would otherwise die with them if they were simply prosecuted through the normal channels. The means employed to extract this information—promises of pardon or mitigation that no one had any intention to fulfill, and/or more threatening kinds of persuasion (torture is not an impossibility)—might not have been strictly according to legal form, but

42. TNA, SP 11/57, fols. 180r–v; PROB 11/28/631.

the ends (the receipt of the information the widows' counsellors sought) justified them more generally. The subsequent step, the bringing of a Star Chamber suit to restore the goods, was clearly "legal" in the sense that it was undertaken through a royal court, but its purpose seems to have been to sidestep the prosecution of the felony of receiving stolen goods in order to avoid felony forfeiture, which would have made the recovery of the goods difficult if not impossible.

Peeling off the layers of a case like this allows us "to tell a story that might otherwise never be told," as Charles Donahue has put it[43]—back-room maneuvers were rarely recorded, and thus when we get an opportunity to see one in action, we should take it. As he has also pointed out, we can only speculate about what lies behind and beyond the written record that remains. This speculation is both "irresistible," as Charlie Donahue puts it,[44] and necessary, for the documents' meaning is not determinable simply by the words inscribed on it but also by the instrumental purposes it served, and we can only approach understanding that through inference about its larger context. In this particular case, for instance, we cannot know why men like Cromwell, Wolsey, and More felt moved to facilitate this unofficial interrogation, a crucial missing piece of the puzzle this record poses: but we can speculate. They might well have been driven by moral outrage at the nature of the crime and thus bent the rules to achieve the goal of a rough justice, with the central perpetrators punished in exemplary fashion and the victims reunited with at least some of their goods. The identity of the robbery victims—a very elderly widow and her daughter, widowed with six children, likely all underage—no doubt contributed to the sense in which "true" justice might be served by these kinds of tactics. If the maid's murder on its own would not likely have sparked this level of outrage, it likely intensified it, if only because it demonstrated how close Mistress Lacey herself came to being slain. Women like Lucy Lacey and Anne Knyvett were seen to be in need of protection, and in the absence of husbands or other male relatives, others must step in; and indeed they *were* in need of help, as in no way could Mistresses Lacey and Knyvett, as women, have orchestrated this on their own. Thus, we could interpret the ad-hockery

43. Charles Donahue, *Law, Marriage, and Society in the Later Middle Ages: Arguments About Marriage in Five Courts* (Cambridge: Cambridge University Press, 2007), 55.

44. Donahue, *Law, Marriage, and Society*, 62.

here as a means to reach a conclusion that was just in a broader sense, if not one that strictly followed the law: this fits in with some scholarship that has emphasized flexibility in legal and para-legal processes in order to carve out appropriate outcomes from an otherwise unwieldy or unyielding system.[45] It is important for us to recognize, however, that such bending of processes did not always contribute to conclusions that would have been viewed then, much less now, as "truly," or even roughly, just. Around the same time, for instance, Cromwell's handling of a wife-murder allowed the perpetrator to escape without prosecution; that murderer, too, had strings to pull.[46] Even if occasionally an elderly (albeit wealthy and well-connected) widow was its beneficiary, such ad-hockery was a tool of power and most benefited the powerful. It was also thickly intertwined in the workings of law and the courts in Tudor England. Although it is often entirely absent from the evidentiary record, we need to think about how the back channels, even more than official processes, constituted and reproduced the powers of the elite.

45. See, for instance, Thomas A. Green, *Verdict According to Conscience: Perspectives on the English Criminal Trial Jury, 1200–1800* (Chicago: University of Chicago Press, 1985), esp. chapters 2 and 3; Cynthia B. Herrup, *The Common Peace: Participation and the Criminal Law in Seventeenth-Century England* (Cambridge: Cambridge University Press, 1987), esp. chapter 8.

46. This is the 1529 case of John Watson; see TNA, SP 1/42, fols. 126–45.

The Admiralty Jurisdiction of the Court of Requests

Emily Kadens

In 1594, six English sailors sued the merchant-owners of the ship the *Hopewell* of Bristol.[1] They alleged that, while they were serving aboard the ship about four years earlier, the ship had taken a Spanish prize laden with "Ollyvantes Teethe Graynes Cyvett and Fower Chestes of goulde beinge of the value of Thirtye Thousande powndes."[2] This value they claimed to be "lawefull pryses and to be devyded accordinge to the usuall Cowrse that allwayes heretofore have beene had & taken in and uppon all lawefull pryses taken at the Sea."[3] Although such a dispute fell under the traditional jurisdiction of the High Court of Admiralty, the sailors were not suing there. Instead, they brought this suit in the Court of Requests, a forum often waived aside as a minor equity court dealing with copyhold land and the small claims of those too poor to sue in Chancery.[4] In fact, Requests served as a subsidiary admiralty jurisdiction, and this essay explores why some litigants chose to use it for that purpose.

During the sixteenth and early seventeenth centuries, Requests played a substantial role within the sphere of the parallel and competing

1. *Pyers, et al. v. Hyggyns, et al.*, 1594, NA, REQ 2/30/64 (bill of complaint).
2. Ibid.
3. Ibid.
4. A. T. Carter, *A History of the English Courts*, 7th ed. (London: Butterworth, 1944), 99; Isaaac Saunders Leadam, *Select Cases in the Court of Requests, A.D. 1497–1569*, Selden Society 12 (London: Bernard Quaritch, 1898), xvi–xvii.

jurisdictions of the Westminster courts.[5] It served as a jack-of-all-trades court, a court of last resort, and a quasi-appellate forum in which a certain subset of litigants could have their cases heard or reheard in what they apparently considered to be a more favorable venue.

Admiralty disputes made up a small but not insignificant part of the Court's docket from the beginning. The Court's judge and first historian, Sir Julius Caesar, wrote at the end of the sixteenth century that Requests had cognizance of "causes... maritime and ultramarine."[6] Caesar had reason to know, since he served simultaneously for fifteen years as an Admiralty judge and a Master of Requests.[7] In 1894, Reginald Marsden, in the first of his Selden Society volumes on the Court of Admiralty, also noted that the Court of Requests "exercised an Admiralty jurisdiction, delegated to it from the Privy Council, in matters of salvage, spoil, piracy, letters of reprisal, and prize...."[8] But this recognition aside, Requests's admiralty cases, like virtually all of its extensive docket,[9] have gone unstudied.

This essay addresses that lacuna in only a small way. It details the types of admiralty disputes heard in Requests and the various ways litigants used the Court, whether as a primary, parallel, or last resort court. In the process, this foray into the Court of Requests scores a Charlie Donahue

5. The most recent and complete discussion of the Court of Requests can be found in chapter four of Tim Stretton, *Women Waging Law in Elizabethan England* (Cambridge: Cambridge University Press, 1998), 70–100. Another work making an important contribution to the scholarship on Requests is *The Ancient State Authoritie, and Proceedings of the Court of Requests by Sir Julius Caesar*, ed. L. M. Hill (Cambridge: Cambridge University Press, 1975). The unpublished dissertation of D. A. Knox provides thorough study of the institutional history of the Court at a crucial moment in its development. D. A. Knox, "The Court of Requests in the Reign of Edward VI 1547–1553" (Ph.D. thesis, Cambridge University, 1974). The author thanks Mr. Knox for supplying a pdf of the dissertation. Finally, Leadam's Selden Society volume cited above is still useful, even if later scholarship has raised questions about some of the conclusions he offers in his introduction.

6. *Ancient State*, 9.

7. Caesar served as an Admiralty judge from 1584–1606 and a Master of Requests from 1591–1606. L. M. Hill, *Bench and Bureaucracy: The Public Career of Sir Julius Caesar, 1580–1636* (Stanford: Stanford University Press, 1988), 69, 88.

8. Reginald G. Marsden, *Select Pleas in the Court of Admiralty*, Selden Society 6 (London: Bernard Quaritch, 1894), 1:lxv.

9. The one exception is marriage cases involving female plaintiffs. Tim Stretton, ed., *Marital Litigation in the Court of Requests 1542–1642* (Cambridge: Cambridge University Press, 2008).

trifecta, following his various publications on court records, commercial law, and equity.[10]

The Court of Requests

Much like the Court of Star Chamber for criminal cases, Requests evolved in the late fifteenth century from the adjudicatory role played by members of the king's council.[11] Its avowed purpose was to hear the suits of those too poor or too lacking in status vis-à-vis the defendant to be able to bring suit or expect justice in another court.[12] Despite this apparent intention, many of the suits in Requests did not in fact involve the poor. Aristocrats and gentry also found the court useful, as did yeoman, artisans, physicians, lawyers, and merchants—both English and foreign.[13]

The timing of the appearance of a formal Court of Requests remains the subject of dispute. Whatever may have been its antecedents during the reigns of Henry VI or Richard III,[14] a separate series of records of a council dealing with requests for justice from the poor exists from 1493.[15] And the evidence suggests that a true court with a dedicated space and a regular rotation of judges evolved incrementally over a number of decades between 1516 and the middle of the sixteenth century.[16] By the reign of Edward VI, Requests had an established presence, hearing cases in the White Hall at Westminster Palace.

10. See e.g., Charles Donahue, ed., *The Records of the Medieval Ecclesiastical Courts Part II: England* (Berlin: Duncker & Humblot, 1994); Mary Beth Basile, Jane Fair Bestor, Daniel R. Coquillette and Charles Donahue, *Lex Mercatoria And Legal Pluralism: A Late Thirteenth-Century Treatise and its Afterlife* (Cambridge, Mass.: Ames Foundation of Harvard Law School, 1998); Charles Donahue, "Equity in the Courts of Merchants," *Tijdschrift voor Rechtsgeschiedenis* 72 (2004), 72.

11. J. H. Baker, *The Oxford History of the Laws of England*, vol. 6, 1483–1558 (Oxford: Oxford University Press, 2003), 203; Leadam, *Select Cases*, x–xi; Stretton, *Women Waging Law*, 71–72.

12. *Ancient State*, 8.

13. Knox, "The Court of Requests," 304; Stretton, *Women Waging Law*, 93–95.

14. Hannes Kleineke, "Richard III and the Origins of the Court of Requests," *The Ricardian* 17 (2007): 24–25; Stretton, *Marital Litigation*, 7.

15. Leadam, *Select Cases*, xii.

16. Knox, "The Court of Requests," 98–108; Stretton, *Marital Litigation*, 7–8.

The Court's procedure generally followed that of Chancery summary procedure. The complainant filed an English bill, which the defendant answered. The pleadings could continue back and forth with replications and rejoinders until the issue was fully explored. A commission to find facts, or for local commissioners to hear and determine, would then issue under the privy seal. Commissioners in the county where the dispute arose, or the Court Examiner in Westminster, would take depositions from witnesses using interrogatories drawn up by one or both of the parties.[17] These interrogatories remained secret until publication, at which time the parties' counsel made arguments to the court.

While a small number of case files include records of arbitrated settlements or draft opinions, and the dorsal notes on pleadings and depositions routinely record procedural steps,[18] the court's interlocutory and final rulings are kept in separate court books. These books are extant, though sometimes badly damaged, for most of the court's history without large gaps.[19] Unfortunately, some gaps do remain, and some suits seem never to have made it into the court books at all despite having generated large files of pleadings and depositions.[20] Thus, it is not always possible to ascertain how the judges ruled in individual disputes.

As a court of equity, the Masters of Requests did not feel compelled to make reasoned rulings based on law. Their decisions tended to recite the facts found in the pleadings and evidence and then to come to a conclusion about blame and remedies.[21] This court, as a consequence, did not play a role in evolving new legal or equitable doctrine. Nonetheless, the rich details provided in the pleadings and depositions offer a panorama of sixteenth- and early seventeenth-century English life. We can learn about lawyers' practice of renting rooms in houses near the inns of court,[22] about

17. Knox, "The Court of Requests," 282; Stretton, *Marital Litigation*, 10–11.

18. Knox, "The Court of Requests," 62.

19. Ibid., 29–41 (providing a detailed overview of the extant court entry books through the reign of Edward VI).

20. Knox, "The Court of Requests," 63; Stretton, *Marital Litigation*, 11.

21. Stretton, *Women Waging Law*, 90–91.

22. *Stone v. Morecrofte*, 1596, NA, REQ 2/273/83.

cheating factors,[23] about levels of literacy and account-keeping,[24] about the Elizabethan theater,[25]and about gambling,[26] embezzling apprentices,[27] and predatory lending practices.[28]

A sample of 518 case files distributed randomly across the reign of Queen Elizabeth I demonstrates how wide a variety of matters came before the Court.[29] About forty percent of these files concern transactions in property, including leases, copyholds, and rents. A large number of varied disputes, around twenty-five percent, involve bonds, including claims that bonds had been satisfied, suits praying relief on bonds, and suits against sureties. Suits against executors, suits seeking stays of proceedings pending in other courts, and suits alleging fraud each make up about ten percent

23. *Foxe v. Sandford*, 1577, NA, REQ 2/34/55 (factor rendering false accounts); *Babington et al. v. Nundy*, 1592, NA, REQ 2/34/19 (factor keeping principals' goods for himself).

24. *Spence v. Tunckes*, 1584, NA, REQ 2/265/43 (pewterer of Gloucester cheated by his apprentice, who kept the accounts because the master was illiterate); *Sulyard v. Raymond*, 1595, NA, REQ 2/266/37 (1595) (practice of keeping accounts by tallies).

25. Charles William Wallace, "Shakespeare and His London Associates As Revealed in Recently Discovered Documents," *University Studies of the University of Nebraska* 10 (1910), 261; idem, "The First London Theater, Materials for a History," *University Studies of the University of Nebraska* 13 (1913): 1.

26. *Pearson v. Hutchinson, et al.*, 1589, NA, REQ 2/34/14 and REQ 2/51/18 (professional gambler preying on apprentice); *Scott v. Riche*, 1600, NA, REQ 2/268/14 (professional gambler preying on law student).

27. Paul Seaver, "A Social Contract? Master Against Servant in the Court of Requests," *History Today* 39/9 (1989), 50, 54.

28. *Countess of Sussex v. Graffignian*, 1571, NA, REQ 2/266/85 (misleading lending practices).

29. This sample comes from volume one of the so-called Atkins Calendar, a two-volume, nineteenth-century manuscript catalogue kept in the reading room of the National Archives in Kew, London. The individual case files are archived in Requests 2 (REQ 2). With the exception of a single abbreviated and largely uninformative published catalogue covering the first 136 bundles of case files, the remaining catalogues, covering bundles 6–10, 137–311, and 387–424, are in manuscript and only available at the National Archives. These catalogues organize the files by reign and within each reign alphabetically by name of the complainant. As a consequence each bundle contains files from different years within a particular reign. The various catalogues overlap in both period covered and letters of the alphabet. See Public Record Office, *List of Proceedings in the Court of Requests, Preserved in the Public Record Office*, vol. 1 (London: His Majesty's Stationery Office, 1906); Stretton, *Marital Litigation*, 15–17; http://www.nationalarchives.gov.uk/help-with-your-research/research-guides/court-of-requests-records-1485-1642/.

of the sample. Another seven percent of entries concern goods, money, or documents unjustly withheld from their rightful owners. In addition to these staple subjects of dispute, this group of cases also includes twenty suits on the sale of goods, and twelve matters purely of debt, including a suit in 1601 by Richard Davies, Treasurer of the Inner Temple, against John Aston of the Inner Temple for a debt of over £14 "for the expenses of a 'Drinking' feast which according to custom Def[endant] was bound to pay for."[30] Thirteen disputes concern marriage matters, including recovery of a marriage portion, claims for subsistence, and return of goods given upon engagement. Another thirteen demand that the defendant be compelled to abide by an arbitration agreement or court order. Five suits seek redress for false imprisonment; nine deal with breach of trust; five claim a right to an office, such as a prebend or bailiff position; and seven deal with disputes about ships. A smattering of other suits concern lost obligations, subornation of witnesses, misbehaving apprentices, tithes, and insolvency.[31]

The Requests records provide such varied material because of the scope and magnitude of the Court's docket. Scholars have estimated that the Court received some 16,500 cases during the reign of Queen Elizabeth alone.[32] For the six-year reign of Edward VI, 933 different suits have been identified.[33] The total number of cases filed during the approximately 150 year lifetime of the Court cannot even be estimated with any accuracy be-

30. "Atkins Calendar," NA, Map and Large Document Reading Room, 1.56 (NA, REQ 2/142/5). See Frederick Andrew Inderwick, ed., *The Inner Temple: Its Early History, as Illustrated by Its Records, 1505–1603* (London: Masters of the Bench, 1896), 434.

31. Cf. Leadam, *Select Cases*, lxxxix: "Questions of title to and possession of land, especially as to copyholds, fines and commons, tithes, annuities, trusts, extents, debt with specialties and without, executorships and administatorships, contracts, villainages, watercourses, leases, covenants generally, highways, wardship, dower, jointure, escape, forfeitures to the king by recognisance or otherwise, riots and routs, forgery and perjury, where goods were seized as forfeited by the lord of any manor, or by force, cosenage or dishonest dealing, questions affecting the conduct of executors, questions of marriage settlements of lands or goods, suits for money due upon account or received by the defendant to the plaintiff's use, damages claimed for injuries sustained from violence—all these were tried by the Court of Requests."

32. Stretton, *Women Waging War*, 73–74.

33. Knox, "The Court of Requests," 63.

cause at least half of the case file archive (about 400 boxes) remains entirely uncatalogued.[34]

Admiralty Matters in Requests

Turning specifically to the Court's admiralty docket, a review of the manuscript catalogues through the reign of Queen Elizabeth, turned up about 120 separate cases that could also have come under the jurisdiction of the High Court of Admiralty. The topics covered in these disputes read like a list of the matters addressed in the Admiralty libel files:[35] shipwreck and pillage of wrecks, prize, charter-parties, overseas contracts, piracy, sale and hire of ships, seizure of ships for debt, capture of ships abroad, salvage, privateers, goods stolen from ships in port and robbery on the high seas, damage to and repair of ships, unseaworthiness, and loss and insurance of cargo.

The common law courts heard disputes concerning some of these matters, so litigants were not confined to the Court of Admiralty.[36] Why then would they choose to bring their suits in Requests? The cases themselves provide a number of explanations.

A very simple reason litigants brought these suits in Requests is that from early in the Court's history they were permitted to do so. In several pre-1547 suits, the complainants petitioned the king, and the matters, as with many petitions, were referred to the Court of Requests. In *Bodley v. Bury, et al.*, for instance, the complainant was an English merchant who freighted goods with an English ship in Lisbon for transport back to England. The defendants, the ships' officers, secretly set sail without waiting for complainant or the other merchants whose goods the ship carried. The complainant claimed to have searched for the ship in Flanders and England without success. He petitioned the king's council to summon the defendants to answer. His petition does not mention the Court of Requests, though the court certainly existed in some form by the time of the suit in the reign of Henry VIII.[37]

34. http://discovery.nationalarchives.gov.uk/details/r/C13323.
35. Marsden, *Select Pleas*, 1.lxi–lxii, lxv–lxxi.
36. Ibid., lxviii.
37. *Bodley v. Bury, et al.*, NA, REQ 2/10/37.

Similarly, in *Derikson v. Orwill, et al.*, the complainant, a "Dutchman" from Mechelen, claimed that linens were unjustly taken from him by a royal officer at the open market of Calais and that two English knights stole his ship. He alleged that King Henry VII promised restitution, which he has never received. He petitioned straight to Henry VIII pleading his extreme poverty and begging the King to keep his father's promise. Again, his petition does not mention Requests.[38] But the fact that the king or his council would refer such cases to Requests indicates that they focused more on the issues of the complainants' poverty or the claims of injustice by ordinary people than on the proper forum for the matter at issue.[39]

In another set of early cases, litigants likely turned to Requests because they had reason to fear that they would not get justice in Admiralty. This is particularly clear in the case of *Gower v. Clynton*. The complainant bought a ship and spent the winter fitting it out. Come spring, when he was ready to set sail, he received a summons from the Lord Admiral to appear in the Court of Admiralty in London. While Gower was on his way to London, the Lord Admiral ordered that the ship be seized. When Gower asked the Admiralty Court why the judge answered that it was the Lord Admiral's will, and that Gower would have to make suit to him to get the ship back. Instead, Gower petitioned the king and the case went to Requests.[40]

Perhaps parties could choose between these courts because the judicial establishment did not see Admiralty and Requests as competitors for

38. *Derikson v. Orwill, et al.*, reign of Henry VIII, NA, REQ 2/10/178.

39. See *Ancient State*, 8 (the Court has jurisdiction "where the cause was specifically recommended from the King, to the examination of his Councell"). *Laynham v. Hall et al.*, *pre-1547*, NA, REQ 2/3/121 (petition to force defendants to return complainants' goods lost by shipwreck); *De Andraca v. Apprice*, ca. 1553–1557, NA, REQ 2/157/13 (petition to obtain assistance in getting redress from Englishman who robbed complainant of his ship and wares and put him and his crew into a dinghy without food or water).

40. *Gower v. Clynton*, ca. 1550–1553, NA, REQ 2/20/21. See also *Symons v. Coke*, ca. 1543/4, NA, REQ 2/7/141 (petition alleging complainant was cheated out of his award in a mediated dispute by defendants who obtained a letter from the Lord Admiral requiring the complainant to surrender the pledge—a ship's sails—that he held from the defendants); Morcombe, et al., 1598, NA, REQ 2/165/162 (bill alleging the defendants, royal messengers of the Court of Admiralty, were supposed to arrest the surety of a sea captain who owed complainants a judgment. Instead the defendants colluded with the surety so he could avoid capture).

admiralty matters. To get into Requests, complainants generally alleged only that they had no remedy at the common law. And in the formulaic objections that began all answers, defendants asserted only that the complainant could, and thus should, have brought suit at common law. This was standard rhetoric that alluded to the role that contemporaries understood the Court to play. As Sir Julius Caesar put it, litigants were permitted to come before the Court because "the cause meerely conteined matter of equity, and had no proper remedy at the Common Law...."[41]

Thus to ensure that one obtained Requests' jurisdiction, and did not have one's suit sent back to the law courts, it made strategic sense to argue that the strictness of the common law prevented one from obtaining justice. This argument took several forms. Most commonly, the complainant alleged that he or she could not produce evidence that met common law requirements.[42] In *Nunez v. Brome & Jobson*, a case brought in 1591 about the sale of an unmerchantable ship to the Spanish-Jewish physician Hector Nunez,[43] Nunez complained that he could not sue in common law because defendants had the only copy of the deed of sale.[44] Without the sealed instrument, the complainant had no suit at covenant.[45] In other instances, the complainant had neither writing nor available witnesses. This was particularly true in admiralty cases, when all of the witnesses "be marriners and all of them at sea in forreigne Countries and doubtfull wether they be livinge so as they cannot have there p[re]sent testimony of the trewth" of the claim.[46] In a statement suggesting perhaps more that the complainant felt the common law court would not understand the issue of general average involved rather than purely a lack of evidence, he asserted that "for &

41. *Ancient State*, 8.

42. Knox, "The Court of Requests," 341.

43. Charles Meyers, "Debt in Elizabethan England: the Adventures of Dr. Hector Nunez, Physician and Merchant," *Jewish Historical Studies* 34 (1994), 125–40.

44. NA, REQ 2/64/32 (bill).

45. J. H. Baker, *An Introduction to English Legal History*, 4th ed. (London: Butterworths, 2002), 327.

46. *Mathew & Goodman v. Callemor et al.*, 1598, NA, REQ 2/241/3 (bill). See also *Heythnyson v Corsini*, 1595, NA, REQ 2/49/12 (Danish ship master claiming that he could not sue at common law for what was owed him under a charterparty after a shipwreck because Corsini had gotten both parts of the charterparty into his possession and all the men who could have acted as witnesses had perished in the wreck).

concerning thes kinde of merchantly dealings whereof yo[ur] said subiect hath noe sufficient testimony he is destitute of remedy by the order of the comon lawe."[47]

Requests solved such problems because the defendant and witnesses were required to testify under oath,[48] a fact complainants sometimes emphasized in expressing their "hope that the sayd [defendants] beinge all of them men of greate welth creditt and good dealinge in other cawses will upon there corporall oathes confesse" the truth.[49] In addition, in admiralty matters, Requests provided an advantage over the common law courts because numerous councilors and Masters of Requests served, often concurrently, as Admiralty judges. The most famous is Sir Julius Caesar, but Sir John Tregonwell, Dr. William Cooke, Dr. Valentine Dale, Dr. David Lewes, and Sir John Harbert also held both positions, their presence in Requests spanning most of the second half of the sixteenth century.[50] Since no more than four Masters of Requests served at a time after the middle of the century, litigants bringing admiralty disputes into Requests probably felt they had a decent chance of appearing before a master who would understand their issues.

Sometimes, however, bringing suit in Requests was a mere tactical move to obtain evidence, usually written, that complainants needed to further their claims at common law.[51] As a court of equity, Requests could examine and require the parties to introduce documentary evidence. Usually this involved getting copies of a deed or charter-party that then became available to the complainant, who could drop his suit in Requests and proceed against the defendant at law. The case of *Somers v. Mordive*, however, demonstrates a different role Requests played in obtaining evidence.[52] Henry Somers, a Dutchman from Zeeland, had a lawsuit against Myles Mordive, an Englishman, pending before the town court of Antwerp. To resolve this dispute, the testimony of certain English witnesses was required, and Somers had a sealed certificate from the Antwerp court

47. *Hickes v. Kytching et al.*, 1588, NA, REQ 2/96/2 (bill).
48. Stretton, *Marital Litigation*, 10–11.
49. Mathew & Goodman v. Callemor, et al., 1598, NA, REQ 2/241/3 (bill).
50. Stretton, *Marital Litigation*, 256, 259–61.
51. Stretton, *Women Waging Law*, 81.
52. *Somers v. Mordive*, 1561, NA, REQ 2/268/56.

to prove the need. He sought to have Requests issue a writ of privy seal to the witnesses commanding them to appear and give testimony. Then he wanted the Court to send sealed copies of these depositions to the court in Antwerp.[53] Requests obliged, at least in part, for depositions survive from the case.

Interestingly, despite Sir Julius Caesar's statement that "causes ecclesiasticall, maritime and ultramarine... are not to bee determined in this Court, unless there bee some matter of equitie in them not remediable in theire proper Courts,"[54] in only a few of the dozens of cases examined did the complainant explain why he or she would be remediless in Admiralty. The 1592 case of *Whiteworth v. Cossyns* is an example of the litany of woes not uncommon in Requests cases.[55] Jeffrey Whiteworth, a yeoman of the Queen's guards, became part owner of a ship, a one-eight part of the interest in which he later sold on credit to Philip Cossyns, a mariner. Cossyns, against Whiteworth's wishes, got himself placed in charge of the ship as master for a trading trip to Barbary. Whiteworth freighted wares on the ship, including sixteen dozen shoes. Cossyns turned out to be every bit as treacherous as Whiteworth had suspected, making off with the goods, convincing French villagers to insure the ship, and then deliberately wrecking it. When he returned home, and Whiteworth sought payment of the bond for the interest in the ship, Cossyns sued him in the Court of Requests, winning his case by forcing his apprentice and servant girl to testify falsely under oath that they had witnessed their master paying off Whiteworth who allegedly never delivered the cancelled bond. Cossyns then fled the country, and now Whiteworth is back in Requests. He explained that

> in the Admiraltie Court [he] can not recover the mony due to him for the said shoes delyvered to him in credit nor for any other the goods aforsaid for that yt is verie probable that the said Cossyns wil never retorne into England but by stealth to carrye and transport his wiefe into the p[ar]tes beyonde the seas... and therfore yo[ur] said subiect

53. Ibid. (petition).
54. *Ancient State*, 9.
55. NA, REQ 2/38/39 (bill).

> is verie like to be remediles, by any help at the Lawe in this yo[ur] Realme.[56]

Knowing that he could not get his money or property from the absent defendant, all Whiteworth wanted was for Requests to undo the result of the earlier lawsuit and let him retain the bond he had been ordered to convey to Cossyns, at least until Cossyns showed up to answer the new charges.[57]

A second case referencing the lack of remedy in Admiralty, *Mathew & Goodman v. Callemor et al.*, concerned the nonpayment of freight charges by merchants.[58] The complainants, a pewterer and a mariner of London, jointly owned a ship, which the defendants had hired to carry goods to São Miguel Island, now part of the Azores, but then "within the dominionns of the now kinge of Spayne."[59] After much confusion, including a second voyage from England to São Miguel Island and an apparently faithless factor there who did not provide a return cargo, the defendants refused to pay the freight and charges. The complainants sued in Admiralty, but their suit was stymied, as Mathew explained in a petition to Sir Julius Caesar as Master of Requests, "by Reason he hathe not such witnesses as the Civill Lawe in that case requireth to p[ro]duce in his behalf to recover."[60] Yet even here, in a matter falling within the jurisdiction of the Admiralty Court, the bill continued to justify the lack of a remedy at common law due to the absence of witnesses.[61]

This same case also provides insight into another reason that admiralty disputes ended up in the Court of Requests. It was the court to hear poor men's suits, and sometimes those suits concerned admiralty matters. Mathew petitioned the Court to be permitted to sue *in forma pauperis*, asking that fees be waived and that the Court appoint counsel and an attorney to represent him.[62] Caesar granted the petition on the grounds that "this

56. Ibid.
57. Ibid.
58. *Mathew & Goodman v. Callemor et al.*, 1598, NA, REQ 2/241/3.
59. Ibid. (bill).
60. Ibid. (petition).
61. Ibid. (bill).
62. Ibid. (petition).

suppliants povertie is not matchable w[i]th the welth of the defend[ants]."[63] The poverty and the lower status of the complainant were both standard arguments justifying the existence of Requests, and at least some admiralty disputes demonstrate that the poor took advantage of the forum.[64]

Thus far the role of Requests conforms to the stereotype: an equity court for the poor hearing admiralty disputes sometimes brought by the poor. But Requests also took part in the contemporary jockeying for position between the various Westminster courts in two other general ways. First, litigants came to Requests when they felt they had nowhere else to turn to resolve a great injustice or when they just wanted to get a second, or third, bite of the apple. Second, Requests served as a back-up or referee when jurisdictional uncertainty raised questions about whether disputes should most properly be brought in Admiralty or common law.

As an admiralty court of last resort Requests heard lawsuits in which complainants unspooled long tales of woe describing the ways in which the defendants had hounded them with unjust suits in other courts and grasping at some way to right the wrongs. Two suits, both involving a foreign merchant party, give the flavor of these sorts of cases.

In *Lubbincke v. Law, Chigler & Redfarne*,[65] the complainant, William Lubbincke, was a German merchant who was robbed on board a ship bound from Germany to Spain by the ship's captain, master, and owner, all Englishmen. Lubbincke sued in Admiralty. The defendants in that case conspired with a certain James Law, who approached Lubbincke just as the Admiralty case was looking like it would come out in his favor, and claimed that the Lubbincke's brothers owed Law money. He promised to lend Lubbincke £100 to further pursue his suit if Lubbincke paid him back that money and the money his brothers allegedly owed with the proceeds from the Admiralty suit. Lubbincke agreed, but knowing neither English nor Latin he could not read either the bond he signed or its penalty clause. He thought Law was translating them accurately and that he would not have to pay until he won his suit, but in fact the bond called for repayment within a month. On top of that, Law never actually handed over the money.

63. Ibid. (petition, dorsal note in Caesar's hand).

64. See also *Pyers, et al. v. Hyggyns, et al.*, 1594, NA, REQ 2/30/64 (petitioning to sue *in forma pauperis*).

65. *Lubbincke v. Law, Chigler & Redfarne*, 1600, NA, REQ 2/166/119.

Law then brought an action of debt against Lubbincke before the sheriff of London and got judgment. Law executed judgment so that Lubbincke ended up in prison in the Poultry Counter. Next, the original thieves conspired with Chigler who promised to lend Lubbincke £20 so he could prosecute his suits in Admiralty and against Law. Not having learned his lesson the first time, Lubbincke again signed a bond he could not read. Chigler, who also did not hand over the money, sold Lubbincke's bond, and then got Redfarne to initiate a suit on his behalf against Lubbincke for the £20. All of which was done, said Lubbincke, to keep him in prison and prevent him from continuing his Admiralty suit on the original theft. With no money left, and nowhere else to turn, Lubbincke sought out justice from the Court of Requests.[66]

The second case is, if anything, even more convoluted.[67] George Hanger, a London clothworker, entered into an agreement with John Van Forden, a shipowner of Elsemere, Denmark that each would give £1000 bond to abide by the decision of four arbitrators if they issued their decision by May 27, or, if not, by the decision of Julius Caesar, judge of the Court of Admiralty, if he issued his decision by the end of May. The arbitrators did not make a ruling in time, but Caesar did. Under the ruling, Hanger had to immediately pay Van Forden £158 5s. plus another £100 after Van Forden put sureties into the Admiralty Court that he would hold Hanger harmless in any suits by Joachim Beldicker, a Dutch mariner, concerning an attachment made of Beldicker's property. Hanger made the initial payment; Van Forden put in the sureties with the Court; Hanger went to Caesar to pay the £100. But Caesar refused to take the money because he knew that Van Forden's sureties were inadequate and had been rejected by the Court. He told Hanger to hold onto the money until he made a new order. Caesar never made that order, however. Meanwhile, Beldinck caused an attachment to be made of the £100 in Hanger's hands by the Mayor's Court of London. This made Hanger liable to answer for £100 in two courts, and he still had no sureties in the Admiralty Court to hold him harmless against Beldinck. Van Forden had left the country, so Hanger could not pursue him, and anyway the bond he had signed with Van Forden prevented him

66. Ibid. (bill).

67. *Hanger v Van Forden, et al.*, 1598, NA, REQ 2/215/11.

from taking the case to the common law. Hanger went to Requests to get this mess sorted out.

Not all examples of litigants using Requests to get a second chance encompassed such alleged extremes of injustice. And in some instances, trying to get review in Requests could backfire on complainants. Where the case had been fully adjudicated in another court, defendants could and did demur to the bill of complaint rather than file an answer. Requests was supposed to throw such cases out, and sometimes it did.[68] This was what happened in the case of the sailors allegedly denied their prize with which this essay began. The defendants replied that the dispute had been litigated and judged in both the High Court of Admiralty and on appeal in the Court of Delegates and that the complainants had lost in both courts.[69] Requests ordered the complainants to respond to this claim, and when they did not make their appearance to do so, dismissed their suit.[70]

In some suits, litigants asked Requests to act as a referee between other courts. Through such cases, the Court found itself injected into the wider sixteenth- and seventeenth-century jurisdictional disputes between law and Admiralty and law and equity in general. For example, in a complex case about a German factor accused of cheating his English principals with regard to trade in Spanish wine, the factor had sued in Admiralty to force an accounting between the parties.[71] Later he wanted to remove the pending suit to Requests because

> his Counsell learned aswell in the Civile as com[m]on lawes of this Realme fyndeth the same not to be a marine cause and not havinge heare in England but beyonde the Seas sufficient witnesses to be p[ro]duced on the p[ar]te of yo[ur] said Suppliant for profe of all the saide p[re]misses is advised to surcesse the saide Suite in the Admerall

68. Knox, "The Court of Requests," 356–357.

69. *Pyers, et al. v. Hyggyns, et al.*, 1594, NA, REQ 2/30/64 (demurrer).

70. Order Book, May 26, 1595, NA, REQ 1/18 fol. 467. However, that the defendants might not have been entirely pure in this matter is suggested by that they were also sued in Exchequer for "unloading the Hopewell secretly, at night and paying no customs or other dues, E 159/400 Hil 26r & v, 180 r & v." Jean Vanes, ed., *Documents Illustrating the Overseas Trade of Bristol in the Sixteenth Century* (n.p.: Bristol Record Society, 1979), 56, n. 12.

71. *Demmer v. Watson & Shawcrofte*, 1590, NA, REQ 2/197/34.

> Courte and to seeke reliefe and remedies for his saide wronge and iniurie in yo[ur] most honorable Courte of requestes.[72]

What might have been driving counsel in this case to change his advice is apparent from the 1576 suit of *Allen v. Dingley*. Allen sold a ship to Dingley, who never paid. Allen then joined Dingley's other creditors in suing for an arrest of the ship in Admiralty. When the ship did not sell at public auction, Allen received permission from the Court to purchase it himself and pay off the other creditors. Dingley then sued Allen in Queen's Bench for detinue of the ship and violation of the Statutes of 13 & 15 Richard II and 2 Henry IV "against suche persones as doe implead or sue any person in [Admiralty] for any matter not rising or done upon the highe Seas."[73] These statutes were commonly referenced as part of the common law justices' late sixteenth- and seventeenth-century push to restrict Admiralty jurisdiction.[74] What this case demonstrates, however, is that the well-known battle between law and Admiralty was not purely binary. In their search for solutions, litigants somehow hoped that Requests could transcend the jurisdictional tug-of-war and provide a forum to resolve their disputes.

In *Michelson v. Baker, et al.*, the complainant described the jurisdictional dilemma more personally. He explained at length in his bill that:

> [I]t is very doubtfull whether your highnes sayd s[er]vant should sewe the sayd [defandants] at or in yo[ur] highness Court of admiraltie or otherwise at the common Lawes.... So that if [complainant]... should com[m]ense his sute for the sayd dett and duties at or in yo[ur] highnes Courte of Admeraltie the [defendants]... wolde then suggest that the cause were tryable at or by the co[m]on lawes of the Realme and so p[ro]hibit [complainant]. And so lykewyse yf [complainant] should com[m]ense his sayd sute at the com[m]on lawes upon a Matter so ambiguous and doubtfull whether it were triable in or by the

72. Ibid. (bill).

73. *Allen v. Dingley*, 1576, NA, REQ 2/168/23 (bill). The statutes referenced are 13 Ric. II c. 5 (1389); 15 Ric. II c. 3 (1391); and 2 Hen. IV c. 11 (1400).

74. M. J. Prichard & D. E. C. Yale, *Hale and Fleetwood on Admiralty Jurisdiction*, Selden Society 108 (London, 1993), l.

> sayd com[m]on lawes the sayd [defendants] woulde stand and demurre to the iurisdicc[i]on of the... course of the Com[m]on law to the greate delay of [complainant] and the utter ympov[er]ishment of [complainant] w[i]th suche delatories upon suche doubtefull sutes.[75]

In other words, the complainant feared that if he sued in either Admiralty or common law the defendants would make jurisdictional objections. Here again, a litigant wanted to see Requests as a compromise forum in which his suit could be heard and he could be protected from his wealthier and "lawyered-up" opponents.

"Collateral litigation was an established feature of lawsuits in the early modern period,"[76] and Requests was an equal participant in the forum shopping in which litigants engaged. From the reign of Queen Elizabeth an increasing number of Requests suits sought stays of proceedings in other courts. This perceived meddling in their business earned Requests the opprobrium of the common law justices. While during much of the sixteenth century common law and Requests judges had worked together,[77] by the end of the century the large numbers of cases seeking stays was "the cause of immense friction."[78] The common law justices retaliated, issuing writs of prohibition to prevent Requests from interfering with its judgments.[79] Most famously, in 1598 in *Stepney v. Flood* the Court of Common Pleas held that Requests was "no court that had power of judicature, but all the proceedings thereupon were *coram non judice*."[80]

And yet, whatever may have been the impact on Requests' ability to enforce its judgments,[81] these prohibitions did not in the end dampen litigants' enthusiasm for the forum. If anything, the Requests docket seems to have expanded during the reigns of Charles I and James I and to still be very active up until a year or two before its disappearance in 1643.[82] A

75. *Michelson v. Baker, et al.*, 1574, NA, REQ 2/31/56.
76. Prichard and Yale, *Hale and Fleetwood*, xlviii.
77. *Ancient State*, xxxi; Knox, "The Court of Requests," 350–352.
78. Knox, "The Court of Requests," 356.
79. *Ancient State*, ix–xi.
80. Sir Edward Coke, *The Fourth Part of the Institutes of the Laws of England* (London: E & R. Brooke, 1797), 97; *Ancient State*, x–xi.
81. Stretton, *Marital Litigation*, 12.
82. Knox, "The Court of Requests," 9–10, 16; Stretton, *Marital Litigation*, 9.

poor person's court serving more than just the poor, a so-called minor court doing brisk business, a court supposedly focused on land matters dealing extensively with commercial and maritime issues, Requests occupied a significant space in the judicial landscape of early modern England.

Quantitative Easing Four Centuries Ago: Juan de Mariana's *De monetae mutatione* (1609)

Wim Decock

Introduction

Professor Donahue has repeatedly defined himself as a "text-based legal historian," combining rigorous philological analysis of legal texts with careful analysis of the historical context from which these texts emerged. He is also firmly committed to the proposition shared by many legal historians that institutions and legal concepts change over time, rendering his research immune from anachronistic interpretations of historical texts.[1] At the same time, Professor Donahue has always seen in the close reading of texts and their contexts an excellent way of improving the dialogue between the past and the present, and, potentially, of offering historical insights to jurists involved in the solution of current issues. Therefore, this contribution will dwell on a particular text by Juan de Mariana (1535–1624), a Jesuit theologian, on monetary debasement (*De monetae mutatione*), an issue of not merely historical interest. While firmly rooted in a specific historical context that remains different from today's world, Mariana's concerns are echoed in today's economic and political debates about monetary policy which have been raging on both sides of the Atlantic in the wake of the recent sovereign debt crises.

1. E.g. Charles Donahue, "A Crisis of Law? Reflections on the Church and the Law over the Centuries," *The Jurist* (2005), 3.

As a matter of fact, Mariana published this tract on the Spanish government's monetary policy in 1607, just two years after the fourth sovereign default of Spain in five decades. The historical context from which Mariana's text emerged, was a particular one, indeed. From the mid-sixteenth until the mid-seventeenth centuries, Spain was not only the dominant colonial empire, it also defaulted six times on its sovereign debt (1557, 1575, 1596, 1607, 1627, 1647), thus laying the basis of what has become a record eleven numbers of state bankruptcies in the preceding five centuries.[2] One of the favorite techniques used by the Spanish monarchs to overcome those crises was to expand the monetary basis, especially by devaluing the currency. While not entirely the same, some will find it fascinating to compare this technique with the modern use of quantitative easing (QE) and other unconventional monetary financing techniques to expand the monetary base.[3]

THE CONTEXT: SPANISH MONETARY POLICY IN TIMES OF CRISIS

A couple of words are needed to explain the historical context from which Mariana's tract on money emerged. Haunted by sovereign defaults and a real economy in decline, Spanish governments in the sixteenth and seventeenth centuries increasingly had recourse to monetary ways of financing the state budget, particularly by debasing the coinage. More specifically, Mariana reacted against King Philip III's repeated efforts to debase copper money (*vellón*) during the first decade of the seventeenth century, only shortly after the state bankruptcy of 1597 and after the king had introduced

2. Figures are based on C. M. Reinhart and K. S. Rogoff, *This Time is Different: A Panoramic View of Eight Centuries of Financial Crises*, NBER Working Paper Series, 13882 (March 2008), 20, available online at http://www.nber.org/papers/w13882.pdf.

3. Technically speaking, QE differs from currency debasement in several regards, for instance because it involves large-scale purchasing of sovereign bonds by a central bank, which did not even exist at the time of the Spanish empire. Practically speaking, though, the effects aimed at were more or less the same: expand the monetary basis, oppose a downward spiral of prices and alleviate the burden of excessive sovereign debt levels. For an introduction to QE, see M. Joyce et al., "Quantitative Easing and Unconventional Monetary Policy—An Introduction," *The Economic Journal: The Journal of the Royal Economic Society* 122 (November 2012), F271–F288.

the *vellón* in 1599.[4] Those debasements increased the Crown's revenue by virtue of the mint fees, but they worsened the inflation of prices which had been rattling the Spanish economy for more than a century.[5]

There are several reasons why King Philip III introduced and subsequently altered copper money instead of gold or silver. First of all, Spain had almost run out of silver by spending it on the war against the independence of the Low Countries.[6] More importantly, however, already back in the middle ages, the kings of Aragon and Castile had renounced their right to mint profits, the so-called seigniorage, on silver and gold coinage.[7] In this regard, Spain was an anomaly in the widespread phenomenon of silver-coinage debasements in early-modern Europe. From 1497 to 1686, no debasement of Castilian and Aragonese silver and gold money occurred. Yet, the surrendering of mint fees did not apply to copper coinage. Accordingly, Philipp III introduced pure copper coins in 1599 and debased them by weight in 1602 to increase royal revenues from minting fees.

The result of the King's monetary policy for the circulation of money can be aptly summarized through Gresham's law that bad money drives out the good. What little remained of silver and gold coinage was exported to foreign countries, while Spain was inundated by cheap *vellones* and foreign debased silver. Purchasing power decreased severely, the real economy was devastated. In 1607, Spain defaulted again.[8]

4. J. H. Munro, ed., *Money in the Pre-Industrial World: Bullion, Debasements and Coin Substitutes* (London: Pickering & Chatto, 2012), 7–8, http://www.economics.utoronto.ca/munro5/IntroductionMoneyPre-IndustrialWorld.pdf. The historical facts in this section are entirely borrowed from John Munro's work.

5. On the explanation of the "price revolution" in sixteenth-century Europe, see above.

6. M. North, *Das Geld und seine Geschichte: Vom Mittelalter bis zur Gegenwart* (1994), 98.

7. Munro, *Money in the Pre-Industrial World*, 7 and idem, "Money, Prices, Wages, and "Profit Inflation" in Spain, the Southern Netherlands, and England during the Price Revolution Era: ca. 1520–ca. 1650," *História e Economia: Revista Interdisciplinar* 4 (2008), 43–44, http://www.economics.utoronto.ca/munro5/HistoriaEconomiaProfitInflation.pdf.

8. North, *Das Geld und seine Geschichte*, 98.

THE TEXT: JUAN DE MARIANA AGAINST MONETARY DEBASEMENT[9]

A "learned extremist"?

Upon its publication in 1609, Juan de Mariana's *De monetae mutatione* stirred immediate controversy and made him subject to prosecution for high treason (*laesio maiestatis*). Even though Mariana managed to avoid punishment, he was held in custody in Madrid and Rome for a while and he was also urged to modify offensive passages in his treatise.[10] In the meantime, Pope Paul V put the first edition of *De monetae mutatione* on the Spanish Index of prohibited books. Moreover, state officials took almost all extant copies out of circulation.[11] This may help explain why Mariana's ideas on money have received relatively scarce attention in the past, despite the abundant literature on his political ideas as expressed in the tract *De rege et regis institutione* (1599).[12] If anything, the episode following the publication of his treatise on monetary debasement seems to add further weight to the popular notion, circulated even by Bluntschli in his *Deutsches Staatswörterbuch*, that Mariana was nothing but an infamous Jesuit proponent

9. The material in this section has previously been published in my "Spanish Scholastics on Money and Credit," in D. Fox and W. Ernst, ed., *Money in the Western Legal Tradition: Middle Ages to Bretton Woods* (Oxford, Oxford University Press, 2016), 267–283, namely 272–277.

10. G. Lewy, *Constitutionalism and Statecraft during the Golden Age of Spain. A Study of the Political Philosophy of Juan de Mariana S.J.* (Geneva: E. Droz 1960), 31.

11. J. Falzberger, ed. and trans., *Juan de Mariana: De monetae mutatione (1609), Über die Munzveränderung* (1996), i–ii. Unless indicated otherwise, this is the modern Latin edition which we used for this investigation. It is also worthwhile mentioning that an English translation of *De monetae mutatione* with annotations has been provided by Patrick T. Brannan in S. J. Grabill, *Sourcebook in Late-Scholastic Monetary Theory: The Contributions of Martín de Azpilcueta, Luis de Molina S.J., and Juan de Mariana S.J.* (Lanham, Md.: Lexington Books, 2007), 248–327.

12. The most recent standard work on Mariana's political thought is H. E. Braun, *Juan de Mariana and Early Modern Spanish Political Thought* (Aldershot: Ashgate, 2007), including references to further literature. An autonomous study of Mariana's *De monetae mutatione* which remains valuable is J. Laures, *The Political Economy of Juan de Mariana* (New York: Fordham University Press, 1928), http://mises.org/books/mariana.pdf.

of tyrannicide.[13] Though this notion has rightly been rejected as untrue by modern scholars such as Harald Braun,[14] Mariana was a fearless thinker, indeed, who did not spare his criticism for the Spanish monarchs Philip II and his successor. In assessing Mariana's liberal economic ideas, Murray Rothbard even called him a "learned extremist."[15]

Medieval constitutionalist ideas

Mariana's tract on monetary debasement is an illustration of the political dimension inherent in scholastic monetary thought. This was not something new. The connection between coinage debasement and political ideas on representation was already at the heart of medieval canon lawyers' discussion of money.[16] In the late medieval period, an influential analogy was established between the kings' conditional power to tax, viz. with the consent of the people, and his power to alter money. Through the work of Nicolas Oresme (c. 1320–1382) and Gabriel Biel (c. 1420–1495), the idea gained ground that money is not the property of the prince alone, as Thomas Aquinas had argued, but of the entire community.[17] Hence, the consent of the representatives of the community was required before a ruler could

13. The "making of Mariana's notoriety" is critically discussed in Braun, *Juan de Mariana and Early Modern Spanish Political Thought*, 7–11. In his introductory note to the translation of Mariana's *De monetae mutatione* in Grabill, *Sourcebook in Late-Scholastic Monetary Theory*, 242. Alejandro Chafuen rightly points out that, despite rumors to the contrary, the French king Henry IV's assassin had never heard of Mariana.

14. Braun, *Juan de Mariana and Early Modern Spanish Political Thought*, 80–91, also reviewed by P. Williams, see: http://www.history.ac.uk/reviews/review/647.

15. M. N. Rothbard, *An Austrian Perspective on the History of Economic Thought. Vol. 1: Economic Thought Before Adam Smith* (Aldershot: Elgar, 1995), 117, http://library.mises.org/books/Murray%20N%20Rothbard/Austrian%20Perspective%20on%20the%20History%20of%20Economic%20Thought.pdf.

16. See Andreas Thier's contribution on the canon law of money in Fox and Ernst, *Money in the Western Legal Tradition*.

17. H. Mäkeler, "Nicolas Oresme und Gabriel Biel. Zur Geldtheorie im späten Mittelalter," *Scripta Mercaturae. Zeitschrift für Wirtschafts- und Sozialgeschichte* 37 (2003), 56, http://www.hendrik.maekeler.eu/oresme-biel.pdf. For further explanation of Oresme's and Biel's monetary theories, see the contributions by Fabian Wittreck and Stefan Kötz in this volume.

debase the coinage.[18] It would seem that Mariana pushed these medieval constitutionalist ideas to their radical conclusion.[19] At the outset of his treatise on money, Mariana dealt with three questions that are indicative of the close connection between coinage debasement, constitutionalist political ideas, and taxation: 1) Is the king the owner of the goods which his subjects possess? (*num rex sit dominus bonorum quae subditi possident*); 2) Is it allowed for the king to impose taxes on his subjects without their consent? (*an rex possit tributa subditis imperare non consentientibus*); 3) Is it allowed for the king to debase the money after the weight or quality have been altered without consulting the people? (*num rex monetam vitiare possit pondere aut bonitate mutatis populo inconsulto*).[20]

Historical evidence

Confronted with the financial plight caused by Philip III's reckless fiscal measures, Mariana wished to assume responsibility and address himself to the king and his counselors. They should not be surprised if, suddenly, an audacious individual like him stood up and wrote to the king about the misery which his subjects suffered and resented in silence.[21] Mariana cynically observed that there had been those who had warned—in vain—against the alteration of money, since they were more cautious by virtue of their historical consciousness and knowledge of past evils (*ex memoria prae-*

18. On the medieval origins of this debate, see P. Spufford, "Assemblies of Estates, Taxation and Control of Coinage in Medieval Europe," in *Etudes presentées à la Commission internationale pour l'histoire des assemblées d'Etats* 31 (1966), also cited by Thier in this volume.

19. Incidentally, this is a widespread evaluation of Mariana's political thought in general reached by scholars who studied his tract *De rege*, e.g. J. Fernández Santamaría, *Reason of State and Statecraft in Spanish Political Thought* (Lanham, Md.: University Press of America, 1983). Against this current, Braun, *Juan de Mariana and Early Modern Spanish Political Thought*, xii stresses that Mariana's political thought is too much indebted to an altogether pessimistic, Augustinian view of man to be called radically constitutionalist.

20. Falzberger, *Juan de Mariana: De monetae mutatione (1609)*, 2.

21. Falzberger, *Juan de Mariana: De monetae mutatione (1609)*, praefatio, 10. The human misery ensuing from this financial catastrophe is reflected in the Spanish literature of the time, see E. Vilches, *New World Gold: Cultural Anxiety and Monetary Disorder in Early Modern Spain* (Chicago: University of Chicago Press, 2010), containing an interesting treatment of Mariana's *De monetae mutatione* on 258–264.

teriti temporis et malorum ex eo cautiores).[22] Hardly, if ever, did debasements of coinage not turn out to be detrimental to the community (*vix umquam pecuniam in peius mutari nisi reipublicae malo*).[23] Mariana's critique, then, was firmly rooted in historical experience, which may be considered as a typical feature of his humanist spirit.[24] Mariana was famous for his critical historical scholarship, although it was certainly not free from partisan tendencies in questions regarding the relation of secular and ecclesiastical authorities or claims to succession of the crown.[25] His History of Spain (*Historiae de rebus Hispaniae*), published in 1592, remained a reference work up to the eighteenth century and earned him the names of the Spanish Thucydides or the Spanish Tacitus.[26] In the manner of those great classical authors, Mariana offered a critical account of the mechanisms of princely politics through the mirror of history. In his eyes, history was a mute teacher of the uses and abuses of power and a warning for the future.

Against political absolutism

The thrust of Mariana's answer to the three above-mentioned questions was to polemicize against political absolutism. He showed himself a staunch defender of private property and limited government, much in the spirit of jurists such as Arias Piñel (1515–1563).[27] Power is bound by certain limits (*potestatis certi quidam fines sunt*).[28] The unrestrained exercise of power is

22. Falzberger, *Juan de Mariana: De monetae mutatione (1609)*, argumentum, 6.

23. Falzberger, *Juan de Mariana: De monetae mutatione (1609)*, argumentum, 8.

24. Compare R. W. Truman, *Spanish Treatises on Government, Society and Religion in the Time of Philip II. The "de regimine principum" and Associated Traditions* (Leiden: Brill, 1999), 322.

25. P. Linehan, *History and the Historians of Medieval Spain* (Oxford: Clarendon Press, 1993), 7 and 407.

26. Braun, *Juan de Mariana and Early Modern Spanish Political Thought*, 2–3.

27. See Decock, *Theologians and Contract Law: The Moral Transformation of the Ius Commune (c. 1500–1650)* (Leiden: M. Nijhoff, 2012), 568–569. The defense of private property against absolutist claims by the crown appears to have been generalized among Spanish jurists of the early modern period; see H. Kamen, *Una sociedad conflictiva: España, 1469–1714* (Madrid: Alianza, 1994), 244, and J. Fernández-Santamaría, *Natural Law, Constitutionalism, Reason of State, and War. Counter-Reformation Spanish Political Thought*, (New York: Peter Lang, 2005–6), 1.349–392.

28. Falzberger, *Juan de Mariana: De monetae mutatione (1609)*, cap. 1, 16.

the sign of a tyrant (*tyranni id proprium est nullis finibus coercere imperium*).[29] The authority to govern the people does not grant a ruler the power to submit his subjects' goods to his judgment and steal them.[30] Mariana adduced the authority of the Roman and canon legal tradition to bolster his argument that kings are prohibited to enact laws without consulting their subjects if those laws are burdensome for the people.[31] Accordingly, in answering the question whether a prince can tax his subjects without their consent, Mariana repeated the idea that

> the private goods of the citizens are not left to the arbitrary will of the king. Consequently, he must not take away all or part of them unless that is the will of those who are the legal owners of those goods. Moreover, if, as the jurists wisely say, the king cannot make laws that are pernicious to private citizens without their consent, then he cannot occupy a part of their goods by creating and imposing new taxes.[32]

No taxation without representation

From the assumption that monetary debasement is a form of taxation, Mariana could easily derive that the king could not alter the money but

29. Falzberger, *Juan de Mariana: De monetae mutatione (1609)*, cap. 1, 20.

30. Falzberger, *Juan de Mariana: De monetae mutatione (1609)*, cap. 1, 18.

31. Falzberger, *Juan de Mariana: De monetae mutatione (1609)*, cap. 1, 18, l. 18–22: "Ita iureconsultorum communis sententia est (quam explicant in cod. Si contra ius vel utilitatem publicam, lege ultima, affertque eam Panormitanus cap. Quanto / De iureiurando), Reges sine consensu populi nihil posse in subditorum detrimentum sancire."

The reference to "cod. Si contra ius" in the Latin text has erroneously been interpreted as a reference to the *Nueva Recopilación* and commentaries on this Spanish compilation of laws in Falzberger, *Juan de Mariana: De monetae mutatione (1609)*, 158 and also in Grabill, *Sourcebook in Late-Scholastic Monetary Theory*, 306. In fact, the passage refers to C. 1,22,6 from Justinian's Code.

32. Falzberger, *Juan de Mariana: De monetae mutatione (1609)*, cap. 2, 26, l. 1–6: "Id satis confirmat, quod paulo ante dicebamus, in Regis arbitrio non esse privata civium bona. Non ergo aut universa aut partem decerpet nisi ex eorum voluntate, quorum in iure sunt. Praeterea si ex iureconsultorum oraculo nihil Rex potest statuere in privatorum perniciem iis recusantibus, non poterit bonorum partem occupare novo tributo excogitato et imposito."

on condition that the people agreed:[33] "If the prince cannot impose taxes against the will of the people, then neither can he institute monopolies or make new profits out of debased money against their will." In Mariana's opinion, "all those tricks, under whatever guise they come, are geared towards one and the same unlawful end, namely to weigh to oppress the people with new burdens and to amass money."[34] In making this argument, Mariana drew heavily on the canon law tradition. His plea against King Philip III's monetary policy abounds with references to the commentaries on title *De iureiurando*, canon *Quanto personam tuam* (X 2.24.18), which was the *sedes materiae* for the canonists' discussion of monetary debasement. Innocent IV, Cardinal Hostiensis, and Abbas Panormitanus figure among Mariana's favorite authorities. In fact, the decretal *Quanto personam tuam* found its origin in a confrontation between Pope Innocent III and the king of Aragon in the late twelfth century.[35] As Mariana deemed worthwhile recalling, Innocent III had invalidated the oath by which James, King of Aragon, promised to preserve the debased coinage minted by Peter II, his father, since the consent of the people was lacking among other reasons.[36] He further admonished that under Ferdinand II of Aragon and Philip II laws concerning money had always been passed in popular assemblies representing the people, namely the *cortes*.[37]

33. Falzberger, *Juan de Mariana: De monetae mutatione (1609)*, cap. 3, 34, l. 13–16: "Quod si Princeps subditis tributa imperare non potest invitis neque rerum venalium monopolia instituere, non poterit ex moneta adulterata novum lucrum captare."

34. Falzberger, *Juan de Mariana: De monetae mutatione (1609)*, cap. 3, 36, l. 8–10: "Artes hae omnes quacumque simulatione eodem omnes pertinent, ad gravandum populum novis oneribus et pecuniam corradendam, quod non licet."

35. For details, see D. Smith, *Innocent III and the Crown of Aragon: The Limits of Papal Authority* (Burlington, Vt.: Ashgate, 2004), 24–26, also quoted by Thier. It is worthwhile noticing that Pope Innocent III's decretal remained a point of reference in discussions on monetary debasement in the early modern period, not only in the works of theologians and canonists, but also for instance in the work of the Swiss jurist Melchior Goldast (1576–1635), cf. *Catholicon rei monetariae sive leges monarchicae generales de rebus nummariis et pecuniariis* (Frankfurt, 1620), tit. 33, 104–105.

36. Falzberger, *Juan de Mariana: De monetae mutatione (1609)*, cap. 3, 34.

37. Falzberger, *Juan de Mariana: De monetae mutatione (1609)*, cap. 3, 36. It has been pointed out by other scholars that Mariana's political thought was naturally conservative and resisting innovation. His conception of legitimate government action relied on history, custom and "the ways of our ancestors," see H. Höpfl, *Jesuit Political Thought. The Society of Jesus and the State, c. 1540–1630* (Cambridge, Cambridge University Press, 2004), 242.

Need for a stable currency

Having laid down the fundamental legal and political principles by which Philip III's alteration of copper money should be judged, Mariana went on to discuss the more technical and economic aspects of the alteration of money. On the theoretical side, his ideas were often influenced by Aristotle and by Reiner Budel (†1530), a jurist in the service of the Duke of Bavaria whose work *De monetis* appeared in 1591 in Cologne.[38] Chapter four of Mariana's tract dealt with the distinction between the legal, or extrinsic, and the natural, or intrinsic, value of money by analogy with the legal and the natural price of a good. Our Jesuit thought that in a well-ordered society the king's administrators made sure that those values coincided as much as possible, but he regretted to find that the opposite policy was practiced in Spain in his time: by having the legal value of copper money largely exceed its natural value, the king temporarily enriched the royal treasure, but created the conditions for financial disaster in the long run.[39] In chapter five, dedicated to money, weights and measures as the foundations of the economy (*commercii fundamenta*), Mariana highlighted the role of money as a unit of account, and, hence, the need for a stable currency:[40] "Just as the foundations of brick buildings must remain firm and stable, weights, measures and money cannot be altered without risk or damage to the economy." Mariana praised the example of the ounce, a unit of weight which had remained unchanged in Spain since Roman times. He dealt with this subject more extensively in his popular work *De ponderibus et mensuris*, published in 1599.

Gresham's law

Historians of economic thought will appreciate Mariana's lucid analysis in chapter nine of the phenomenon whereby "bad money drives out the good,"

38. Scant biographical notices on Budel are contained in Falzberger, *Juan de Mariana: De monetae mutatione (1609)* (1996), 162.

39. Falzberger, *Juan de Mariana: De monetae mutatione (1609)*, cap. 4, 38 and 42.

40. Falzberger, *Juan de Mariana: De monetae mutatione (1609)*, cap. 5, 46, l. 7–10: "Quae eo pertinent ut sit omnibus persuasum, uti in structuris fundamenta immota manent et intacta, non secus pondera, mensuras, pecuniam sine periculo non moveri et commercii detrimento."

known as "Gresham's law" after the name of the English businessman Thomas Gresham (c. 1519–1579), but actually observed already by Oresme.[41] The truth and reality is, according to Mariana, that "when copper is very abundant, silver radically disappears among the citizens, and this should be numbered among the major disadvantages."[42] Our Jesuit goes on to explain why this happens:[43] "The silver flows into the royal treasure, since the king orders citizens to pay their taxes in that coinage. The silver money does not return to circulation, since the king himself pays his debts, if any, to his subjects in copper coinage. Indeed, it is easy to pay with copper and there will be plenty of it, while he will export the silver. Whatever remains of the silver among the citizens disappears, since all first spend the copper coinage while hiding the silver, unless necessity forces them to produce the silver." Apart from this economic disadvantage, though, what mattered even more to Mariana was the unlawful character of King Philip's alteration of the copper money.

Monetary debasement as robbery

Among many other disadvantages of monetary debasement discussed in chapter ten, Mariana rehearsed the principal objection already raised at the beginning of his tract: it goes against reason and natural law (*cum recta ratione et cum naturae ipsius legibus pugnat*). The following quote summarized Mariana's major objection against the alteration of money:

41. For critical observations regarding both the history and validity of "Gresham's law," see R. Mundell, "Uses and Abuses of Gresham's Law in the History of Money," *Zagreb Journal of Economics* 2 (1998), http://www.columbia.edu/~ram15/grash.html.

42. Falzberger, *Juan de Mariana: De monetae mutatione (1609)*, cap. 9, 82–84: "Verum ut fateamur, quod res est: aeris quando copia nimia est, argentum certe inter cives evanescit et perit, quod in praecipuis incommidis debet numerari."

43. Falzberger, *Juan de Mariana: De monetae mutatione (1609)*, cap. 9, 84: "Nempe in regium aerarium confluit argentum, quoniam tributa in ea moneta solvi mandat, neque in orbem recurrit, quoniam ipse, si quid subditis debet, aerea moneta satisfacit, cuius facultas magna et copia erit, argentum per eum ad exteros deferetur. Sed et quod argentum inter cives manet, disparet cunctis prius aeream monetam expendentibus, recondentibus argenteam, nisi re necessaria cogantur illam proferre."

> It is not up to the king to rush upon his subjects' goods to snatch them away from their rightful owners according to his will. Look: would a prince be allowed to break into his subjects' granaries, take half of the grain stored there for himself, and by way of compensation let the owners to sell the remainder at the same price as the original whole? I do not think that there would be anyone so preposterous as to condone such an act. But that is precisely what happened with the old copper coins.[44]

Beneath the sarcasm lay the central message of Mariana's *De monetae mutatione*: debasing the *vellones* without the consent of the people was a form of disguised robbery which violated the natural rights of the citizens. It should be mentioned, though, that our Jesuit did not limit himself to a scathing deconstruction of King Philip III's monetary policy. In the last three chapters of his tract, he did his best to suggest alternative ways to fill the royal treasury and to revive the Spanish economy.

CONCLUDING REMARKS

Mariana's text was an audacious attempt to tackle one of the big issues in economic and monetary policy of his time. In Mariana's treatment we witness the close interconnectedness between economic, legal and political arguments. Mariana rebuked the debasement of the currency by King Philip III on the grounds that it violated the fundamental rights of the people. In his view, altering the currency required the approval of the citizens, just as levying taxes. Otherwise, monetary debasement risked to be a disguised form of robbery. Apart from historical experience, Mariana adduced arguments from canon law to oppose King Philip III's monetary debasement. As many economists would have predicted, the cure was mostly worse than the disease. In resorting to techniques of monetary financing without solving the underlying economic problems, the Spanish monarchs temporarily

44. Falzberger, *Juan de Mariana: De monetae mutatione (1609)*, cap. 10, 92, l. 10–16: "In regis arbitrio non esse in subditorum bona involare, ut ea pro voluntate dominis legitimis detrahat. Nunc age: an liceat Principi in horrea singula irrumpere, dimidium frumenti reconditi sibi sumere, nocumentum compensare facultate dominis lata vendendi, quod relinquitur, quanti integrum cumulum ante? Non arbitror fore tam praepostero iudicio hominem, qui factum excusaret. At in moneta aerea vetere hoc ipsum est factum."

ended one crisis but prepared the next. This was precisely the point which Juan de Mariana wished to make. Whether this means that Mariana's critique on currency debasement can be read as an outright rejection of today's quantitative easing policies, is another question. At least, it puts the arguments used by opponents of unconventional monetary policies used by governments in the latest sovereign debt crisis into perspective.

The Mystery of the "Charitable Arbitrator," or Reflections on a Neglected Old Regime Text and the Intersection Between Status and Practices of Arbitration and Mediation

Amalia D. Kessler

Some years back, Charlie Donahue did what he does so often and so well: He posed a fundamental question about legal history whose resolution, like the proverbial peeling of the onion, turns out to reveal layers of depth and complexity all too rarely explored. As Charlie inquired, "granted how important procedure is for any predictive theory of law, and granted how much prediction is a part of every lawyer's equipment, how is it that procedure is sometimes forgotten," the neglected stepchild of substance?[1] Indeed, he went on to query, "[h]ow did [the substance/procedure] distinction" come about" at all?[2] This is not the place to detail Charlie's very interesting comparative overview of the emergence of this distinction—a question that has also been of much interest to me of late.[3] But it is important to note

1. Charles Donahue, Jr., "'The Hypostasis of a Prophecy': Legal Realism and Legal History," in *Law and Legal Process: Substantive Law and Procedure in English Legal History*, eds. Matthew Dyson and David Ibbetson (Cambridge: Cambridge University Press, 2013), 6.

2. Ibid.

3. Amalia D. Kessler, *Inventing American Exceptionalism: The Origins of American Adversarial Legal Culture, 1800–1877* (New Haven: Yale University Press, forthcoming 2017).

that, in asking why such little attention is devoted to procedure, he (inadvertently) highlighted one of the great virtues of his own remarkable body of research—namely, that it gives due weight to procedure.

Charlie has written about a great many areas of substantive law, ranging from the law of marriage and the family, to property law, to the law merchant. But while the subject matter that he has studied is admirably broad and varied, his writings as a whole are marked by a dogged determination to understand how the law actually plays out in practice, so as to shape lived experience. This determination, in turn, translates into a focus on how procedure operates to make possible (or impossible) the vindication of particular legal claims. In his words, "[i]f one adopts the predictive theory of law" and thereby concerns oneself with the question of what courts are likely in fact to decide, one must attend to "the entire procedural system."[4] Indeed, "if we go this far, why should we confine ourselves just to the institutions as they are conceived and the rules of procedure as they are stated?"[5] A complete analysis requires attention to "factors that are not explicitly recognised by the system but that likely, or perhaps certainly, are going to affect the result."[6] Providing such a complete account of any legal system in operation therefore requires painstaking work of reconstruction—a kind of total immersion into the world of the past that attends to all the possible factors, legal and non-legal, acknowledged and hidden, that together work to shape the system's outcomes. Needless to say, this is a tremendously daunting task, at least for those of us lacking Charlie's vast erudition.

In the spirit of celebrating Charlie and his longstanding interest in questions of procedure, I turn now to a remarkable but surprisingly forgotten book published in Paris in 1666: *L'arbitre charitable*.[7] According to

4. Donahue, 3

5. Ibid.

6. Ibid.

7. Alexandre de la Roche, *L'arbitre charitable, et un moyen facile pour accorder les procez promptement, sans peine, et sans frais* (Paris: L. Raveneau, 1668). The book's first edition, published in 1666, does not list a place of publication. But the second edition, issued in 1668, identifies a Paris-based publisher. Derek Roebuck, *The Charitable Arbitrator: How to Mediate and Arbitrate in Louis XIV's France* (Oxford: HOLO Books/The Arbitration Press, 2002), 86. Roebuck provides both a facsimile of the original 1666 edition and a translation into English of the 1668 edition. For purposes of this paper, I have relied

the book's title page, its author was Alexandre de la Roche, the Prior of Saint Pierre—a man about whom, unfortunately, nothing today is known.[8] But while the book has largely fallen into oblivion, it enjoyed considerable success in its day, such that it was reissued in three more editions within five years from when it first appeared. And if de la Roche is to be believed, it was also translated into English, German, Danish and Latin by various governmental ministers and ambassadors eager to encourage a readership back home.[9] But why exactly was the book so successful? And more generally, what did its author hope to achieve with its publication? The mystery here is that what de la Roche presented as a plea for reform appears in many ways simply to capture what we now know to be the reality of dispute resolution in mid-to-late-seventeenth- (and eighteenth-) century France.

The core goals of the book are set forth in an epistle to the then king, Louis XIV, that appears in the introduction to the second (1668) edition and those that followed. According to de la Roche, it was in the best interest of both "the people" and "the Prince" that the latter should "forb[id] suits and disputes, or at least finish[] them off at birth" by promoting arbitration and mediation.[10] But as his subsequent discussion makes clear, what he described as his "manual" was not directed primarily at the king,

---

on his translation, cross-checked against the original. The only scholarly works that I have found addressing *L'arbitre charitable* are Roebuck's book and an article by Stuart Carroll. Roebuck's introduction provides valuable contextual information concerning *L'arbitre charitable*, but little analysis. His interest in the book appears to stem from his view that it serves as a statement of the timeless, universal virtues of arbitration. Ibid., 96. In contrast, Stuart Carroll explores what the book can teach us about early-modern France and provides a sharper analytical frame. Stuart Carroll, "The Peace in the Feud in Sixteenth- and Seventeenth-Century France," *Past & Present* 178 (2003): 86–97. In his account, the book should be viewed as "a practical handbook" aimed at promoting peace during an era in which widespread feuding remained common—or rather was only just declining. Ibid., 87. From this perspective, the publication of *L'arbitre charitable* reflected the emergence of a new era in which noblemen shifted away from a culture of chivalric honor and vengeance towards one structured around norms of civility, as these played out most importantly at court. Ibid., 111–14. But while Carroll's analysis may be correct as far as it goes, it is overly narrow. As discussed below, de la Roche sought to target a much broader readership than merely the noble elite. Moreover, Carroll neglects the scholarly literature suggesting that practices of arbitration and mediation were quite common in early modern France.

8. Roebuck, 78–84.
9. De la Roche, 131–32.
10. Ibid., 101.

but instead at French society itself.[11] More particularly, it was his goal to reach two distinct categories of readers. First, he sought to persuade disputants themselves to pursue arbitration and/or mediation—ideally as an alternative to litigation, but at least as a means of settling lawsuits already filed: "[T]he author intends to speak to those poor litigants who are looking for a way to bring their lawsuits and their woes to a quick end; they will find here the means to help them."[12] Second, he hoped that his manual would convince those who might serve as either arbitrators or mediators to embrace this role. Towards this end, he himself sent the book to French bishops with an eye toward encouraging them and the local village priests who served under them (the *curés*) to take on such informal, dispute-resolution responsibilities.[13] De la Roche's aspiration to appeal both to disputants and to potential arbitrators and mediators is evident, moreover, in the overarching structure of the manual, which addresses itself (largely on a chapter-by-chapter basis) to particular categories of French subject—including, local *curés*, bishops, monks and nuns, abbots, provincial governors, great lords, judges, and members of the lower orders. The author urged all of these groups to settle their disputes by means of arbitration or mediation. So too, he insisted that all but members of the lowest orders ought to assume responsibility for settling the disputes of those within their charge.

As for how to go about promoting extrajudicial dispute resolution, de la Roche advocated a two-fold approach—one tending to blend together both arbitration and mediation. The process would begin with the intervention of a "mediator," charged with persuading the disputants that it was in their best interest to settle the dispute out of court. If the mediator succeeded, the parties would sign an agreement to have their dispute resolved by a set of three arbitrators—with one arbitrator to be selected by each disputant and the mediator assisting in the disputants' efforts to decide on a third. The mediator would then require both parties to deposit with him a sum of money, to be held as a bond committing them to abide by any arbitral award issued.[14]

11. Ibid., 131.
12. Ibid.
13. Ibid., 132.
14. Ibid., 194–99.

At times, the very process of preparing for an eventual arbitration resulted in a mediated settlement: "I have known mediators, and even the parties themselves, at this stage propose ways which allowed them to bring the matter to a successful settlement."[15] But should this not occur, all requisite documentation was to be sent by the mediator to the three arbitrators for purposes of review.[16] These arbitrators themselves might then engage in mediation, rather than arbitration—seeking to persuade the parties to agree to some kind of mutually acceptable resolution of their dispute, instead of issuing a binding decision. As de la Roche observed, "[b]ecause it should be the arbitrators' intention to bring peace and as far as possible prevent any occasion for a lawsuit, it is better to get the parties to make a compromise rather than making an arbitral award."[17] Not surprisingly, given the fluidity of the distinction between arbitration and mediation, he claimed that effective arbitrators and mediators shared many of the same core qualities. More particularly, the arbitrator "should be patient like the good mediator and prudent like him, and above all charitable like him."[18]

In justifying his decision thus to prepare a manual urging the widespread use of arbitration and mediation, de la Roche insisted that nothing short of the kingdom's very survival was at stake: "[C]hicanery is the worst of all France's evils."[19] The chicanery that encouraged the emergence of "passionate and never-ending lawsuits" bred duels and blood feud among the noble elite[20] and caused *curés* to be absent from "their parishes for three or four years under the pretext that they have been involved in a miserable lawsuit."[21] Such litigation served no purpose other than to "empt[y] the pocket and bring[] the merchant into disrepute"[22] and resulted in a situation in which "the land is not worked... and the artisan does no work."[23]

15. Ibid., 195–96.
16. Ibid.
17. Ibid., 204.
18. Ibid., 200.
19. Ibid., 101.
20. Ibid.
21. Ibid., 167.
22. Ibid., 238.
23. Ibid., 177.

And for the poor, litigation was simply a nonstarter: "[T]he poor man complains that he has no hope of justice."[24]

Such complaints about the evils of litigation (and the lawyers who thrive on it) were not unique in mid-to-late seventeenth-century France, any more than they are in much of the world today. Indeed, as we will see, at precisely the same time that de la Roche published his manuscript urging the vital necessity of employing arbitration and mediation as an alternative to litigation, the French monarchy itself—under the guidance of Comptroller General Jean-Baptiste Colbert—undertook another, very different initiative directed at the perceived evils of litigation. As early as 1664, Colbert wrote to the king, complaining that law produced "chicanery," which in turn, "occupies a million men and gnaws away at a million others," thus "reducing them to... misery."[25] And indeed, the scholarly consensus is that early-modern French men and women were in fact quite litigious.[26] De la Roche's complaints about excessive litigation are thus hardly surprising. What requires explanation is his proposed remedy—or rather his insistence that this remedy marked some kind of radical reform.

Despite the existence of a sizable and growing scholarly literature, there is still far too little that we know about the nature of dispute resolution in early modern France—and in particular, about practices of arbitration and mediation. Part of the problem is that many such practices took place outside the courtroom and never resulted in formalized agreements of any kind—or at least none that were registered with a court and thereby preserved in what ultimately became state archives. Moreover, while it was possible to notarize arbitral awards and then register them with the court (such that failure to comply could lead to court-based enforcement), many disputants never took this additional step. There is thus a dearth of documentation.[27] Also problematic is the existence of what appear to be signif-

24. Ibid., 104.

25. Roebuck, 47 (quoting Colbert's letter).

26. For a summary of the literature discussing "early modern litigiousness" throughout Western Europe, including especially France, see Rafe Blaufarb, "Conflict and Compromise: *Communauté* and *Seigneurie* in Early Modern Provence," *The Journal of Modern History* 82 (2010), 520–23.

27. Zoë A. Schneider, *The King's Bench: Bailiwick Magistrates and Local Governance in Normandy, 1670–1740* (Rochester, N.Y.: University of Rochester Press, 2008), 181; Blaufarb, 532. But see Jeremy Hayhoe, *Enlightened Feudalism: Seigneurial Justice and Village*

icant regional differences in the nature and extent of both arbitration and mediation. Scholars studying different provinces have thus reached different conclusions about such key questions as the frequency of arbitration and mediation vis-à-vis formal litigation and the extent to which arbitral awards were enforced by formal court judgment.[28]

But despite evidence of regional variability, the overall portrait that scholars have drawn of dispute resolution in early modern France is one that suggests that—whether in Burgundy, Normandy, or Provence—methods of both arbitration and mediation were very commonly employed. Moreover, those responsible for conducting arbitration and mediation appear to have been precisely the kinds of people whom de la Roche was trying to target—namely, various "kinds of local authorities," such as "priests, . . . dames, sieurs, or other local notables."[29] The surviving documentation and regional variability are such that we cannot conclude whether these practices of arbitration and mediation complied with de la Roche's proposed methods in every respect. But in key ways, his contemporaries appear to have been already doing what he was so insistent in presenting as a radical plan for reform.

Society in Eighteenth-Century Northern Burgundy (Rochester, N.Y.: University of Rochester Press, 2008), 116 (suggesting that such court-based ratification was common in Burgundy).

28. Hayhoe's study of Burgundy suggests that formal litigation was much more common than arbitration and that arbitration, when practiced, frequently led to court-based judgments. Hayhoe, 114–20. In contrast, Schneider's study of Normandy suggests that arbitration "dwarfed the activities of the official courts" and that such arbitral awards were rarely ratified by court order. Schneider, 181–84. Brigitte Maillard, in turn, emphasizes in her discussion of the Loire Valley the extent to which arbitration and mediation took place within the formal court system. Brigitte Maillard, "Les hautes justices seigneuriales, agents actifs des régulations sociales dans les campagnes de la moyenne vallée de la Loire au XVIIIe siècle," in *Les justices de village: administration et justice locale de la fin du moyen âge à la révolution* (Rennes: Presses Universitaires de Rennes, 2002), 294–95.

29. Schneider, 182. See also Hayhoe, 120. Although Hayhoe's account focuses primarily on the eighteenth century, other scholarship suggests that the nature and prevalence of arbitration and mediation did not change significantly during the transition from the late seventeenth century into the eighteenth. See generally Schneider; Blaufarb; Benoît Garnot, "Justice, infrajustice, parajustice et extrajustice dans la France de l'Ancien Régime," *Crime, Histoire & Sociétés* 4 (2000), 103–20 (providing holistic accounts of dispute-resolution practices that extend from the mid-to-late-seventeenth through eighteenth centuries).

Is it possible that de la Roche simply had no understanding of the contemporary dispute-resolution landscape? This seems highly improbable. His manuscript discusses details of arbitration practice and legislation that suggest a significant degree of familiarity with the rules and realities of dispute resolution. But if ignorance is not the explanation, then what is? De la Roche's insistence that there was a significant divide between the formal justice system and the informal methods of arbitration and mediation that he recommended provides a hint. And it does so precisely because scholarship on dispute-resolution in early-modern France has firmly rejected the existence of such a divide. Jeremy Hayhoe, for example, observes that judges in Burgundy frequently engaged in mediation rather than judgment (or rather issued judgments that simply reflected the results of mediations they had conducted).[30] Similarly, Zoë Schneider notes that arbitration in Normandy was often undertaken by the very same lawyers and judges responsible for operating the local courts, such that "[t]his blending of personnel" led to a partial "merging of community practices into the royal system" of courts.[31] And Rafe Blaufarb claims that in Provence, arbitration and formal litigation worked hand in hand, such that the norm was long cycles of renegotiation pursued through some combination of "formal lawsuits and out-of-court settlement," with one constantly giving way to the other.[32]

Given that litigation, on the one hand, and arbitration and mediation, on the other, commonly intermingled in practice, de la Roche's insistence that they were radically distinct may in fact constitute his core intervention. His goal, in other words, seems to have been to delineate clearly between these (actually intersecting) practices. But if so, why? The timing of his publication is suggestive. Just as the book was first issued in 1666, Colbert was in the process of launching his massive and remarkably successful campaign to reform French law with an eye towards producing greater standardization, and thus centralized control—a campaign whose first real fruit took the form of the Civil Procedure Ordinance of 1667. While the Ordinance itself was not formally promulgated until 1667, the law reform commission responsible for drafting it was appointed as far back as May

30. Hayhoe, 123–24.

31. Schneider, 181–82.

32. Blaufarb, 532, 543. See also Garnot, 110 (arguing much the same concerning Old Regime France as a whole).

1665 and began to meet regularly that September. Those sitting on the commission did not work in isolation but, to the contrary, widely solicited the views of interested parties—including by appointing officers, known as *maîtres des requêtes*, to go out to the country's leading royal courts (the *parlements*) to seek guidance and respond to concerns.[33] Elite contemporaries, like de la Roche, thus likely had opportunities to become familiar with the commission's activities and aspirations well prior to the Ordinance's formal promulgation in 1667.

Within this context, one way of reading *L'arbitre charitable*—and, in particular, de la Roche's effort to promote arbitration and mediation at the expense of litigation—is as a critique of Colbert's reform plans and the ambitions for top-down, centralized control that motivated them. As the Preamble to the Civil Procedure Ordinance would go on to detail, the fact that procedure differed across the country "brings ruin on families by the multiplicity of proceedings, the cost of the actions and the inconsistency of judgments."[34] Accordingly, the ordinance sought to "establish[] uniformity of procedure in all our courts and sessions."[35] Uniformity of procedure would encourage uniformity in the application of substantive law, thus eliminating the inequities of arbitrariness and the costs of unpredictability, while also facilitating the monarchy's efforts to establish centralized, absolutist rule. In contrast, de la Roche's plea for arbitration and mediation aimed to preserve a long, corporatist tradition of local pockets of power and self-regulation. In relying on dispersed local elites, rather than a centralized, top-down system, and in endowing these actors with a great deal of

33. Roebuck, 49–50; Alfred Aymé, *Colbert, promoteur des grandes ordonnances de Louis XIV* (Paris: W. Remquet, Goupy et Cie, 1860), 13–20. Roebuck is wise to suggest that there is likely some connection between the appearance of de la Roche's book in 1666 and Colbert's Civil Procedure Ordinance one year later. But his argument that de la Roche's goal was to persuade the Ordinance's drafters to include language encouraging arbitration lacks evidentiary support and fails to account for many of the particulars of *L'arbitre charitable*, including the text's most distinctive feature—namely, its focus on the interrelation between status, on the one hand, and practices of arbitration and mediation, on the other.

34. Roebuck, 51 (quoting the preamble to the Ordinance). See also *Ordonnance de Louis XIV, roy de France et de Navarre, donnée à S. Germain en Laye au mois d'avril 1667* (Paris: Chez les associez choisis par ordre de sa majesté pour l'impression de ses nouvelles ordonnances, 1667), 2.

35. Roebuck, 51; *Ordonnance*, 2.

case-specific discretion, arbitration and mediation marked a very different vision of justice than did Colbert's new, absolutist plan.

But it was not only the top-down, centralized nature of the formal legal system urged by Colbert that so troubled de la Roche about contemporary litigation. At least as worrisome, he suggested, was the relatively recent (and increasingly harmful) rise of what he called the "unfortunate *Vénalité des Charges*"—namely, venal officeholding, including within the judiciary.[36] The royal court system had been profoundly reshaped by the 1604 implementation of the Paulette tax, which entitled royal officeholders to bequeath their offices to their offspring. While the Paulette did not apply in the seigneurial courts, judgeships in these as well were not infrequently sold for a substantial fee.[37] The end result was the rise of an increasingly hereditary judiciary operating under little supervision and largely immune to discipline.[38] Although the monarchy repeatedly sought to regain control of its courts by eliminating the practice of venal officeholding, its desperate need for readily available funds, combined with the growing power of the entrenched interests it had created were such that it could do little to promote meaningful reform.

Seeking to avoid royal wrath (as well as the ill will of censors who might prohibit the publication of his book), de la Roche claimed that his critique of venality was aimed only at noblemen (and thus at the sale of judgeships in the seigneurial, rather than royal courts). As he observed, when the French kings introduced the practice of venality as a key tool of state finance, they did so "in spite of themselves"—driven by their need to finance "the misfortune of wars."[39] But while the kings adopted venality against their better judgment and because they had no choice but to do so, the noblemen who followed suit had no such excuse for their actions. The embrace of venality "may be excused in our Sovereigns but not in their Lords."[40] Indeed, de la Roche insisted, "the wars have not altered the nature

36. De la Roche, 178.

37. The extent to which seigneurial judgeships were sold appears to vary on a regional basis as well. Hayhoe, 35–36; Schneider, 130–32.

38. Schneider argues, however, that at least in Normandy, the selling of judgeships did not lead them to become hereditary. Schneider, 131–32.

39. De la Roche, 178.

40. Ibid.

of their holding of estates, fiefs, and jurisdictions," which they continued to hold as vassals of the king.[41] As such, one of their main obligations—one that ran with the land—was "to provide justice free, as they did during the term of the first grant to them."[42]

But while de la Roche was careful to exonerate the king, his critique of a court system grounded in venality would seem to apply just as much to royal as to seigneurial judges. As he reminded readers, the traditional role of the king was to do justice—with justice understood to be the personal, discretion-laden equity of the arbitrator and mediator, rather than the formal, law-bound judgment that Colbert envisioned. Thus, Saint Louis, "one of the greatest of our kings," took "singular pleasure in rendering justice to his people and in finding ways of settling their differences"—and in so acting, he assumed the role of "arbitrator."[43] But under the new system of venality that had emerged, the court system had ceased to provide justice as an extension of the sovereign's status and power (and of that bestowed by him on a noble elite), but instead simply for monetary gain. Calling for arbitration and mediation was thus a way of trying to return to this older vision of justice—to a world in which, as argued by the historian Michel Antoine, the king's function was to serve as a "royal dispenser of justice."[44] In such a world, de la Roche claimed, "the responsibilities, the discussions, the advice and the good management of their estate, and the protection of their vassals' interests would be more important to [noblemen] than the prices for which they could sell their offices."[45]

What exactly was so terrible about the new venal approach to justice? Part of the answer was that the sale of judgeships led to the appointment of incompetent officials: "The mischief has got so bad that there are some who can neither read nor write."[46] So too, de la Roche complained, judges who expended a fortune to purchase their offices were interested in recouping their costs and making a profit—a mentality that, in turn, encouraged

41. Ibid.

42. Ibid.

43. Ibid., 206

44. Michel Antoine, "La monarchie française de François Ier à Louis XVI," in *Les monarchies* (Paris: Presses Universitaires de France, 1986), 185–208.

45. De la Roche, 178.

46. Ibid., 180.

them to search for ways of charging (usually excessive) fees. Justice had thus been transformed into an "enormous number of locusts which feed on the people."[47] But there are hints of yet a third critique of these new practices of venal officeholding—one that reflected contemporary anxieties about the growing commercialization of the French state in an era in which the monarchy was becoming increasingly dependent on commercial wealth and finance.[48] Since doing justice was central to traditional conceptions of sovereign power and status, the notion that anyone with the requisite funds could buy a judgeship suggested the possibility of a frightening upending of the corporatist hierarchy that had long structured Old Regime society. Thus, for example, while noblemen had once understood that by virtue of their status they were obligated to "render justice free to their vassals," the newly commercialized conception of justice that had arisen had led them to forget basic principles of *noblesse oblige*.[49] In de la Roche's view, one of the great virtues of arbitration and mediation was that these practices thrived on—and indeed, served to reinforce—status differentiation.

L'arbitre charitable is premised on the assumption that arbitration and mediation operate most effectively when the disputants differ in status and thus power. As de la Roche explained, "[s]ettlement between equals is more difficult than with superiors or inferiors."[50] When the disputants were equal, each one was afraid that showing a willingness to arbitrate or mediate and thereby settle out of court would be read as evidence of inferiority, leading "the opposing party" to "boast that the other is afraid and is begging for mercy."[51] In contrast, when the disputants occupied clearly different rungs in the status hierarchy, there was no risk that the mere fact of settlement might somehow change the balance of power. To the contrary, differences in status afforded guidelines concerning the kinds of disputing behavior expected of each party. As set forth in the title to Chapter XIX, "the Lower Classes and the Weak can usually settle any Lawsuits they may

47. Ibid.

48. Henry C. Clark, "Commerce, the Virtues, and the Public Sphere in Early-Seventeenth-Century France," *French Historical Studies* 21 (1998), 415–40.

49. De la Roche, 181.

50. Ibid., 191.

51. Ibid.

have with those more powerful than the[y], and... they ought to do so."[52] It was the weaker man's obligation to grovel (and thereby reaffirm his own inferiority), just as it was the powerful man's obligation to show mercy to the weak (and thereby reaffirm his position of high standing). Accordingly, de la Roche advised the man of lower standing to "address himself directly to the lord in writing," and beg that the latter desist in his claim: "Explain to him by letter... that you have far too much respect for him to want to have a fight with him; but, because he is just and equitable, and would never wish to crush the weak, that you beg him to name arbitrators...."[53] The powerful man, in turn, would likely agree, since it was a mark of high status to bestow compassion on the weak and the poor:

> [H]ow can a great lord, duke, marquis, or other, who is more powerful than his opponent, dare to refuse to come to a settlement with the weaker party who has begged him, who has offered to pay or do whatever the arbitrators award? If the great lord should refuse, he will be taken for... a scoundrel who wants to devour the poor....[54]

Even to the extent that the dispute was between great lords, de la Roche claimed that status was key to successful arbitration and mediation. All great lords had an incentive to settle litigation quickly for the simple reason that, as everyone recognized, "[w]hat is more undignified than a great lord with a lawsuit?"[55] Noblemen were meant to fight real battles, not to waste their time on an "unhappy war of the desk."[56] Moreover, in arbitrating and mediating disputes between themselves, great lords could take advantage of small differences in status to facilitate settlement. If the action of great lords "is against their inferiors, they have only to ask them to settle and they will agree with pleasure: the weak want peace with the stronger."[57] But so too, great lords could settle with their superiors by reminding the latter that it was their obligation as men of high status to try

52. Ibid., 188.
53. Ibid.
54. Ibid., 189.
55. Ibid., 182.
56. Ibid.
57. Ibid., 183.

"to find a peaceful solution" and that, as long as they made such an effort, "neither equals nor inferiors will be able to complain."[58]

De la Roche's commitment to developing a system of arbitration and mediation that was deeply attuned to—and capable of reinforcing—the fine-grained forms of status differentiation put at risk by absolutist standardization and growing commercialization is perhaps most obvious, however, in the sample forms that he provided at the end of his manual. Among these forms is a series of "summons[es] to arbitration."[59] De la Roche included three in total, each carefully calibrated to the relative status of the two disputants. The first was for "Arbitration between Equals," and it afforded the standard, default language to which additional verbiage would have to be added, if the disputants in fact differed in status.[60] A second sample form was for the situation in which the summons is directed "from a Superior to an Inferior."[61] In this circumstance, the superior had to include language indicating that it was precisely because he "is more powerful than [the inferior] is, in property, credit or connexions" that he was seeking arbitration.[62] More particularly, "it was "to show that the said deponent does not intend to take advantage of his birth, property, credit or connexions, and that his only desire is to preserve what is his, [that] the said deponent makes an offer to agree to arbitrators &c."[63] Finally, the third summons was to be sent by "an Inferior to one more Powerful than h[e]" and thus contained language by means of which the inferior pleaded for mercy:

> [I]n so far as the pursuit of the said action will cause the ruin of the said [proponent of arbitration] and of his poor family, who have not the property, nor the credit, nor connexions of the said [superior], the said proponent begs and entreats him to terminate the said action promptly, without trouble and without cost, and to have the charity to nominate arbitrators, &c.[64]

58. Ibid., 184.
59. Ibid., 233–35.
60. Ibid., 233.
61. Ibid., 234.
62. Ibid.
63. Ibid.
64. Ibid., 235.

To some extent, of course, all communication in the Old Regime was tailored so as to acknowledge and reinforce status differentiation. In this respect, de la Roche's guidance concerning summonses for purposes of arbitration was of a kind with broader trends reflected elsewhere, including both practices of letter-writing and pleadings in formal litigation. But de la Roche believed that arbitration and mediation were distinctive in their dependence on (and concomitant tendency to reinforce) status hierarchy; and this was precisely their appeal. The local control and discretion that undergirded the old Regime's corporatist hierarchy—and that the new Civil Procedure Ordinance and venal officeholding threatened to undermine—were the very lifeblood of practices of arbitration and mediation.

As time would tell, de la Roche's struggle proved largely for naught. In ushering in a new era of rule of law, the French Revolution brought to fruition the absolutist monarchy's longstanding goal of top-down centralization and standardization. While the monarchy itself never aimed to achieve equality under the law, its efforts to subjugate the entirety of French society to centralized, state control served, as de Tocqueville recognized long ago, to undermine status differentiation, thereby facilitating the revolutionary project of equality.[65] The end result, we can see in retrospect, was to make arbitration and mediation troubling in a way that had never before been the case. What was once a natural corollary of status differentiation—of *noblesse oblige*—was thus reframed as a kind of egalitarian, bottom-up justice of the people. This can be seen most clearly in the figure of the *justice de paix*, created by the revolutionaries in 1790 and imagined as reinforcing norms of democratic equality by virtue of the fact that he was a layman elected by locals to help mediate their disputes.[66] In reality, however, recent scholarship suggests that the *justices de paix* were a carryover from a long tradition of seigneurial justice, such that an established institutional apparatus (including clerks and files) was rechristened, but

65. Alexis de Tocqueville, *The Old Regime and the French Revolution*, trans. Stuart Gilbert (New York: Doubleday, 1955).

66. Amalia D. Kessler, "Marginalization and Myth: The Corporatist Roots of France's Forgotten Elective Judiciary," *American Journal of Comparative Law* 58 (2010), 698–701; Jean Léonnet, "Une Creation de l'Assemblée Constituante: La Conciliation judiciaire," in *Une autre justice: Contributions à l'histoire de la justice sous la Révolution française* (Paris: Fayard, 1989), 267–81, at 273; Isser Woloch, *The New Regime: Transformations of the French Civic Order, 1789–1820s* (New York: W. W. Norton, 1994), 307–08.

otherwise largely preserved. Moreover, in practice, these courts appear to have relied extensively on traditions of deference within the community of the same sort that had long facilitated seigneurial judges' efforts to mediate local disputes.[67] As this suggests, although we moderns have found ways to preserve arbitration and mediation, we are much less willing than our early-modern predecessors to acknowledge how these practices may thrive on (and reinforce) differences in status and power. While de la Roche was able to imagine a world full of charitable arbitrators delivering justice for free as a corollary of their positions of high standing, our arbitrators and mediators most decidedly work for a fee—even as we tell ourselves that justice is resolutely equal.[68]

67. Antoine Follain, "De la justice seigneuriale à la justice de paix," in *Une justice de proximité: la justice de paix, 1790–1958*, ed. Jacques-Guy Petit (Paris: Presses Universitaires de France, 2003), 19–33; Serge Bianchi, "La justice de paix pendant la Révolution, acquis et perspectives," in *Une justice de proximité*, 39; Gilles Rouet, "La justice de paix en France entre 1834 et 1950: une exploration spatiale," in *Une justice de proximité*, 98–99; Steven G. Reinhardt, *Justice in the Sarladais, 1770–1790* (Baton Rouge: Louisiana State University Press, 1991), 150–52.

68. For a discussion of the complex intersection between status and practices of arbitration and mediation in the Progressive Era United States (and its enduring legacy), see Amalia D. Kessler, "Arbitration and Americanization: The Paternalism of Progressive Procedural Reform," *Yale Law Journal* 124 (2015), 2961–73, 2991–93.

Lights Hidden Under *Bushel's Case*

Thomas A. Green[1]

Some forty years ago, Charlie Donahue created a course which he titled "Law, Morals and Society." Designed for undergraduates, and situated among the offerings of the University of Michigan's interdisciplinary Medieval and Renaissance Collegium, the course reflected the approach to doing history that, as this volume recognizes, Charlie has followed throughout his long and enormously influential career as scholar, teacher, lecturer, and irrepressible master of well-timed interventions during conference-panel discussion periods. "LMS" was composed of four units. Charlie, who taught two of them, led off with the legal basis for the deposition of Richard II; I followed with the law of homicide in medieval England; Charlie returned with a unit on the law of marriage; Tom Tentler anchored the relay with the law relating to witchcraft. In each unit, we began with documents that expressed the law involved, and just as the students began to feel comfortable with those documents and the way what they expressed seemingly helped to organize a bit of the premodern world, we subjected the law to an investigation based on political, social and cultural contexts that rudely upset initial conceptions of how that bit of the world was organized—of just what constituted the law, and in what way whatever was the law can be said to have gone about its organizing work. A very Charlie sort of course.

1. I thank Elizabeth Papp Kamali and Michael Lobban for insightful comments on an earlier draft of this essay and Brittany Harrison for excellent editorial help.

At the time, I was teaching a seminar on the history of the criminal trial jury in England and America. Jury independence, and even jury nullification, played a large role. Hence my interest in *Bushel's Case* and, thanks in large part to Charlie, my interest in the light that its context shone on the opinion. So what *was* its context? A very Charlie sort of question, but I don't recall what Charlie said one ought to do if it didn't appear to have an answer. Surely he didn't advise turning one's musings about it into a *Festschrift* essay! Mea culpa, Charlie.

THE TEXT INTRODUCED

Bushel's Case (1670)[2] was mysterious to me some thirty years ago, when I devoted a long chapter to the case and its context, and I am even more perplexed by it today.[3] That it was a mystery was not quite my point in 1985; it is, however, the point of this brief return to the case by way of comment on some recent work that aims to shed light on the opinion of John Vaughan, Chief Judge of Common Pleas, writing for all of the active high judges of England. Directed at the opinion itself, which held that jurors could not be fined or imprisoned on the grounds that their verdict was against fact or law, the new light plays on the soil out of which the opinion arose. We are left to speculate about whether, and to what extent, what the light reveals actually nourished one of the stateliest of growths in the forest of English law.

On the face of it, there is little mystery as to the reasons Vaughan adduced for his holding. A judge could not be certain jurors had gone against the facts as they perceived them; therefore, as law arises from the facts, the judge could not be certain jurors went against the law. Why could the judge not know jurors abused their fact-finding authority? Because the jurors might have out-of-court knowledge of their own regarding the facts or reliability of witnesses in a particular case; because the jurors might reach a different understanding than the judge with respect to in-court testimony ("even then the Judge and jury might honestly differ in the result from the

2. Vaughan 135, 124; *English Reports* 1006 (1670).

3. Thomas Andrew Green, *Verdict According to Conscience: Perspectives on the English Criminal Trial Jury, 1200–1800* (Chicago: University of Chicago Press, 1985), ch. 6.

evidence"[4]), and it was the jurors' understanding that counted. Why was it the jurors' understanding that counted? Because the common law, by long tradition, proceeded by trial by jury, which would be a waste of time if judges could supplant jurors' understandings with their own, and it would be unreasonable to make jurors swear to what they did not believe.[5]

This seems tolerably clear as a set of general propositions that effectively establish a plenary rule. All cases short of those involving provable ministerial wrongdoing—i.e., verdicts tainted by bribery, coercion, etc.—are shielded from inquiry by the very logic of such a rule. There might be thought a weakness here. If the assumption is that jurors are not permitted to reject the judge's instructions as to law, why is their compliance with that instruction not subject to investigation? Possibly it is subject, up to a point—by having jurors state on oath that they did not reject those instructions (According to the logic of the rule, such an oath would leave no basis for certainty of their non-compliance). But why only up to that point? Why not require jurors to state the facts found (or the opinions they entertained as to witness credibility) that led them to acquittal within the parameters of the instructions? The answer, one supposes, is that judges can't judge the veracity of such sworn responses, for the very reasons underlying the rule. There is also the possibility of an unstated broader consideration here: such close questioning might amount to a form of coercion. Jurors might be led into swearing what they did not believe "though the [induced/coerced] verdict be right."[6]

The breadth and conclusiveness of the ruling in *Bushel's Case* are apparent when one considers the immediate context in which the case arose. Edward Bushel was one of the jurors imprisoned (until they paid a heavy fine) for their verdict of acquittal in the prosecution, in 1670, of William Penn and William Mead for unlawful assembly and disturbance of the peace. The two Quaker preachers had preached in Gracechurch Street, London, and had not desisted when ordered to do so, at which point a tu-

4. Vaughan, 147; *English Reports*, 1012.

5. Vaughan, 143; *English Reports* 1010; Vaughan, 148; *English Reports*, 1012–13. Also, importantly—but without explanation—Vaughan ventured that to "omit" or "abolish" the criminal trial jury would be "the greater mischief to the people, than to abolish them in civil tryals." Vaughan, 144; *English Reports*, 1010.

6. Vaughan, 148; *English Reports*, 1013.

mult had ensued. According to those trial accounts that we have (mainly one by Penn[7] and one by Samuel Starling, Lord Mayor of London, who presided at the trial),[8] Penn questioned the law underlying the indictment and exhorted his jurors to adjudge that law insufficient, against the laws of England.[9] Penn was removed from the courtroom proper for his statements and behavior; within his hearing, the trial continued, over his outcries from the bale dock to which he had been consigned. The jury divided, eight for guilty, four not, and was sent out to reconsider, whereupon the jurors returned a verdict of "Guilty of speaking in Gracechurch Street." Sent out again, upon orders to reach a general verdict, the jurors agreed on acquittal. Bushel, deemed one of the leaders of a court-room insurrection, refused to pay the fine and sued out a writ of habeas corpus addressed to the Court of Common Pleas, Vaughan presiding. After some doubts—Vaughan expressing them for his own part—about whether Common Pleas was the proper venue for such a writ, the Court accepted the case based upon the return to the writ, which alleged that the prisoners had, as jurors, found against the fact and against the law. After a plenary session with the other common law judges (save for John Kelyng, Chief Judge of King's Bench, whose illness had sidelined him), Vaughan authored the ruling outlined above.

It is, I suppose, imaginable that the jurors could agree only that Penn and Mead had preached in Gracechurch Street, but not that they had caused an unlawful assembly or a disturbance of the peace, even under the law as it was understood by the bench. One doesn't need to blot out Penn's exhortations regarding the law, or the possibility that they had some effect upon the jurors. One might suppose it possible that those pleas to the jurors merely reinforced their sincere inclination to view the facts as unproved. Or reinforced their doubts about the credibility of crown witnesses, or their susceptibility to believe out-of-court evidence—e.g., statements by some of those present at the preaching that had come to the attention of some of the

7. William Penn and William Mead, *The People's Antient and Just Liberties* (London: n.p. 1670), printed in *State Trials*, 6.951–1000. (References hereinafter are to *State Trials*.)

8. Sir Samuel Starling, *An Answer to the Seditious and Scandalous Pamphlet, entitled, The Trial of W. Penn and W. Mead* (London: W.G., 1671).

9. *State Trials*, 6.959.

jurors. Conceptually, at least, it is possible that Penn and Mead's case fell within the logic of the ruling in *Bushel's Case*, including, importantly, the logic that an inquiry to determine whether or not it did was itself precluded. The rule in *Bushel's Case* was that conclusive.

Wider Contexts Introduced

Two recent and important discussions of *Bushel's Case* attempt to explain Vaughan's opinion—either what he really had in mind or what led him, perhaps subconsciously, to think about jury trial in the way that he did. Neither account denies the possible influence of the immediate political and legal context that scholars have sometimes emphasized. The main (and by now familiar) elements of that context include: worries about the restored monarchy's manipulation of the judiciary and suppression of liberties; the spate of jury finings in the 1660s (King's Bench Judges Hyde, Twisden, and Kelyng being the most commonly cited); Commons' censure of Kelyng on grounds of fining and disrespect for Magna Carta; Vaughan's leading role in Commons' anti-fining campaign.[10] What the new accounts intend, rather, is the supplying of a philosophical framework for Vaughan's and others' opposition to fining, one that helps to explain that opposition and is not merely the plaything of the politics of the day.

James Whitman comes at the opinion from the perspective of what he terms a "moral comfort" rule, that, from the Middle Ages forward, applied to judges and jurors: according to theological prescript, one's soul was imperiled by wrongful conviction in cases involving the blood sanction (and perhaps even more broadly), but honest belief that guilt was beyond a reasonable doubt protected one against such peril.[11] This, Whitman claims, is key to understanding the importance of, and the respect accorded to, verdicts according to conscience throughout the common law period, at least into the eighteenth century, and especially in felony, which was almost uni-

10. This background is discussed in, e.g., Green, *Verdict According to Conscience*, 208–21; John A. Phillips and Thomas C. Thompson, "Jurors v. Judges in Later Stuart England: The Penn/Mead Trial and *Bushell's Case*," *Law and Inequality* 4 (1986), 189–229.

11. James Q. Whitman, *The Origins of Reasonable Doubt: Theological Roots of the Criminal Trial* (New Haven: Yale University Press, 2008), ch. 6.

formly capital. There is great power in this account. The challenge it poses for our understanding of the medieval English criminal law is only now being met.[12] Whitman invites the reader to consider Vaughan's opinion in light of this longstanding context, the theology of "moral comfort," still, he argues, both identifiable and broadly influential in late-seventeenth-century legal-moral thought. It helps us to understand judicial reticence to take the verdict-rendering act into their own hands; to see that the creation and retention of trial by jury had a deep underlying logic—indeed, a moral dimension; to recognize that the too-close questioning of jurors' motivations threatened to disturb what was thought best left between them and their own consciences—that is, between them and God. Armed with these insights, we are able to appreciate Vaughan's invocation of what might otherwise seem an insincere—because no-longer often applicable—claim that jurors might (for all the judge can ever know) have brought to bear private knowledge in their fact-finding process.

Kevin Crosby, too, focuses on "the role of conscience in jury deliberations" in his enterprising article, "Bushell's Case and the Juror's Soul."[13] Crosby recognizes the foundational importance of Whitman's work, but he sees Whitman's perspective as limited:

> Whitman's focus on the moral dangers of judging, and the concomitant need to find ways of soothing judges' consciences, means that the focus in his account is on how criminal justice systems have coaxed cautious judges (which here includes jurors) into convicting. This is an important perspective. However, it downplays the capacity of the later seventeenth-century criminal jury to do something other than what the other actors involved in the administration of the criminal law would have liked it to do.[14]

The period in fact witnessed a flowering of jury-independence theory, a concept of the jury wherein the individual juror's conscience—his "soul"—was paramount: "*Bushell's Case,* taken together with the concur-

12. See Elizabeth Papp Kamali, "A Felonious State of Mind: Mens Rea in Thirteenth- and Fourteenth-Century England" (Ph.D. dissertation, University of Michigan, 2015).

13. Kevin Crosby, "Bushell's Case and the Juror's Soul," *The Journal of Legal History* 33 (2012), 251–290, at 253.

14. Ibid., 253–54.

rent pamphlet literature, offers a positive model of jury trial which downplays the jury's relationship either with the judge's or with the sovereign's laws in favour of a focus on the juryman's soul."[15] Once we see this, we see "moral comfort" relative to convicting a defendant as only one aspect of a verdict according to conscience at the time of *Bushell's Case* and of less importance than the contemporary reconceptualization of the relationships among institutions of governance. We see that jury theory now embraced a positive and constitutive idea of the "juror's soul." This development marked a significant departure from traditional theory, according to which the jury was understood precisely in relation to the monarch and/or judge. Crosby draws clear contrasts between late-seventeenth-century jury theory and those of Coke (who emphasized the role of the judge in relation to the jury) and Hobbes (who emphasized the role of the sovereign), and whose own great differences pale alongside the differences between them and the "soul"-based radical jury independence that was to follow: jurors' primary duty was to themselves, not to the bench or crown. We are invited not only to read Vaughan's opinion in light of this new model of jury trial and jury theory, but to see that opinion as expounding the new positions.[16]

It is useful, I think, to view Whitman's and Crosby's approaches to the context of Vaughan's opinion in *Bushel's Case* both separately and conjointly. These are both highly sophisticated, intricately woven accounts of jury theory extending over lengthy periods, each deserving fuller consideration than it will receive here, as my main objective is to think out loud about their relation to Vaughan's opinion. Whitman begins his English-side account with the thirteenth century and carries down to modern times, focusing on *Bushel's Case* at one turn in his story. Crosby, though aiming at and ending with that case, interprets late seventeenth-century jury theory in relation to currents of that theory dating from the fifteenth century. Crosby's account may be said to fit into Whitman's at the macro level: conscience and duty in the eyes of God forms a background for him. But his study grows outward from there. Crosby postulates that from the concern identified by Whitman, and other more political-theory-based strains of thought, came a positive conception of jury independence that

15. Ibid., Abstract.
16. Ibid., 270–80.

affected the rendering of verdicts generally in criminal cases. The implications of this difference seem modest when one focuses on their more or less equal concern with what they take to be a distinctly contemporary resonance in Vaughan's invocation of conscience. They differ, however, in the particular contemporary writings upon which they focus in providing context for that invocation (a matter not discussed here). As already noted, their differing approaches produce different proposed insights into either what Vaughan was really thinking or why Vaughan—perhaps unselfconsciously—came out the way he did.

THE TEXT IN RELATION TO THE PROPOSED CONTEXT(S)

Personal Knowledge

Even one who would assert that the true basis for the opinion remains a matter of Vaughan's *own* personal knowledge would quickly agree that jurors' personal knowledge played a significant role in the Chief Judge's thinking. The questions that historians are left with have to do with how Vaughan mainly defined personal knowledge and his reasons for giving various forms of that knowledge real or apparent weight. The classic form of such knowledge—and the one that seems to dominate the opinion—is pre-formed, out-of-court knowledge concerning the facts of the case at hand. These might be physical or mental facts, that is, facts about what the defendant did or thought that were not brought forward at the trial. They might also be "background" facts about the defendant or witnesses that a juror (or jurors) thought affected the credibility of what parties said in court.[17]

This kind of knowledge has obvious roots in "self-informing," long assumed to be a staple of early-jury process. It is generally agreed that by the late seventeenth century—indeed, well before—self-informing in the literal sense was a relatively rare feature of criminal process. But if one expands the literal meaning to something like an awareness of community-based understandings—even rumors—the situation is more difficult to assess. Pre-trial process, including coroners' inquests (in homicide), depositions, and grand jury proceedings, yielded information available to the bench

17. See especially Vaughan, 147; *English Reports*, 1012.

and, where read aloud in court, to jurors, but those records were not taken to include most discordant minority views, including some that might have been in circulation. Of course, they needn't be comprehensive so long as jurors were legally bound to render a verdict solely on the evidence given at the trial. But just where such a rule stood in that regard as of the late seventeenth century is open to question. For his part, Vaughan did not deem there to be such a rule; that's the basis of his stated reliance—to whatever extent genuine[18]—on this kind of personal knowledge.

The second form of personal knowledge might better be termed a right to make an independent assessment (interpretation) of in-court testimony (sworn and unsworn). This assessment involved what facts were truly in play, which in turn involved an assessment of narratives and, importantly, of the credibility of narrators. The two forms of personal knowledge overlap at a point: that is, where pre-formed knowledge/impressions colored assessment of in-court narratives/narrators. But Vaughan can certainly be

18. Focusing on Vaughan's heavy reliance on the literal form of personal knowledge, John Langbein has characterized Vaughan's opinion as "wilfully anachronistic" and "dishonest nonsense." John H. Langbein, "The Criminal Trial before the Lawyers," *University of Chicago Law Review* 45 (1978), 299, nn. 105 and 298; see also John H. Langbein, *The Origins of Adversary Criminal Trial* (New York: Oxford University Press, 2003), 324. Langbein aptly criticizes Vaughan's handling of sixteenth-century precedent regarding jurors' personal knowledge and rightly mocks Vaughan's hardly credible claim, that (in his own day) "the better and greater part of the evidence may be wholly unknown [to the judge]; and this may happen in most cases, and often doth...." Vaughan, 149; *English Reports*, 1013. Langbein, *Criminal Trial before the Lawyers*, 299, n. 105. Langbein also notes contemporary evidence for the fining of jurors which Vaughan omits from his opinion, and he explains the opinion largely in terms of its political context. Ibid., 299–30, 106–108. Those who have recently sought to relate Vaughan's text to a broader (and more high-minded) context have not fully rebutted Langbein's arguments for treating it as mere pretext. Whitman, *Origins of Reasonable Doubt*, 176–78 makes a compelling case that Vaughan's stress on out-of-court personal knowledge fit into a well-known tradition in moral theology writings that still carried weight and that related closely to "moral comfort" concerns. Vaughan's claim that such knowledge was a commonplace, however, strikes a distinctly false note and perhaps calls into question Vaughan's motivations in effecting this fit. In any event, as the text that follows suggests, I myself wonder whether this form of personal knowledge was in fact Vaughan's main concern. For an important article on the centrality of literal personal knowledge in post-*Bushel's Case* jury writings, see Simon Stern, "Between Local Knowledge and National Politics: Debating Rationales for Jury Nullification After *Bushel's Case*," *Yale Law Journal* 111 (2002), 1815–2002.

read to countenance the second form as operating entirely separately from the first. Such a reading appears to rest upon the famous words:

> A man cannot see by another's eye, nor hear by another's ear, no more can a man conclude or infer the thing to be resolved by another's understanding or reasoning; and though the verdict be right the jury give, yet their not being assured it is so from their own understanding, are foresworn, at least *in foro conscientiae*.[19]

It rests, as well, on Vaughan's observation that, even were the jury to have no evidence other than that deposed in court, even then the Judge and jury might honestly differ in the result from the evidence, as well as two Judges may, which often happens.[20]

Vaughan's language here clearly embraces "understanding" of what is seen and heard, and might go no further than what one would consider sheer cognitive and/or intuitive powers, thus not embracing assessment based on credibility. Or, more broadly, it might embrace credibility based on tone and demeanor. But this particular language does not embrace credibility that was based (as other and more prominent parts of his opinion are) on out-of-court personal knowledge about the parties. Those other parts of the opinion are open to the objection that Vaughan well knew such personal knowledge was mostly obsolete. This language is not open to that objection.

And it is this language that shades off into intuition, impression regarding fact or psychology that might be thought the ultimate defense of jury independence. One could rule against out-of-court personal knowledge—require jurors to swear to such knowledge in open court, thus converting it to in-court testimony. But could a judge, as a purely practical matter, identify and rule against in-court personal understandings on the basis that he could be certain that they were insincere, or sincere but wrong, misguided, overly sympathetic? Vaughan claimed the judge could not. Can the historian, as judge, claim with certainty that *he* was being insincere?

This is not to say that, over and above the practical impossibility of such a ruling, there were not moral or ethical bases for precluding such a

19. Vaughan, 148; *English Reports*, 1012–13.
20. Vaughan, 147; *English Reports*, 1012.

rule, ones that rose to the level of legal mandate—even to what might be called constitutional mandate.

The Moral Bases for Independence

Purely as a matter of theory, Whitman's "moral comfort," Crosby's independence-based-on-juror's-soul, and constitutionalism are analytically separable but also eminently analytically conjoinable. They can be brought together because a sheer constitutionalism begs questions as to just why the constitution stands as it does. And the answers given to this query at any particular time—and in any particular context—might be various, ranging from "It just is" to any of a number of considerations, some of which might have always been present in thinking about the jury, some of which might have been of more recent vintage, from some time ago to the virtual present.

Vaughan, of course, did not settle for "It just is." His opinion is devoted to listing the many reasons why the jury's verdict (and the jurors themselves) could not be assailed. I have previously examined those reasons in detail, so shall not repeat myself here. What remains a bit puzzling about Vaughan's opinion is not only his failure (as I have earlier stressed)[21] to advert to (and dismiss) the arguments for true law-finding that Penn made at his trial and that surfaced in numerous writings of the day, nor is it only Vaughan's total erasure of Restoration precedents for fining and the politics in which he himself had played a prominent role. One might now add to those puzzling matters Vaughan's silence about the awkward position (regarding "moral comfort") that Whitman shows some contemporary observers recognized the jury as being in.[22] One might wonder, as well, why Vaughan said so little—if anything—about the juror's "soul" and nothing explicit about the idea that the jury occupied a position independent of bench and sovereign.

One response to these new puzzles is simply that judges usually hewed to the law, stating it in "black-letter" terms and explicating it along

21. Green, *Verdict According to Conscience*, 249.

22. The jury in Penn and Mead's trial was, of course, dealing with a misdemeanor, not with a capital offense. That might be thought an answer to this particular conundrum. Because Vaughan wrote about the jury in criminal cases quite generally, however, I do not think the context of the case necessarily disposes of the matter.

traditionalist lines. Even new ideas were commonly made to appear time-out-of-mind, or were hinted at only implicitly and in veiled language, especially if, when broadly stated, they might pose collateral threats to the stability of the formal law. At that point, they were not only beneath notice but beneath contempt. This legalist approach, when applied to issues central to the legal system as a whole, represented a constrained form of constitutionalism—not the "just-is" variety, but something still far short of a full airing of the considerations that lay behind the decision. Given the resulting opacity, Whitman's and Crosby's important contributions to context might well inform the historian about what really moved Vaughan, then again they might not. They might instead, by multiplying the possibilities regarding what really moved Vaughan, *increase* the mystery, making the old chestnut that is the opinion even more difficult to crack.

Now one might fairly insist that what the opinion in *Bushel's* Case stood for was not strictly—or even mainly—a matter of what really *and consciously* moved Vaughan. Judicial opinions have meanings beyond that. Those meanings depend upon the eyes and ears, the reasoned inferences, the informed intuitions of those who read and/or hear them. A judge does not control the meaning of the law embedded in a living opinion, merely that of his own personal intentions embedded in his writing that opinion, which remain personal to him and are not thereby necessarily the "law" he has produced. This makes context crucial to our understanding of the law, of the contemporary understanding of the meaning of Vaughan's opinion. But whatever they might think about this perspective, I suspect Whitman and Crosby would say that what really moved Vaughan is indeed of importance and, further, that context tells us what really and consciously moved him, so that the only question left to be resolved is why he was so indirect, so implicit—so opaque.

In resisting the conclusion that the newly proposed contexts necessarily reveal Vaughan's thinking (or, even, his subconscious motivations), I want to return to what I think we all take to be the crux of the opinion, the issue of personal knowledge. The out-of-court variety has ancient roots and increasingly diminished importance; it thus seems least affected by late-seventeenth century trends of thought. Still, a possible link between the out-of-court and the in-court variety remained: jurors might have been thought to assess credibility and even the meaning of factual narratives in light of what they knew, not of the "facts" as such, but generally of local life, mores, and circumstances. That was—and remains—an oft-cited reason for (what remains of) the vicinage rule.

Jury assessment of in-court testimony and demeanor lies at the heart of the matter, and always had. It could be defended on its own terms. It connected seamlessly with the fact that the defendant had put himself "on the country" rather than on the bench. It connected, too, with the politics of central versus local control, and, with the political economy of the taking of life by command of the law. Its connection with another of Vaughan's apparently leading reasons—that if the judge may decide fact, what is the point in using a jury—of course begs the question, why, indeed, use a jury. But from Vaughan's perspective the fact that the English did use juries, and had for the past 450 years (rather than the instrumental considerations just noted), might have—for all we know—rendered conjectures as to the answer of the begged question *ultra vires*. Legalism/constitutionalism had, as it were, a life of its own. I myself wonder whether it is entirely fanciful to suggest that this "life of its own" led Vaughan to erase the Restoration, to consider its politics irrelevant (except in so far as they reflected what he deemed a proper respect for the constitutional position of the jury) and the recent instances of fining not "precedents" but, instead, judicial actions whose legality were themselves *sub judice* in *Bushel's Case*.

None of this denies that "moral comfort"—in this case that of the bench—helps to explain why the English adopted and then clung to the jury, especially in cases of blood. Nor does it deny that judges, Vaughan included, were well aware of this, despite their reticence about listing it as a reason for using the jury, much less specifying it as a reason for allowing discretion to the juries on which the bench had off-loaded the "peril" involved in judging. Nor does it deny that, by the late-seventeenth century, the sort of de facto jury independence that had always been a corollary of its powers of in-court assessment of testimony and demeanor had, as Crosby would have it, been theorized in some quarters in terms of a new form of constitutional independence. And those who might conjecture that Vaughan's attention to "eyes and ears," etc., bespeaks the influence of late-seventeenth-century science (here, epistemology) might also have a point.[23] All that it denies is that we can yet know from context what the text meant, as Vaughan created and understood it.

The Text in the Context of Doing History

I have fenced off, for lack of space, some important issues of context. So too did Vaughan fence them off, and one of my central points has been that we don't yet know just why he did so. There is still plenty of room for further assessment of the context of *Bushel's Case*. I mean to encourage that assessment, but, as is clear, I hope also to encourage further discussion of Vaughan's opinion—of the text itself. It has always struck me as an odd composition, at a few points tantalizingly of its day, but mainly resolutely a voice from the past that resonates far less than we might expect with Restoration events and thought.[24] In that regard, it remains something of a mystery, and just why it remains so is a question worthy of historians' interest, even if one of less moment than questions about Restoration jury theory more generally.

The form and content of Vaughan's opinion bear relation not only to what Vaughan thought about the questions raised by *Bushel's Case* but also to a broader matter not yet addressed in this essay. That matter is what might be called the "silent power" of the criminal trial jury, evident from its inception down to modern times. Like almost any institution or process, the criminal trial jury produced unintended effects, and given its place in the political and social order, the jury's effects were bound to be of special importance. Some thirty years ago, I noted—by way of tentative hypotheses—some of these effects. For example, de facto jury law-finding (or, if you prefer, highly discretionary fact-finding) created a rough-and-ready distinction between murder and manslaughter well before the law began to give formal recognition to that distinction in the sixteenth century. I sug-

23. On the theme of the new epistemology, see Barbara J. Shapiro, *Probability and Certainty in Seventeenth-Century England: A Study of the Relationships Between Natural Science, Religion, History, Law and Literature* (Princeton, Princeton University Press, 1983), ch. 5.

24. I have, for lack of space, omitted discussion of Vaughan's fascinating handling of the question whether the writ of attaint pertained to criminal cases. He concluded that it did not, thus depriving himself of an easy out: if attaint was available, the fining of jurors would raise the possibility of "double jeopardy."

gested that centuries of trial-jury practice were influential in the emergence of this formal legal development, whether or not those who legislated the change were aware of that influence, so that what came from "above" ultimately derived from what existed "below." In similar fashion, longstanding jury practice might well have played a "silent" role in the legislating of clergyability for much simple larceny. And so on.[25]

At another level, the criminal trial jury played a role in the production of its own staying power. To be sure, this institutional permanence resulted from a matrix of decisions by legal, political, and social actors in accordance with their interests. The jury, in this regard, was object not subject; it was acted upon. Yet the power of the idea of the jury might be said to have emanated in part simply from the jury's being what it was—from its having become an inviolable part of the constitution. This is difficult to separate conceptually from the "interest" possessed by that other legal actor, the judge, in remaining true to the law, and certainly to constitutional principles. It is perhaps a matter of taste whether or not we ascribe to the jury itself some power in the maintenance of the particular judicial fidelity to the robe that manifested itself in the bench's legitimation of the jury, but Vaughan's opinion, which at points reads a bit like settled conviction in search of a rationale, might be deemed testimony to this particular silent power of the jury.

Present ideas can be born from age-old practices originally created to serve distinct interests. Those practices, and indeed those interests, might live on, but so might a later-emerged but by now well-aged idea of the appropriateness—even constitutionally-required essence—of the practice itself. The constitutional requirement of determination of criminal guilt by a lay jury under instructions from the judge as to the law the jury must apply to the facts it found was an idea that lived on alongside the idea that it was in the interest of judges as individuals and of the state as defender of the law that a lay jury be seen to have shouldered the civil duty of determining criminal responsibility.[26] That Vaughan did not invoke the latter idea hardly means that it didn't occur to him, or, even, that it wasn't the driving force behind his opinion. It suffices to say, however, that the form and substance

25. Green, *Verdict According to Conscience*, especially 125, 147, 314–15, n. 146, 377–82.

26. Whitman, *Origins of Reasonable Doubt*, 178–84, rightly emphasizes the idea of duty in writings in the aftermath of *Bushel's Case*.

of that opinion leave open the possibility that little more than the appeal of a vital abstraction was at work. And the question of the proportional influence of the many forces (political, social, religious, or otherwise philosophical) driving the appeal of that abstraction is still open for historical investigation.

Conclusion

There can be no certainty about the ultimate success of such investigation. The text, taken by itself, might prove forever unyielding, and as for the hope that study of the context will elucidate the text, it might turn out that one just can't get here from there. Of course, historians wouldn't necessarily know that success was utterly foreclosed, so they likely would go on trying to unveil the meaning of the text via new insights regarding context. I think Charlie would count the possibility of ultimate irresolution part of the challenge and not a bad thing—anyway, not a tragedy. I wonder, though, whether he would go a further step. Is he sufficiently perverse—as I surely am—to think that, in this particular context, absolute certainty would be regrettable?

Suppose, for example, an historian discovered a letter verifiably from Vaughan to a friend that explained the "true" rationale of his opinion in laborious detail. Such a document would be a real find. It would merit publication, and were the finder a junior in the profession, it would make a nice contribution to his or her tenure file. We would, finally, *really* know what Vaughan was thinking. Bliss!

But would we not have lost something? One more old chestnut down the drain. There aren't many such cases that so powerfully test the historian's archival skills and imagination. It is true that Vaughan's actual motivations, once learned, might be of considerable interest and might themselves spin off new problems that would go part way to off-set the loss. I can't help feeling, however, that they would go only part of the way, and no more.

The Relevance of Colonial Appeals to the Privy Council

Mary Sarah Bilder[1]

The famous case of *Perrin v. Blake* may have begun with a hurricane. On 28 August 1722, a terrible hurricane hit Jamaica, almost precisely ten years after an earlier one. Port Royal was destroyed and hundreds of people died, including several hundred enslaved Africans when a slave ship sank in the harbor. Within a year or two, perhaps amidst the disease that followed, William Williams died. He thought his wife might be pregnant. He left a will attempting to provide for that possibility. The words chosen—and a series of later unfortunate events—gave rise to an appeal from Jamaica to the Privy Council. This appeal proved so troubling to English lawyers and judges that it was transferred into the regular English legal system. After decades, on the eve of a hearing in the House of Lords, the appeal was settled in 1777, leaving in its wake centuries of debate over the proper application of the rule in *Shelley's Case*.[2]

1. Thanks to Jim Oldham for sharing an informative 2002 memo by Avedis H. Sefarian about the Ambler and Eldon manuscripts on *Perrin*; Yvonne Fraser-Clarke, Head of Special Collections, National Library of Jamaica, for assistance with Jamaican materials; Sharon O'Connor for reading various drafts; and to Charlie Donahue for making it all possible.

2. On the 1722 hurricane, see David Longshore, *Encyclopedia of Hurricanes, Typhoons, and Cyclones* (New York: Facts on File, 2008), 267–268; Matthew Mulcahy, *Hurricanes and Society in the British Greater Caribbean, 1624–1783* (Baltimore: Johns Hopkins Press, 2008), 121; John Atkins, *Voyage to Guinea, Brazil and the West Indies* (1735; repr. London: Routledge, 2013), 236; Edward Long, *History of Jamaica*, 2 vols. (London: T. Lowndes, 1774), 2.145.

The appeal raises the question of the relationship between appeals to the Privy Council and English law. The question is appropriate in a volume honoring Charlie Donahue. Over the last decade, he found himself in a position analogous to eighteenth-century English legal figures confronted with colonial appeals. Charlie has served as the Literary Director of the Ames Foundation and oversaw the publication of the *Appeals to the Privy Council from the American Colonies: An Annotated Digital Catalogue*.

For the past two centuries, the colonial appeals to the Privy Council fell between the cracks on both sides of the Atlantic. For Americans, the creation of the Supreme Court and the absence of published reports of appeals implied legal discontinuity between "American" (post-1787) law and the pre-1787 British imperial world. For the British, the loss of the Atlantic colonies and the lack of printed precedents in appeals implied legal discontinuity between English common law and the colonial appeals. Elsewhere I have written about the importance of the appeals for colonial American legal history and the history of the development of the global law of the colonial world. Here I want to focus on the importance of the appeals for English legal history.[3]

This essay follows two narratives: first, an account of Charlie's work with the Ames Foundation and his increasing involvement with the Privy Council Appeals project; second, a story about the overlooked history of *Perrin* as an appeal to the Privy Council. This essay does not attempt to exhaustively explore the case but to raise a few questions about the ways in which appeals to the Privy Council altered English law and lawyers.

THE COLONIAL APPEALS CATALOGUE

For much of Charlie's career, he served in the multiple roles of English legal historian, property professor, and Literary Director of the Ames Foundation. When Charlie became Literary Director of the Ames Foundation, he stepped into quite large shoes. The Foundation had been established in 1910 by friends of James Barr Ames. The stated mission was "for the purpose of

3. Mary Sarah Bilder, *The Transatlantic Constitution: Colonial Legal Culture and the Empire* (Cambridge: Harvard University Press, 2004); Sharon Hamby O'Connor and Mary Sarah Bilder, "Appeals to the Privy Council before American Independence: An Annotated Digital Catalogue," *Law Library Journal* 104, no. 1 (2012), 83–97.

continuing the advancement of legal knowledge and aiding the improvement of the law." The Foundation had interpreted that mission by focusing on English legal history publications. Under the guidance of John Henry Beale, T. F. T. Plucknett, and Samuel E. Thorne, the Foundation ensured that the previously unpublished Yearbooks of Richard II appeared. Under Charlie's leadership, the Foundation continued this tradition with the print publication of a variety of unpublished legal manuscripts from the thirteenth to fifteenth centuries, the digital publication of significant early legal manuscripts in the collection of Harvard Law Library, as well as supporting David Seipp's Yearbook Abridgement database.[4]

Nonetheless, at the outset of the twenty-first century, Charlie agreed to step beyond the boundaries of traditional early English legal history and support a project about law on the other side of the Atlantic and several centuries beyond the focus of his scholarly interests. The goal was to make accessible materials related to important appellate cases that helped define American colonial constitutional law and the larger constitutional law of the British Empire—to create a modern bibliography of the Appeals to the Privy Council from the American colonies with extant records. Charlie later noted that the project was "at once quite far from what we have traditionally done but also quite closely related to it." He emphasized, it "has been quite a trip for the undersigned."[5]

By this fortuity, relatively late in Charlie's remarkable career as an English legal historian, he became a collaborator on the Appeals to the Privy Council from the American Colonies—and, in coming years, the Caribbean and Canada. Charlie was an enthusiastic, albeit occasionally exasperated, Literary Director. The Appeals project challenged the assumptions and approaches of traditional English legal history.

The British Privy Council heard appeals from the 13 colonies that became the United States and from the other colonies in Canada and the Caribbean. Over 700 cases were appealed from various American jurisdictions: Barbados; Bermuda, Connecticut, Dominica, Georgia, Jamaica, the

4. Ames Foundation Publication Series Brochure, W. S. Hein & Co.; Ames Foundation, http://amesfoundation.law.harvard.edu/.

5. *Appeals to the Privy Council from the American Colonies: An Annotated Digital Catalogue*, ed. Sharon Hamby O'Connor, Mary Sarah Bilder, and Charles Donahue Jr. (William S. Hein & Co., 2015), v–vi.

Leeward Islands, the lower counties on the Delaware, Maryland, Massachusetts, New Hampshire, New Jersey, New York, Nova Scotia, Pennsylvania, Quebec, Rhode Island, St. Vincent, and Virginia. For two centuries, the records lay scattered in repositories on both sides of the Atlantic. Nearly one-third of these cases came from the thirteen colonies that became the United States.[6]

As an initial matter, the Appeals project presented an opportunity for the Ames Foundation to move beyond the conventional print approach to publication of original legal records. The gold standard for publication of primary source legal materials long had been an elegant hardbound print volume in which manuscripts were typeset, scholarly annotations provided context, detailed footnotes pointed researchers to additional primary resources, and a lengthy introduction by the editor explained the significance of the source. Often a facsimile of portions of the manuscript was included. Since the late nineteenth century, the Selden Society embodied this approach with distinctive navy blue bindings and gold lettering. The Ames Foundation had followed in the Selden Society's footsteps.

The Foundation's volumes comprised part of the invaluable tradition of documentary editions, catalogues, and bibliography. The strength of these older print resources arose from their clearly defined scope, the meticulous care of presentation, and the compilation and annotation of information without intermingling historical interpretation. The best of these volumes illuminated inaccessible primary sources. This publishing tradition countered the bias inevitable in histories that relied predominantly or exclusively on contemporaneously printed sources. The Ames Foundation and the Selden Society supported scholarship for which there was no obvious commercial market. Behind these volumes stood a remarkable belief in the importance of a scholarly community over time. The hours expended as a Literary Director overseeing and supporting projects and years spent as an editor laboriously preparing a volume were all worthy endeavors because at some time—perhaps long after the lifetime of those involved—these volumes would help others understand and write secondary scholarship about the past.

6. Joseph Henry Smith, *Appeals to the Privy Council from the American Plantations* (1950; repr. New York: Octagon Publishing, 1965), 667–671. I have excluded vice-admiralty cases.

In the twenty-first century, the new digital age raised the possibility that this endeavor would be abandoned. An increasing number of historical websites uploaded images of primary sources from archives. Digitization radically altered the economics of scholarship. A scholar could now sit in her office anywhere in theory in the world and see the images. Travel funds did not have to be obtained; the conflicts of family and job obligations were minimized. And the images of entire primary documents—not a single facsimile—reminded scholars to think about manuscript culture. Yet this digitization was often bereft of accompanying information—now often referred to as metadata. One could see the primary source but not come any closer to understanding it.

In the first decade of the twenty-first century, Charlie, Sharon O'Connor, and I found ourselves trying to chart a path through this new frontier of electronic publishing and digital humanities. We wanted to combine the best of the print publication tradition with the image accessibility of new media. In the end, the project became a new genre of historical website, what we call an "annotated digital catalogue." At the core, the catalogue is a simple list of colonial appeals to the Privy Council (the "catalogue"). The list is extensively annotated to create multiple entry points for researchers and to refer to related documents and information. The digital format permits flexibility in access and direct viewing of documents, the vast majority of which are in England or scattered across the United States. The catalogue provides links to original documents for these appeals available in England and the United States. Most significantly, as of 2015, it includes images of surviving briefs filed in 54 appeals. These briefs—known as "printed cases"—provide the reasons for the appeals. The reasons reveal the principles underlying colonial constitutional law and eighteenth-century British common and statutory law.[7]

At every turn, Charlie insisted on honoring both the experience of working in the archives and the precise editing tradition of the print volumes. We thus paid to have photographed many blank verso sides of printed cases. We even discussed—but ultimately abandoned as impractical—including measurements and possible watermarks. In overseeing our

7. The conceptual framework for the catalogue was discussed in O'Connor and Bilder, "Appeals."

preparation of the editorial metadata, Charlie focused on the smallest nuances. We debated was it more appropriate to use the term "not extant" or "not found" to describe the absence of printed cases. We spent hours discussing where to list cases that were not "true appeals." Charlie was highly particular about the style. We went back and forth, seemingly endlessly, over whether en-dashes should be followed by spaces; whether vessels should be set in italics. He was vigilant on behalf of the small budget of the Ames Foundation. Historical societies and libraries found themselves negotiating reduced rates and favors to allow us to create the entire original database for under $10,000. In advocating for reasonable digital fees, Charlie also set an important precedent in ensuring that digitization for scholarly projects be considered part of a long tradition in aid by non-profit primary source repositories to researchers, as opposed to an opportunity to raise revenue.

Charlie gradually found himself pulled into the world of the colonial Appeals. At the moment, there are no digital publishers akin to print publishers. In the past, the Literary Director could send the completed manuscript off to professional publishers to produce. But no such analogy existed. Charlie thus decided to become the technical creator of the website and database. He spent the Christmas vacation of 2010 creating and coding the first version of the database. Over the next five years, Charlie became the "techie" for the site. He agreed to a dual access approach to give the user the best of modern and traditional research tools. The site was built to encourage a wide variety of possible entry points. The home page has a standard search engine. Two additional contents lists arrange the appeals by colony and by year. Furthermore, a series of "useful lists" were created (e.g., appeals about vessels; appeals with printed cases, a list of counsel). When hyperlinks did not work, Charlie fixed them. When fonts were hard to read, Charlie fixed them. To ensure that the site could be navigated, Charlie wrote detailed instructions and supported the addition of a special memorandum for students and enthusiasts, which offers advice on how to use the Catalogue for developing a course paper or for advancing research in the field.

As Charlie was pulled deeper and deeper into the project, his natural curiosity and knowledge of English law drew him inexorably to the substance of the appeals. For example, in certain cases, one of the parties was given a peculiarly suspicious name: Thomas Turf or William Thrustout.

(Charlie particularly liked the Virginia lawyers' use of Thrustout.) Charlie wanted to ensure that the names of the cases make evident that the person was a likely fictional person. As he wrote to us, "The Ames Foundation is not going to publish something, even on the web, that is likely to provoke the wrong kind of smiles from those who know something about English legal history." As we worried about whether to list as a participant a fictional party, Charlie wrote, "A note allows us to express doubts, or to distinguish between a fictitious person and a fictitious lease and to express our degree of certainty about the fiction." This insistence was the deep strength of Charlie's work as historian and editor.

Before we knew it, Charlie begun to puzzle his way through ejectment cases. Charlie discovered that some of the colonial cases followed the English form in which there was often a fictional lease and lessee. But far more (thirty-seven cases) did not use the fiction at all. He began to imagine how the "colonial action in trespass and ejectment worked." Charlie drew on records that I had for two cases from Rhode Island and then journeyed to the Massachusetts State Archives to investigate the colonial case files for two others. The results of his research appear in a note on the website and in the printed volume, "Additional Research in Ejectment Cases." By the time Charlie had completed his investigation, he had also decided that efforts must be undertaken to attempt to have the colonial court records made digitally available.

Charlie only slowly accepted credit for his significant involvement in the Appeals project. He agreed that his name could be listed as "with the assistance of" in the print edition of the Appeals catalogue. Eventually, Charlie agreed that he had become a full co-author. In 2015, the American Association of Law Libraries awarded all three co-authors its important Joseph L. Andrews Legal Literature award to the *Appeals to the Privy Council from the American Colonies: An Annotated Digital Catalogue.*

The Plantation Case

In the journey from benevolent Literary Director to co-author, Charlie traveled the path that English lawyers and judges also traveled in participating in colonial appeals. Because the records of appeals were not easily accessible and because the appeals fell literally between modern legal jurisdictions, English legal historians have overlooked their importance and influence to leading English lawyers and judges. *Perrin v. Blake,* originally known as "The Plantation Case," raises these questions. It is particularly appropriate in this essay as it involves the Rule in *Shelley's Case,* a matter Charlie addressed in some depth in his property casebook.[8]

Nothing about the facts of *Perrin* foretold its future as a case that "divided the profession of law into bitter factions for many years." William Williams owned a large plantation in the English plantations, specifically, Dean's Valley, in Westmoreland, Jamaica. It was a "sugar works" and of sufficient wealth that the English lawyers described Williams as "possessed of a very large personal Estate" and "considerable real Estates." The plantation was 2862 acres. From the late eighteenth to early nineteenth centuries, Westmoreland was the location of "some sixty sugar estates" with "10,000 slaves in the 1760s."[9]

Williams was married to Mary Williams and had three daughters and a son. He made a will on March 13, 1722. According to the later legal documents, he died on February 3, 1723. Williams' will was complicated. Lord Mansfield later would imply that the testator had written the will and "unwarily and ignorantly used" the words. The pervasive legal terminology and formality of the will, however, suggests that it was drafted by someone

8. Charles Donahue, Jr., Thomas E. Kauper, and Peter W. Martin, *Property: An Introduction to the Concept and the Institution* (St. Paul: West Publishing Co., 1974), 558–559. For a summary of *Perrin* and relevant sources, see James Oldham, *English Common Law in the Age of Mansfield* (Chapel Hill: University of North Carolina Press, 2004), 356–363. *Plantation Case, The Biographical History of Sir William Blackstone* (London, 1782), vii n.§. The most succinct summary appears in the notes to "An Argument by Mr. Justice Blackstone," *A Collection of Tracts Relative to the Law of England,* ed. Francis Hargrave (London: T. Wright, 1787), 489–490.

9. *Divided:* J. Campbell, *The Lives of the Chief Justices of England,* 3 vols. (London: John Murray, 1849–1857), 2.430. The facts throughout have been drawn from the three printed cases: *Norwood Witter, Esq. and Others v. John Doe, the Lessee of John Sharpe...* (Respondent's Case; William Murray and Alexander Hume-Campbell) (21 Nov. 1752) (Law Library of Congress); *John Doe v. Hannah Blake* (1765) (Appellant's Case; Charles Yorke and William de Grey); *William Perrin and Thomas Vaughan... v. Hannah Blake* (1765) (Respondent's Case; Fletcher Norton and Alexander Wedderburn) (British Library Add. MS 36219, fol. 236). The appellant's case in the 1752 appeal has not yet been located. *Some sixty:* Richard Dunn, *A Tale of Two Plantations: Slave Life and Labor in Jamaica and Virginia* (Cambridge, Mass.: Harvard University Press, 2014), 7.

with either some legal knowledge or access to an English form book for estates and property.[10]

At the time of Williams' death, his young son, John, was about six. In succeeding years, one daughter died and the two elder daughters came of age and married. Bonella married Norwood Witter. Hannah married Benjamin Blake. John grew up and traveled to England for his education. There he met and became engaged to Sarah Knight. They married apparently sometime in late 1739.

Sarah's father attempted to protect her in the marriage. She was the daughter of another wealthy English-Jamaican merchant, James Knight. James Knight had returned to London and was in the process of composing a history of Jamaica. In London, lawyers drafted and negotiated the settlement. John Williams agreed to settle of jointure of 1000 pounds a year on Sarah. In January 1739, a marriage settlement was agreed to. Under the terms of the settlement, Sarah's family were made trustees and the Dean's Valley plantation and sugar works were entailed on the future sons of the marriage. If Sarah survived John, she was to receive an annuity of 1000 pounds sterling paid from the Royal Exchange in four payments. Apparently, John was only twenty years old at the time he executed the articles.[11]

The will of William Williams was not in England and "it was thought prudent" according to Sarah's later lawyers to insert additional protection for Sarah. As they later would explain, it was not "then known how the

10. The death date of February 3, 1723 was listed in the legal cases. The 1723 death date assumes that references to his death in 3 February 1723 were new style. If it were old-style, then Williams did not die until 3 February 1724. The death date does not match the death date for the William Williams of Dean's Valley. Records of headstone inscriptions for the Dean's Valley Dryworks Estates describe a William Williams who died on November 19, 1723 when Williams was 35 years old. This monument mentions the hurricane and also appears to describe Williams as holding the office of *custos rotulorum*. J. H. Lawrence-Archer, *Monumental Inscriptions: The British West Indies* (London: Chatto and Windus, 1875), 337. For example, as the title page of George Billingshurst, *Arcana Clericalia: Or the Mysteries of Clerkship Explained* (London, 1705) noted, it provided forms for "conveying, limiting and settling estates by deeds, fine, and recoveries, in fee, in tail, for life...." Henry Swinburne's *A brief Treatise of Testaments and Last Wills* (reprinted from 1590 on) provided commonly adapted forms.

11. On James Knight, see Kenneth Morgan, *Materials on the History of Jamaica in the Edward Long Papers* (Wakefield: Microform Academic Publishers, 2006). The underage fact comes from the Appellant's Case (1764).

Right" of John stood and whether he would be able to settle Dean's Valley as he promised. Thus he also granted to the Knights in trust for her one half of his personal estate in Jamaica and one half of the profits of his "several Plantations, messuages, lands, negroes, stock of cattle, hereditaments" and property. In return, Sarah—as was standard practice—agreed to relinquish her claim to dower.[12]

In February and March 1743, John Williams executed documents necessary in Jamaica to break any entail created by his father's will. James Knight apparently had lent John Williams money and settled an additional sum on him in his will for carrying out the settlement. As far as Sarah and John were concerned, her sons would inherit the estate and, in the case of John's death, she would have a jointure. If a son had been born, events might have played out differently. John might have planned to return or, like many English heirs to the sugar plantations, he might have thought to spend the rest of his life in England living off the profits of the highly abusive sugar plantation economy. The value of his estate was later estimated at upwards of 3000 pounds a year.[13]

John Williams died in England on the last day of December 1744. Sarah was left a childless widow. She remained in London, never traveling to Jamaica. Meanwhile, in Jamaica, Bonella and Hannah and their husbands took—or more plausibly remained—in possession of Dean's Valley.

What followed was decades of litigation by Sarah to attempt to receive her jointure. In 1752, her brother, John Knight, wrote her that he was attempting to acquire by replevin "the Negroes upon Dean's Valley." The local court, however, needed an affidavit that the "Negroes are in the Possession of Messrs. Witter & Blake" and Knight was not sure when he could do it. Although he was attempting to send her funds, he worried about her.

12. Norwood Witter (Respondent's Case), 1. On marriage settlements, see, e.g., Barbara English and John Saville, *Strict Settlement: A Guide for Historians* (Hull: University of Hull Press, 1983); A. W. B. Simpson, *A History of the Land Law*, 2nd ed. (Oxford: Clarendon Press, 1986), 204–241; Eileen Spring, *Law, Land, & Family: Aristocratic Inheritance in England, 1300 to 1800* (Chapel Hill: University of North Carolina Press, 1993).

13. For will of James Knight, see James Knight's will (22 May 1743), PRO. On return to England, see Dunn, *Tale of Two Plantations*, 30; Richard Dunn, *Sugar and Slaves: The Rise of the Planter Class in the English West Indies, 1624–1813* (New York: W. W. Norton, 1972); *Mathew Parker, The Sugar Barons: Family, Corruption, Empire, and War in the West Indies* (New York: Walker & Co., 2011).

He hoped she would "go into the Country during the summer months." She should rent a house and he would "pay for it." He was at great "Trouble & expense" with respect to her affairs in Jamaica and he counseled, "preserve your health for the enjoyment of your fortune." By 1765, her London lawyers described her as "supported by the Assistance she has received from her own Friends" without which she would have "been reduced to a State of Want."[14]

Over the many cases and appeals, the multiple arguments raised by the lawyers were simplified. For example, for some time, the lawyers puzzled over whether the relevant provision was a joint life estate to John and a supposed posthumous son and therefore all the remainders were dependent on the posthumous son's birth; they were thus all void. Similarly, the lawyers argued over whether the bargain and sale deed executed in Jamaica was sufficient to bar the entail, although it did not follow the approach required in England.[15]

Eventually, Sarah Williams' effort to obtain her jointure was turned into a case about the meaning of the will and, eventually, the application of the rule in *Shelley's Case*. When Charles Yorke and William de Grey submitted the printed case for Sarah in 1765 as appellant, the four reasons did not directly raise the rule. The respondent's case, however, did raise the issue, arguing that William Williams' will gave John only "an Estate for Life." The lawyers claimed that it represented the "Intention of the Testator," although the will was "not framed with much legal Precision." As John Campbell later explained, the "great question, was whether he took an estate for life or in tail?" If John took a life estate, he could do nothing. If he took an entailed estate, then he could break it and convert it to fee simple, out of which Sarah would have her jointure.[16]

The mortality of life in Jamaica took its toll on the suit. In 1751, Bonella died, leaving her husband, Norwood Witter, to pursue the suit on behalf of their son, William Witter. Eventually Benjamin Blake also died, leaving

14. John Knight to Mrs. Sarah Williams (February 1752), Documents Pertaining to Jamaica, 1720–1775 MST 1651, No. 31; *supported*: Appellant's Case (1765), 8.

15. Appellant's Case (1765), 2–3 N.B.

16. Respondent's Case (1765), 5. For a recent careful discussion of the Rule, see David A. Smith, "Was There a Rule in *Shelley's Case*?," *Journal of Legal History* 30 (2009), 53–70. *Great question*: Campbell, 2.431.

Hannah (Williams) Blake to pursue the suit. In 1765, Norwood Witter died. In London, Sarah Williams survived—and remained a widow.

Perrin is famous because of a contretemps between Mansfield and the other judges. In 1769, Mansfield decided against Sarah Williams obtaining anything from the estate and, as she had waived her dower, anything at all after her marriage. Judge Yates dissented. Mansfield's decision was then overruled in 1772 by William Blackstone and six other judges of the Exchequer Chamber. Only Justice de Grey favored the Mansfield position. As James Oldham notes, it "was among the handful of major defeats for Lord Mansfield." Before the case was heard by the House of Lords, it was settled.[17]

Mansfield's role was complicated. When the case arrived at the Committee for hearing Appeals, Lord Mansfield found himself the only "law lord" at the hearing. Francis Hargrave explained that Mansfield "did not chuse, that a question, of so general a tendency in respect to all the landed property in England, should be decided by his single opinion." The lawyers agreed to stay the appeal and obtain a "solemn adjudication" of the issue in Westminster Hall. The parties brought a "feigned action of trespass" with the "benefit of a writ of error to the exchequer chamber, and from then to the house of lords." Mansfield therefore was held responsible for preventing the appeal as a mere Caribbean appeal.[18]

Mansfield's decision ironically improved Sarah Williams's chances. A 1775 letter from defendant William Blake insisted that the Council had decided that John Williams was merely a tenant for life. It had been thought, however, that "there was something very nice in the Case" and so it was sent over to King's Bench. The subsequent reversal in the Exchequer gave her considerable bargaining power. She offered to settle for 400 pounds sterling per year. As the personal estate was "near Fifty thousand Pounds in Bonds, Mortgages &c," Blake apparently agreed, although he

17. James Oldham, *English Common Law in the Age of Mansfield* (Chapel Hill: University of North Carolina Press, 2004), 356. On *Perrin*, see Francis Hargrave, *Collectanea Juridica*, 2 vols. (London: For E. and R. Brooke, 1791–1792); *A Collection of Tracts Relative to the Law of England*, ed. Francis Hargrave (London, T. Wright, 1787). The 1769 decision was Mansfield, Aston, Willes against Yates.

18. Hargrave, "Mr. Justice Blackstone," 492 n.

then noted that he had "since thought better" of it. The eventual settlement is not presently known.[19]

After the decision, controversy developed over Mansfield's earlier role in the appeal. Charles Fearne accused Mansfield of giving Sarah Williams advice contrary to his later decision. Some advice apparently was given before the 1743 settlement, presumably either to John Williams or to James Knight. In April 1747, while Solicitor General, Mansfield allegedly wrote an opinion that stated the remainder was in tail and he could suffer a recovery. Mansfield declared that he had not offered such an opinion. Fearne insisted that he had.[20]

Regardless of the opinion that Mansfield gave, the printed case reveals that Mansfield represented Sarah Williams in the 1752 appeal. Intriguingly, William de Grey, the only Exchequer justice to join Mansfield, represented Sarah Williams in the 1765 appeal. Because commentators on *Perrin* judged these appeals to be irrelevant, Mansfield's rather extensive participation has been overlooked.

In general, modern legal commentators have favored the Mansfield position, taking for granted that the intention of William Williams was not to leave anything beyond a life estate to his son. Contemporary legal commentators tended to favor the entail interpretation, permitting the son to convert the property to fee simple and to provide the widow with a jointure. The contemporaries—more familiar with conveyancing practices such as strict settlement—may have the better instinct about the testator's likely substantive intent and general conveyancing practices.

19. William Blake to Samuel Wilkinson Gordon, 18 June 1775 (copy), in Documents Pertaining to Jamaica, 1720–1775 MST 1651, No. 32 (described by Ingram as No. 31), National Library of Jamaica (the end of the letter was missing). The settlement was to be structured by investing 6000 pounds sterling.

20. Charles Fearne, *An Essay on the Learning of Contingent Remainders and Executory Devises* (London, W. Stahan and M. Woodfall for P. Uriel, 1772); Charles Fearne, *Copies of Opinions ascribed to Eminent Council on the Will which was the Subject of the case of Perrin v. Blake* (London: W. Strahan and M. Woodfall, 1780). On pre-1743 advice, see Fearne, *Copies*, 10–11 (statement of the case). For Solicitor General's opinion as copied from Booth's copy, see ibid., 15. Other opinions included D. Ryder (Attorney General), Bev. Filmer, and James Booth. Filmer and Booth were noted conveyancers. For discussion favoring Mansfield, including the January 1746 Murray opinion for life estate, and suggestion that Booth was influenced by client advice, see John Holliday, *The Life of William, Late Earl of Mansfield* (London: P. Elmsly, 1797), 199–209.

Francis Hargrave criticized Mansfield's decision. Hargrave thought it unfortunate that "a lady should not be able to know, whether her jointure was good or not without waiting upwards of thirty years." He declared it was "certainly a misfortune to the lady, whose interests were at stake, that the case took such a turn." What bothered Hargrave was that her case had been interpreted "as a final precedent for explaining a rule of law of general importance: one, about which there has latterly prevailed amongst professional persons an uncommon diversity of sentiments, and by the mode of applying which the titles to all the real property of the country are ever liable to most essentially affected." In brief, Hargrave may have believed the appeal should have been decided simply as a particular appeal.[21]

Why did Mansfield decide that this particular appeal could not be decided without affecting all of English law? What was the relationship between the law and legal principles as argued in the reasons in the printed cases of appeals and as argued in King's Bench, Common Pleas, Exchequer, and the House of Lords? Were there other legal questions raised in appeals that formally or informally were transferred into the regular law courts? How did appeals affect the development of English law? We do not know the answer to any of these questions.

How did arguing the appeals affect Mansfield's legal thought? How did arguing appeals alter the legal thought of the many English lawyers listed on the printed cases? William Murray argued fifteen colonial American cases between 1732 and 1754. Dudley Ryder argued another twelve. Charles Yorke argued twenty-eight between 1753 and 1766. William DeGrey and Charles Pratt similarly appear on the printed cases. These numbers do not include appeals from the Caribbean and Canada—as well as appeals in which there was no extant printed case. The law argued in the appeals was not bound by English common law in the same way as in King's Bench or Common Pleas. Actions developed in the colonies followed different rules than technical English procedural law. Outcomes permitted in the colonies were not always the same as those under English law. When they went on to become judges, did this type of legal argument stay with them? To what

21. Hargrave, "Mr. Justice Blackstone," 493 n.

extent are the appeals from the colonies responsible for the extraordinary development of late eighteenth-century English law?[22]

How did the appeals from the colonies alter these lawyers, politicians, and judges' view of the expanding empire? In 1976, K. E. Ingram suggested that the Jamaican appeals were important in understanding the relationship between England and the Caribbean. He found thirty-one printed cases relating to Jamaican appeals in the Hardwicke collection at the British Library. They "illustrate the extremely litigious nature of the Jamaican planter class and the tedious and very slow processes whereby lawsuits were settled." After decades of searching for manuscript sources relating to Jamaica, Ingram emphasized that the dominance of Jamaican plantation papers as part of the estate papers of "one or other titled member of the British landowning class is quite remarkable." A preliminary glance at the appeals from the Caribbean reveals the repeated involvement of slavery. What was the role of the London lawyers and judges in the development of laws relating to slavery? Furthermore, both Sarah Williams and Hannah Blake participated in additional appeals. How did women use the appeals system to obtain property and financial security? How did they interact with the London legal profession and with local attorneys? For example, a note on a copy of the 1757 order of the Committee of Council for hearing Appeals from the plantations stated "Copy made for Mrs. Williams to send to Jamaica" with two printed cases with remarks. How did the English legal system configure wealthy white women's property interests and slavery? How was English law influenced by the economic interests of Caribbean slaveholders?[23]

22. Bilder, *Appeals*, 527–532. For an excellent article discussing the appeals to the House of Lords and Scots lawyers, see John Finlay, "Scots Lawyers and House of Lords Appeals in Eighteenth-Century Britain," *Journal of Legal History* 34 (2011), 249–277.

23. K. E. Ingram, *Sources of Jamaican History, 1655–1838: A Bibliographic Survey* (Zug: Inter Documentation Co., 1976), 30–31. Manuscripts records in Jamaica include, for example, letter in 1771 from Peter Ramsey to Sarah Williams and Ms. Ann Barrett relating to litigation over the Knight plantation, Molynes. SWIS 679, National Library of Jamaica. Sarah Williams was also involved in James Barclay v. Daniel Munro (25 March 1757), Add. MS 36217 fol. 132, British Library (relating to the estate of John Knight and James Knight; Vere Langford Oliver, *Caribbeana*, 6 vols. (London: Mitchell, Hughes and Clarke, 1910–1919), 6.71. *Copy*: J. Barclay appeal re the estate of James Knight, MS 492, National Library of Jamaica.

Charlie Donahue's work behind the scenes with the Appeals catalogue will help scholars begin to answer these questions. In coming years, we will finally learn what interested the great eighteenth-century English lawyers about the appeals. It may be some of what interested Charlie—a place where English law was freed slightly from its historical, printed precedential moorings.

Prosecuting Polygamy in Early Modern England

John Witte, Jr.

Once or twice a semester when I was his student, and every two or three years thereafter when I visited Cambridge, I would stop by Charlie Donahue's office. He was always gracious and welcoming. His office was always covered with books and manuscripts. An old folio volume or two usually lay open on his reading desk; leather leavings flecked the floor; pipe tobacco aroma hung in the air. Charlie always cleared a chair for me, told me about his latest work and asked me about mine. On one such visit, some two decades ago, he urged me to write about the history of "real polygamy" (*polygamia vera*), as Hostiensis had called it—having two or more spouses at the same time.[1] "There's just not enough good work done on this topic," he said memorably. "And nobody seems to have done much at all about all the old cases on point."

In the ensuing years, Charlie himself,[2] his student Sara McDougall,[3] and several others have taken up the medieval prosecution of real polygamy and the private law consequence of precontract impediments.[4] I have tried

1. Hostiensis, *Summa Aurea in titulos decretalium* [1537 Lyon ed.], ed. and ann. Nicolas Superantii (repr. Aalen: Scientia Verlag, 1962), fol. 40v.

2. See Charles Donahue, Jr., *Law, Marriage, and Society in the Later Middle Ages* (Cambridge: Cambridge University Press, 2007).

3. Sara McDougall, *Bigamy and Christian Identity in Late Medieval Champagne* (Philadelphia: University of Pennsylvania Press, 2012).

4. See Donahue, *Law, Marriage, and Society*, 70–72; see also R. H. Helmholz, *Marriage Litigation in Medieval England* (Cambridge: Cambridge University Press, 1974), 57–66, and the chapter by Paul Brand herein.

my hand at the topic, too.[5] In this chapter, I present some evidence of the prosecution of polygamy under a new 1604 Act of Parliament that, for the first time since Anglo-Saxon days, declared polygamy to be a capital crime in England prosecuted in the secular courts. Before then, as Charlie has shown definitively, polygamy questions remained within the jurisdiction of the English church courts. The English church courts annulled second marriages and engagements when there was still a valid first marriage, and ordered spiritual sanctions on intentional polygamists and their accomplices—public penance, various shame punishments, and excommunication in serious cases. They looked to the secular courts to make appropriate marital property settlements for innocent duped fiancées, spouses, and children. In serious cases of brazen polygamy, secular courts could also impose corporal punishments—flogging, prison, mutilation, banishment, even execution. But the crime for which these parties were punished was usually not polygamy, but perjury or adultery. Unlike Continental lands, medieval England did not have separate secular statutes prohibiting polygamy.

This began to change in the sixteenth century. Alarmed by the polygamous experiments and speculations unleashed by the Protestant Reformation, notably during Henry VIII's battles with the papacy, church courts and Parliament alike pressed for ever sterner punishment of polygamy. In 1604, Parliament made intentional polygamy a capital crime. Other laws passed in the same decade sought to rein in easy annulments, easy desertion, and self-divorce, especially among the lower classes. Still other laws sought to nullify private or secretly contracted marriages and second marriages that lacked parental consent, two witnesses, civil registration, and the church's blessing. Together, these new laws raised the threshold for valid marriage formation but closed the door firmly on divorce, save by a rare private bill passed by Parliament. Once validly married, spouses were stuck for life. Those who took a second fiancée or wife, in defiance of these new laws, now did so at their peril.

5. John Witte, Jr., *The Western Case for Monogamy over Polygamy* (Cambridge: Cambridge University Press, 2015). This chapter is drawn in part from chapter 7 of this volume and used with the publisher's permission.

The New Criminalization of Polygamy

Before 1604, the formation of a valid marriage in England required only a mutual promise of marriage stated in the present tense ("I take you for my husband/wife") between a man and woman with freedom, fitness, and capacity to marry each other. A future promise ("I promise to take you as my wife/husband") followed by consensual sexual intercourse also constituted a valid marriage. No parental consent, testimony of witnesses, publication of banns, or religious ceremonies were necessary, although some couples did marry with all these formalities. In 1604, a comprehensive new set of Canons and Constitutions Ecclesiastical required parental consent for parties under 21 years old, and public banns and church consecration for all prospective couples. But these same Canons also confirmed the traditional "licensing exception," which eventually undercut these publicity rules and again allowed for clandestine "licensed" marriages.[6] Only in 1753 did Parliament try to put a stop to this clandestine marriage industry for good by passing Lord Hardwicke's Act that made banns, witnesses, parental consent for minors, and consecration prerequisites for every valid marriage, and voided marriages that defied these formation steps.[7]

Marriages, once validly contracted could be dissolved either by annulment (which allowed remarriage) or divorce (which did not). An order of *annulment* required proof of one of the impediments to marriage that survived Tudor statutory reform—a blood or family relationship between the parties prohibited by Leviticus, a precontract to an earlier marriage by one of the parties, coercion, fraud or mistake in the formation of the marriage, or proven impuberty, frigidity, or impotence discovered shortly after the wedding. Once a marriage was annulled, the parties were generally free to remarry, at least the innocent and healthy party. Annulments had hidden costs, however, beyond the costs of litigation. The annulment dissolved a woman's right to collect dower interests in her former husband's estate, and it could lead to the illegitimation of any children born of the first union.[8]

6. Edward Cardwell, ed., *Synodalia: A Collection of Articles of Religion, Canons, and Proceedings of Convocations in the Province of Canterbury*, 2 vols. (Oxford: Oxford University Press, 1842), 1.305, Canons 100, 101; 2.580–83.

7. 26 Geo. II, c. 33.

8. See Cardwell, ed., *Synodalia*, 1.152–155, 161–163; Sir Edward Coke, *The First Part of the Institutes of the Lawes of England* (London: Societie of Stationers, 1628), folios 32,

A decree of *divorce* required proof of adultery, desertion (for more than seven years), or protracted ill treatment by one's spouse. Until the mid-nineteenth century, a decree of divorce in England was an order for separation from bed and board alone, with no right of remarriage for either party while the other spouse was still alive. Only if the party could get a rare private bill for divorce passed by Parliament could they remarry before the death of their estranged spouse. The 1604 Canons underscored this traditional rule by ordering church court judges to enjoin divorced parties to "live chastely and continently" and with no other mate, until the death of their estranged spouse.[9] Divorced parties who did remarry prior to the (presumed) death of their ex-spouse faced prosecution. Before 1604, the criminal charges were usually for adultery or perjury. After 1604, the new crime was called "polygamy" or "bigamy."[10]

The 1604 Act of Parliament that initiated this new regime was entitled: "An act to restrain all persons from marriage until their former wives and former husbands be dead." The full Act reads:

> Forasmuch as diverse evil disposed persons being married, run out of one country into another, or into places where they are not known, and there become to be married, having another husband or wife living, to the great dishonour of God, and utter undoing of diverse honest men's children, and others;
>
> [I.] Be it therefore enacted... that any person or persons within His Majesty's dominions of England and Wales, being married, or which hereafter shall marry, do at any time at the end of the said session

33v, 235; id., *The Third Part of the Institutes of the Lawes of England* (London: M. Flesher, 1644), 93; Richard Burn, *Ecclesiastical Law*, 8th ed., 4 vols. (London: A. Strahan, 1824), 1.118–135; John Godolphin, *Repertorium Canonicurn*, 3rd ed. (London: Assigns of R. & E. Atkins, 1687), 508–13.

9. Cardwell, ed., *Synodalia*, Canon 107.

10. Coke urged his fellow common lawyers to use the term "polygamy" to describe only the crime of having two or more spouses at the same time and "bigamy" to refer to "clerical bigamy," the canon law rule that prohibited prospective priests from having two or more wives in a row before their ordination, or from marrying even one non-virginal wife. Coke, *The First Part of the Institutes*, 80a–80b, n.1. See also William Blackstone, *Commentaries on the Laws of England*, 4 vols. (Oxford: Oxford University Press, 1765), 4.13.2.

of this present Parliament, marry any person or persons, the former husband or wife being alive; that then every such offence shall be [a] felony, and the person and persons so offending shall suffer death as in cases of felony, and the party and parties so offending shall receive such and the like proceeding, trial, and execution in such county where such person or persons shall be apprehended, as if the offence had been committed in such county where such person or persons shall be take or apprehended.

II. Provided always, that this Act, nor anything therein contained, shall extend to any person or persons whose husband or wife shall be continually remaining beyond the seas by the space of seven years together, or whose husband or wife shall absent him or herself the one from the other by the space of seven years together, in any parts of within His Majesty's dominions, the one of them not knowing the other to be living within that time.

III. Provided also, and be it enacted by the authority aforesaid, that this Act, nor anything herein contained, shall extend to any person or persons that are or shall be at the time of such marriage divorced by any sentence had or hereafter to be had in the ecclesiastical court; or to any person or persons where the former marriage hath been or hereafter shall be by sentence in the ecclesiastical court declared to be void and of no effect; nor to any person or persons for or by reason of any former marriage had or made, or hereafter to be had or made, within [the] age of consent.

IV. Provided also, that no attainder for this offence, made [a] felony this act, shall make or work any corruption of blood, loss of dower, or disinhersion of heir or heirs.[11]

11. 1 Jac. 1, c. 11 (spelling and capitalization modernized). See Coke, *The Third Part of the Institutes*, cap. 27, page 88.

This 1604 Polygamy Act remained on the books until it was replaced by new acts of 1828 and 1861 which made polygamy a non-capital crime, punishable by up to seven years of "transportation" or two years of prison.[12]

The 1604 Polygamy Act created a new relationship between church courts and state courts in the prosecution of polygamy. English state courts, for the first time since Anglo-Saxon days, now had jurisdiction over polygamy, with power to punish convicted polygamists with a range of criminal sanctions, including execution in grave cases. But church courts still retained jurisdiction over marital formation and dissolution, with power to judge the validity of a marriage, to issue orders of annulment or divorce, and to impose a range of spiritual sanctions on delinquent parties, including excommunication in cases of serious sin. This continued into the nineteenth century.

This created three possible scenarios in a typical polygamy case. (1) If it was clear from the evidence, or if the church court on request found that a defendant had two or more valid intact marriages, that defendant was a polygamist and subject to prosecution and criminal punishment by the secular court. (2) If the church court had properly *annulled* or "voided" one of the defendant's two marriages, the defendant's second marriage was not an act of polygamy. The defendant would be acquitted of any crime of polygamy and free from both church court discipline and secular court punishment. (3) If the church court had properly granted the defendant a *divorce* (meaning a separation) but the first spouse was still alive, the defendant's second marriage was still an act of polygamy, albeit a less serious crime. Absent aggravating factors, such defendants were usually not criminally punished much but sent to a church court for spiritual discipline and for the annulment of their second marriage.[13] The secular courts, in turn, would make the necessary adjustments to dower and other marital property. Those three scenarios seem to have been the intent of the Polygamy Act, and that was how the English courts came to interpret and apply it.

The 1604 Polygamy Act was designed to provide relief to long deserted spouses who wanted the freedom to remarry. The medieval canon law had required such parties to furnish absolute proof of the death of

12. 9 Geo. 4, c. 31.

13. Coke, *Third Part of the Institutes*, cap. 29, page 89; Matthew Hale, *Pleas of the Crown* (London: Richard Atkyns et al. 1678), 1.693ff.

their long-gone spouse before they could remarry—an impossible burden of proof in many cases. This posed a "heartbreaking dilemma" for many lonely spouses, and especially for mothers with young children.[14] If they remained single, these mothers and their children were often condemned to poverty and exploitation. If they remarried without proof of their first husband's death, they were vulnerable to charges of bigamy and the spiritual sanctions that followed, including the illegitimating of any children born from the second marriage. The 1604 Act sought to resolve this dilemma by building in a clear statute of limitations on desertion. If deserters remained hidden somewhere within Great Britain for seven years, or if even good faith travelers "beyond the seas" remained away for more than seven years, the abandoned spouse at home could remarry with impunity. Those who remarried within the seven-year window on the good faith assumption that their first spouse had died sometimes could still face charges of polygamy if the spouse unexpectedly turned up.[15] It was prudent to wait seven years before remarriage, but at least there was now relief available to the patient.

The 1604 Polygamy Act was also designed to shield minors from youthful marital mistakes or arranged marriages that might later put them in the frame for polygamy. If a person of the age of consent (12 for girls, 14 for boys) but under 21 years old got consensually married and had procured their parents' consent to the marriage as well, that marriage was valid, and would count against them if they were charged with polygamy. But if the minor had been forced into an arranged marriage by their parents, or had contracted their marriage without parental consent, that first marriage was presumptively invalid. If later charged with polygamy, those parties could defend themselves by challenging the validity of this first premature marriage. That defense became stronger still after Lord Hardwicke's Act of 1753 made parental consent for a minor's marriage a clear requirement for the validity of the marriage.

In application, the 1604 Polygamy Act did allow a polygamist to escape capital punishment on the technical grounds of "benefit of clergy." By this point, both clergy and laity, and both men and (after 1691) wom-

14. R. H. Helmholz, *Roman Canon Law in Reformation England* (Cambridge: Cambridge University Press, 1990), 166.

15. *R. v. Gibbons*, 12 Cox 237 (holding bigamy); cf. *R. v. Moore*, 13 Cox 544 (holding no bigamy).

en, too, could plea "benefit of clergy."[16] The success of their plea turned on their ability to read the opening verse of Psalm 51: "Have mercy on me, O God, according to thy steadfast love...." If the plea succeeded, the convicted defendant was branded on the thumb with a "B" for bigamist, or "P" for polygamy (though peers and Anglican priests escaped even that). A 1717 statute allowed courts to condemn convicted polygamists and other felons, even if they had successfully pled benefit of clergy, to transport for up to seven years.[17] An 1827 statute abolished the "benefit of clergy" for all persons in all crimes, including polygamy.[18]

A new 1828 polygamy statute, however, declared polygamy to be a non-capital felony punishable by up to seven years of transport or two years of prison.[19] This was confirmed in the 1861 Offenses Against the Persons Act, a comprehensive criminal law that remains on the books in England, and is echoed in many countries in the British Commonwealth.[20]

The Prosecution of Polygamy in the Old Bailey

In the 224 years that the 1604 Polygamy Act was the law of England, the Old Bailey in London and various assize and appellate courts around England heard hundreds if not thousands of criminal cases of polygamy—though exactly how many is unclear. The *All English Law Reports* lists 368 cases touching "bigamy" and 51 more cases touching "polygamy" from 1604 until the new statute of 1828 was enacted. These *Reports* are far from complete, however: a great number of court records from these earlier centuries did not survive, and many cases went unreported officially by the courts, even if sometimes reported by local chroniclers, newspapers, or private diarists.

A superb on-line collection of cases from 1674 to 1913 in the Old Bailey, London's central criminal court, holds a total of 2,384 criminal cases of bigamy or polygamy (out of a grand total of 197,000 plus criminal cases).[21]

16. 21 Jas. 1, c. 6 for larceny, and extended to all felonies by 3 & 4 W. & M., c. 9 and 4 & 5 W. & M., c. 24.

17. 5 Geo. 1, c. 11.

18. 7 & 8 Geo. 4, c. 28, s. 6.

19. 9 Geo. 4, c. 31.

20. U.K. Stat. 1861, c. 100, s. 57.

21. See http://www.oldbaileyonline.org/ [hereafter "OB"], which provides transcripts, and many facsimiles of all the criminal cases reported in the *Old Bailey Proceedings*

Of all these bigamy cases, 507 were brought under the 1604 Act before the 1828 statutory reform.[22] Of these 507 cases, 6 of them ended with execution—2 women, 4 men. In 110 cases, the defendants successfully pled benefit of clergy and were branded—14 women, 96 men. In 59 cases, the defendants were sentenced to transport for seven years—1 woman, 58 men. In 32 cases, they were sent to prison from two weeks to two years—2 women, 30 men. In 5 cases, they were simply fined—all men. In 211 cases, the defendants were found not guilty—67 women, 144 men. Eight cases, all involving men, ended inconclusively.

Several patterns are clear in this 500 plus case sample. First, polygamy remained very much "a male crime," in Sara McDougall's apt phrase, as it had been in the Middle Ages.[23] Both men and women were equally subject to the 1604 Act. But only 19% of the Old Bailey cases (95/507) were brought against women. Fully 70% of these women defendants (67/95) were acquitted; an additional 15% of them (14/95) successfully pled benefit of clergy, escaping with a branded thumb. Fewer than 5% of these women defendants faced harsh punishment: 2 went to prison, 1 was transported, and 2 were executed (both in the seventeenth century). Men were prosecuted much more frequently, and punished much more severely for polygamy. More than 81% of the polygamy cases were brought against men. Men were severely punished through imprisonment, transportation, or execution in 22% of these cases, compared to 5% of the women. And men were acquitted in only 35% of these cases, women in more than 70%.

Second, though the 1604 Polygamy Act declared polygamy to be a capital felony, executions for polygamy were rare. Only 6 out of the 507 defendants in the Old Bailey were executed, and all these took place before 1693. There were no doubt more executions ordered for convicted bigamists by the Old Bailey from 1604 to 1674, the year the first records have survived. There were certainly more executions ordered by criminal courts outside of London. But the number of executions for polygamy is very small—perhaps surprisingly so, given the moral outrage heaped upon this crime by

---

from 1674 to 1913, and of the *Ordinary of Newgate's Accounts* between 1676 and 1772.

22. I have omitted the 23 cases in 1828, because they do not make clear whether they are applying the 1604 act or the 1828 act.

23. Sara McDougall, "Bigamy: A Male Crime in Medieval Europe," *Gender and History* 22 (2010), 430–46.

early modern jurists and theologians alike. "Benefit of clergy" was the real safety net: 22% (110/507) of Old Bailey defendants successfully pled benefit of clergy and escaped execution.

Third, transportation for seven years was the preferred harsh punishment for particularly brazen polygamists. Some 11% (58/507) of the defendants, all but one of them men, were so sentenced. Transportation was usually a form of banishment to a penal colony—often North America, after 1787 Australia as well, and occasional other outposts in the vast British Empire. Convicts were often put to hard work on the "hulks"—think of Charles Dickens' *Great Expectations*—that provided passage over, and they could be sold as indentured servants, a few times as slaves, to the ship captains on arrival to their grim new home.[24]

Fourth, imprisonment was a relatively rare form of punishment in these cases, imposed on only 6% (32/507) of the defendants, with sentences rarely over a year. Imprisonment for any crime was not a common form of long-term punishment in England before the nineteenth century, and a good number of such convicts were held in private prisons or had their sentences commuted into indentured servitude.[25]

Fifth, the vast majority of cases involved a party with two spouses only, rather than multiple spouses. A few traveling cads did keep multiple wives in different cities, or just rotated through a series of wives without bothering to end their prior marriages. They were the ones who were usually sentenced to death, although most pled benefit of clergy. A good example is the 1676 case against an unnamed handsome charlatan who ultimately seduced 17 different wives around England. He "inveigled them to marry him, and for some small time enjoyed their persons, and got possession of their more beloved Estates, he would march off in Triumph with what ready money and other portable things of value he could get, to another strange place, and there lay a new plot" to seduce another wife. He was finally caught and prosecuted, foolishly waived benefit of clergy in hopes of a sentence of transportation, but was instead sentenced to be hung.[26] Mary Stokes presented a comparable case, albeit a rarer one for women in the

24. J. M. Beattie, *Crime and the Courts in England, 1660–1800* (Princeton: Princeton University Press, 1986), 450–618.

25. Ibid., 573–610.

26. *Case of May* 10, 1676, OB no. t16760510-1.

day. She married four men in the space of five years, slept with them a few nights—the second husband got just one night—and then made off with their property. She then moved down the road and took up with the next handsome wealthy man she could find. A scandalized judge accused her of being "an idle kind of a Slut," and ordered her executed.[27]

While these sensational cases made for good gossip, news, and occasional plays and novels, most polygamy cases involved rather ordinary people who had gotten remarried and were now charged with bigamy or polygamy. The cases were often brought at the instigation of their first or second spouse, or of an interested family member or third party. Occasionally an aggressive church or state official instigated prosecution. Many of the cases turned on the simple factual question whether the defendant had two valid marriages intact at once. Defendants' honest and reasonable mistakes of fact or law did not exonerate them, but these mistakes often mitigated their punishment. Defendants who were impoverished, abused, manipulated, or otherwise victimized by their first spouses and were trying to make thin ends meet by forming a second marriage, tended to get more sympathy. The more knowing and deliberate the defendant was in entering a second illegal marriage the more likely it was that severe punishment would follow. Defendants who compounded their crime by stealing marital property, abandoning their minor children or pregnant wife, or leaving massive debts for the abandoned spouse and family to cover generally faced harsher punishments. Those who bragged about their multiple marriages or defamed their abandoned spouses and families also got harsher punishment. So did those who changed their names, posted false banns, or manipulated the legal process to gain the hand of their second spouse.

Female Defendants

A typical case against a woman brought under the 1604 Polygamy Act was the Crown's prosecution of Mary Picart in 1725.[28] Mary had been properly married more than twenty years before to Jean Gandon—in a church wedding with witnesses. Jean's brother testified that the couple had two or

27. *Case of Mary Stokes* (December 6, 1693), OB no. t16961206-14.

28. *Case of Mary Picart, alias Gandon* (1725), in James Montagu, ed., *The Old Bailey Chronicle*, 4 vols. (London: S. Smith, 1788), 1:377–78.

three children, but Jean had since become old and decrepit. Mary was livelier. One day, she went into London, and got drunk with one Philip Bouchain. They went to a Fleet Street marriage licensor, and Philip paid a license fee for them to marry on the spot which they did in a brief ceremony. The drunken couple then collapsed into bed together, only to be interrupted loudly a few hours later by Mary's relatives who ordered her home and him out. Philip had evidently passed out, because he remembered nothing of getting married. Mary, too, denied any second marriage though she remembered vaguely the brief ceremony. Both insisted that they had not had sex with each other. Because the second marriage was not consummated, the jury acquitted her. They could well have convicted her, since consummation was not a condition for a valid marriage. But execution for an interrupted one night drunken tryst was evidently too much for the jury.

A 1726 case against Mary Jane Bennett also ended in acquittal, this time because the first marriage was declared void.[29] When she was fourteen, Mary had gone to live with an Italian man, named Dr. Letart, to serve as his interpreter. He "debauched" her, getting her pregnant. He then threatened to kill her or to "send her to Brideswell" if she would not marry his friend Peter Dorfille. If she would marry Peter, Letart promised to maintain and compensate her handsomely. She married Peter, but Letart then abandoned her and "never took the least notice of her." Peter proved to be a "poor weakly Thing," a "Tool of a Husband," who did nothing and took whatever she earned. Despondent, Mary eventually took up with Thomas Smith, was impregnated by him, and now wanted to marry him. She told Thomas she was a widow, and they were promptly married by a Fleet licensor. Mary was then indicted for bigamy under the 1604 Act. The jury acquitted her, finding no evidence of a lawful first marriage to Peter given Letart's coercion and extortion, and probably taking pity on her for being so exploited.

Pity was also evident in a later case against a destitute woman, Mary Burns.[30] Seven years earlier, Mary had wed Richard Winter. They lived as husband and wife for a few months. He then enlisted in the military

29. *Select Trials at the Session-House in the Old-Bailey for Murder, Robberies, Rapes, Sodomy, Coining, Frauds, Bigamy, and other Offences*, 4 vols. (London: J. Applebee, 1742), 3:32–33.

30. *The Case of Tywning*, Gloucestershire, 106 Eng. Rep. 407 (1819).

and went away on foreign service, never to return. Just over a year after Richard's departure, a desperately poor Mary wed one Francis Burns, and the new couple produced two children. After the seven year statute of limitations for desertion built into the 1604 Act had expired, Mary must have thought she was free. But an ambitious local official had her prosecuted for bigamy, since she had married within a year of her first husband's departure, not after seven years of waiting. The trial court evidently convicted her, but the case was appealed to the King's Bench, whose judges were divided. The dissent thought the 1604 Polygamy Act created a presumption that the absent party was alive for the first seven years, and could only be presumed dead thereafter. Any other rule, the dissent said, would allow a woman to "marry a week after her husband's departure" but leave her free from prosecution unless and until her first husband returned within seven years of the first wedding. The majority ruled in Mary's favor, holding that the first husband Richard could be presumed dead, which the ensuing seven years of his absence confirmed. That was a more defendant-friendly reading of the statute than many courts offered.[31]

Not all women defendants escaped liability. Mary Stoakes compounded her crime with fraud and was more severely punished.[32] In 1688, she married Thomas Adams before several witnesses. In 1692, she left Thomas and married William Carter, again before several witnesses. But she soon left William, too, changing her name to Mary Elliott, and holding herself out to yet another man as a single maid with an estate. She was tried and convicted for polygamy. She escaped execution by claiming benefit of clergy, newly available to women, and was branded.

Elizabeth Wood Lloyd proved even more brazen.[33] In 1812, she had married Thomas Lloyd, a baker. Around 1816, she began consorting with a sailor, suspiciously named Captain Bligh, and the couple would take a room together when he was between voyages. Thomas found her out, and told her in front of Bligh and other witnesses: "If you like the sailor better than me, you had better go with him." Bligh gave Thomas five shillings and made off with Elizabeth. Whether Bligh and Elizabeth ever formally

31. See comparable result in *Case of Rebecca How* (July 5, 1749), OB no. t17490705-85.

32. *The Trials of all the Felon Prisoners, Tried, Cast, and Condemned, This Session at the Old Bailey* (London: n.p., 1798), 6.

33. *Case of Elizabeth Wood Lloyd* (April 6, 1826), OB no. t18260406-790

married is unclear, but in 1822 she was formally married to William Henry Truss, signing the marriage registration as "Betty Wood Louther Bligh, the widow of Captain Bligh." Truss later found out about her prior marriage to Thomas, and he promptly left her, albeit after giving her a rather handsome severance. But seeking to end the marriage, and recoup his settlement, Truss had Elizabeth prosecuted for polygamy. She was convicted and sentenced to seven years transport.

Male Defendants

While most courts gave women charged with bigamy the benefit of the doubt—particularly before they could plead the benefit of clergy—they tended to treat male defendants more firmly, even when the facts seemed to call for leniency. Take the case of William Morgan Manners.[34] He had married Eliza Redkison in a proper church wedding. Shortly after their honeymoon, Eliza took up with an old boyfriend. William moved their marital home to another town in an effort to end the affair. But one day, when William was traveling, Eliza returned to her old flame, taking much of their marital property with her. William made sixteen attempts to persuade her to come back home, but Eliza's boyfriend threatened to shoot him if he returned. William waited three years, and then got remarried to Susan Anderson. He was convicted for bigamy. An unsympathetic court sentenced him to seven years transport.[35]

John Fisher lost any hope of getting the court's sympathy because of his perjury and premarital sex.[36] In June, 1812, he had married Mary Arlett in a church wedding. She was apparently already pregnant because in November that year, John testified that she promptly "left her home with all the child's clothes, and everything she could lay h[o]ld of, and left me only just enough to put on in the morning." He spent time settling their ample debts and then sought to start over by changing his name to John Ingram.

34. *Case of William Morgan Manners* (September 12, 1821), OB no. t18210912-95.

35. See same results on similar facts in *Case of Henry Sanders* (April 17, 1822), OB no. t18220417; *Case of Thomas Sale Denby* (May 22, 1822), OB no. t18220522-165. But see *Case of John W. K. Kitchingmam* (July 3, 1822), OB no. t18220703-23 who received only one year of prison on similar facts.

36. *Case of John Fisher* (July 10, 1816), OB no. t18160710-77.

Holding himself out as a bachelor, he married Ruth Elcock four years after his first marriage to Mary. His bigamy and perjury were discovered, and he was convicted for seven years of transport.[37]

Brazen polygamists, particularly those who compounded their offense with serious crimes, found no sympathy from the Old Bailey and other criminal courts.[38] The case of Thomas Brown provides a good example. Brown, a tobacconist in London, had properly married a maidservant named Ann Mussels in February, 1747. Six months later, he picked up a second woman, Susannah Watts, in a local pub, courted her briefly, and then promptly married her in a proper ceremony. They went on a honeymoon, and he then took her home. His first wife Ann raised the roof when Thomas arrived with his new wife, and a mortified Susannah had him prosecuted for bigamy. Given his long criminal record already, which included earlier charges of robbery and rape, the court said "they hoped they should live to see this crime punished with death." But Thomas successfully pled benefit of clergy.

Samuel Taylor aggravated his bigamy with fraud, theft, and desertion of his pregnant wife.[39] Seventeen years earlier, he had properly married Mary Hayter, but the couple had separated by mutual consent, and Mary had then taken in another woman and did not want him back. Sixteen years after that first marriage, Taylor held himself out as a widower and married Harriet le Sturgeon. She got pregnant, and he left her in her seventh month, taking some of her goods, too. He was convicted for bigamy and got seven years of transport. John Maude left his wife Harriet of 13 years and their six children. He pretended to be a bachelor and married Esther Barrett, and sired another child by her. He was convicted for bigamy and perjury and sentenced to seven years transport.[40] John Crooks left his pregnant wife once, returned to impregnate her again, and then left her and their two young boys for good, rendering them impoverished

37. Same result in another perjury *Case of John Harwood* (December 6, 1820), OB no. t18201206-156.

38. *Case of Thomas Brown* (Sept. 9, 1747), OB no. t17470909-22.

39. *Case of Samuel Taylor* (October 28, 1818), OB no. t18181028-148.

40. *Case of John Maude* (December 1, 1789), OB no. t18191201-109. See similar result in *Case of John Mackiah Collins* (April 17, 1782), OB no. t18220417-121.

wards of the local parish.[41] Crooks then bragged to someone that "he had a great many wives." Local authorities began to look into his case and found an earlier marriage still intact. They prosecuted John for bigamy, and he was sentenced to seven years transport.[42] All three men were lucky to have escaped with their lives.

Lewis Houssart, a French emigrant barber living in England, was not so lucky.[43] In 1723, Lewis had married Elizabeth Heren in a church wedding before several witnesses. A parish clerk testified to the new marriage with Elizabeth, but he also mentioned that Lewis was rather nervous after the wedding for no seeming reason. That raised the court's suspicions. They subpoenaed another pastor serving in the French émigré community who testified that he had, in fact, several years earlier married Lewis to another woman named Ann Rondeau. That name was familiar to the court because Ann had just been murdered. Lewis was called back for investigation, now on suspicion both of bigamy and murder. He eventually admitted knowing Ann, but denied that they were ever married. He also cast ample aspersions on Ann's character and chastity to the great chagrin of her family. Ann's brother testified that Ann and Lewis had been married, and claimed that Lewis in fact had murdered her. Lewis was then tried for murder, too. The evidence was largely circumstantial, but the court had lost all sympathy for him. He was convicted and hung. It was not clear whether he tried to plead benefit of clergy, but his broken English testimony recorded in the case suggests that he could not have recited Psalm 51 accurately enough to escape.

Robert Fielding, Esq. was also convicted for polygamy, but he escaped execution by successfully pleading benefit of clergy.[44] The facts sound like a Jane Austen novel. Fielding, a handsome bachelor but also a high society rake, was in hot pursuit of a new widow, Barbara, the Duchess of Cleavland and former mistress of King Charles II. Using his legal connections, he had checked on her will, and found her legacy of some 80,000 pounds inducement enough. He began pursuing her through intermediaries and

41. *Case of John Crooks* (January 9, 1822), OB no. t18220109-134.

42. See similar result in *Case of William Guy* (April 9, 1923), OB no. t18230409-175.

43. *Select Trials at the Session-House in the Old-Bailey*, 2.72–87.

44. *The Arraignment, Trial, and Conviction of Robert Fielding, Esq. for Felony in Marrying Her Grace, the Duchess of Cleavland; His First Wife, Mrs. Mary Wadsworth Being Then Alive as the Session of the Old-Bailey* (London: John Morphew, 1708).

letters in August, 1704. The Duchess's servants evidently did not like Robert, because they secretly protected her against his pursuits, burning one of his letters of inquiry and blocking his agent's efforts to see her. Robert was not so easily put off. When he took up his pursuit in person, one of the servants, the comely Mary Wadsworth, dressed up like the Duchess, and allowed Robert to see her through a window on one of Robert's frequent visits to the home. This made Robert doubly eager to meet the Duchess, and he kept trying to find a way. The servants then had Mary go to meet Robert at his home, holding herself out as the Duchess. Robert was infatuated, and after a lengthy interview, proposed marriage to her. A demur Mary eventually accepted. Robert collected a Roman Catholic priest who married them on the spot. They consummated their marriage that night, and slept together several more times in coming weeks as she prepared her move into his home. Robert gave Mary gifts, money, furniture, and clothing. He also gave her an expensive wedding ring. He wrote her several letters thereafter always addressed to "his wife," "the countess of Fielding," and the like. Mary became pregnant. The pretense continued for the next six months. Robert then discovered that Mary was in fact a penniless maidservant, and he promptly threw her out. He then resumed his pursuit of the Duchess, whom he married in November, 1705. But when he began to abuse his new wife, the Duchess, and was then found sleeping with her granddaughter as well, whom he impregnated, the Duchess sued him and brought him up on criminal charges.[45]

Robert was charged with bigamy as well. Part way through the case, the judge seemed to be leaning in favor of Robert's argument that his first marriage to Mary was void because of his mistake of marrying "this false woman." There was also a serious question of whether the Catholic priest could officiate at a proper English wedding, and whether he had even administered the proper marital vows.[46] But then Robert overplayed his hand. He argued that Mary couldn't validly marry him anyway, since she had already been married for two years to another man, Lilly Brady. Robert triumphantly produced a copy of her marriage registration from the Fleet

45. See Amanda Foreman, "Valentine's Revenge," *Smithsonian* (February, 2014), 29–31, 102.

46. See Rebecca Probert, *Marriage Law and Practice in the Long Eighteenth Century* (Cambridge: Cambridge University Press, 2009), 136–37.

and urged the court to charge her with bigamy, not him. Counsel for Mary cleverly turned that argument against Robert: for him to charge Mary with bigamy was to admit that he had married her, too, since his marriage to her was the indictable second marriage. Robert sought to escape his dilemma by petitioning a church court to annul his marriage with Mary on grounds of precontract, fraud, or mistake. The church court eventually did so, but not before the criminal court convicted him under the 1604 Polygamy Act. He pled benefit of clergy, was branded on the thumb, and sent away on payment of bail in lieu of prison.

Sometimes an irregularity in the formation of one of the marriages allowed the court at least to mitigate the punishment of a defendant rather than exonerate him. This can be seen in a 1794 case of John Taylor in the Old Bailey.[47] In 1771, John had married Sara Marshall in a proper church wedding. The marriage was evidently never consummated, and Sara, who was incapable of sexual intercourse, eventually persuaded the long suffering John to marry another younger woman. In 1792, John married Margery Sophia Richardson, with his first wife's approval. All was going well until "some great reformer of morals," as the defense called him, had John prosecuted for the "abominable and atrocious felony" of bigamy. There was enough dispute about the character and motivations of the prosecutor and the quality of the evidence against the defendant to give the court pause. But they hung their light sentence on the stated suspicion that the second marriage had not been properly formed. John was given a two-week prison sentence and small fine.

Thomas Wardropper, a butcher, was also very lightly punished on suspicion that his first marriage was invalid.[48] In 1787 he had married Ann Archer, but there was some evidence he was coerced to marry her and that he was drunk on the wedding day, further impeding his consent. This was evidently a shotgun wedding, because the couple had a child shortly before or after the wedding. They were soon estranged, and Anne seems to have gone to France, leaving Thomas to care for the child. In 1791, Thomas was persuaded to marry the "beautiful" Alice Doyle, who was the ward of one of his friends and eager to have Alice married off. Thomas and Alice were

47. *R. v. John Taylor* (November 11, 1794), OB no. t17941111-44.

48. *Case of Thomas Wardropper* (December 6, 1797), OB no. t17971206-2.

properly married, and lived together with the child for more than a year. But then Alice discovered Thomas's prior marriage to Ann and moved out on her own. Alice then began taking up with a Mr. Douglas, who provided her with ample furnishings, and evidently came over regularly to test the bed. Douglas wrote Thomas letters trying to force him to end his marriage with Alice so he could marry her. With that failing, he instigated the prosecution of Thomas for bigamy. After hearing all this tawdry and self-serving testimony, the court concluded that this "is not one of those cases in which severe punishment ought to be inflicted." Thomas was fined one shilling and discharged.

Summary and Conclusions

Already in Anglo-Saxon times, England condemned polygamy as a serious moral offense. But until 1604, it was left to church courts to punish polygamists using spiritual punishments. During the sixteenth century Anglican Reformation, Parliament took firmer control of marital formation and dissolution, though church courts were still left to administer much of England's family law. Parliament and Convocation worked hard to stamp out the medieval practice of self-marriage and self-divorce. They instituted firm new marital formation rules of parental consent, two witnesses, civil registration, and church consecration for valid marriage. They restricted divorce to very rare cases that could occasion a special bill in Parliament, and truncated impediments to rein in a runaway annulment practice. When private licensing arrangements to make marriage, and simple desertion and remarriage practices continued, Parliament enacted the 1604 Polygamy Act that made polygamy a serious crime, punishable by the secular courts. But the Act also provided relief for long-deserted parties, by allowing them to remarry if abandoned for more than seven years.

Using this 1604 law, both individual victims of desertion or double marriage as well as church or state officials could initiate indictment of parties for polygamy. Other interested parties also had standing to press polygamy claims, effectively as private attorneys-general. Thousands of polygamy cases came before the criminal tribunals of England, not least the famous Old Bailey, which heard more than 500 such polygamy cases under the 1604 Act. Convicted parties faced punishments ranging from fines and short imprisonment, to transportation to a penal colony or execution orders, though almost all those convicted for a capital felony successfully pled benefit of clergy. The vast majority of polygamy cases were brought against men, and they were punished far more severely than women if convicted. The 1604 Polygamy Act—while eventually replaced by Acts of Parliament in 1828 and 1861 that made felony a non-capital crime—was a model for the common law world and broader British Commonwealth. Particularly North American colonies used the basic structure of the 1604 Polygamy Act, and it continues to shape American and Canadian criminal laws against polygamy still today.

www.ingramcontent.com/pod-product-compliance
Lightning Source LLC
Chambersburg PA
CBHW021428180326
41458CB00001B/172

* 9 7 8 1 8 8 2 2 3 9 2 4 5 *